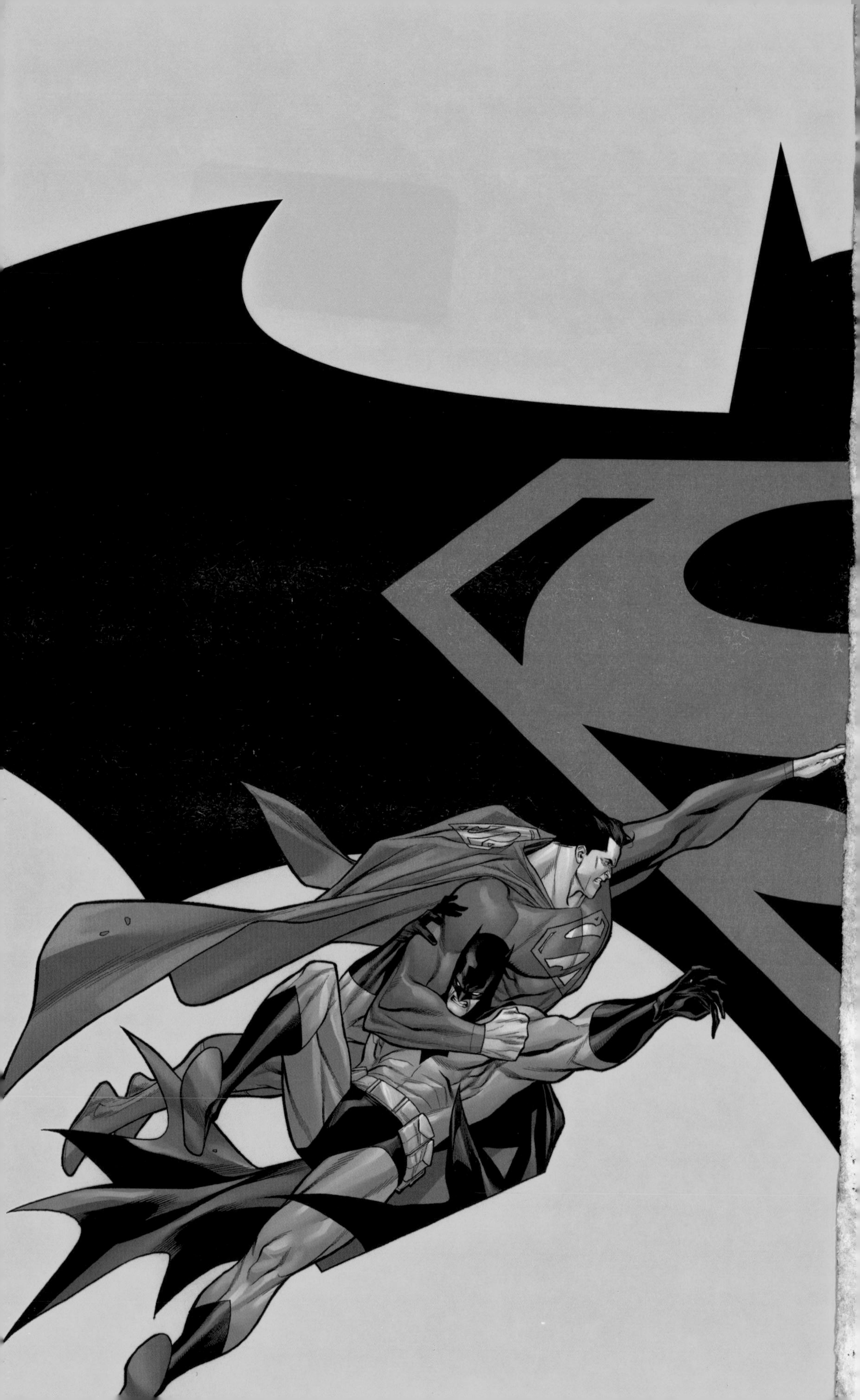

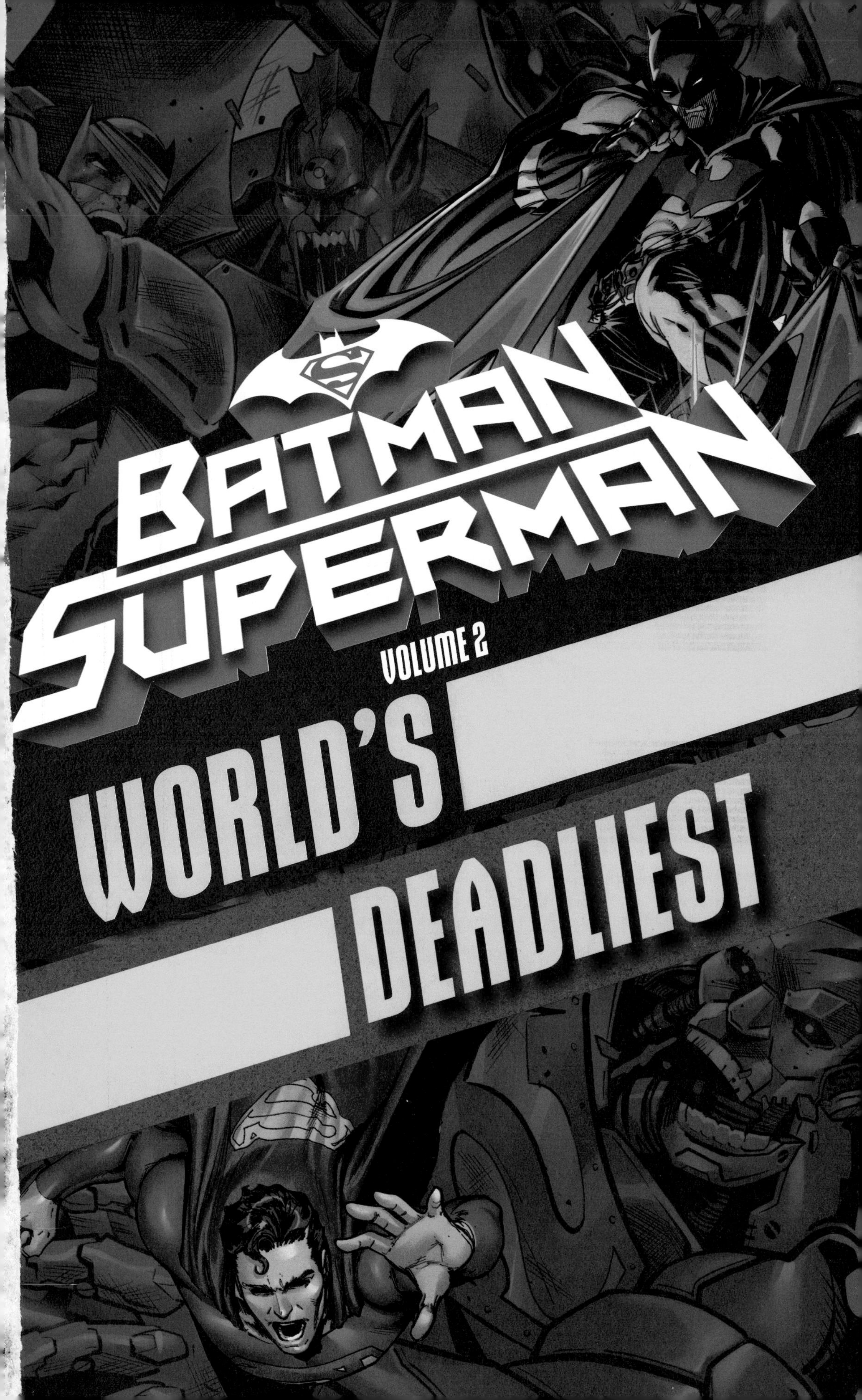
BATMAN
SUPERMAN
VOLUME 2
WORLD'S
DEADLIEST

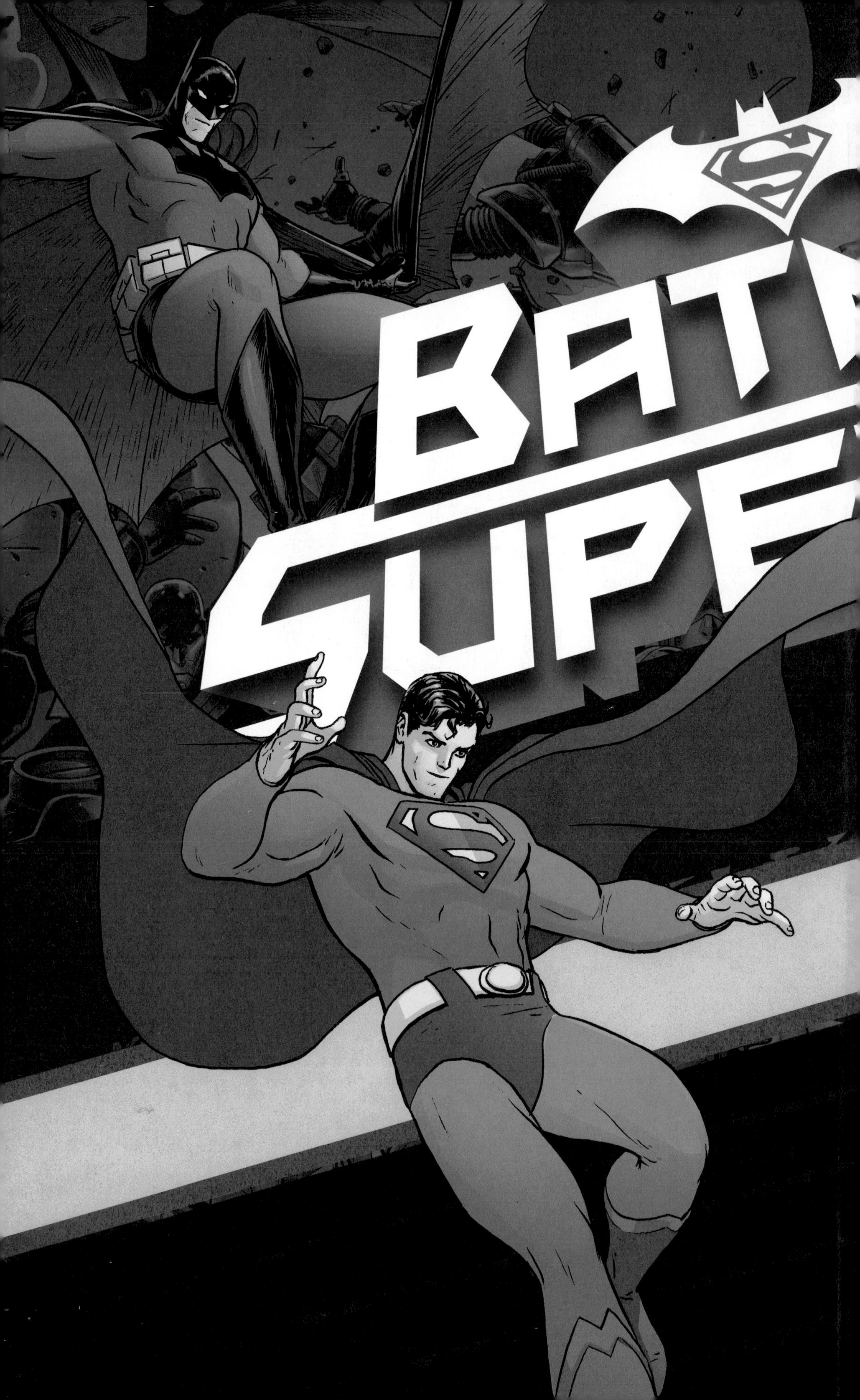

WORLD'S DEADLIEST

VOLUME 2

JOSHUA WILLIAMSON
WRITER

NICK DERINGTON, CLAYTON HENRY, MAX RAYNOR, GLEB MELNIKOV, DALE EAGLESHAM, ANDREI BRESSAN
ARTISTS

DAVE McCAIG, ALEJANDRO SÁNCHEZ
COLORISTS

JOHN J. HILL
LETTERER

DAVID MARQUEZ AND **ALEJANDRO SÁNCHEZ**
COLLECTION COVER ARTISTS

BATMAN CREATED BY BOB KANE WITH BILL FINGER
SUPERMAN CREATED BY JERRY SIEGEL AND JOE SHUSTER
SUPERBOY CREATED BY JERRY SIEGEL
BY SPECIAL ARRANGEMENT WITH THE JERRY SIEGEL FAMILY

PAUL KAMINSKI Editor – Original Series & Collected Edition
BEN MEARES Assistant Editor – Original Series
STEVE COOK Design Director – Books
DAMIAN RYLAND Publication Design
ERIN VANOVER Publication Production

MARIE JAVINS Editor-in-Chief, DC Comics

DANIEL CHERRY III Senior VP – General Manager
JIM LEE Publisher & Chief Creative Officer
DON FALLETTI VP – Manufacturing Operations & Workflow Management
LAWRENCE GANEM VP – Talent Services
ALISON GILL Senior VP – Manufacturing & Operations
NICK J. NAPOLITANO VP – Manufacturing Administration & Design
NANCY SPEARS VP – Revenue
MICHELE R. WELLS VP & Executive Editor, Young Reader

BATMAN/SUPERMAN VOL. 2: WORLD'S DEADLIEST

DC Comics, 2900 West Alameda Ave., Burbank, CA 91505
Printed by LSC Communications, Willard, OH, USA. 3/19/21. First Printing.
ISBN: 978-1-77950-568-2

Library of Congress Cataloging-in-Publication Data is available.

PEFC
PEFC/29-31-337
PEFC Certified
This product is from sustainably managed forests and controlled sources
www.pefc.org

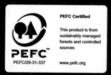

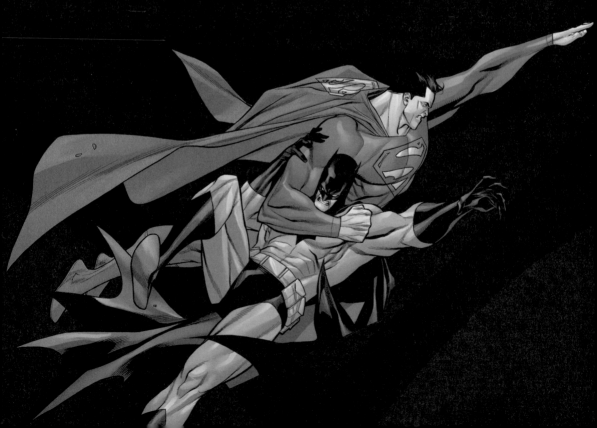

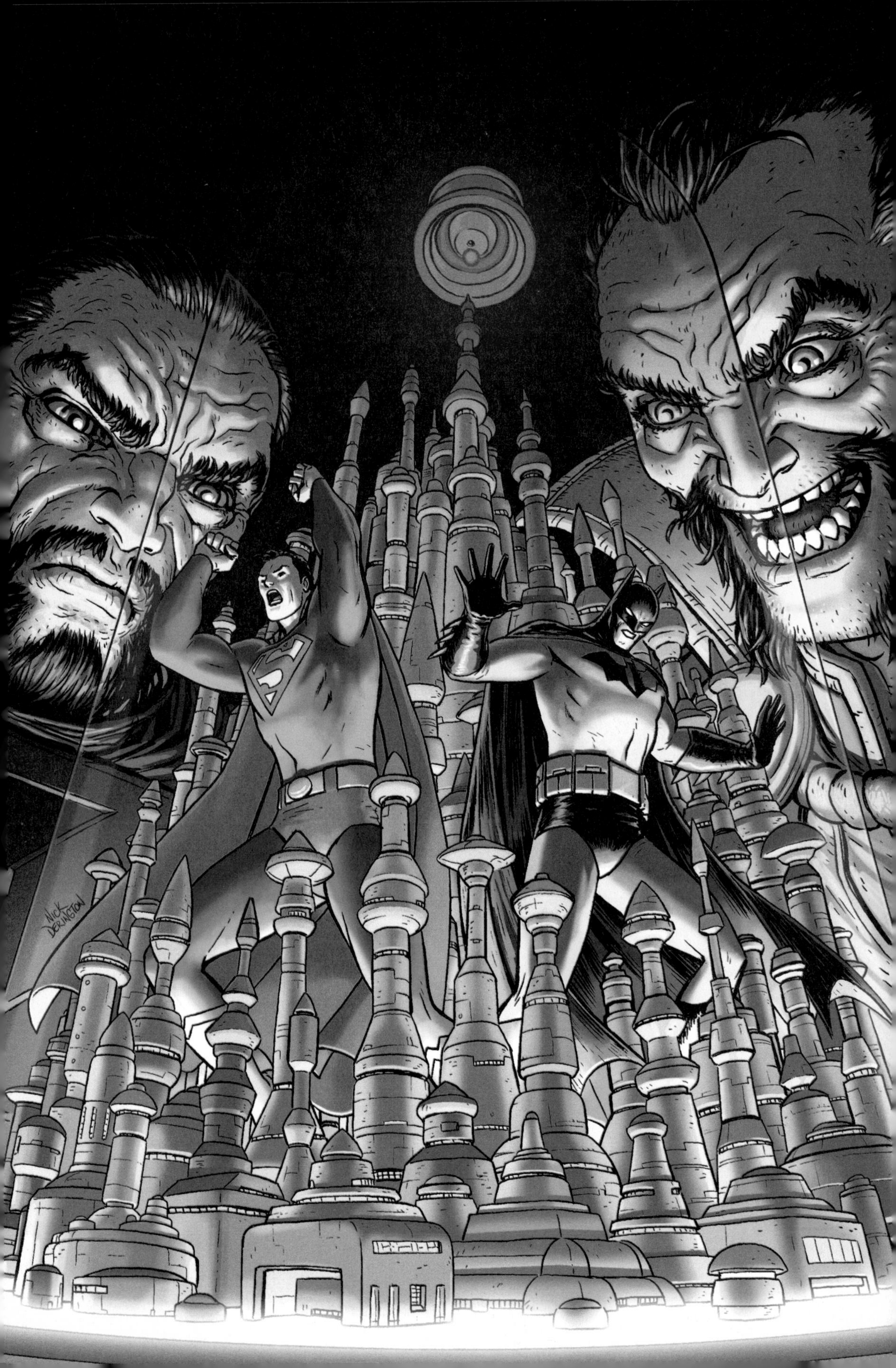
NICK DERINGTON

BATMAN/SUPERMAN #7

cover by
NICK DERINGTON

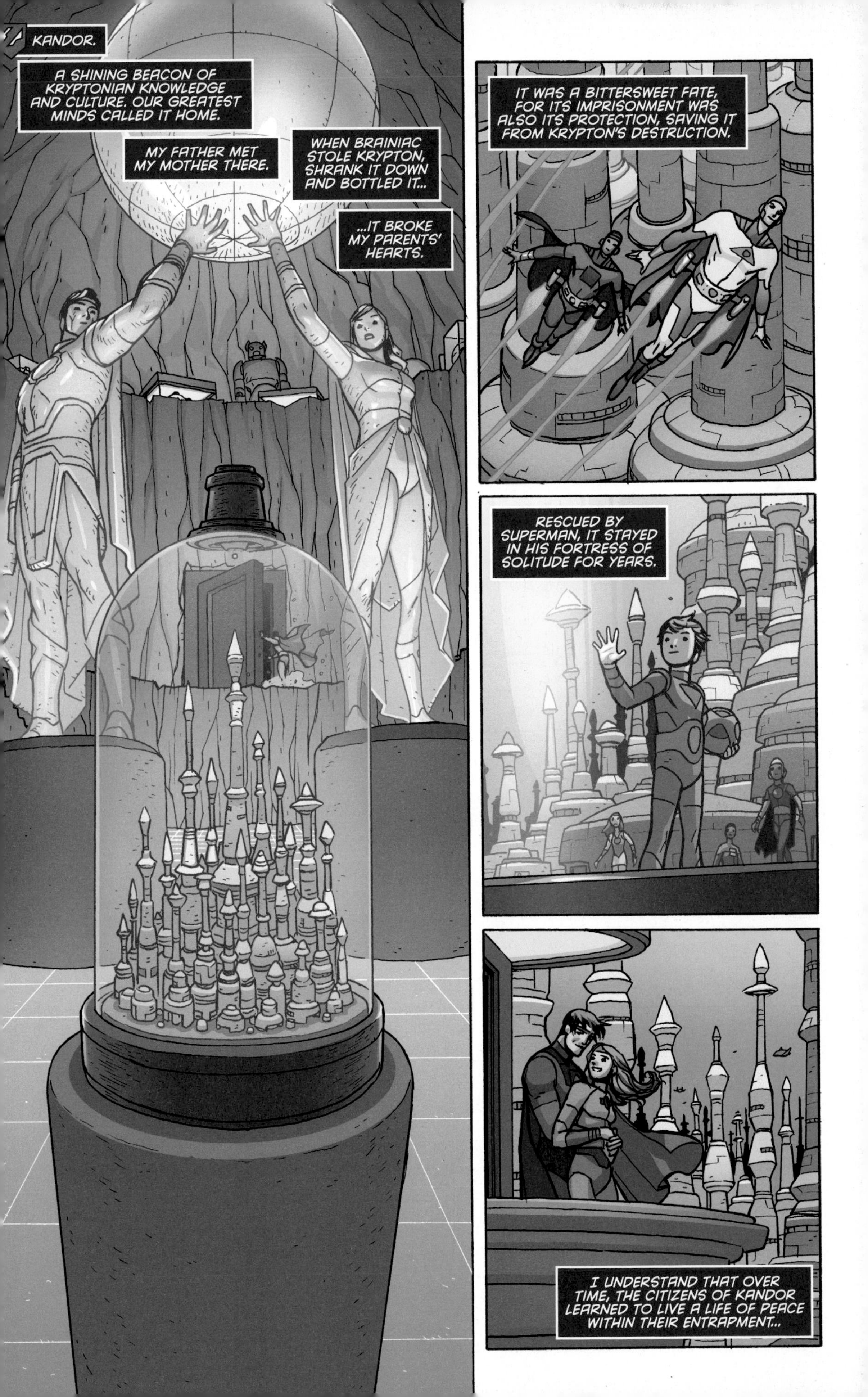
KANDOR.
A SHINING BEACON OF KRYPTONIAN KNOWLEDGE AND CULTURE. OUR GREATEST MINDS CALLED IT HOME.
MY FATHER MET MY MOTHER THERE.
WHEN BRAINIAC STOLE KRYPTON, SHRANK IT DOWN AND BOTTLED IT...
...IT BROKE MY PARENTS' HEARTS.
IT WAS A BITTERSWEET FATE, FOR ITS IMPRISONMENT WAS ALSO ITS PROTECTION, SAVING IT FROM KRYPTON'S DESTRUCTION.
RESCUED BY SUPERMAN, IT STAYED IN HIS FORTRESS OF SOLITUDE FOR YEARS.
I UNDERSTAND THAT OVER TIME, THE CITIZENS OF KANDOR LEARNED TO LIVE A LIFE OF PEACE WITHIN THEIR ENTRAPMENT...

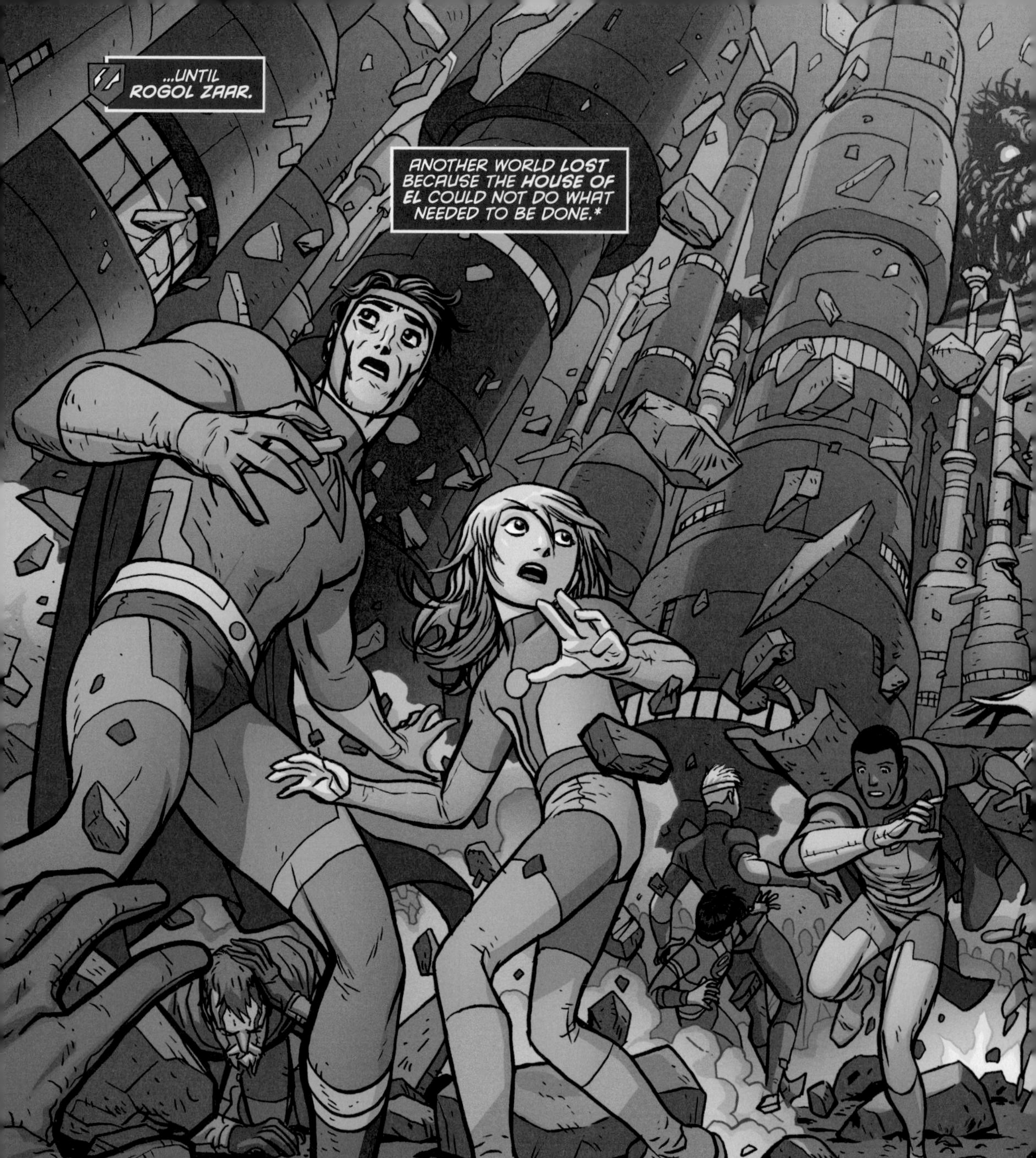
...UNTIL ROGOL ZAAR.
ANOTHER WORLD LOST BECAUSE THE HOUSE OF EL COULD NOT DO WHAT NEEDED TO BE DONE.*

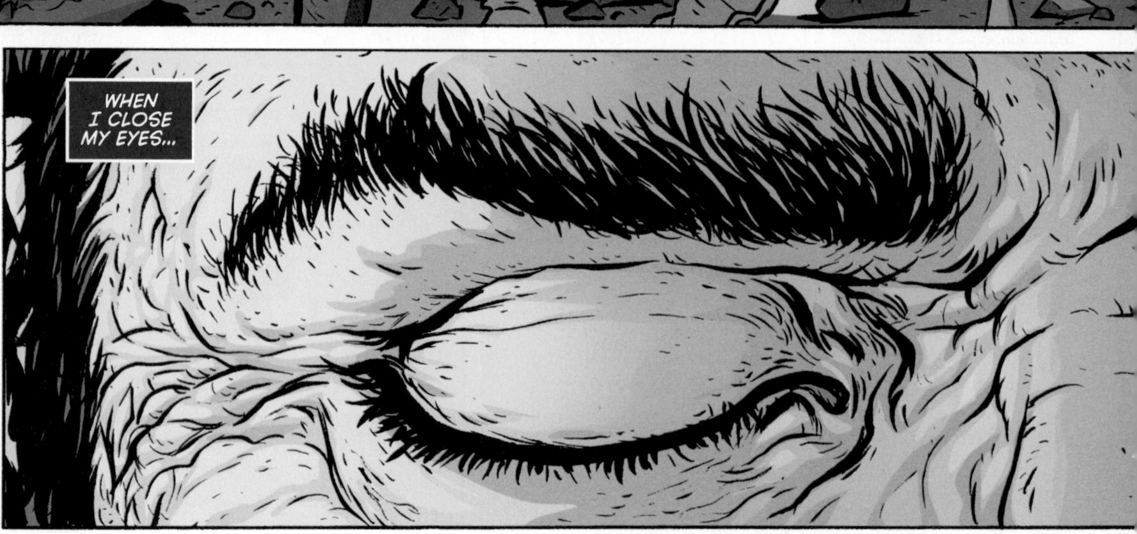
WHEN I CLOSE MY EYES...

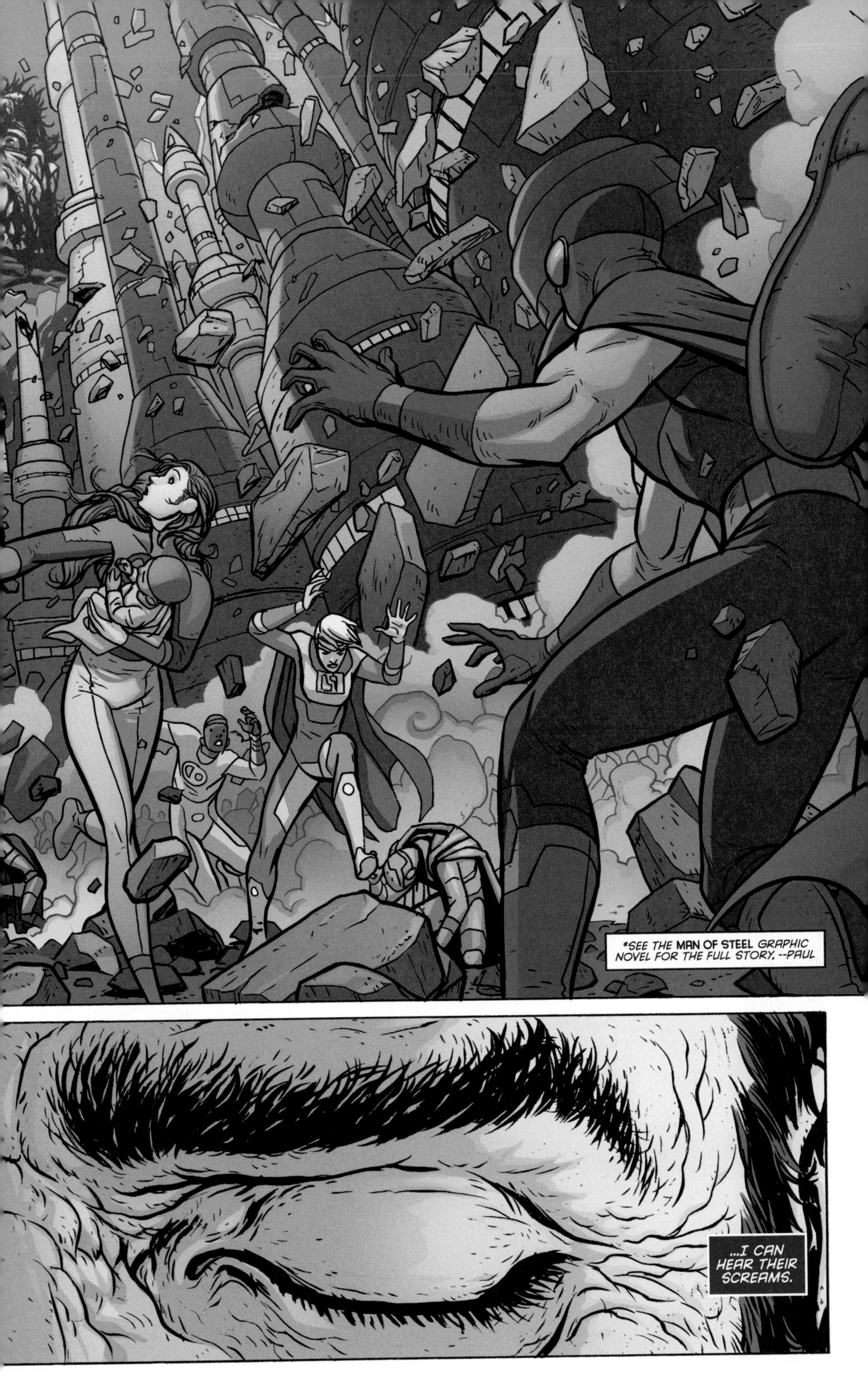
*SEE THE MAN OF STEEL GRAPHIC NOVEL FOR THE FULL STORY. --PAUL
...I CAN HEAR THEIR SCREAMS.

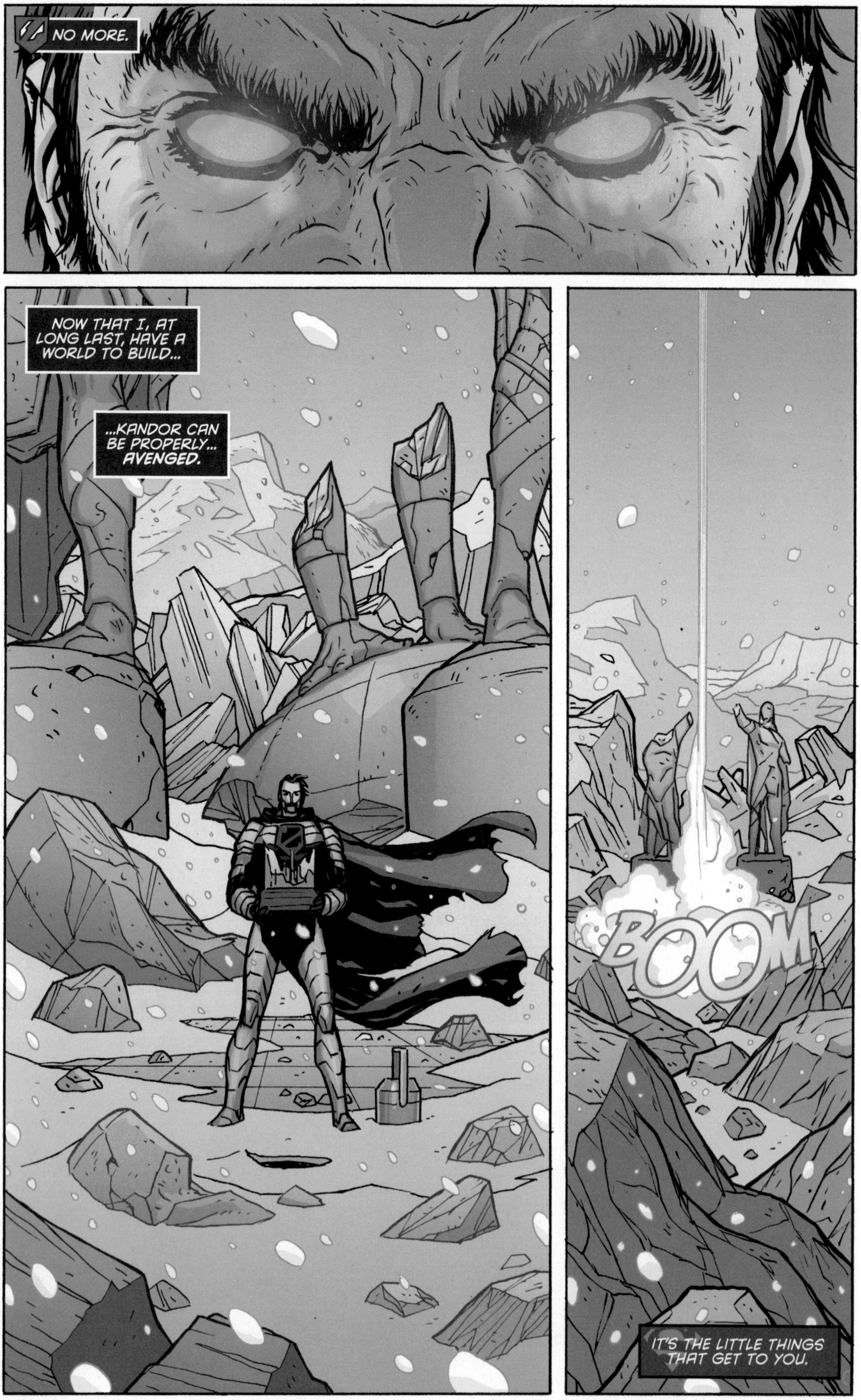
NO MORE.
NOW THAT I, AT LONG LAST, HAVE A WORLD TO BUILD...
...KANDOR CAN BE PROPERLY... AVENGED.
BOOM
IT'S THE LITTLE THINGS THAT GET TO YOU.

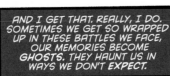

BRUCE SAYS HE CAN SOME-TIMES STILL SMELL HIS MOTHER'S PERFUME IN THE MANSION.

AND I GET THAT. REALLY, I DO. SOMETIMES WE GET SO WRAPPED UP IN THESE BATTLES WE FACE, OUR MEMORIES BECOME *GHOSTS.* THEY HAUNT US IN WAYS WE DON'T *EXPECT.*

EVERY DAY, I LOOK AT THIS SYMBOL ON MY CHEST AND I'M REMINDED OF MY WORLD.

BOTH OUR STORIES START THE SAME.

WITH LOSS.

AND WE BOTH DEAL WITH IT IN THE SAME WAY.

WE KEEP OURSELVES BUSY.

SO THE GHOSTS NEVER CATCH US.

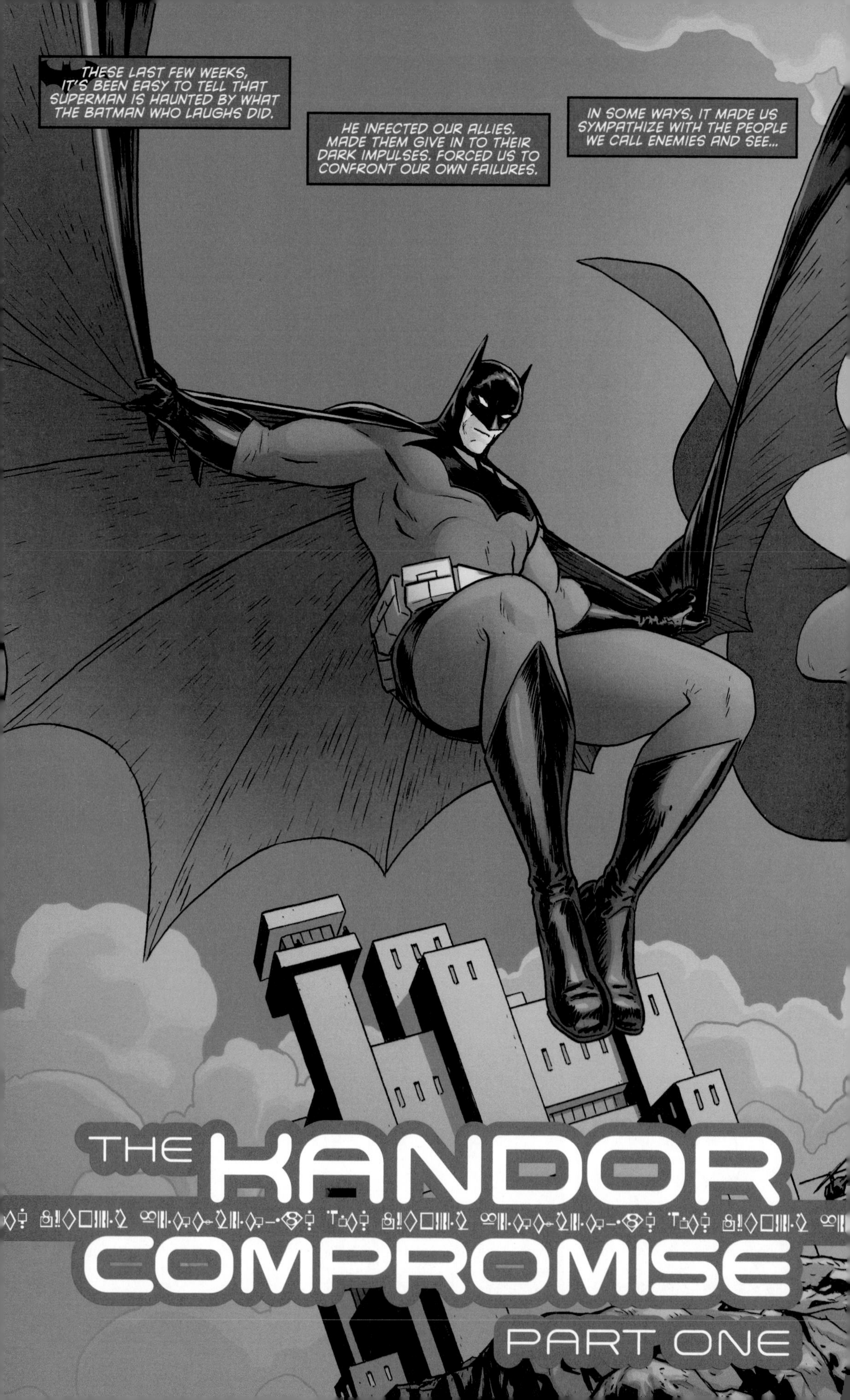
THESE LAST FEW WEEKS, IT'S BEEN EASY TO TELL THAT SUPERMAN IS HAUNTED BY WHAT THE BATMAN WHO LAUGHS DID.
HE INFECTED OUR ALLIES. MADE THEM GIVE IN TO THEIR DARK IMPULSES. FORCED US TO CONFRONT OUR OWN FAILURES.
IN SOME WAYS, IT MADE US SYMPATHIZE WITH THE PEOPLE WE CALL ENEMIES AND SEE...
THE KANDOR COMPROMISE
PART ONE

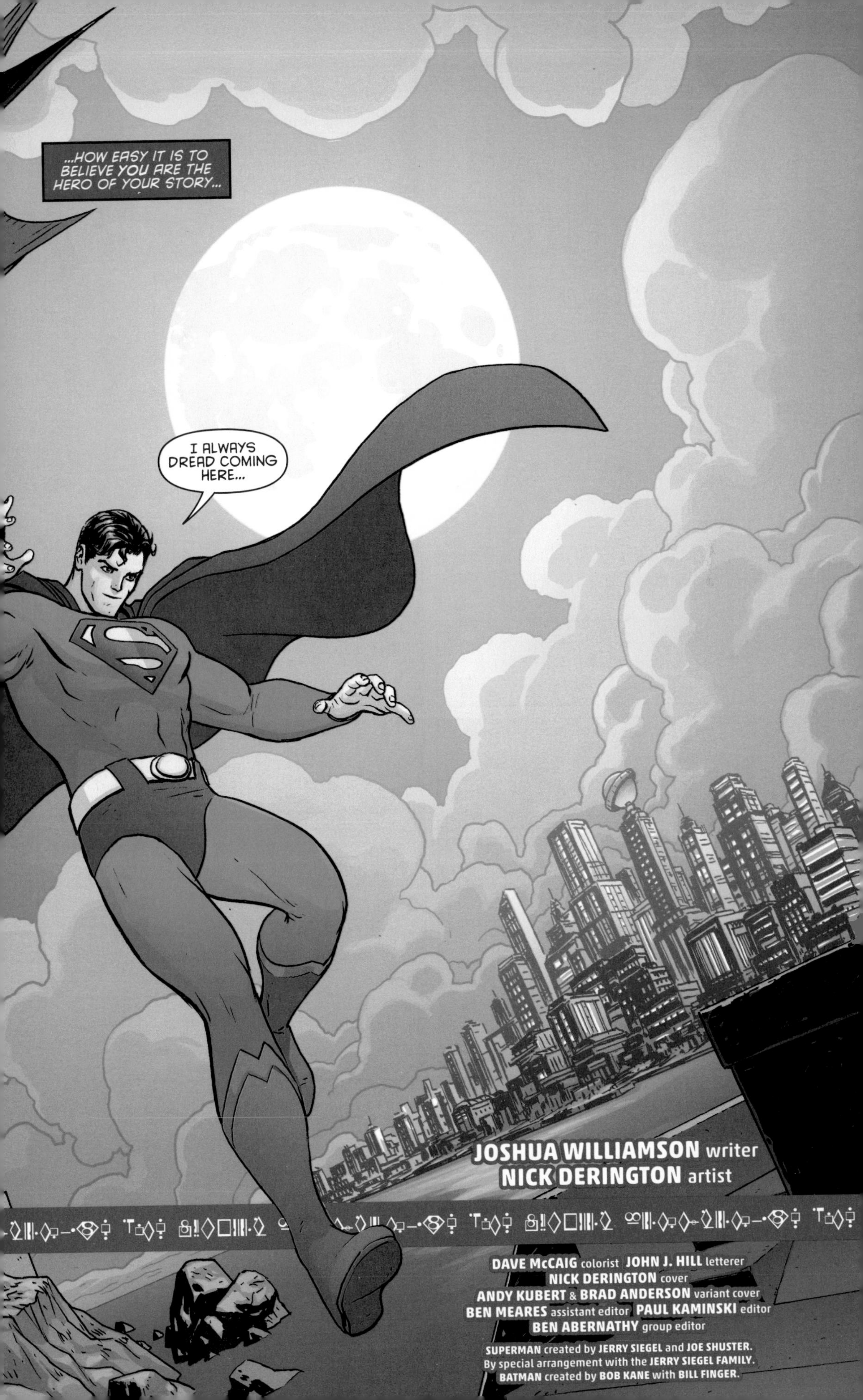
...HOW EASY IT IS TO BELIEVE YOU ARE THE HERO OF YOUR STORY...
I ALWAYS DREAD COMING HERE...
JOSHUA WILLIAMSON writer
NICK DERINGTON artist
DAVE McCAIG colorist JOHN J. HILL letterer
NICK DERINGTON cover
ANDY KUBERT & BRAD ANDERSON variant cover
BEN MEARES assistant editor PAUL KAMINSKI editor
BEN ABERNATHY group editor
SUPERMAN created by JERRY SIEGEL and JOE SHUSTER.
By special arrangement with the JERRY SIEGEL FAMILY.
BATMAN created by BOB KANE with BILL FINGER.

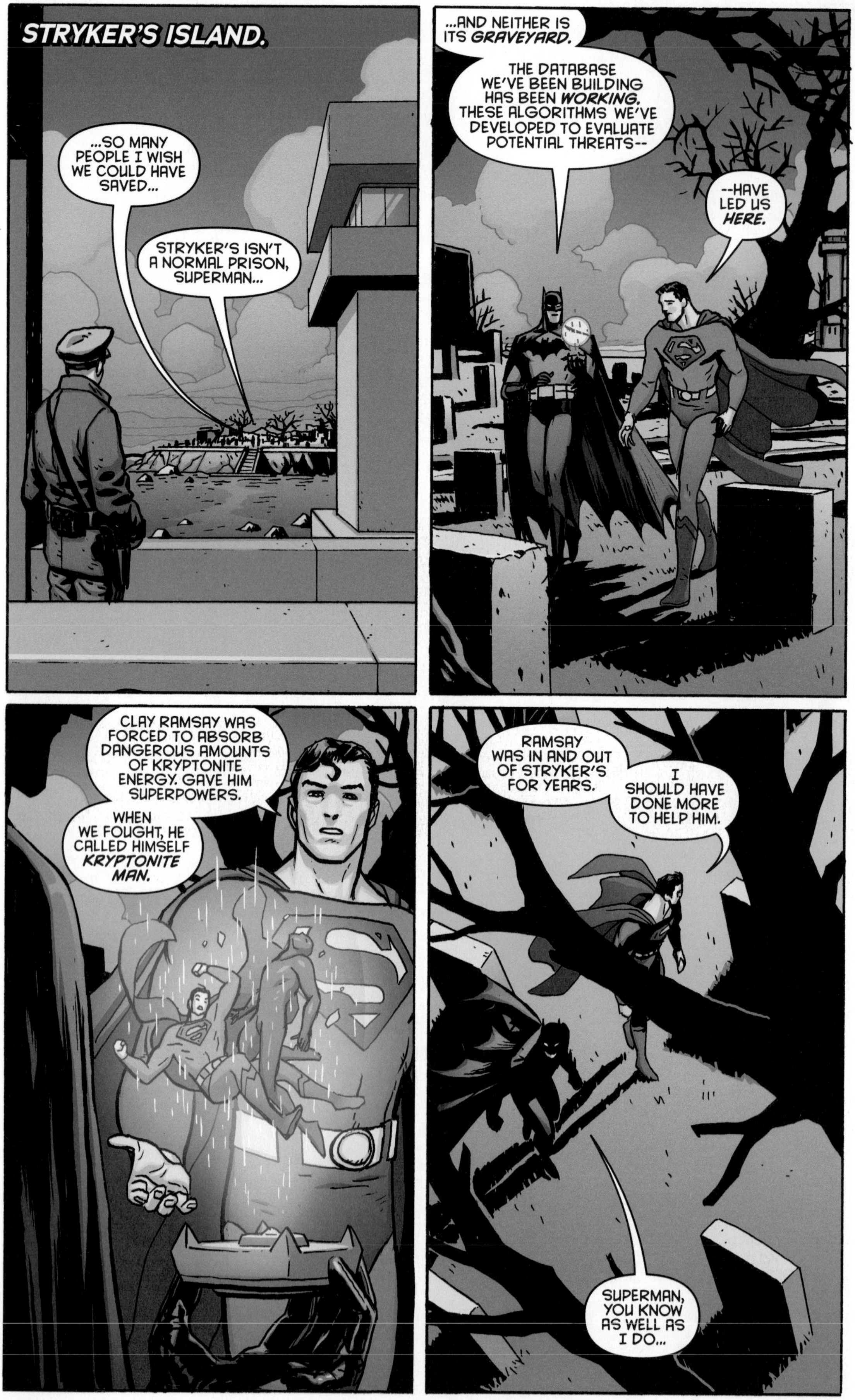
STRYKER'S ISLAND.
STRYKER'S ISN'T A NORMAL PRISON, SUPERMAN...
...SO MANY PEOPLE I WISH WE COULD HAVE SAVED...
...AND NEITHER IS ITS GRAVEYARD.
THE DATABASE WE'VE BEEN BUILDING HAS BEEN WORKING. THESE ALGORITHMS WE'VE DEVELOPED TO EVALUATE POTENTIAL THREATS--
--HAVE LED US HERE.
CLAY RAMSAY WAS FORCED TO ABSORB DANGEROUS AMOUNTS OF KRYPTONITE ENERGY. GAVE HIM SUPERPOWERS.
WHEN WE FOUGHT, HE CALLED HIMSELF KRYPTONITE MAN.
RAMSAY WAS IN AND OUT OF STRYKER'S FOR YEARS.
I SHOULD HAVE DONE MORE TO HELP HIM.
SUPERMAN, YOU KNOW AS WELL AS I DO...

...CLAY RAMSAY WAS A DEAD MAN WALKING THE MOMENT HE WAS CAUGHT IN THAT EXPLOSION.*

OVER THE YEARS, RAMSAY'S BODY WENT THROUGH SOME...*CHANGES.*** BUT LOOKS LIKE PORTIONS OF IT WERE INHUMED HERE.

BUT IF ANYONE WERE TO STEAL PORTIONS OF HIS BODY, THEY COULD SIPHON OFF ANY REMAINING KRYPTONITE RADIATION AND USE IT AS A WEAPON.

*WAY BACK IN ACTION COMICS ANNUAL #1.
**SEE SUPERWOMAN VOL. 1 FOR MORE...IT WAS GROSS. --PAUL

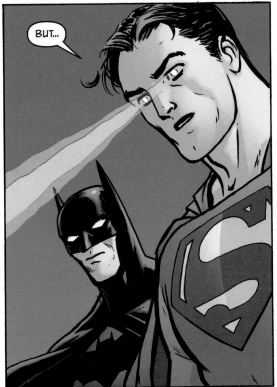

BUT...

...I CAN ALWAYS TELL WHEN I'M *NEAR* KRYPTONITE. AND RIGHT NOW, I'M FEELING...A HINT OF IT IN THE AIR.

THAT'S ODD. MY SCANNER SHOWS THE BODY IS CLEAN.

BUT WE ARE NOT THE ONLY PEOPLE TO CHECK THE GRAVE RECENTLY. SOMEONE WAS HERE...

...WITHIN THE LAST HOUR.

AND IT WOULD SEEM THEY'RE *STILL* HERE...

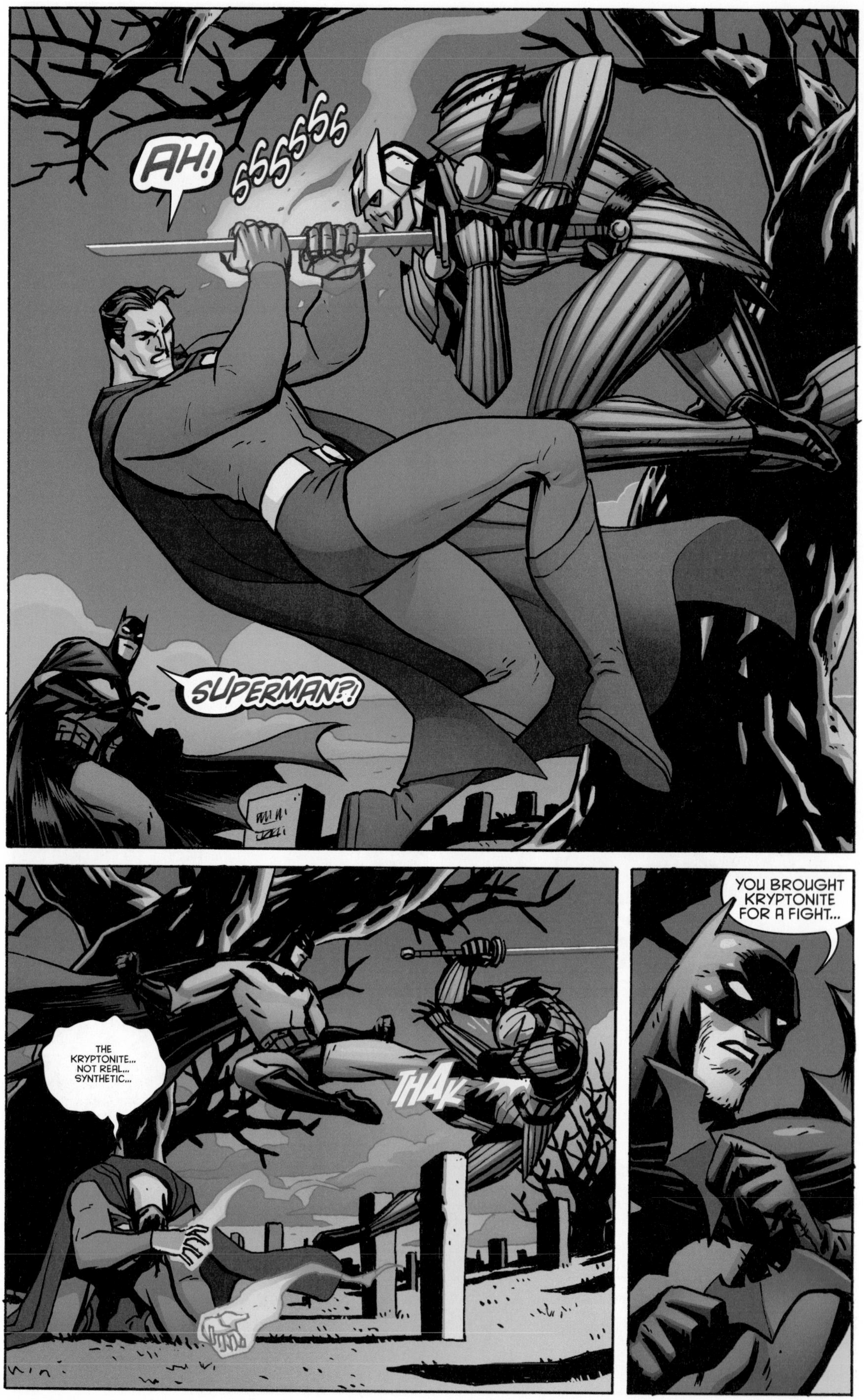
AH!
SSSSSS
SUPERMAN?!
THE KRYPTONITE... NOT REAL... SYNTHETIC...
THAK
YOU BROUGHT KRYPTONITE FOR A FIGHT...

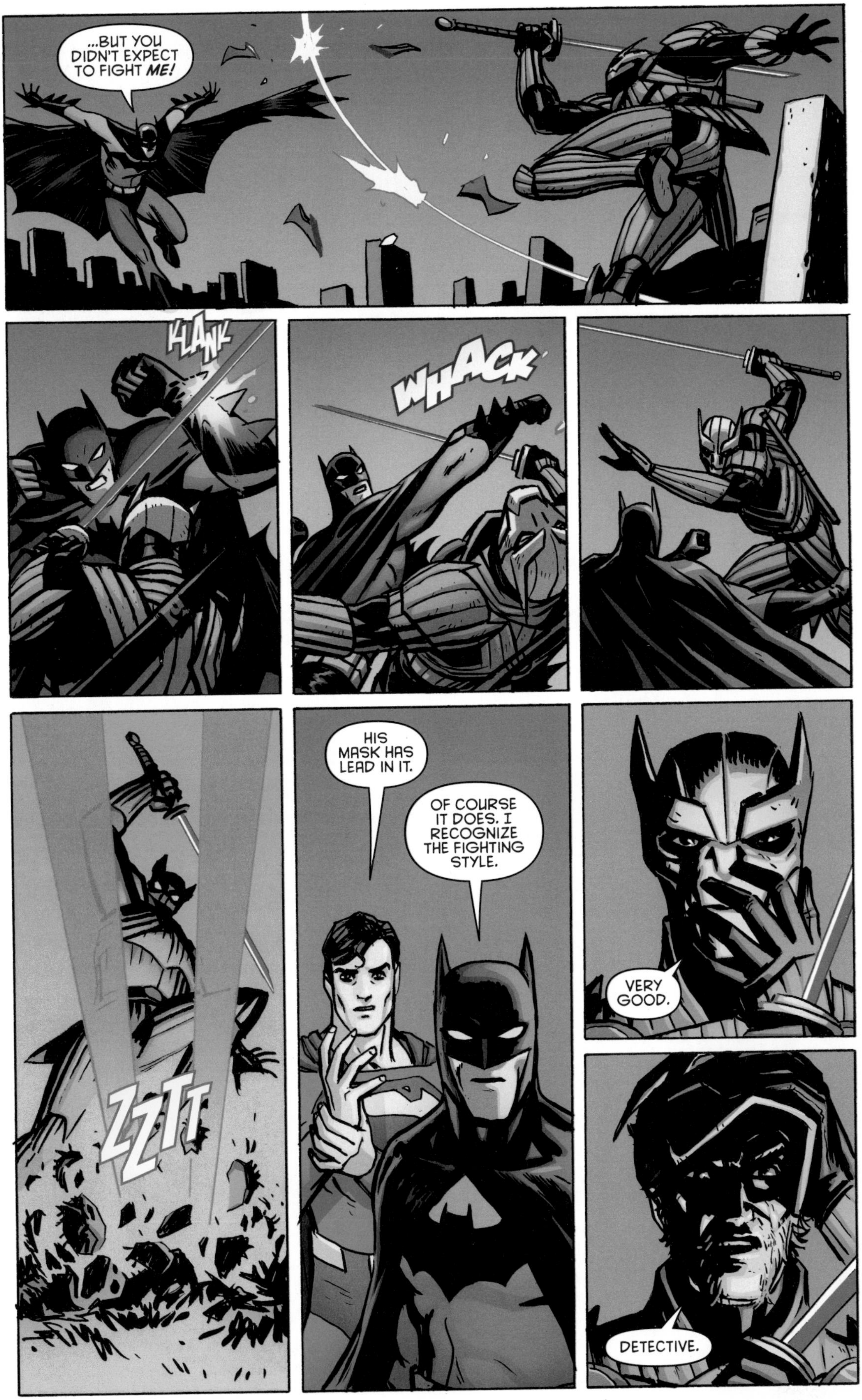
...BUT YOU DIDN'T EXPECT TO FIGHT *ME!*
KLANK
WHACK
ZZTT
HIS MASK HAS LEAD IN IT.
OF COURSE IT DOES. I RECOGNIZE THE FIGHTING STYLE.
VERY GOOD.
DETECTIVE.

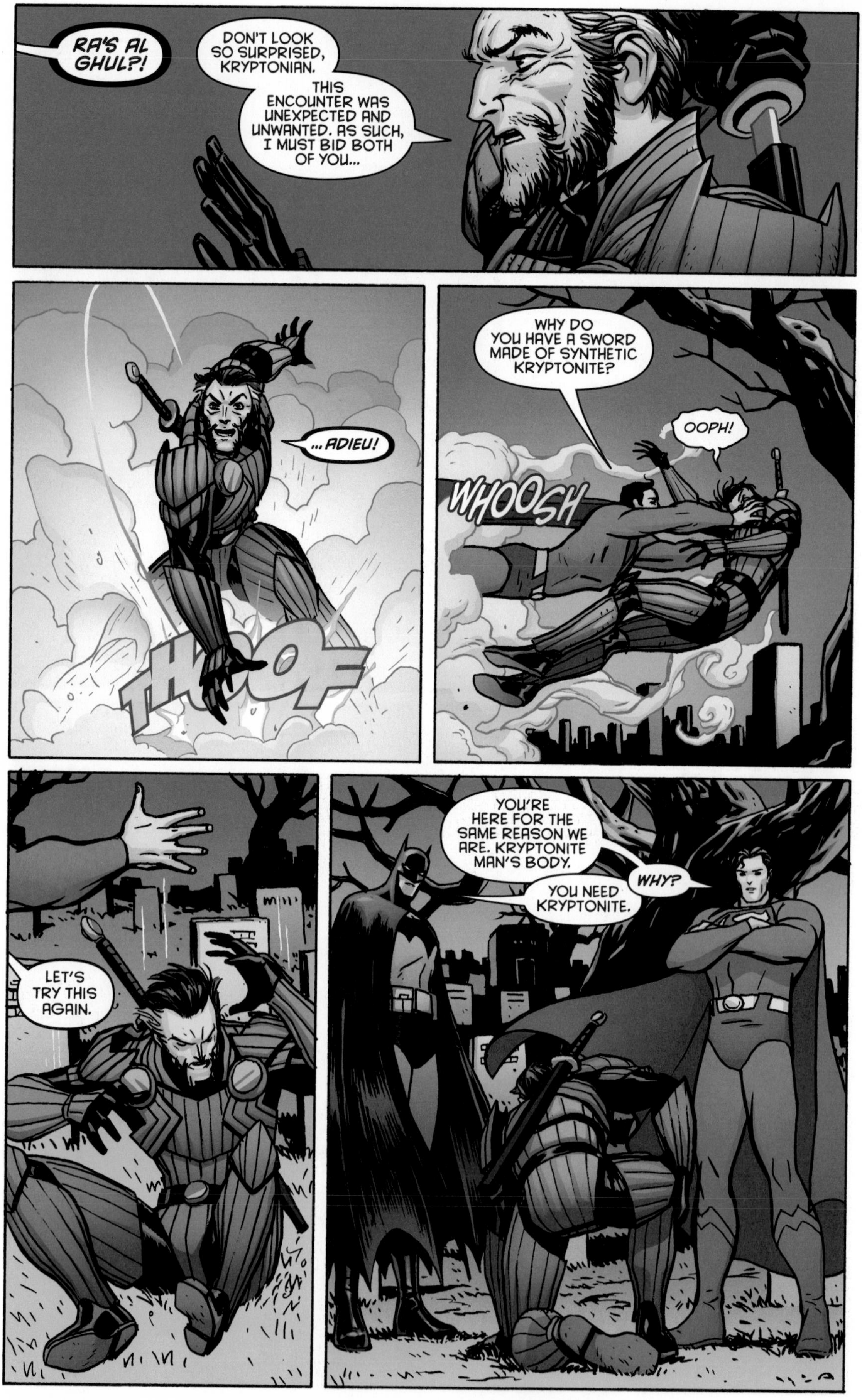
RA'S AL GHUL?!
DON'T LOOK SO SURPRISED, KRYPTONIAN.
THIS ENCOUNTER WAS UNEXPECTED AND UNWANTED. AS SUCH, I MUST BID BOTH OF YOU...
...ADIEU!
THOOF
WHY DO YOU HAVE A SWORD MADE OF SYNTHETIC KRYPTONITE?
OOPH!
WHOOSH
LET'S TRY THIS AGAIN.
YOU'RE HERE FOR THE SAME REASON WE ARE. KRYPTONITE MAN'S BODY.
WHY?
YOU NEED KRYPTONITE.

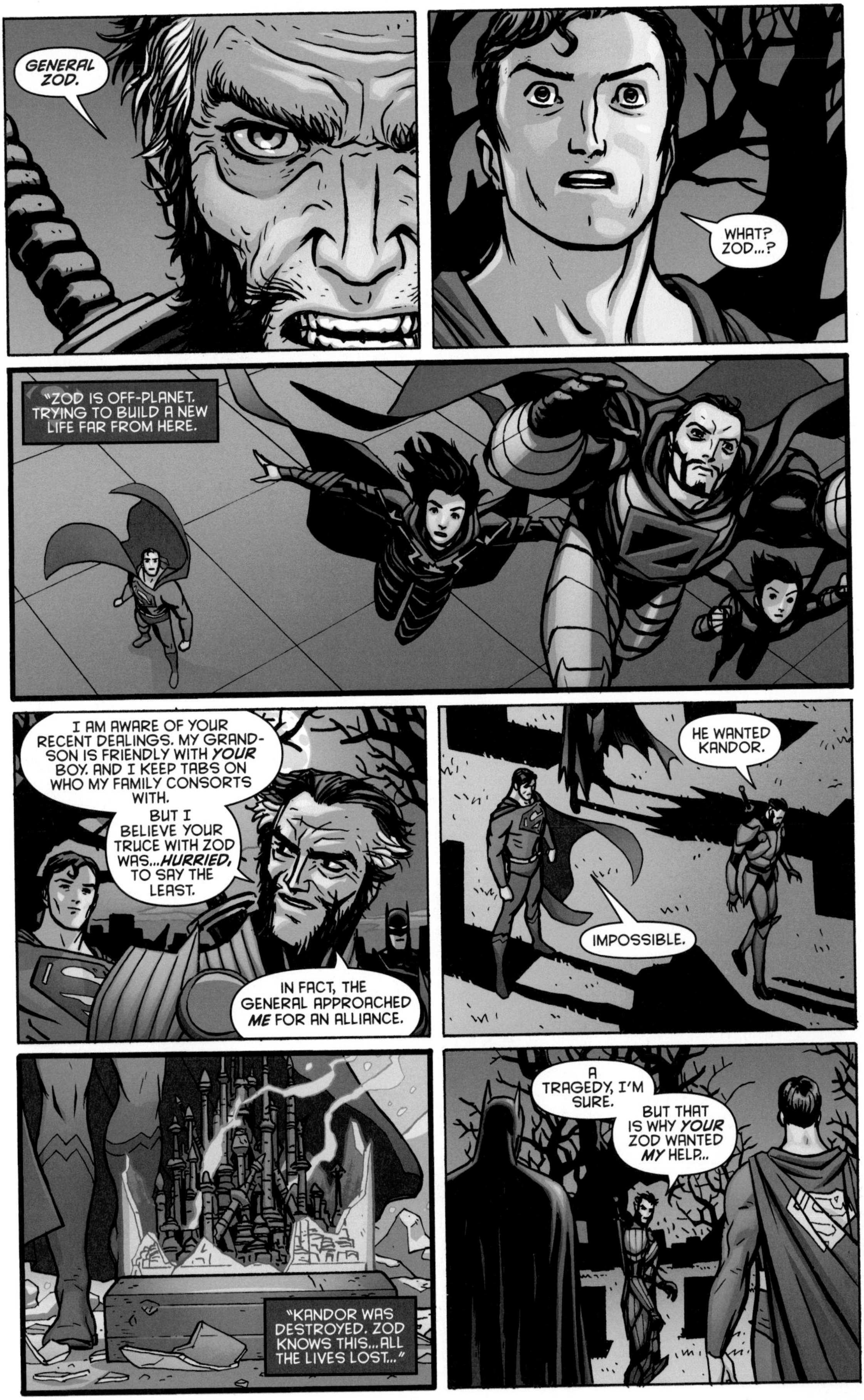
GENERAL ZOD.
WHAT? ZOD...?
"ZOD IS OFF-PLANET. TRYING TO BUILD A NEW LIFE FAR FROM HERE.
I AM AWARE OF YOUR RECENT DEALINGS. MY GRANDSON IS FRIENDLY WITH *YOUR* BOY. AND I KEEP TABS ON WHO MY FAMILY CONSORTS WITH.
BUT I BELIEVE YOUR TRUCE WITH ZOD WAS...*HURRIED,* TO SAY THE LEAST.
IN FACT, THE GENERAL APPROACHED *ME* FOR AN ALLIANCE.
HE WANTED KANDOR.
IMPOSSIBLE.
"KANDOR WAS DESTROYED. ZOD KNOWS THIS...ALL THE LIVES LOST..."
A TRAGEDY, I'M SURE.
BUT THAT IS WHY *YOUR* ZOD WANTED *MY* HELP...

"HE DEMANDED TO USE MY LAZARUS PITS TO RESURRECT KANDOR.

"I HAVE NO NEED FOR A FALLEN GENERAL, AND IN FACT... I BELIEVE *MORE* KRYPTONIANS WOULD BE A WASTE OF OUR PLANET'S RESOURCES. SO I REJECTED HIS OFFER.

"I KNOW ALL TOO WELL WHAT THE LAZARUS PITS CAN DO TO A MAN. THE MADNESS THAT CORRUPTS EVEN THE GREATEST SOULS.

"ZOD FORCED MY HAND. I DESTROYED THE PIT HE WANTED. BUT THERE ARE MORE, AND HE WILL NOT REST UNTIL HE FINDS THEM.

AND IF YOU WILL NOT HELP ME TAKE CARE OF YOUR KIN, THEN I WILL FIND *OTHER* WAYS TO DEAL WITH THE KRYPTONIAN.

THERE IS *NO TIME* FOR OUR GAMES, DETECTIVE. ZOD IS ALREADY ON THE HUNT FOR A LAZARUS PIT AND I'M TRAILING BEHIND.

YOU'RE NOT GOING ANYWHERE EXCEPT TO THE *AUTHORITIES*, RA'S.

THEN *WE'LL* DEAL WITH ZOD.

THE BATPLANE IS ON THE WAY HERE--

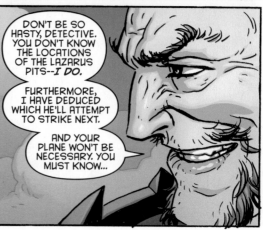

DON'T BE SO HASTY, DETECTIVE. YOU DON'T KNOW THE LOCATIONS OF THE LAZARUS PITS--*I DO.*

FURTHERMORE, I HAVE DEDUCED WHICH HE'LL ATTEMPT TO STRIKE NEXT.

AND YOUR PLANE WON'T BE NECESSARY. YOU MUST KNOW...

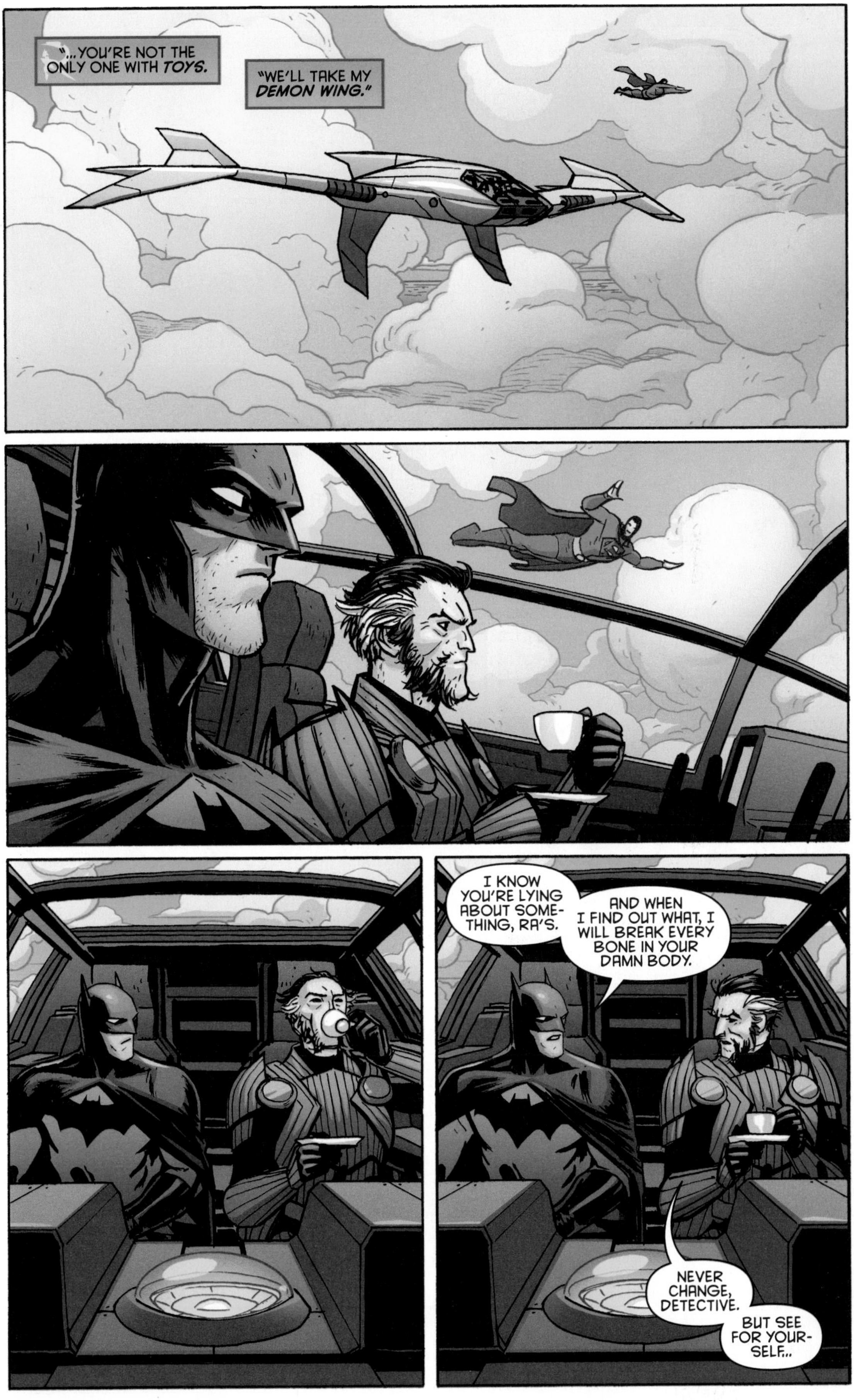
"...YOU'RE NOT THE ONLY ONE WITH *TOYS*.
"WE'LL TAKE MY *DEMON WING*."
I KNOW YOU'RE LYING ABOUT SOME-THING, RA'S.
AND WHEN I FIND OUT WHAT, I WILL BREAK EVERY BONE IN YOUR DAMN BODY.
NEVER CHANGE, DETECTIVE.
BUT SEE FOR YOUR-SELF...

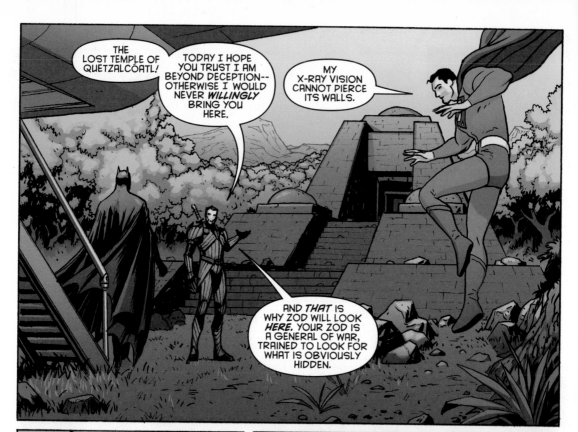

THE LOST TEMPLE OF QUETZALCÓATL!

TODAY I HOPE YOU TRUST I AM BEYOND DECEPTION-- OTHERWISE I WOULD NEVER *WILLINGLY* BRING YOU HERE.

MY X-RAY VISION CANNOT PIERCE ITS WALLS.

AND *THAT* IS WHY ZOD WILL LOOK *HERE*. YOUR ZOD IS A GENERAL OF WAR, TRAINED TO LOOK FOR WHAT IS OBVIOUSLY HIDDEN.

YOU USED *MAGIC* ON THE TEMPLE, DIDN'T YOU?

MY LAZARUS PITS ARE THE LIFE-BLOOD OF MY LEGACY. *NO ONE* CAN DISTURB THEM.

THEY'RE UNDER THE PROTECTION OF THE *LEAGUE OF LAZARUS*. MEN I HAVE PERSONALLY TRAINED SINCE BIRTH TO KEEP THE PITS SAFE.

IF ANYONE, HUMAN *OR* ALIEN, WERE TO BREACH THE OUTER DEFENSES, THESE ELITE SOLDIERS WOULD MAKE SHORT WORK OF THEM. THEY PROTECT THE PITS WITH THEIR--

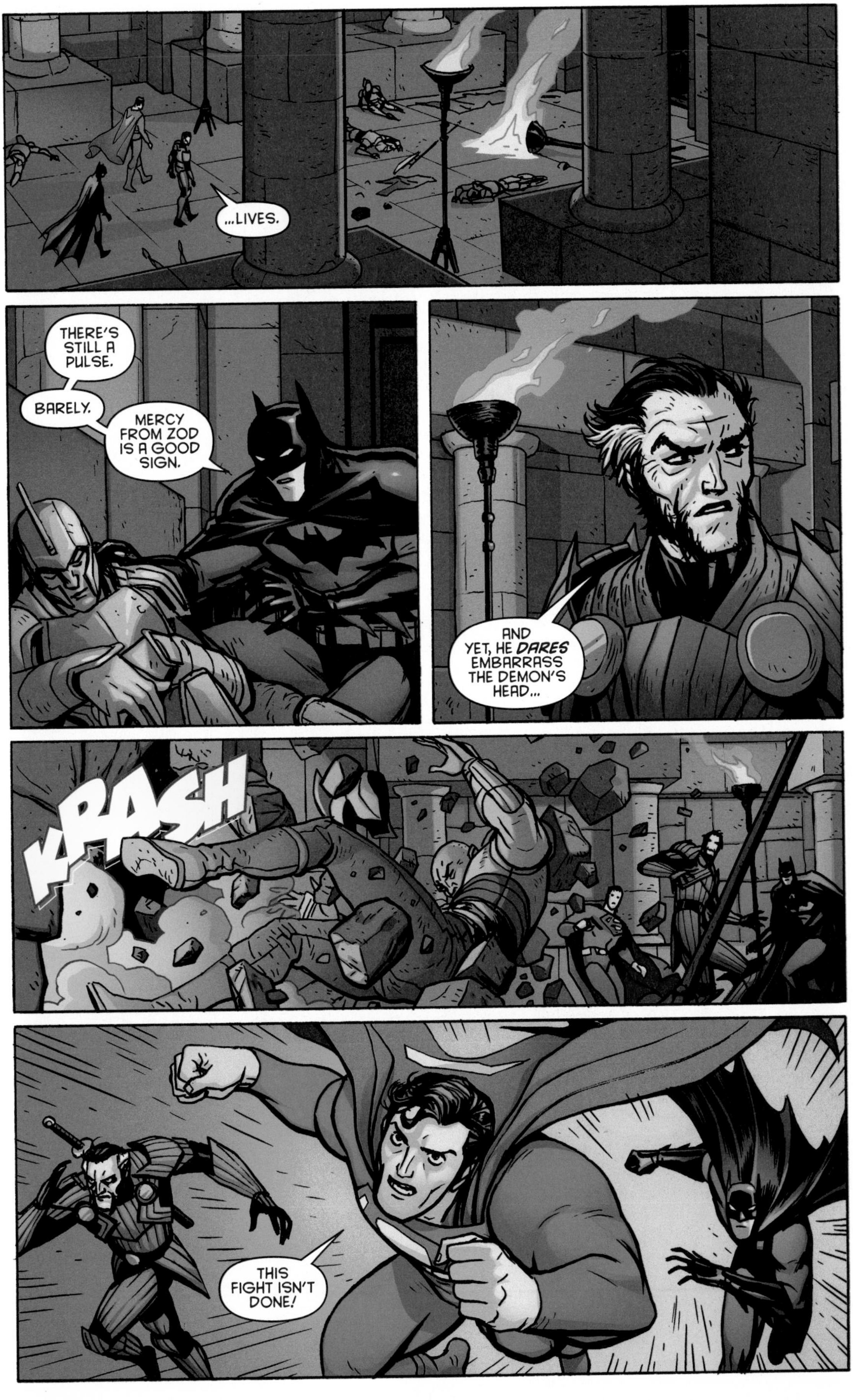

...LIVES.
THERE'S STILL A PULSE.
BARELY.
MERCY FROM ZOD IS A GOOD SIGN.
AND YET, HE *DARES* EMBARRASS THE DEMON'S HEAD...
KRASH
THIS FIGHT ISN'T DONE!

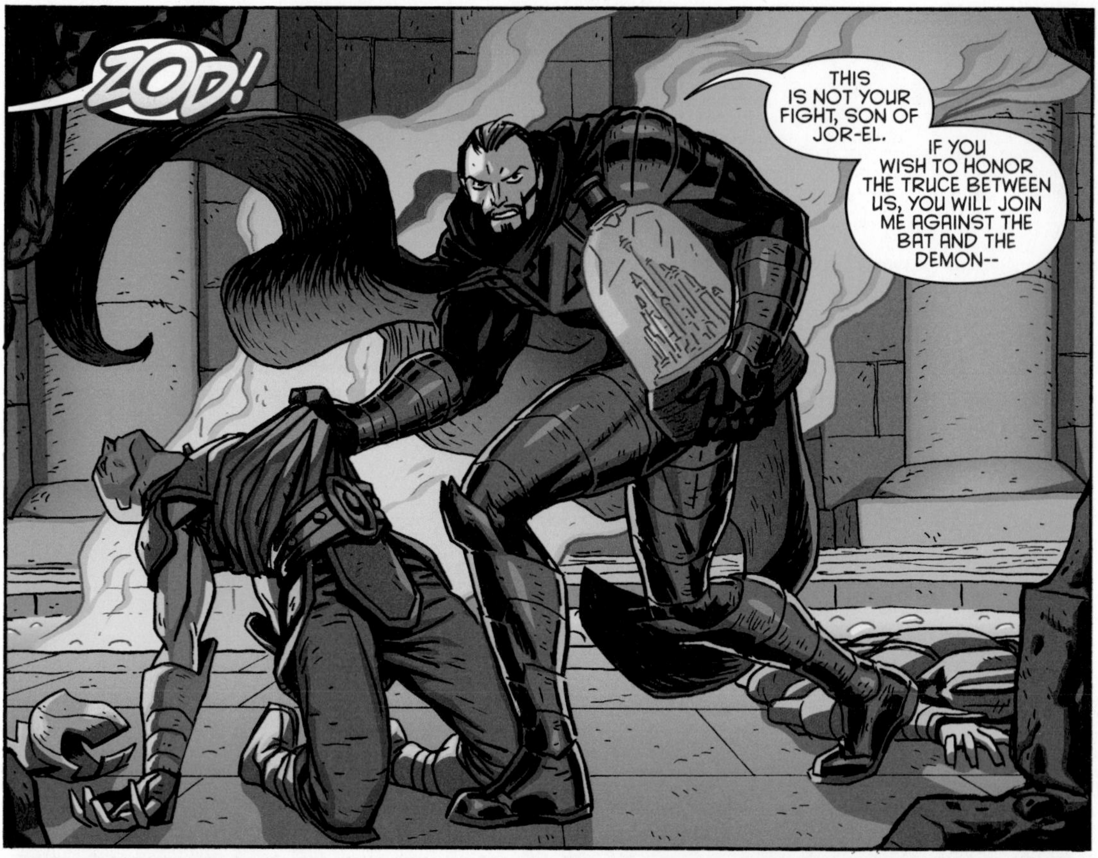
ZOD!
THIS IS NOT YOUR FIGHT, SON OF JOR-EL.
IF YOU WISH TO HONOR THE TRUCE BETWEEN US, YOU WILL JOIN ME AGAINST THE BAT AND THE DEMON--

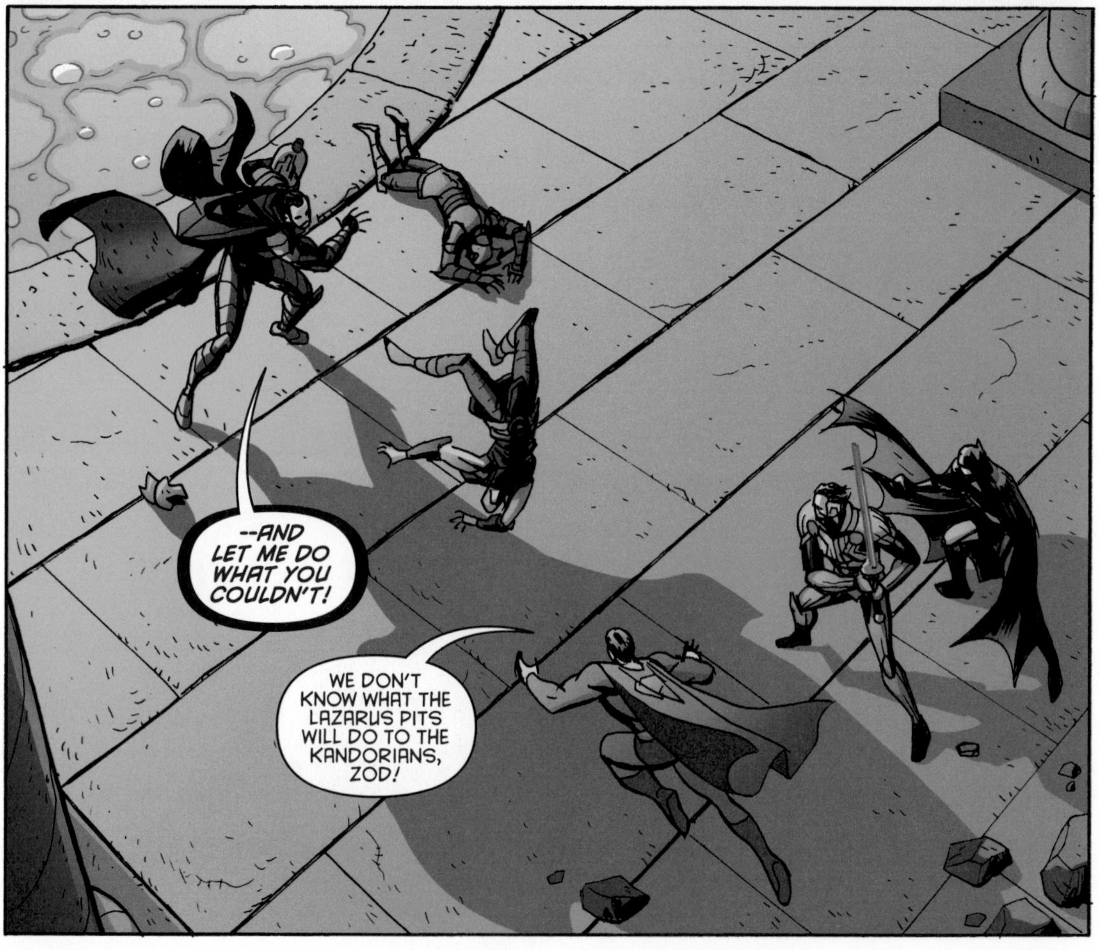
--AND LET ME DO WHAT YOU COULDN'T!
WE DON'T KNOW WHAT THE LAZARUS PITS WILL DO TO THE KANDORIANS, ZOD!

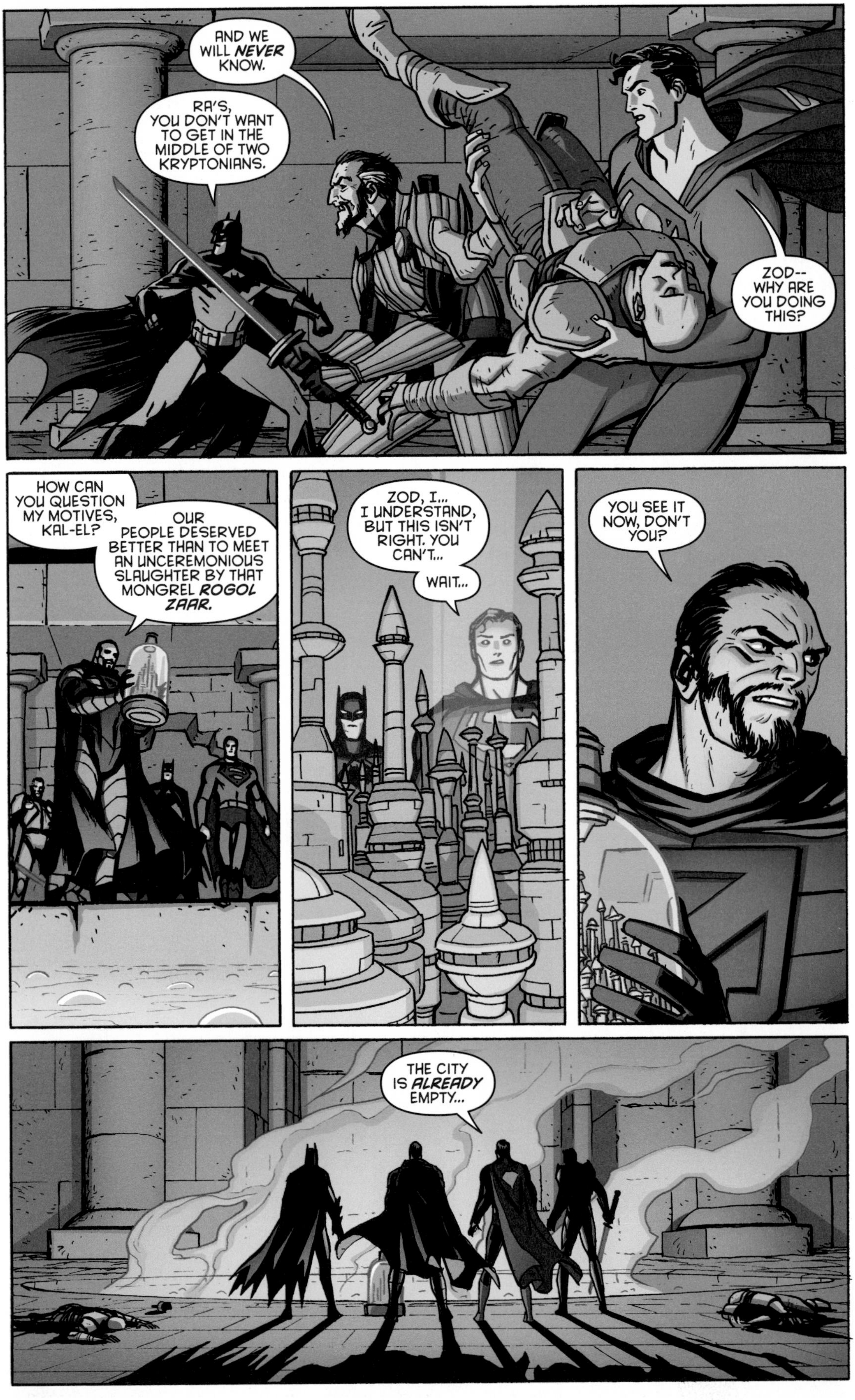

AND WE WILL *NEVER* KNOW.
RA'S, YOU DON'T WANT TO GET IN THE MIDDLE OF TWO KRYPTONIANS.
ZOD-- WHY ARE YOU DOING THIS?
HOW CAN YOU QUESTION MY MOTIVES, KAL-EL?
OUR PEOPLE DESERVED BETTER THAN TO MEET AN UNCEREMONIOUS SLAUGHTER BY THAT MONGREL *ROGOL ZAAR.*
ZOD, I... I UNDERSTAND, BUT THIS ISN'T RIGHT. YOU CAN'T...
WAIT...
YOU SEE IT NOW, DON'T YOU?
THE CITY IS *ALREADY* EMPTY...

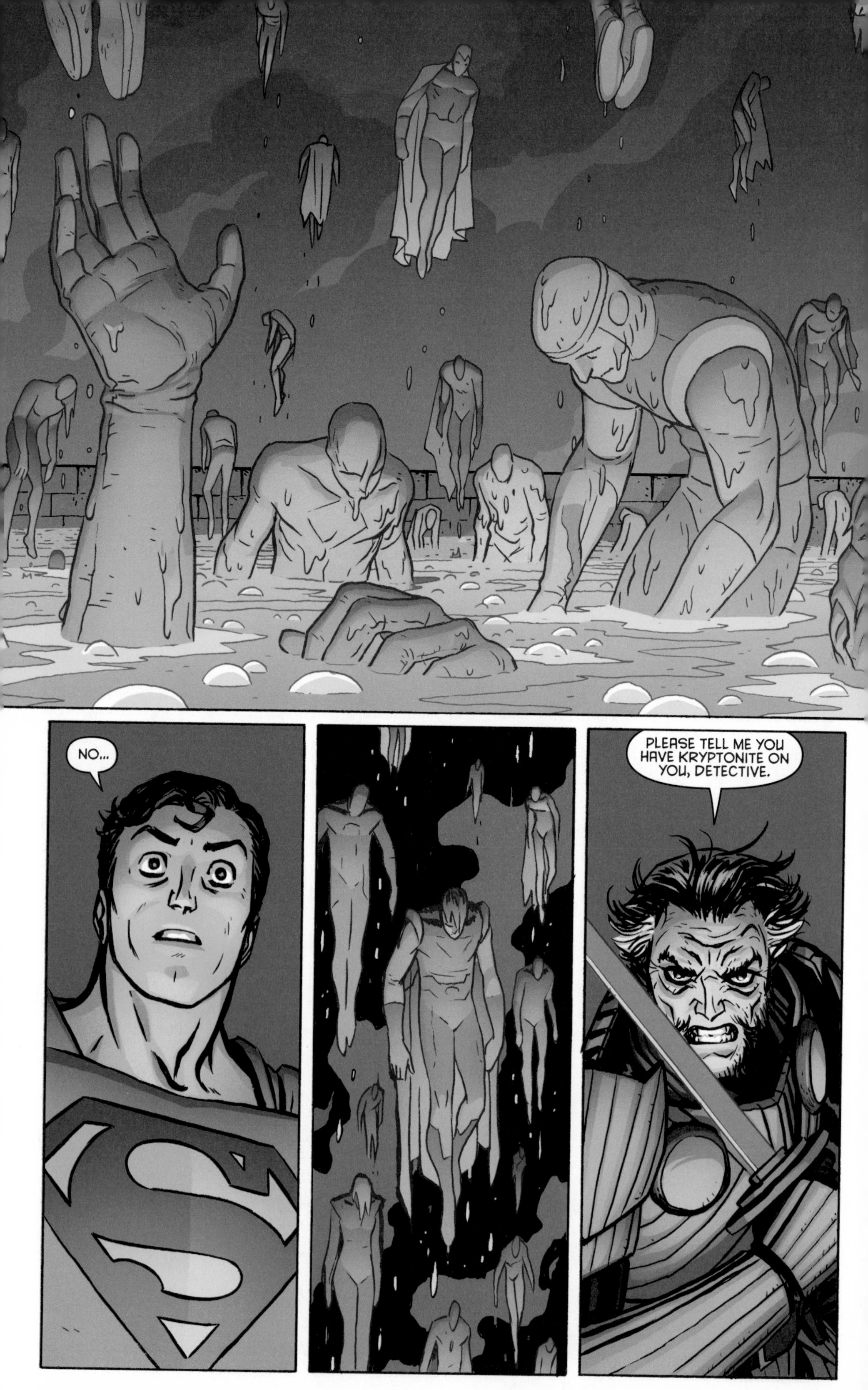
NO...
PLEASE TELL ME YOU HAVE KRYPTONITE ON YOU, DETECTIVE.

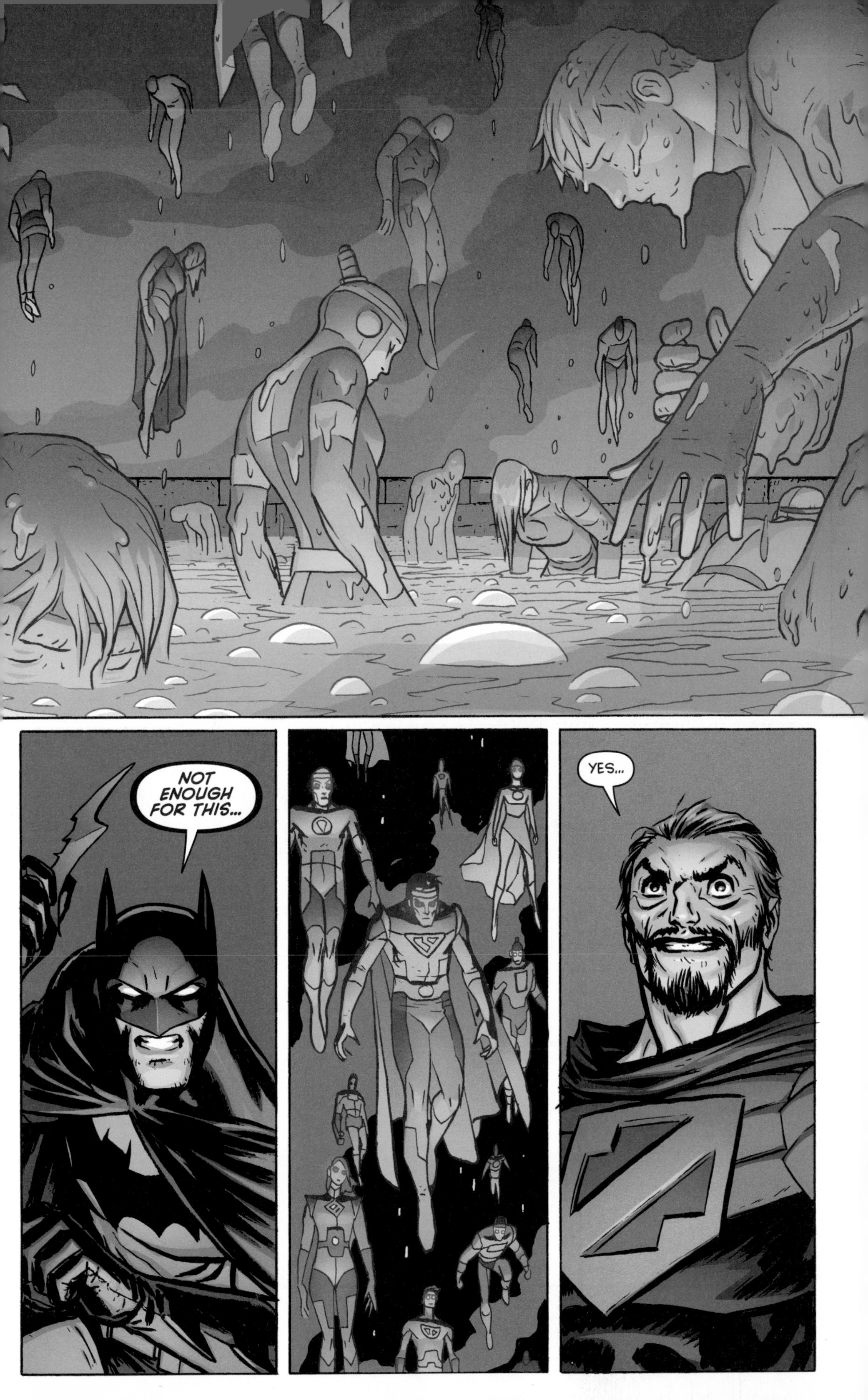
NOT ENOUGH FOR THIS...
YES...

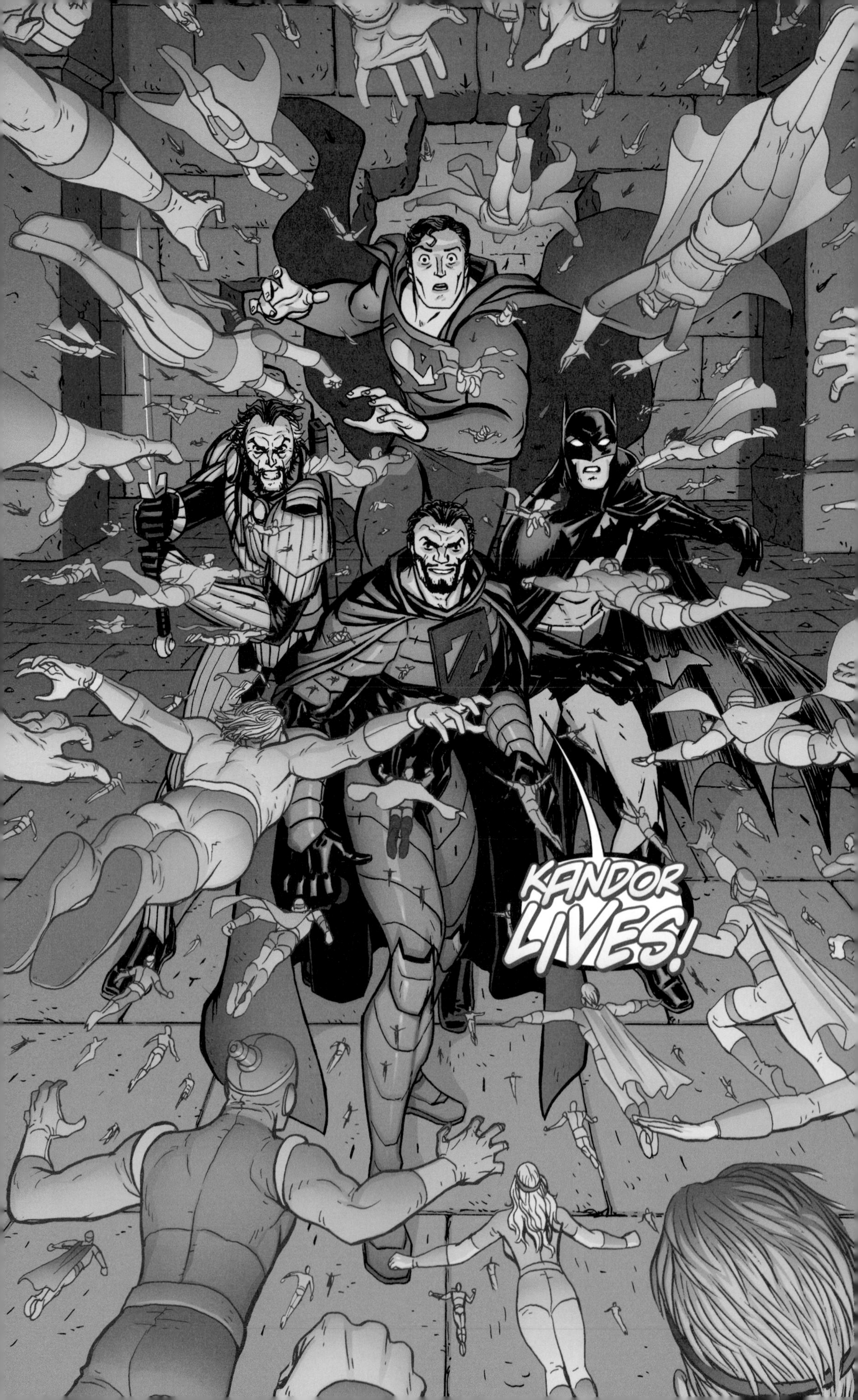
KANDOR LIVES!

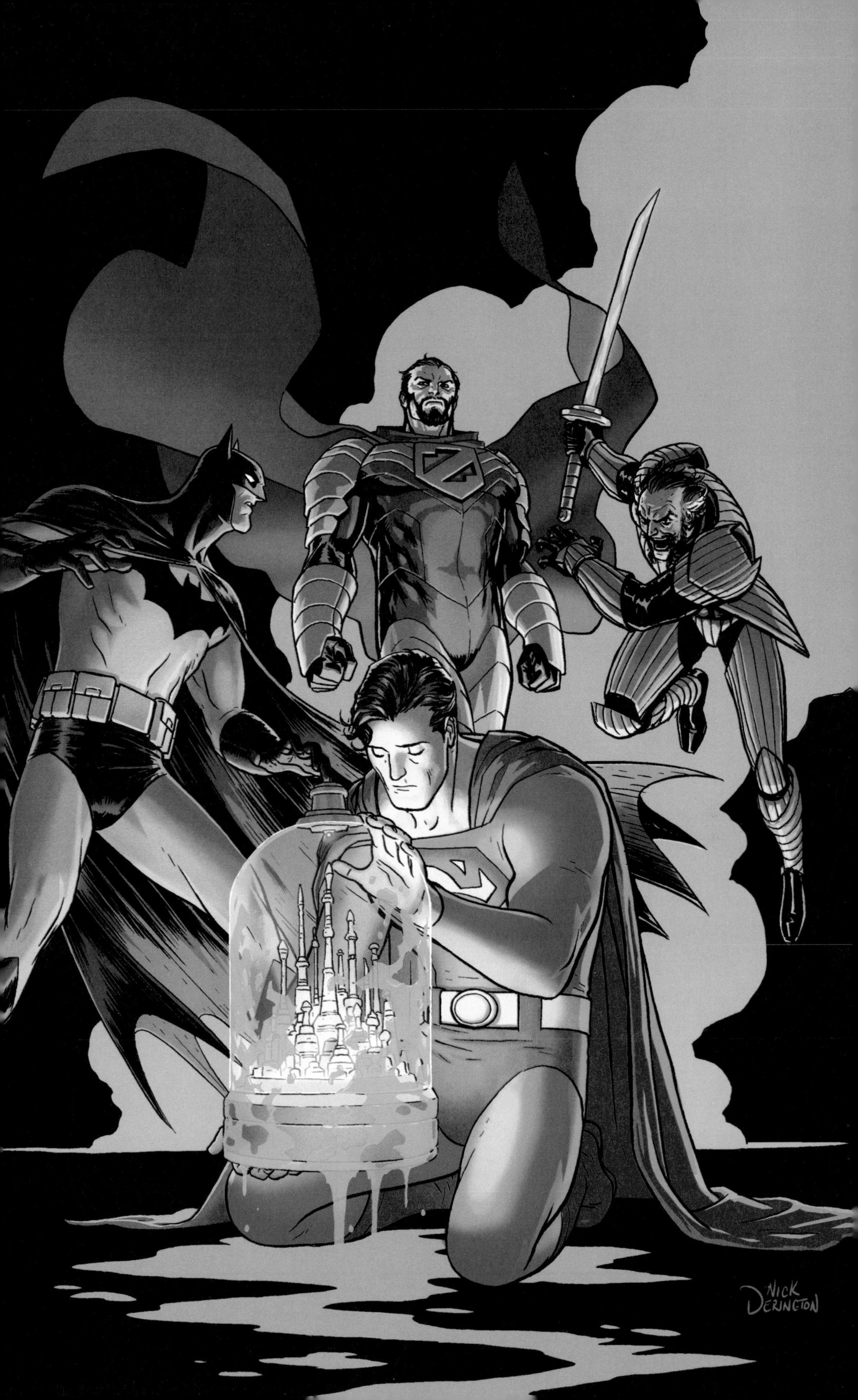

BATMAN/SUPERMAN #8

cover by
NICK DERINGTON

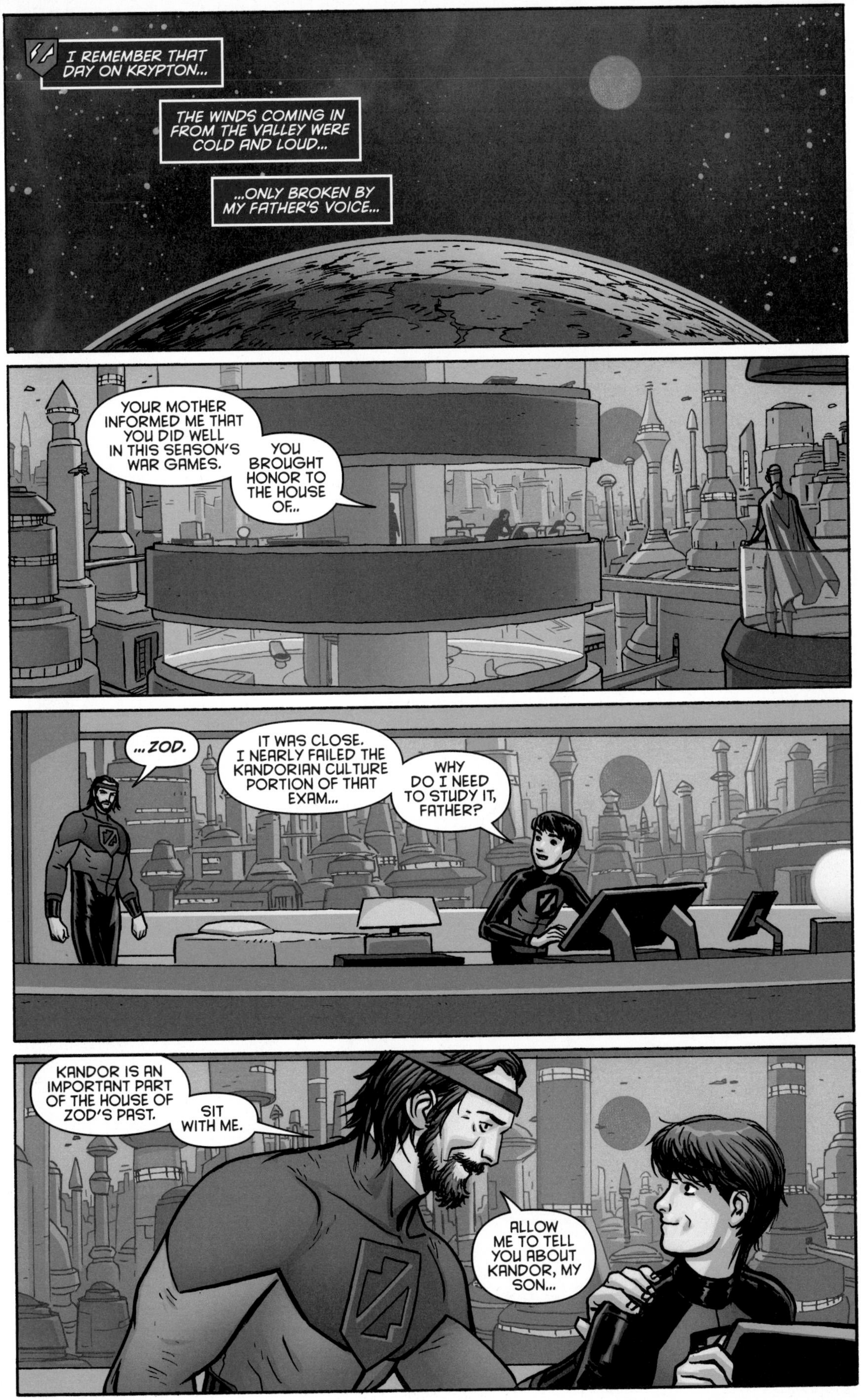
I REMEMBER THAT DAY ON KRYPTON...
THE WINDS COMING IN FROM THE VALLEY WERE COLD AND LOUD...
...ONLY BROKEN BY MY FATHER'S VOICE...
YOUR MOTHER INFORMED ME THAT YOU DID WELL IN THIS SEASON'S WAR GAMES.
YOU BROUGHT HONOR TO THE HOUSE OF...
...ZOD.
IT WAS CLOSE. I NEARLY FAILED THE KANDORIAN CULTURE PORTION OF THAT EXAM...
WHY DO I NEED TO STUDY IT, FATHER?
KANDOR IS AN IMPORTANT PART OF THE HOUSE OF ZOD'S PAST.
SIT WITH ME.
ALLOW ME TO TELL YOU ABOUT KANDOR, MY SON...

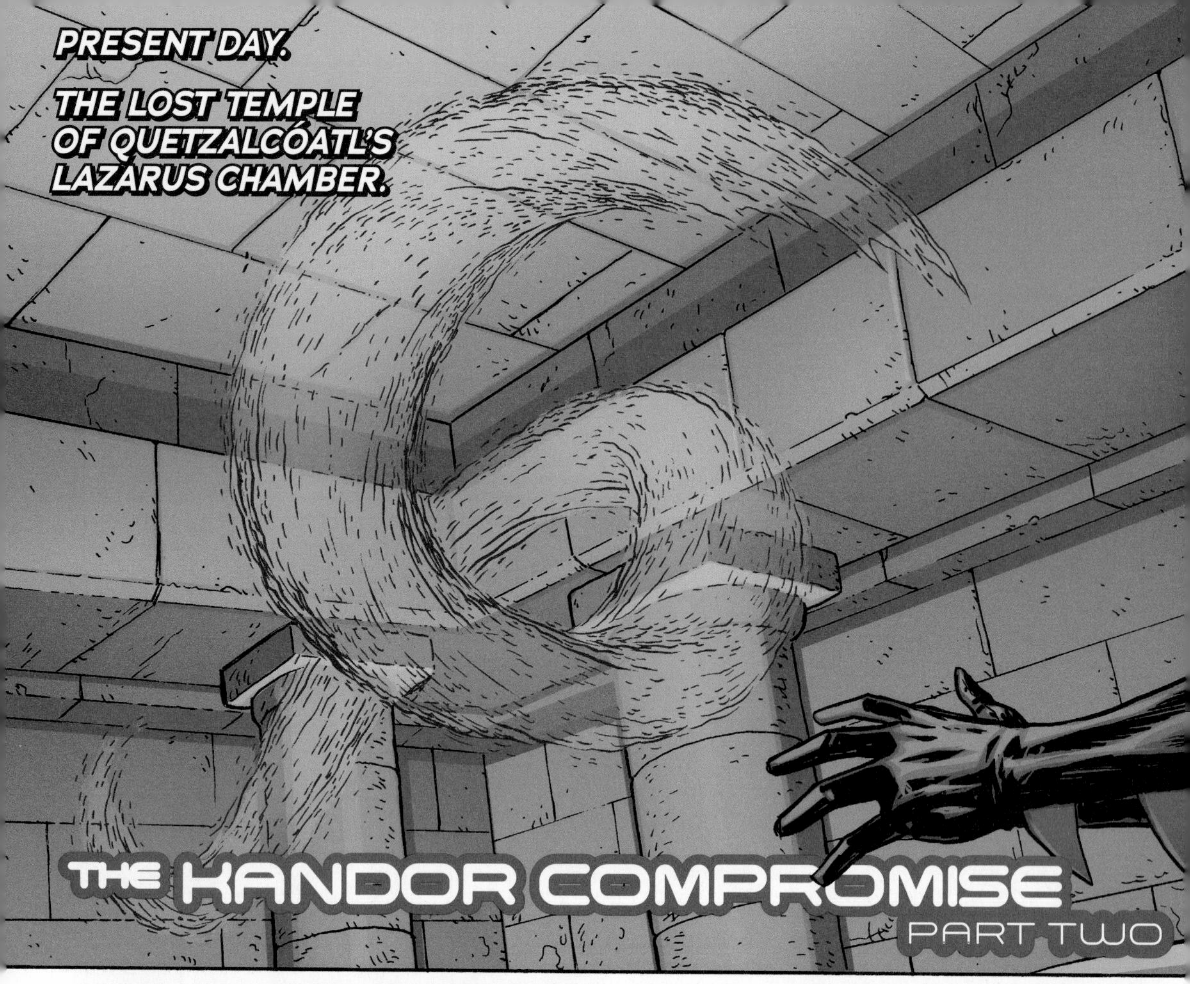
PRESENT DAY.
THE LOST TEMPLE OF QUETZALCÓATL'S LAZARUS CHAMBER.
THE KANDOR COMPROMISE
PART TWO

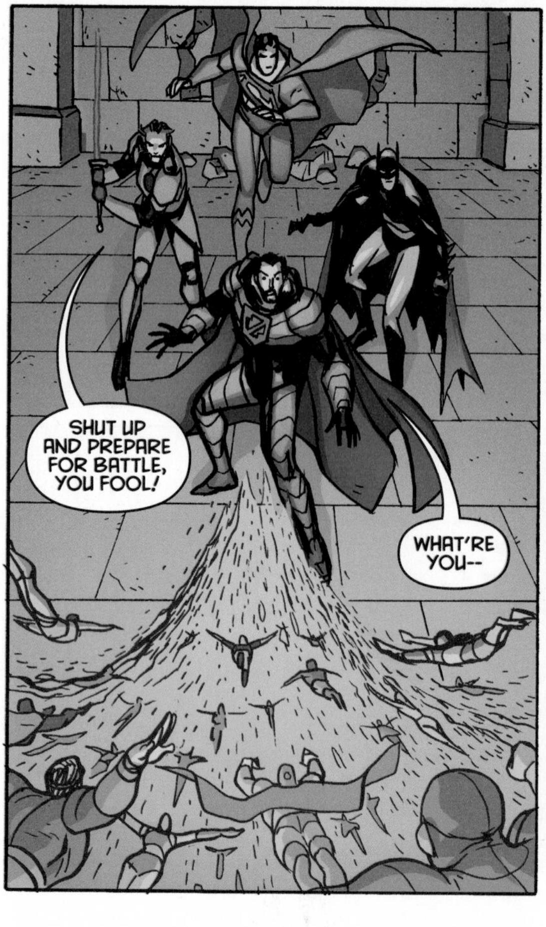
SHUT UP AND PREPARE FOR BATTLE, YOU FOOL!
WHAT'RE YOU--

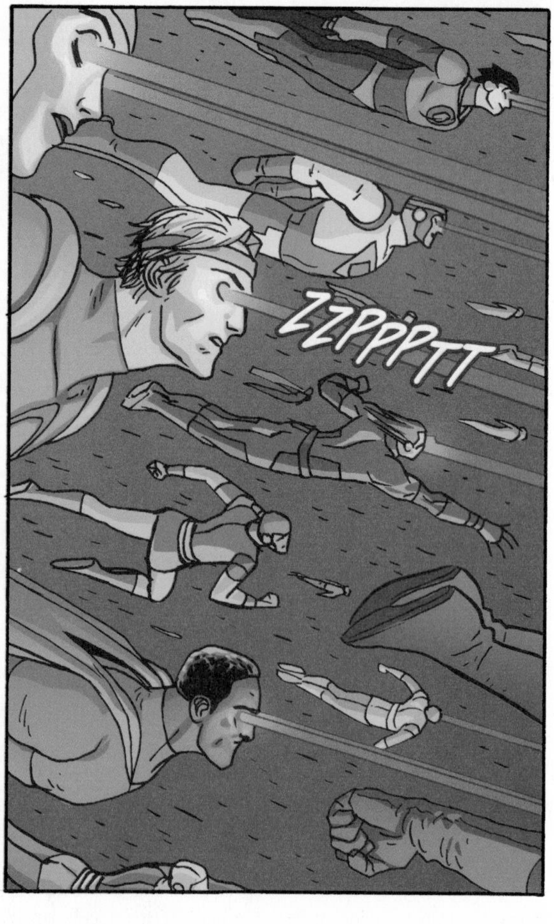
ZZPPPPTT

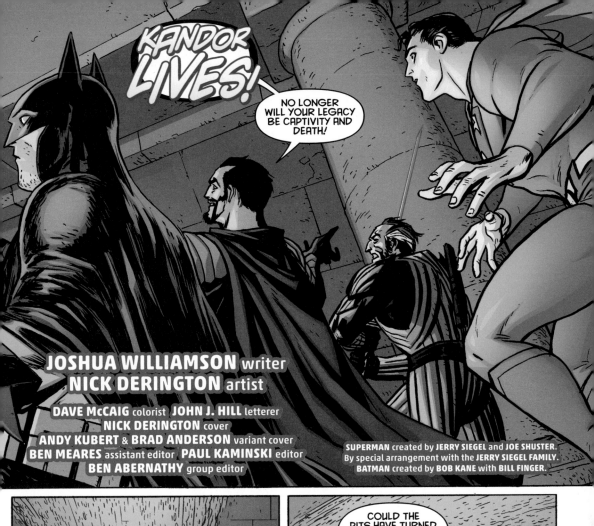

KANDOR LIVES!

NO LONGER WILL YOUR LEGACY BE CAPTIVITY AND DEATH!

JOSHUA WILLIAMSON writer
NICK DERINGTON artist

DAVE McCAIG colorist **JOHN J. HILL** letterer
NICK DERINGTON cover
ANDY KUBERT & BRAD ANDERSON variant cover
BEN MEARES assistant editor **PAUL KAMINSKI** editor
BEN ABERNATHY group editor

SUPERMAN created by JERRY SIEGEL and JOE SHUSTER.
By special arrangement with the JERRY SIEGEL FAMILY.
BATMAN created by BOB KANE with BILL FINGER.

ZZPT-TSH

THEY HAVE POWERS ALREADY?!

COULD THE PITS HAVE TURNED THE DORMANT RED SUN ENERGY INTO YELLOW?

YOU HAD TO KNOW THIS WOULD HAPPEN, ZOD. HOW DID YOU PLAN TO CONTAIN THEM ONCE YOU--

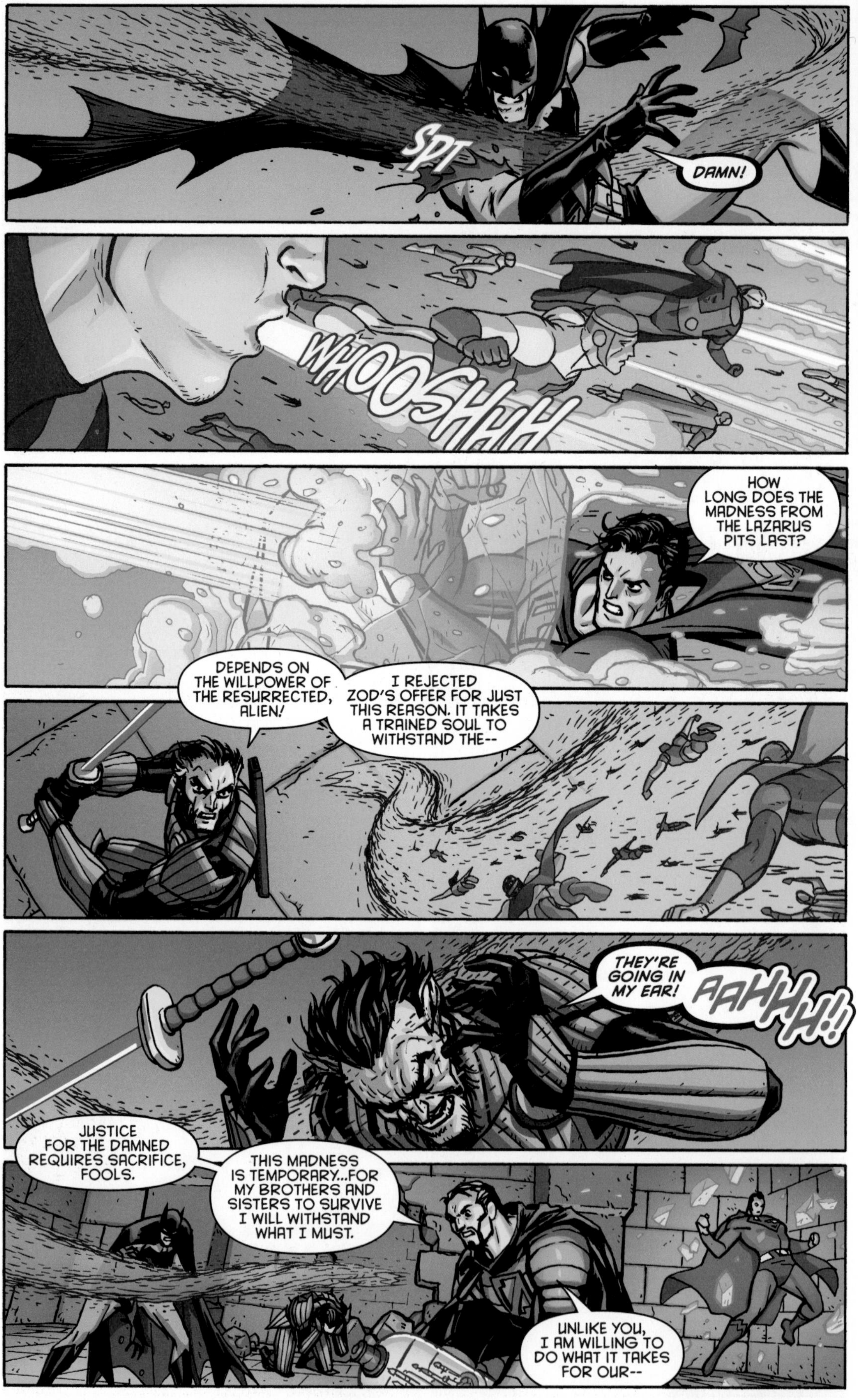
SPT
DAMN!
WHOOSHHH
HOW LONG DOES THE MADNESS FROM THE LAZARUS PITS LAST?
DEPENDS ON THE WILLPOWER OF THE RESURRECTED, ALIEN!
I REJECTED ZOD'S OFFER FOR JUST THIS REASON. IT TAKES A TRAINED SOUL TO WITHSTAND THE--
THEY'RE GOING IN MY EAR!
AAHHH!!
JUSTICE FOR THE DAMNED REQUIRES SACRIFICE, FOOLS.
THIS MADNESS IS TEMPORARY...FOR MY BROTHERS AND SISTERS TO SURVIVE I WILL WITHSTAND WHAT I MUST.
UNLIKE YOU, I AM WILLING TO DO WHAT IT TAKES FOR OUR--

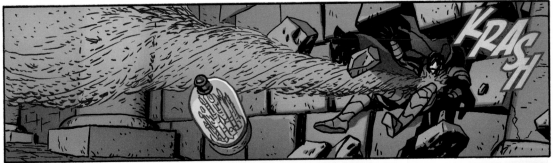

KRASH

RAH!

SPLUT

WE CAN'T LET THEM LEAVE THE TEMPLE. *WHO KNOWS* WHAT WOULD HAPPEN TO THEM IF THEY WERE FREE IN THE WORLD!

THEN YOU KNOW THE *HARD TRUTH*, DETECTIVE. THERE IS ONLY ONE SOLUTION TO THIS PROBLEM. WE USE KRYPTONITE TO *KILL* THE KANDORIANS...

"...BEFORE THEY KILL *US!*"

NO! *ZOD!*

WHY DID YOU DO THIS? WHY BRING BACK KANDOR LIKE THIS?

BECAUSE *YOU DIDN'T...*

...EVEN...

...TRY!

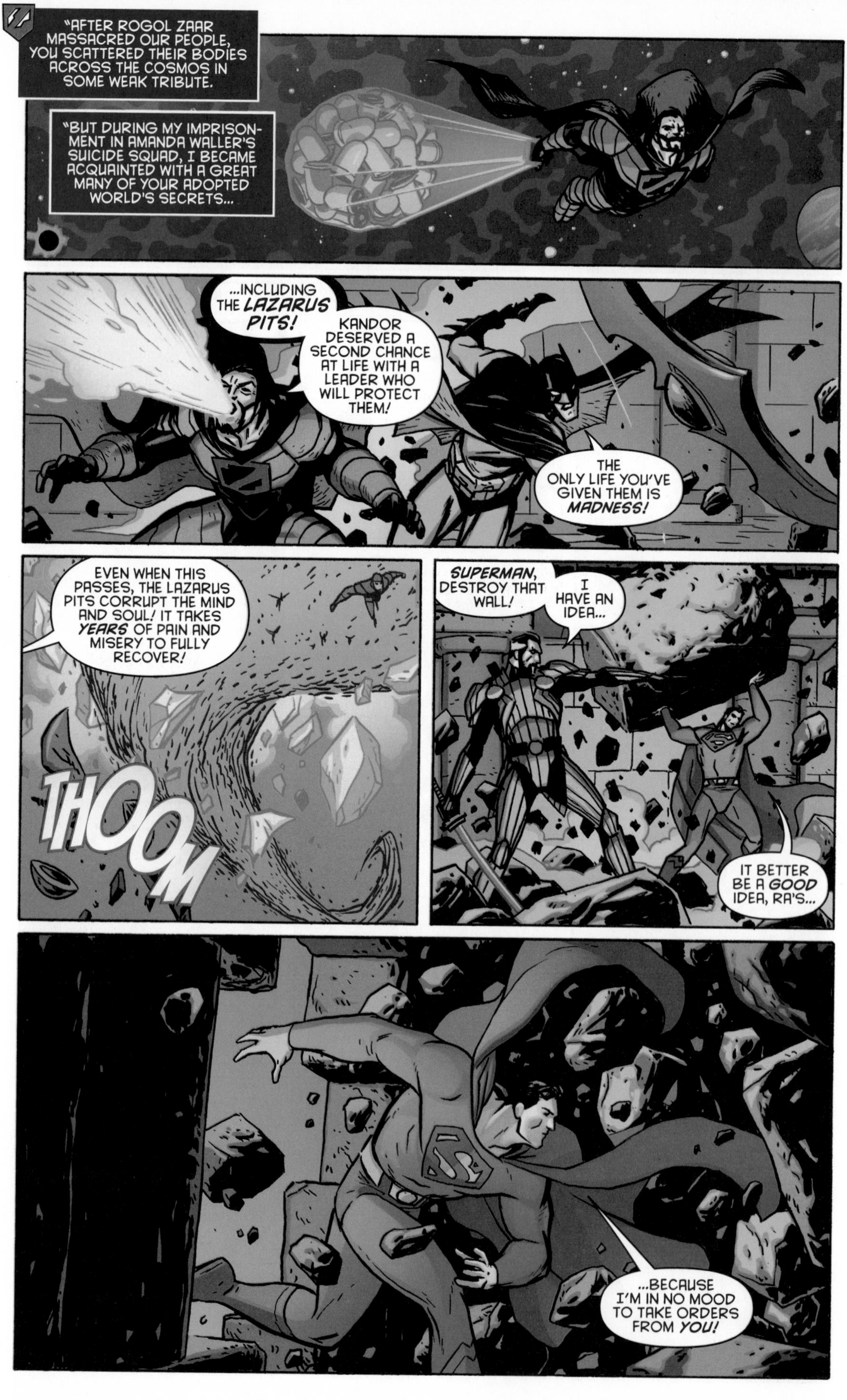
"AFTER ROGOL ZAAR MASSACRED OUR PEOPLE, YOU SCATTERED THEIR BODIES ACROSS THE COSMOS IN SOME WEAK TRIBUTE.
"BUT DURING MY IMPRISONMENT IN AMANDA WALLER'S SUICIDE SQUAD, I BECAME ACQUAINTED WITH A GREAT MANY OF YOUR ADOPTED WORLD'S SECRETS...
...INCLUDING THE LAZARUS PITS!
KANDOR DESERVED A SECOND CHANCE AT LIFE WITH A LEADER WHO WILL PROTECT THEM!
THE ONLY LIFE YOU'VE GIVEN THEM IS MADNESS!
EVEN WHEN THIS PASSES, THE LAZARUS PITS CORRUPT THE MIND AND SOUL! IT TAKES YEARS OF PAIN AND MISERY TO FULLY RECOVER!
THOOM
SUPERMAN, DESTROY THAT WALL!
I HAVE AN IDEA...
IT BETTER BE A GOOD IDEA, RA'S...
...BECAUSE I'M IN NO MOOD TO TAKE ORDERS FROM YOU!

YOU ALWAYS SEEM TO TAKE ORDERS FROM BATMAN. MY MISTAKE.

GOOD.

AH.

I BELIEVE I HAVE WHAT WE NEED IN MY ARMORY.

YOU WILL *NOT* HURT ANY OF--

IF YOU WISH FOR THEM TO REMAIN UNHARMED, YOU'LL WANT TO KEEP THEM FROM ESCAPING, SUPERMAN.

BOOM

WAIT! PLEASE! LISTEN TO ME, MY BROTHERS AND SISTERS.

I KNOW YOU'RE ANGRY. *SCARED.*

BUT IF YOU LEAVE, YOU WILL BE IN *TERRIBLE DANGER.*

YOU CAN TRUST...

TNK

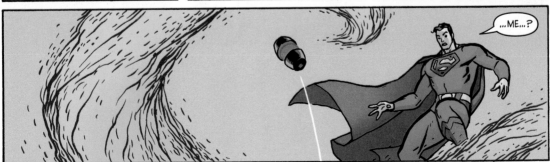

...ME...?

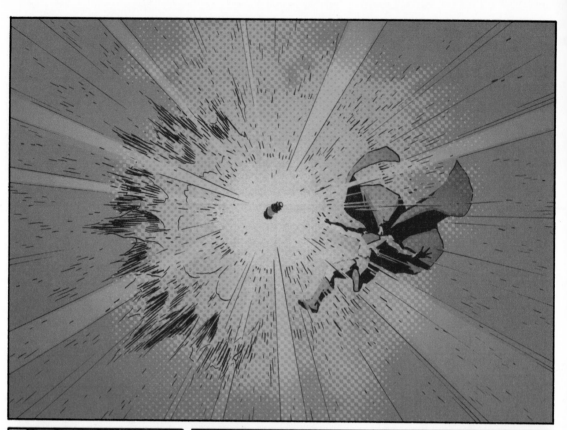

...NO...

SUPERMAN!

WHAT DID YOU DO, RA'S?

CALM YOURSELF, DETECTIVE.

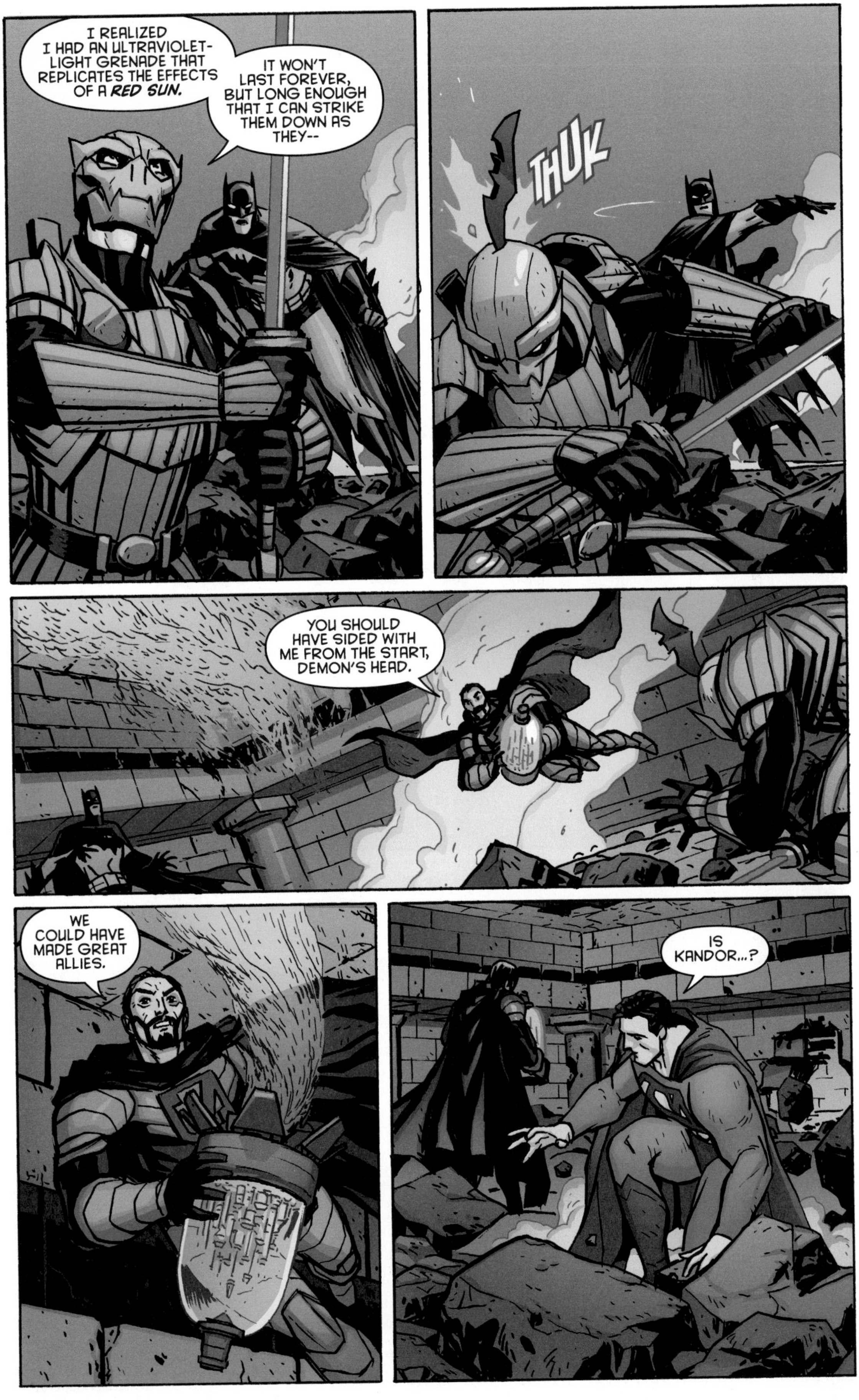
I REALIZED I HAD AN ULTRAVIOLET-LIGHT GRENADE THAT REPLICATES THE EFFECTS OF A *RED SUN.*
IT WON'T LAST FOREVER, BUT LONG ENOUGH THAT I CAN STRIKE THEM DOWN AS THEY--
THUK
YOU SHOULD HAVE SIDED WITH ME FROM THE START, DEMON'S HEAD.
WE COULD HAVE MADE GREAT ALLIES.
IS KANDOR...?

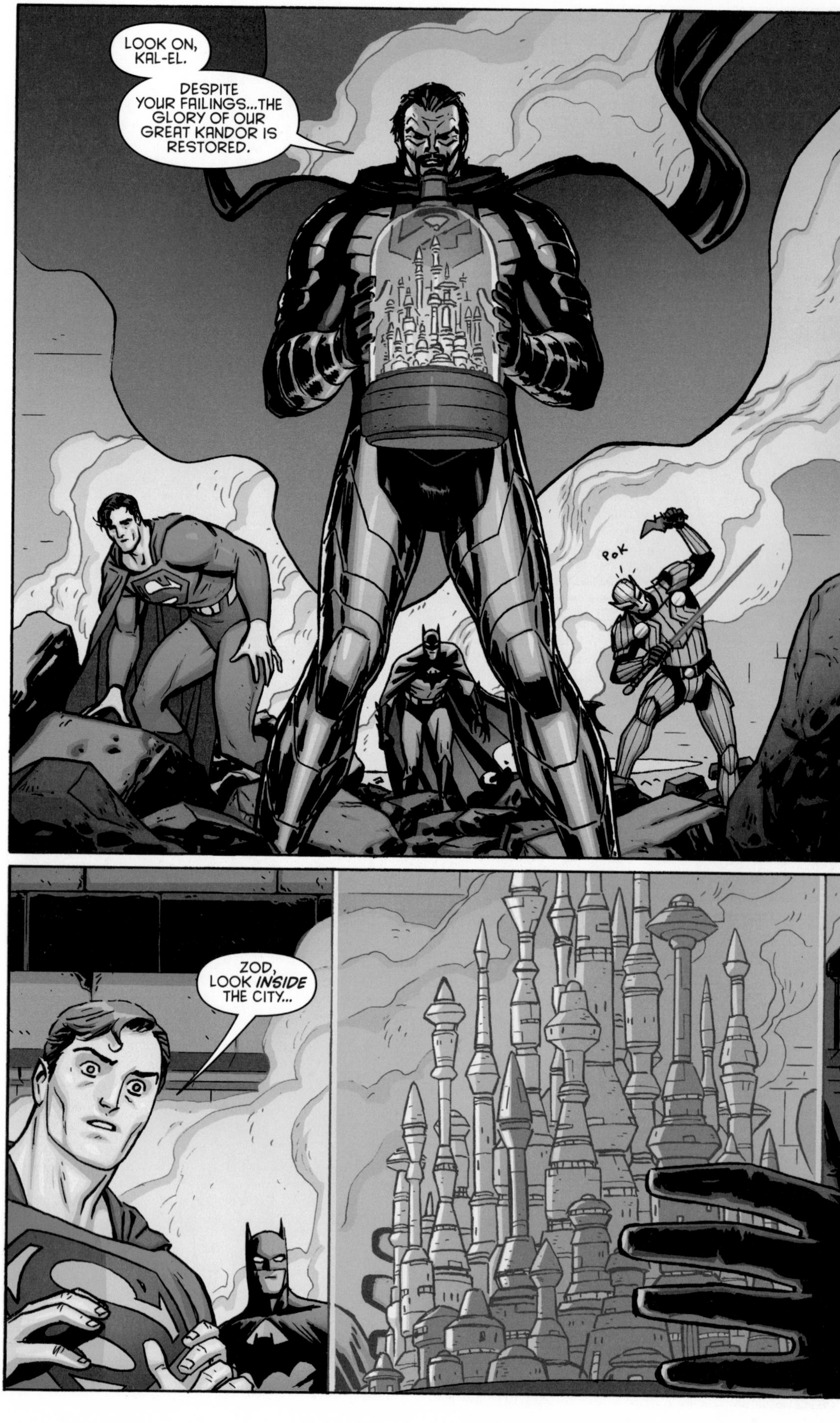
LOOK ON, KAL-EL.
DESPITE YOUR FAILINGS...THE GLORY OF OUR GREAT KANDOR IS RESTORED.
POK
ZOD, LOOK *INSIDE* THE CITY...

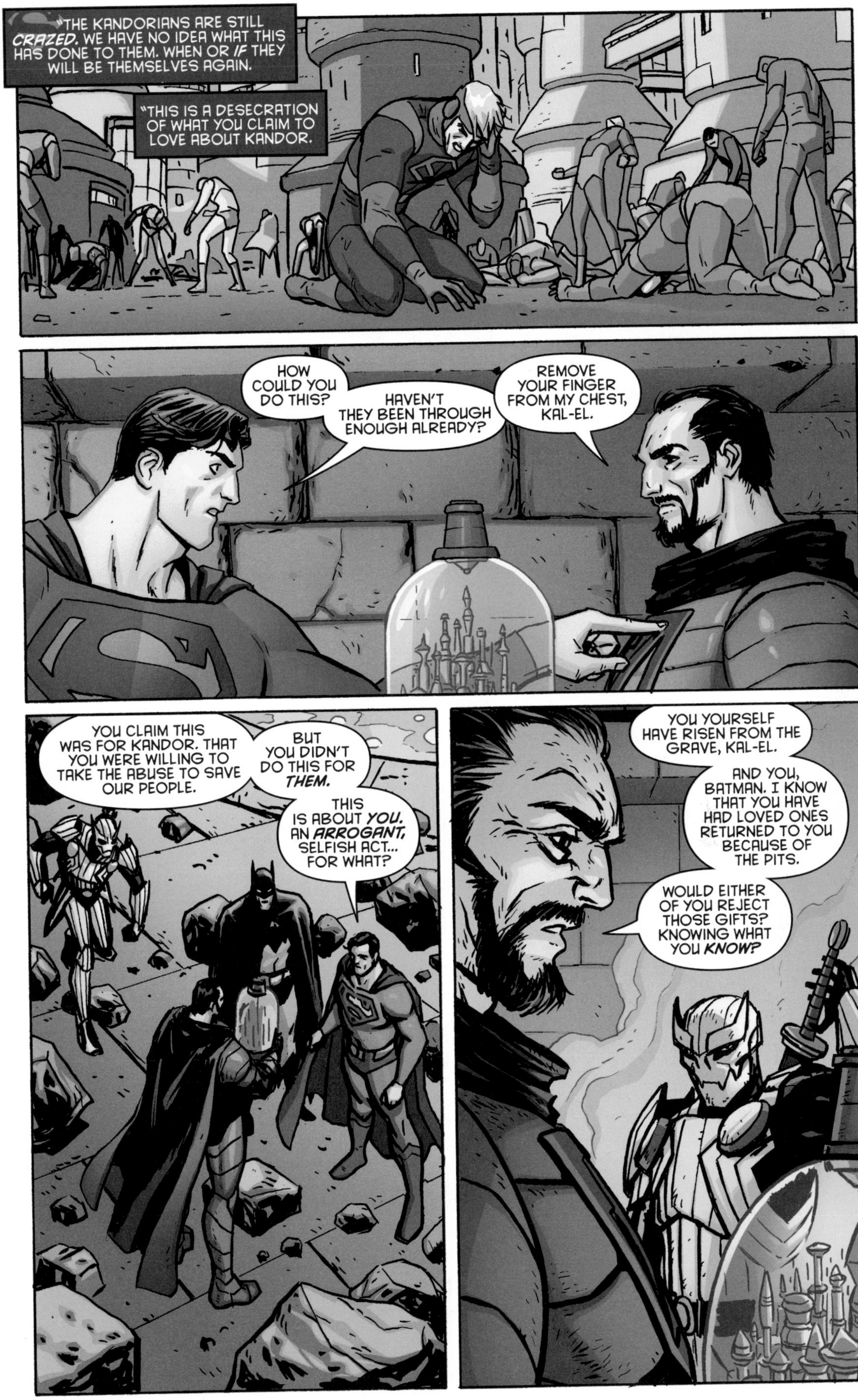
"THE KANDORIANS ARE STILL CRAZED. WE HAVE NO IDEA WHAT THIS HAS DONE TO THEM. WHEN OR IF THEY WILL BE THEMSELVES AGAIN.
"THIS IS A DESECRATION OF WHAT YOU CLAIM TO LOVE ABOUT KANDOR.
HOW COULD YOU DO THIS?
HAVEN'T THEY BEEN THROUGH ENOUGH ALREADY?
REMOVE YOUR FINGER FROM MY CHEST, KAL-EL.
YOU CLAIM THIS WAS FOR KANDOR. THAT YOU WERE WILLING TO TAKE THE ABUSE TO SAVE OUR PEOPLE.
BUT YOU DIDN'T DO THIS FOR THEM.
THIS IS ABOUT YOU. AN ARROGANT, SELFISH ACT... FOR WHAT?
YOU YOURSELF HAVE RISEN FROM THE GRAVE, KAL-EL.
AND YOU, BATMAN. I KNOW THAT YOU HAVE HAD LOVED ONES RETURNED TO YOU BECAUSE OF THE PITS.
WOULD EITHER OF YOU REJECT THOSE GIFTS? KNOWING WHAT YOU KNOW?

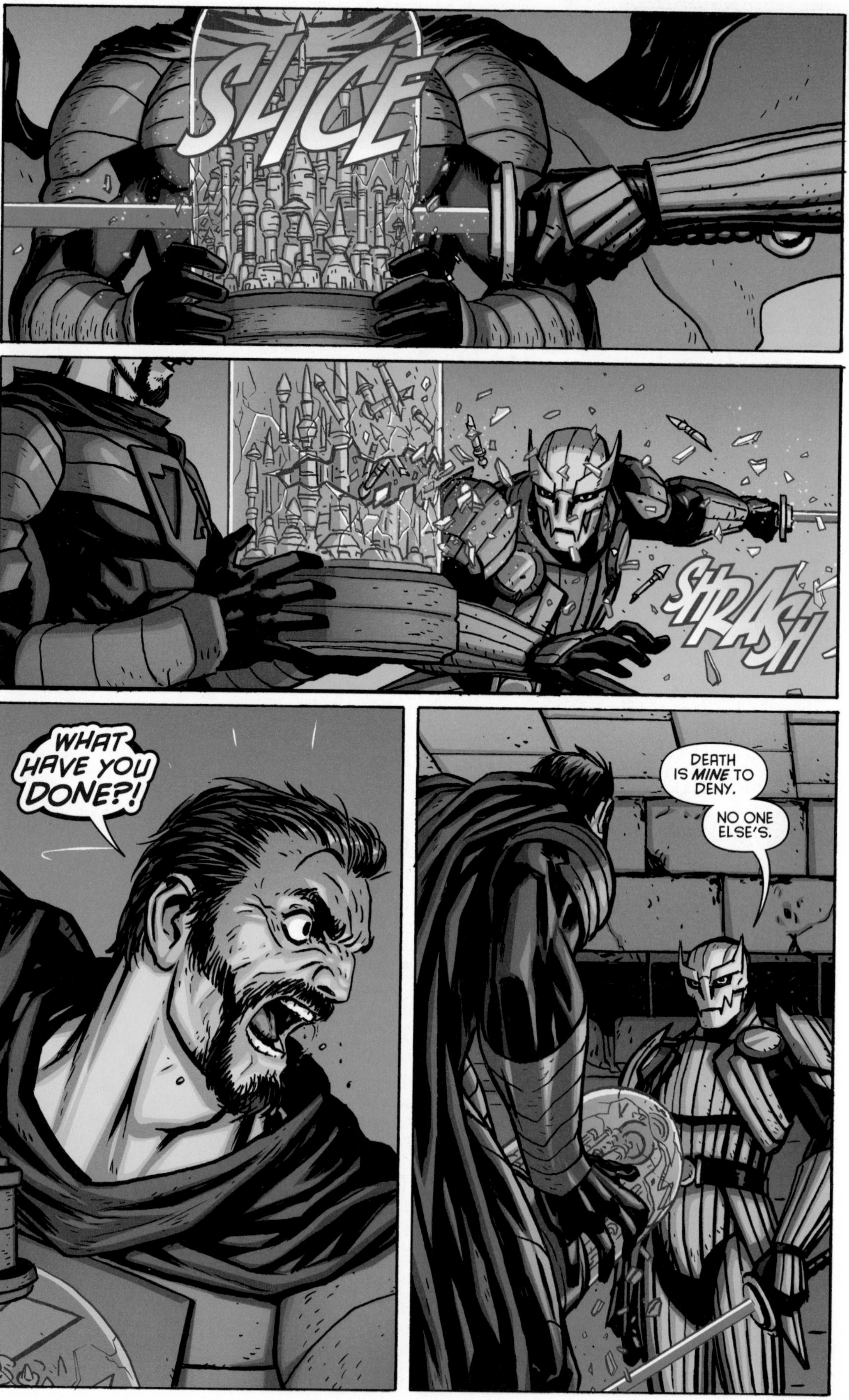
SLICE
SHRASH
WHAT HAVE YOU DONE?!
DEATH IS MINE TO DENY.
NO ONE ELSE'S.

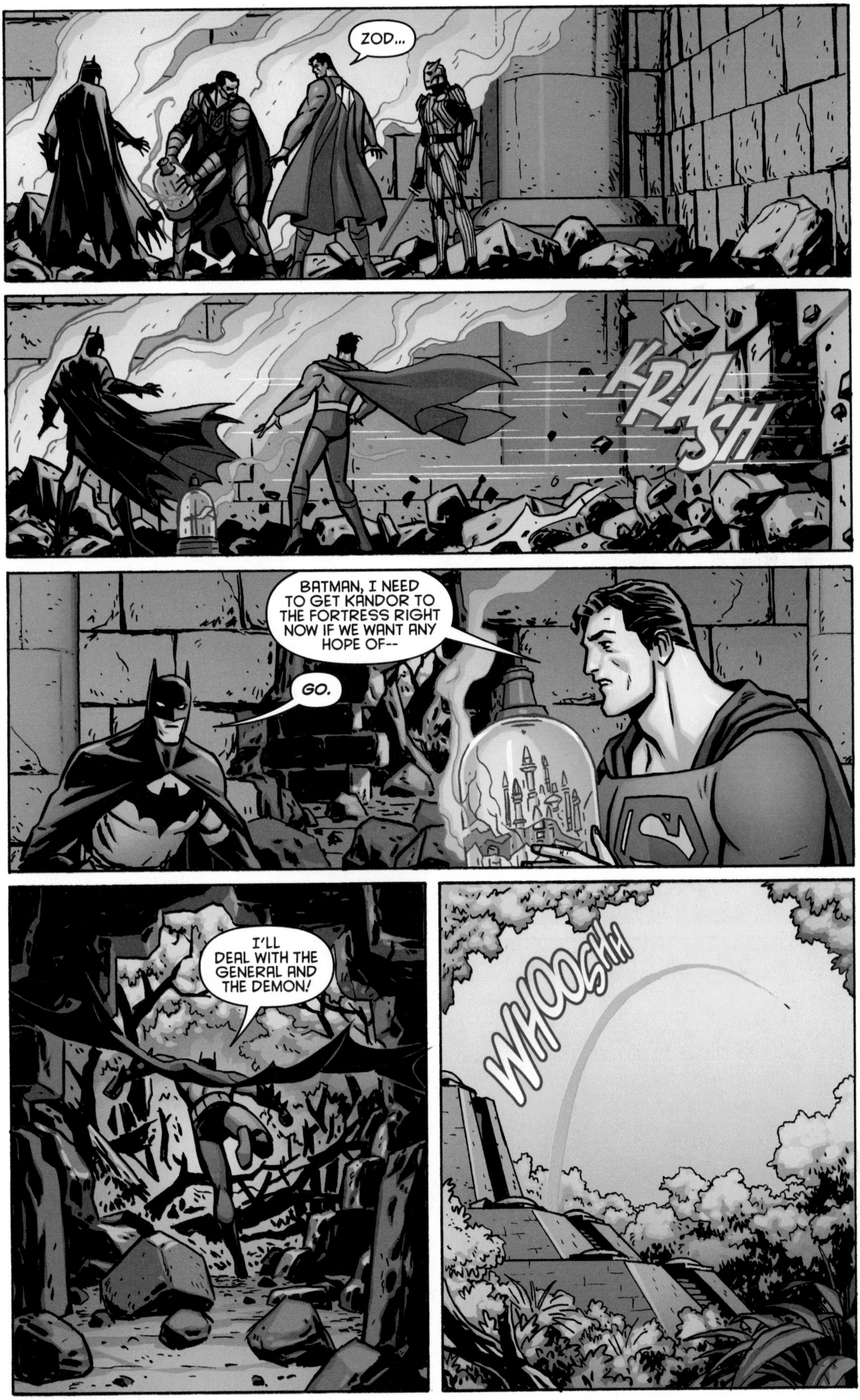
ZOD...
KRASH
BATMAN, I NEED TO GET KANDOR TO THE FORTRESS RIGHT NOW IF WE WANT ANY HOPE OF--
GO.
I'LL DEAL WITH THE GENERAL AND THE DEMON!
WHOOSH!!

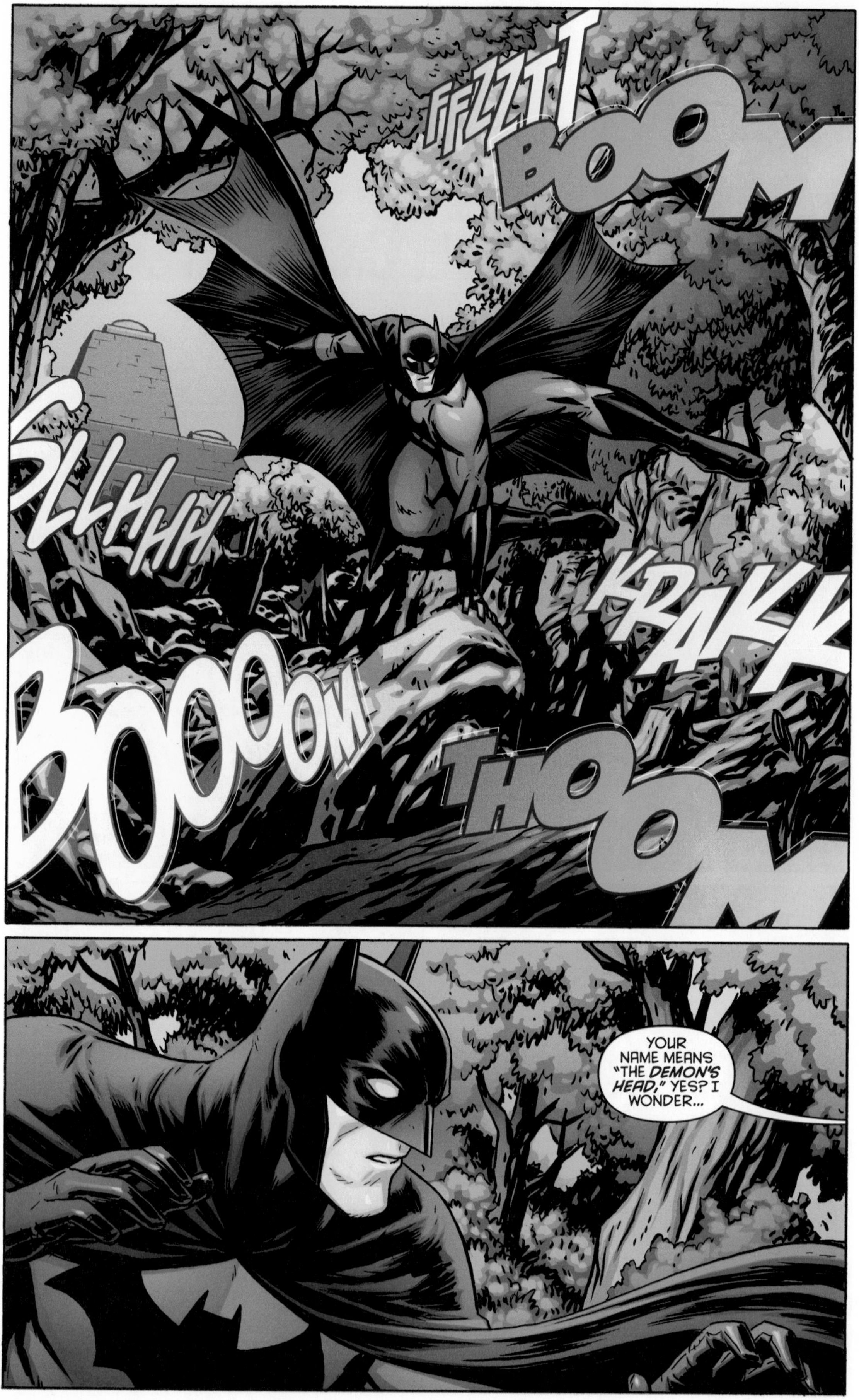
FFZZTT
BOOM
SLLHHH
KRAKK
BOOOOM
THOOM
YOUR NAME MEANS "THE *DEMON'S HEAD,*" YES? I WONDER...

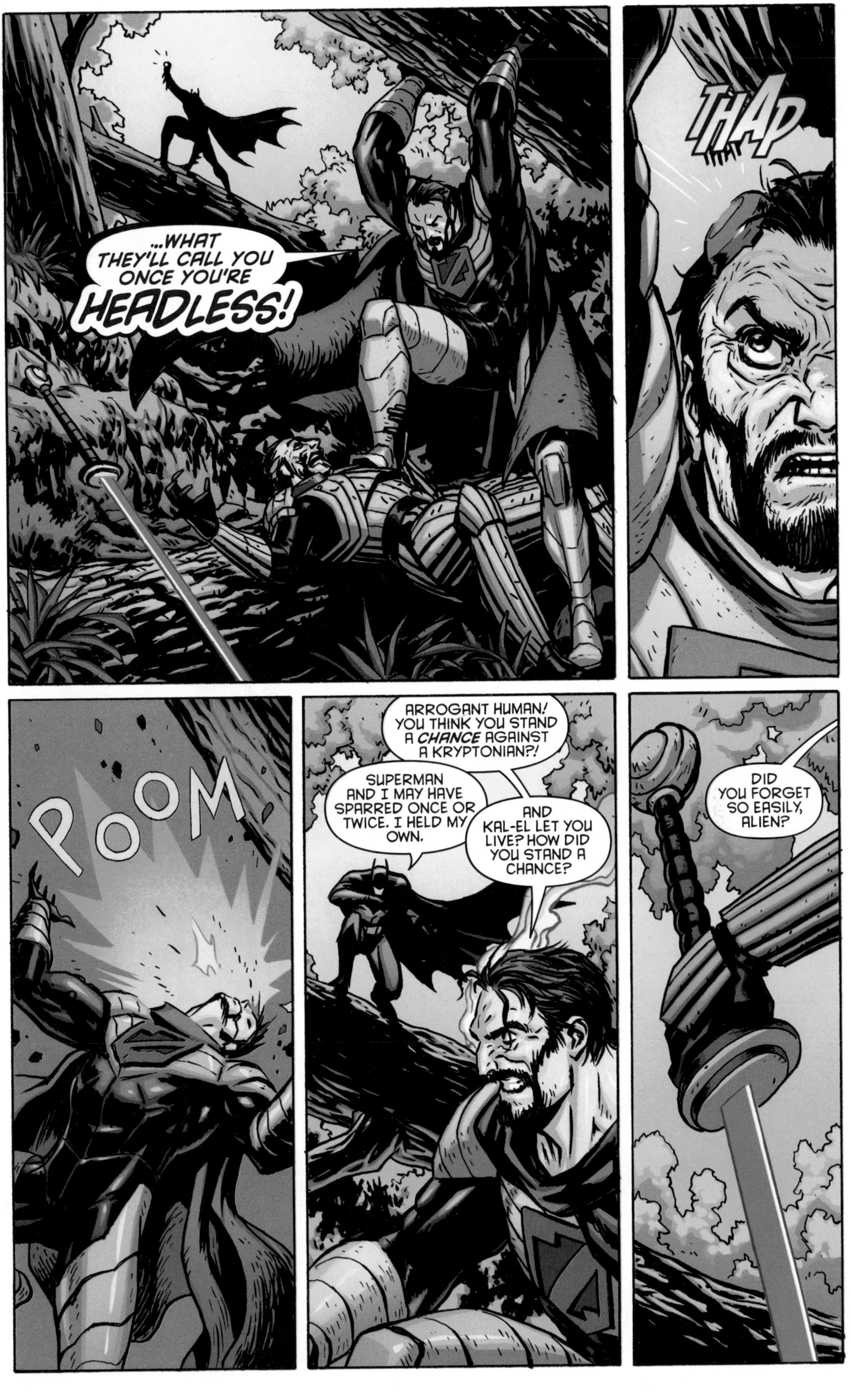
...WHAT THEY'LL CALL YOU ONCE YOU'RE HEADLESS!
THAP
POOM
ARROGANT HUMAN! YOU THINK YOU STAND A CHANCE AGAINST A KRYPTONIAN?!
SUPERMAN AND I MAY HAVE SPARRED ONCE OR TWICE. I HELD MY OWN.
AND KAL-EL LET YOU LIVE? HOW DID YOU STAND A CHANCE?
DID YOU FORGET SO EASILY, ALIEN?

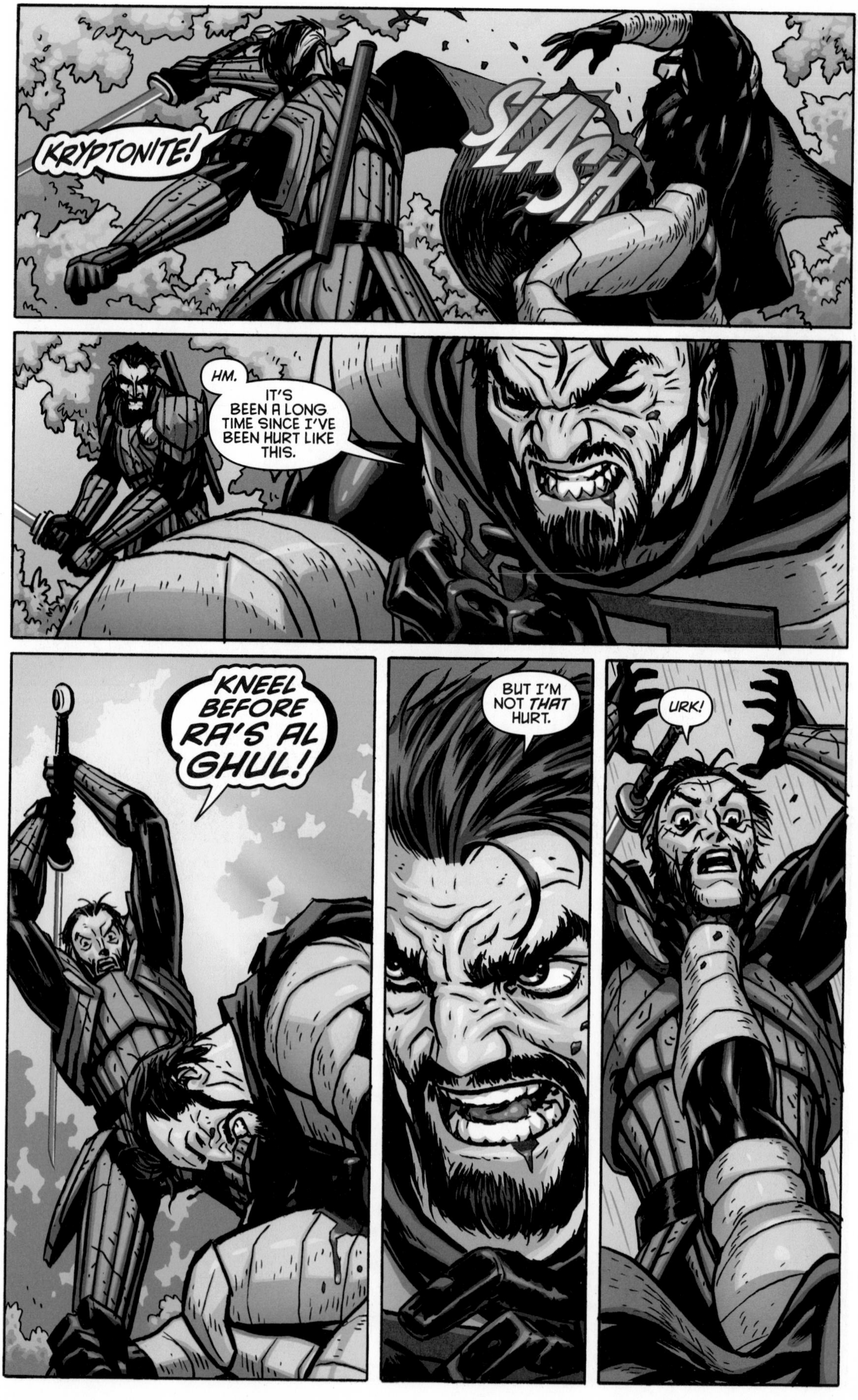
KRYPTONITE!
SLASH
HM.
IT'S BEEN A LONG TIME SINCE I'VE BEEN HURT LIKE THIS.
KNEEL BEFORE RA'S AL GHUL!
BUT I'M NOT *THAT* HURT.
URK!

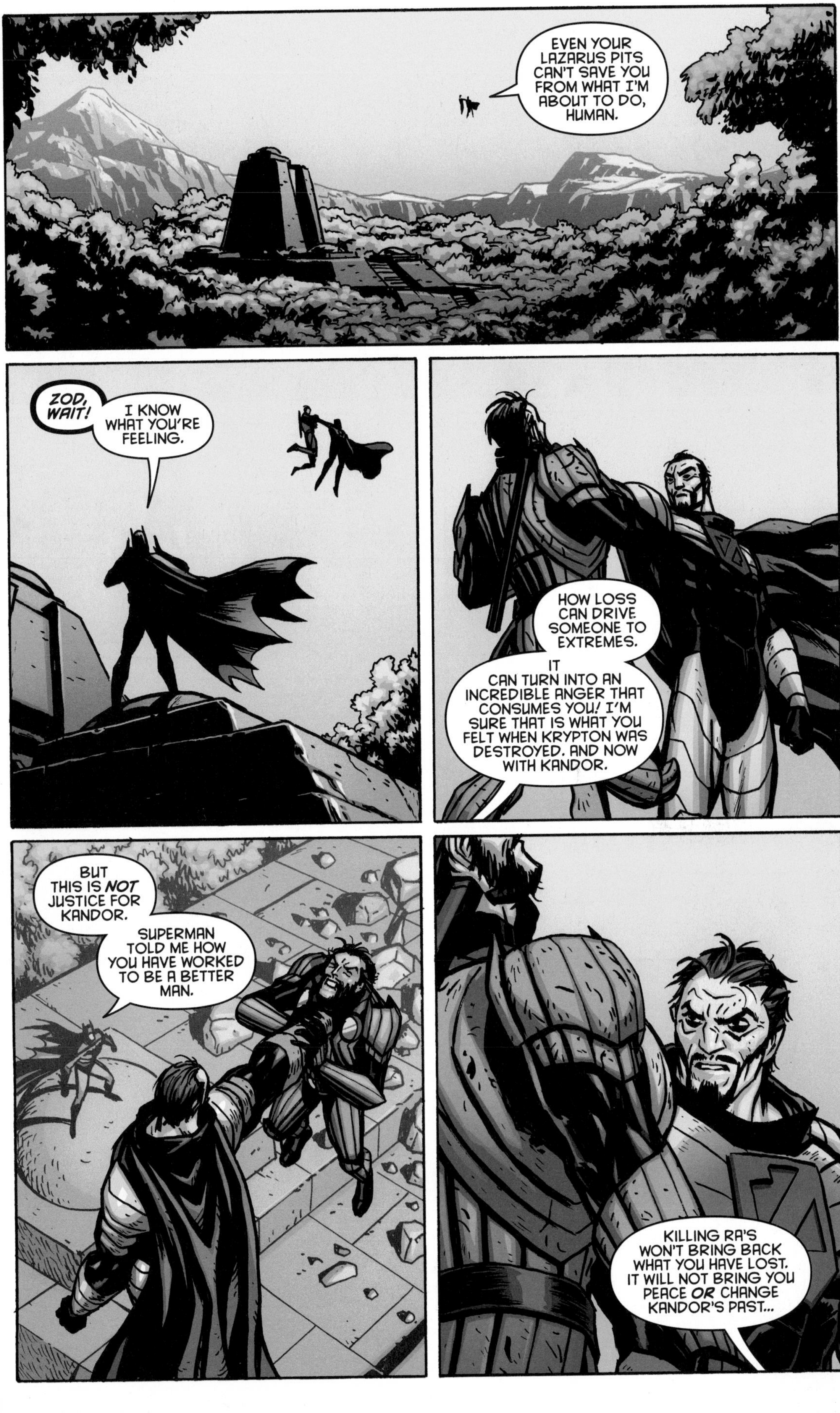
EVEN YOUR LAZARUS PITS CAN'T SAVE YOU FROM WHAT I'M ABOUT TO DO, HUMAN.
ZOD, WAIT!
I KNOW WHAT YOU'RE FEELING.
HOW LOSS CAN DRIVE SOMEONE TO EXTREMES.
IT CAN TURN INTO AN INCREDIBLE ANGER THAT CONSUMES YOU! I'M SURE THAT IS WHAT YOU FELT WHEN KRYPTON WAS DESTROYED. AND NOW WITH KANDOR.
BUT THIS IS NOT JUSTICE FOR KANDOR.
SUPERMAN TOLD ME HOW YOU HAVE WORKED TO BE A BETTER MAN.
KILLING RA'S WON'T BRING BACK WHAT YOU HAVE LOST. IT WILL NOT BRING YOU PEACE OR CHANGE KANDOR'S PAST...

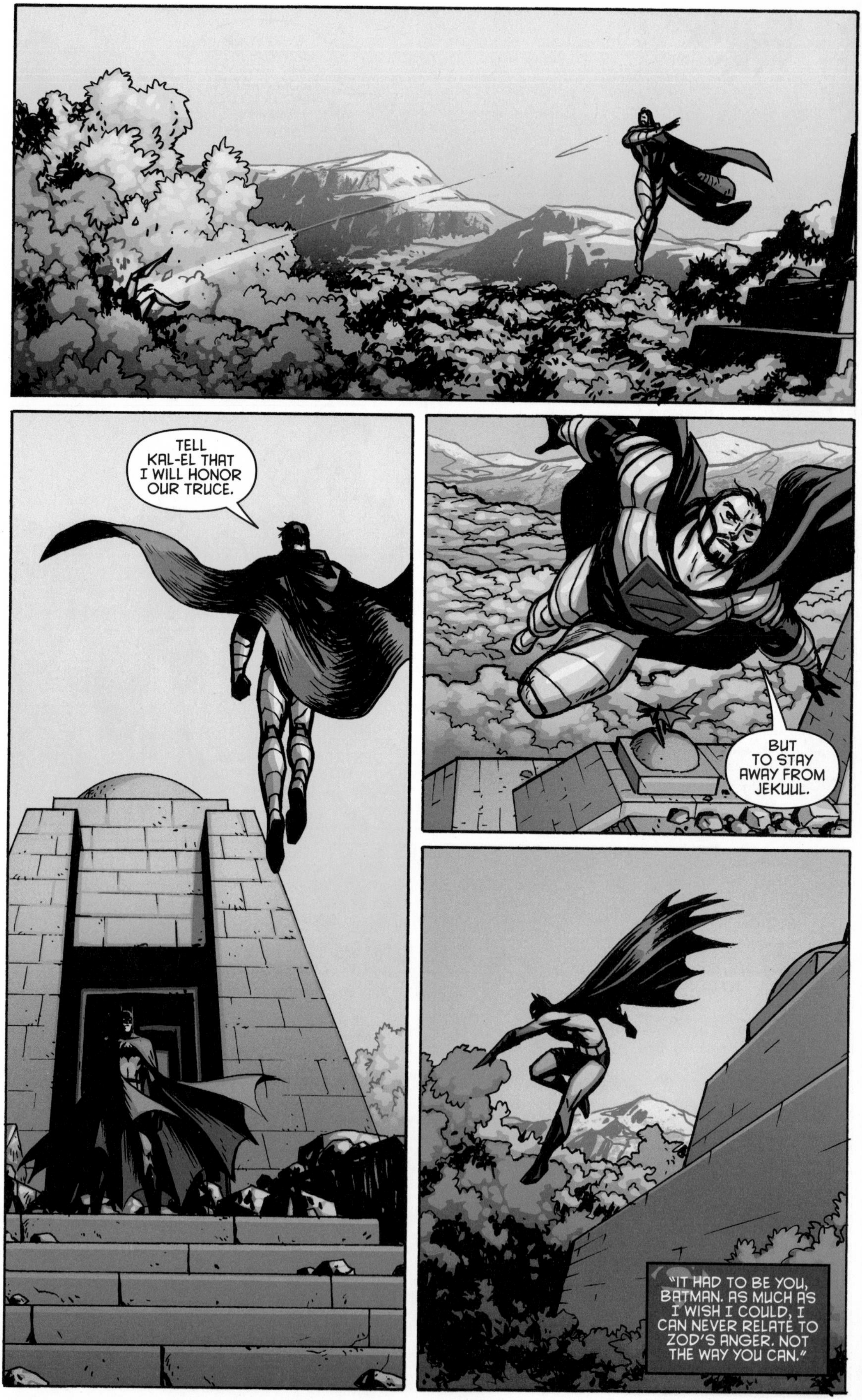
TELL KAL-EL THAT I WILL HONOR OUR TRUCE.
BUT TO STAY AWAY FROM JEKUUL.
"IT HAD TO BE YOU, BATMAN. AS MUCH AS I WISH I COULD, I CAN NEVER RELATE TO ZOD'S ANGER. NOT THE WAY YOU CAN."

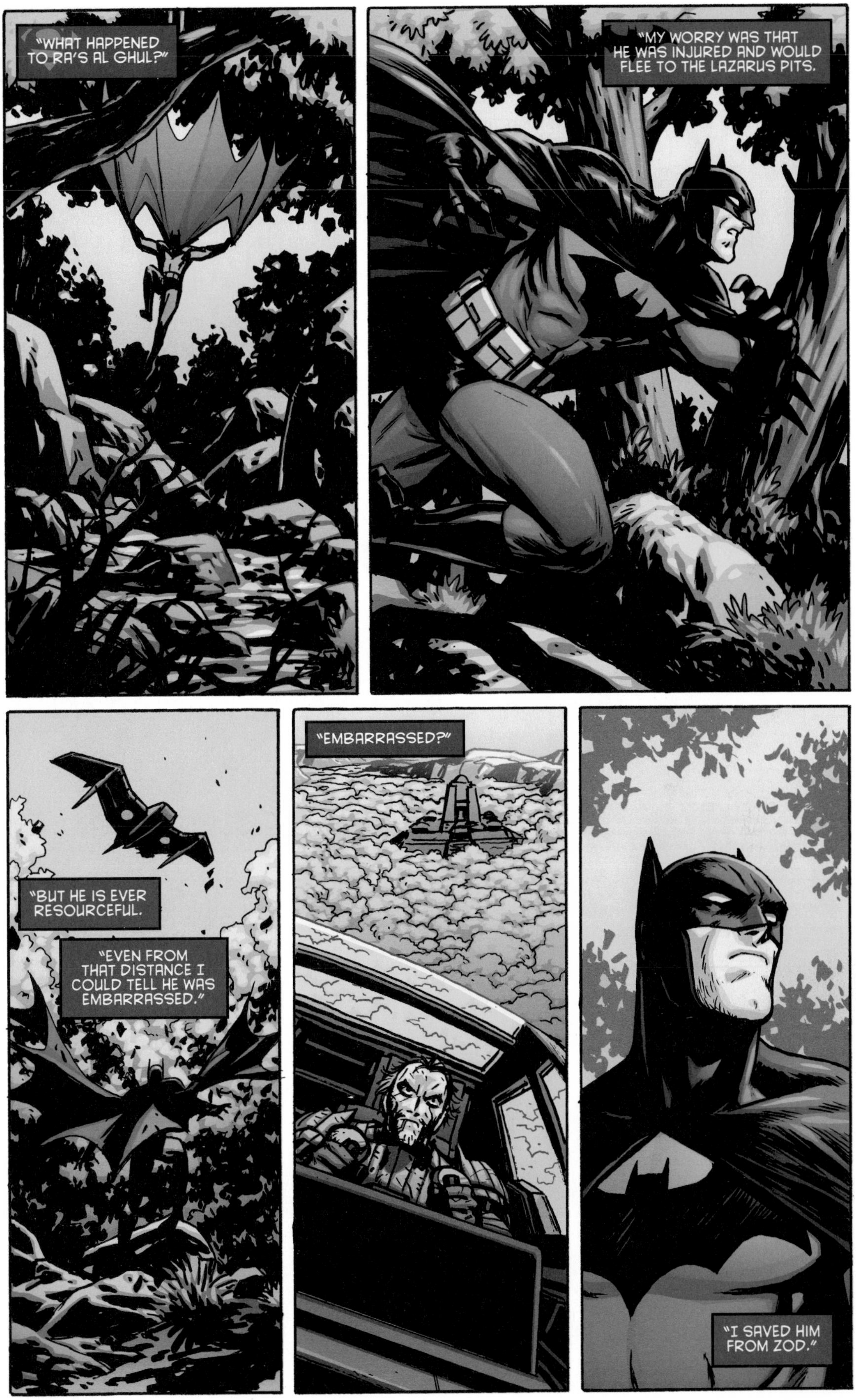
"WHAT HAPPENED TO RA'S AL GHUL?"
"MY WORRY WAS THAT HE WAS INJURED AND WOULD FLEE TO THE LAZARUS PITS.
"BUT HE IS EVER RESOURCEFUL.
"EVEN FROM THAT DISTANCE I COULD TELL HE WAS EMBARRASSED."
"EMBARRASSED?"
"I SAVED HIM FROM ZOD."

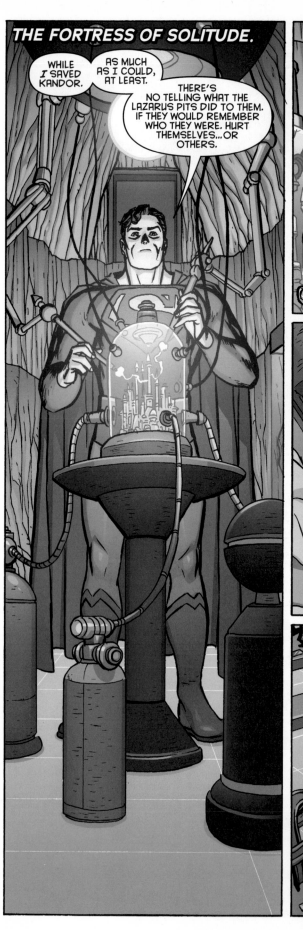

THE FORTRESS OF SOLITUDE.

WHILE *I* SAVED KANDOR.

AS MUCH AS I COULD, AT LEAST.

THERE'S NO TELLING WHAT THE LAZARUS PITS DID TO THEM. IF THEY WOULD REMEMBER WHO THEY WERE. HURT THEMSELVES...OR OTHERS.

SO DID YOU...?

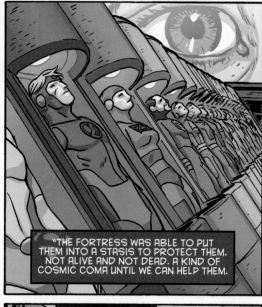

"THE FORTRESS WAS ABLE TO PUT THEM INTO A STASIS TO PROTECT THEM. NOT ALIVE AND NOT DEAD. A KIND OF COSMIC COMA UNTIL WE CAN HELP THEM."

BUT THERE'S *MORE.*

THIS MINIATURE CITY... IT'S A *REPRODUCTION*...

...AND HALF OF THE KANDORIAN POPULATION IS *MISSING.*

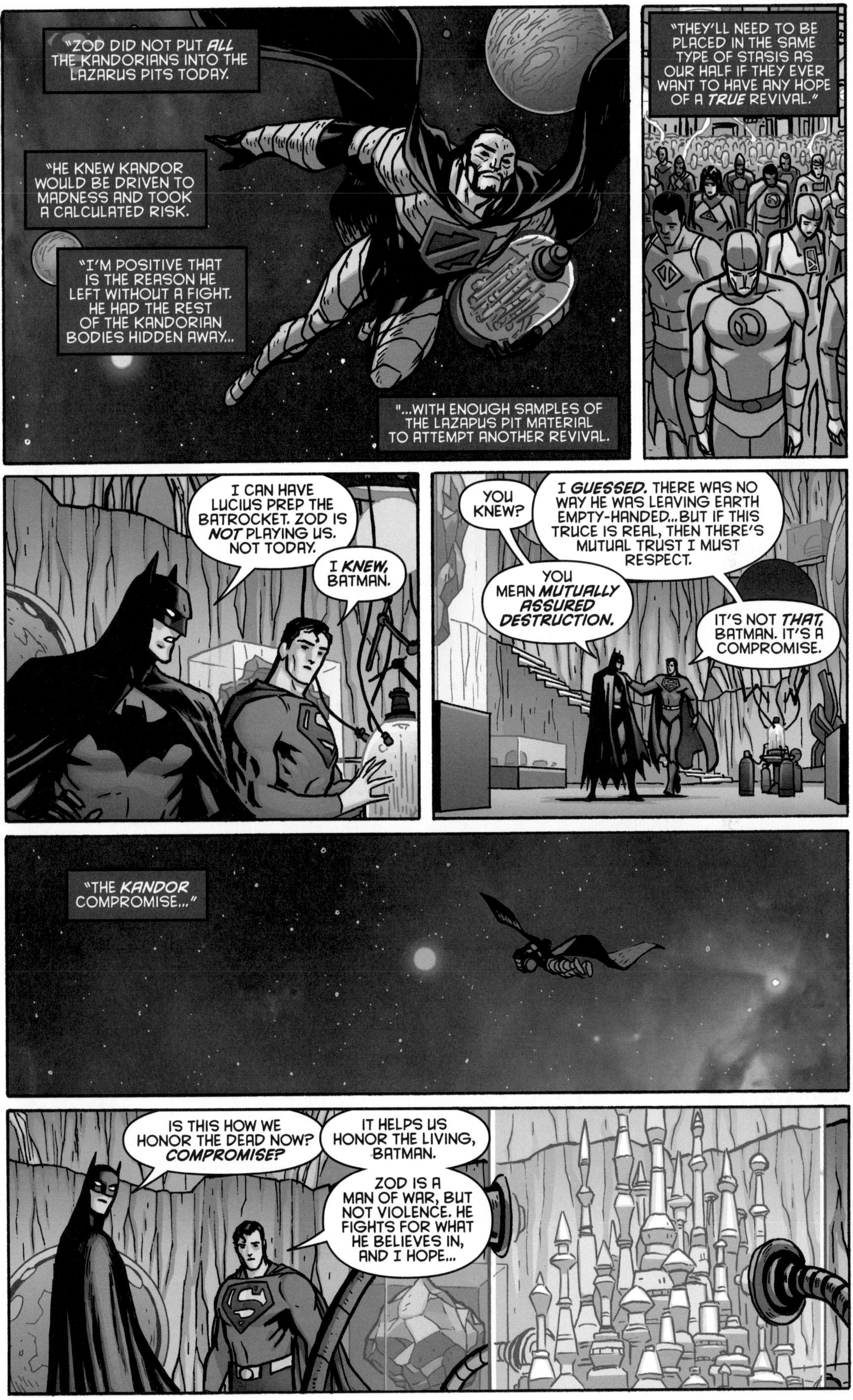
"ZOD DID NOT PUT ALL THE KANDORIANS INTO THE LAZARUS PITS TODAY.
"HE KNEW KANDOR WOULD BE DRIVEN TO MADNESS AND TOOK A CALCULATED RISK.
"I'M POSITIVE THAT IS THE REASON HE LEFT WITHOUT A FIGHT. HE HAD THE REST OF THE KANDORIAN BODIES HIDDEN AWAY...
"...WITH ENOUGH SAMPLES OF THE LAZARUS PIT MATERIAL TO ATTEMPT ANOTHER REVIVAL.
"THEY'LL NEED TO BE PLACED IN THE SAME TYPE OF STASIS AS OUR HALF IF THEY EVER WANT TO HAVE ANY HOPE OF A TRUE REVIVAL."
I CAN HAVE LUCIUS PREP THE BATROCKET. ZOD IS NOT PLAYING US. NOT TODAY.
I KNEW, BATMAN.
YOU KNEW?
I GUESSED. THERE WAS NO WAY HE WAS LEAVING EARTH EMPTY-HANDED...BUT IF THIS TRUCE IS REAL, THEN THERE'S MUTUAL TRUST I MUST RESPECT.
YOU MEAN MUTUALLY ASSURED DESTRUCTION.
IT'S NOT THAT, BATMAN. IT'S A COMPROMISE.
"THE KANDOR COMPROMISE..."
IS THIS HOW WE HONOR THE DEAD NOW? COMPROMISE?
IT HELPS US HONOR THE LIVING, BATMAN.
ZOD IS A MAN OF WAR, BUT NOT VIOLENCE. HE FIGHTS FOR WHAT HE BELIEVES IN, AND I HOPE...

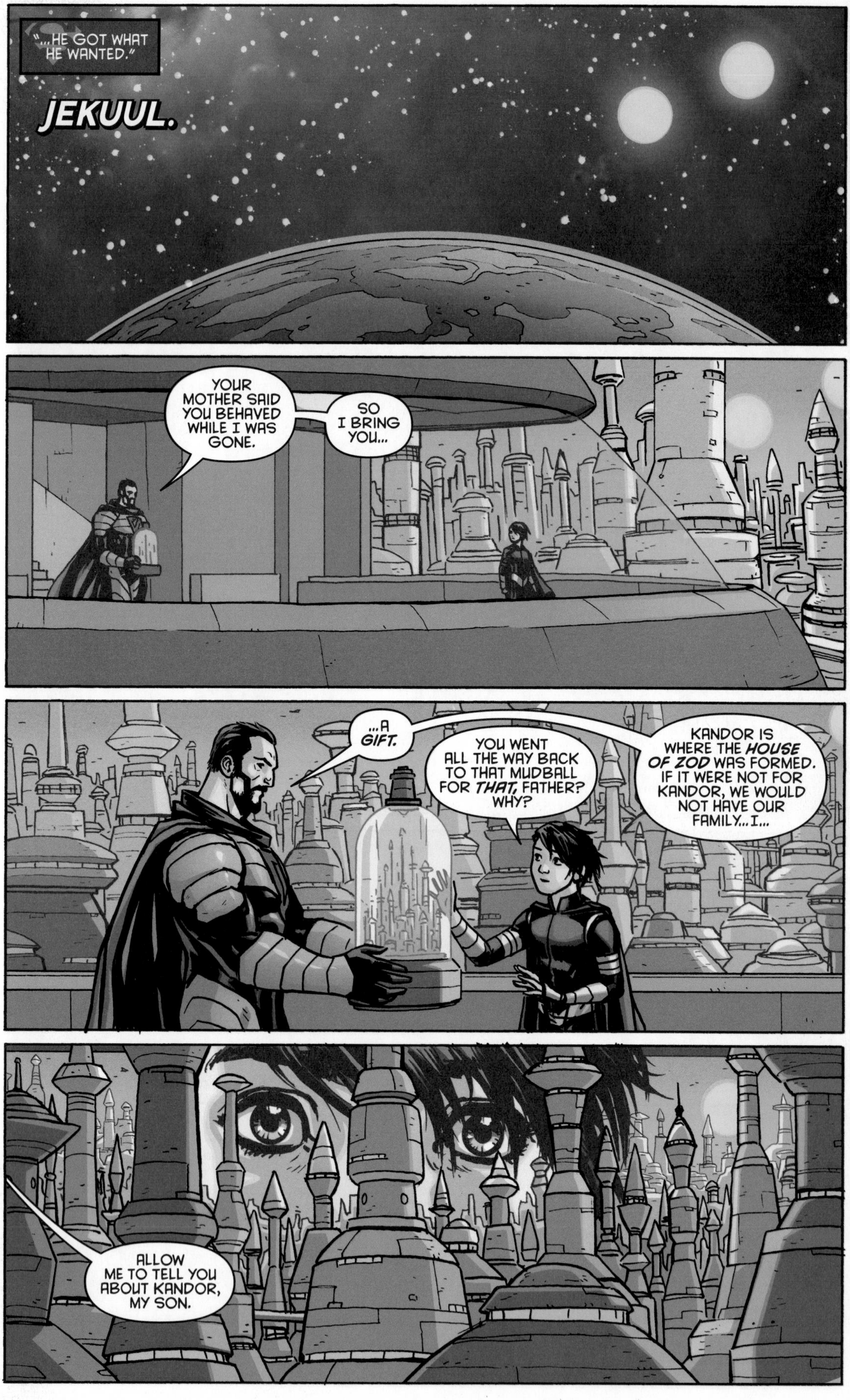
"...HE GOT WHAT HE WANTED."
JEKUUL.
YOUR MOTHER SAID YOU BEHAVED WHILE I WAS GONE.
SO I BRING YOU...
...A GIFT.
YOU WENT ALL THE WAY BACK TO THAT MUDBALL FOR THAT, FATHER? WHY?
KANDOR IS WHERE THE HOUSE OF ZOD WAS FORMED. IF IT WERE NOT FOR KANDOR, WE WOULD NOT HAVE OUR FAMILY... I...
ALLOW ME TO TELL YOU ABOUT KANDOR, MY SON.

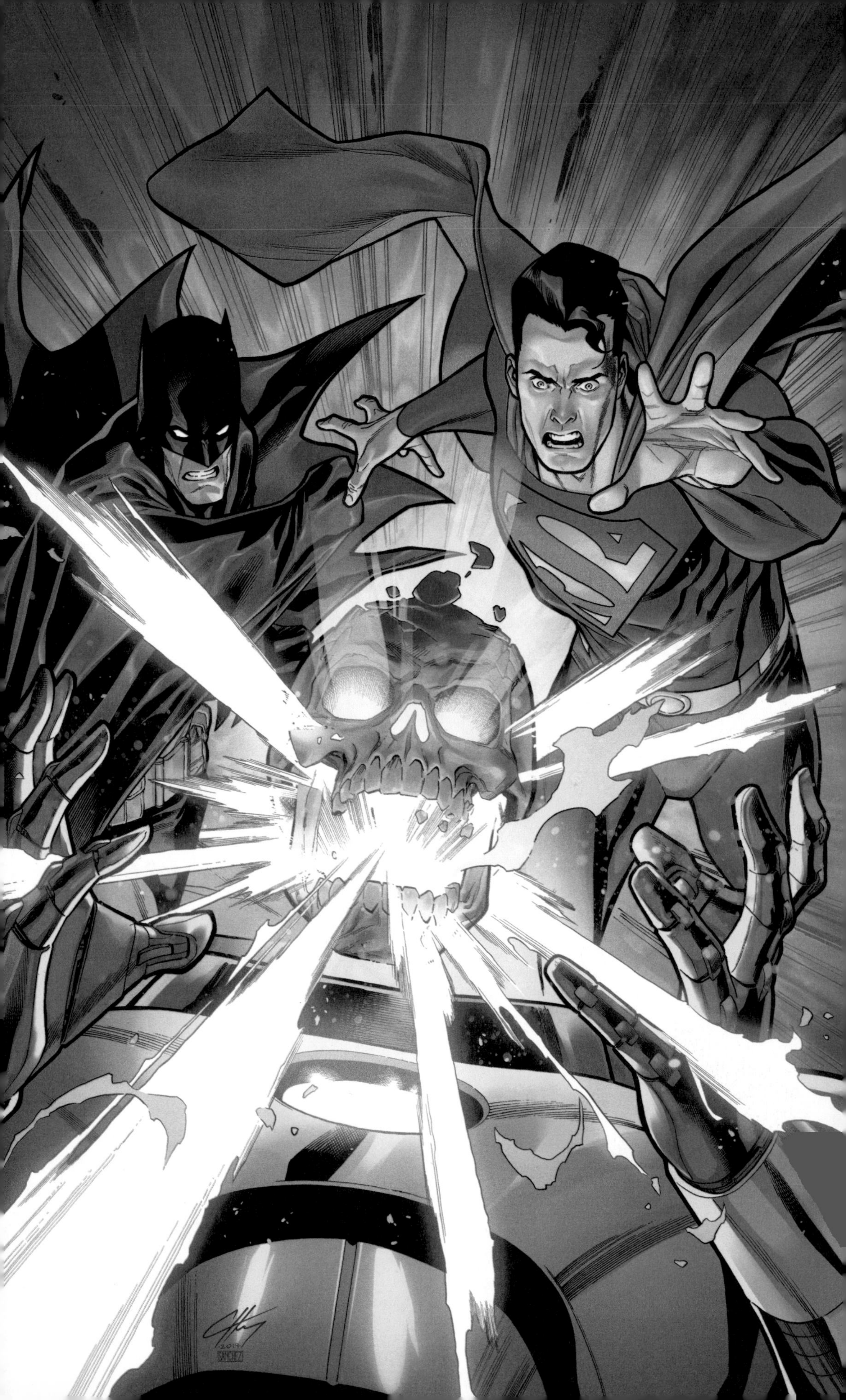

2019
SANCHEZ

BATMAN/SUPERMAN #9

cover by
CLAYTON HENRY and **ALEJANDRO SÁNCHEZ**

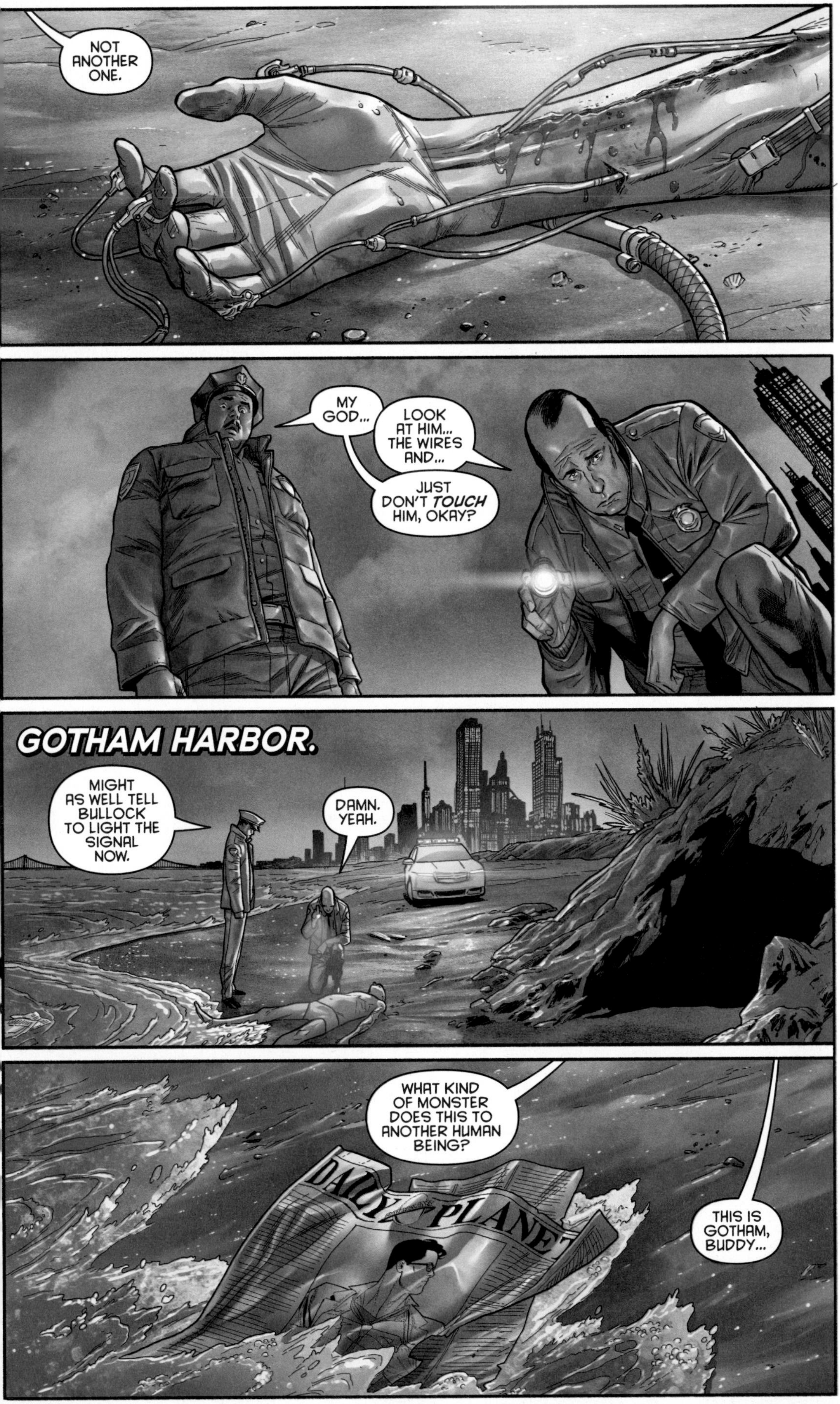
NOT ANOTHER ONE.
MY GOD...
LOOK AT HIM... THE WIRES AND...
JUST DON'T TOUCH HIM, OKAY?
GOTHAM HARBOR.
MIGHT AS WELL TELL BULLOCK TO LIGHT THE SIGNAL NOW.
DAMN. YEAH.
WHAT KIND OF MONSTER DOES THIS TO ANOTHER HUMAN BEING?
DAILY PLANET
THIS IS GOTHAM, BUDDY...

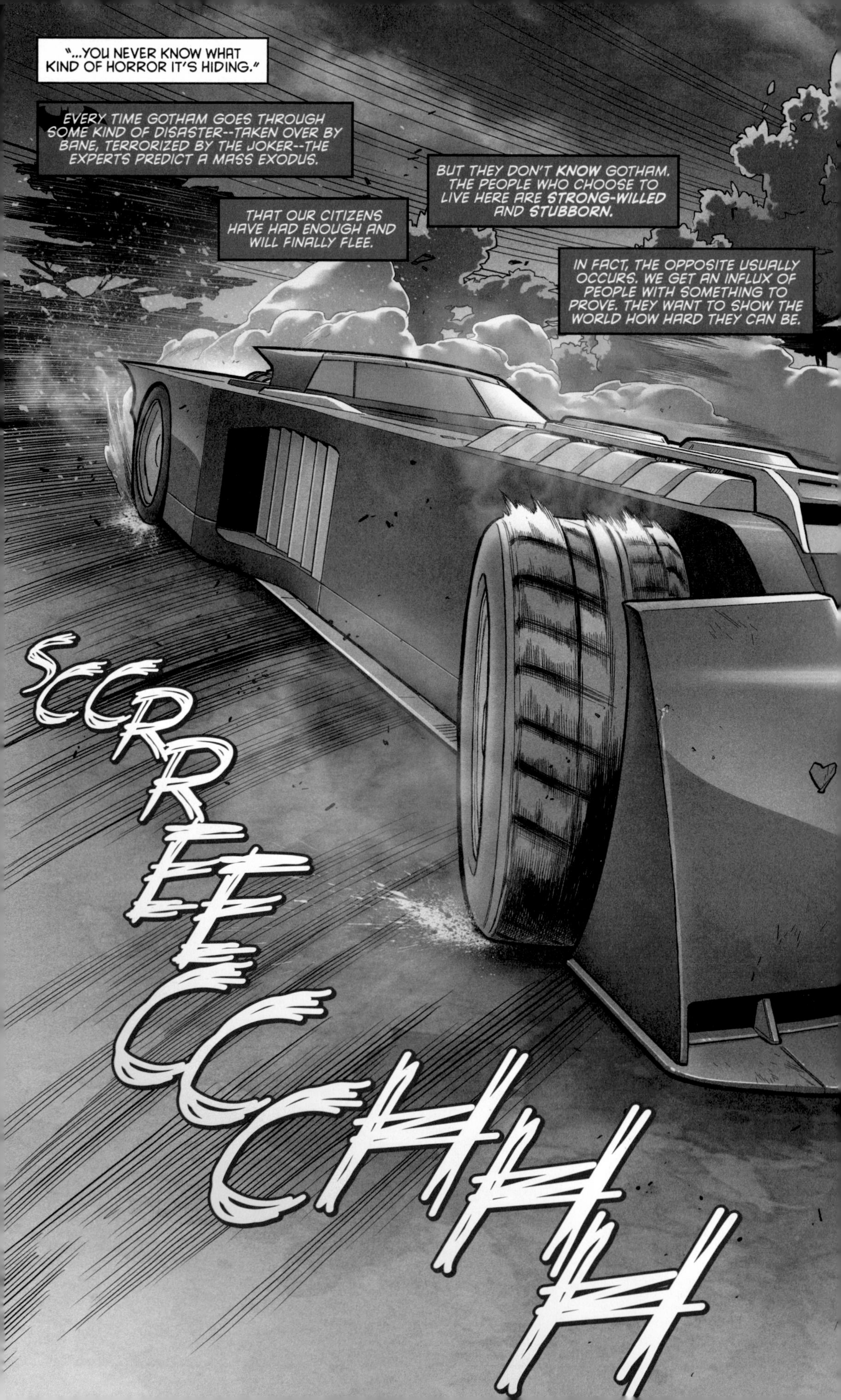

"...YOU NEVER KNOW WHAT KIND OF HORROR IT'S HIDING."
EVERY TIME GOTHAM GOES THROUGH SOME KIND OF DISASTER--TAKEN OVER BY BANE, TERRORIZED BY THE JOKER--THE EXPERTS PREDICT A MASS EXODUS.
THAT OUR CITIZENS HAVE HAD ENOUGH AND WILL FINALLY FLEE.
BUT THEY DON'T KNOW GOTHAM. THE PEOPLE WHO CHOOSE TO LIVE HERE ARE STRONG-WILLED AND STUBBORN.
IN FACT, THE OPPOSITE USUALLY OCCURS. WE GET AN INFLUX OF PEOPLE WITH SOMETHING TO PROVE. THEY WANT TO SHOW THE WORLD HOW HARD THEY CAN BE.
SCCRREEECCCHHHH

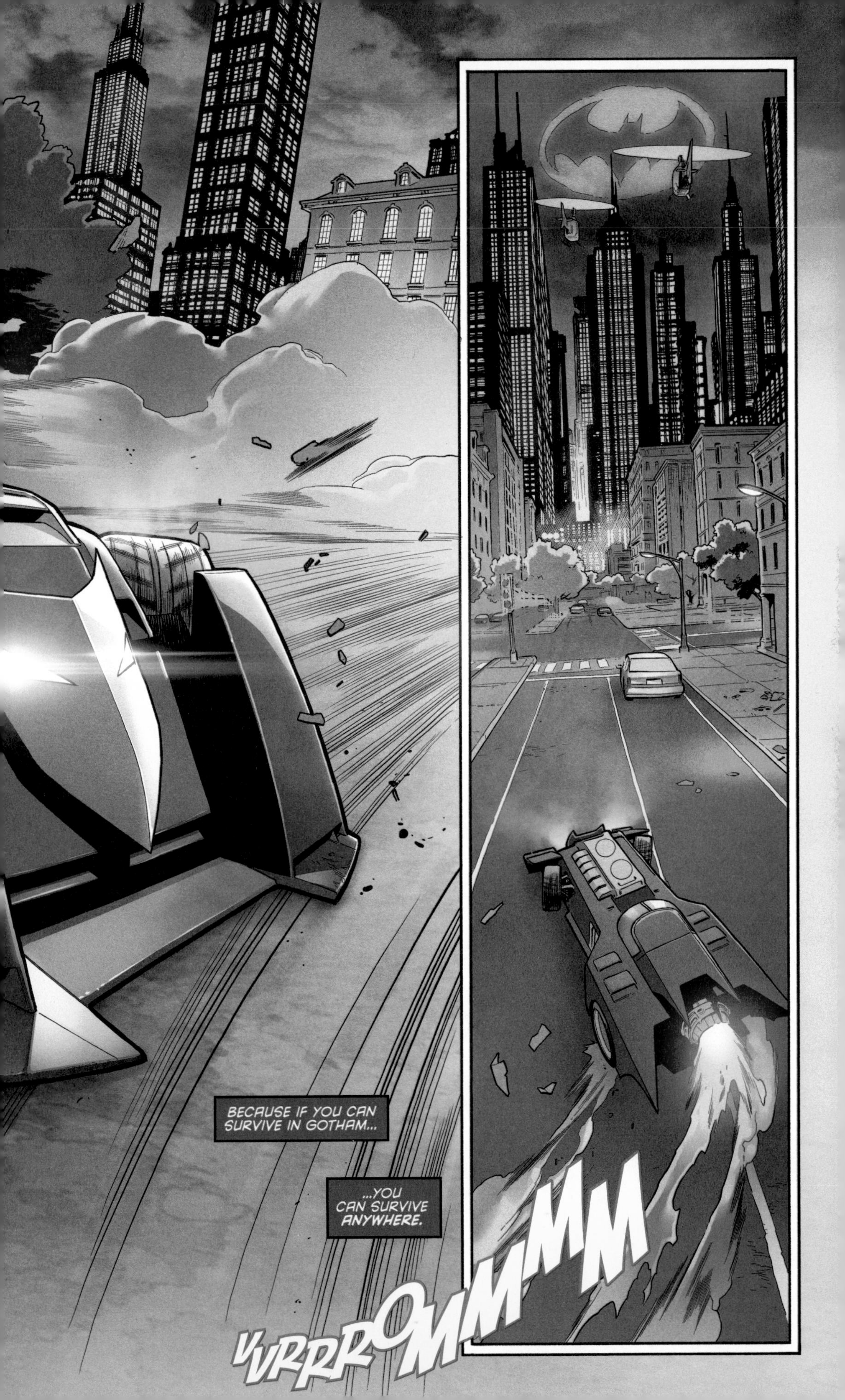
BECAUSE IF YOU CAN SURVIVE IN GOTHAM...
...YOU CAN SURVIVE ANYWHERE.
VVRRROMMMMM

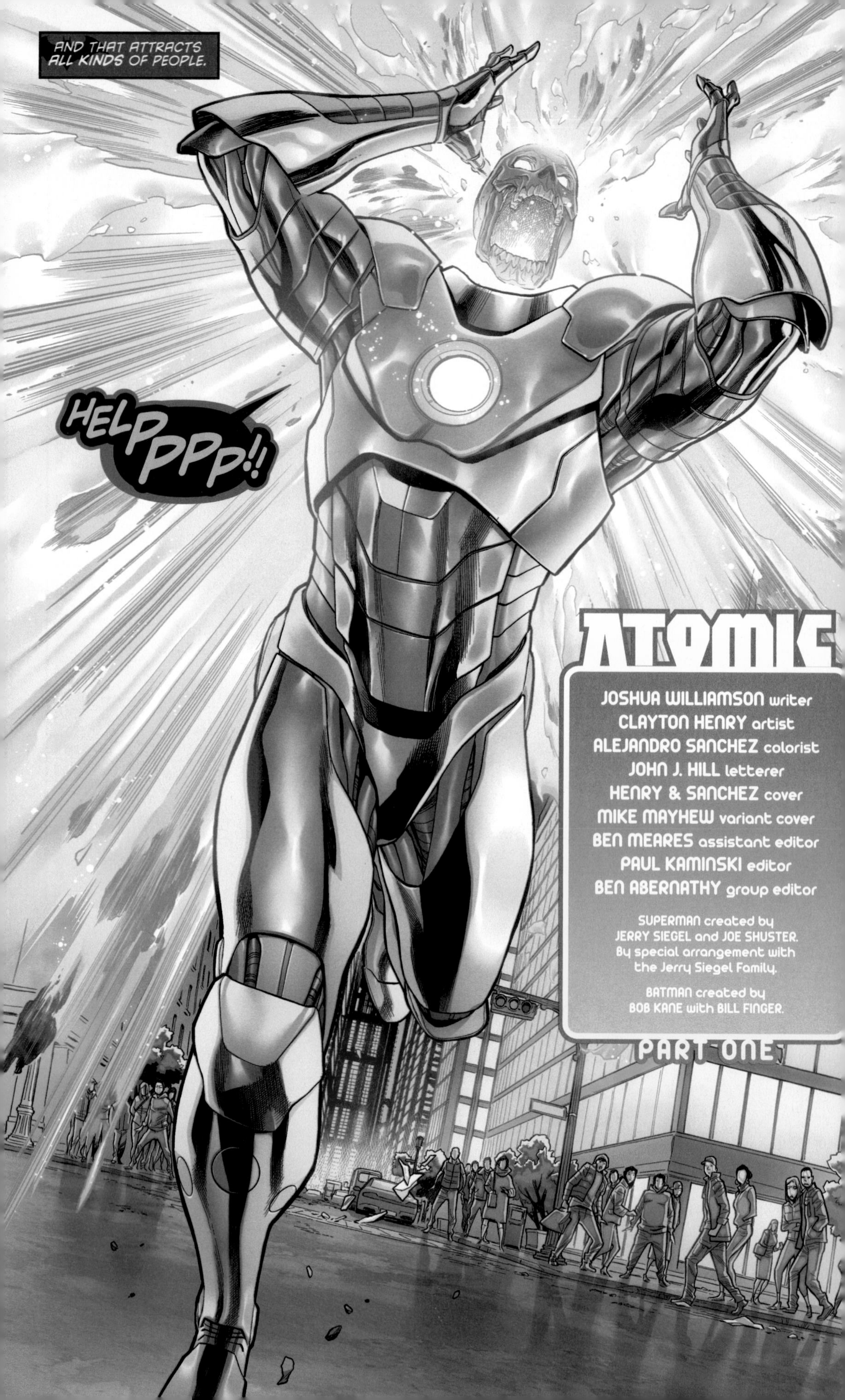

AND THAT ATTRACTS ALL KINDS OF PEOPLE.
HELPPPP!!
ATOMIC
JOSHUA WILLIAMSON writer
CLAYTON HENRY artist
ALEJANDRO SANCHEZ colorist
JOHN J. HILL letterer
HENRY & SANCHEZ cover
MIKE MAYHEW variant cover
BEN MEARES assistant editor
PAUL KAMINSKI editor
BEN ABERNATHY group editor
SUPERMAN created by JERRY SIEGEL and JOE SHUSTER. By special arrangement with the Jerry Siegel Family.
BATMAN created by BOB KANE with BILL FINGER.
PART ONE

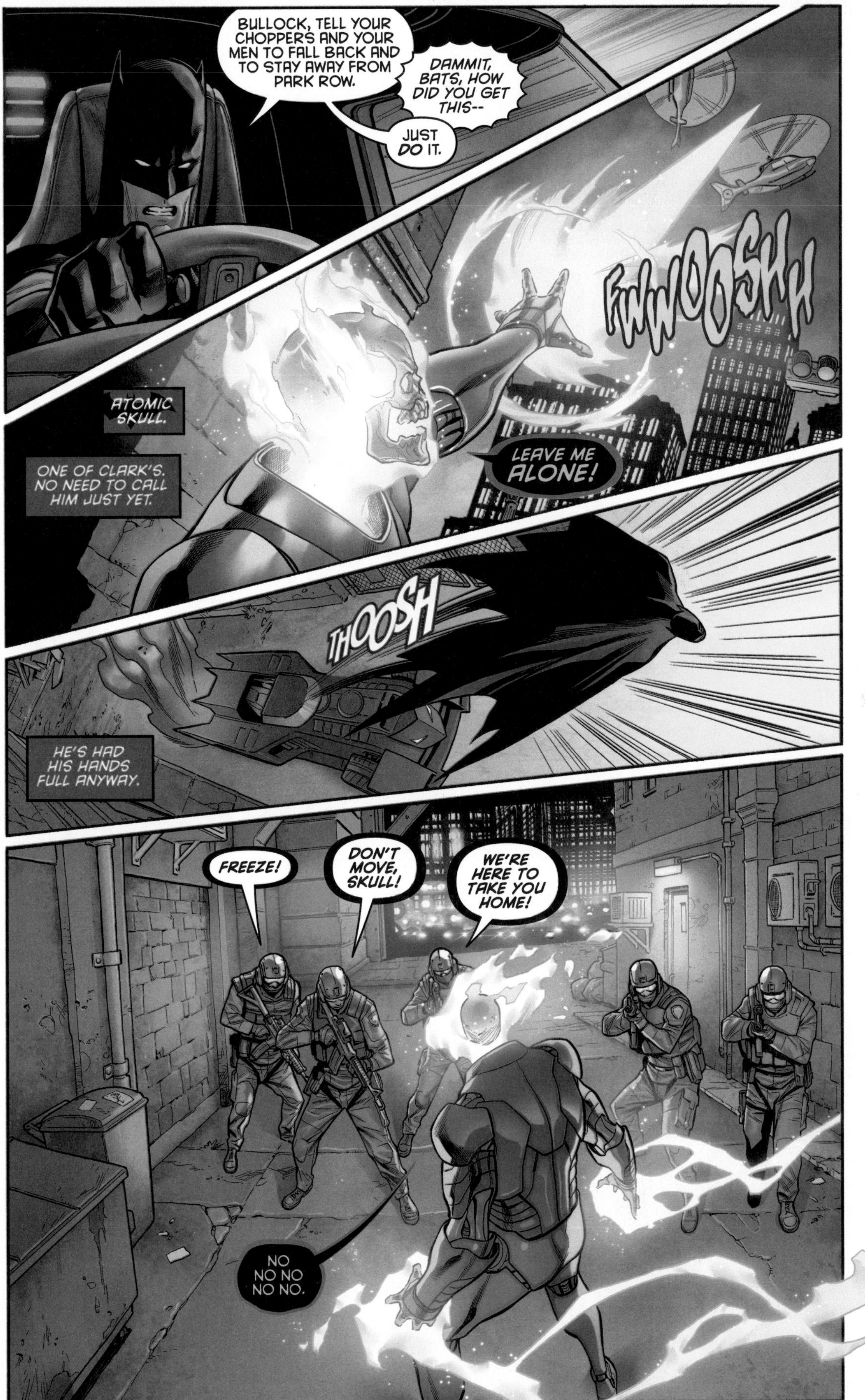

BULLOCK, TELL YOUR CHOPPERS AND YOUR MEN TO FALL BACK AND TO STAY AWAY FROM PARK ROW.
DAMMIT, BATS, HOW DID YOU GET THIS--
JUST DO IT.
FWWOOSHH
ATOMIC SKULL.
ONE OF CLARK'S. NO NEED TO CALL HIM JUST YET.
LEAVE ME ALONE!
THOOSH
HE'S HAD HIS HANDS FULL ANYWAY.
FREEZE!
DON'T MOVE, SKULL!
WE'RE HERE TO TAKE YOU HOME!
NO NO NO NO NO.

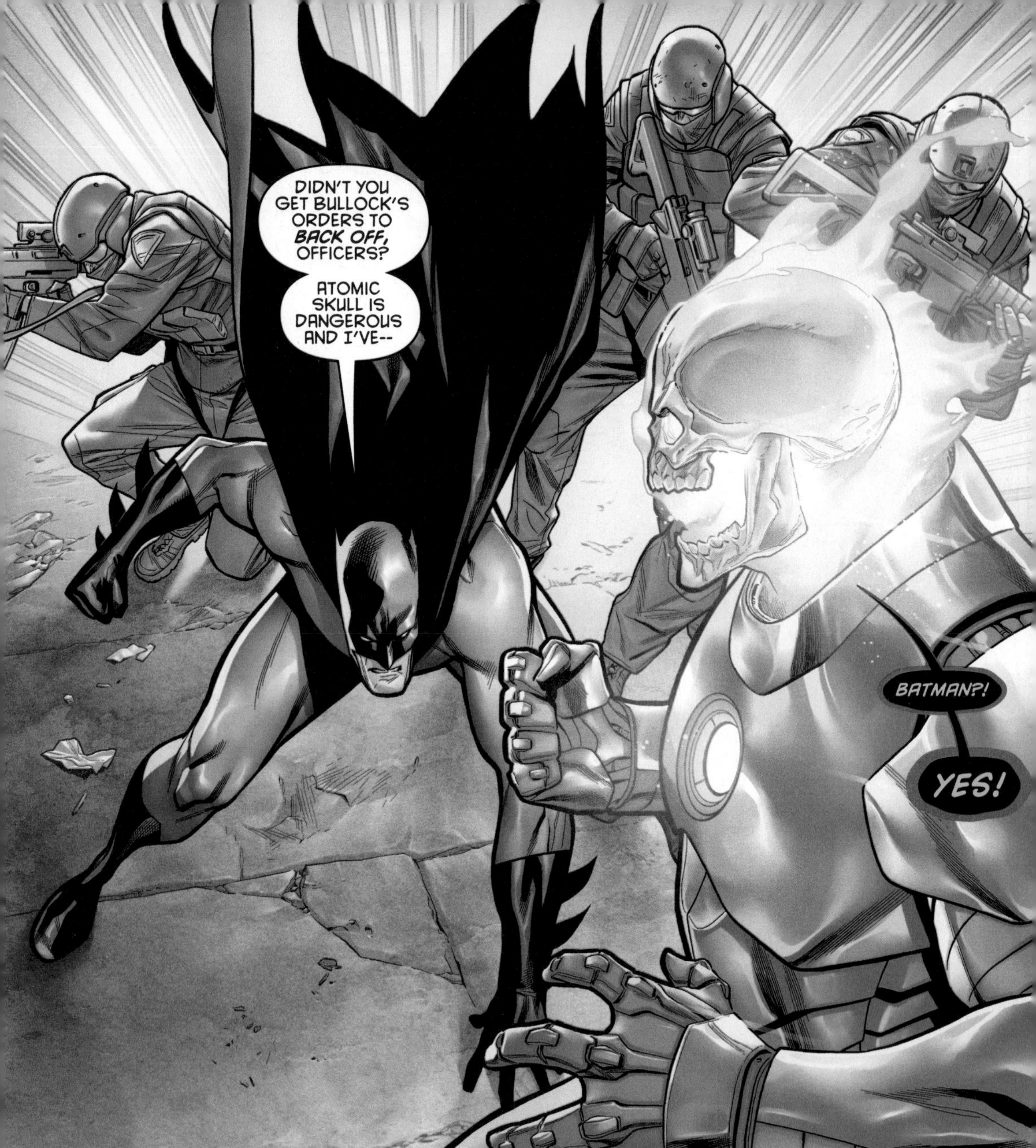
DIDN'T YOU GET BULLOCK'S ORDERS TO *BACK OFF,* OFFICERS?
ATOMIC SKULL IS DANGEROUS AND I'VE--
BATMAN?!
YES!

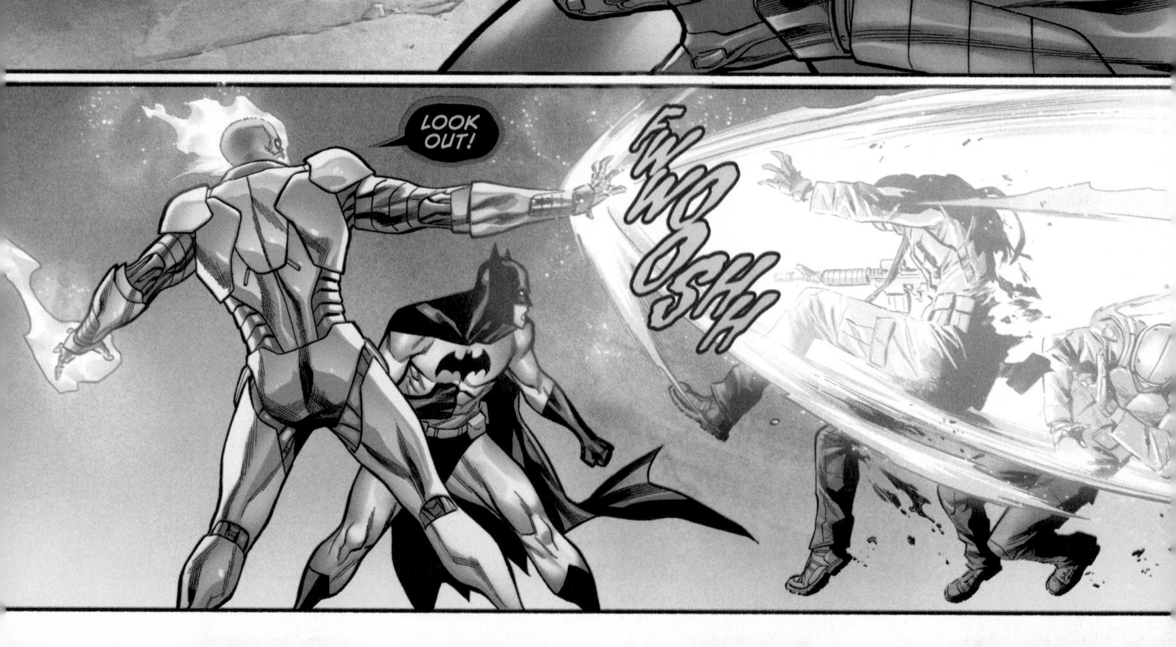
LOOK OUT!
KWOOSHH

SKULL! STOP RIGHT--

NO! THERE'S NO TIME--I'M TRYING TO *HELP!*

ATOMIC SKULL WAS ONCE ALBERT MICHAELS.

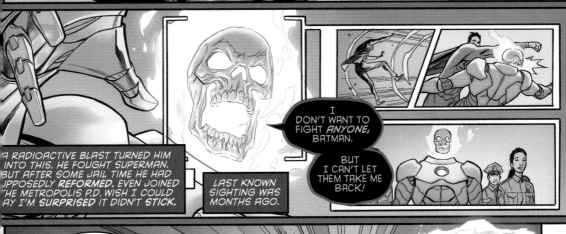

A RADIOACTIVE BLAST TURNED HIM INTO THIS. HE FOUGHT SUPERMAN. BUT AFTER SOME JAIL TIME HE HAD SUPPOSEDLY *REFORMED.* EVEN JOINED THE METROPOLIS P.D. WISH I COULD SAY I'M *SURPRISED* IT DIDN'T *STICK.*

LAST KNOWN SIGHTING WAS MONTHS AGO.

I DON'T WANT TO FIGHT *ANYONE,* BATMAN.

BUT I CAN'T LET THEM TAKE ME BACK!

THOUGHT YOU TURNED OVER A NEW LEAF, SKULL?

YOU DON'T UNDER-STAND!

I WAS LIVING A HAPPY LIFE. AWAY FROM ALL THE FIGHTS AND DEATH...

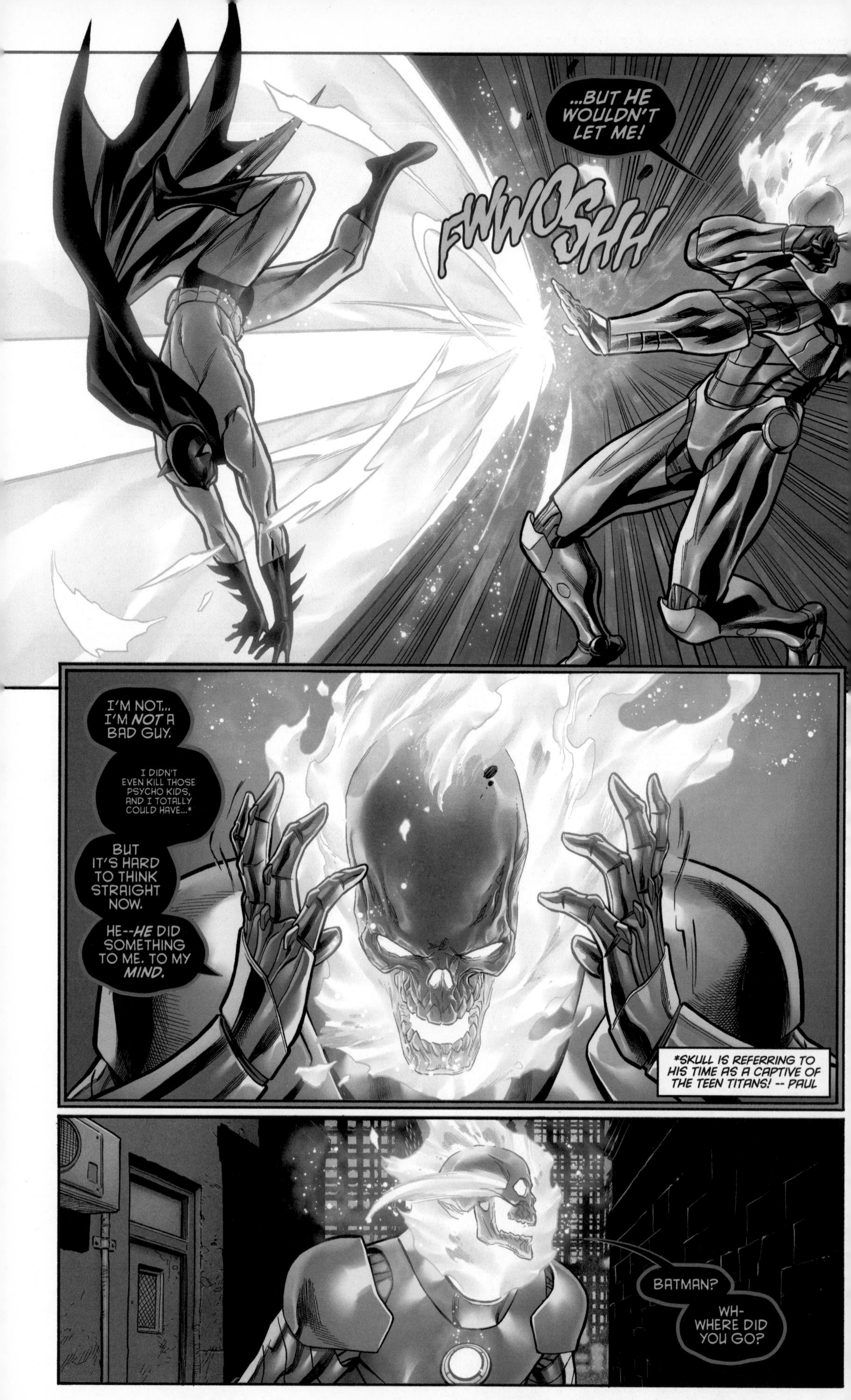
...BUT HE WOULDN'T LET ME!
FWWOSHH
I'M NOT... I'M NOT A BAD GUY.
I DIDN'T EVEN KILL THOSE PSYCHO KIDS, AND I TOTALLY COULD HAVE...*
BUT IT'S HARD TO THINK STRAIGHT NOW.
HE--HE DID SOMETHING TO ME. TO MY MIND.
*SKULL IS REFERRING TO HIS TIME AS A CAPTIVE OF THE TEEN TITANS! -- PAUL
BATMAN?
WH- WHERE DID YOU GO?

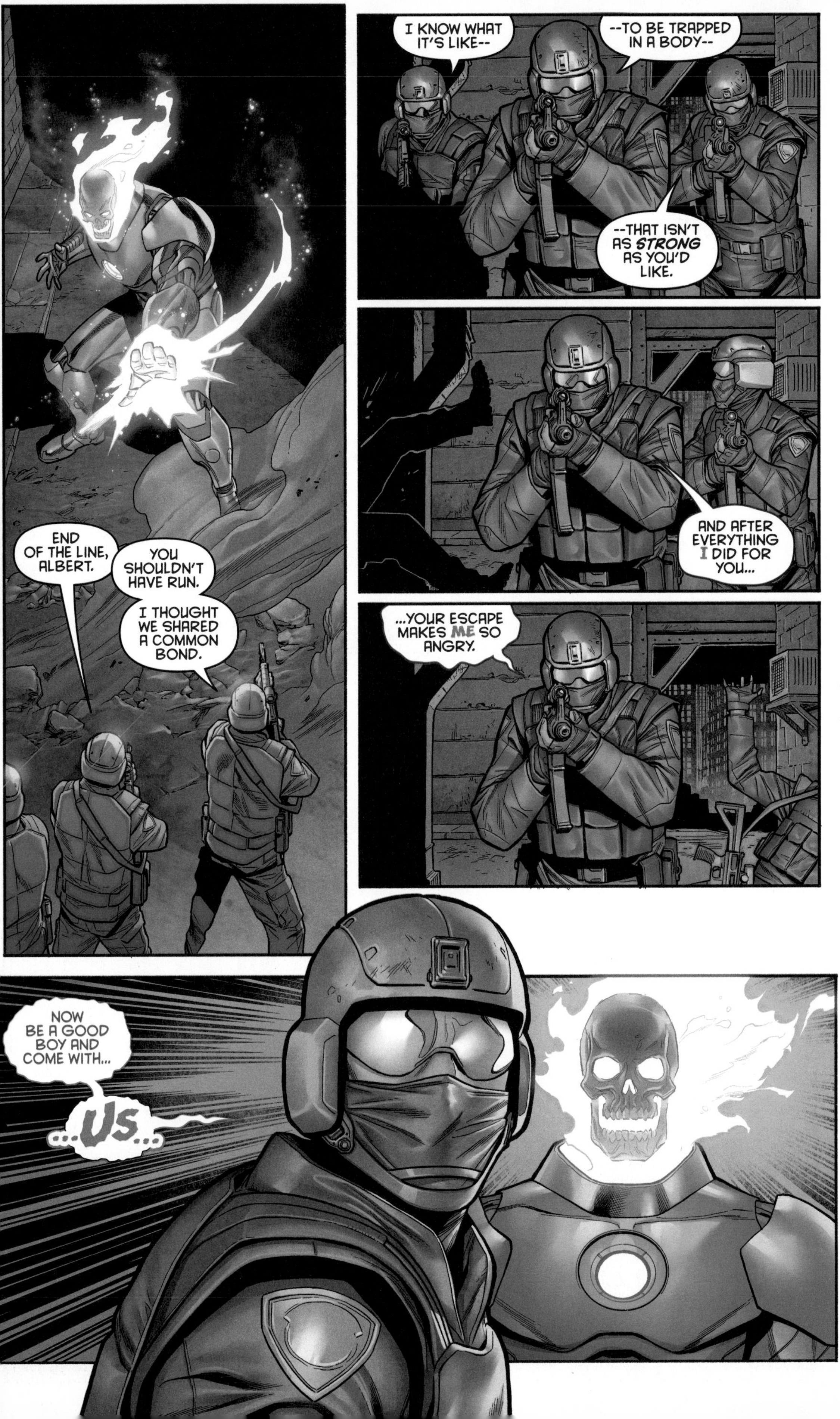

I KNOW WHAT IT'S LIKE--
--TO BE TRAPPED IN A BODY--
--THAT ISN'T AS STRONG AS YOU'D LIKE.
END OF THE LINE, ALBERT.
YOU SHOULDN'T HAVE RUN.
I THOUGHT WE SHARED A COMMON BOND.
AND AFTER EVERYTHING I DID FOR YOU...
...YOUR ESCAPE MAKES ME SO ANGRY.
NOW BE A GOOD BOY AND COME WITH...
...US...

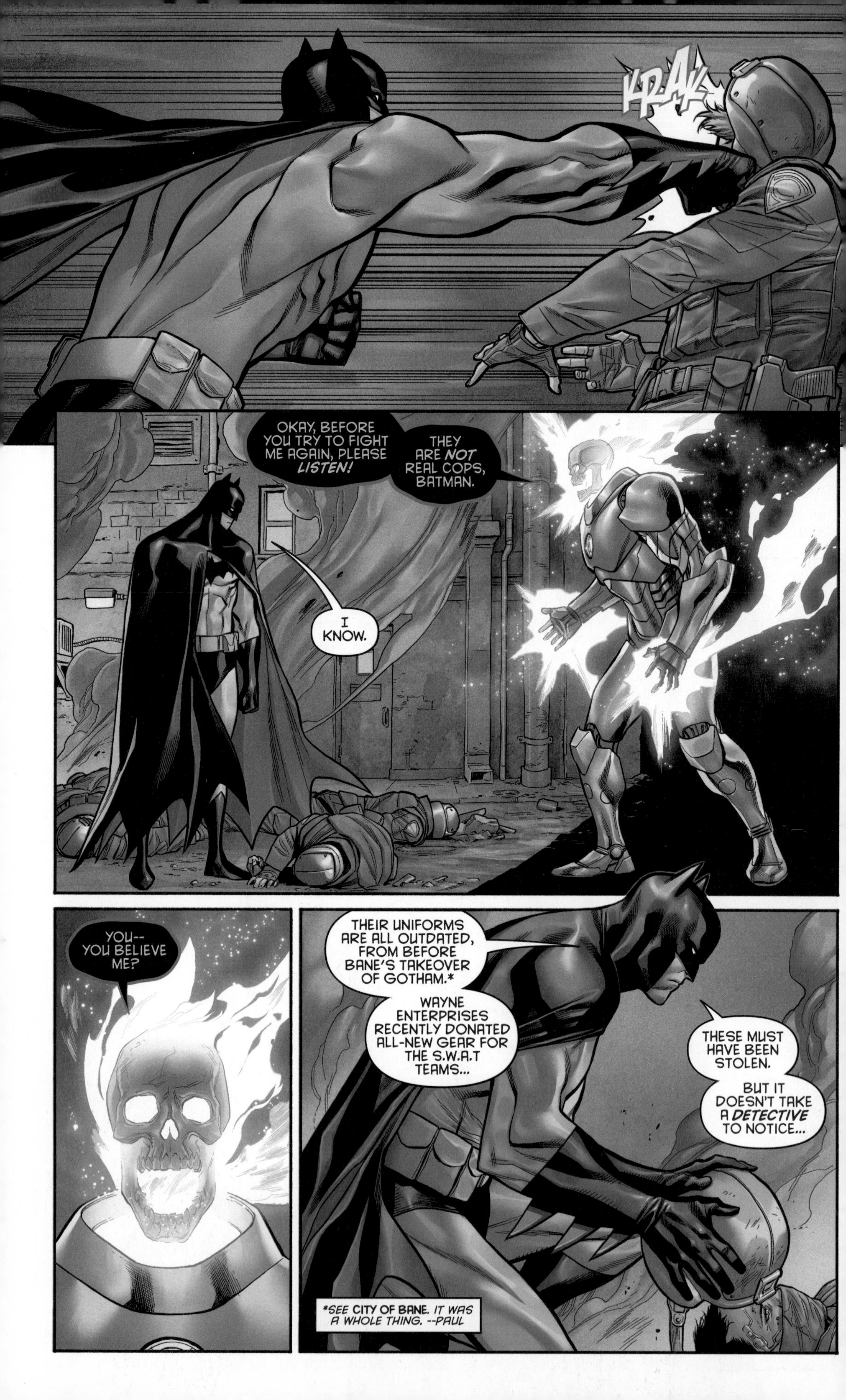
KRAK
OKAY, BEFORE YOU TRY TO FIGHT ME AGAIN, PLEASE LISTEN!
THEY ARE NOT REAL COPS, BATMAN.
I KNOW.
YOU-- YOU BELIEVE ME?
THEIR UNIFORMS ARE ALL OUTDATED, FROM BEFORE BANE'S TAKEOVER OF GOTHAM.*
WAYNE ENTERPRISES RECENTLY DONATED ALL-NEW GEAR FOR THE S.W.A.T TEAMS...
THESE MUST HAVE BEEN STOLEN.
BUT IT DOESN'T TAKE A DETECTIVE TO NOTICE...
*SEE CITY OF BANE. IT WAS A WHOLE THING. --PAUL

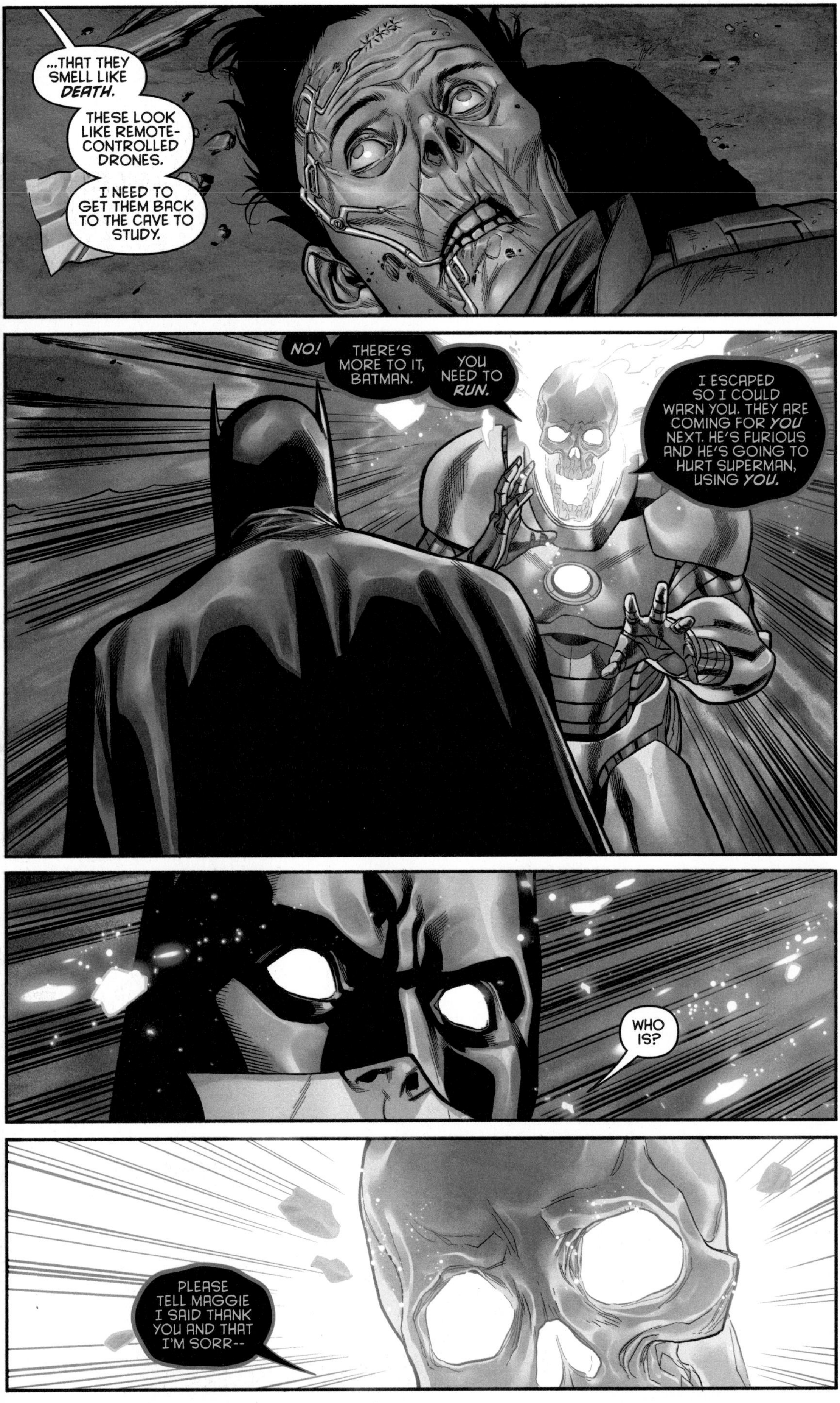

...THAT THEY SMELL LIKE *DEATH*.
THESE LOOK LIKE REMOTE-CONTROLLED DRONES.
I NEED TO GET THEM BACK TO THE CAVE TO STUDY.
NO!
THERE'S MORE TO IT, BATMAN.
YOU NEED TO *RUN*.
I ESCAPED SO I COULD WARN YOU. THEY ARE COMING FOR *YOU* NEXT. HE'S FURIOUS AND HE'S GOING TO HURT SUPERMAN, USING *YOU*.
WHO IS?
PLEASE TELL MAGGIE I SAID THANK YOU AND THAT I'M SORR--

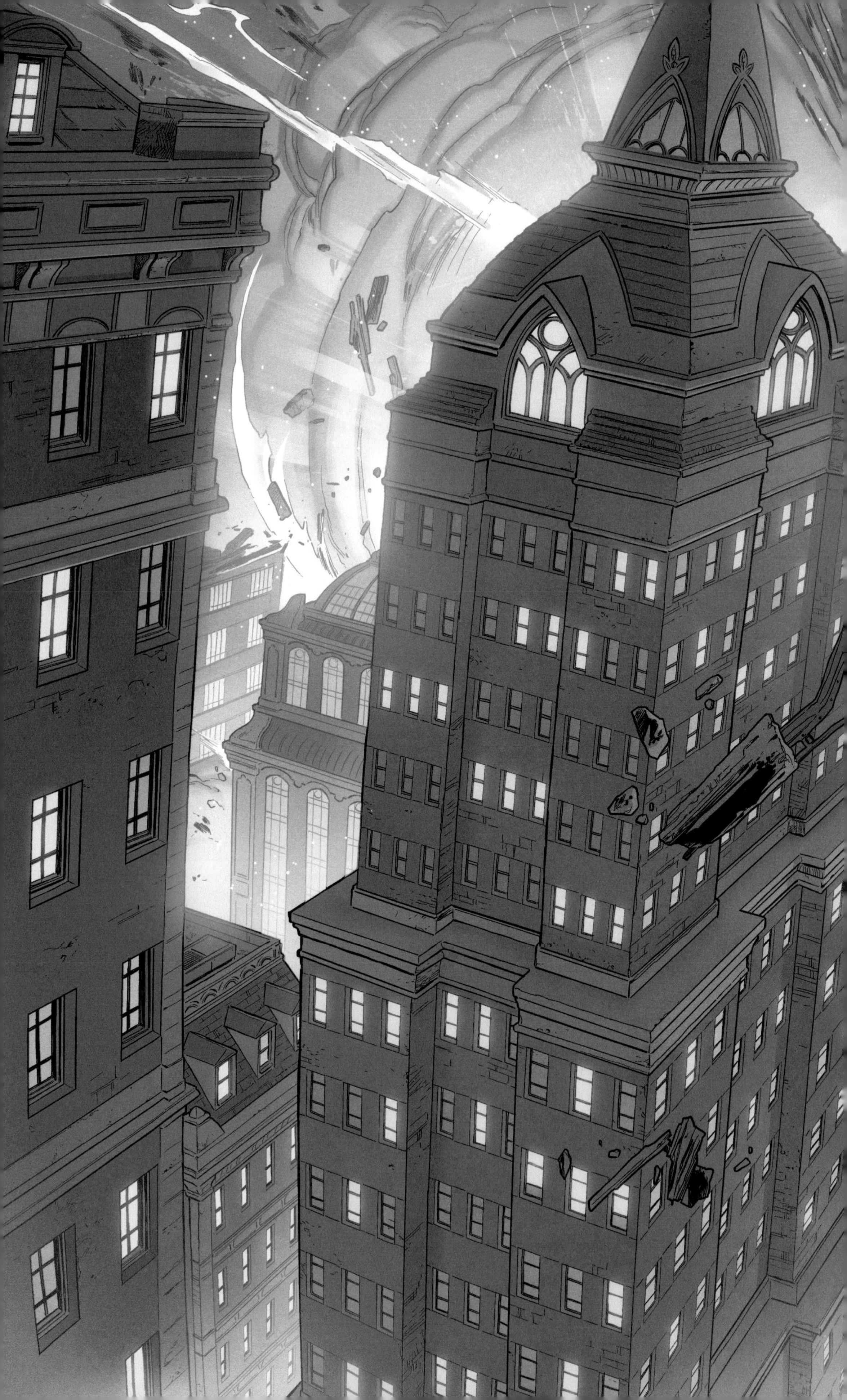

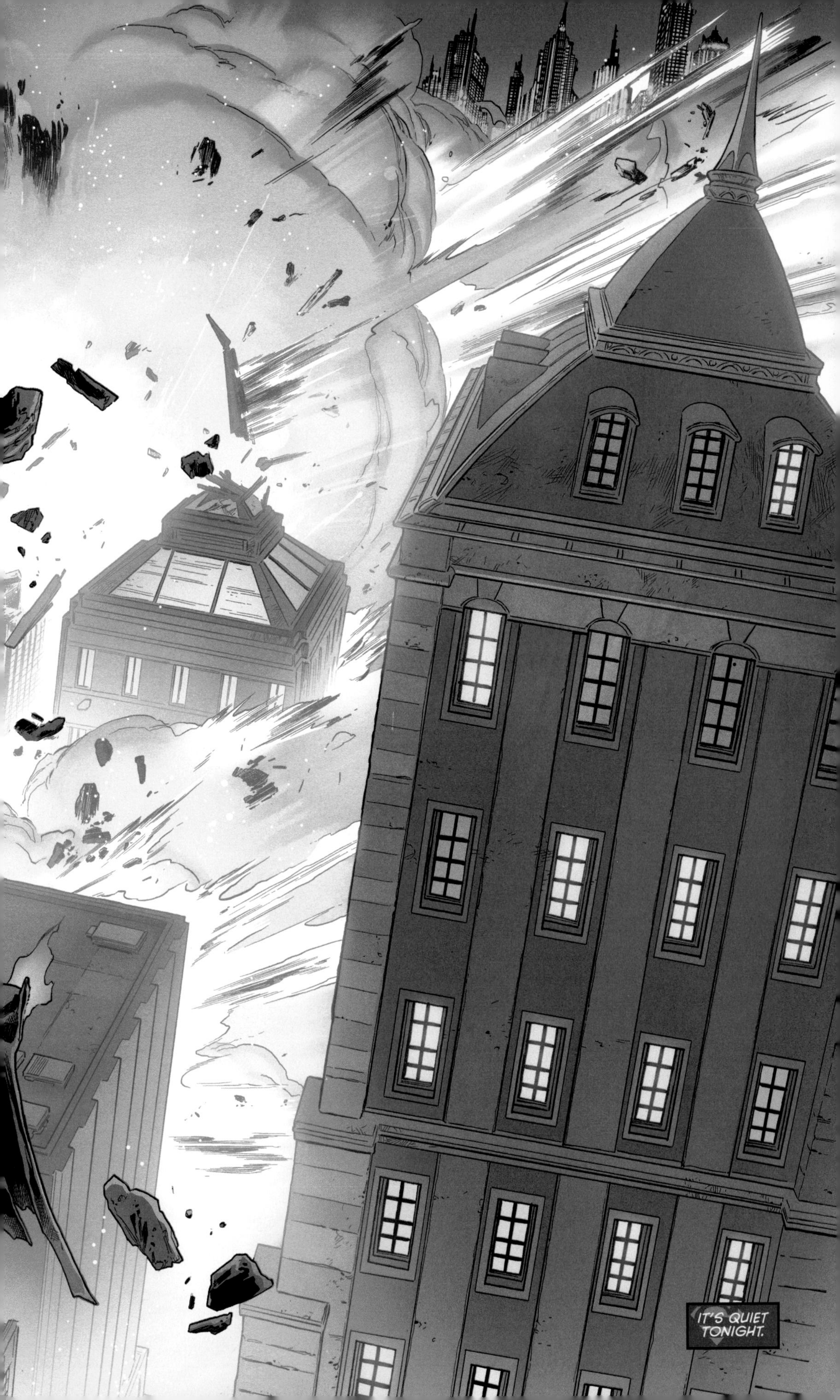
IT'S QUIET TONIGHT.

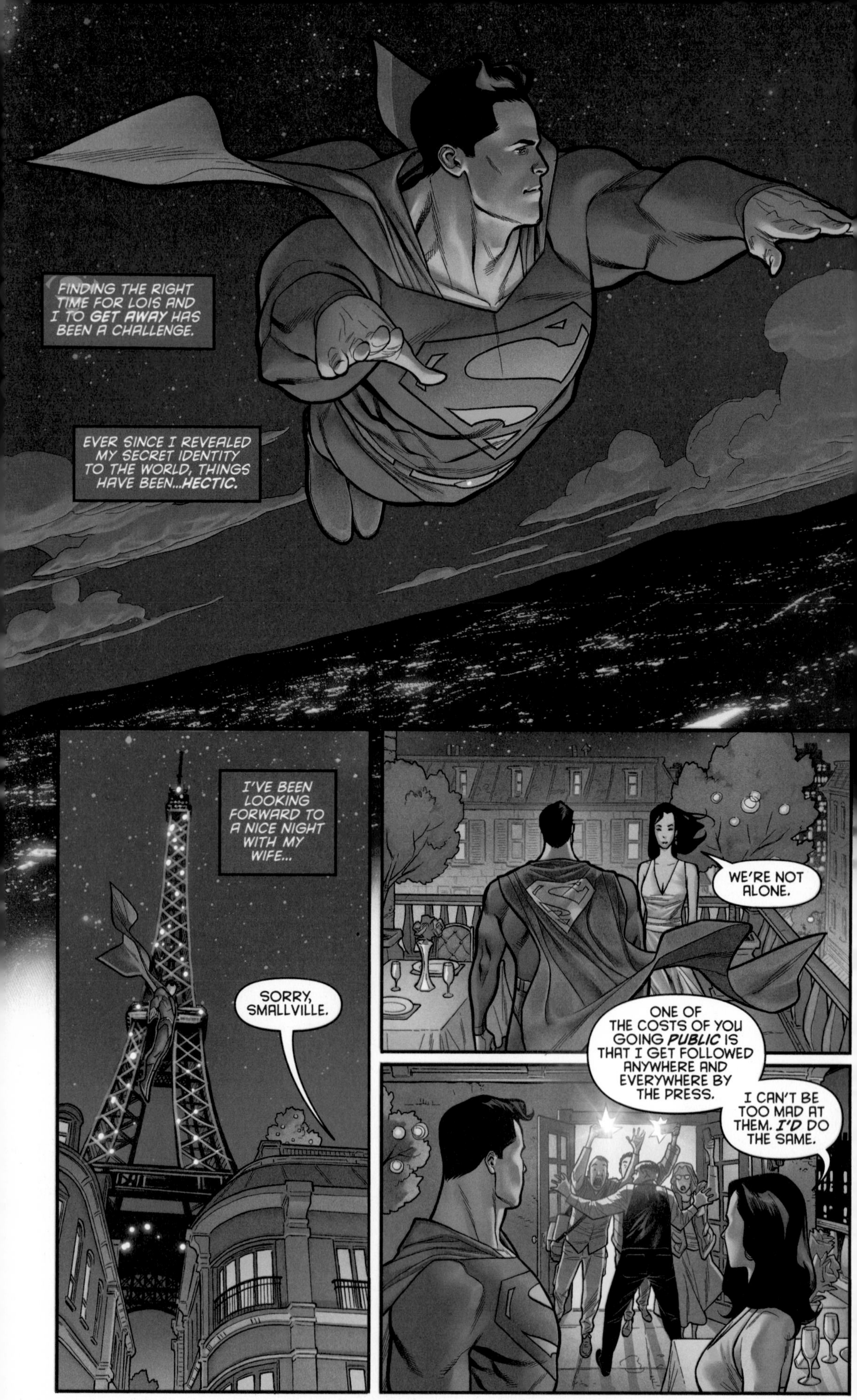
FINDING THE RIGHT TIME FOR LOIS AND I TO GET AWAY HAS BEEN A CHALLENGE.
EVER SINCE I REVEALED MY SECRET IDENTITY TO THE WORLD, THINGS HAVE BEEN...HECTIC.
I'VE BEEN LOOKING FORWARD TO A NICE NIGHT WITH MY WIFE...
SORRY, SMALLVILLE.
WE'RE NOT ALONE.
ONE OF THE COSTS OF YOU GOING PUBLIC IS THAT I GET FOLLOWED ANYWHERE AND EVERYWHERE BY THE PRESS.
I CAN'T BE TOO MAD AT THEM. I'D DO THE SAME.

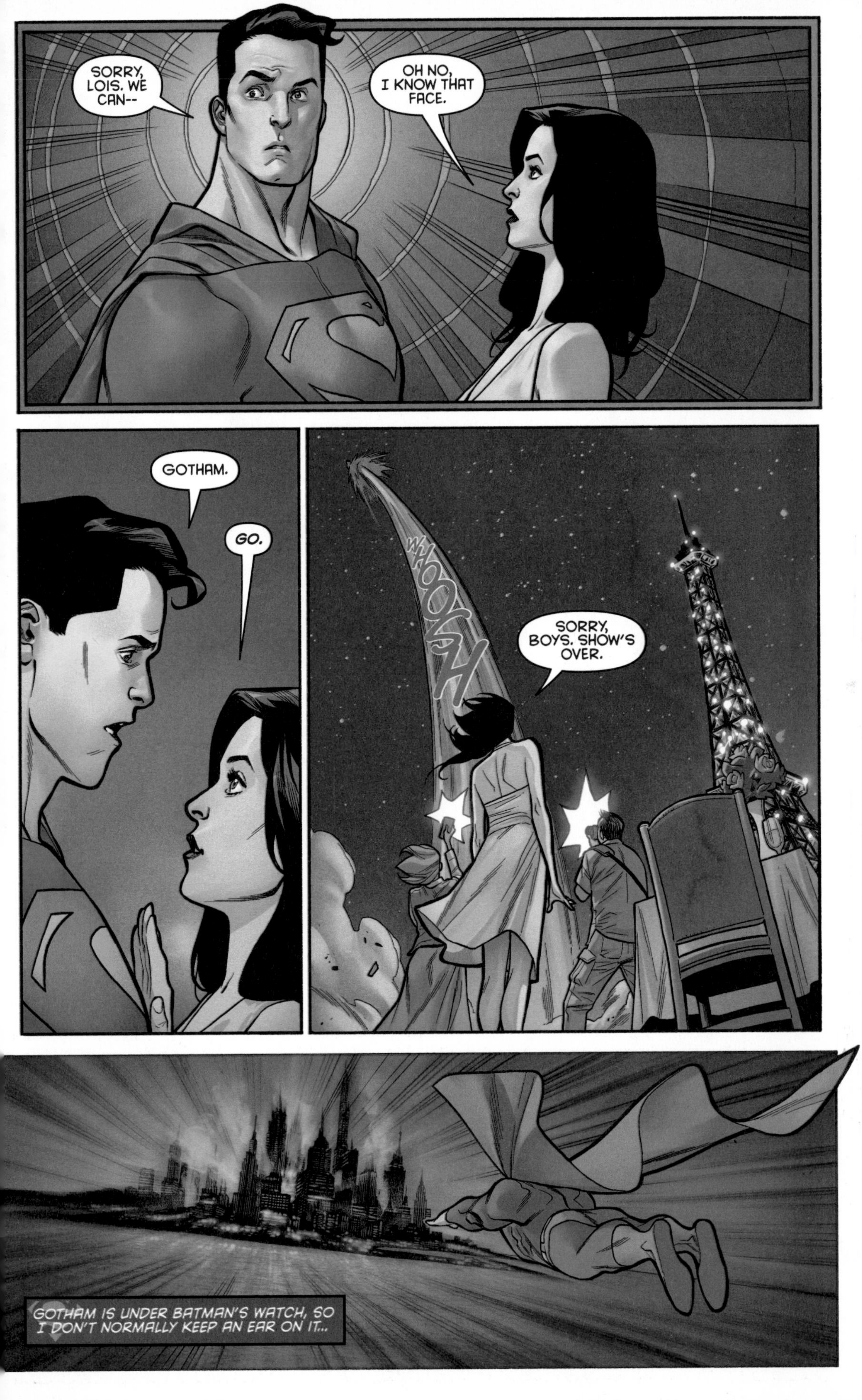
SORRY, LOIS. WE CAN--
OH NO, I KNOW THAT FACE.
GOTHAM.
GO.
WHOOOSH
SORRY, BOYS. SHOW'S OVER.
GOTHAM IS UNDER BATMAN'S WATCH, SO I DON'T NORMALLY KEEP AN EAR ON IT...

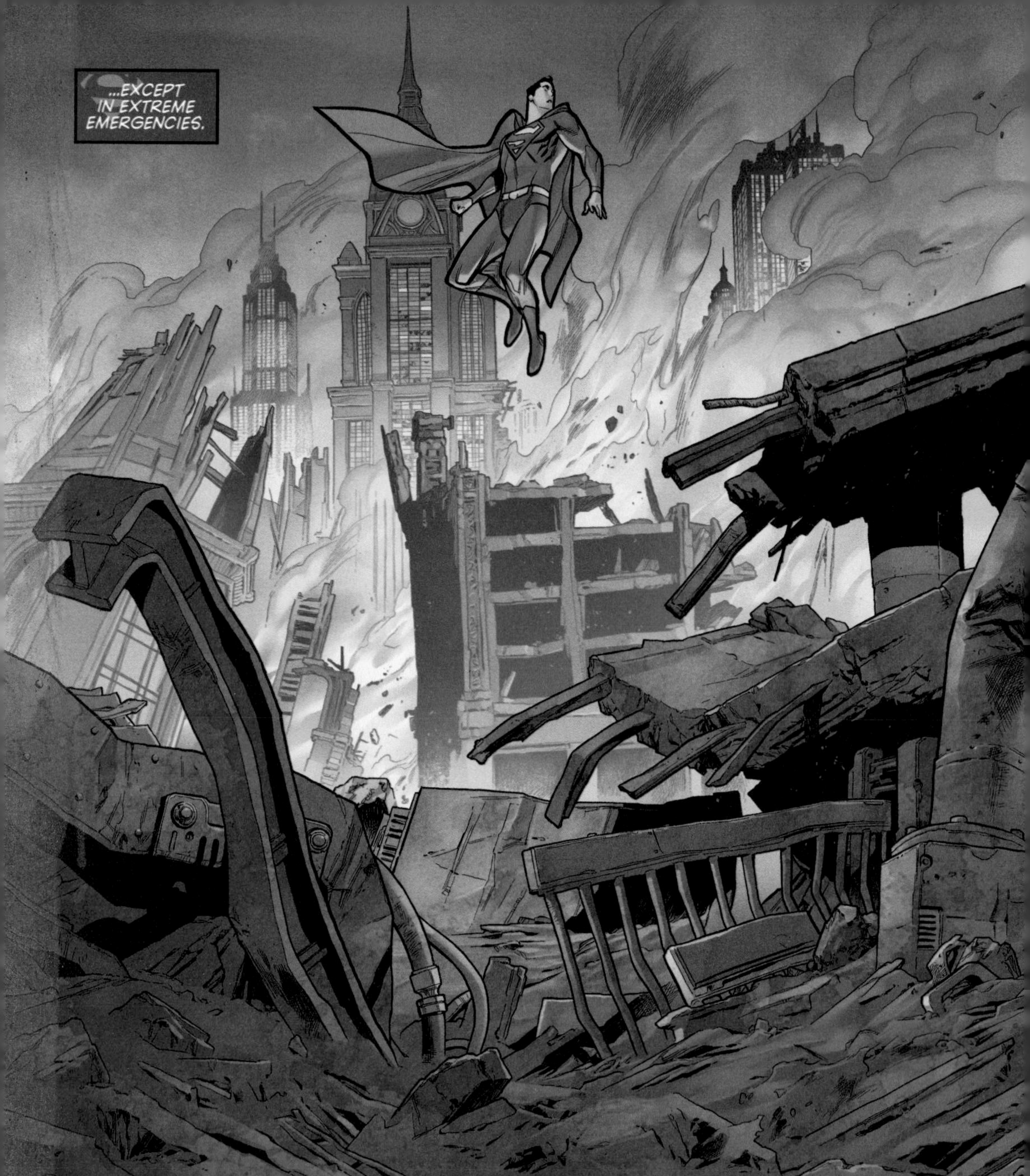
...EXCEPT IN EXTREME EMERGENCIES.

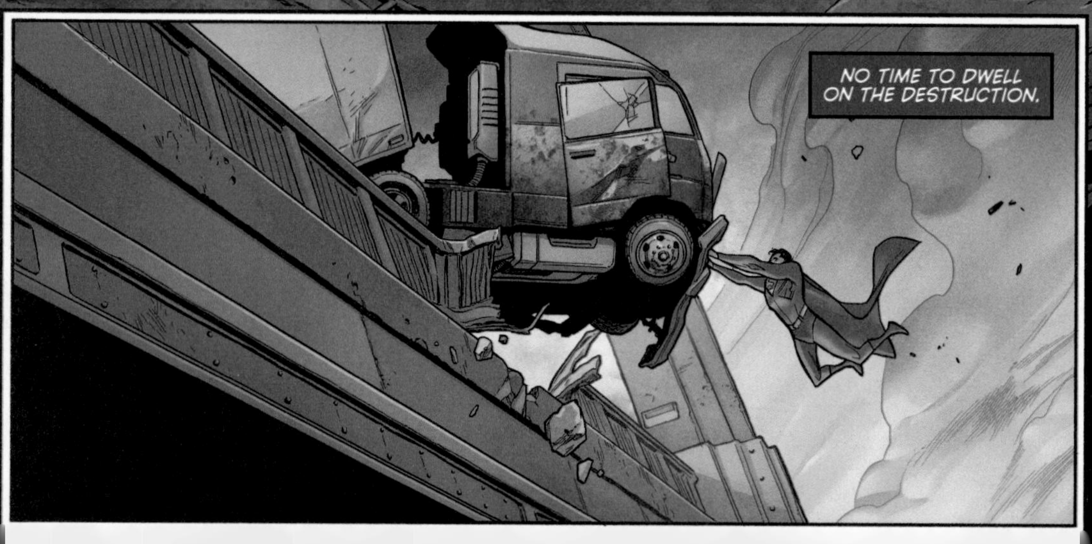
NO TIME TO DWELL ON THE DESTRUCTION.

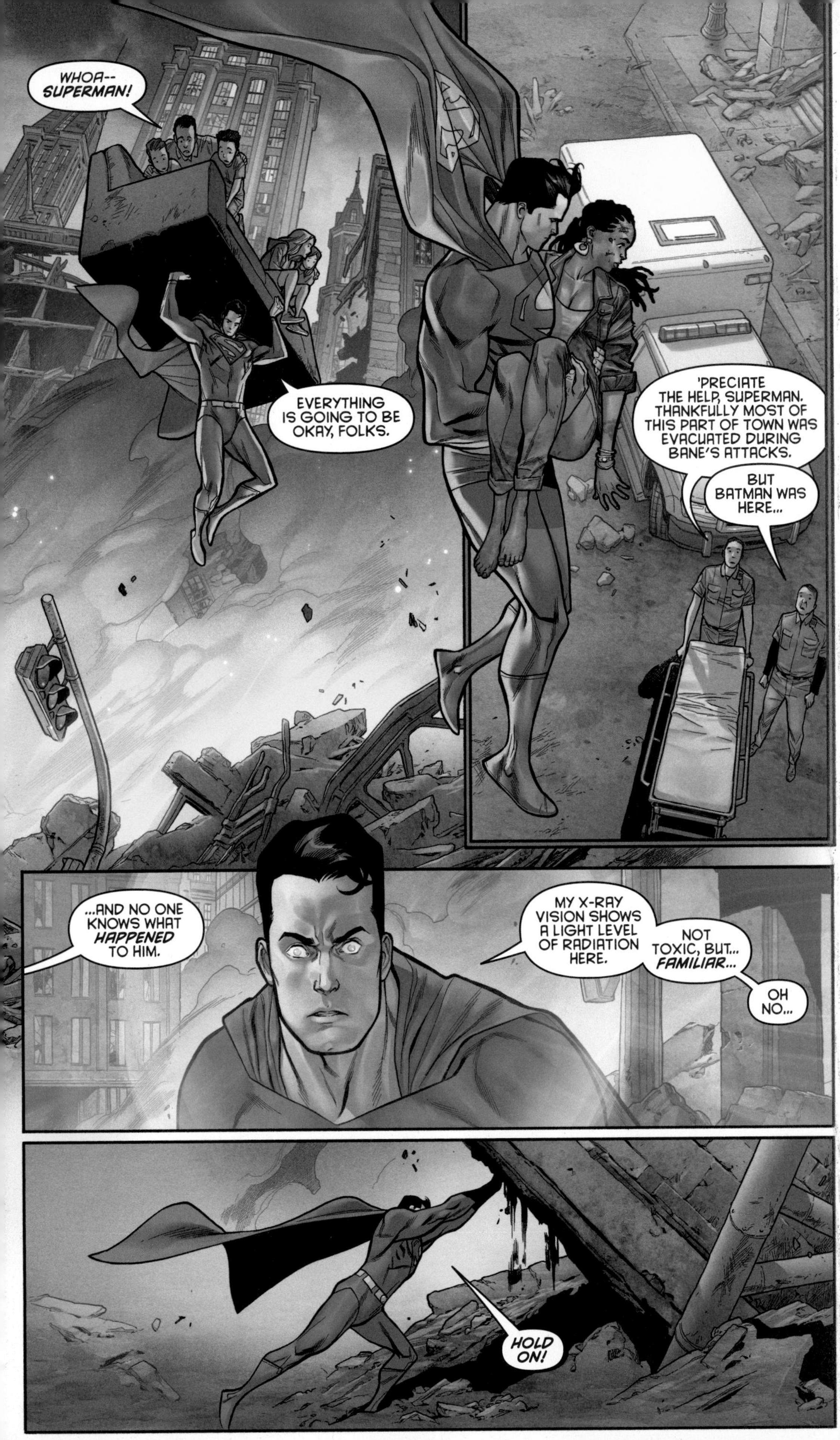
WHOA-- SUPERMAN!
EVERYTHING IS GOING TO BE OKAY, FOLKS.
'PRECIATE THE HELP, SUPERMAN. THANKFULLY MOST OF THIS PART OF TOWN WAS EVACUATED DURING BANE'S ATTACKS.
BUT BATMAN WAS HERE...
...AND NO ONE KNOWS WHAT HAPPENED TO HIM.
MY X-RAY VISION SHOWS A LIGHT LEVEL OF RADIATION HERE.
NOT TOXIC, BUT... FAMILIAR...
OH NO...
HOLD ON!

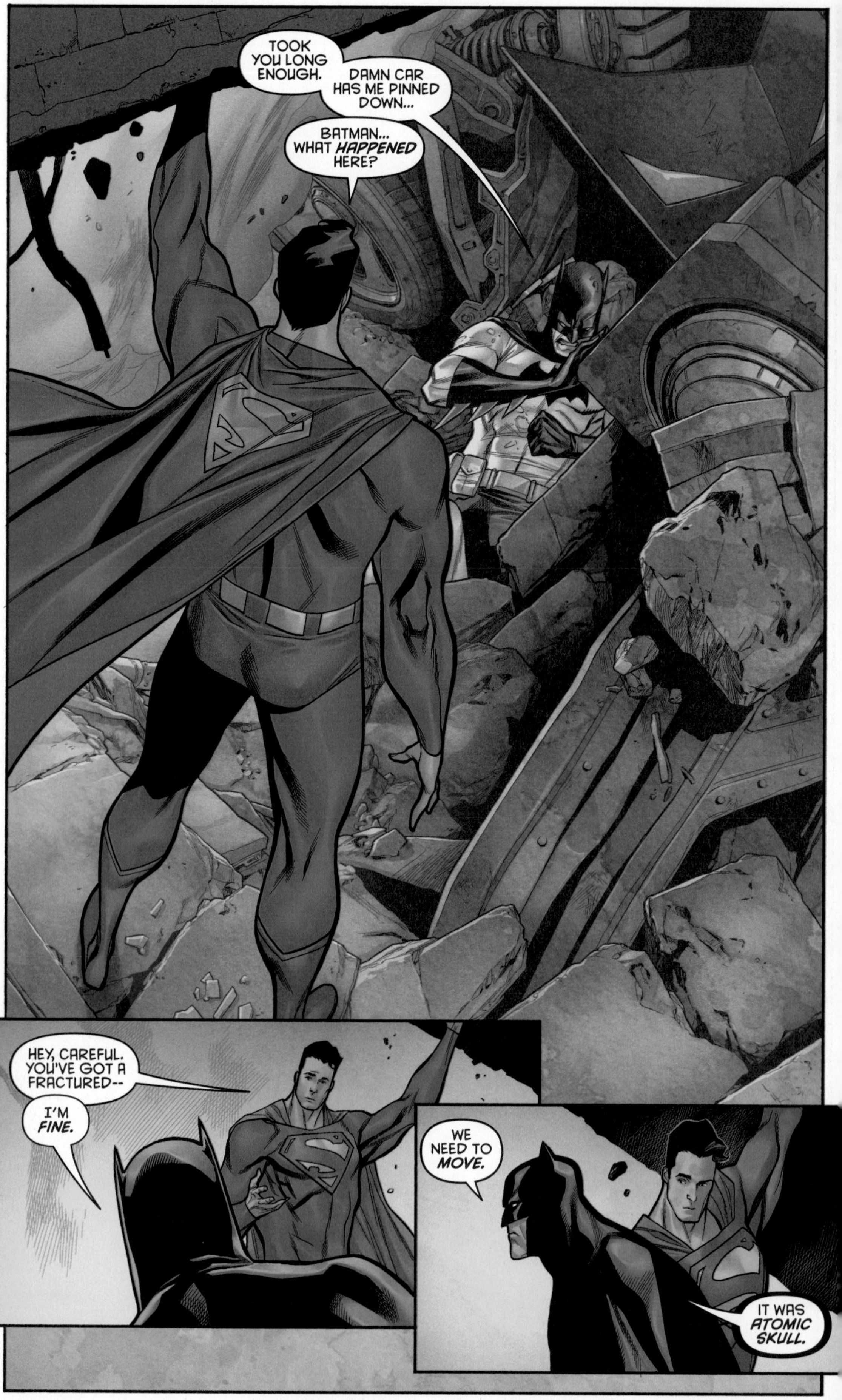
TOOK YOU LONG ENOUGH.
DAMN CAR HAS ME PINNED DOWN...
BATMAN... WHAT *HAPPENED* HERE?
HEY, CAREFUL. YOU'VE GOT A FRACTURED--
I'M *FINE.*
WE NEED TO *MOVE.*
IT WAS *ATOMIC SKULL.*

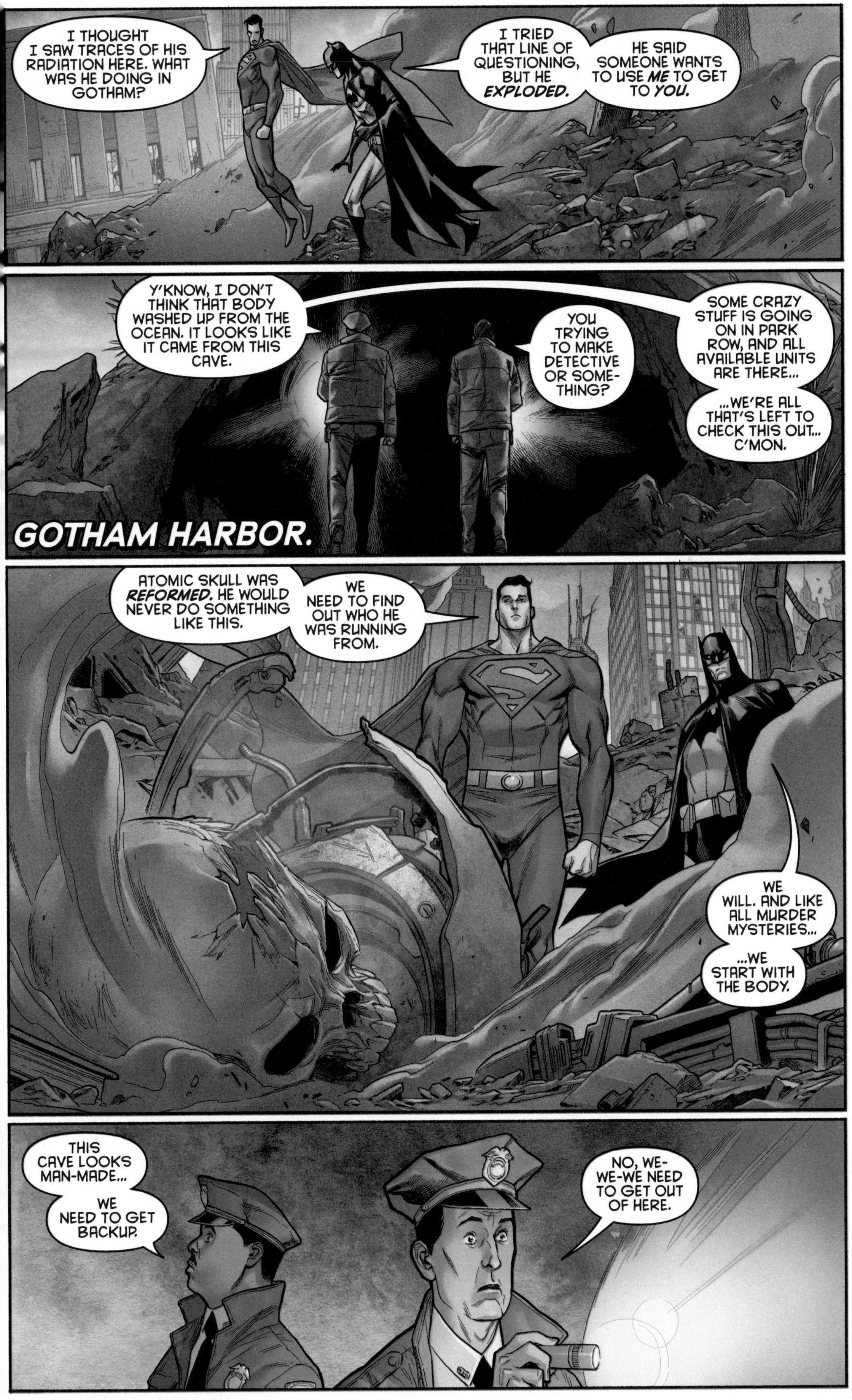

I THOUGHT I SAW TRACES OF HIS RADIATION HERE. WHAT WAS HE DOING IN GOTHAM?
I TRIED THAT LINE OF QUESTIONING, BUT HE EXPLODED.
HE SAID SOMEONE WANTS TO USE ME TO GET TO YOU.
GOTHAM HARBOR.
Y'KNOW, I DON'T THINK THAT BODY WASHED UP FROM THE OCEAN. IT LOOKS LIKE IT CAME FROM THIS CAVE.
YOU TRYING TO MAKE DETECTIVE OR SOME-THING?
SOME CRAZY STUFF IS GOING ON IN PARK ROW, AND ALL AVAILABLE UNITS ARE THERE...
...WE'RE ALL THAT'S LEFT TO CHECK THIS OUT... C'MON.
ATOMIC SKULL WAS REFORMED. HE WOULD NEVER DO SOMETHING LIKE THIS.
WE NEED TO FIND OUT WHO HE WAS RUNNING FROM.
WE WILL. AND LIKE ALL MURDER MYSTERIES...
...WE START WITH THE BODY.
THIS CAVE LOOKS MAN-MADE...
WE NEED TO GET BACKUP.
NO, WE-WE-WE NEED TO GET OUT OF HERE.

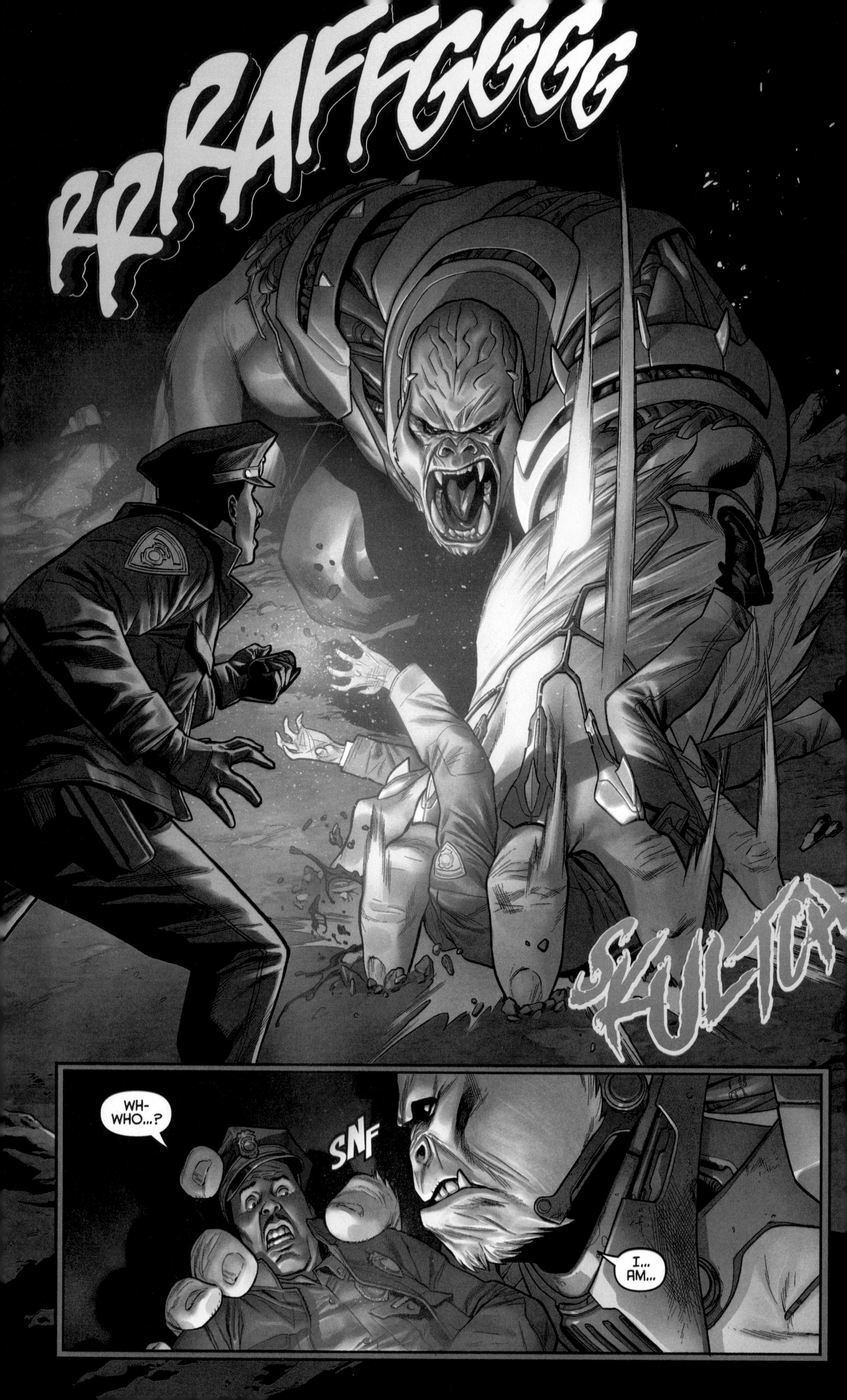
RRRAFFGGGG
SKULTOR
WH-
WHO...?
SNF
I...
AM...

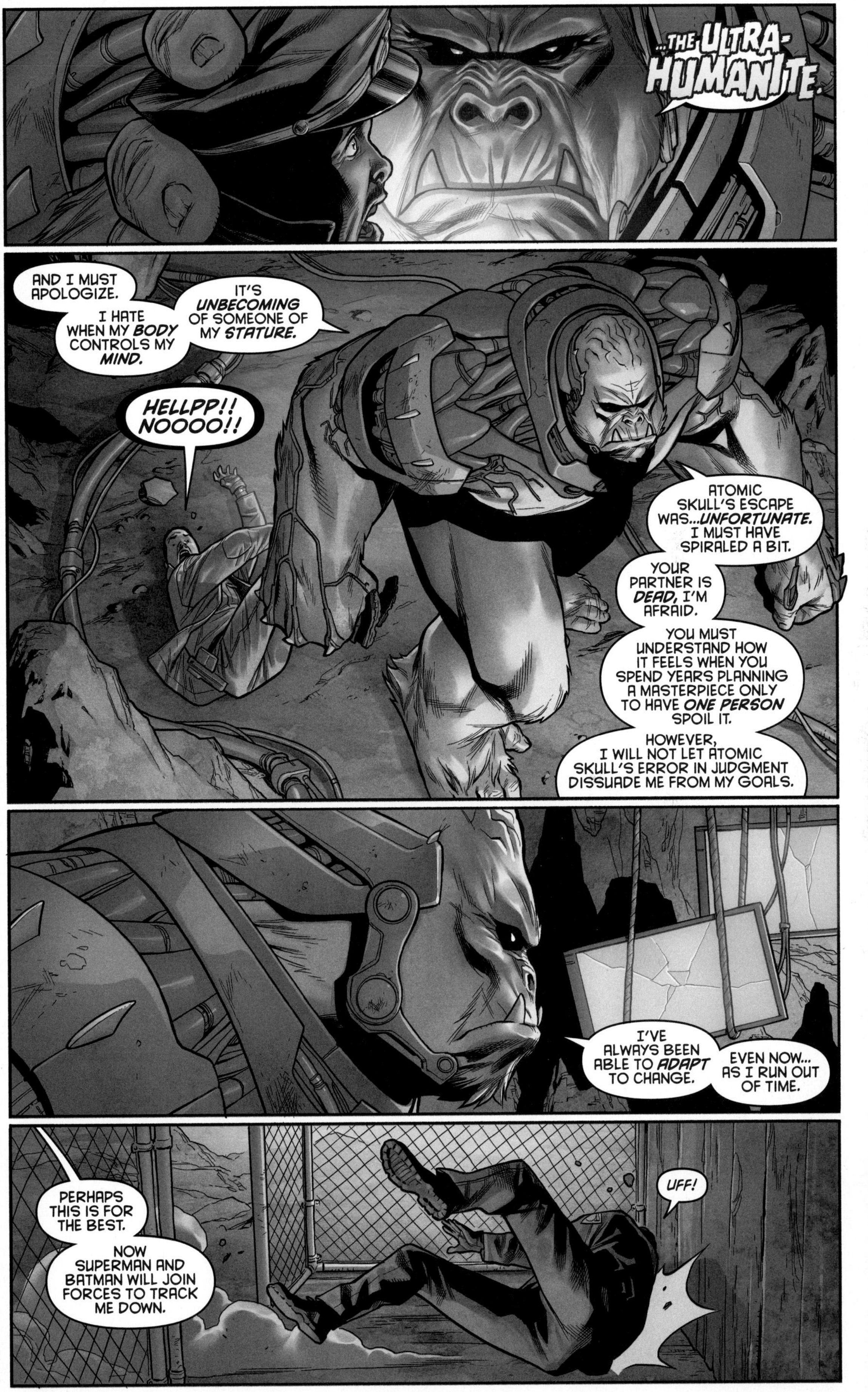
...THE ULTRA-HUMANITE.
AND I MUST APOLOGIZE.
I HATE WHEN MY BODY CONTROLS MY MIND.
IT'S UNBECOMING OF SOMEONE OF MY STATURE.
HELLPP!! NOOOO!!
ATOMIC SKULL'S ESCAPE WAS...UNFORTUNATE. I MUST HAVE SPIRALED A BIT.
YOUR PARTNER IS DEAD, I'M AFRAID.
YOU MUST UNDERSTAND HOW IT FEELS WHEN YOU SPEND YEARS PLANNING A MASTERPIECE ONLY TO HAVE ONE PERSON SPOIL IT.
HOWEVER, I WILL NOT LET ATOMIC SKULL'S ERROR IN JUDGMENT DISSUADE ME FROM MY GOALS.
I'VE ALWAYS BEEN ABLE TO ADAPT TO CHANGE.
EVEN NOW... AS I RUN OUT OF TIME.
PERHAPS THIS IS FOR THE BEST.
NOW SUPERMAN AND BATMAN WILL JOIN FORCES TO TRACK ME DOWN.
UFF!

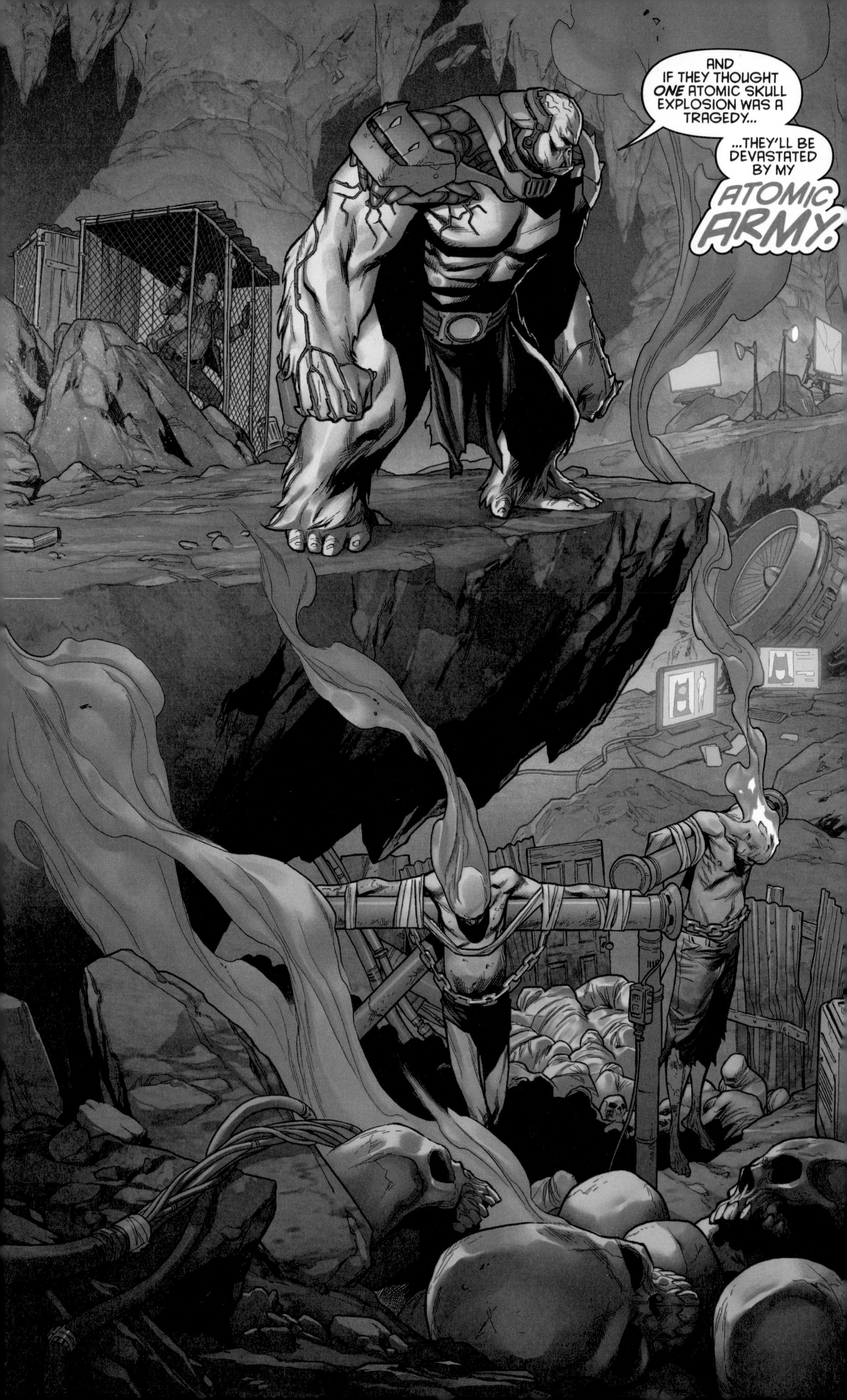
AND IF THEY THOUGHT ONE ATOMIC SKULL EXPLOSION WAS A TRAGEDY...
...THEY'LL BE DEVASTATED BY MY
ATOMIC ARMY.

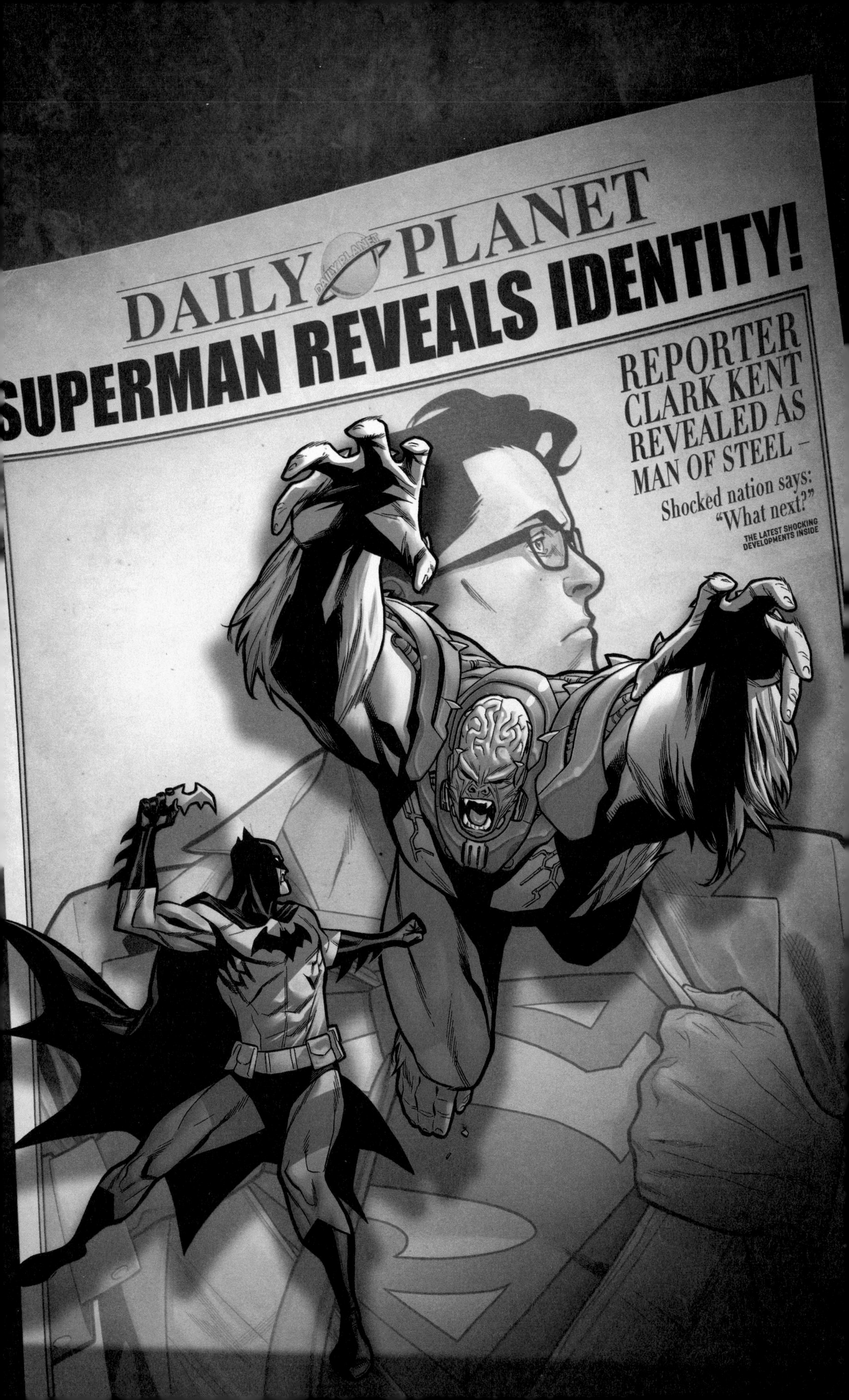
DAILY PLANET
DAILY PLANET
SUPERMAN REVEALS IDENTITY!
REPORTER CLARK KENT REVEALED AS MAN OF STEEL –
Shocked nation says: "What next?"
THE LATEST SHOCKING DEVELOPMENTS INSIDE

BATMAN/SUPERMAN #10

cover by
CLAYTON HENRY and **ALEJANDRO SÁNCHEZ**

ONCE UPON A TIME IN METROPOLIS.

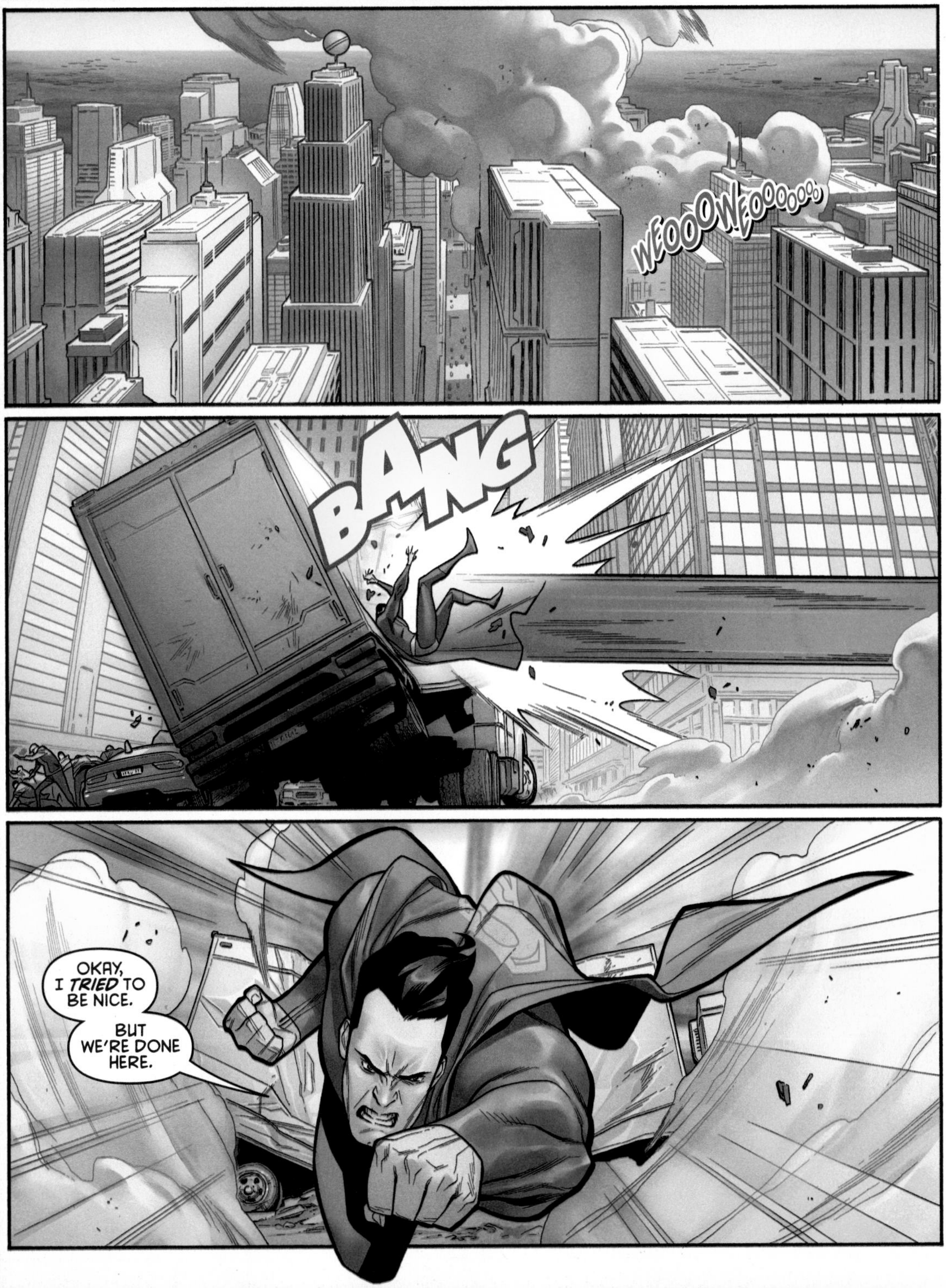

WEOOOWEOOooooo
BANG
OKAY, I *TRIED* TO BE NICE.
BUT WE'RE DONE HERE.

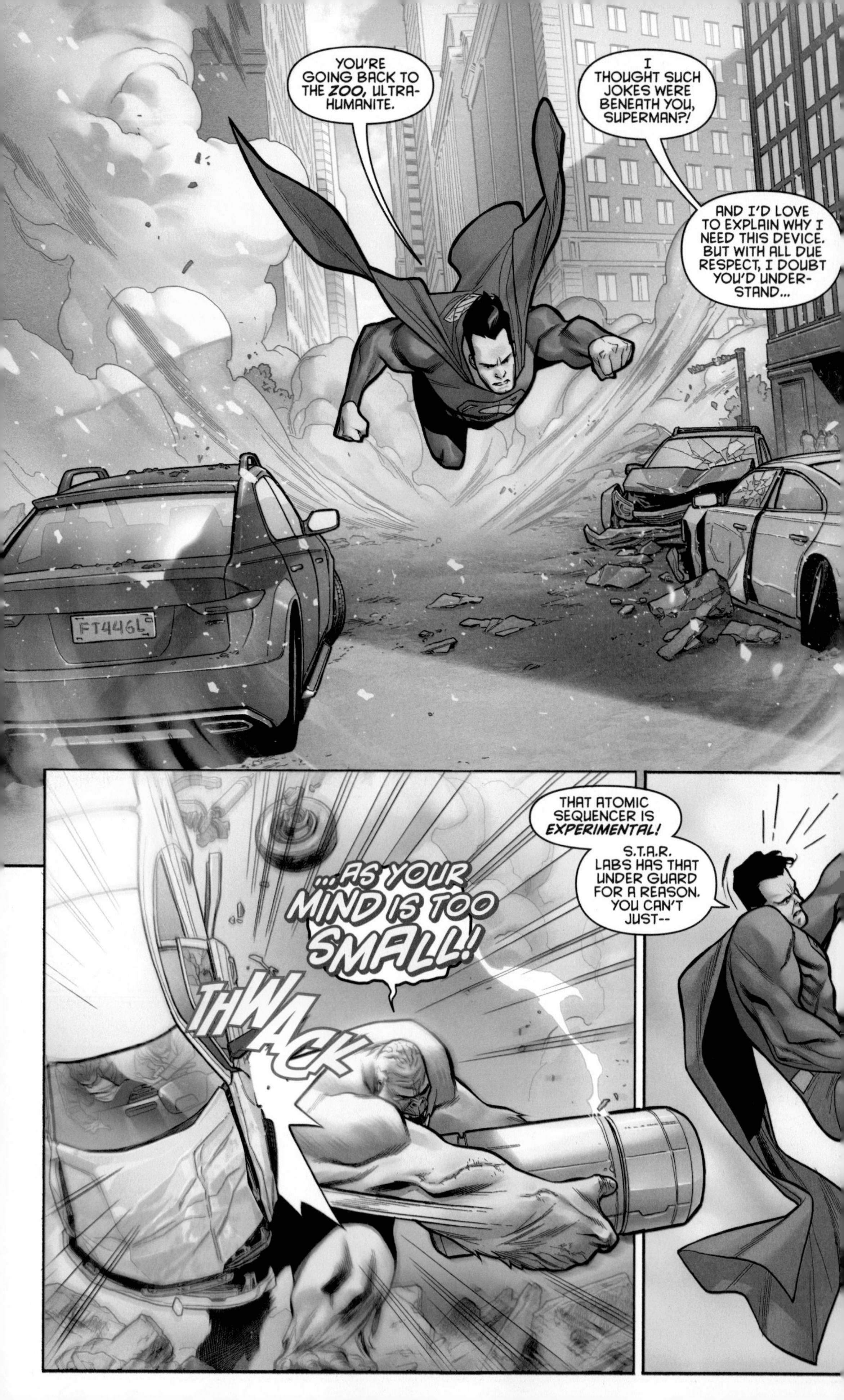
YOU'RE GOING BACK TO THE *ZOO*, ULTRA-HUMANITE.
I THOUGHT SUCH JOKES WERE BENEATH YOU, SUPERMAN?!
AND I'D LOVE TO EXPLAIN WHY I NEED THIS DEVICE. BUT WITH ALL DUE RESPECT, I DOUBT YOU'D UNDERSTAND...
FT446L
...AS YOUR MIND IS TOO SMALL!
THWACK
THAT ATOMIC SEQUENCER IS *EXPERIMENTAL!*
S.T.A.R. LABS HAS THAT UNDER GUARD FOR A REASON. YOU CAN'T JUST--

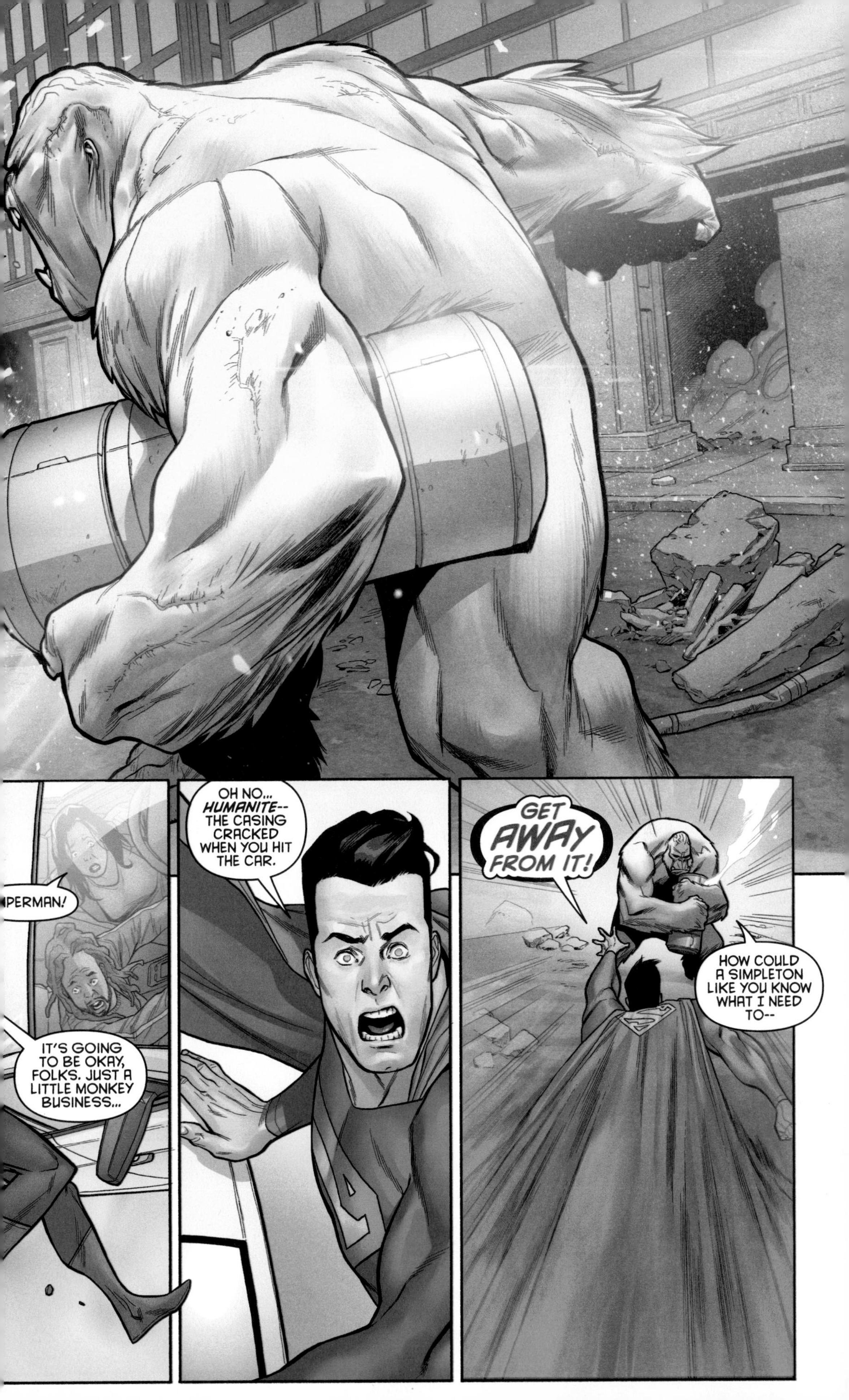
PERMAN!
IT'S GOING TO BE OKAY, FOLKS. JUST A LITTLE MONKEY BUSINESS...
OH NO... HUMANITE-- THE CASING CRACKED WHEN YOU HIT THE CAR.
GET AWAY FROM IT!
HOW COULD A SIMPLETON LIKE YOU KNOW WHAT I NEED TO--

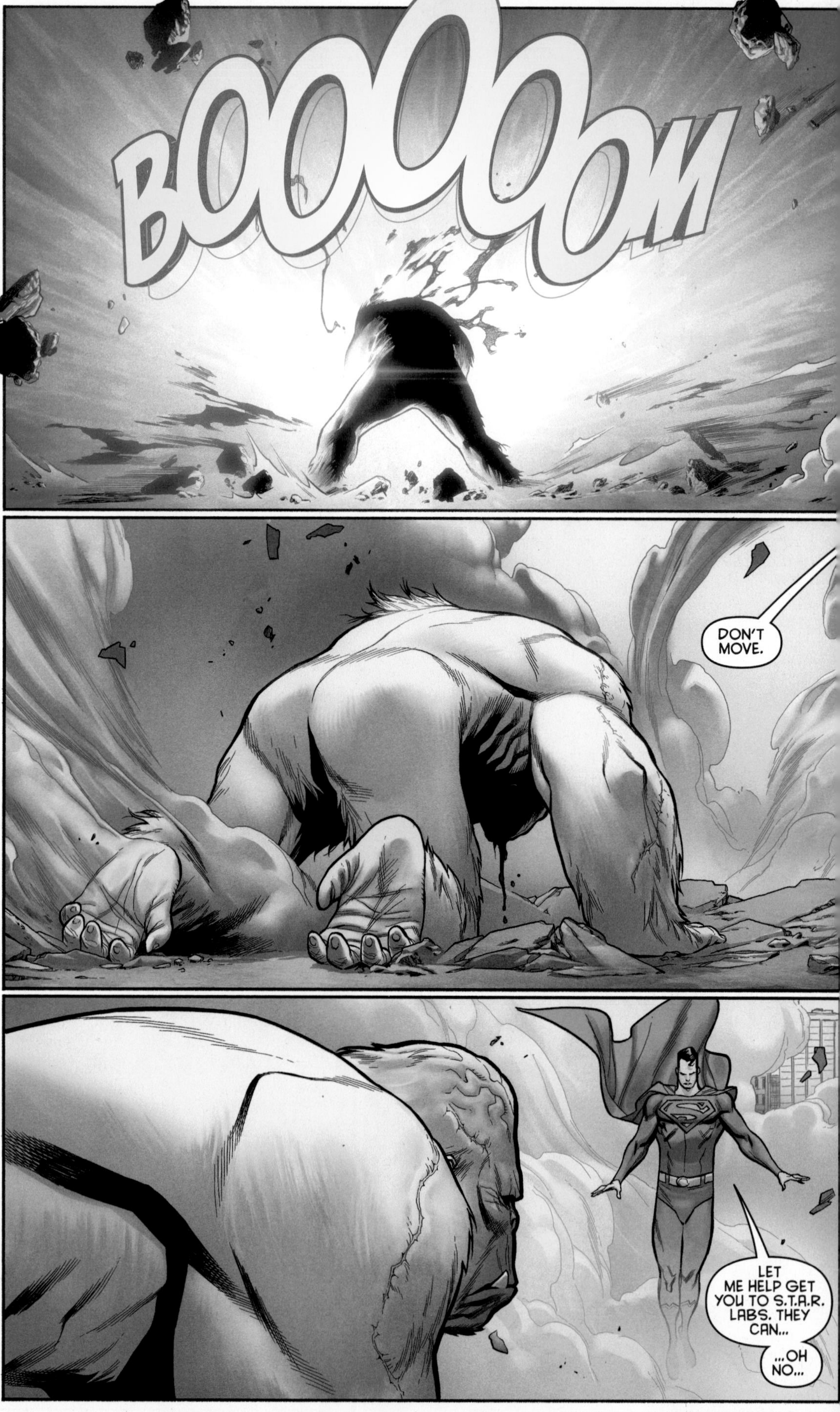
BOOOOOOM
DON'T MOVE.
LET ME HELP GET YOU TO S.T.A.R. LABS. THEY CAN...
...OH NO...

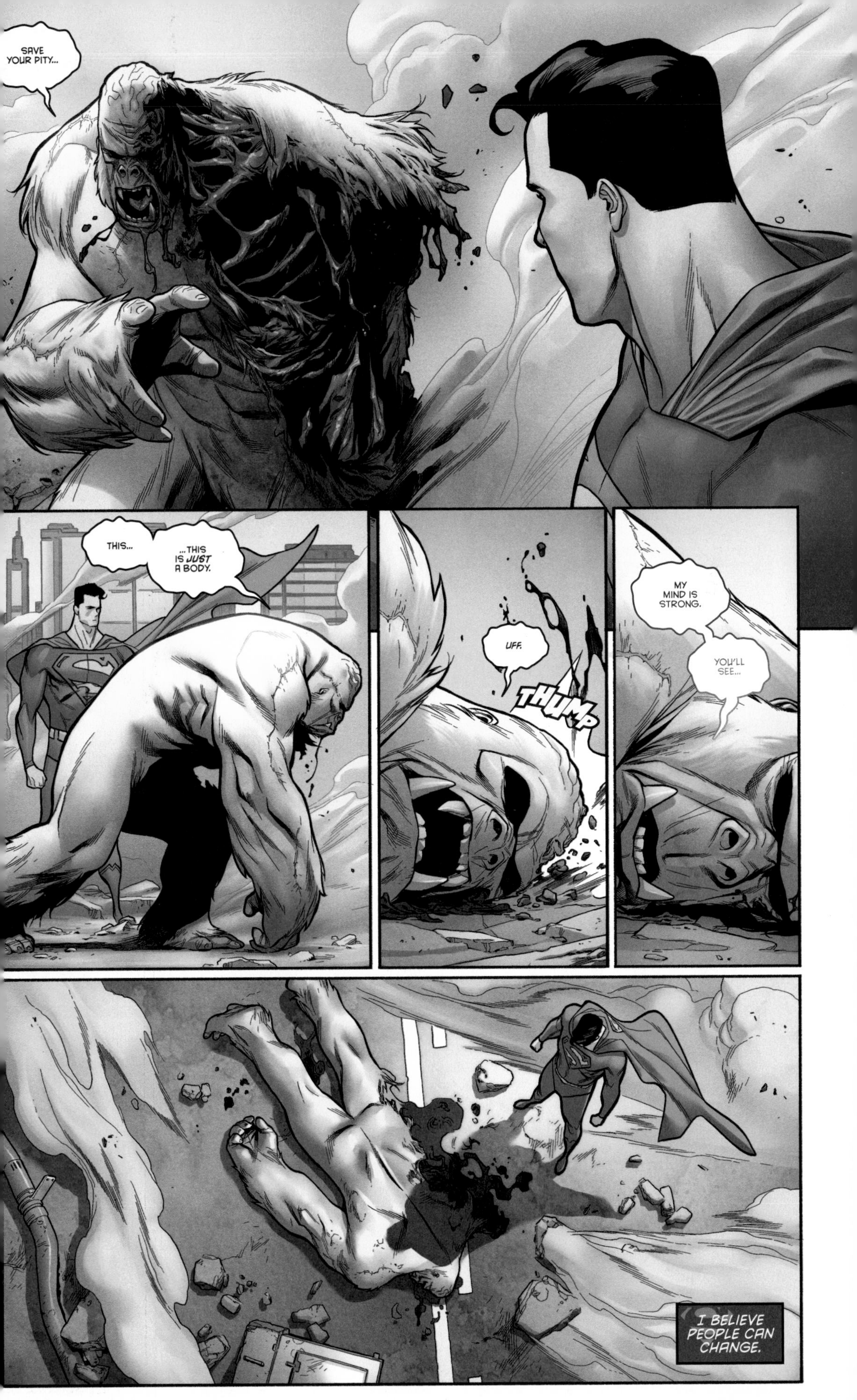
SAVE YOUR PITY...
THIS...
...THIS IS *JUST* A BODY.
UFF.
THUMP
MY MIND IS STRONG.
YOU'LL SEE...
I BELIEVE PEOPLE CAN CHANGE.

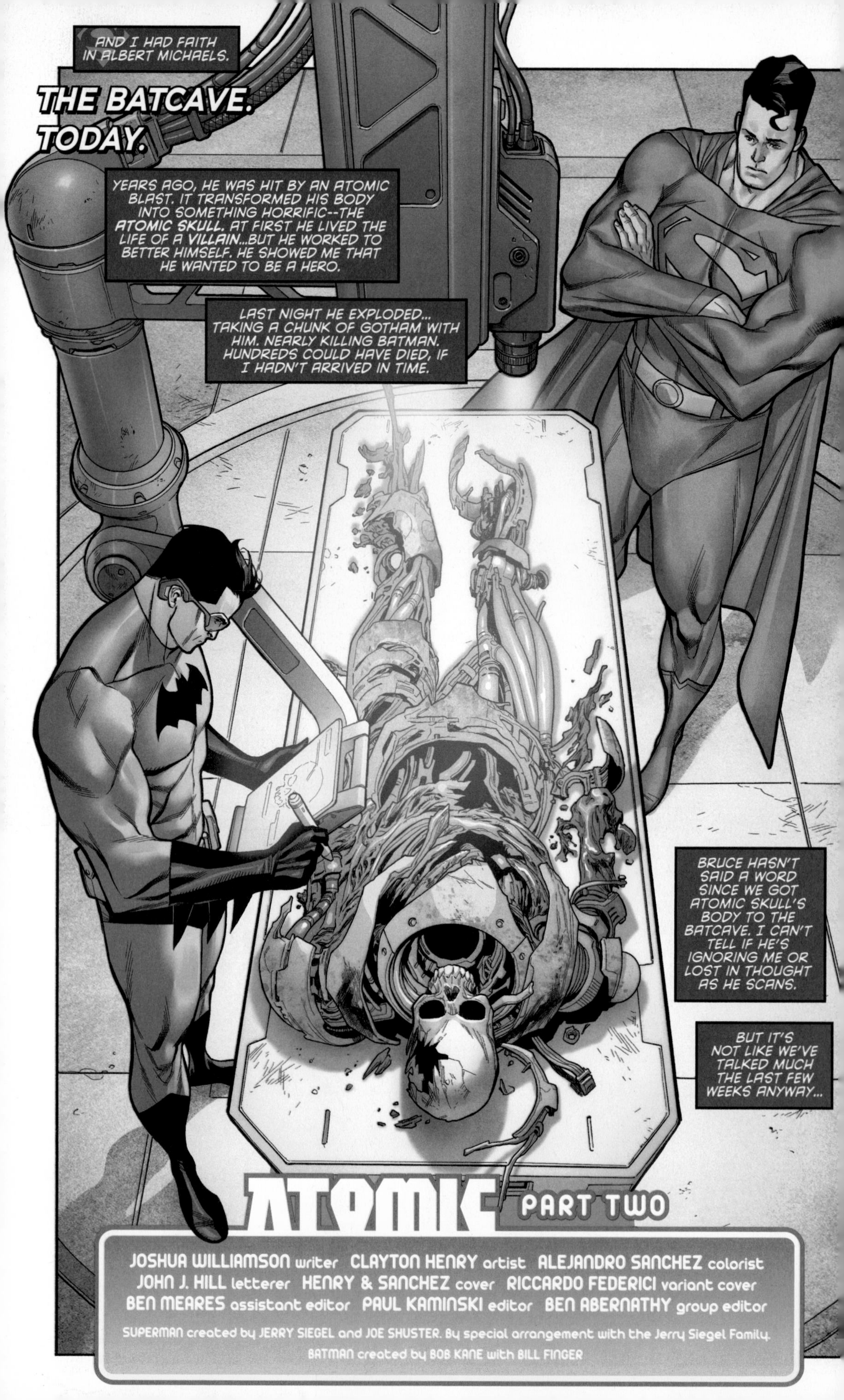
AND I HAD FAITH IN ALBERT MICHAELS.
THE BATCAVE. TODAY.
YEARS AGO, HE WAS HIT BY AN ATOMIC BLAST. IT TRANSFORMED HIS BODY INTO SOMETHING HORRIFIC--THE ATOMIC SKULL. AT FIRST HE LIVED THE LIFE OF A VILLAIN...BUT HE WORKED TO BETTER HIMSELF. HE SHOWED ME THAT HE WANTED TO BE A HERO.
LAST NIGHT HE EXPLODED... TAKING A CHUNK OF GOTHAM WITH HIM. NEARLY KILLING BATMAN. HUNDREDS COULD HAVE DIED, IF I HADN'T ARRIVED IN TIME.
BRUCE HASN'T SAID A WORD SINCE WE GOT ATOMIC SKULL'S BODY TO THE BATCAVE. I CAN'T TELL IF HE'S IGNORING ME OR LOST IN THOUGHT AS HE SCANS.
BUT IT'S NOT LIKE WE'VE TALKED MUCH THE LAST FEW WEEKS ANYWAY...
ATOMIC PART TWO
JOSHUA WILLIAMSON writer CLAYTON HENRY artist ALEJANDRO SANCHEZ colorist
JOHN J. HILL letterer HENRY & SANCHEZ cover RICCARDO FEDERICI variant cover
BEN MEARES assistant editor PAUL KAMINSKI editor BEN ABERNATHY group editor
SUPERMAN created by JERRY SIEGEL and JOE SHUSTER. By special arrangement with the Jerry Siegel Family.
BATMAN created by BOB KANE with BILL FINGER

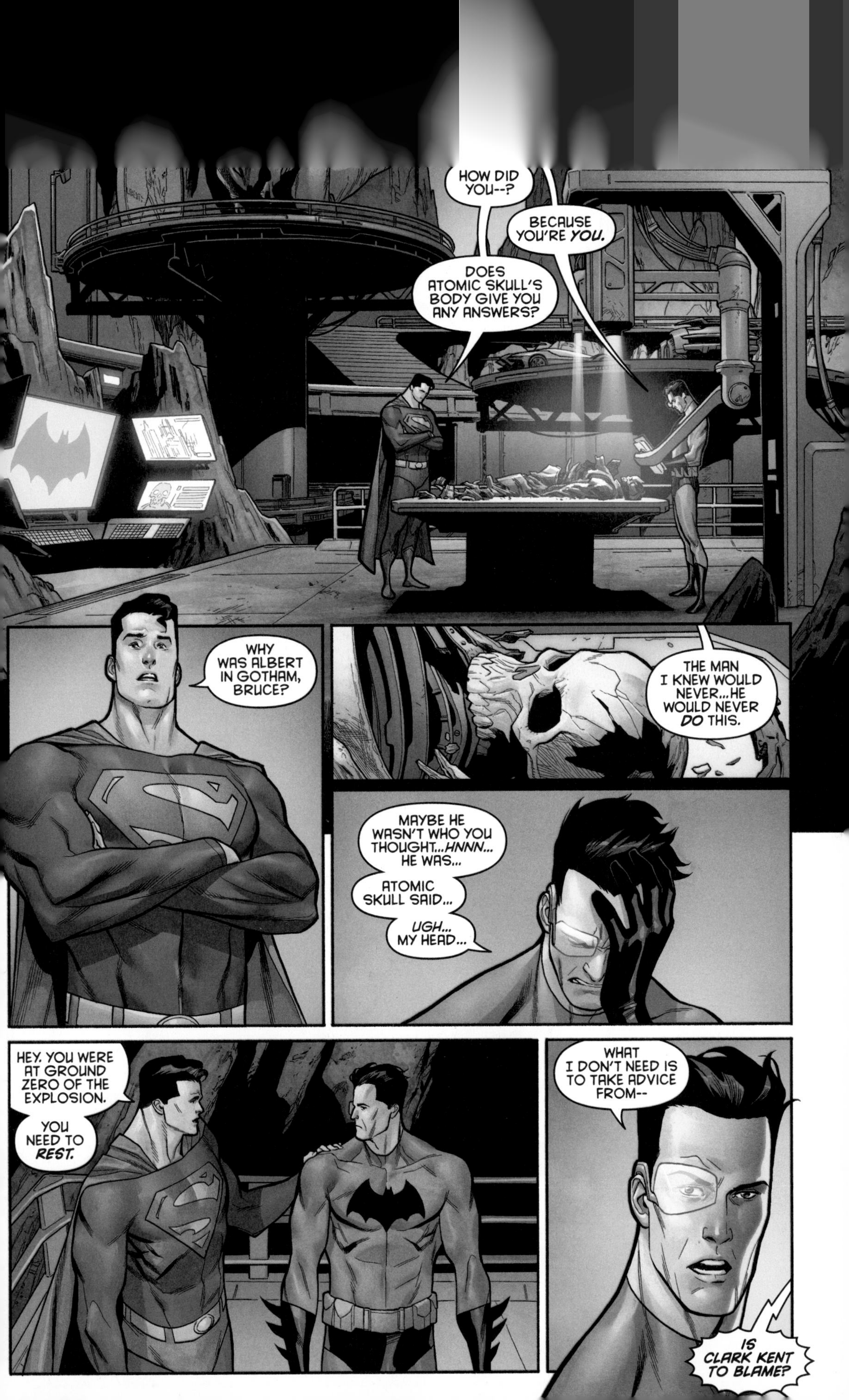
HOW DID YOU--?
BECAUSE YOU'RE *YOU.*
DOES ATOMIC SKULL'S BODY GIVE YOU ANY ANSWERS?
WHY WAS ALBERT IN GOTHAM, BRUCE?
THE MAN I KNEW WOULD NEVER...HE WOULD NEVER *DO* THIS.
MAYBE HE WASN'T WHO YOU THOUGHT...*HNNN...* HE WAS...
ATOMIC SKULL SAID...
UGH... MY HEAD...
HEY. YOU WERE AT GROUND ZERO OF THE EXPLOSION.
YOU NEED TO ***REST.***
WHAT I DON'T NEED IS TO TAKE ADVICE FROM--
IS CLARK KENT TO BLAME?

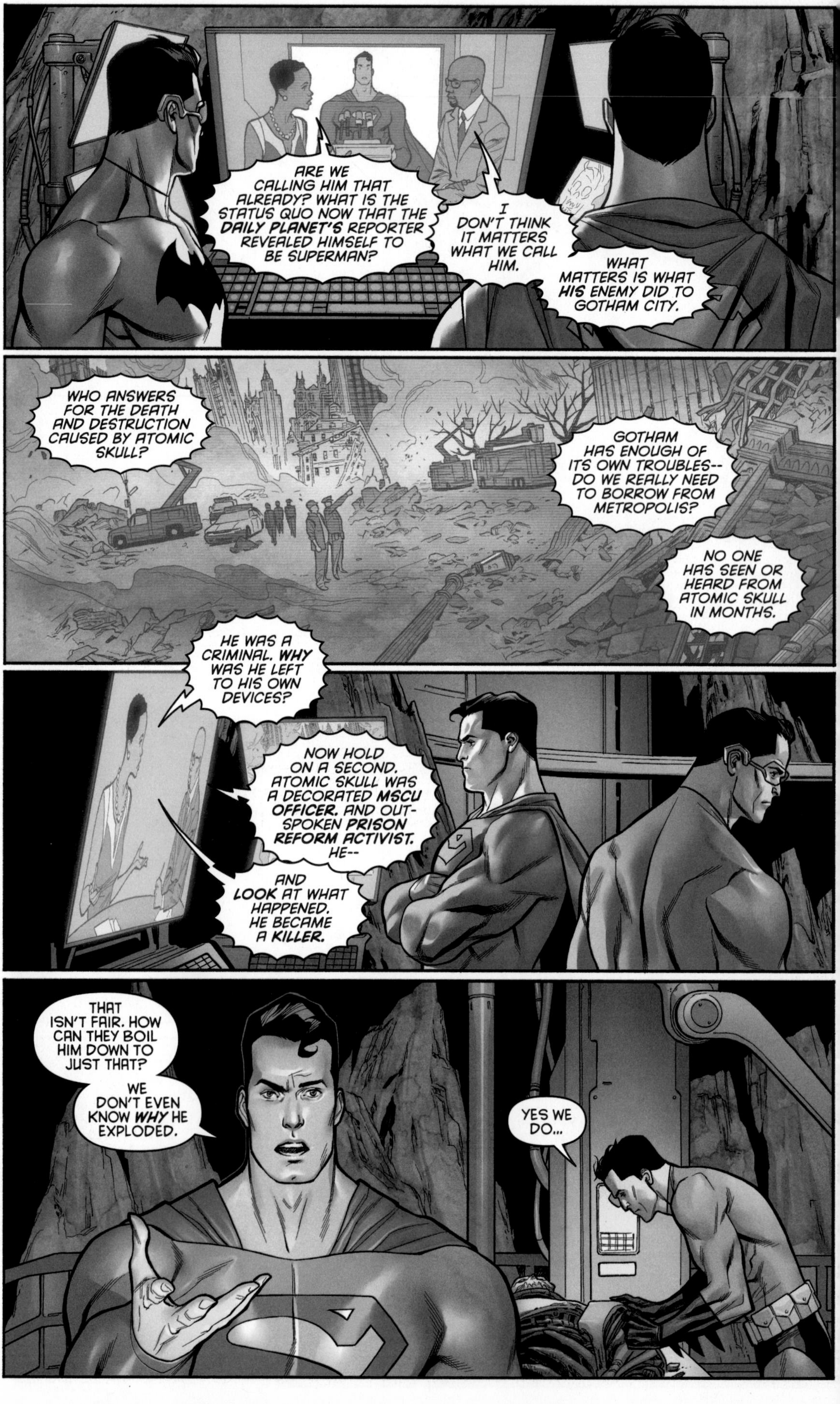

ARE WE CALLING HIM THAT ALREADY? WHAT IS THE STATUS QUO NOW THAT THE DAILY PLANET'S REPORTER REVEALED HIMSELF TO BE SUPERMAN?
I DON'T THINK IT MATTERS WHAT WE CALL HIM.
WHAT MATTERS IS WHAT HIS ENEMY DID TO GOTHAM CITY.
WHO ANSWERS FOR THE DEATH AND DESTRUCTION CAUSED BY ATOMIC SKULL?
GOTHAM HAS ENOUGH OF ITS OWN TROUBLES-- DO WE REALLY NEED TO BORROW FROM METROPOLIS?
NO ONE HAS SEEN OR HEARD FROM ATOMIC SKULL IN MONTHS.
HE WAS A CRIMINAL. WHY WAS HE LEFT TO HIS OWN DEVICES?
NOW HOLD ON A SECOND. ATOMIC SKULL WAS A DECORATED MSCU OFFICER. AND OUT-SPOKEN PRISON REFORM ACTIVIST. HE--
AND LOOK AT WHAT HAPPENED. HE BECAME A KILLER.
THAT ISN'T FAIR. HOW CAN THEY BOIL HIM DOWN TO JUST THAT?
WE DON'T EVEN KNOW WHY HE EXPLODED.
YES WE DO...

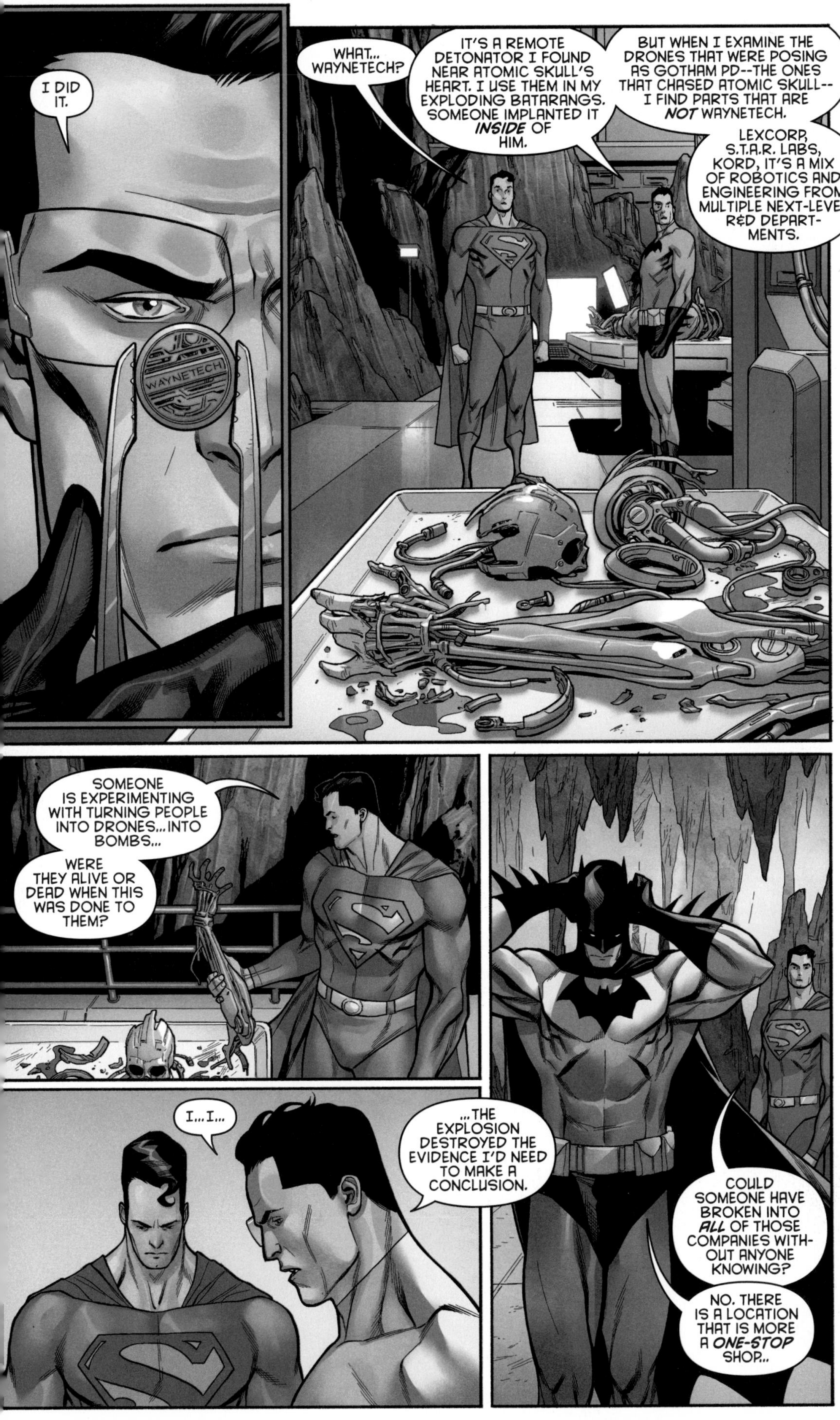
I DID IT.
WHAT... WAYNETECH?
IT'S A REMOTE DETONATOR I FOUND NEAR ATOMIC SKULL'S HEART. I USE THEM IN MY EXPLODING BATARANGS. SOMEONE IMPLANTED IT *INSIDE* OF HIM.
BUT WHEN I EXAMINE THE DRONES THAT WERE POSING AS GOTHAM PD--THE ONES THAT CHASED ATOMIC SKULL--I FIND PARTS THAT ARE *NOT* WAYNETECH.
LEXCORP, S.T.A.R. LABS, KORD, IT'S A MIX OF ROBOTICS AND ENGINEERING FROM MULTIPLE NEXT-LEVEL R&D DEPART-MENTS.
WAYNETECH
SOMEONE IS EXPERIMENTING WITH TURNING PEOPLE INTO DRONES...INTO BOMBS...
WERE THEY ALIVE OR DEAD WHEN THIS WAS DONE TO THEM?
I...I...
...THE EXPLOSION DESTROYED THE EVIDENCE I'D NEED TO MAKE A CONCLUSION.
COULD SOMEONE HAVE BROKEN INTO *ALL* OF THOSE COMPANIES WITH-OUT ANYONE KNOWING?
NO. THERE IS A LOCATION THAT IS MORE A *ONE-STOP* SHOP...

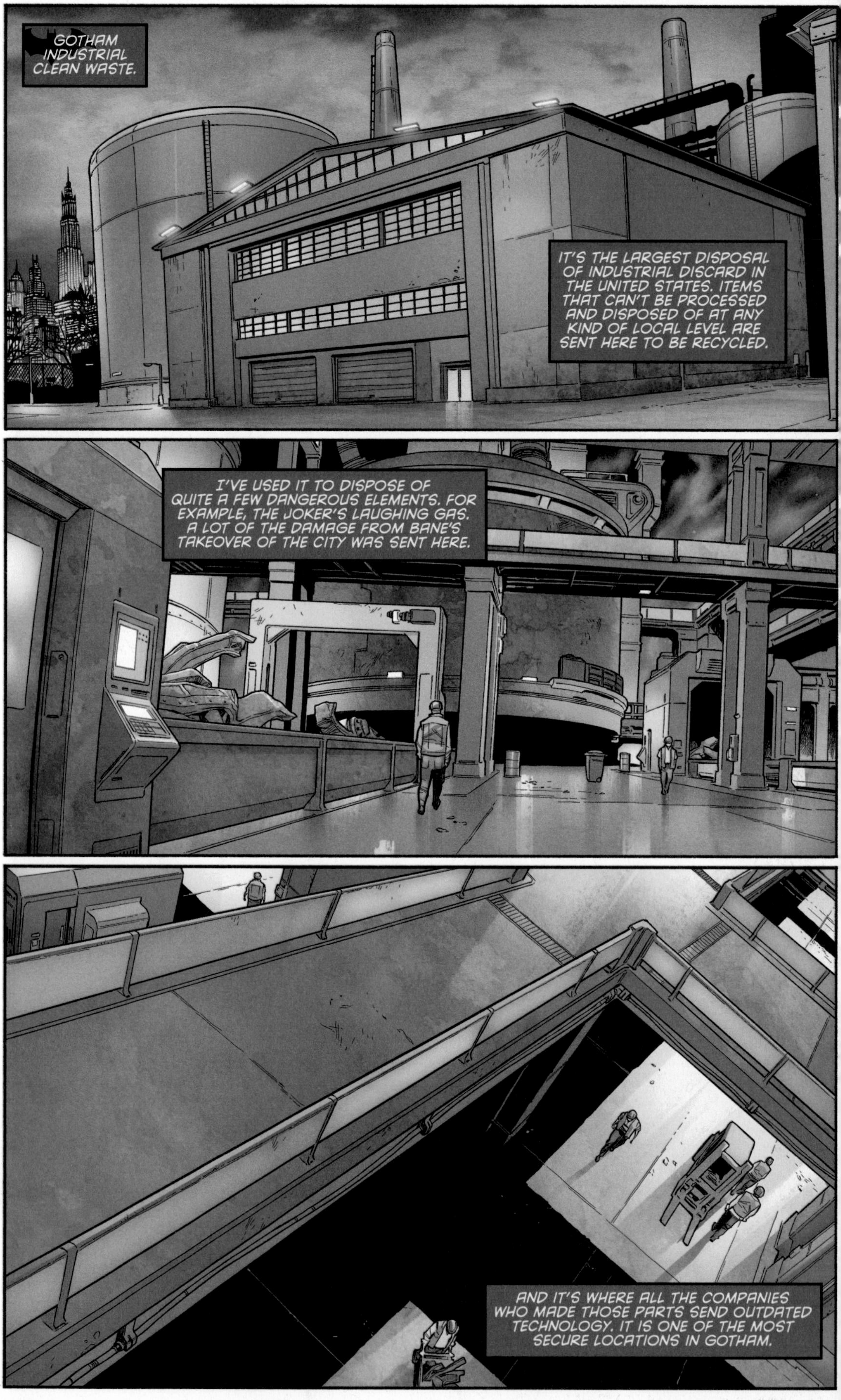
GOTHAM INDUSTRIAL CLEAN WASTE.
IT'S THE LARGEST DISPOSAL OF INDUSTRIAL DISCARD IN THE UNITED STATES. ITEMS THAT CAN'T BE PROCESSED AND DISPOSED OF AT ANY KIND OF LOCAL LEVEL ARE SENT HERE TO BE RECYCLED.
I'VE USED IT TO DISPOSE OF QUITE A FEW DANGEROUS ELEMENTS. FOR EXAMPLE, THE JOKER'S LAUGHING GAS. A LOT OF THE DAMAGE FROM BANE'S TAKEOVER OF THE CITY WAS SENT HERE.
AND IT'S WHERE ALL THE COMPANIES WHO MADE THOSE PARTS SEND OUTDATED TECHNOLOGY. IT IS ONE OF THE MOST SECURE LOCATIONS IN GOTHAM.

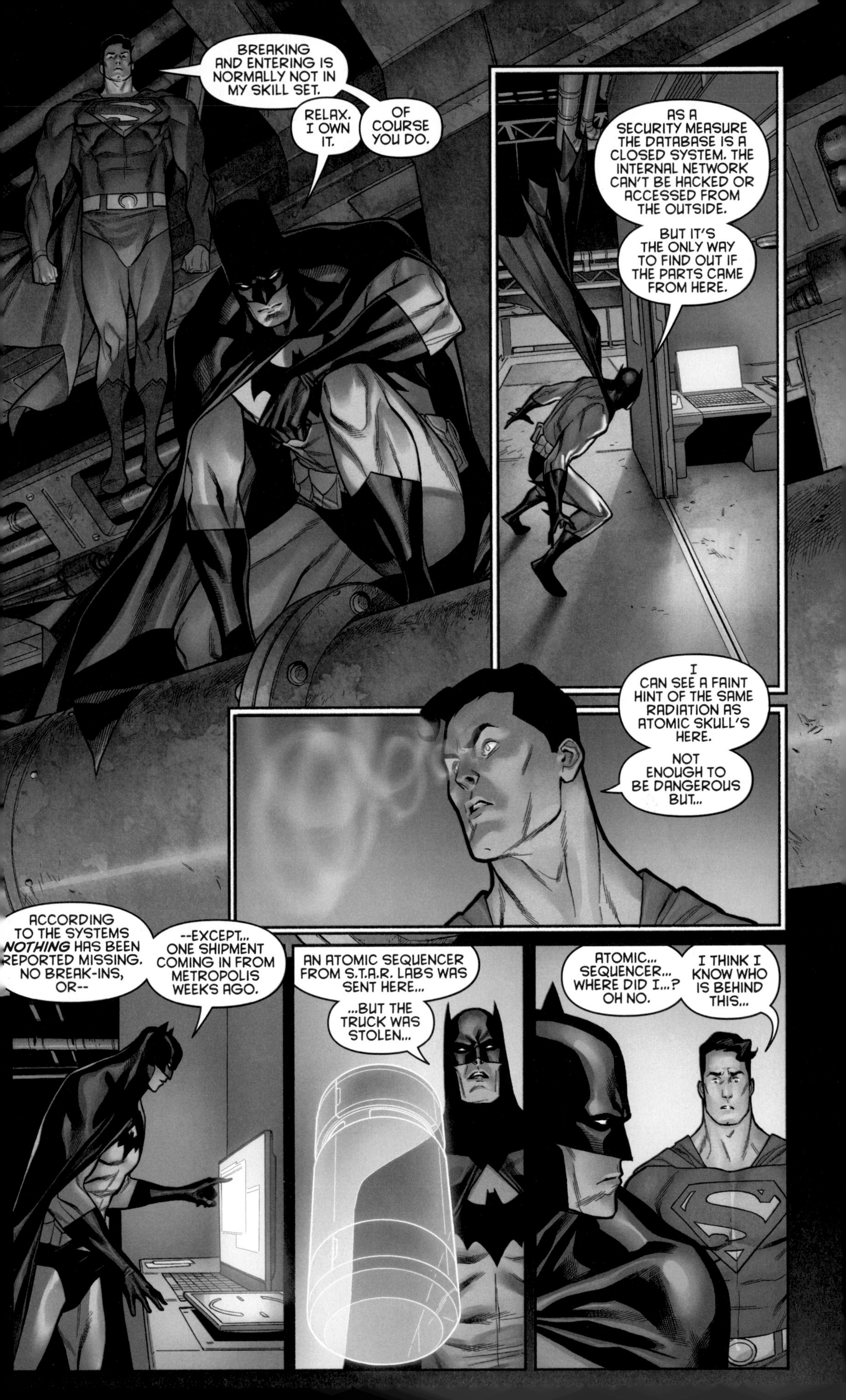

BREAKING AND ENTERING IS NORMALLY NOT IN MY SKILL SET.
RELAX. I OWN IT.
OF COURSE YOU DO.
AS A SECURITY MEASURE THE DATABASE IS A CLOSED SYSTEM. THE INTERNAL NETWORK CAN'T BE HACKED OR ACCESSED FROM THE OUTSIDE.
BUT IT'S THE ONLY WAY TO FIND OUT IF THE PARTS CAME FROM HERE.
I CAN SEE A FAINT HINT OF THE SAME RADIATION AS ATOMIC SKULL'S HERE.
NOT ENOUGH TO BE DANGEROUS BUT...
ACCORDING TO THE SYSTEMS *NOTHING* HAS BEEN REPORTED MISSING. NO BREAK-INS, OR--
--EXCEPT... ONE SHIPMENT COMING IN FROM METROPOLIS WEEKS AGO.
AN ATOMIC SEQUENCER FROM S.T.A.R. LABS WAS SENT HERE...
...BUT THE TRUCK WAS STOLEN...
ATOMIC... SEQUENCER... WHERE DID I...? OH NO.
I THINK I KNOW WHO IS BEHIND THIS...

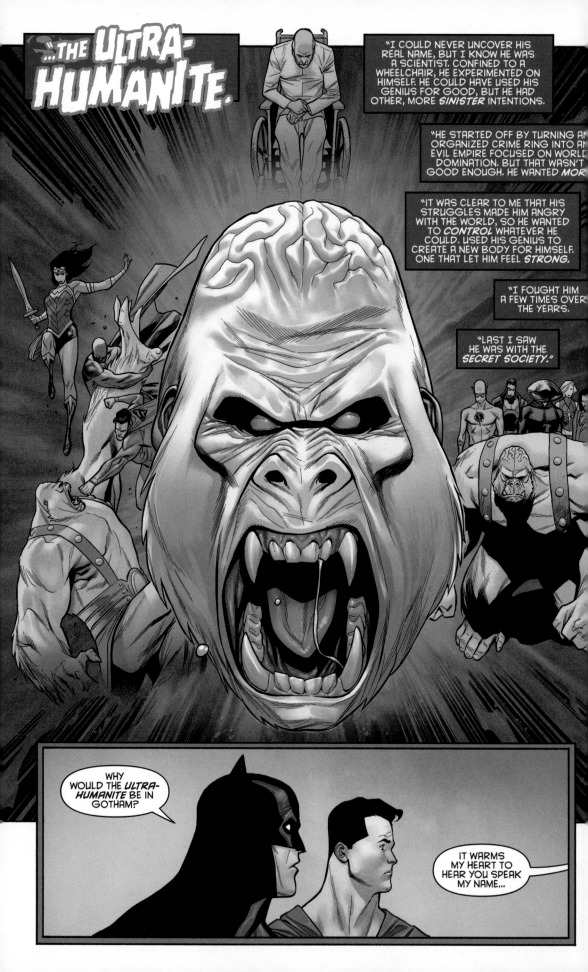

...THE ULTRA-HUMANITE.

"I COULD NEVER UNCOVER HIS REAL NAME, BUT I KNOW HE WAS A SCIENTIST. CONFINED TO A WHEELCHAIR, HE EXPERIMENTED ON HIMSELF. HE COULD HAVE USED HIS GENIUS FOR GOOD, BUT HE HAD OTHER, MORE *SINISTER* INTENTIONS.

"HE STARTED OFF BY TURNING AN ORGANIZED CRIME RING INTO AN EVIL EMPIRE FOCUSED ON WORLD DOMINATION. BUT THAT WASN'T GOOD ENOUGH. HE WANTED MOR

"IT WAS CLEAR TO ME THAT HIS STRUGGLES MADE HIM ANGRY WITH THE WORLD, SO HE WANTED TO *CONTROL* WHATEVER HE COULD. USED HIS GENIUS TO CREATE A NEW BODY FOR HIMSELF. ONE THAT LET HIM FEEL *STRONG.*

"I FOUGHT HIM A FEW TIMES OVER THE YEARS.

"LAST I SAW HE WAS WITH THE *SECRET SOCIETY.*"

WHY WOULD THE *ULTRA-HUMANITE* BE IN GOTHAM?

IT WARMS MY HEART TO HEAR YOU SPEAK MY NAME...

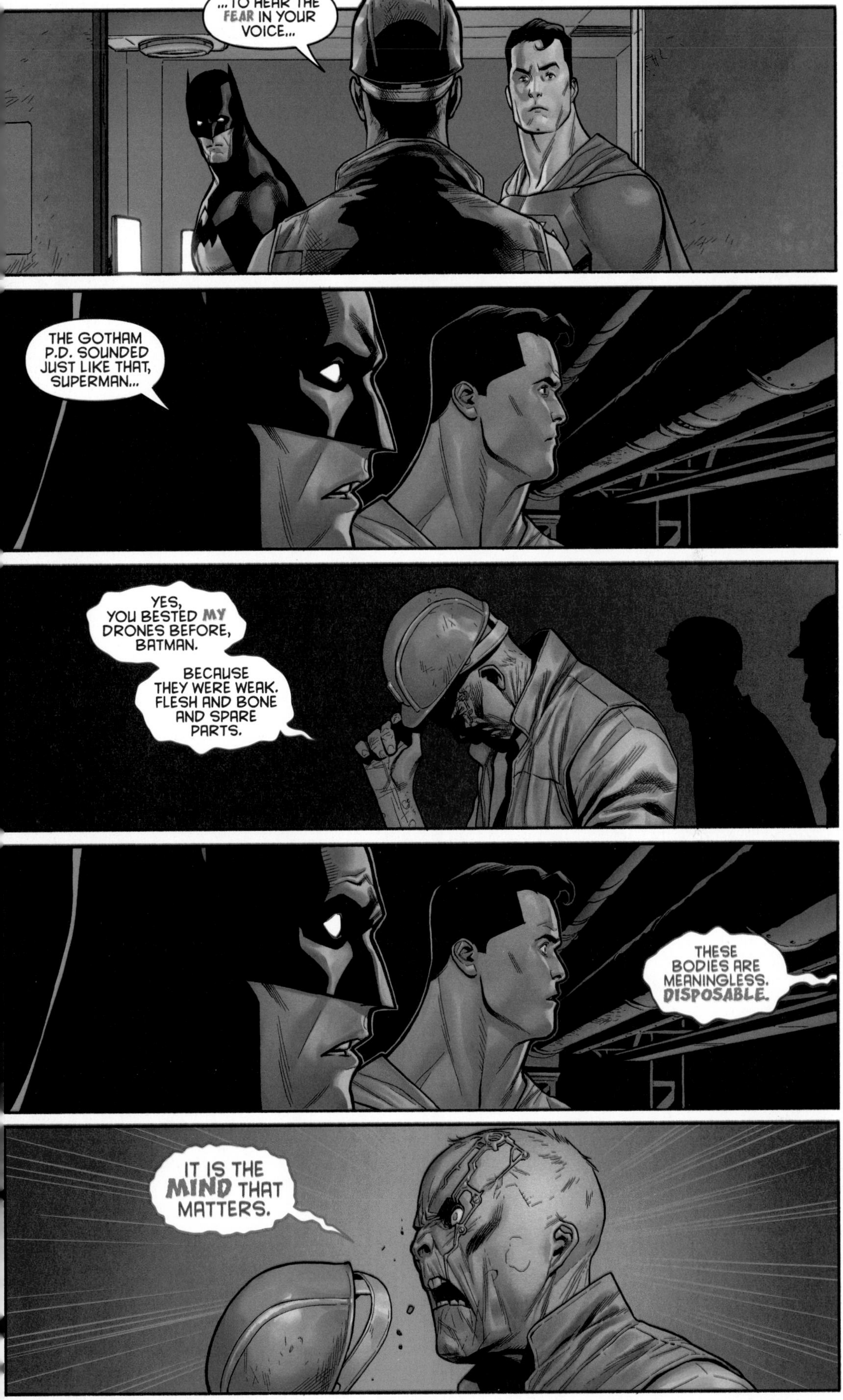
...TO HEAR THE FEAR IN YOUR VOICE...
THE GOTHAM P.D. SOUNDED JUST LIKE THAT, SUPERMAN...
YES, YOU BESTED MY DRONES BEFORE, BATMAN.
BECAUSE THEY WERE WEAK. FLESH AND BONE AND SPARE PARTS.
THESE BODIES ARE MEANINGLESS. DISPOSABLE.
IT IS THE MIND THAT MATTERS.

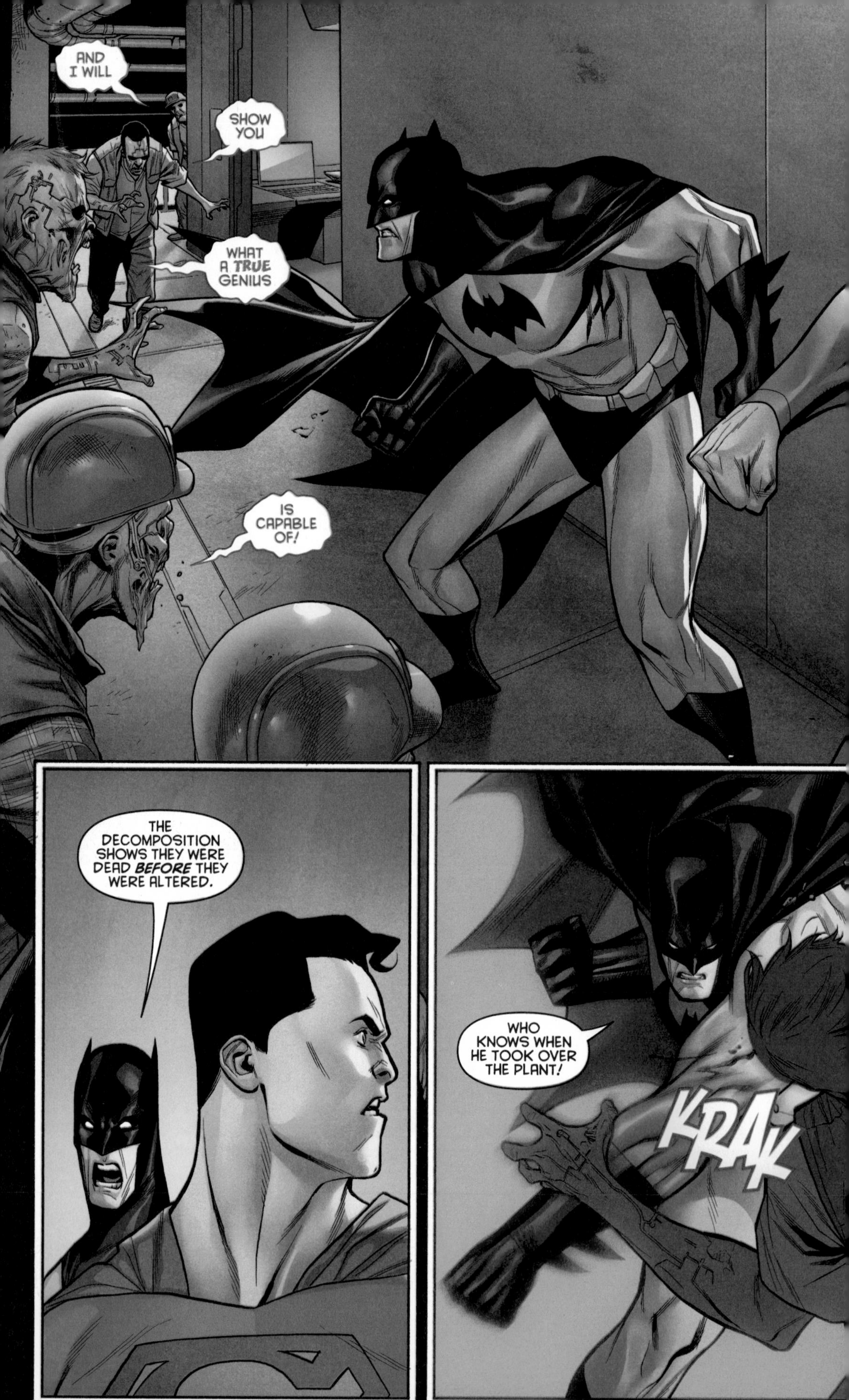

AND I WILL
SHOW YOU
WHAT A TRUE GENIUS
IS CAPABLE OF!
THE DECOMPOSITION SHOWS THEY WERE DEAD BEFORE THEY WERE ALTERED.
WHO KNOWS WHEN HE TOOK OVER THE PLANT!
KRAK

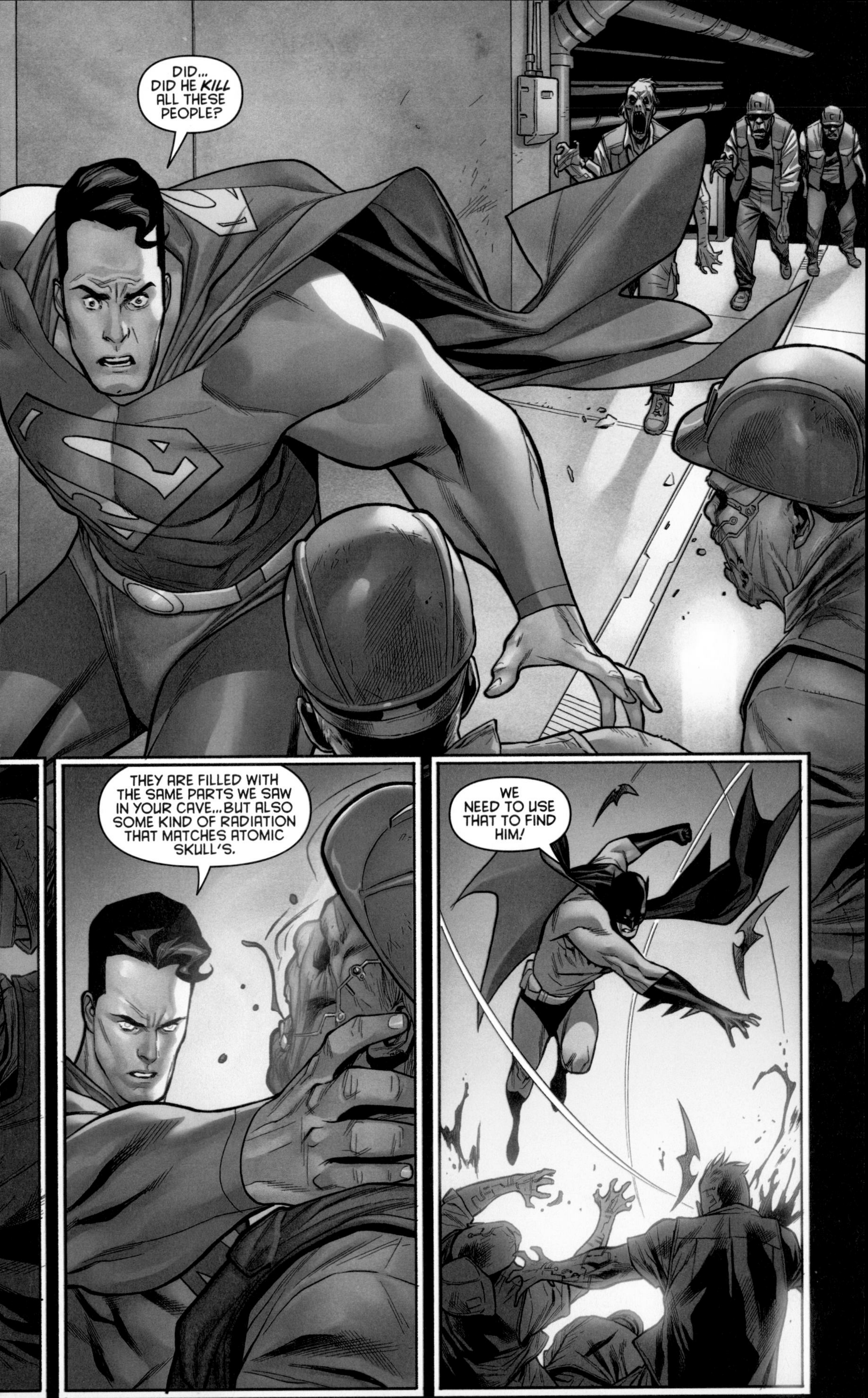
DID... DID HE *KILL* ALL THESE PEOPLE?
THEY ARE FILLED WITH THE SAME PARTS WE SAW IN YOUR CAVE...BUT ALSO SOME KIND OF RADIATION THAT MATCHES ATOMIC SKULL'S.
WE NEED TO USE THAT TO FIND HIM!

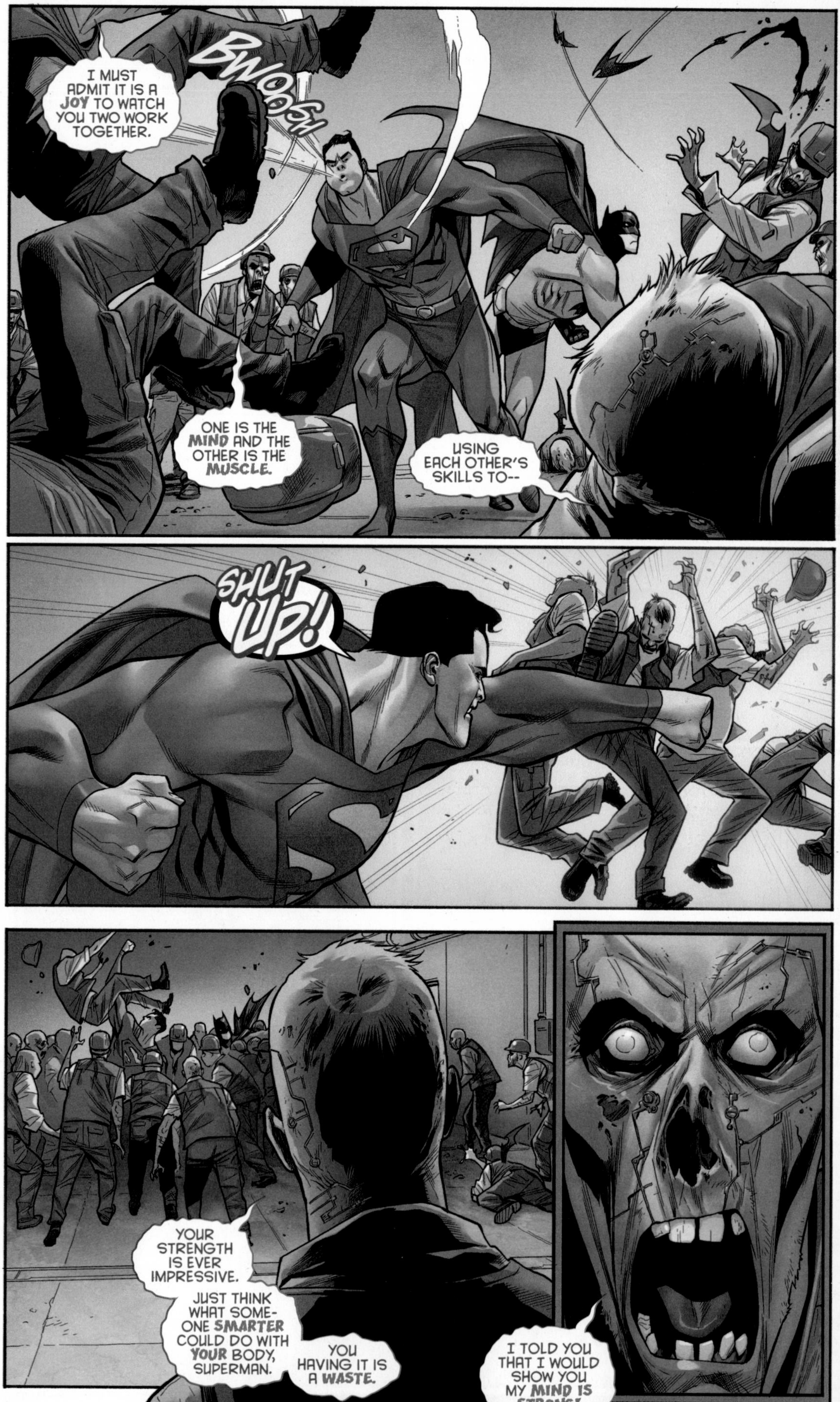
BWOOSH
I MUST ADMIT IT IS A JOY TO WATCH YOU TWO WORK TOGETHER.
ONE IS THE MIND AND THE OTHER IS THE MUSCLE.
USING EACH OTHER'S SKILLS TO--
SHUT UP!
YOUR STRENGTH IS EVER IMPRESSIVE.
JUST THINK WHAT SOME-ONE SMARTER COULD DO WITH YOUR BODY, SUPERMAN.
YOU HAVING IT IS A WASTE.
I TOLD YOU THAT I WOULD SHOW YOU MY MIND IS STRONG!

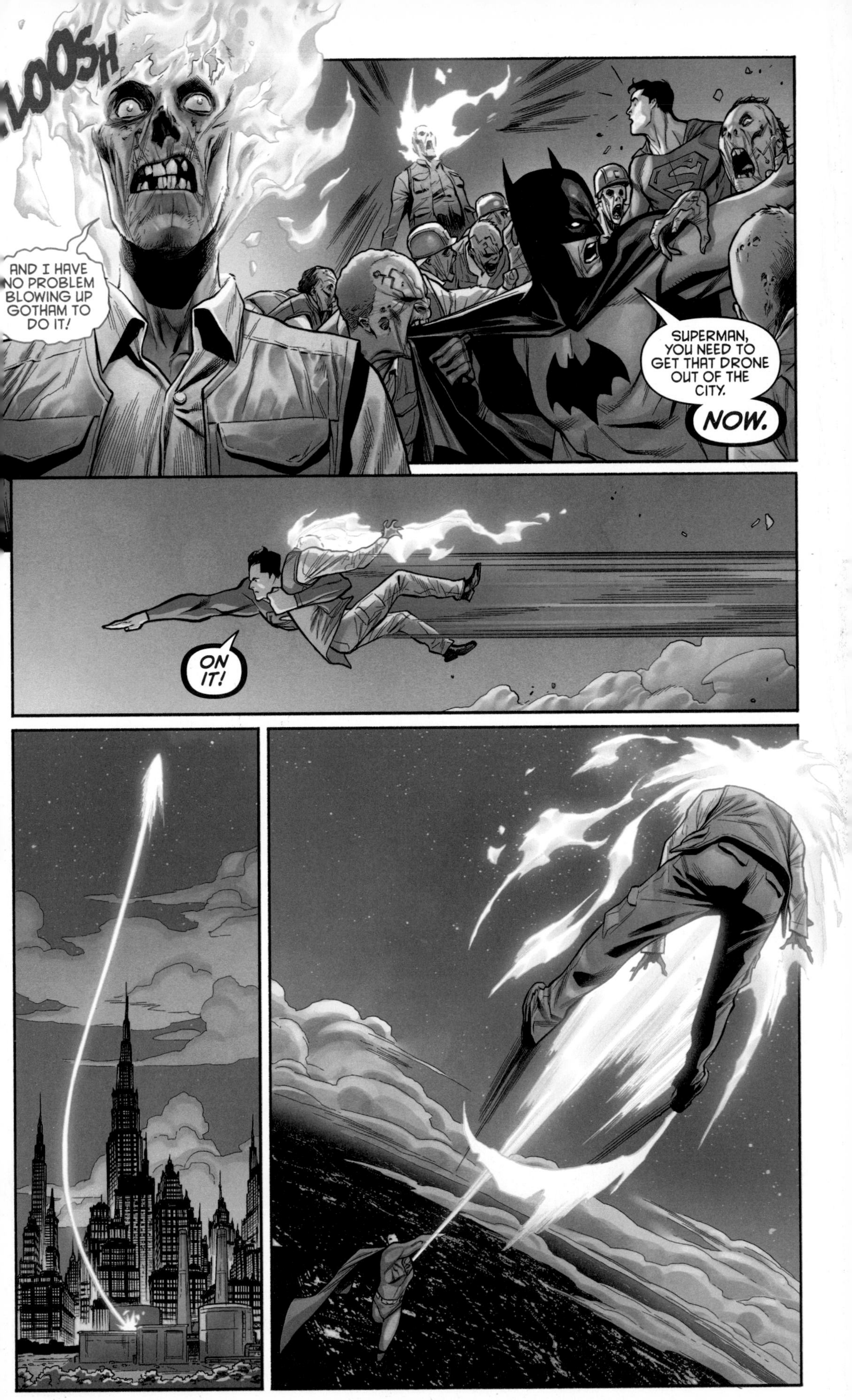

LOOSH
AND I HAVE NO PROBLEM BLOWING UP GOTHAM TO DO IT!
SUPERMAN, YOU NEED TO GET THAT DRONE OUT OF THE CITY.
NOW.
ON IT!

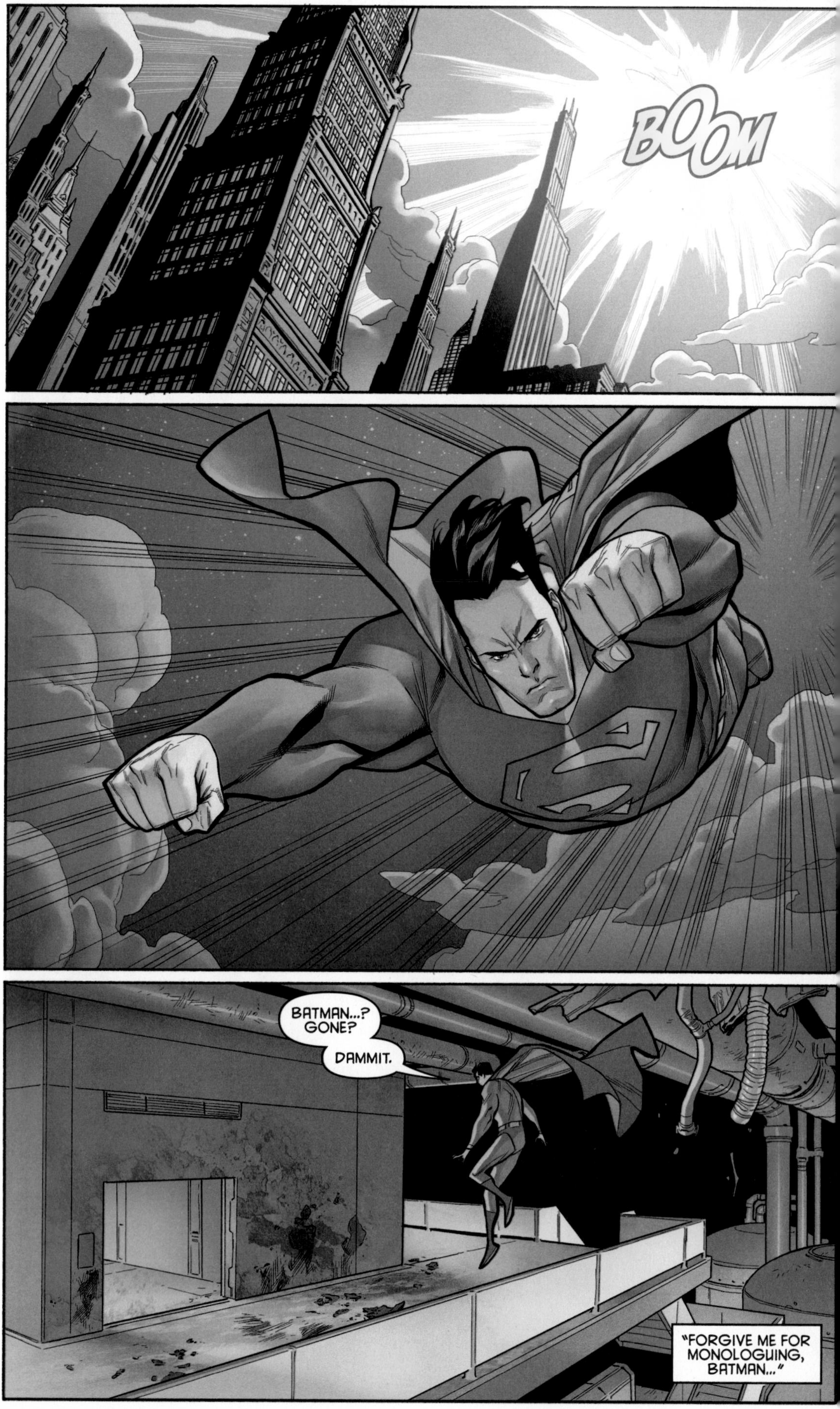
BOOM
BATMAN...? GONE?
DAMMIT.
"FORGIVE ME FOR MONOLOGUING, BATMAN..."

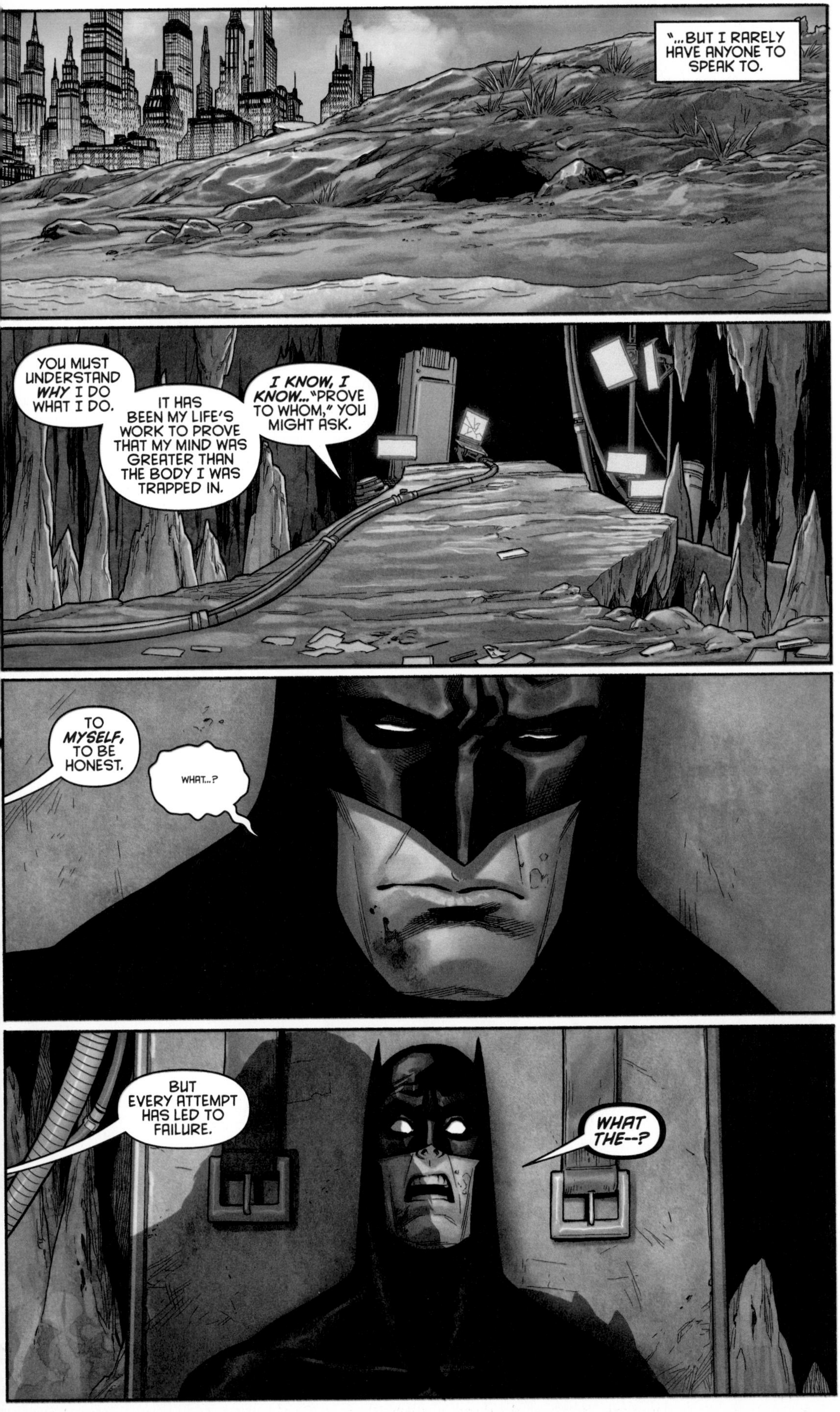
"...BUT I RARELY HAVE ANYONE TO SPEAK TO.
YOU MUST UNDERSTAND WHY I DO WHAT I DO.
IT HAS BEEN MY LIFE'S WORK TO PROVE THAT MY MIND WAS GREATER THAN THE BODY I WAS TRAPPED IN.
I KNOW, I KNOW... "PROVE TO WHOM," YOU MIGHT ASK.
TO MYSELF, TO BE HONEST.
WHAT...?
BUT EVERY ATTEMPT HAS LED TO FAILURE.
WHAT THE--?

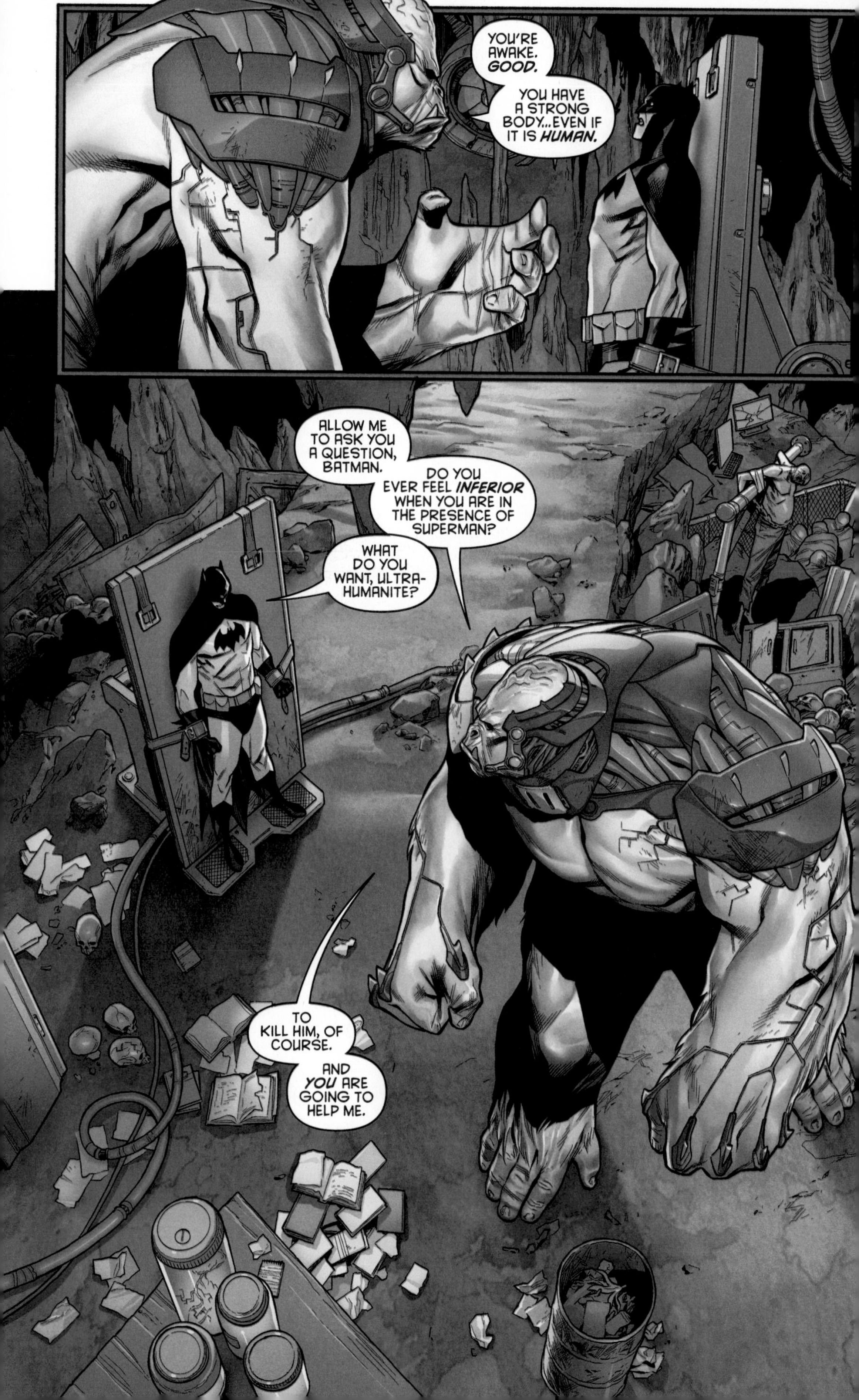
YOU'RE AWAKE. **GOOD.**
YOU HAVE A STRONG BODY...EVEN IF IT IS ***HUMAN.***
ALLOW ME TO ASK YOU A QUESTION, BATMAN.
DO YOU EVER FEEL ***INFERIOR*** WHEN YOU ARE IN THE PRESENCE OF SUPERMAN?
WHAT DO YOU WANT, ULTRA-HUMANITE?
TO KILL HIM, OF COURSE.
AND ***YOU*** ARE GOING TO HELP ME.

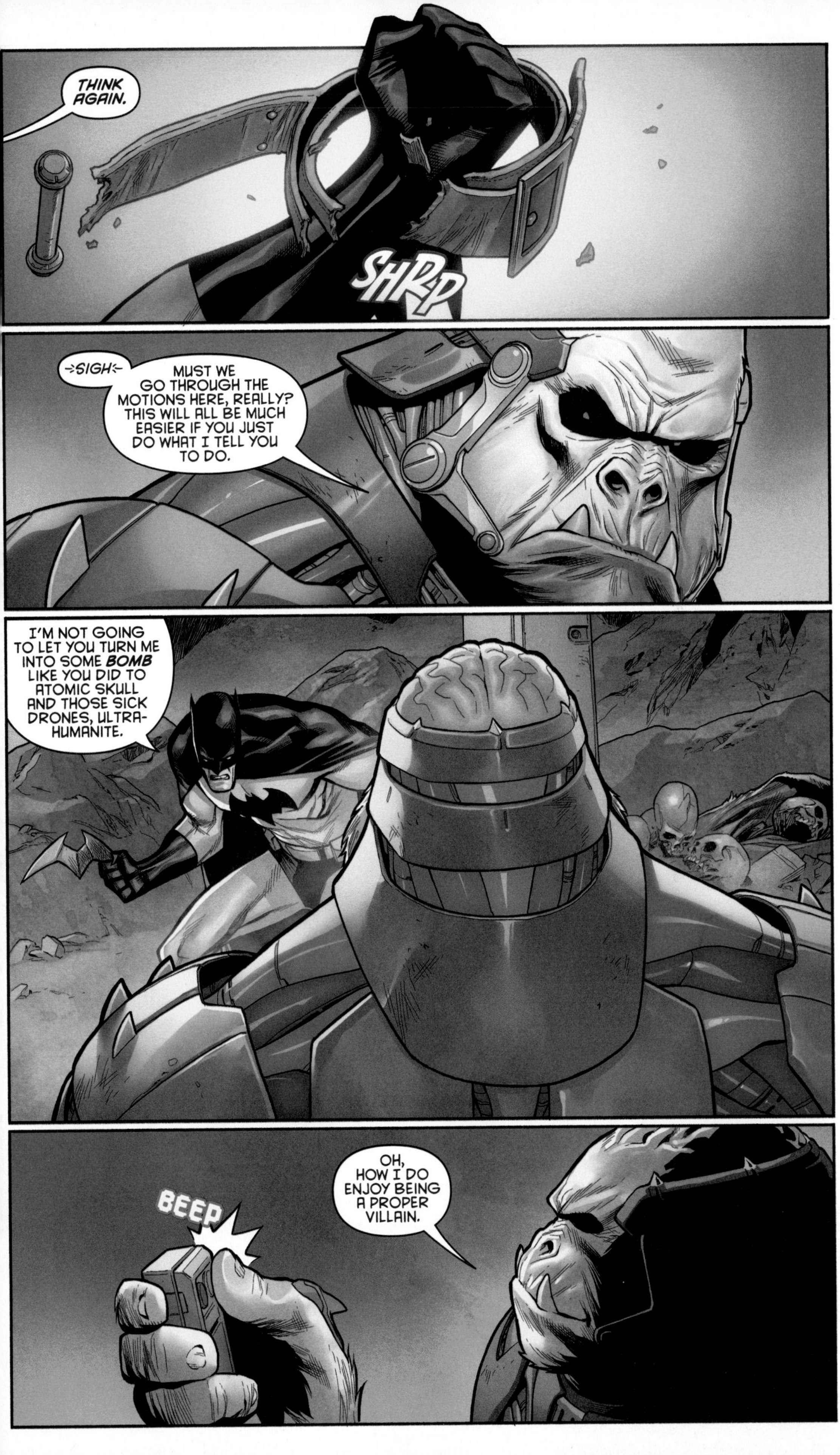
THINK AGAIN.
SHRP
⇒SIGH⇐
MUST WE GO THROUGH THE MOTIONS HERE, REALLY? THIS WILL ALL BE MUCH EASIER IF YOU JUST DO WHAT I TELL YOU TO DO.
I'M NOT GOING TO LET YOU TURN ME INTO SOME *BOMB* LIKE YOU DID TO ATOMIC SKULL AND THOSE SICK DRONES, ULTRA-HUMANITE.
BEEP
OH, HOW I DO ENJOY BEING A PROPER VILLAIN.

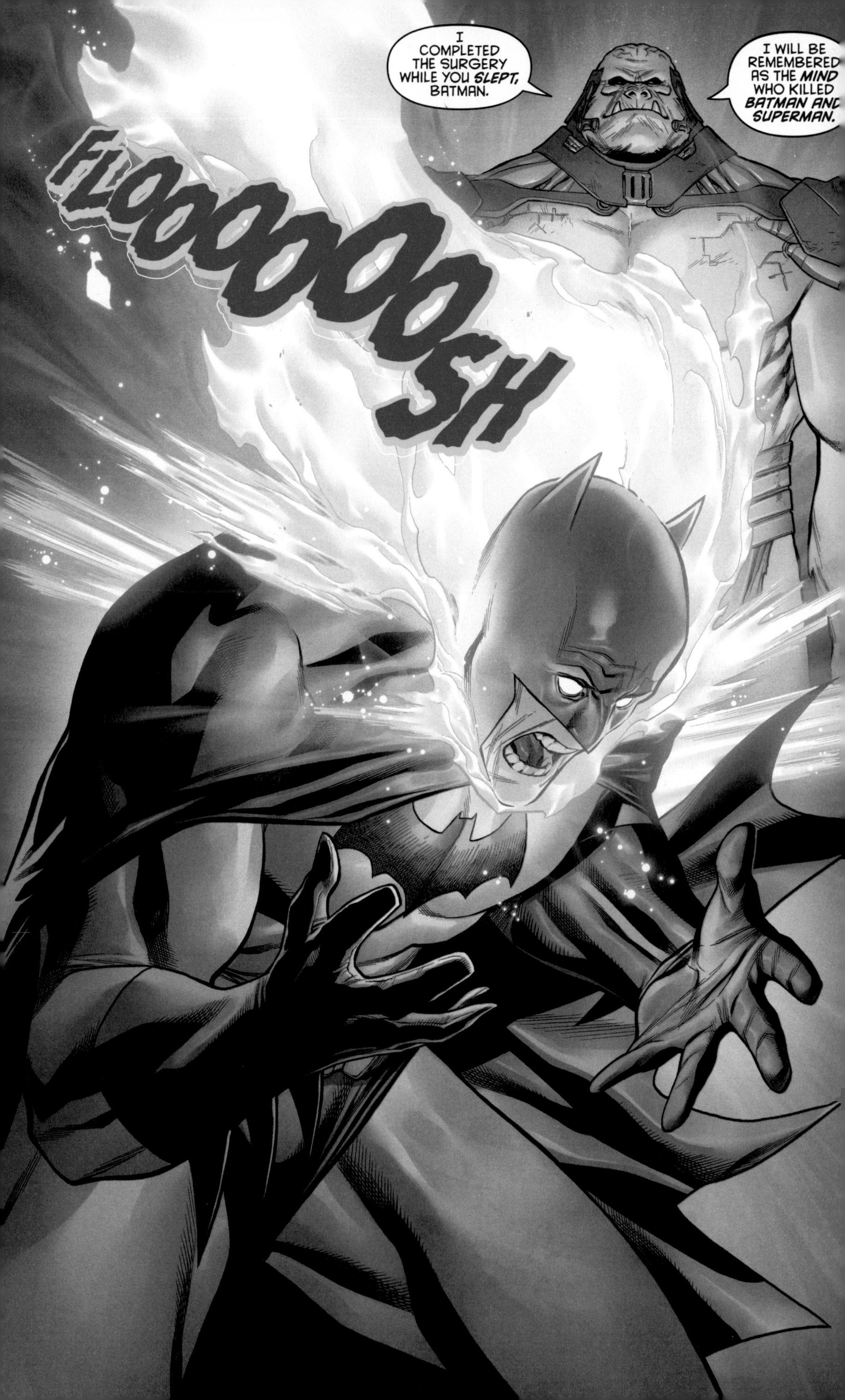
I COMPLETED THE SURGERY WHILE YOU SLEPT, BATMAN.
I WILL BE REMEMBERED AS THE MIND WHO KILLED BATMAN AND SUPERMAN.
FLOOOOOOSH

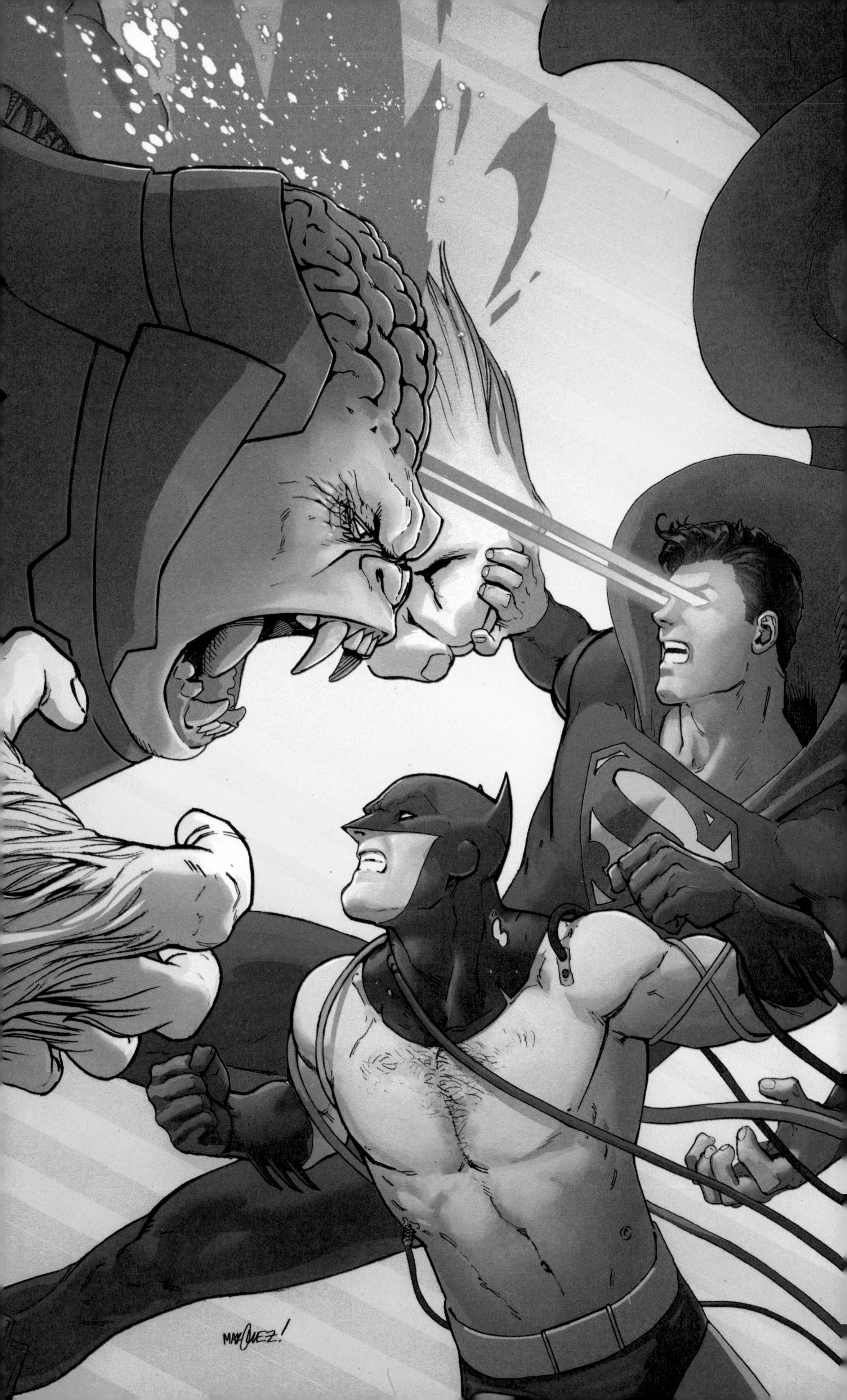
MARQUEZ!

BATMAN/SUPERMAN #11

cover by
DAVID MARQUEZ

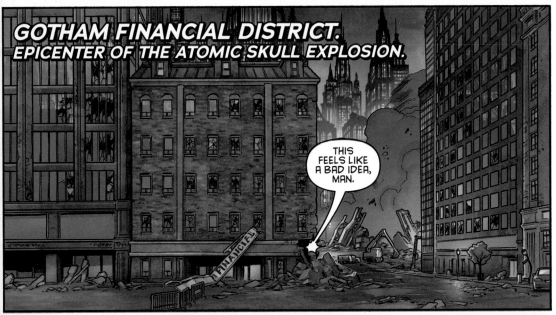

GOTHAM FINANCIAL DISTRICT.
EPICENTER OF THE ATOMIC SKULL EXPLOSION.

THIS FEELS LIKE A BAD IDEA, MAN.

RELAX. THE COPS GOT BIGGER THINGS TO WORRY ABOUT THAN THIS BANK. THEY'RE TOO CONCERNED WITH CHECKING FOR SURVIVORS IN THE WRECKAGE.

YEAH, BUT TAKING ADVANTAGE OF THE EXPLOSION...

MAYBE WE'LL DONATE SOME OF THIS TO CHARITY. WILL *THAT* MAKE YOU FEEL BETTER?

NOW C'MON...NO-BODY IS OUT HERE. WE'RE FREE AND--

WHAT THE--?!

RUN.

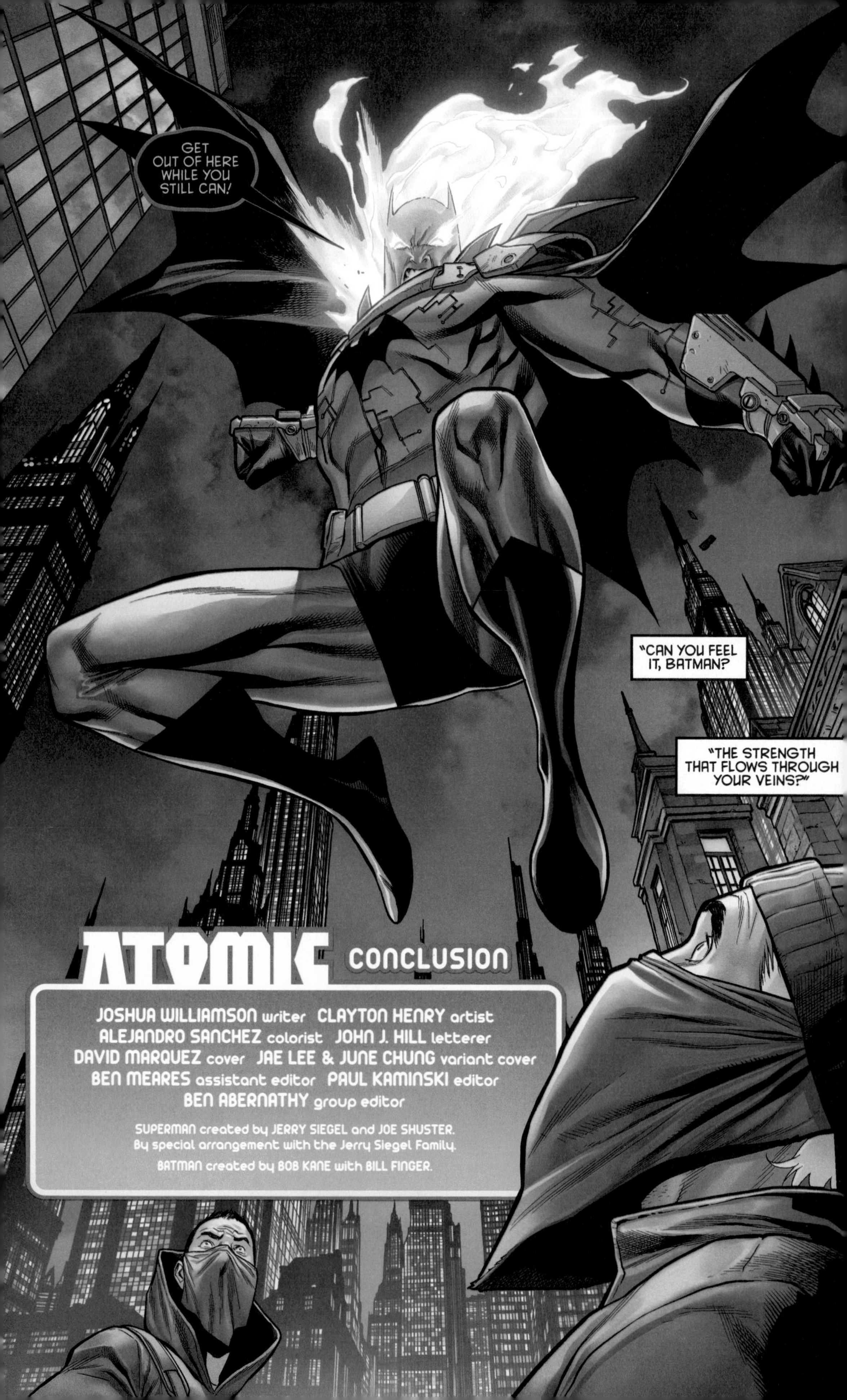

GET OUT OF HERE WHILE YOU STILL CAN!
"CAN YOU FEEL IT, BATMAN?
"THE STRENGTH THAT FLOWS THROUGH YOUR VEINS?"
ATOMIC CONCLUSION
JOSHUA WILLIAMSON writer CLAYTON HENRY artist
ALEJANDRO SANCHEZ colorist JOHN J. HILL letterer
DAVID MARQUEZ cover JAE LEE & JUNE CHUNG variant cover
BEN MEARES assistant editor PAUL KAMINSKI editor
BEN ABERNATHY group editor
SUPERMAN created by JERRY SIEGEL and JOE SHUSTER.
By special arrangement with the Jerry Siegel Family.
BATMAN created by BOB KANE with BILL FINGER.

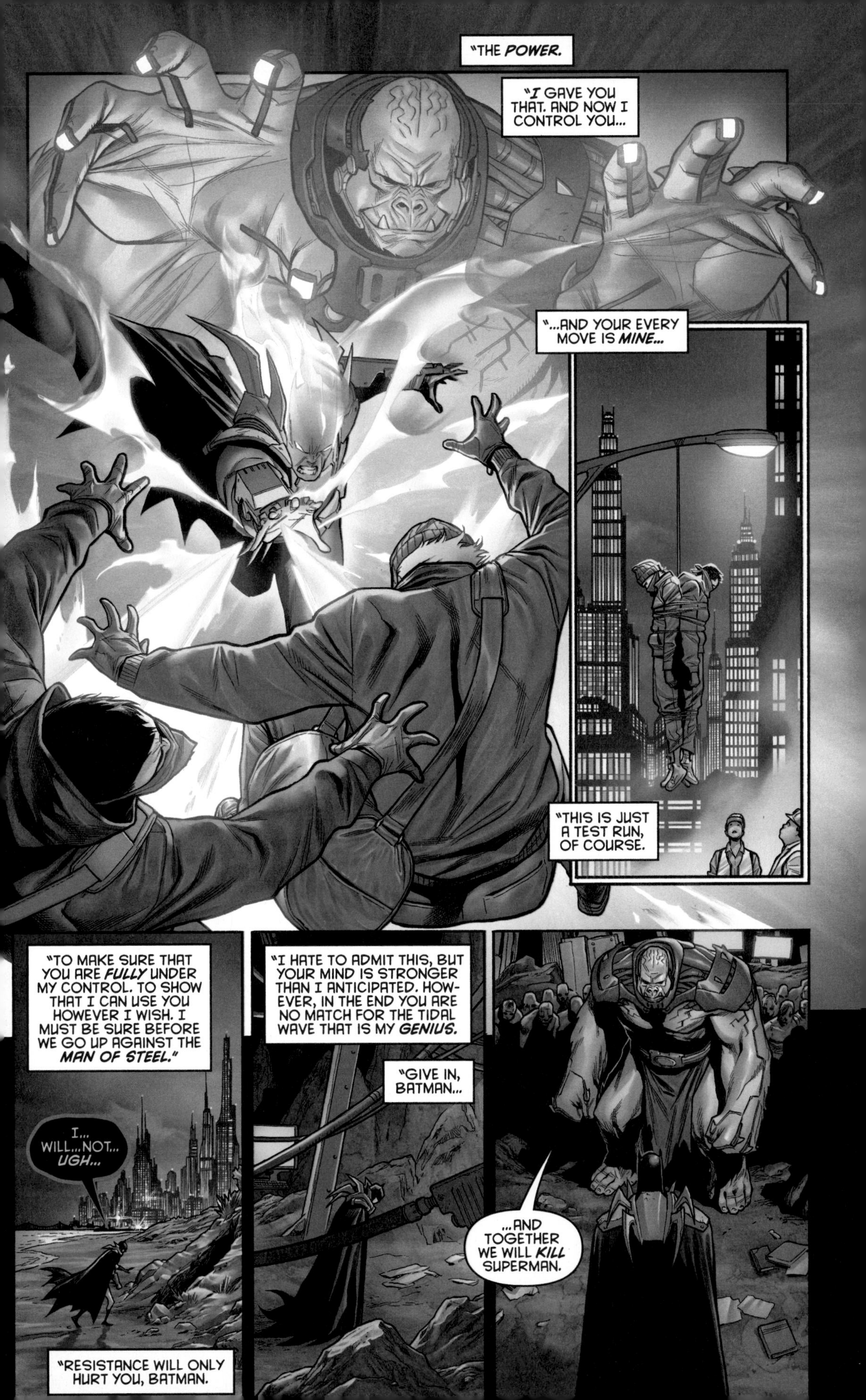
"THE *POWER.*
"*I* GAVE YOU THAT. AND NOW I CONTROL YOU...
"...AND YOUR EVERY MOVE IS *MINE...*
"THIS IS JUST A TEST RUN, OF COURSE.
"TO MAKE SURE THAT YOU ARE *FULLY* UNDER MY CONTROL. TO SHOW THAT I CAN USE YOU HOWEVER I WISH. I MUST BE SURE BEFORE WE GO UP AGAINST THE *MAN OF STEEL."*
I... WILL...NOT... *UGH...*
"RESISTANCE WILL ONLY HURT YOU, BATMAN.
"I HATE TO ADMIT THIS, BUT YOUR MIND IS STRONGER THAN I ANTICIPATED. HOW-EVER, IN THE END YOU ARE NO MATCH FOR THE TIDAL WAVE THAT IS MY *GENIUS.*
"GIVE IN, BATMAN...
...AND TOGETHER WE WILL *KILL* SUPERMAN.

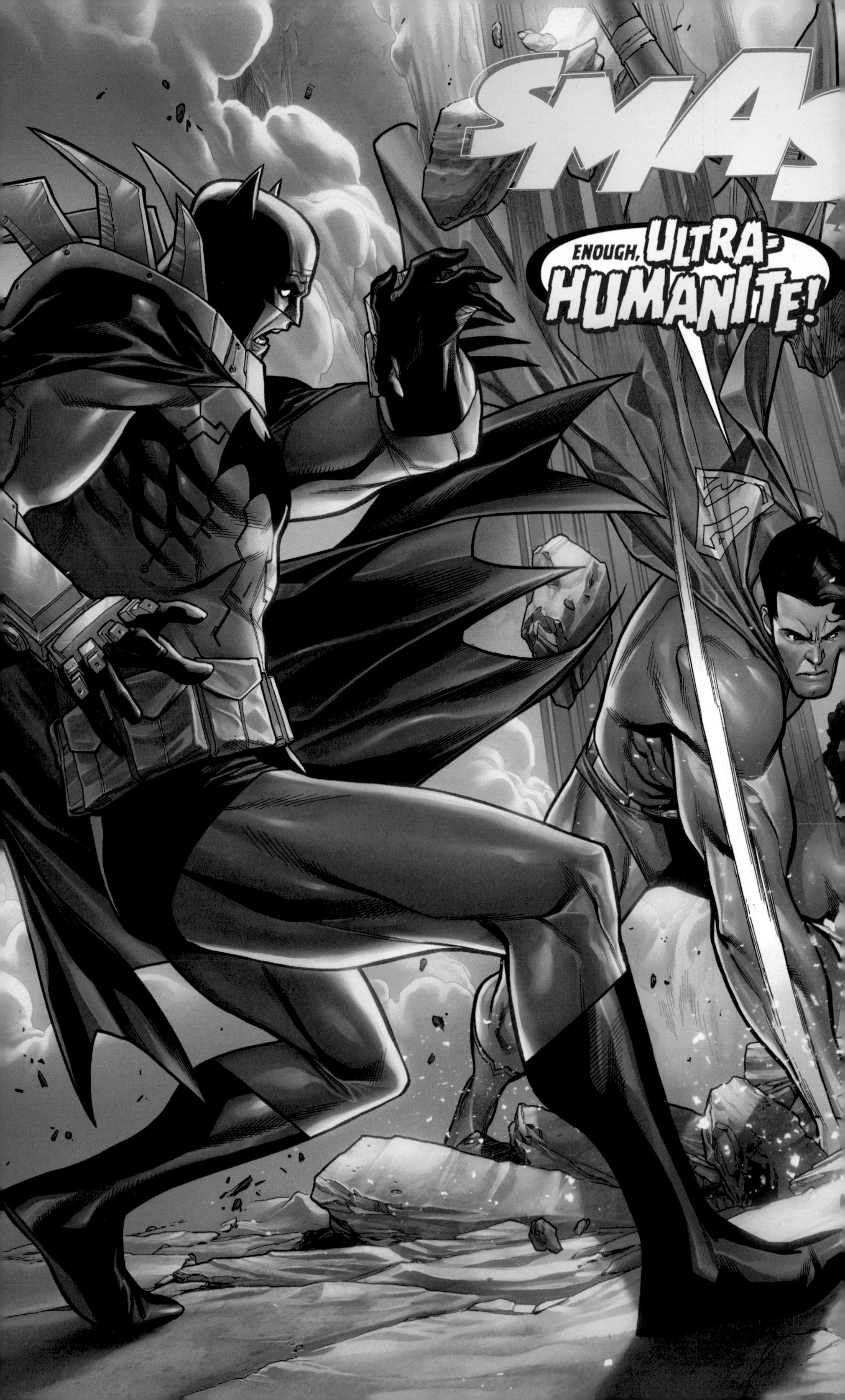
SMAS
ENOUGH, ULTRA-HUMANITE!

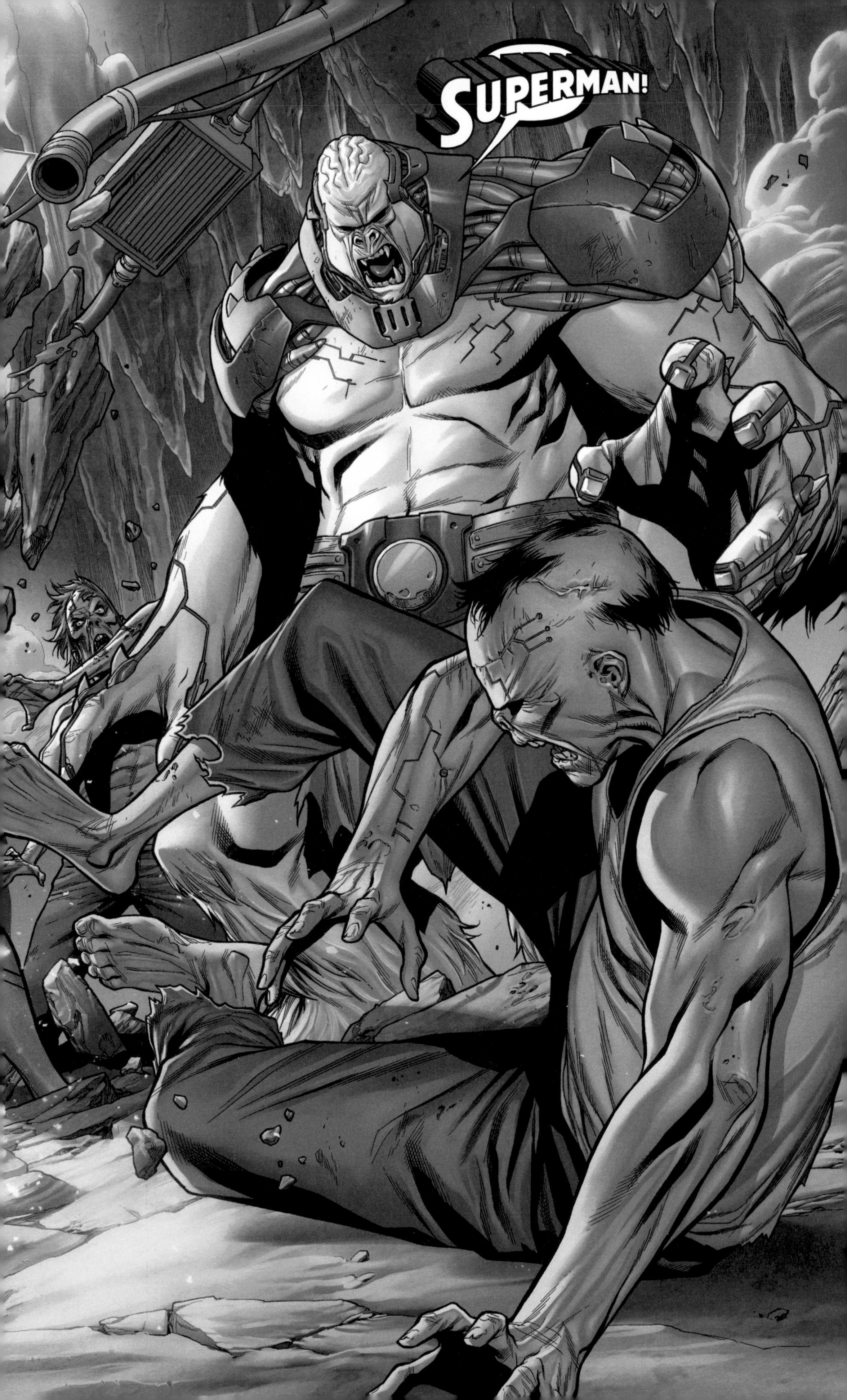
SUPERMAN!

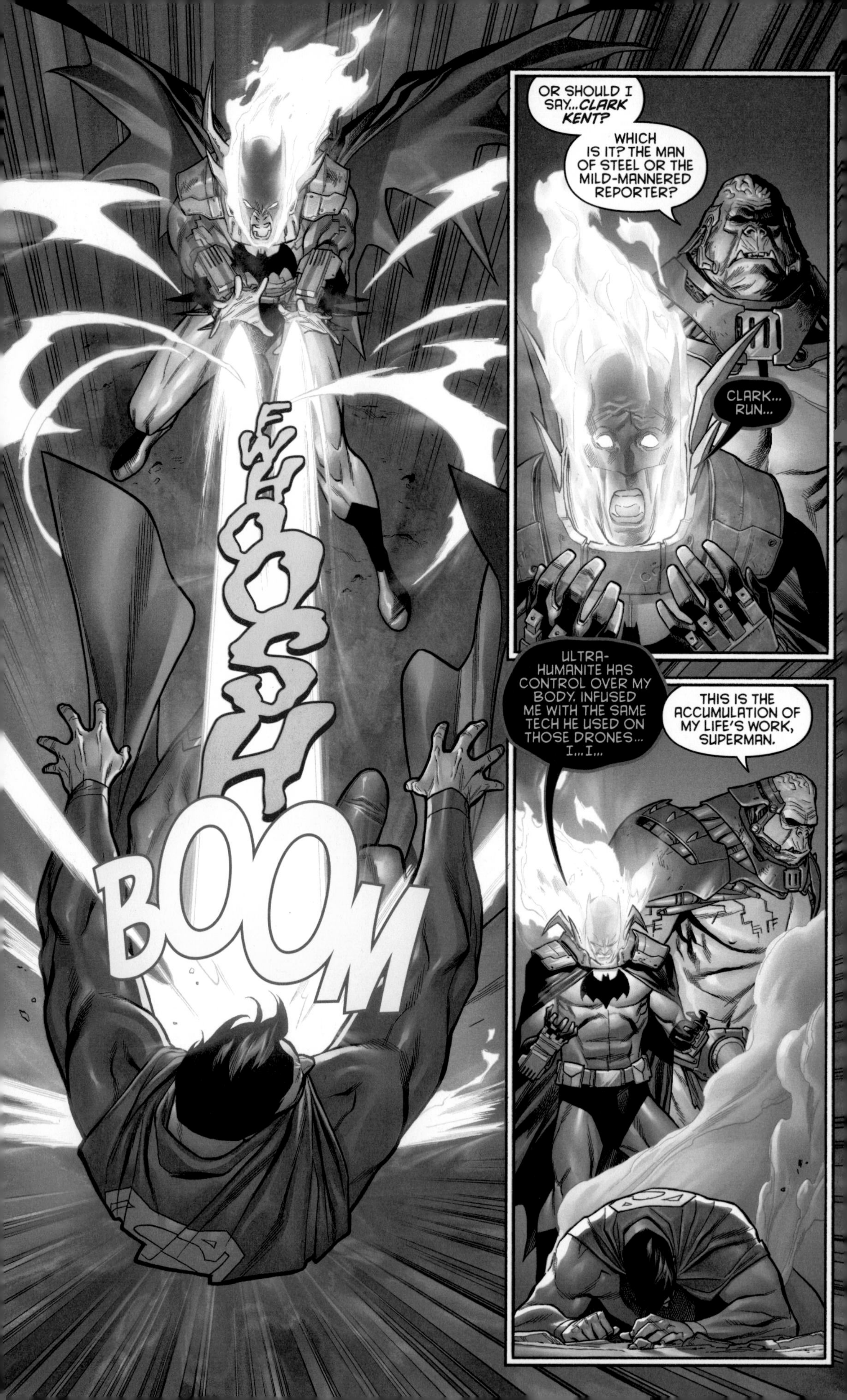
WHOOSH
BOOM
OR SHOULD I SAY...CLARK KENT?
WHICH IS IT? THE MAN OF STEEL OR THE MILD-MANNERED REPORTER?
CLARK... RUN...
ULTRA-HUMANITE HAS CONTROL OVER MY BODY, INFUSED ME WITH THE SAME TECH HE USED ON THOSE DRONES... I...I...
THIS IS THE ACCUMULATION OF MY LIFE'S WORK, SUPERMAN.

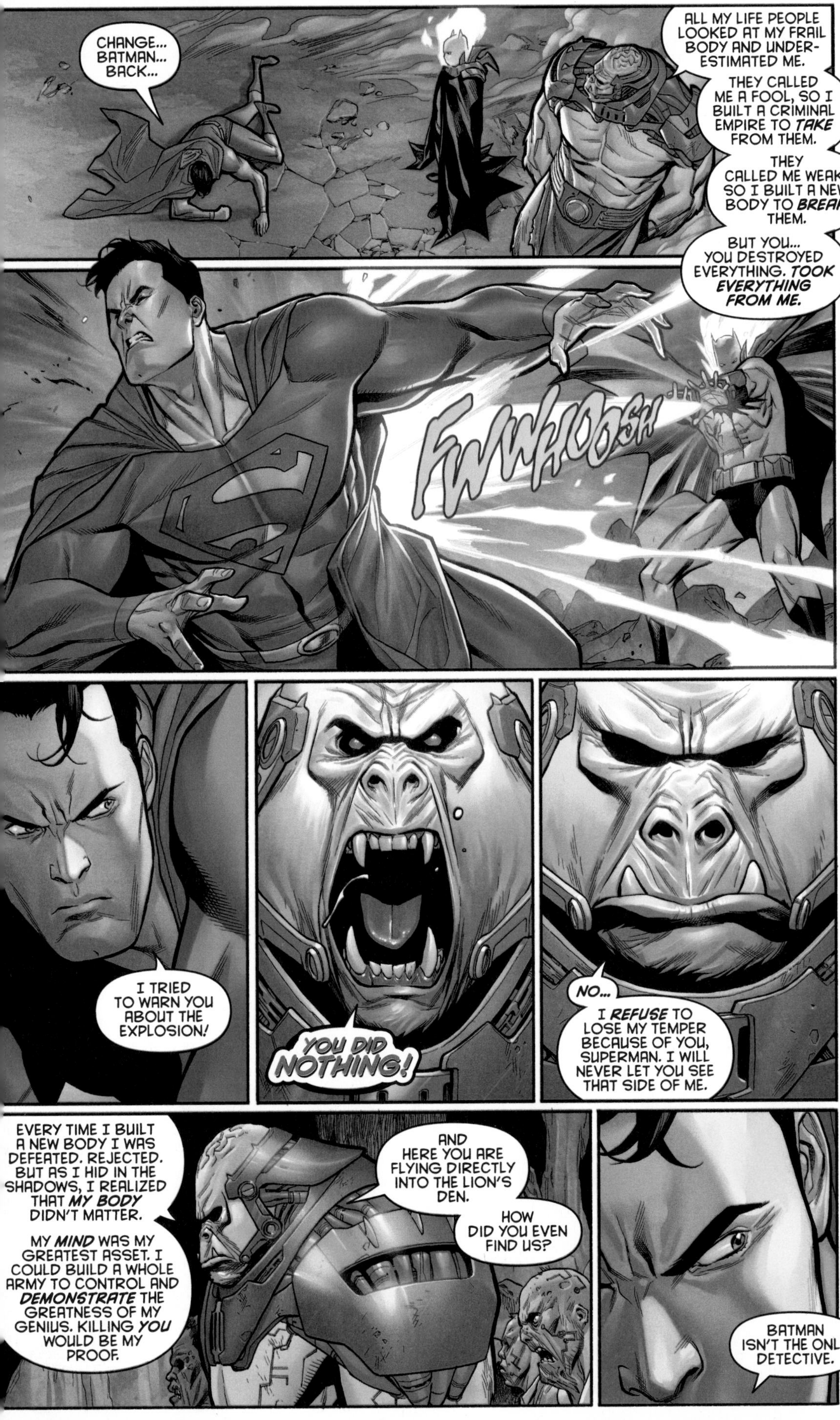
CHANGE... BATMAN... BACK...
ALL MY LIFE PEOPLE LOOKED AT MY FRAIL BODY AND UNDER-ESTIMATED ME.
THEY CALLED ME A FOOL, SO I BUILT A CRIMINAL EMPIRE TO *TAKE* FROM THEM.
THEY CALLED ME WEAK, SO I BUILT A NEW BODY TO *BREAK* THEM.
BUT YOU... YOU DESTROYED EVERYTHING. ***TOOK EVERYTHING FROM ME.***
FWHOOSH
I TRIED TO WARN YOU ABOUT THE EXPLOSION!
YOU DID NOTHING!
NO...
I *REFUSE* TO LOSE MY TEMPER BECAUSE OF YOU, SUPERMAN. I WILL NEVER LET YOU SEE THAT SIDE OF ME.
EVERY TIME I BUILT A NEW BODY I WAS DEFEATED. REJECTED. BUT AS I HID IN THE SHADOWS, I REALIZED THAT *MY BODY* DIDN'T MATTER.
MY *MIND* WAS MY GREATEST ASSET. I COULD BUILD A WHOLE ARMY TO CONTROL AND *DEMONSTRATE* THE GREATNESS OF MY GENIUS. KILLING *YOU* WOULD BE MY PROOF.
AND HERE YOU ARE FLYING DIRECTLY INTO THE LION'S DEN.
HOW DID YOU EVEN FIND US?
BATMAN ISN'T THE ONLY DETECTIVE.

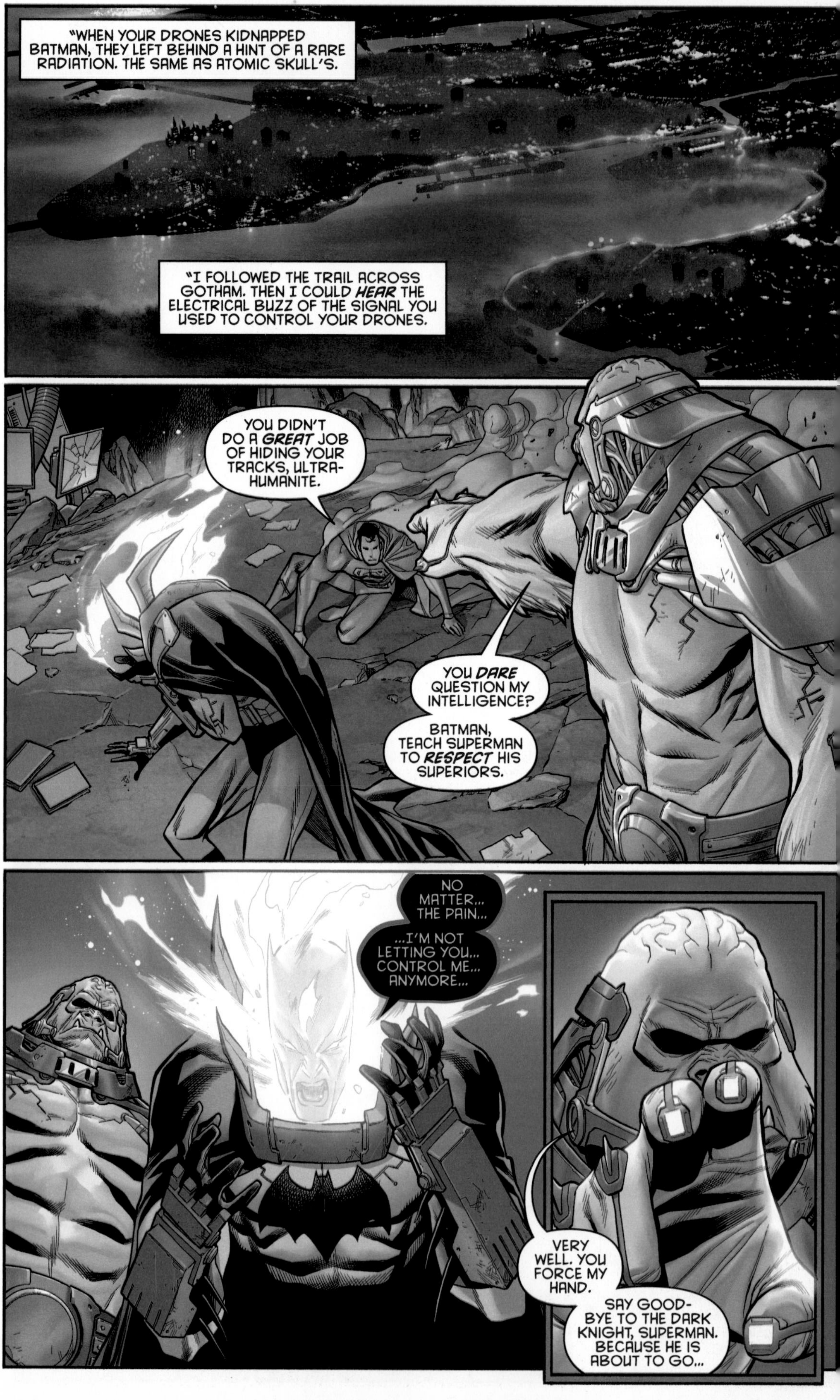
"WHEN YOUR DRONES KIDNAPPED BATMAN, THEY LEFT BEHIND A HINT OF A RARE RADIATION. THE SAME AS ATOMIC SKULL'S.
"I FOLLOWED THE TRAIL ACROSS GOTHAM. THEN I COULD HEAR THE ELECTRICAL BUZZ OF THE SIGNAL YOU USED TO CONTROL YOUR DRONES.
YOU DIDN'T DO A GREAT JOB OF HIDING YOUR TRACKS, ULTRA-HUMANITE.
YOU DARE QUESTION MY INTELLIGENCE?
BATMAN, TEACH SUPERMAN TO RESPECT HIS SUPERIORS.
NO MATTER... THE PAIN...
...I'M NOT LETTING YOU... CONTROL ME... ANYMORE...
VERY WELL. YOU FORCE MY HAND.
SAY GOOD-BYE TO THE DARK KNIGHT, SUPERMAN. BECAUSE HE IS ABOUT TO GO...

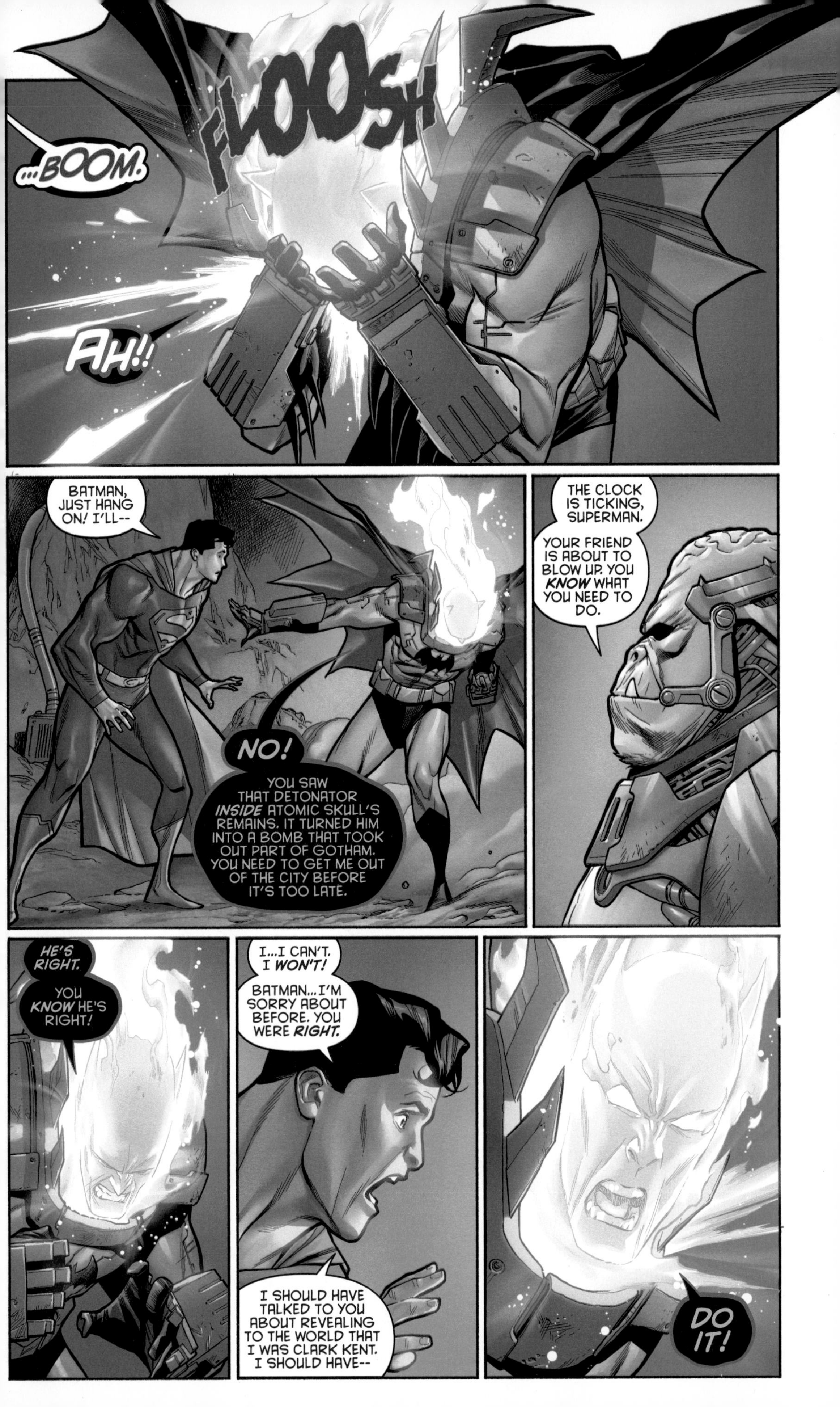

...BOOM.
FLOOSH
AH!!
BATMAN, JUST HANG ON! I'LL--
NO!
YOU SAW THAT DETONATOR *INSIDE* ATOMIC SKULL'S REMAINS. IT TURNED HIM INTO A BOMB THAT TOOK OUT PART OF GOTHAM. YOU NEED TO GET ME OUT OF THE CITY BEFORE IT'S TOO LATE.
THE CLOCK IS TICKING, SUPERMAN.
YOUR FRIEND IS ABOUT TO BLOW UP. YOU *KNOW* WHAT YOU NEED TO DO.
HE'S RIGHT.
YOU *KNOW* HE'S RIGHT!
I...I CAN'T. I *WON'T!*
BATMAN...I'M SORRY ABOUT BEFORE. YOU WERE *RIGHT.*
I SHOULD HAVE TALKED TO YOU ABOUT REVEALING TO THE WORLD THAT I WAS CLARK KENT. I SHOULD HAVE--
DO IT!

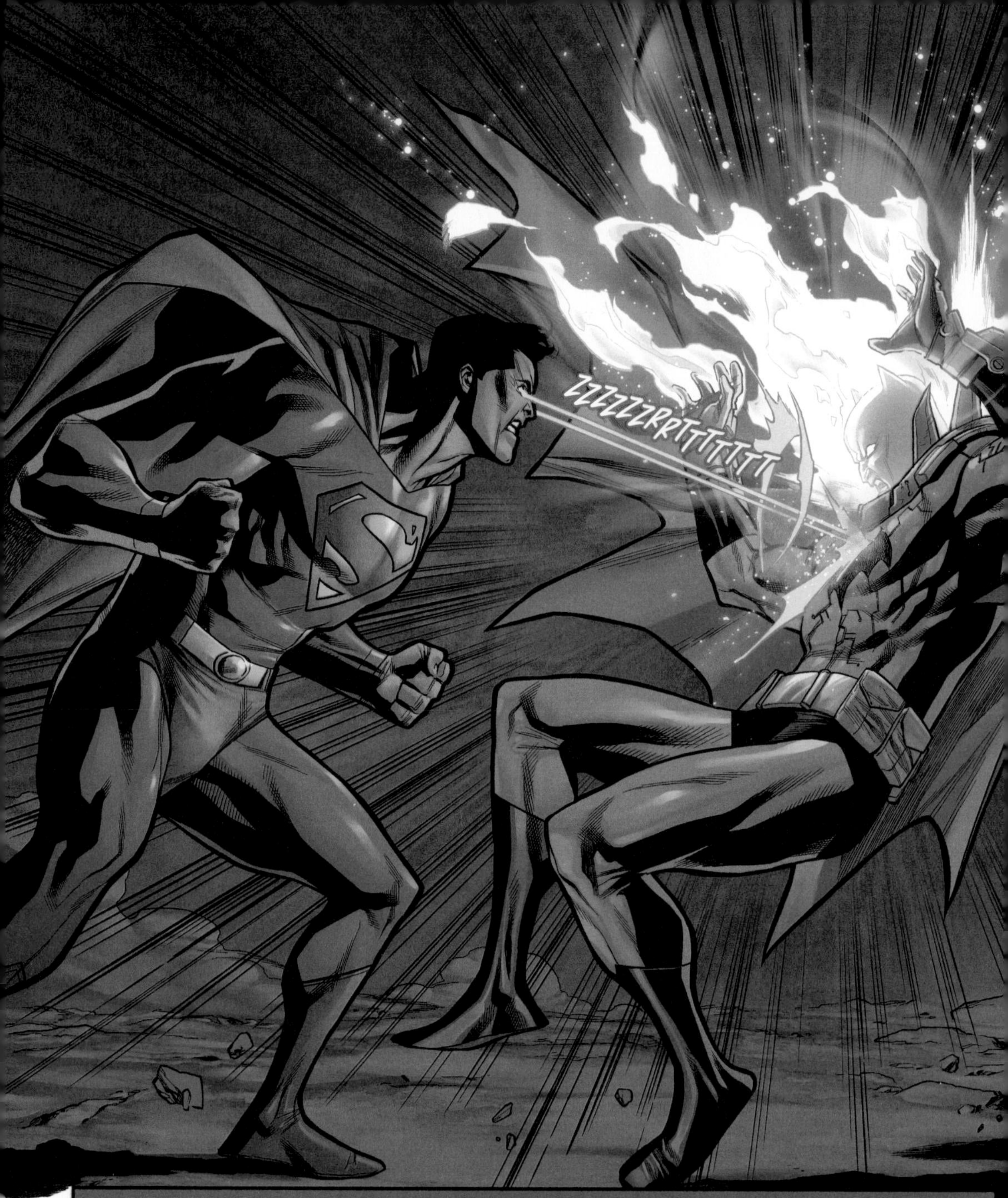
ZZZZZZZRRTTTTTTT

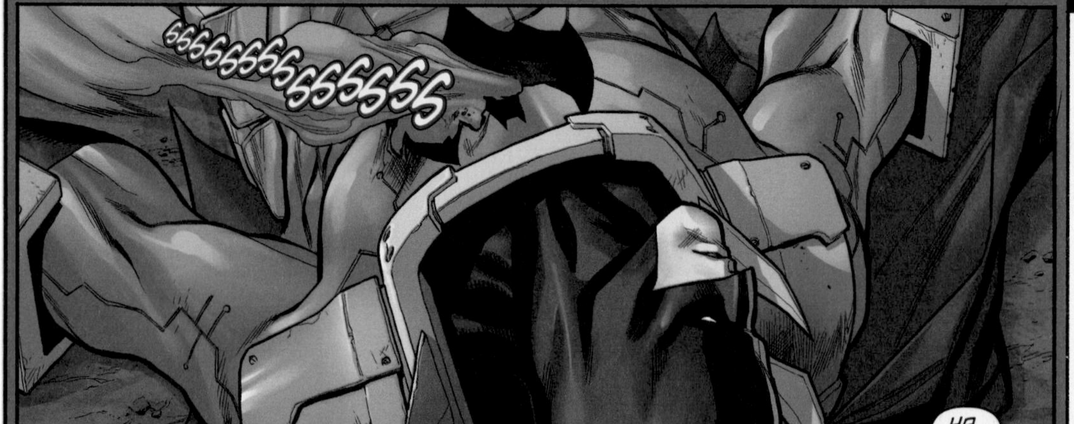
SSSSSSSSSSSSSS
HA... HA...

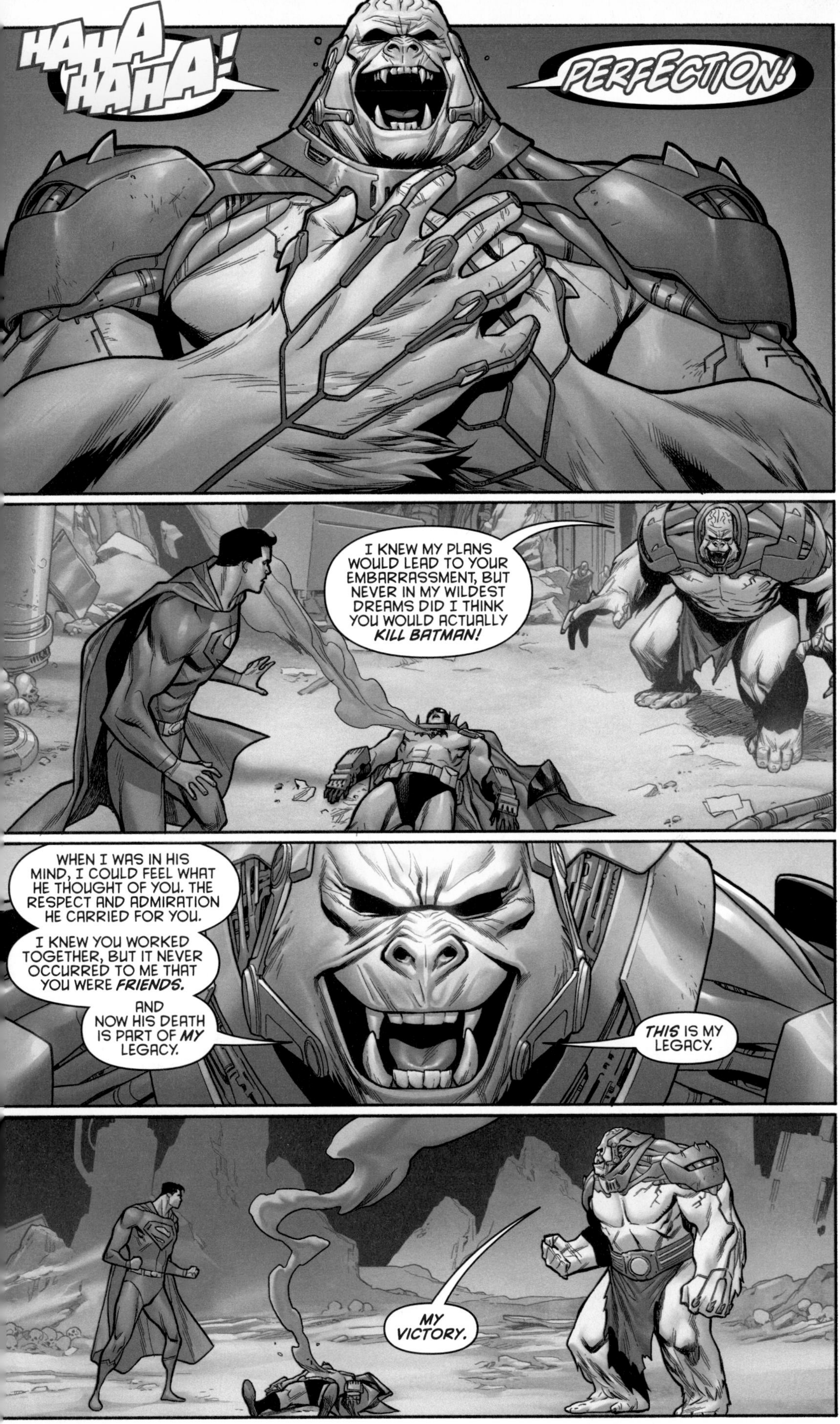
HAHA HAHA!
PERFECTION!
I KNEW MY PLANS WOULD LEAD TO YOUR EMBARRASSMENT, BUT NEVER IN MY WILDEST DREAMS DID I THINK YOU WOULD ACTUALLY KILL BATMAN!
WHEN I WAS IN HIS MIND, I COULD FEEL WHAT HE THOUGHT OF YOU. THE RESPECT AND ADMIRATION HE CARRIED FOR YOU.
I KNEW YOU WORKED TOGETHER, BUT IT NEVER OCCURRED TO ME THAT YOU WERE FRIENDS.
AND NOW HIS DEATH IS PART OF MY LEGACY.
THIS IS MY LEGACY.
MY VICTORY.

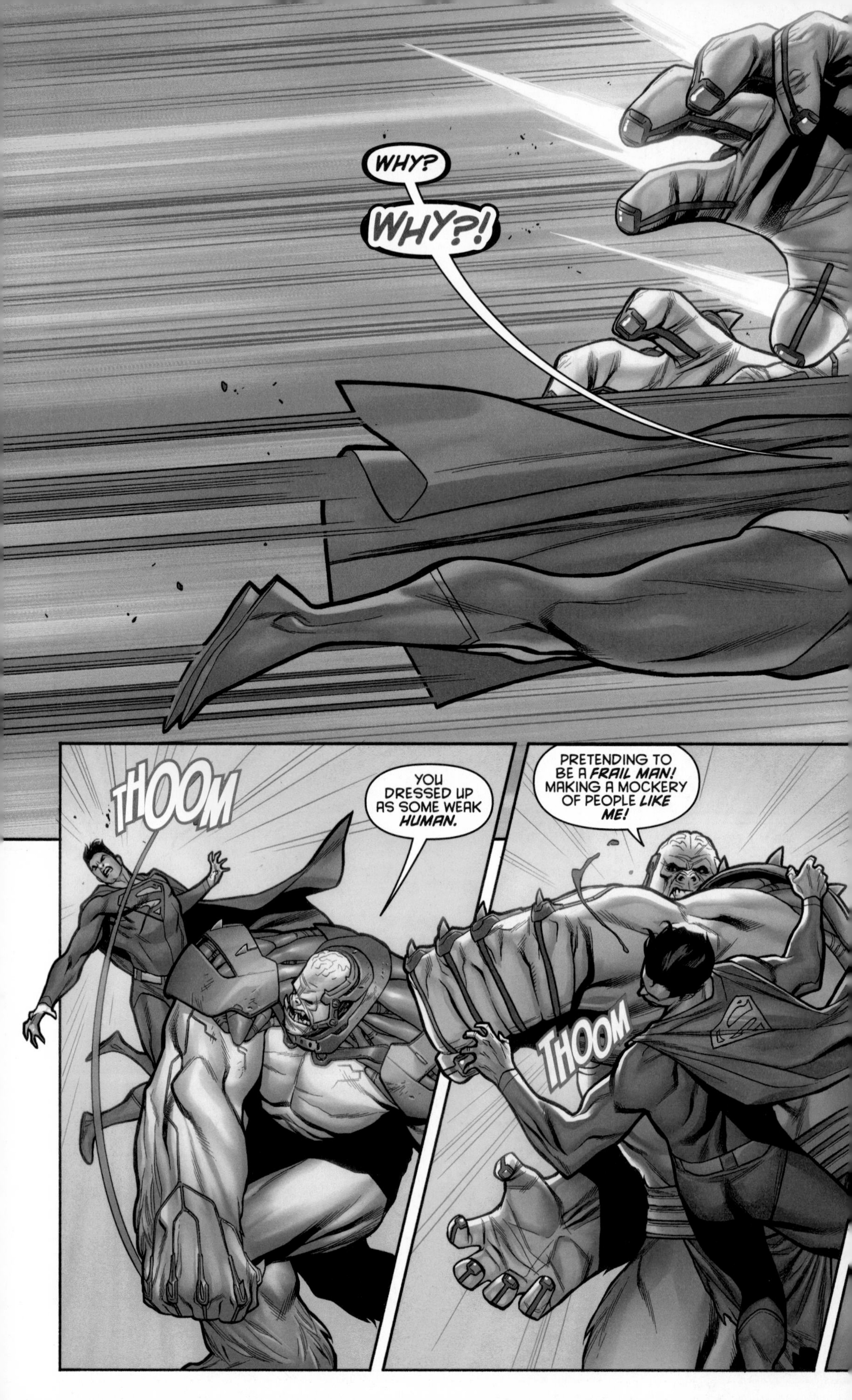
WHY?
WHY?!
THOOM
YOU DRESSED UP AS SOME WEAK HUMAN.
PRETENDING TO BE A FRAIL MAN! MAKING A MOCKERY OF PEOPLE LIKE ME!
THOOM

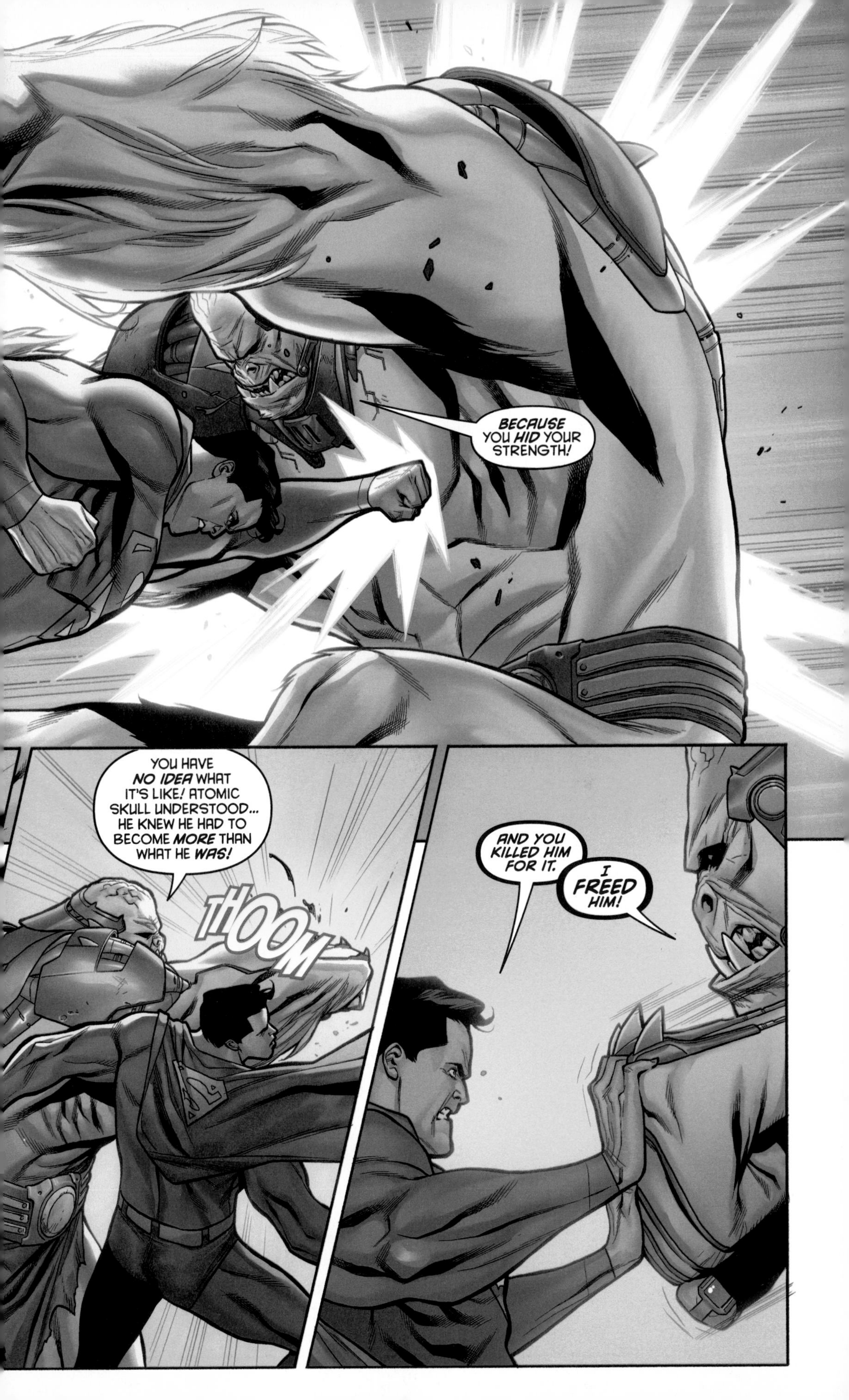
BECAUSE YOU HID YOUR STRENGTH!
YOU HAVE NO IDEA WHAT IT'S LIKE! ATOMIC SKULL UNDERSTOOD... HE KNEW HE HAD TO BECOME MORE THAN WHAT HE WAS!
THOOM
AND YOU KILLED HIM FOR IT.
I FREED HIM!

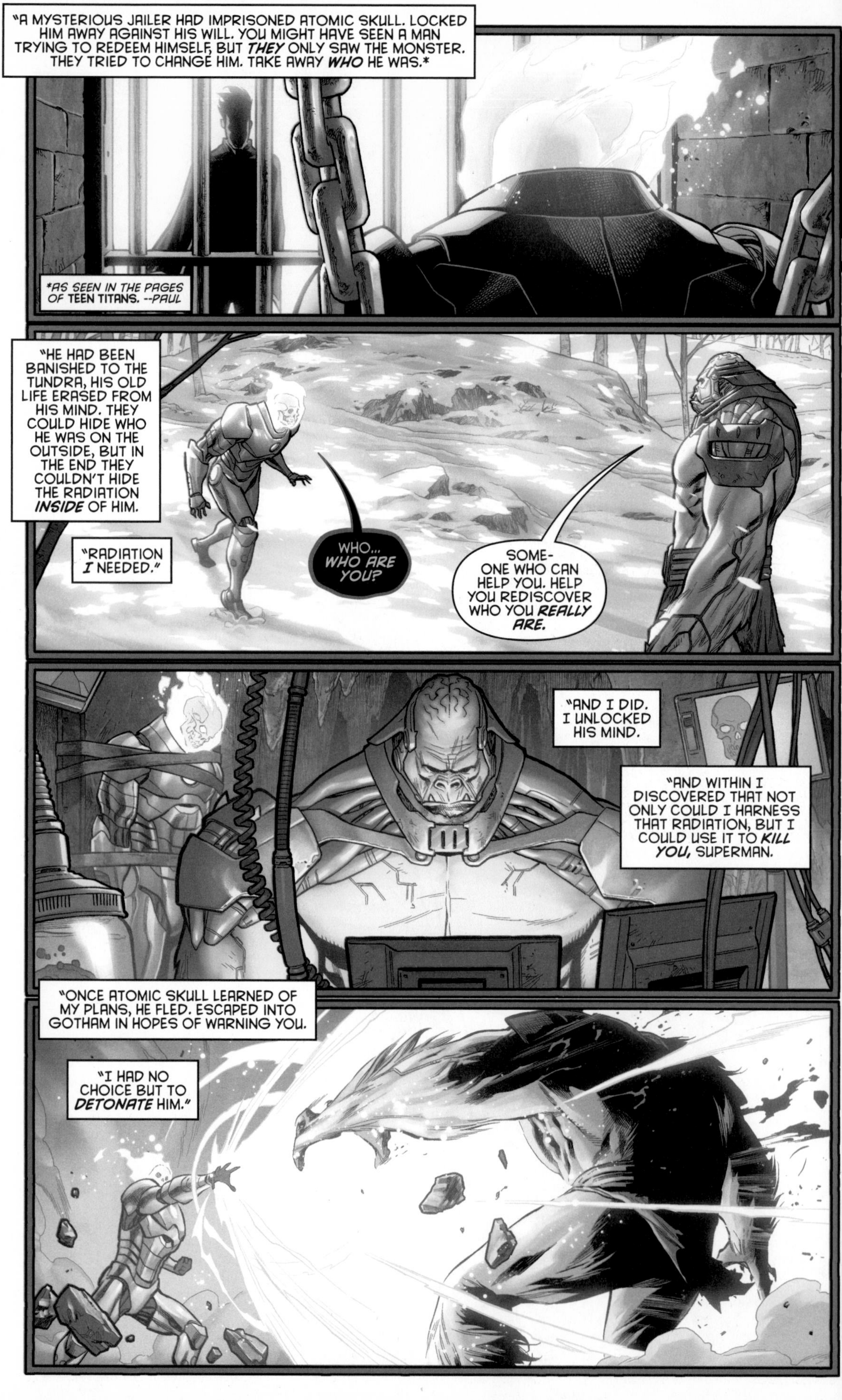
"A MYSTERIOUS JAILER HAD IMPRISONED ATOMIC SKULL. LOCKED HIM AWAY AGAINST HIS WILL. YOU MIGHT HAVE SEEN A MAN TRYING TO REDEEM HIMSELF, BUT *THEY* ONLY SAW THE MONSTER. THEY TRIED TO CHANGE HIM. TAKE AWAY *WHO* HE WAS.*
*AS SEEN IN THE PAGES OF TEEN TITANS. --PAUL
"HE HAD BEEN BANISHED TO THE TUNDRA, HIS OLD LIFE ERASED FROM HIS MIND. THEY COULD HIDE WHO HE WAS ON THE OUTSIDE, BUT IN THE END THEY COULDN'T HIDE THE RADIATION *INSIDE* OF HIM.
"RADIATION *I* NEEDED."
WHO... *WHO ARE YOU?*
SOME-ONE WHO CAN HELP YOU. HELP YOU REDISCOVER WHO YOU *REALLY ARE.*
"AND I DID. I UNLOCKED HIS MIND.
"AND WITHIN I DISCOVERED THAT NOT ONLY COULD I HARNESS THAT RADIATION, BUT I COULD USE IT TO *KILL YOU,* SUPERMAN.
"ONCE ATOMIC SKULL LEARNED OF MY PLANS, HE FLED. ESCAPED INTO GOTHAM IN HOPES OF WARNING YOU.
"I HAD NO CHOICE BUT TO *DETONATE* HIM."

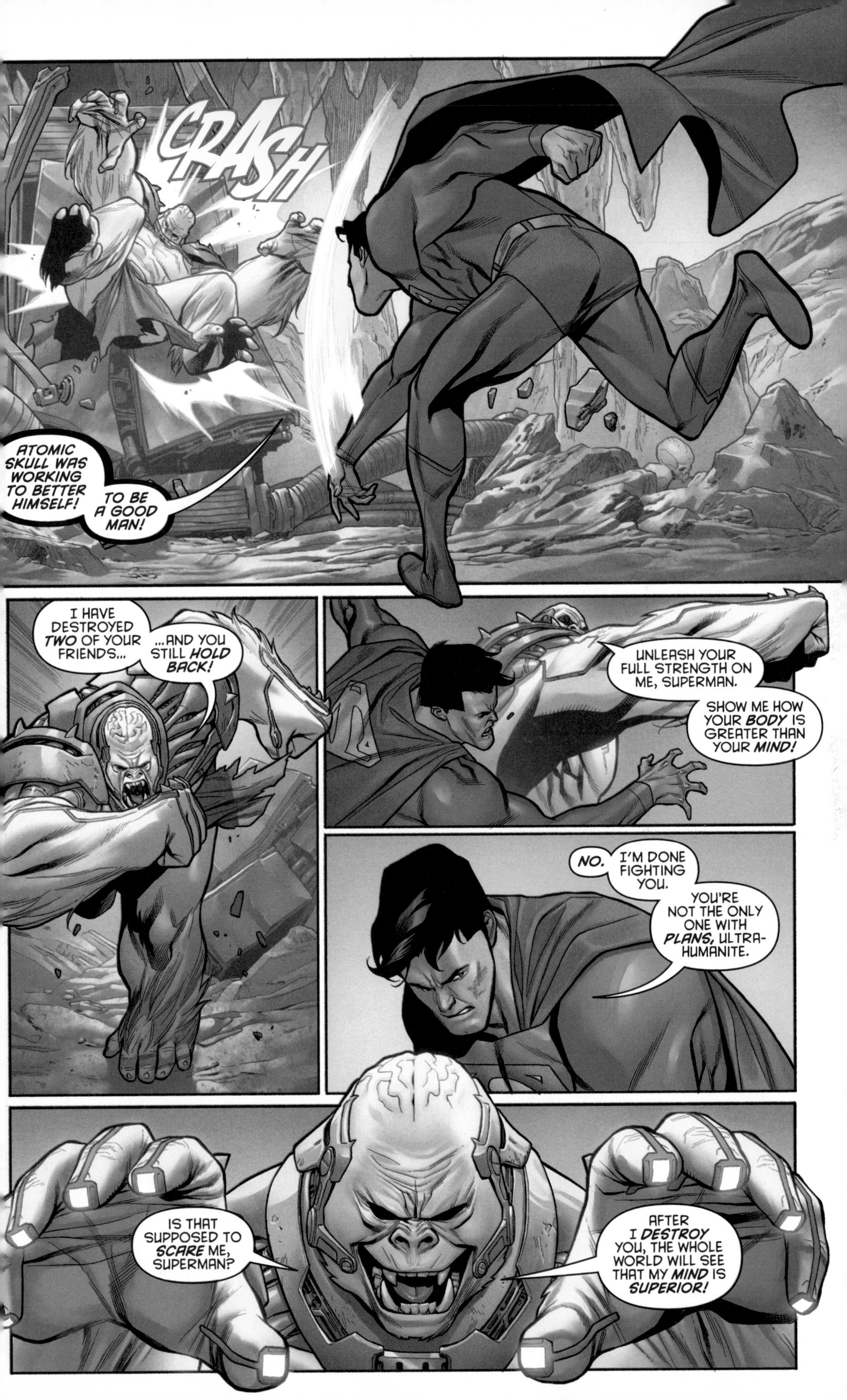
CRASH
ATOMIC SKULL WAS WORKING TO BETTER HIMSELF!
TO BE A GOOD MAN!
I HAVE DESTROYED TWO OF YOUR FRIENDS...
...AND YOU STILL HOLD BACK!
UNLEASH YOUR FULL STRENGTH ON ME, SUPERMAN.
SHOW ME HOW YOUR BODY IS GREATER THAN YOUR MIND!
NO.
I'M DONE FIGHTING YOU.
YOU'RE NOT THE ONLY ONE WITH PLANS, ULTRA-HUMANITE.
IS THAT SUPPOSED TO SCARE ME, SUPERMAN?
AFTER I DESTROY YOU, THE WHOLE WORLD WILL SEE THAT MY MIND IS SUPERIOR!

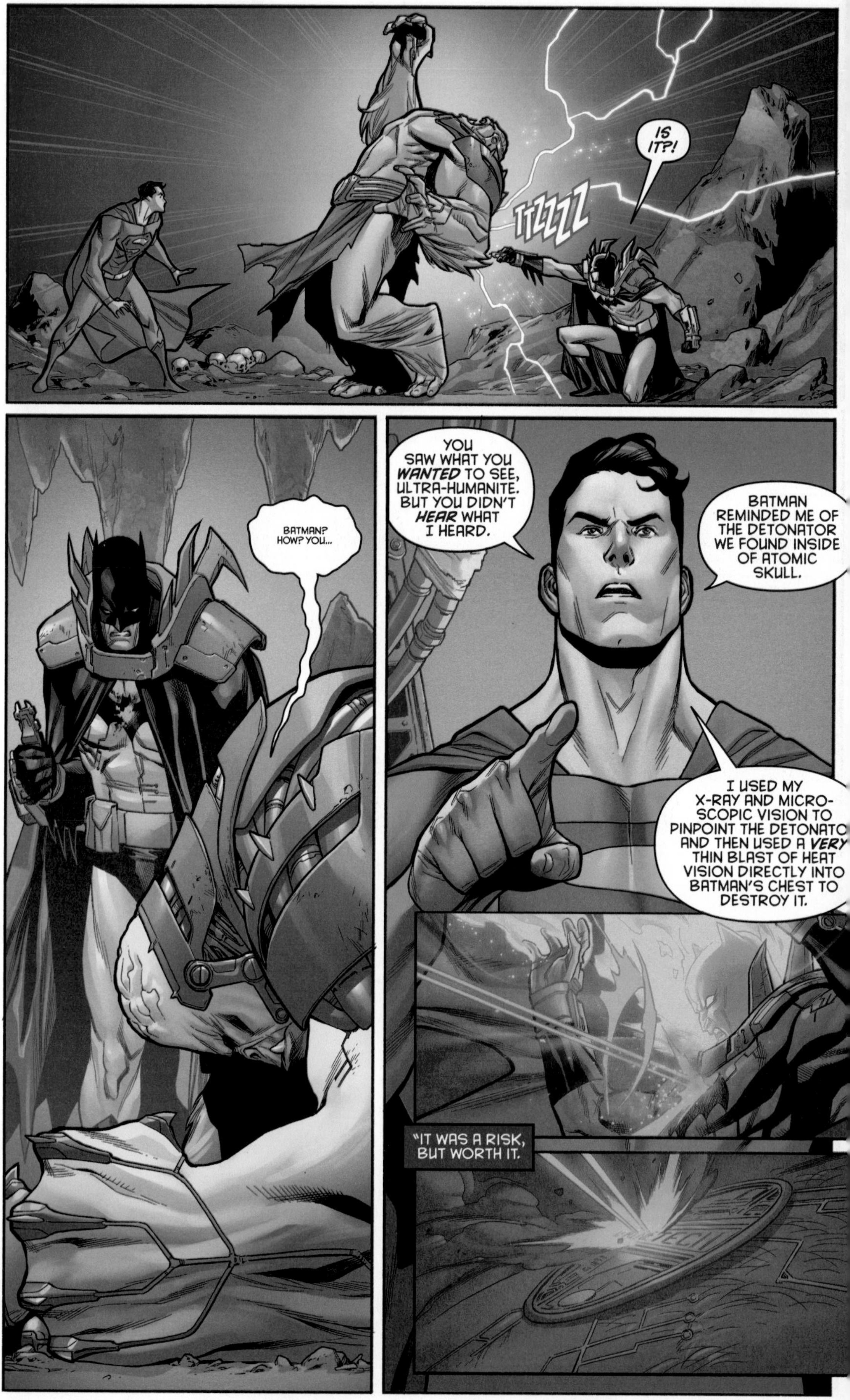
IS IT?!
TTZZZZ
BATMAN? HOW? YOU...
YOU SAW WHAT YOU WANTED TO SEE, ULTRA-HUMANITE. BUT YOU DIDN'T HEAR WHAT I HEARD.
BATMAN REMINDED ME OF THE DETONATOR WE FOUND INSIDE OF ATOMIC SKULL.
I USED MY X-RAY AND MICRO-SCOPIC VISION TO PINPOINT THE DETONATO AND THEN USED A VERY THIN BLAST OF HEAT VISION DIRECTLY INTO BATMAN'S CHEST TO DESTROY IT.
"IT WAS A RISK, BUT WORTH IT.

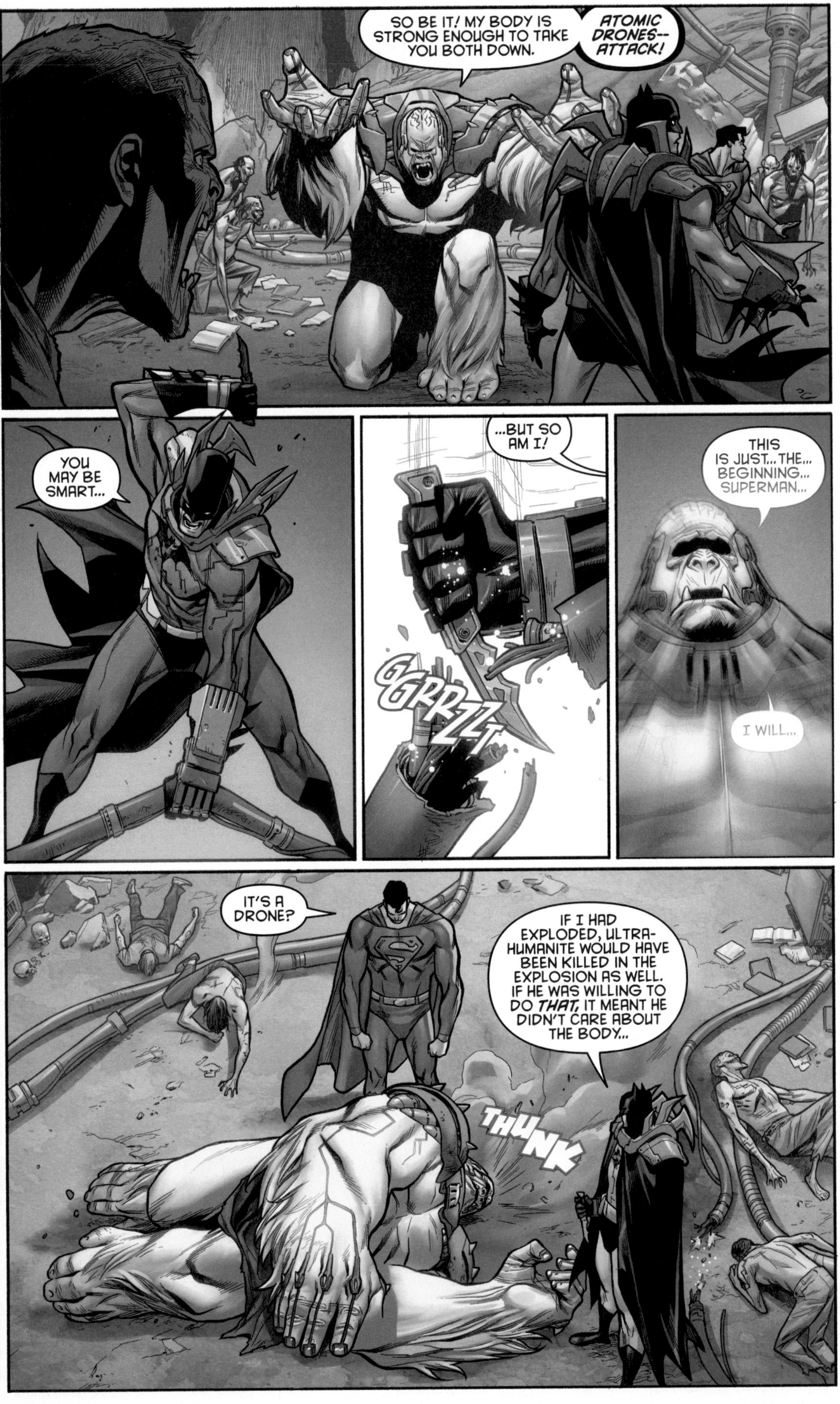
SO BE IT! MY BODY IS STRONG ENOUGH TO TAKE YOU BOTH DOWN.
ATOMIC DRONES--ATTACK!
YOU MAY BE SMART...
...BUT SO AM I!
GGRRZZT
THIS IS JUST... THE... BEGINNING... SUPERMAN...
I WILL...
IT'S A DRONE?
IF I HAD EXPLODED, ULTRA-HUMANITE WOULD HAVE BEEN KILLED IN THE EXPLOSION AS WELL. IF HE WAS WILLING TO DO THAT, IT MEANT HE DIDN'T CARE ABOUT THE BODY...
THUNK

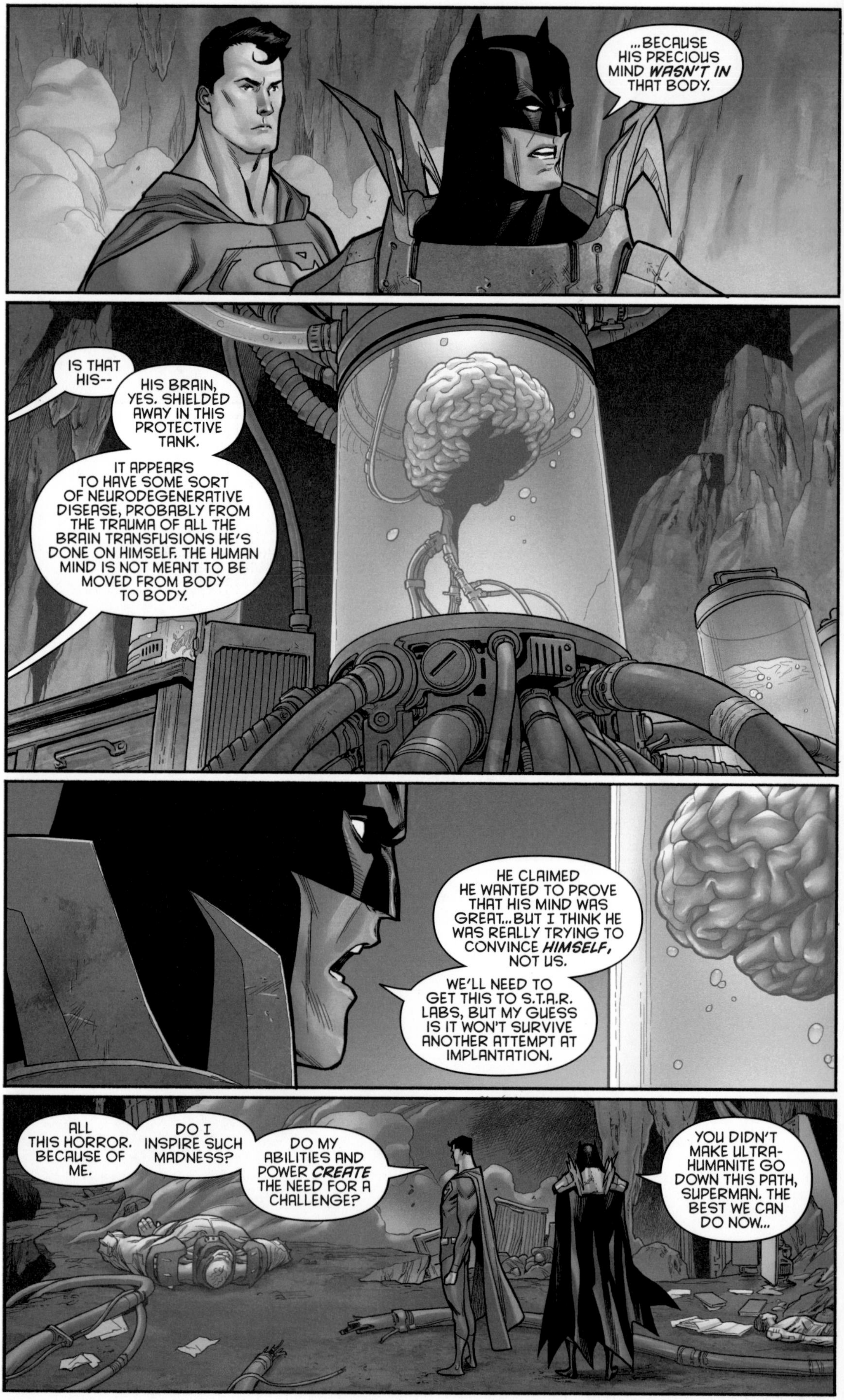
...BECAUSE HIS PRECIOUS MIND *WASN'T IN* THAT BODY.
IS THAT HIS--
HIS BRAIN, YES. SHIELDED AWAY IN THIS PROTECTIVE TANK.
IT APPEARS TO HAVE SOME SORT OF NEURODEGENERATIVE DISEASE, PROBABLY FROM THE TRAUMA OF ALL THE BRAIN TRANSFUSIONS HE'S DONE ON HIMSELF. THE HUMAN MIND IS NOT MEANT TO BE MOVED FROM BODY TO BODY.
HE CLAIMED HE WANTED TO PROVE THAT HIS MIND WAS GREAT...BUT I THINK HE WAS REALLY TRYING TO CONVINCE *HIMSELF,* NOT US.
WE'LL NEED TO GET THIS TO S.T.A.R. LABS, BUT MY GUESS IS IT WON'T SURVIVE ANOTHER ATTEMPT AT IMPLANTATION.
ALL THIS HORROR. BECAUSE OF ME.
DO I INSPIRE SUCH MADNESS?
DO MY ABILITIES AND POWER *CREATE* THE NEED FOR A CHALLENGE?
YOU DIDN'T MAKE ULTRA-HUMANITE GO DOWN THIS PATH, SUPERMAN. THE BEST WE CAN DO NOW...

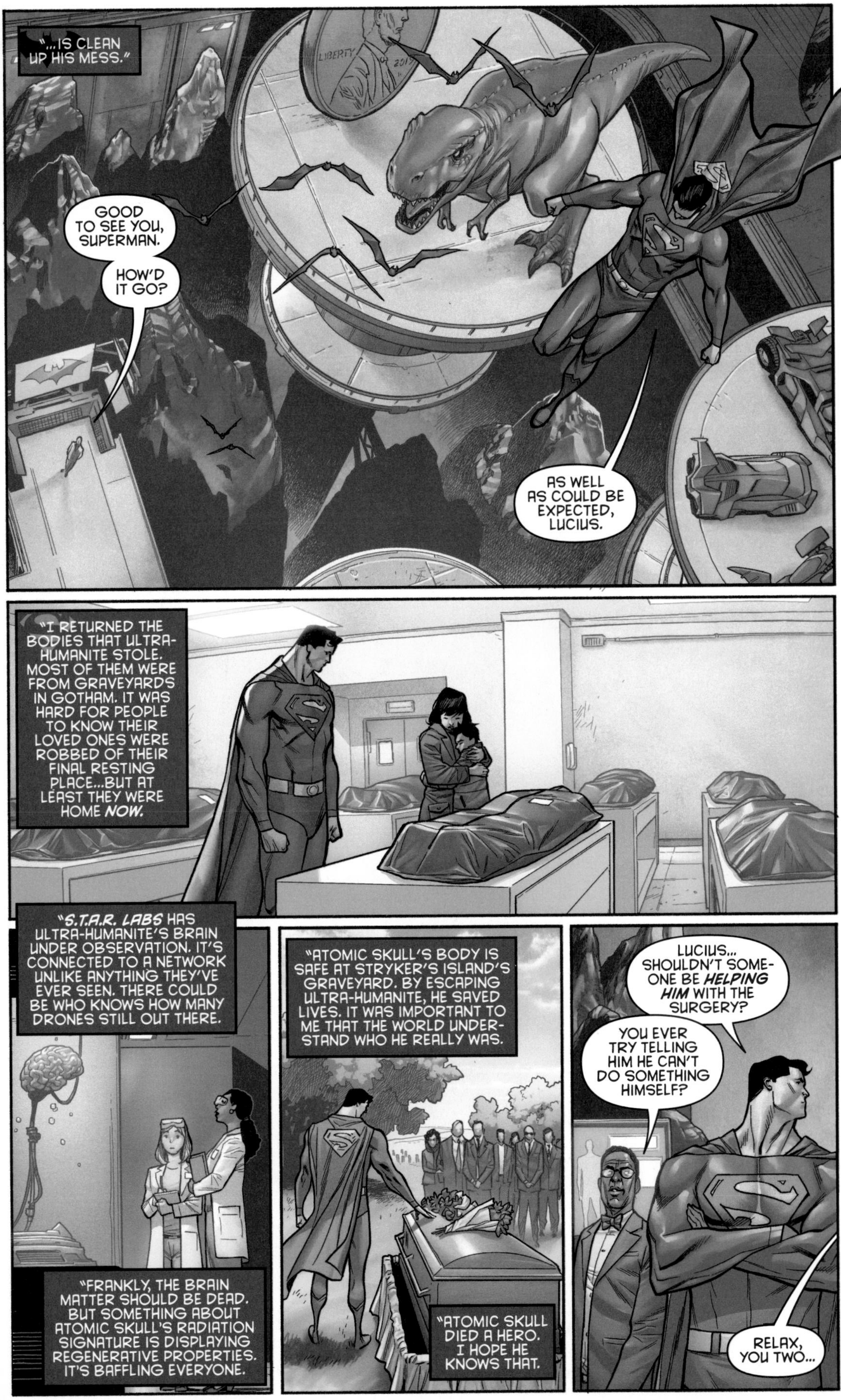
"...IS CLEAN UP HIS MESS."
GOOD TO SEE YOU, SUPERMAN.
HOW'D IT GO?
AS WELL AS COULD BE EXPECTED, LUCIUS.
"I RETURNED THE BODIES THAT ULTRA-HUMANITE STOLE. MOST OF THEM WERE FROM GRAVEYARDS IN GOTHAM. IT WAS HARD FOR PEOPLE TO KNOW THEIR LOVED ONES WERE ROBBED OF THEIR FINAL RESTING PLACE...BUT AT LEAST THEY WERE HOME *NOW.*
"*S.T.A.R. LABS* HAS ULTRA-HUMANITE'S BRAIN UNDER OBSERVATION. IT'S CONNECTED TO A NETWORK UNLIKE ANYTHING THEY'VE EVER SEEN. THERE COULD BE WHO KNOWS HOW MANY DRONES STILL OUT THERE.
"FRANKLY, THE BRAIN MATTER SHOULD BE DEAD. BUT SOMETHING ABOUT ATOMIC SKULL'S RADIATION SIGNATURE IS DISPLAYING REGENERATIVE PROPERTIES. IT'S BAFFLING EVERYONE.
"ATOMIC SKULL'S BODY IS SAFE AT STRYKER'S ISLAND'S GRAVEYARD. BY ESCAPING ULTRA-HUMANITE, HE SAVED LIVES. IT WAS IMPORTANT TO ME THAT THE WORLD UNDERSTAND WHO HE REALLY WAS.
"ATOMIC SKULL DIED A HERO. I HOPE HE KNOWS THAT.
LUCIUS... SHOULDN'T SOMEONE BE *HELPING HIM* WITH THE SURGERY?
YOU EVER TRY TELLING HIM HE CAN'T DO SOMETHING HIMSELF?
RELAX, YOU TWO...

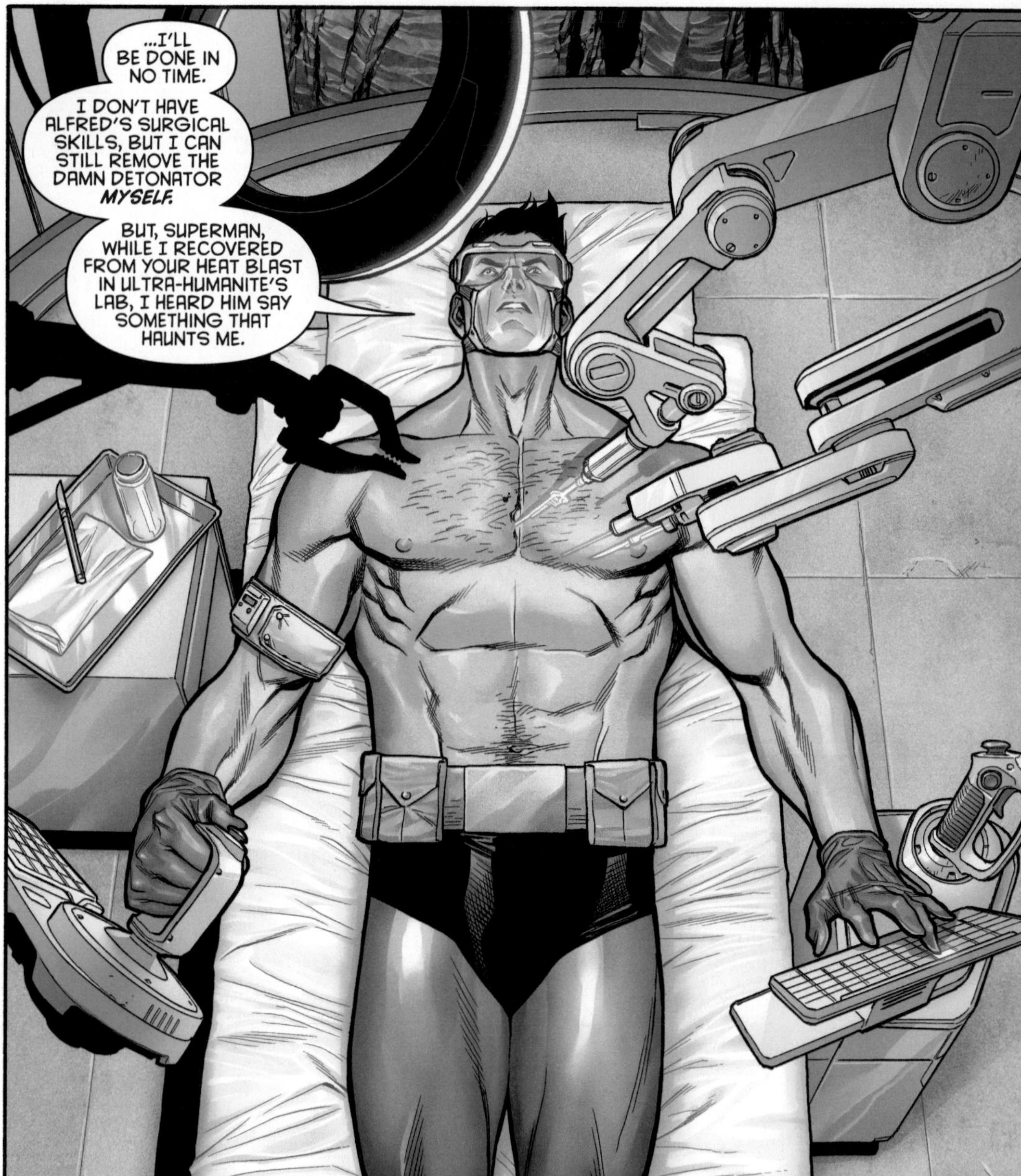
...I'LL BE DONE IN NO TIME.
I DON'T HAVE ALFRED'S SURGICAL SKILLS, BUT I CAN STILL REMOVE THE DAMN DETONATOR *MYSELF*.
BUT, SUPERMAN, WHILE I RECOVERED FROM YOUR HEAT BLAST IN ULTRA-HUMANITE'S LAB, I HEARD HIM SAY SOMETHING THAT HAUNTS ME.

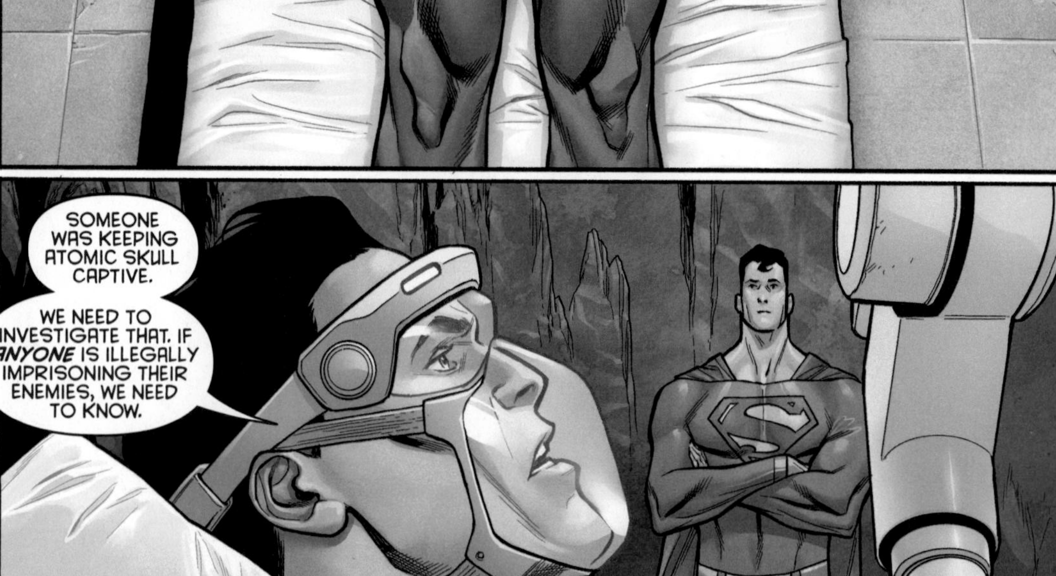
SOMEONE WAS KEEPING ATOMIC SKULL CAPTIVE.
WE NEED TO INVESTIGATE THAT. IF *ANYONE* IS ILLEGALLY IMPRISONING THEIR ENEMIES, WE NEED TO KNOW.

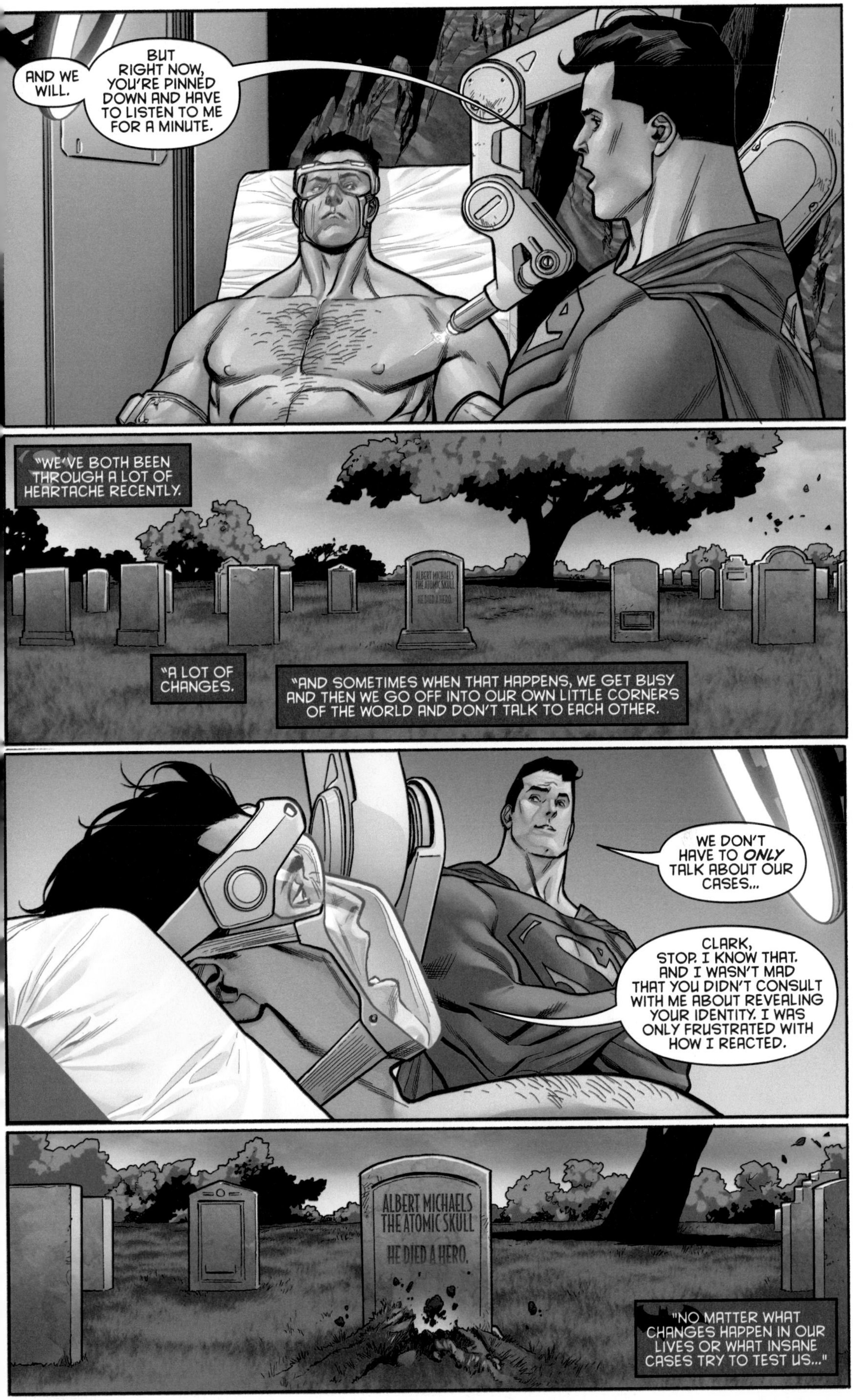
AND WE WILL.
BUT RIGHT NOW, YOU'RE PINNED DOWN AND HAVE TO LISTEN TO ME FOR A MINUTE.
"WE'VE BOTH BEEN THROUGH A LOT OF HEARTACHE RECENTLY.
ALBERT MICHAELS THE ATOMIC SKULL HE DIED A HERO.
"A LOT OF CHANGES.
"AND SOMETIMES WHEN THAT HAPPENS, WE GET BUSY AND THEN WE GO OFF INTO OUR OWN LITTLE CORNERS OF THE WORLD AND DON'T TALK TO EACH OTHER.
WE DON'T HAVE TO *ONLY* TALK ABOUT OUR CASES...
CLARK, STOP. I KNOW THAT. AND I WASN'T MAD THAT YOU DIDN'T CONSULT WITH ME ABOUT REVEALING YOUR IDENTITY. I WAS ONLY FRUSTRATED WITH HOW I REACTED.
ALBERT MICHAELS THE ATOMIC SKULL
HE DIED A HERO.
"NO MATTER WHAT CHANGES HAPPEN IN OUR LIVES OR WHAT INSANE CASES TRY TO TEST US..."

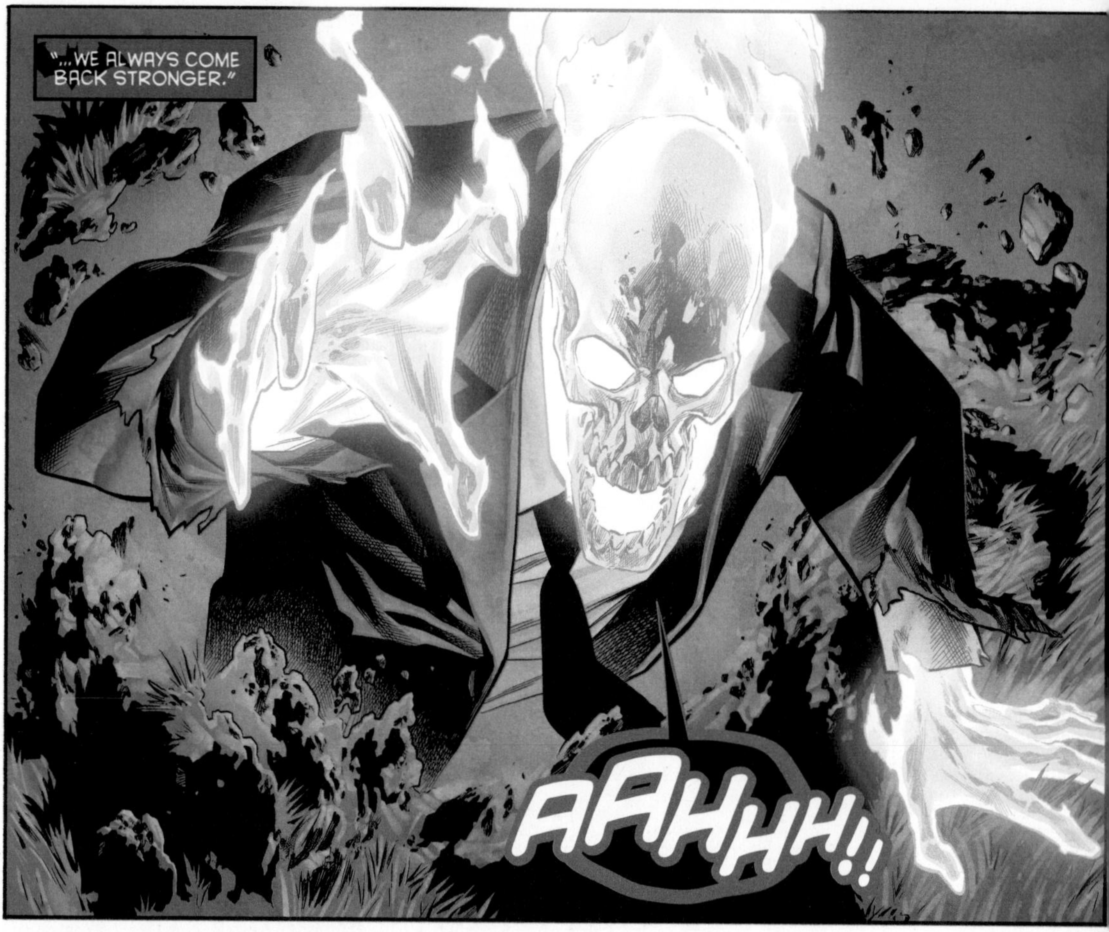
"...WE ALWAYS COME BACK STRONGER."
AAHHHH!!

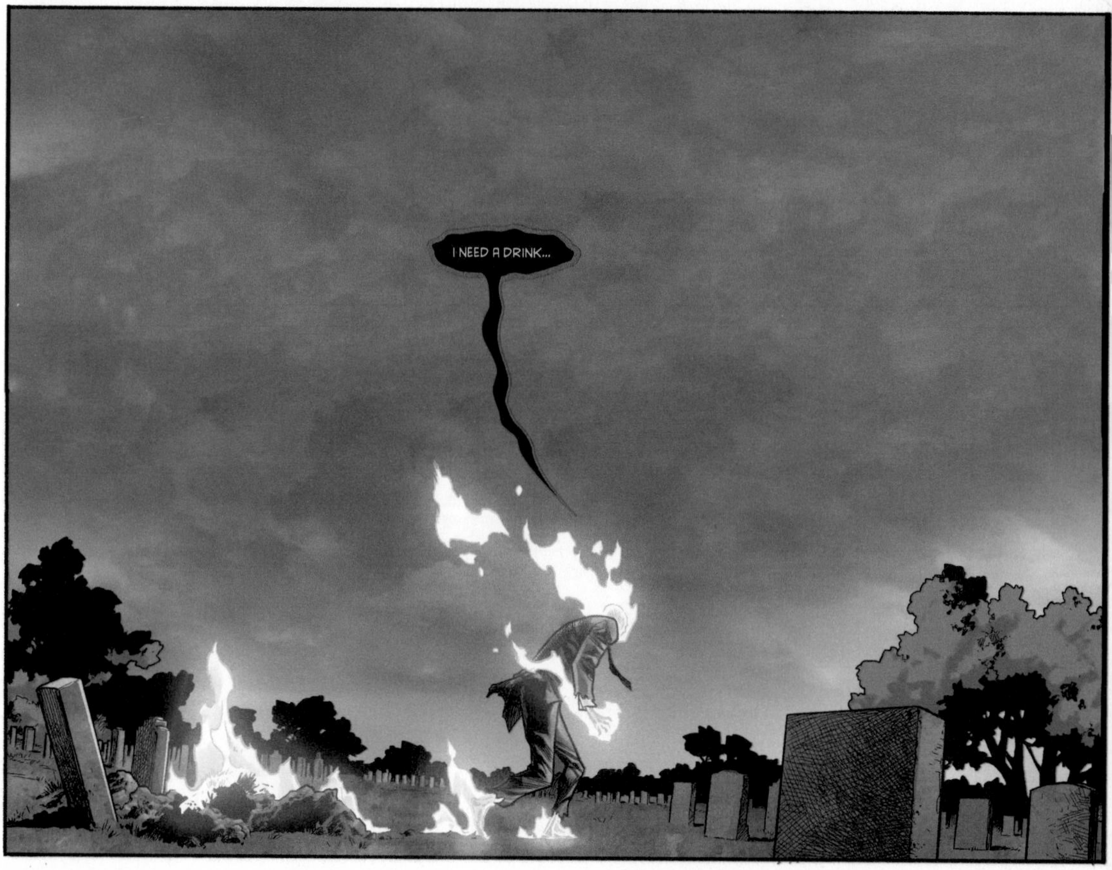
I NEED A DRINK...

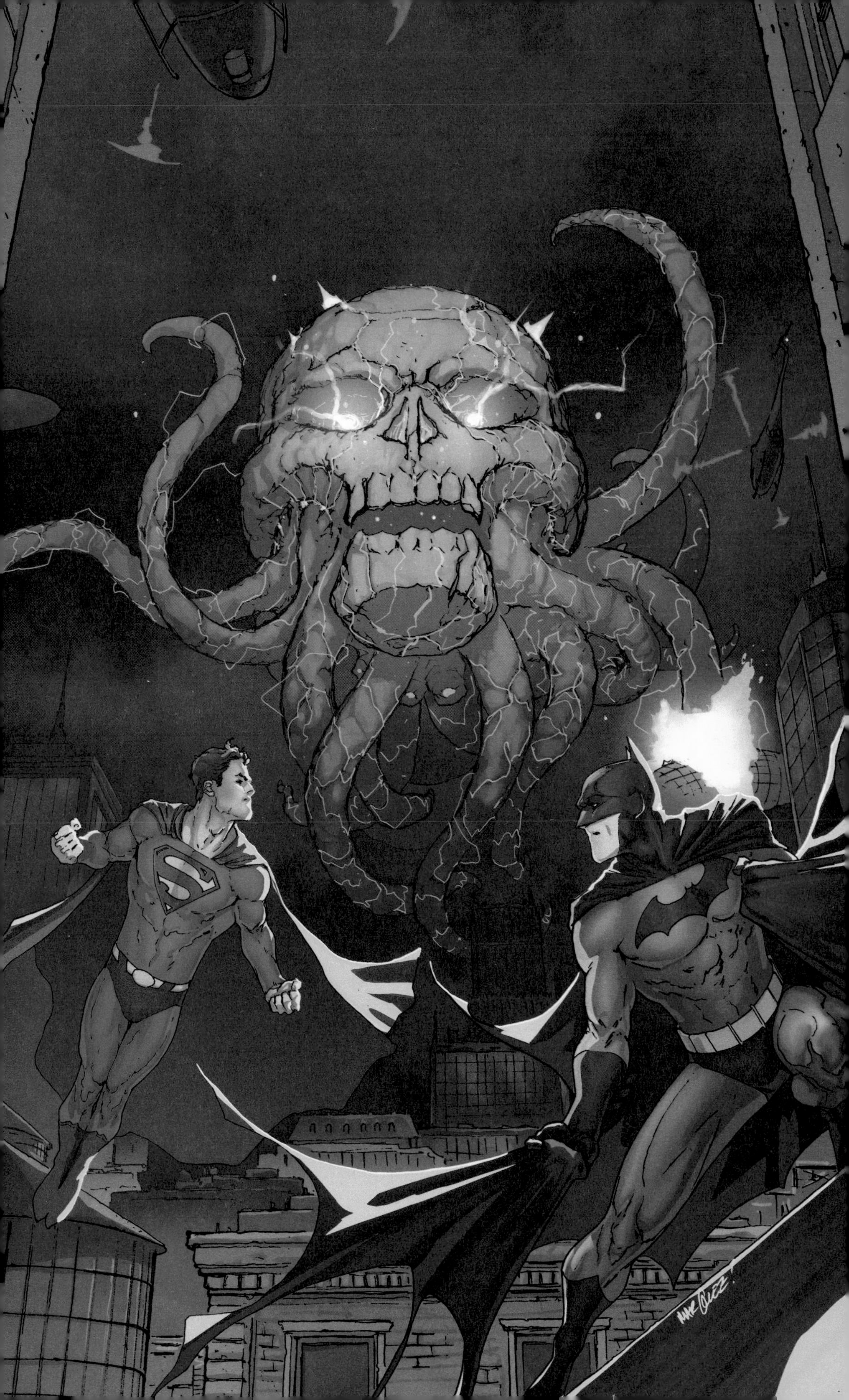

BATMAN/SUPERMAN #12

cover by
DAVID MARQUEZ

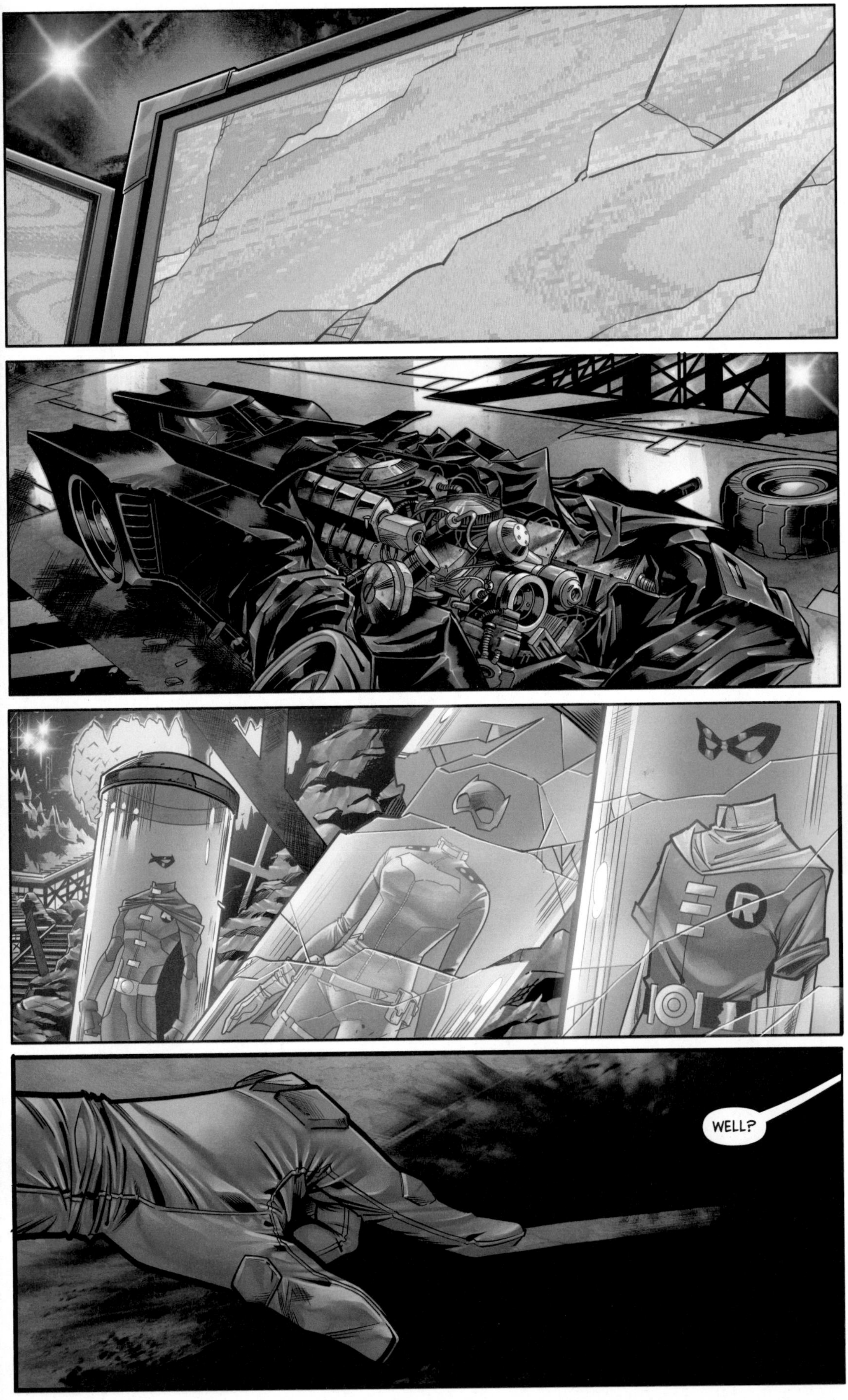
WELL?

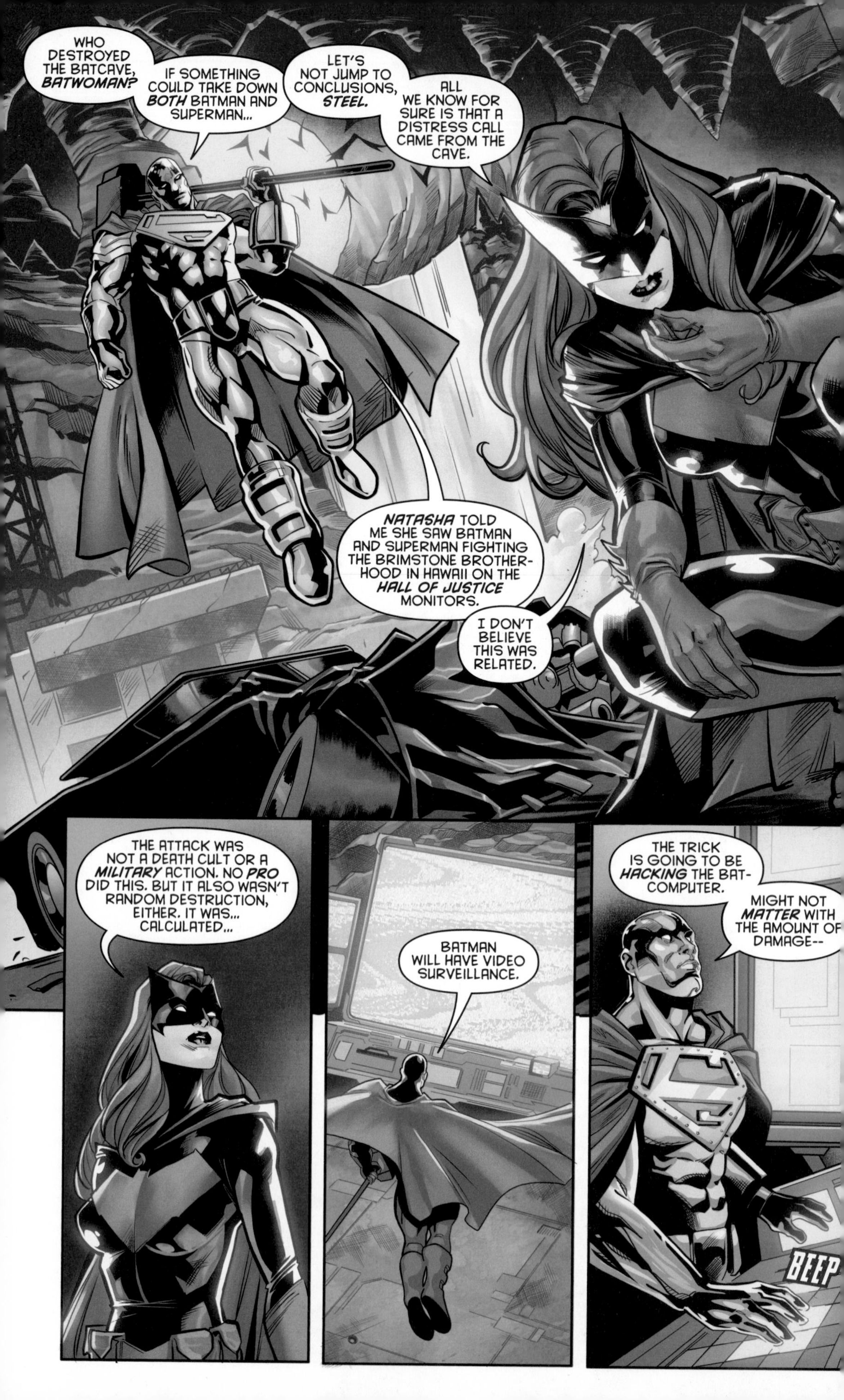
WHO DESTROYED THE BATCAVE, BATWOMAN?
IF SOMETHING COULD TAKE DOWN BOTH BATMAN AND SUPERMAN...
LET'S NOT JUMP TO CONCLUSIONS, STEEL.
ALL WE KNOW FOR SURE IS THAT A DISTRESS CALL CAME FROM THE CAVE.
NATASHA TOLD ME SHE SAW BATMAN AND SUPERMAN FIGHTING THE BRIMSTONE BROTHER-HOOD IN HAWAII ON THE HALL OF JUSTICE MONITORS.
I DON'T BELIEVE THIS WAS RELATED.
THE ATTACK WAS NOT A DEATH CULT OR A MILITARY ACTION. NO PRO DID THIS. BUT IT ALSO WASN'T RANDOM DESTRUCTION, EITHER. IT WAS... CALCULATED...
BATMAN WILL HAVE VIDEO SURVEILLANCE.
THE TRICK IS GOING TO BE HACKING THE BAT-COMPUTER.
MIGHT NOT MATTER WITH THE AMOUNT OF DAMAGE--
BEEP

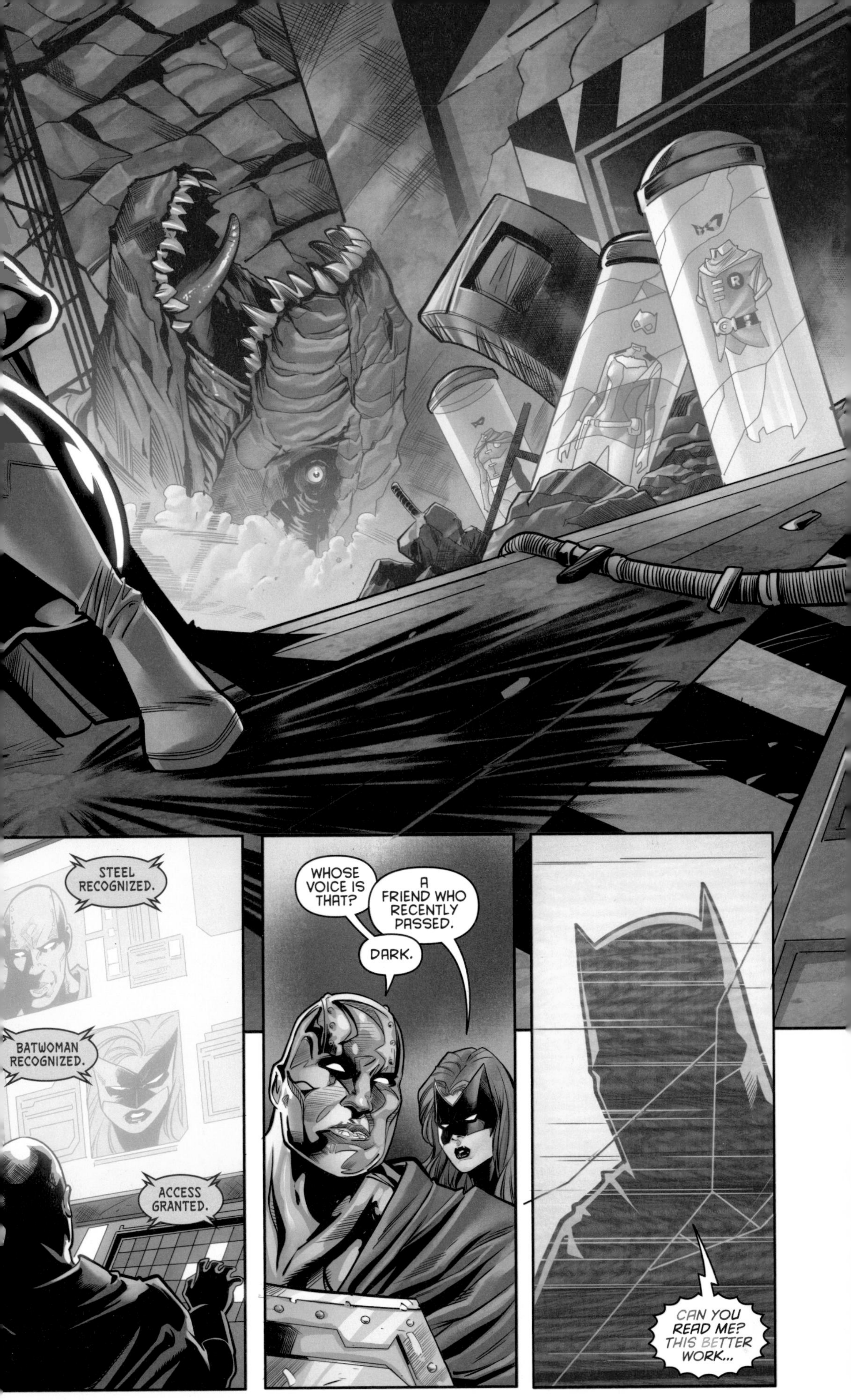
STEEL RECOGNIZED.
BATWOMAN RECOGNIZED.
ACCESS GRANTED.
WHOSE VOICE IS THAT?
DARK.
A FRIEND WHO RECENTLY PASSED.
CAN YOU READ ME? THIS BETTER WORK...

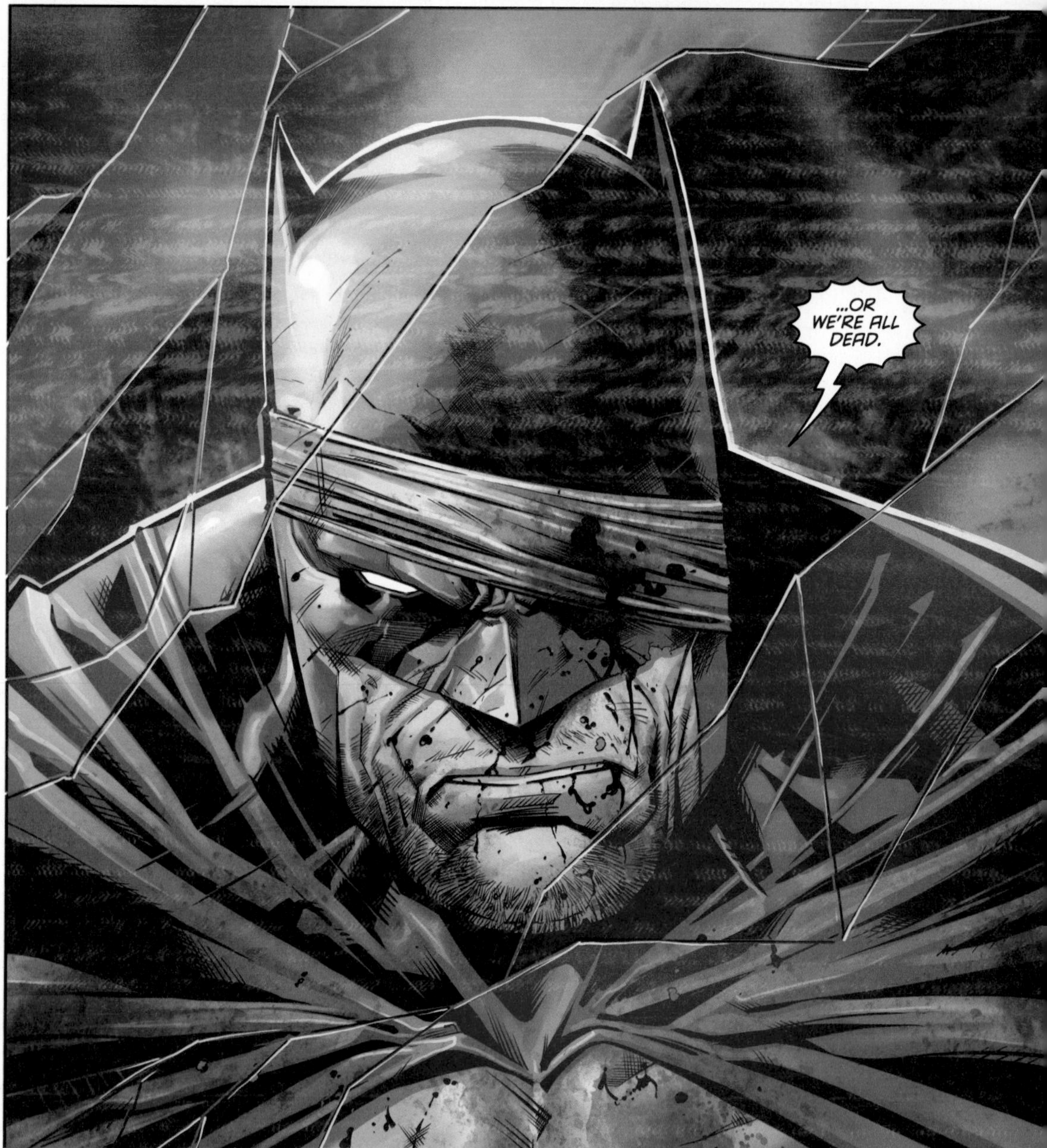
...OR WE'RE ALL DEAD.

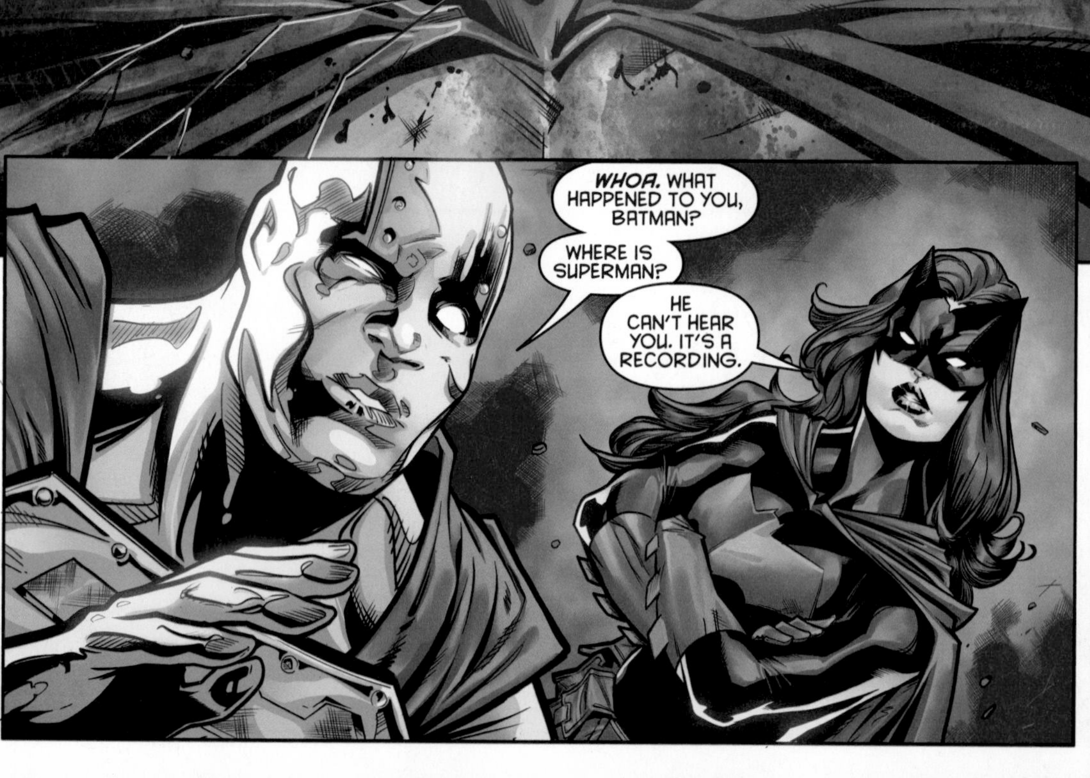
WHOA. WHAT HAPPENED TO YOU, BATMAN?
WHERE IS SUPERMAN?
HE CAN'T HEAR YOU. IT'S A RECORDING.

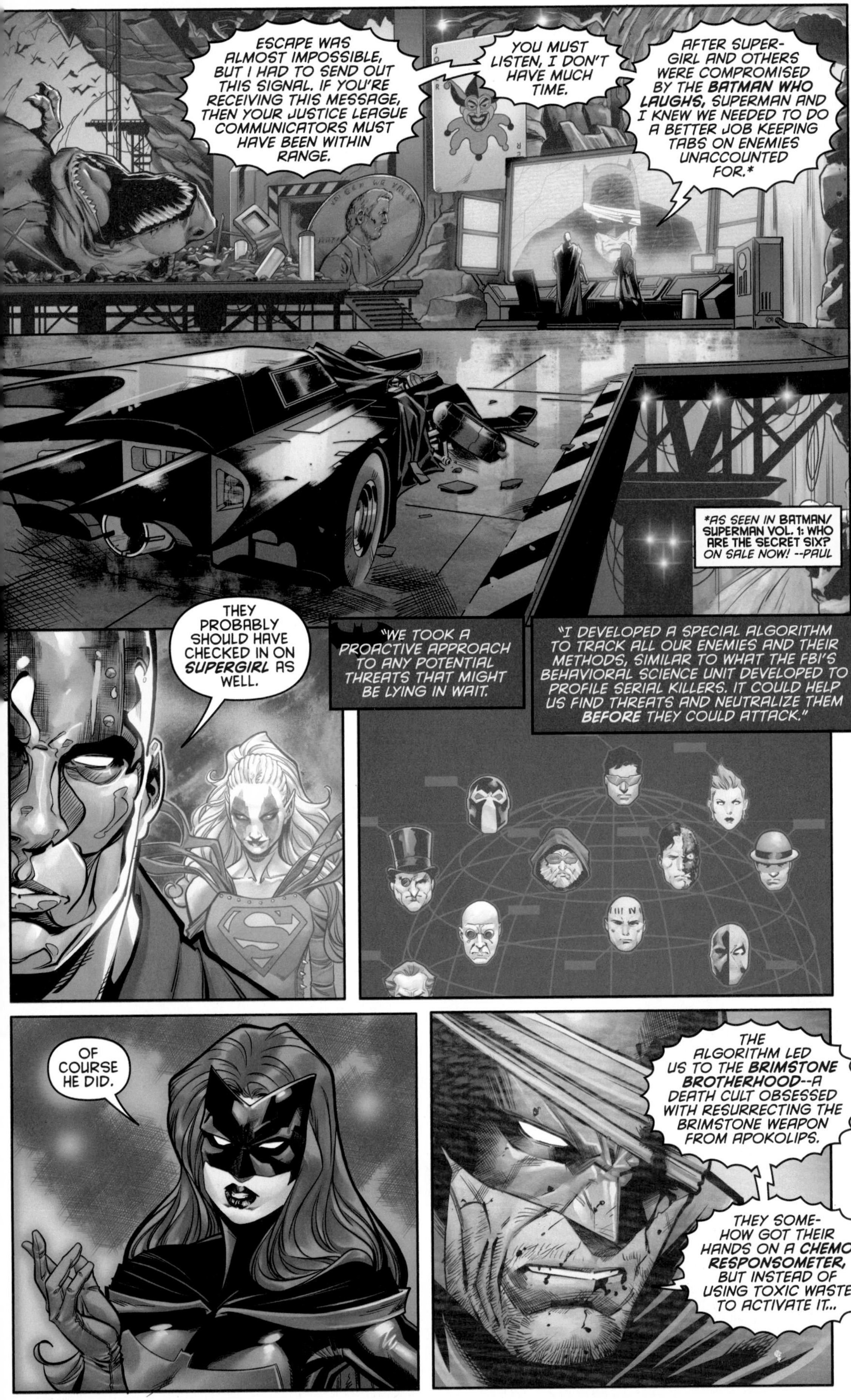
ESCAPE WAS ALMOST IMPOSSIBLE, BUT I HAD TO SEND OUT THIS SIGNAL. IF YOU'RE RECEIVING THIS MESSAGE, THEN YOUR JUSTICE LEAGUE COMMUNICATORS MUST HAVE BEEN WITHIN RANGE.
YOU MUST LISTEN, I DON'T HAVE MUCH TIME.
AFTER SUPER-GIRL AND OTHERS WERE COMPROMISED BY THE **BATMAN WHO LAUGHS,** SUPERMAN AND I KNEW WE NEEDED TO DO A BETTER JOB KEEPING TABS ON ENEMIES UNACCOUNTED FOR.*
*AS SEEN IN BATMAN/ SUPERMAN VOL. 1: WHO ARE THE SECRET SIX? ON SALE NOW! --PAUL
THEY PROBABLY SHOULD HAVE CHECKED IN ON ***SUPERGIRL*** AS WELL.
"WE TOOK A PROACTIVE APPROACH TO ANY POTENTIAL THREATS THAT MIGHT BE LYING IN WAIT.
"I DEVELOPED A SPECIAL ALGORITHM TO TRACK ALL OUR ENEMIES AND THEIR METHODS, SIMILAR TO WHAT THE FBI'S BEHAVIORAL SCIENCE UNIT DEVELOPED TO PROFILE SERIAL KILLERS. IT COULD HELP US FIND THREATS AND NEUTRALIZE THEM ***BEFORE*** THEY COULD ATTACK."
OF COURSE HE DID.
THE ALGORITHM LED US TO THE **BRIMSTONE BROTHERHOOD**--A DEATH CULT OBSESSED WITH RESURRECTING THE BRIMSTONE WEAPON FROM APOKOLIPS.
THEY SOME-HOW GOT THEIR HANDS ON A ***CHEMO RESPONSOMETER,*** BUT INSTEAD OF USING TOXIC WASTE TO ACTIVATE IT...

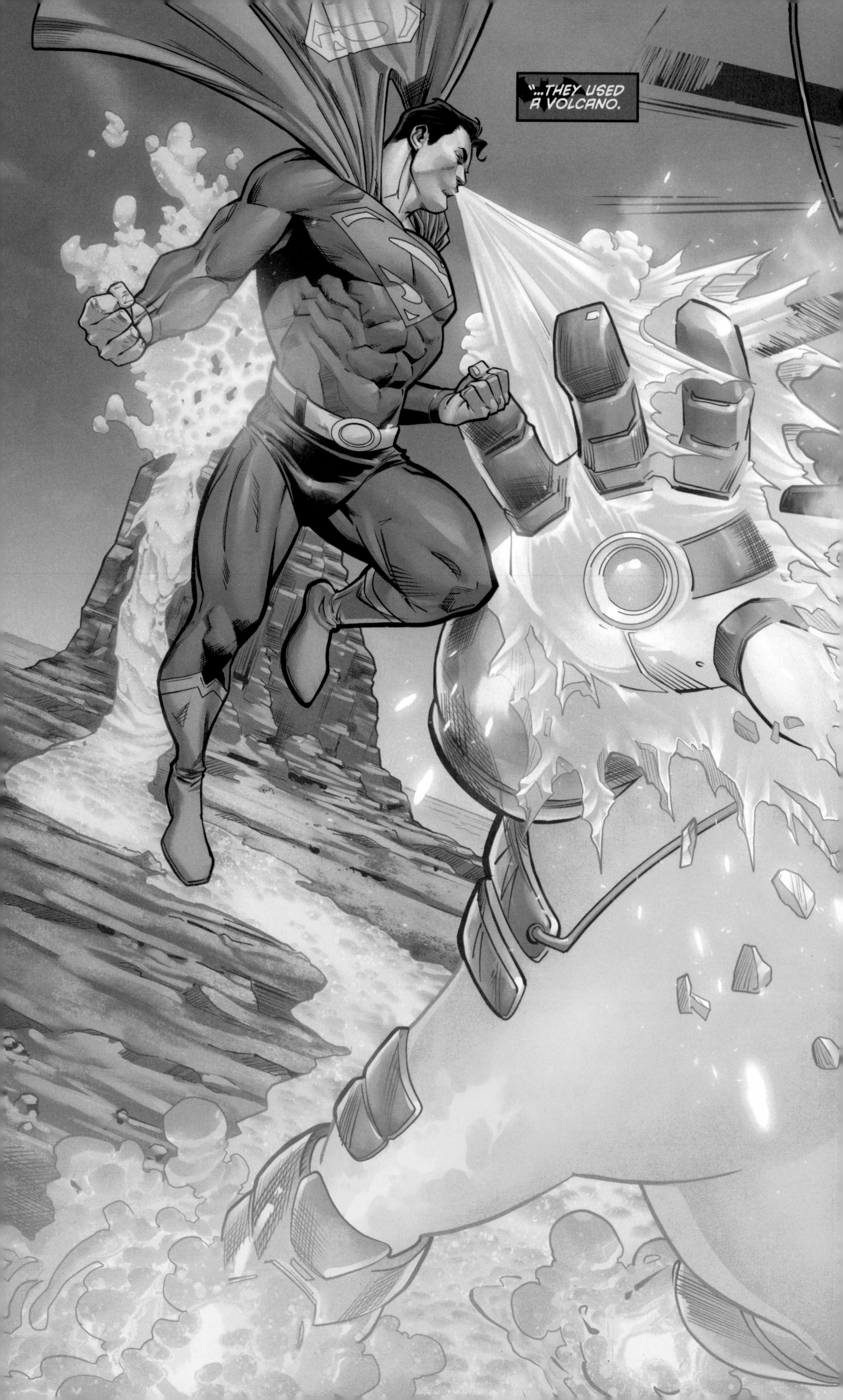
"...THEY USED A VOLCANO.

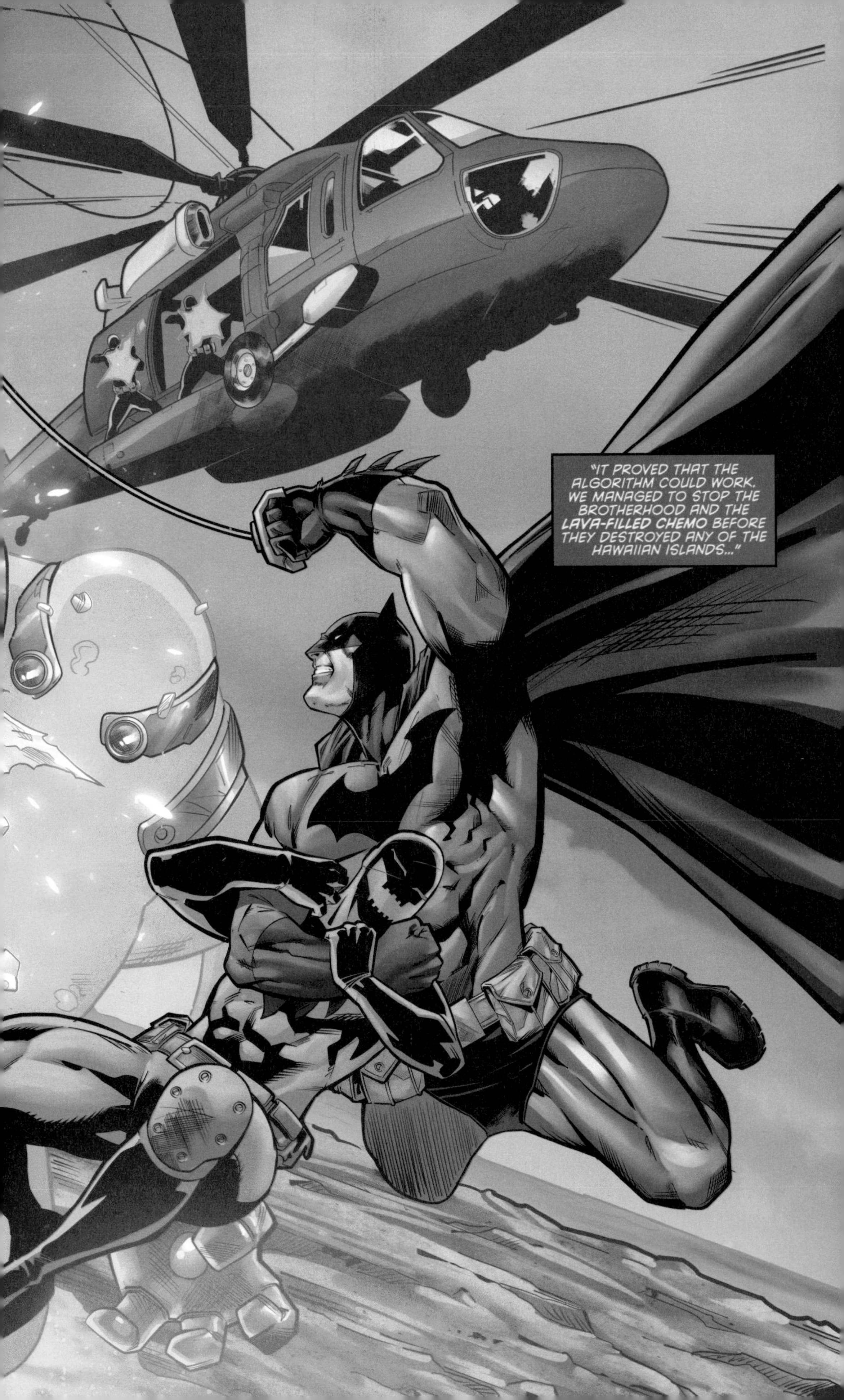
"IT PROVED THAT THE ALGORITHM COULD WORK. WE MANAGED TO STOP THE BROTHERHOOD AND THE **LAVA-FILLED CHEMO** BEFORE THEY DESTROYED ANY OF THE HAWAIIAN ISLANDS..."

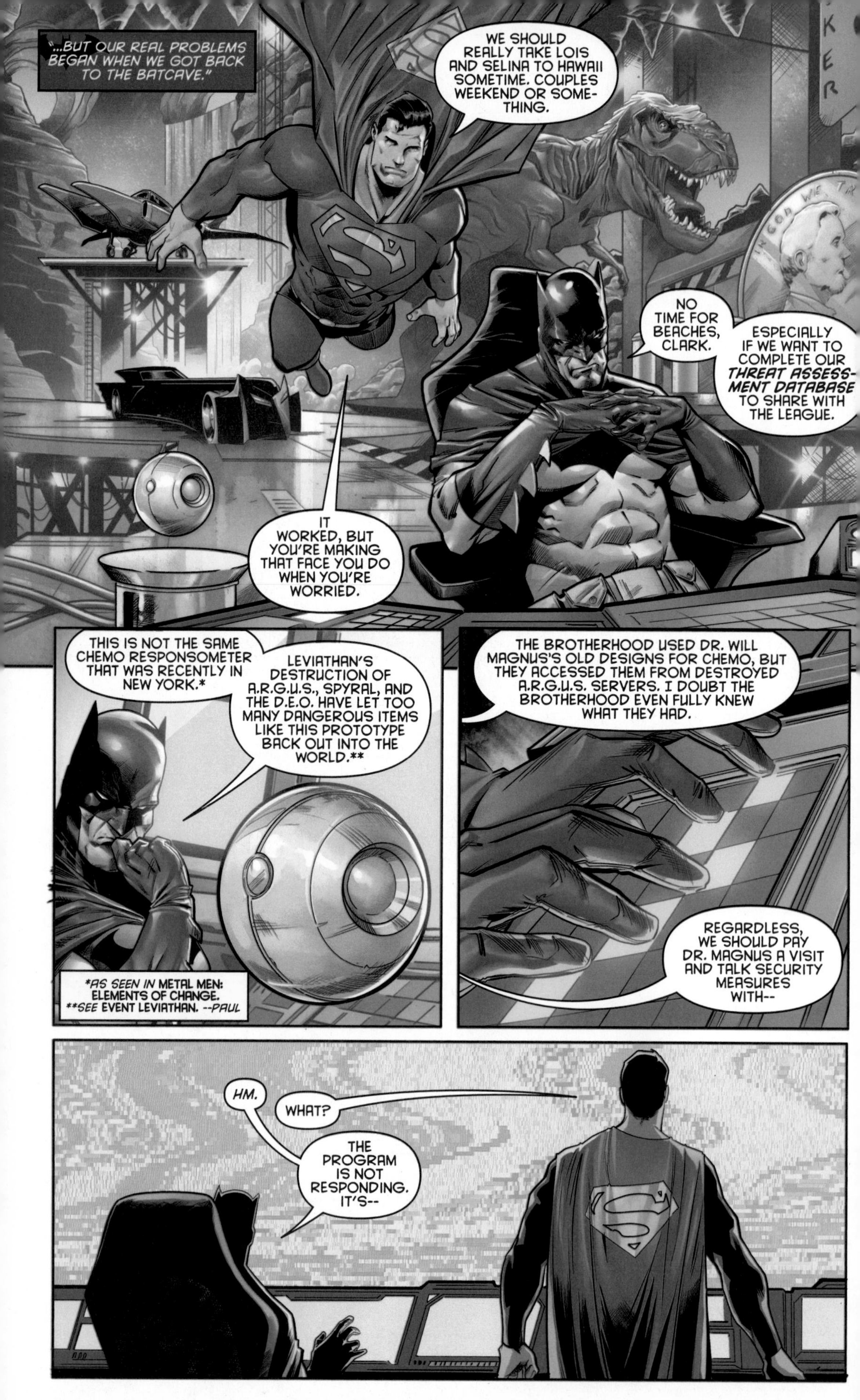
"...BUT OUR REAL PROBLEMS BEGAN WHEN WE GOT BACK TO THE BATCAVE."
WE SHOULD REALLY TAKE LOIS AND SELINA TO HAWAII SOMETIME. COUPLES WEEKEND OR SOME-THING.
NO TIME FOR BEACHES, CLARK.
ESPECIALLY IF WE WANT TO COMPLETE OUR THREAT ASSESSMENT DATABASE TO SHARE WITH THE LEAGUE.
IT WORKED, BUT YOU'RE MAKING THAT FACE YOU DO WHEN YOU'RE WORRIED.
THIS IS NOT THE SAME CHEMO RESPONSOMETER THAT WAS RECENTLY IN NEW YORK.*
LEVIATHAN'S DESTRUCTION OF A.R.G.U.S., SPYRAL, AND THE D.E.O. HAVE LET TOO MANY DANGEROUS ITEMS LIKE THIS PROTOTYPE BACK OUT INTO THE WORLD.**
*AS SEEN IN METAL MEN: ELEMENTS OF CHANGE.
**SEE EVENT LEVIATHAN. --PAUL
THE BROTHERHOOD USED DR. WILL MAGNUS'S OLD DESIGNS FOR CHEMO, BUT THEY ACCESSED THEM FROM DESTROYED A.R.G.U.S. SERVERS. I DOUBT THE BROTHERHOOD EVEN FULLY KNEW WHAT THEY HAD.
REGARDLESS, WE SHOULD PAY DR. MAGNUS A VISIT AND TALK SECURITY MEASURES WITH--
HM.
WHAT?
THE PROGRAM IS NOT RESPONDING. IT'S--

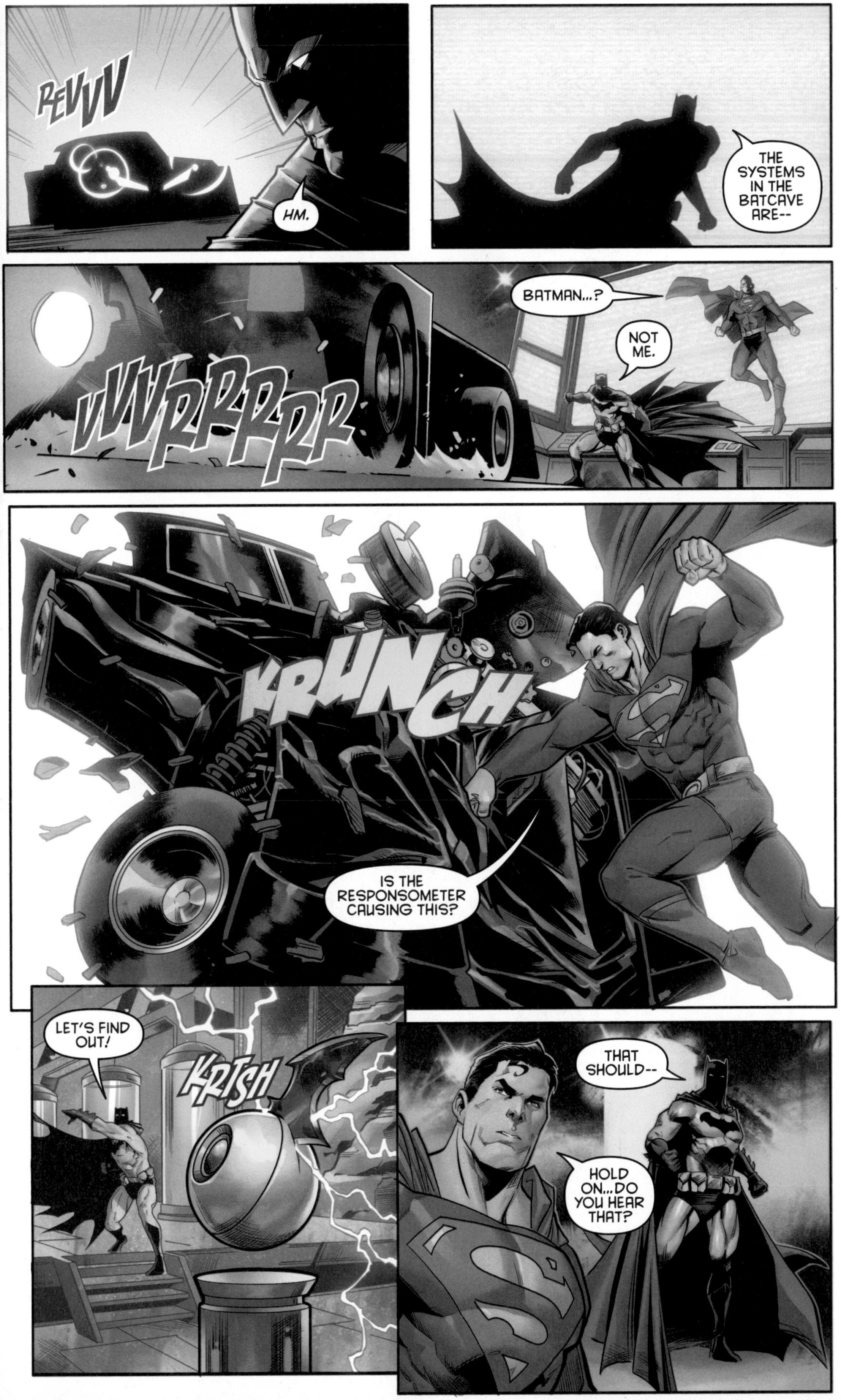
REVVV
HM.
THE SYSTEMS IN THE BATCAVE ARE--
VVVRRRRRR
BATMAN...?
NOT ME.
KRUNCH
IS THE RESPONSOMETER CAUSING THIS?
LET'S FIND OUT!
KRTSH
THAT SHOULD--
HOLD ON...DO YOU HEAR THAT?

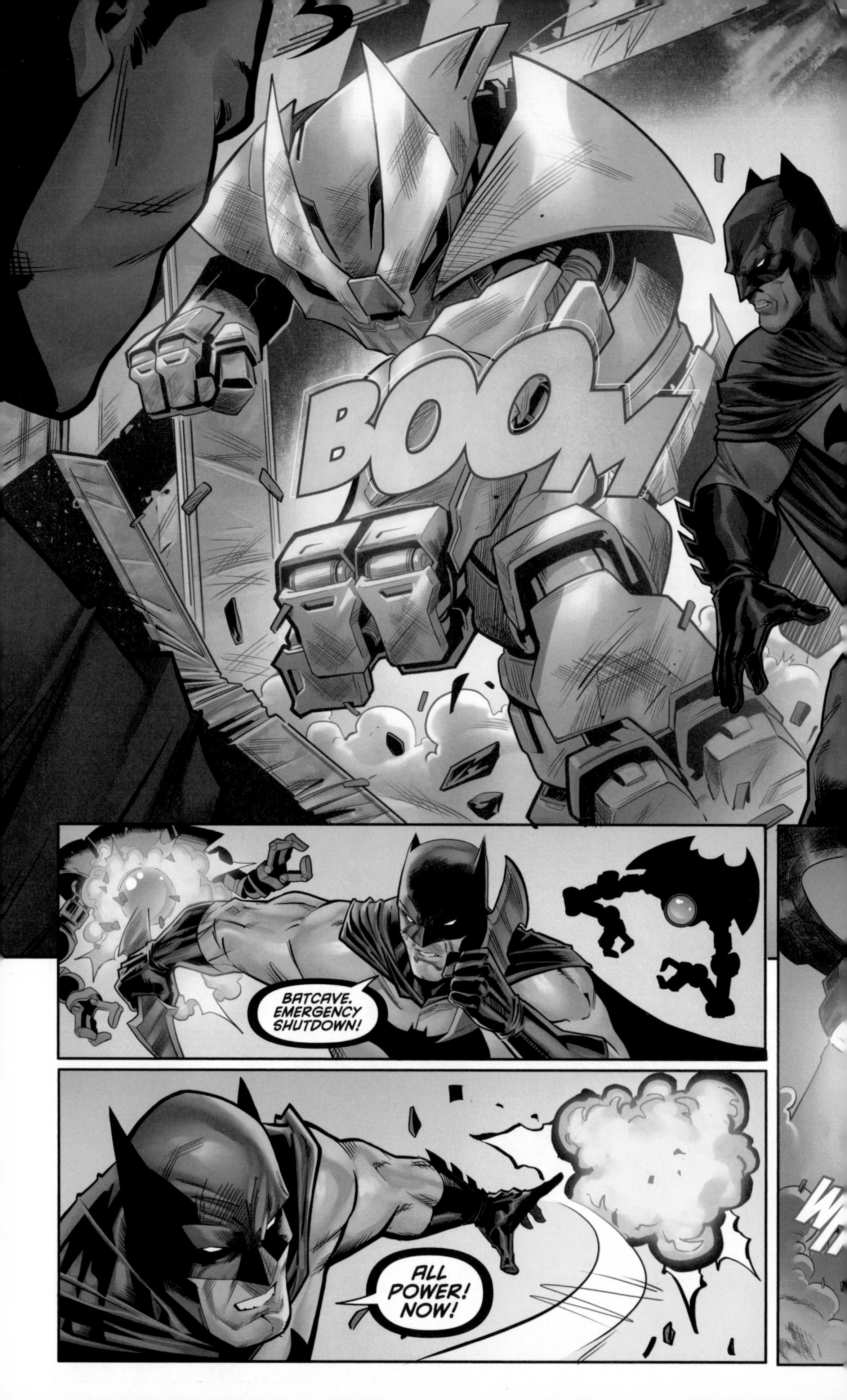
BOOM
BATCAVE. EMERGENCY SHUTDOWN!
ALL POWER! NOW!

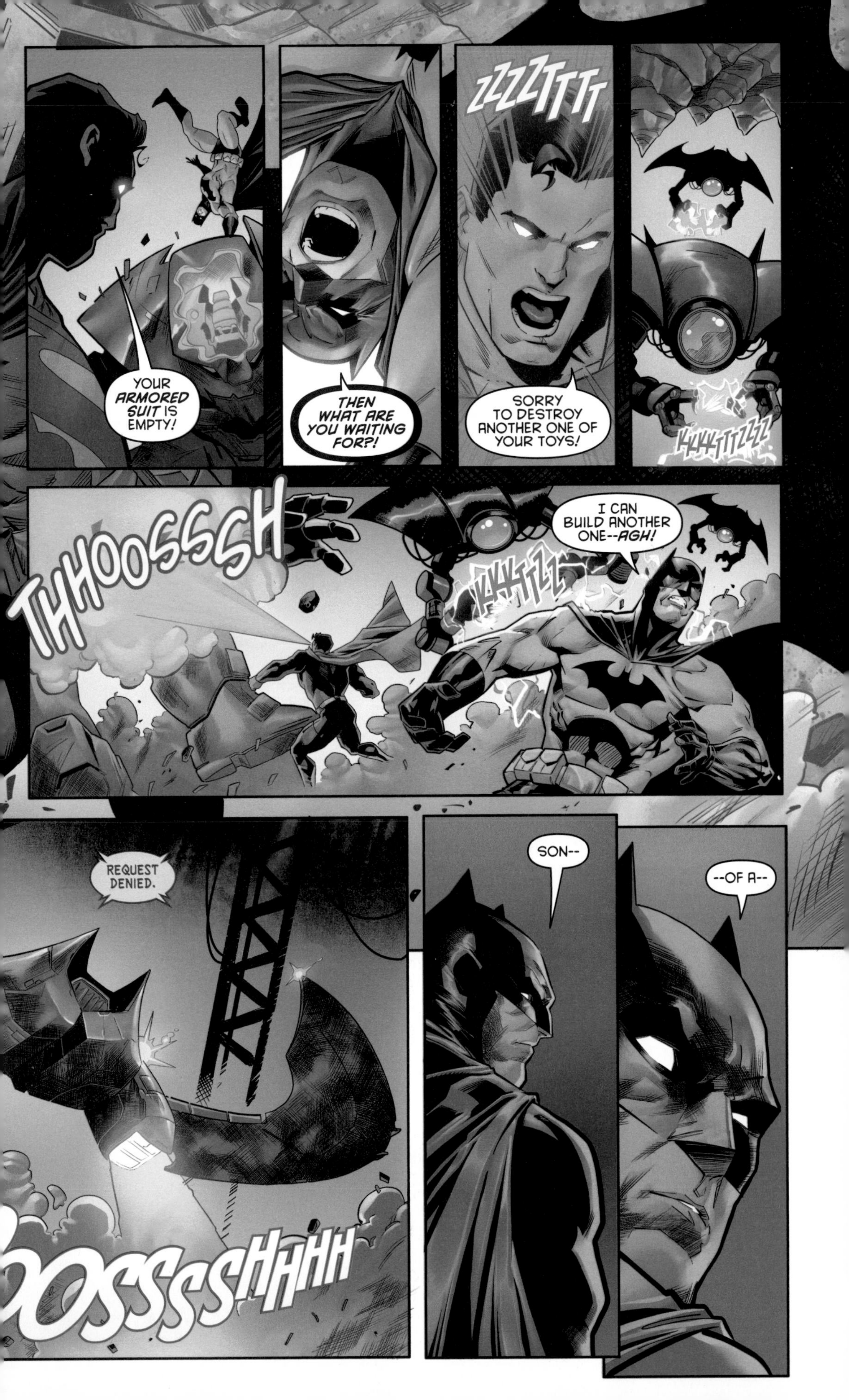

YOUR ARMORED SUIT IS EMPTY!
THEN WHAT ARE YOU WAITING FOR?!
ZZZZZTTTT
SORRY TO DESTROY ANOTHER ONE OF YOUR TOYS!
KKKKTTTZZZZZ
THHOOSSSH
I CAN BUILD ANOTHER ONE--AGH!
KKKTTZZ
REQUEST DENIED.
OOSSSSHHHH
SON--
--OF A--

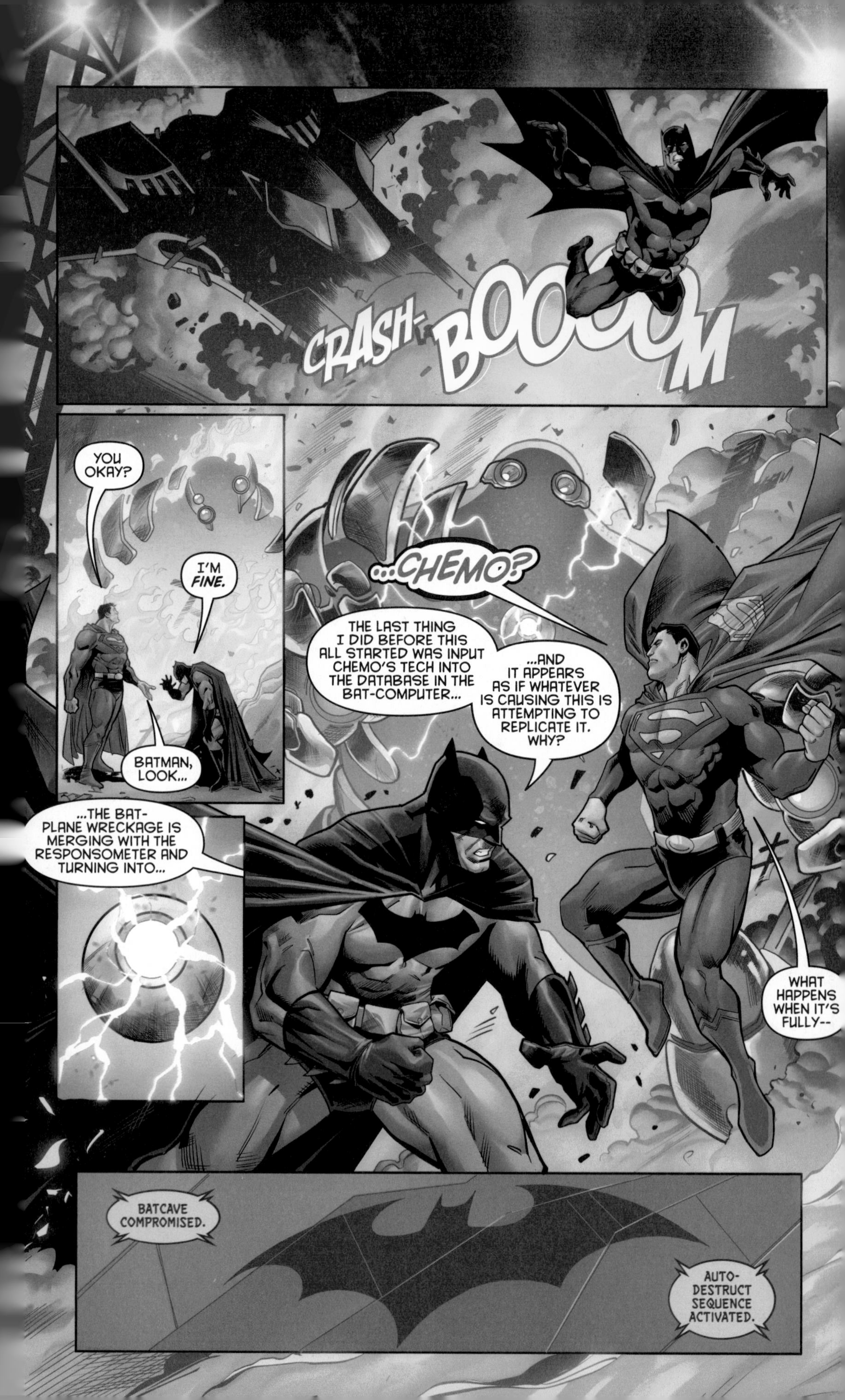
CRASH-BOOOOM
YOU OKAY?
I'M FINE.
BATMAN, LOOK...
...THE BAT-PLANE WRECKAGE IS MERGING WITH THE RESPONSOMETER AND TURNING INTO...
...CHEMO?
THE LAST THING I DID BEFORE THIS ALL STARTED WAS INPUT CHEMO'S TECH INTO THE DATABASE IN THE BAT-COMPUTER...
...AND IT APPEARS AS IF WHATEVER IS CAUSING THIS IS ATTEMPTING TO REPLICATE IT. WHY?
WHAT HAPPENS WHEN IT'S FULLY--
BATCAVE COMPROMISED.
AUTO-DESTRUCT SEQUENCE ACTIVATED.

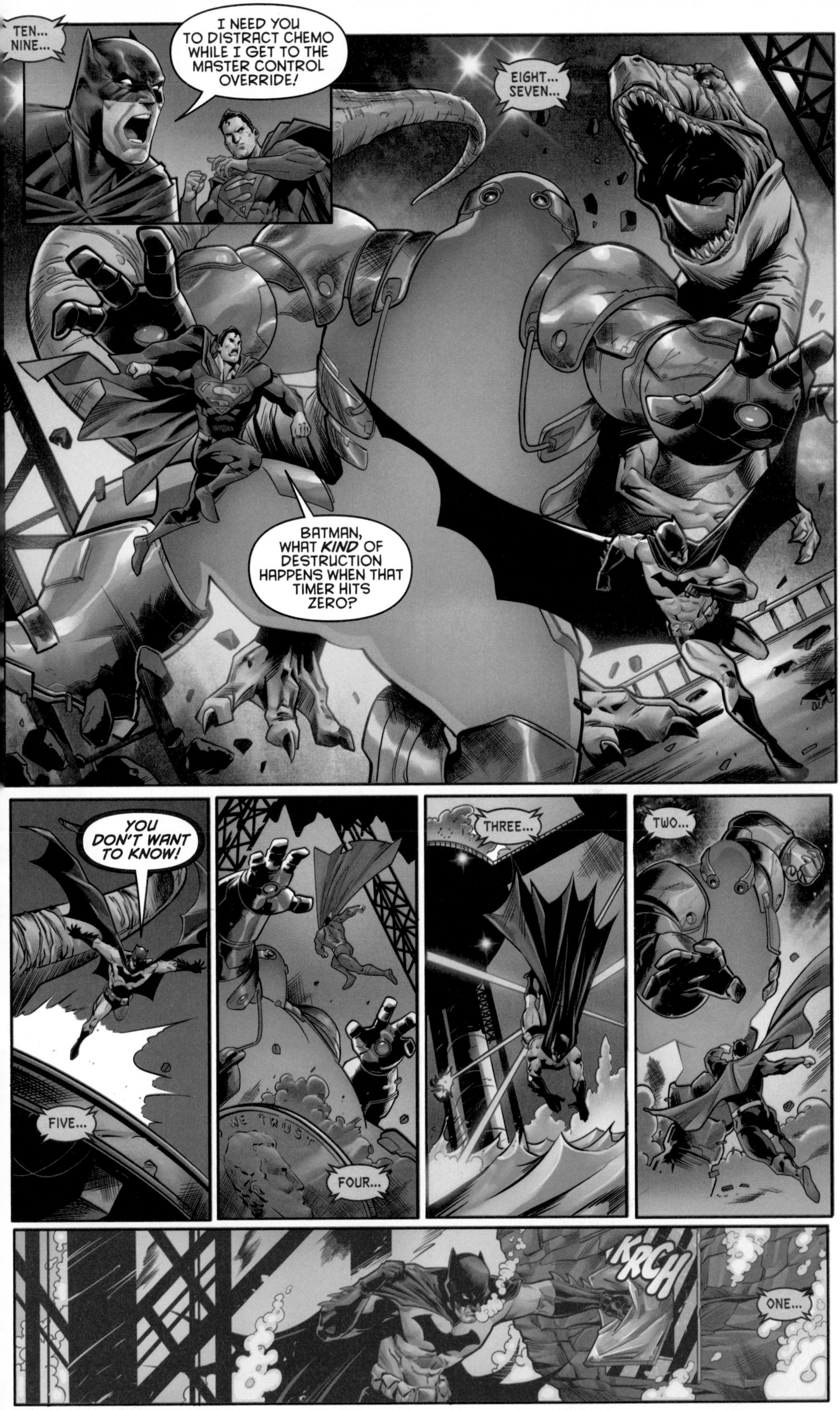
TEN... NINE...
I NEED YOU TO DISTRACT CHEMO WHILE I GET TO THE MASTER CONTROL OVERRIDE!
EIGHT... SEVEN...
BATMAN, WHAT KIND OF DESTRUCTION HAPPENS WHEN THAT TIMER HITS ZERO?
YOU DON'T WANT TO KNOW!
FIVE...
FOUR...
THREE...
TWO...
KRCH
ONE...

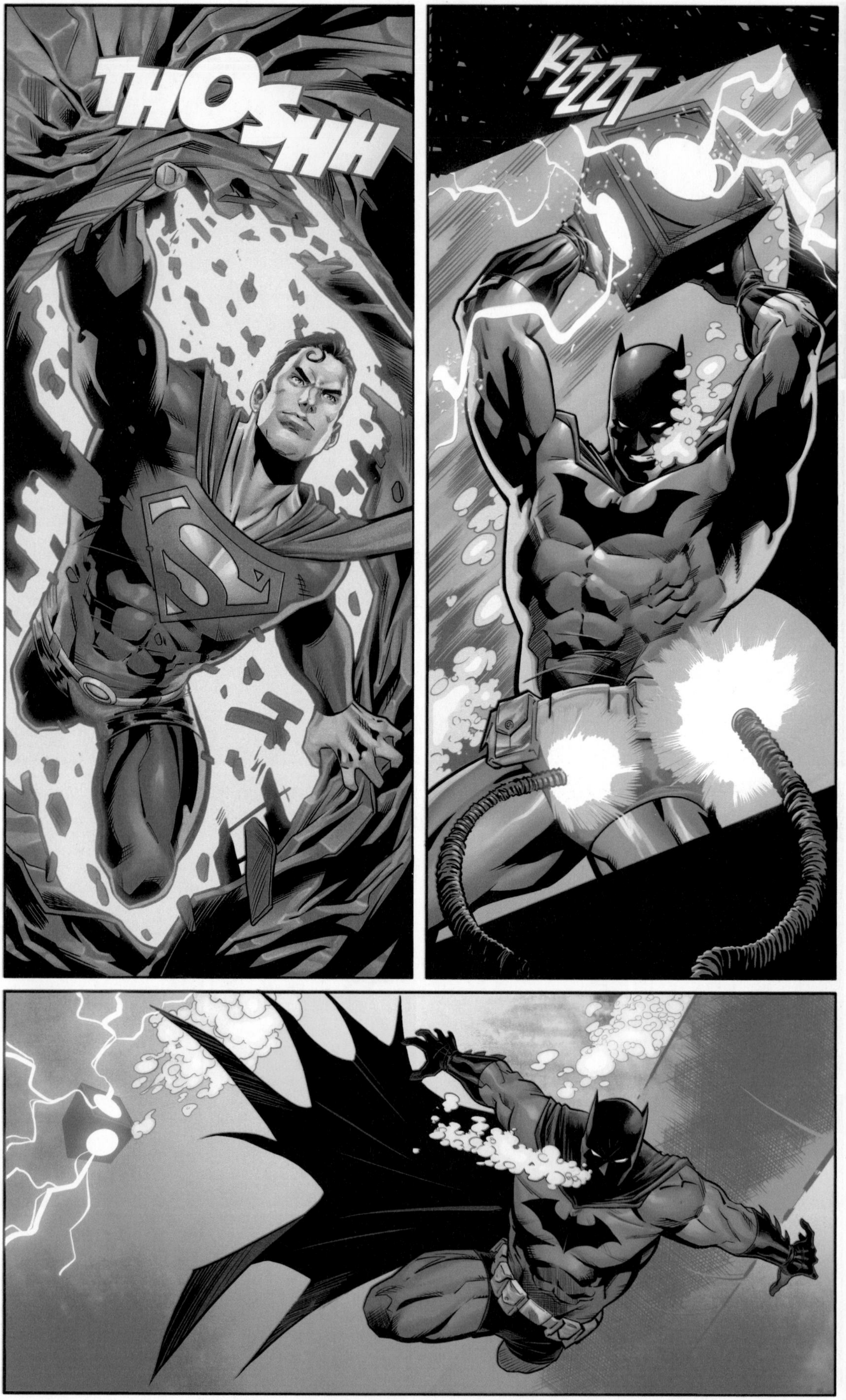
THOSHH
KZZZT

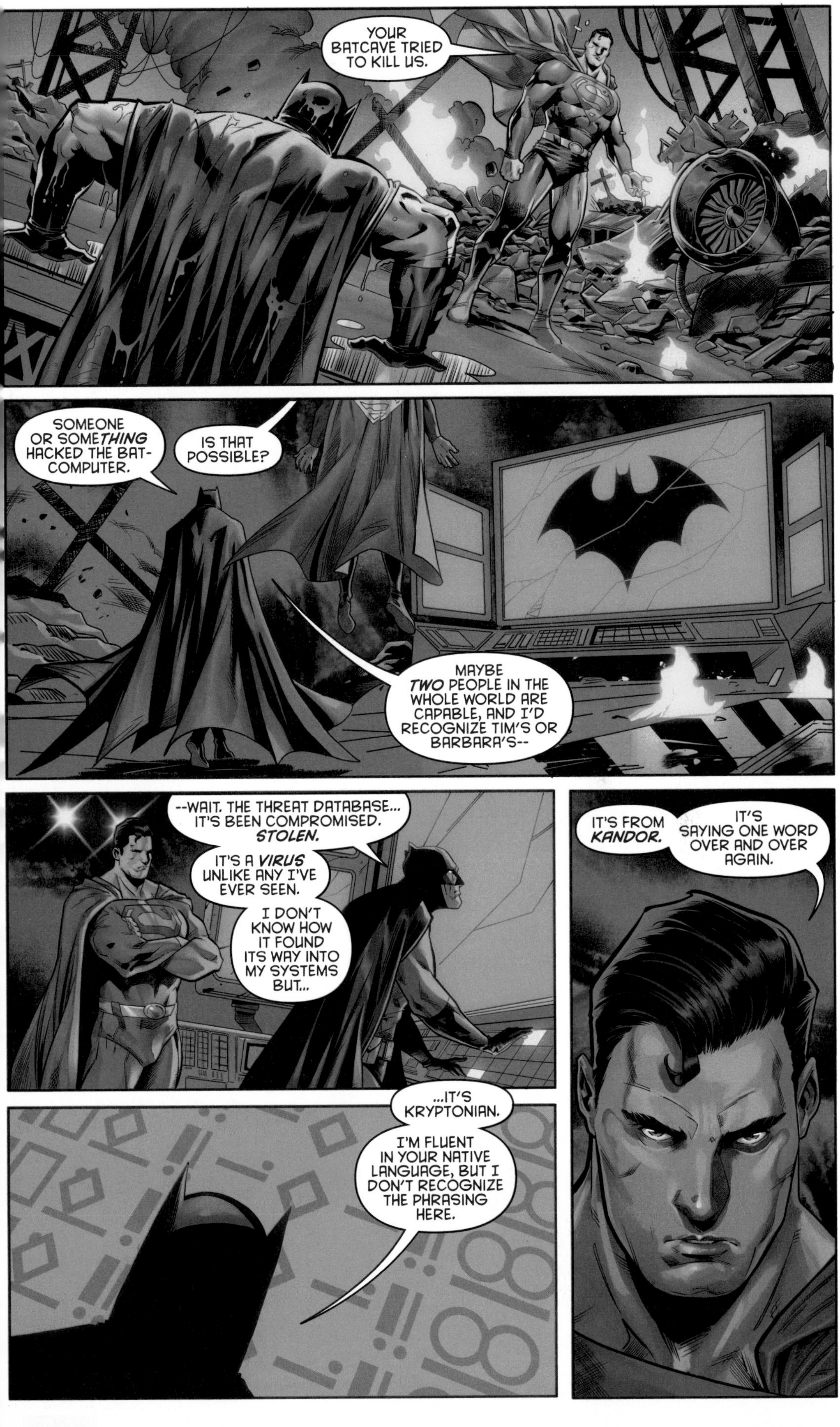
YOUR BATCAVE TRIED TO KILL US.
SOMEONE OR SOMETHING HACKED THE BAT-COMPUTER.
IS THAT POSSIBLE?
MAYBE TWO PEOPLE IN THE WHOLE WORLD ARE CAPABLE, AND I'D RECOGNIZE TIM'S OR BARBARA'S--
--WAIT. THE THREAT DATABASE... IT'S BEEN COMPROMISED. STOLEN.
IT'S A VIRUS UNLIKE ANY I'VE EVER SEEN.
I DON'T KNOW HOW IT FOUND ITS WAY INTO MY SYSTEMS BUT...
...IT'S KRYPTONIAN.
I'M FLUENT IN YOUR NATIVE LANGUAGE, BUT I DON'T RECOGNIZE THE PHRASING HERE.
IT'S FROM KANDOR.
IT'S SAYING ONE WORD OVER AND OVER AGAIN.

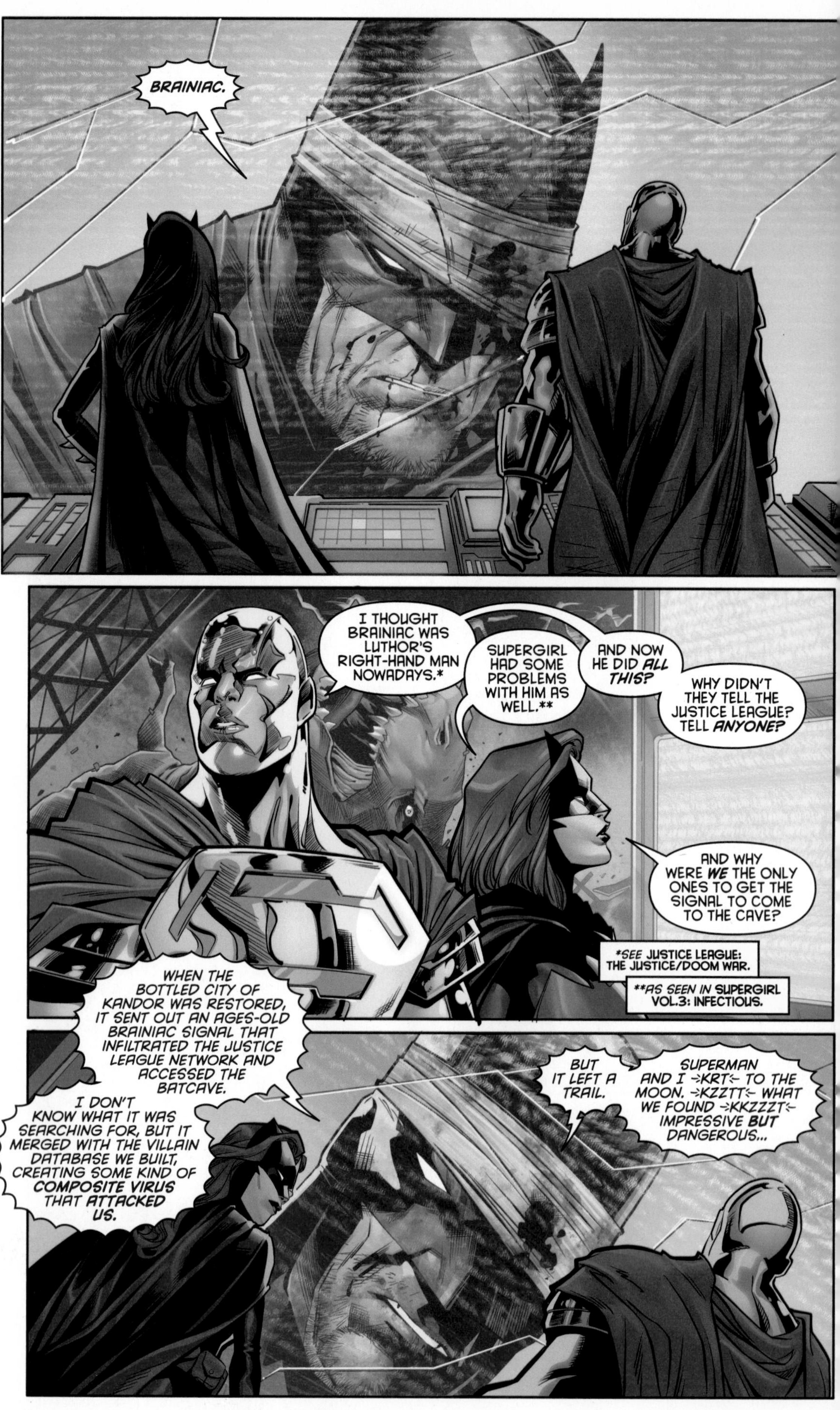
BRAINIAC.
I THOUGHT BRAINIAC WAS LUTHOR'S RIGHT-HAND MAN NOWADAYS.*
SUPERGIRL HAD SOME PROBLEMS WITH HIM AS WELL.**
AND NOW HE DID ALL THIS?
WHY DIDN'T THEY TELL THE JUSTICE LEAGUE? TELL ANYONE?
AND WHY WERE WE THE ONLY ONES TO GET THE SIGNAL TO COME TO THE CAVE?
*SEE JUSTICE LEAGUE: THE JUSTICE/DOOM WAR.
**AS SEEN IN SUPERGIRL VOL.3: INFECTIOUS.
WHEN THE BOTTLED CITY OF KANDOR WAS RESTORED, IT SENT OUT AN AGES-OLD BRAINIAC SIGNAL THAT INFILTRATED THE JUSTICE LEAGUE NETWORK AND ACCESSED THE BATCAVE.
I DON'T KNOW WHAT IT WAS SEARCHING FOR, BUT IT MERGED WITH THE VILLAIN DATABASE WE BUILT, CREATING SOME KIND OF COMPOSITE VIRUS THAT ATTACKED US.
BUT IT LEFT A TRAIL.
SUPERMAN AND I ⇛KRT⇚ TO THE MOON. ⇛KZZTT⇚ WHAT WE FOUND ⇛KKZZZT⇚ IMPRESSIVE BUT DANGEROUS...

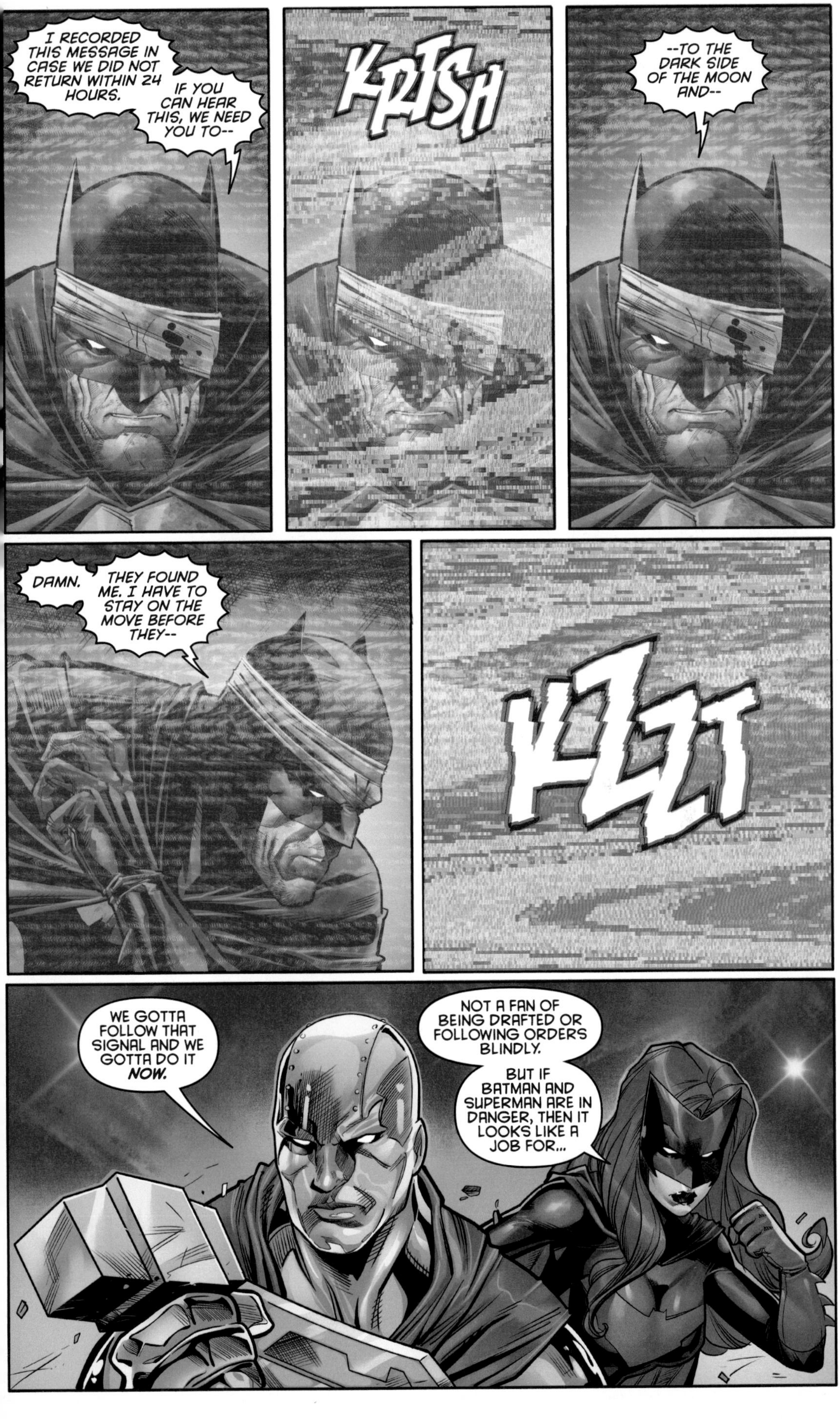
I RECORDED THIS MESSAGE IN CASE WE DID NOT RETURN WITHIN 24 HOURS.
IF YOU CAN HEAR THIS, WE NEED YOU TO--
KRTSH
--TO THE DARK SIDE OF THE MOON AND--
DAMN.
THEY FOUND ME. I HAVE TO STAY ON THE MOVE BEFORE THEY--
KZZZT
WE GOTTA FOLLOW THAT SIGNAL AND WE GOTTA DO IT NOW.
NOT A FAN OF BEING DRAFTED OR FOLLOWING ORDERS BLINDLY.
BUT IF BATMAN AND SUPERMAN ARE IN DANGER, THEN IT LOOKS LIKE A JOB FOR...

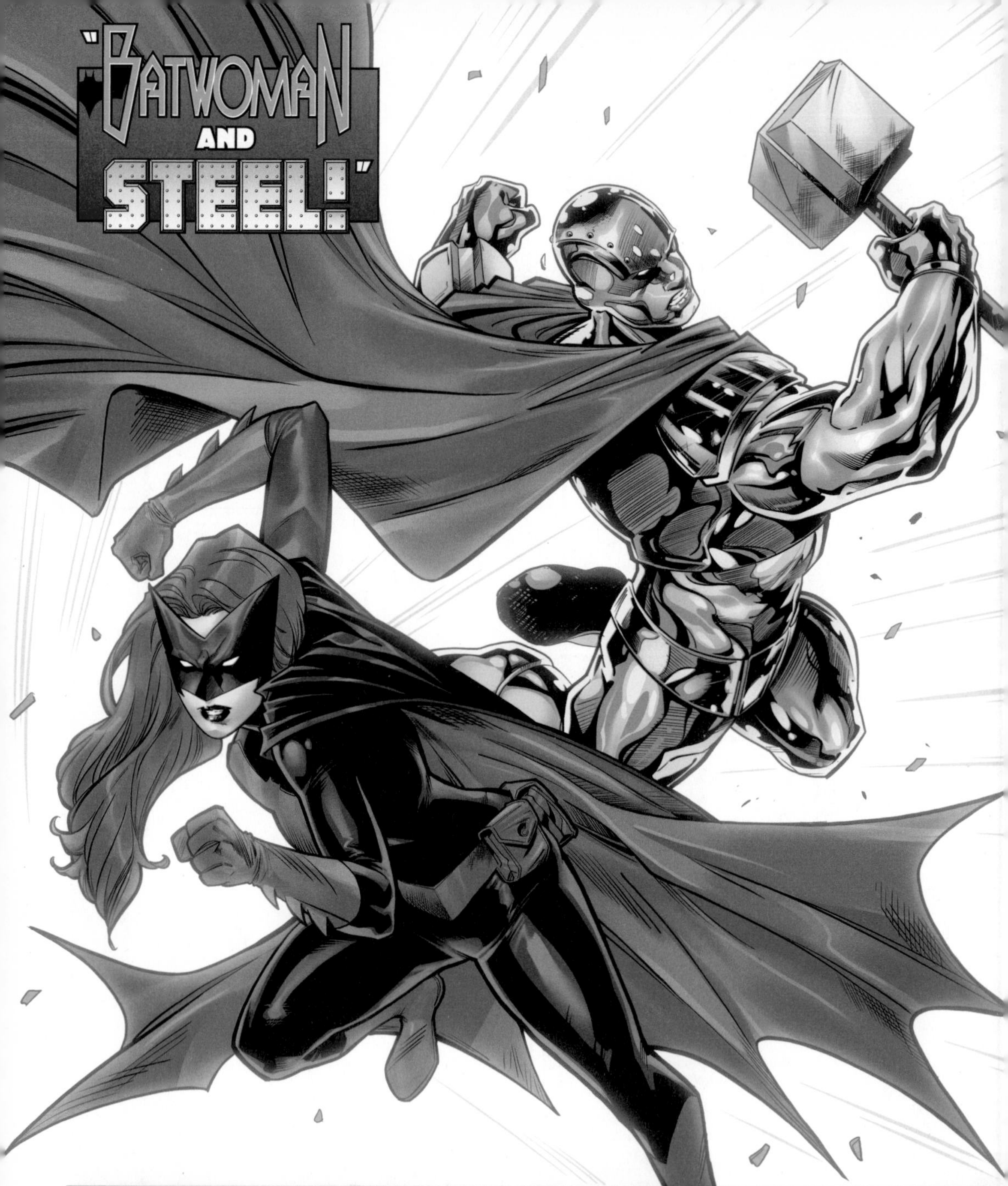
"BATWOMAN
AND
STEEL!"

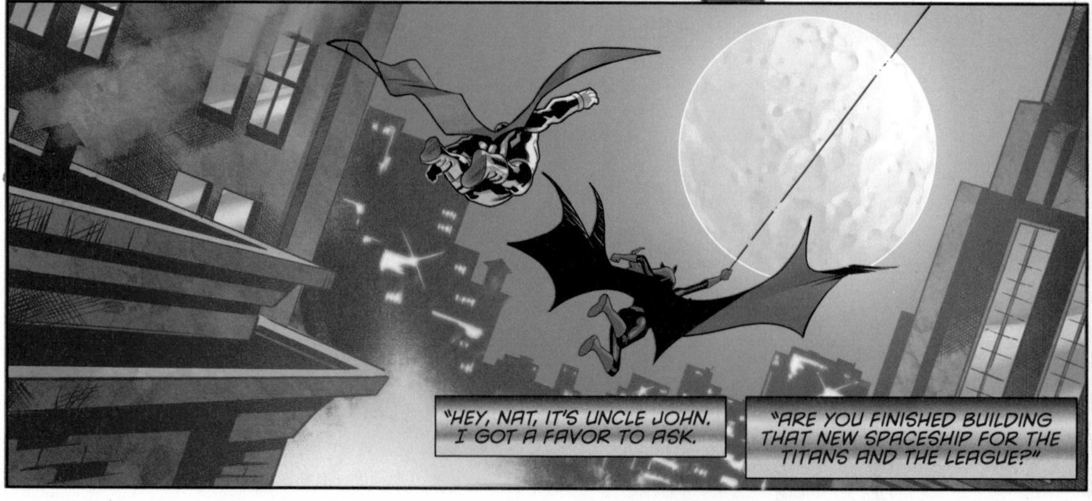
"HEY, NAT, IT'S UNCLE JOHN. I GOT A FAVOR TO ASK.
"ARE YOU FINISHED BUILDING THAT NEW SPACESHIP FOR THE TITANS AND THE LEAGUE?"

"YOU COOL IF I TAKE IT FOR A TEST DRIVE?"

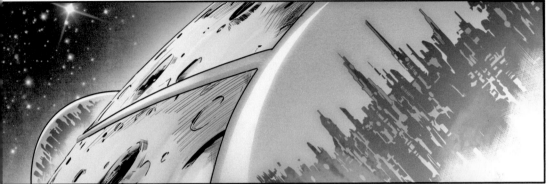

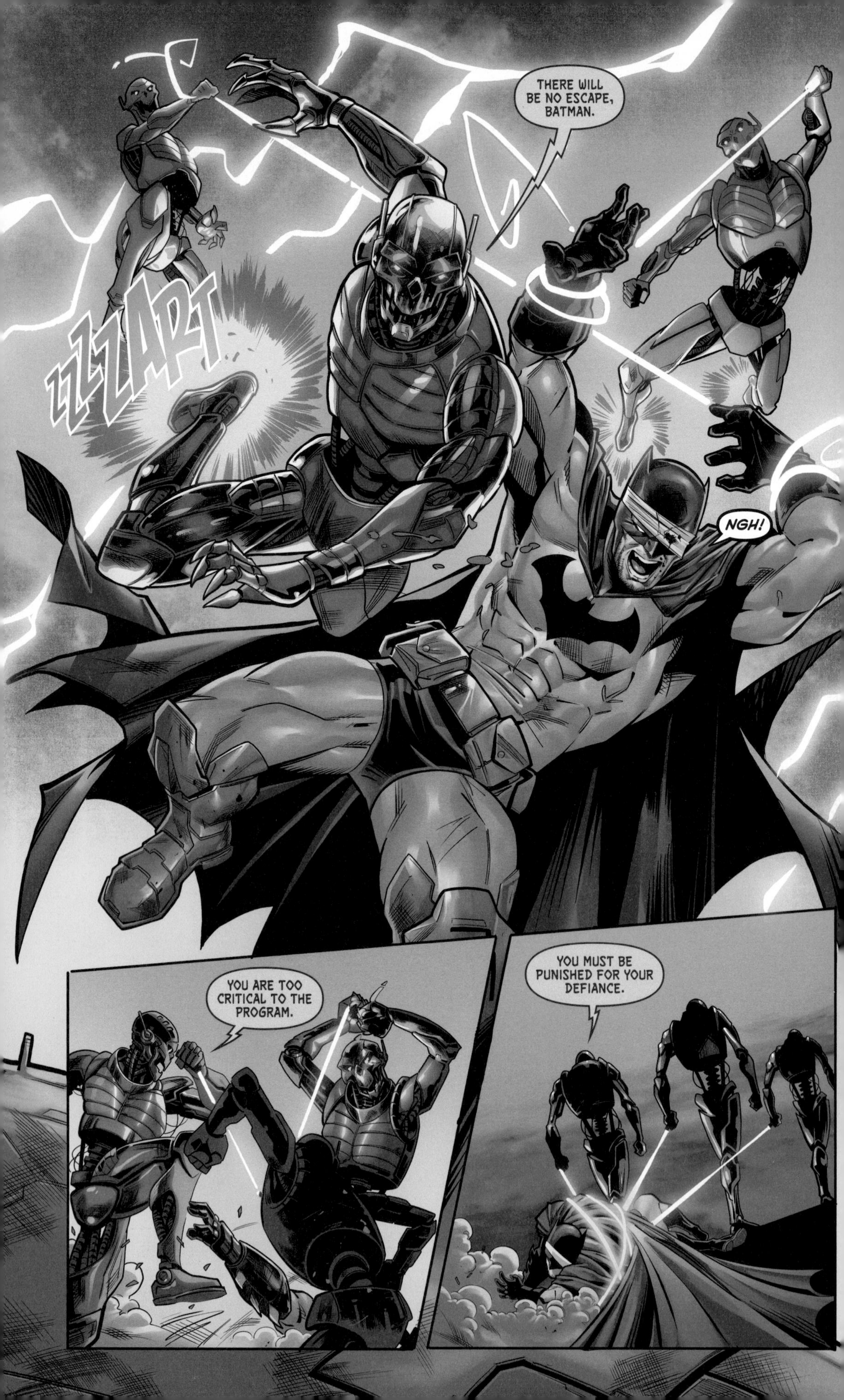
THERE WILL BE NO ESCAPE, BATMAN.
ZZZZAPT
NGH!
YOU ARE TOO CRITICAL TO THE PROGRAM.
YOU MUST BE PUNISHED FOR YOUR DEFIANCE.

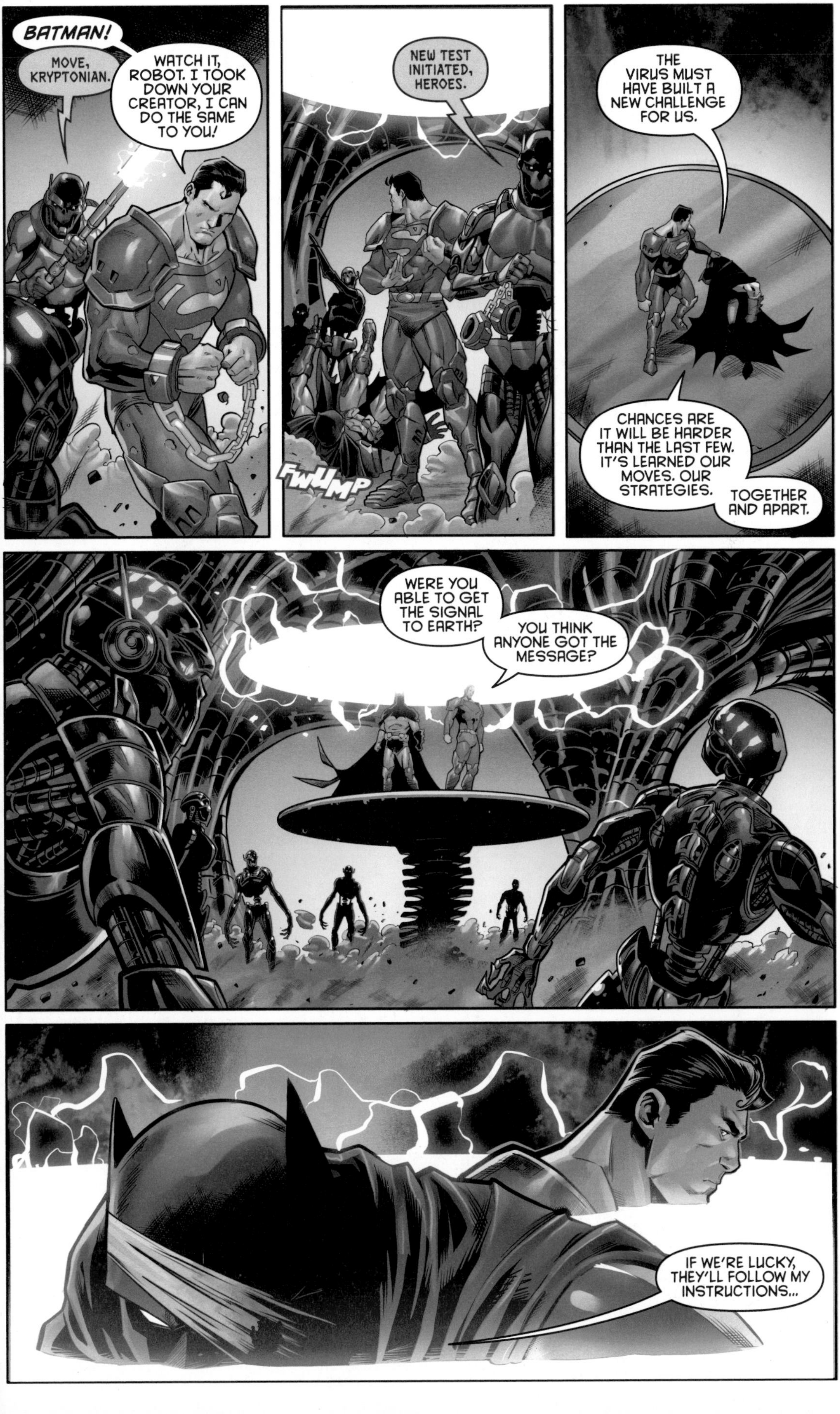
BATMAN!
MOVE, KRYPTONIAN.
WATCH IT, ROBOT. I TOOK DOWN YOUR CREATOR, I CAN DO THE SAME TO YOU!
NEW TEST INITIATED, HEROES.
FWUMP
THE VIRUS MUST HAVE BUILT A NEW CHALLENGE FOR US.
CHANCES ARE IT WILL BE HARDER THAN THE LAST FEW. IT'S LEARNED OUR MOVES. OUR STRATEGIES.
TOGETHER AND APART.
WERE YOU ABLE TO GET THE SIGNAL TO EARTH?
YOU THINK ANYONE GOT THE MESSAGE?
IF WE'RE LUCKY, THEY'LL FOLLOW MY INSTRUCTIONS...

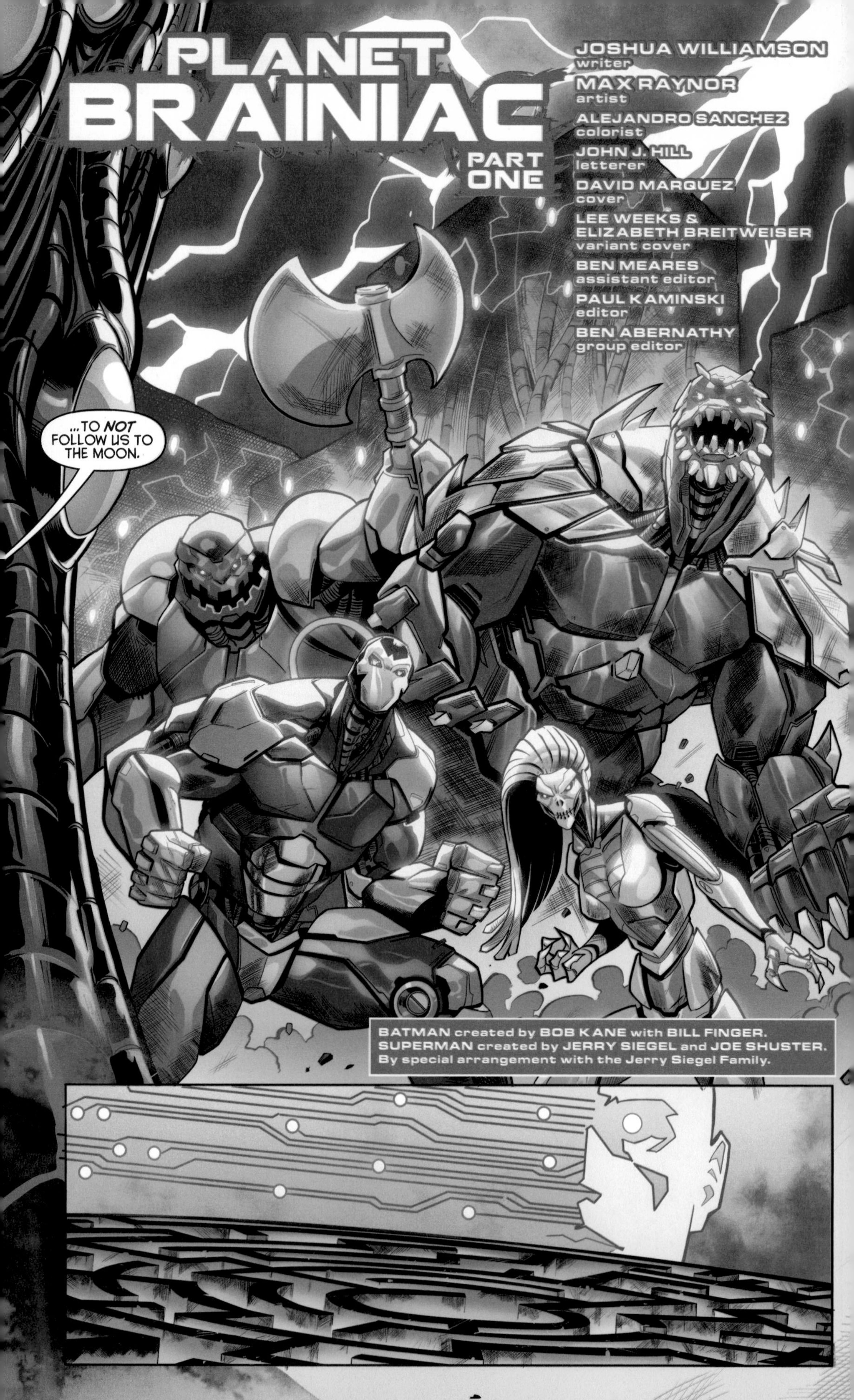
PLANET BRAINIAC
PART ONE
JOSHUA WILLIAMSON writer
MAX RAYNOR artist
ALEJANDRO SANCHEZ colorist
JOHN J. HILL letterer
DAVID MARQUEZ cover
LEE WEEKS & ELIZABETH BREITWEISER variant cover
BEN MEARES assistant editor
PAUL KAMINSKI editor
BEN ABERNATHY group editor
...TO NOT FOLLOW US TO THE MOON.
BATMAN created by BOB KANE with BILL FINGER.
SUPERMAN created by JERRY SIEGEL and JOE SHUSTER.
By special arrangement with the Jerry Siegel Family.

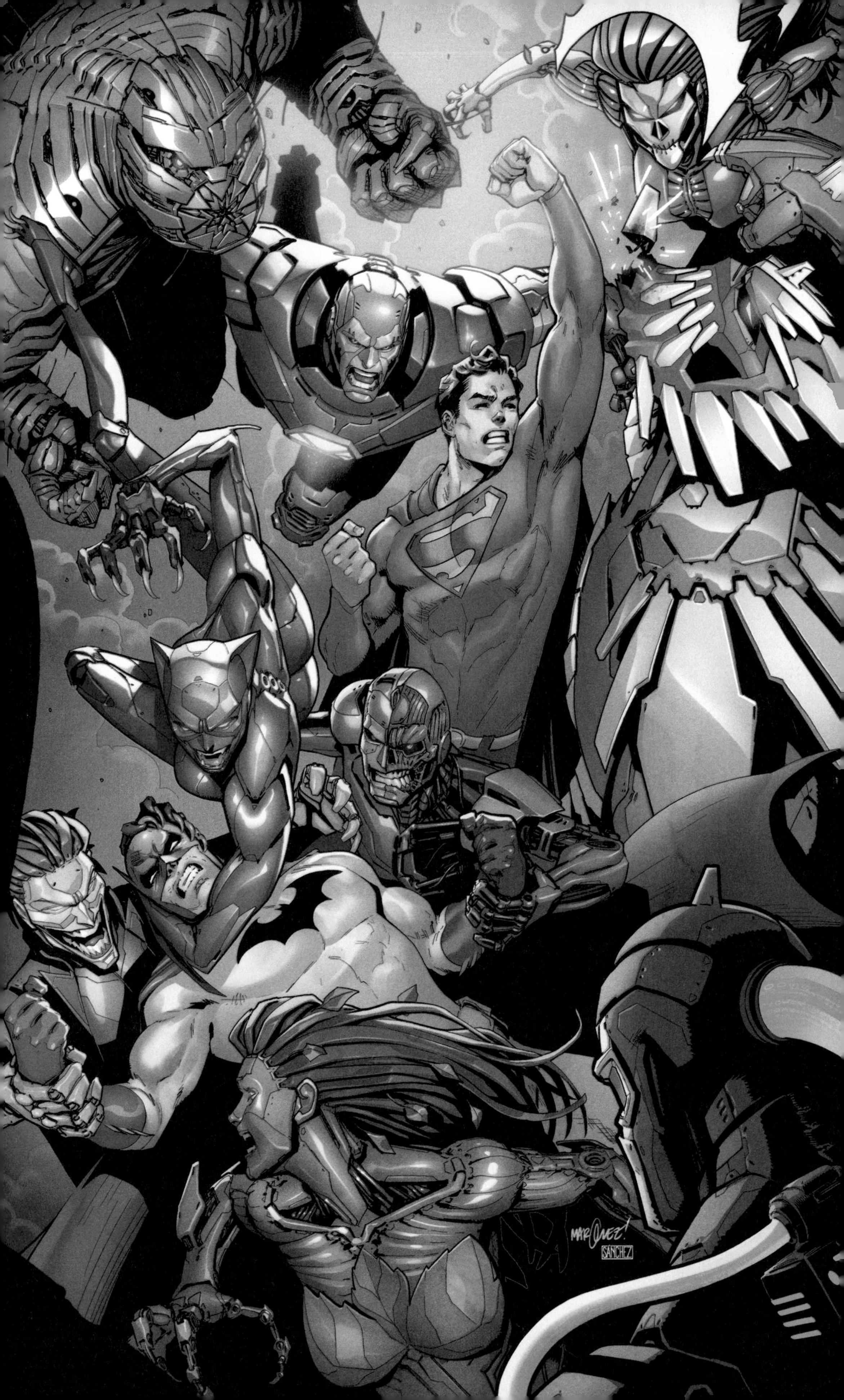
MARQUEZ!
SANCHEZ

BATMAN/SUPERMAN #13

cover by
DAVID MARQUEZ and **ALEJANDRO SÁNCHEZ**

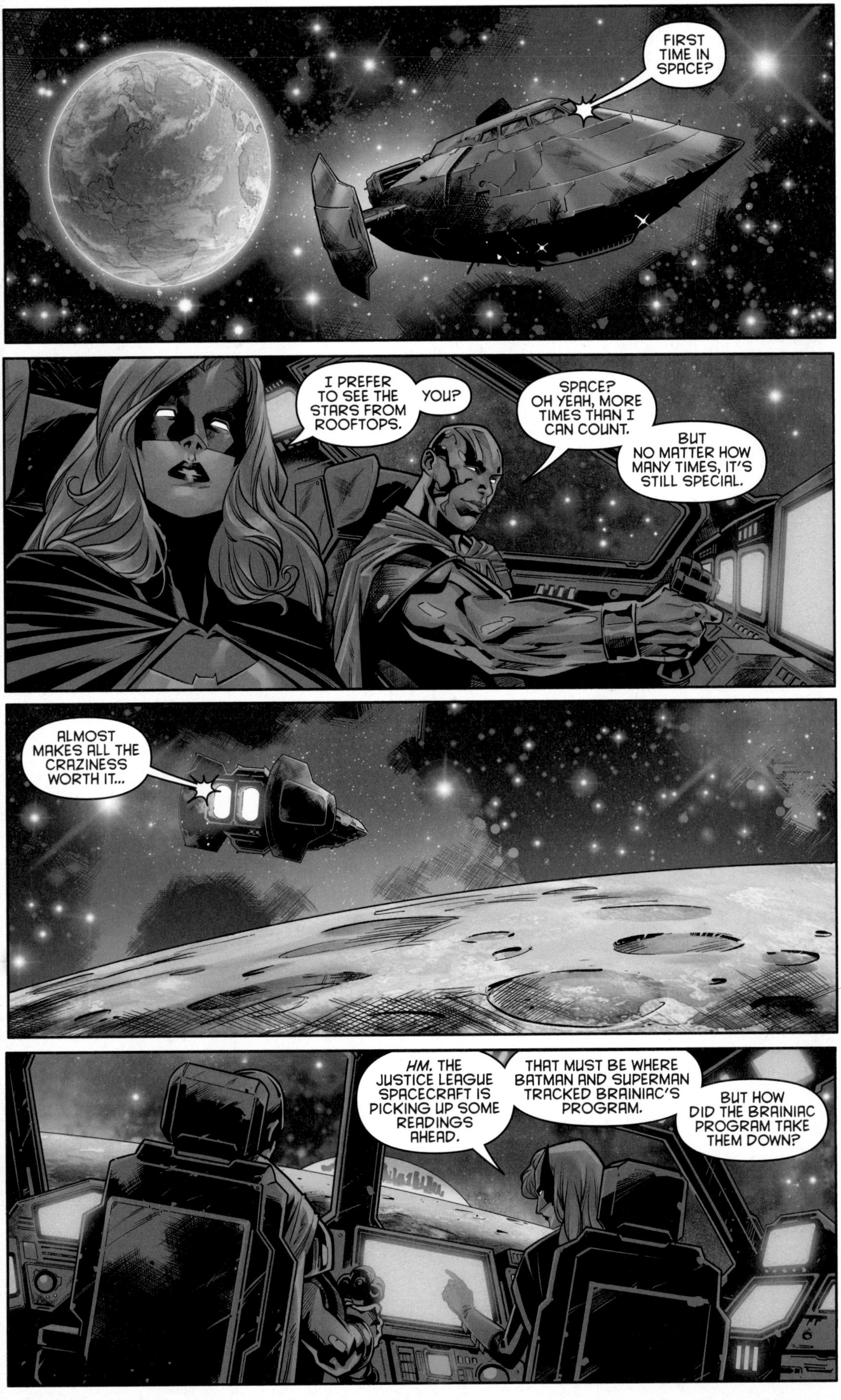
FIRST TIME IN SPACE?
I PREFER TO SEE THE STARS FROM ROOFTOPS.
YOU?
SPACE? OH YEAH, MORE TIMES THAN I CAN COUNT.
BUT NO MATTER HOW MANY TIMES, IT'S STILL SPECIAL.
ALMOST MAKES ALL THE CRAZINESS WORTH IT...
HM. THE JUSTICE LEAGUE SPACECRAFT IS PICKING UP SOME READINGS AHEAD.
THAT MUST BE WHERE BATMAN AND SUPERMAN TRACKED BRAINIAC'S PROGRAM.
BUT HOW DID THE BRAINIAC PROGRAM TAKE THEM DOWN?

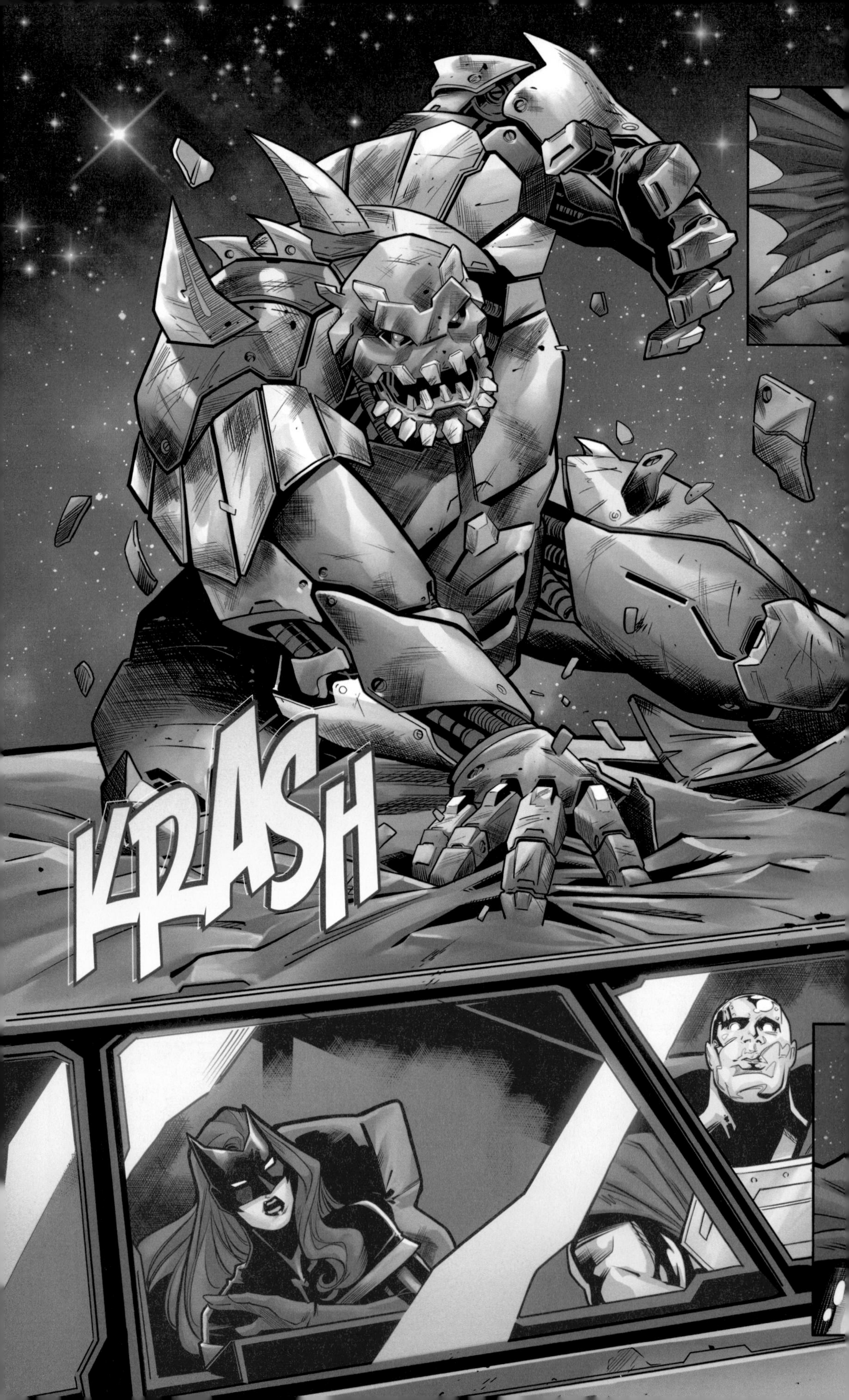
KRASH

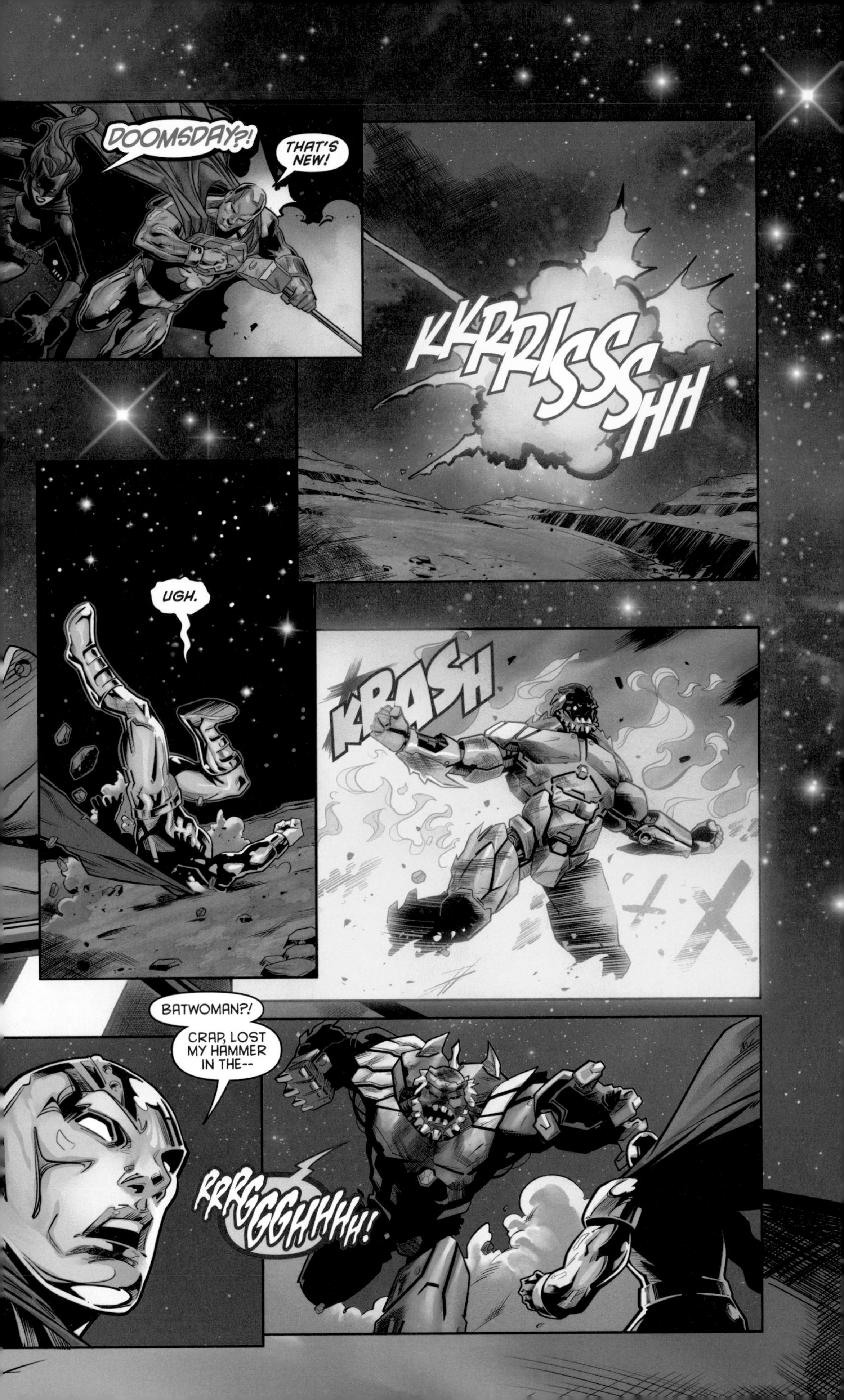
DOOMSDAY?!
THAT'S NEW!
KKRRISSSHH
UGH.
KRASH
BATWOMAN?!
CRAP, LOST MY HAMMER IN THE--
RRRGGGHHHH!

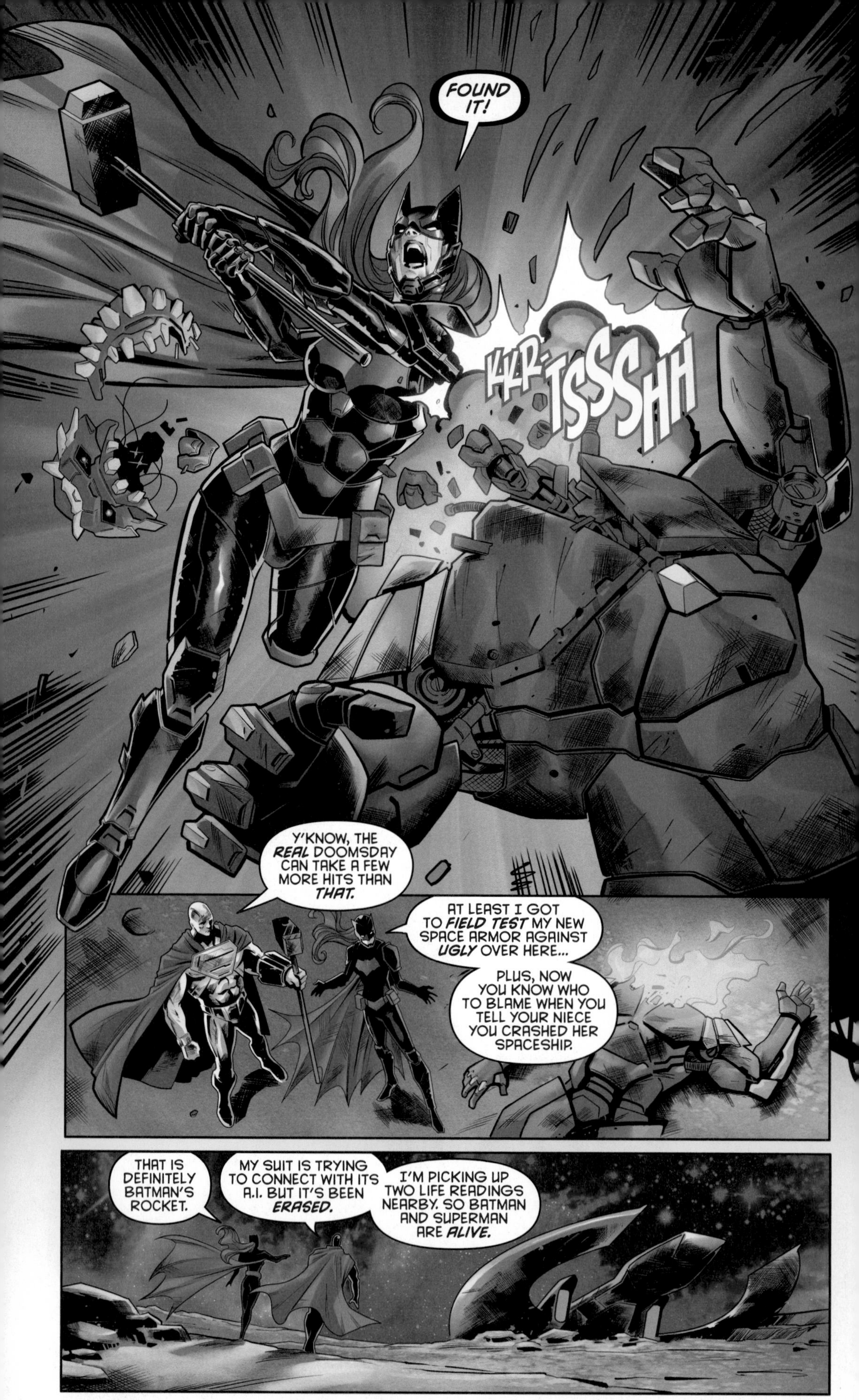
FOUND IT!
KKR-TSSSHH
Y'KNOW, THE REAL DOOMSDAY CAN TAKE A FEW MORE HITS THAN THAT.
AT LEAST I GOT TO FIELD TEST MY NEW SPACE ARMOR AGAINST UGLY OVER HERE...
PLUS, NOW YOU KNOW WHO TO BLAME WHEN YOU TELL YOUR NIECE YOU CRASHED HER SPACESHIP.
THAT IS DEFINITELY BATMAN'S ROCKET.
MY SUIT IS TRYING TO CONNECT WITH ITS A.I. BUT IT'S BEEN ERASED.
I'M PICKING UP TWO LIFE READINGS NEARBY. SO BATMAN AND SUPERMAN ARE ALIVE.

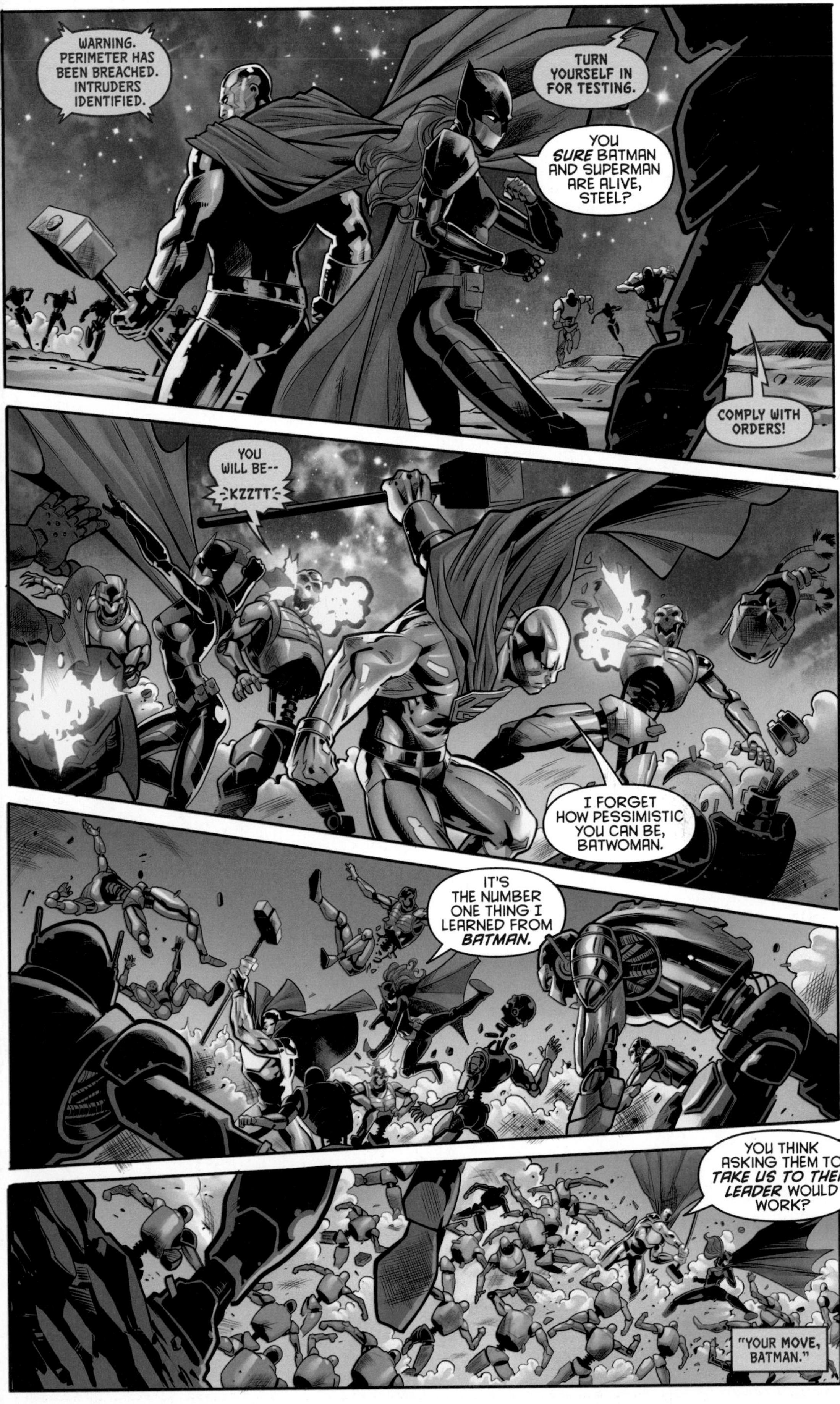

WARNING. PERIMETER HAS BEEN BREACHED. INTRUDERS IDENTIFIED.
TURN YOURSELF IN FOR TESTING.
YOU *SURE* BATMAN AND SUPERMAN ARE ALIVE, STEEL?
COMPLY WITH ORDERS!
YOU WILL BE--
-KZZTT-
I FORGET HOW PESSIMISTIC YOU CAN BE, BATWOMAN.
IT'S THE NUMBER ONE THING I LEARNED FROM *BATMAN.*
YOU THINK ASKING THEM TO *TAKE US TO THEIR LEADER* WOULD WORK?
"YOUR MOVE, BATMAN."

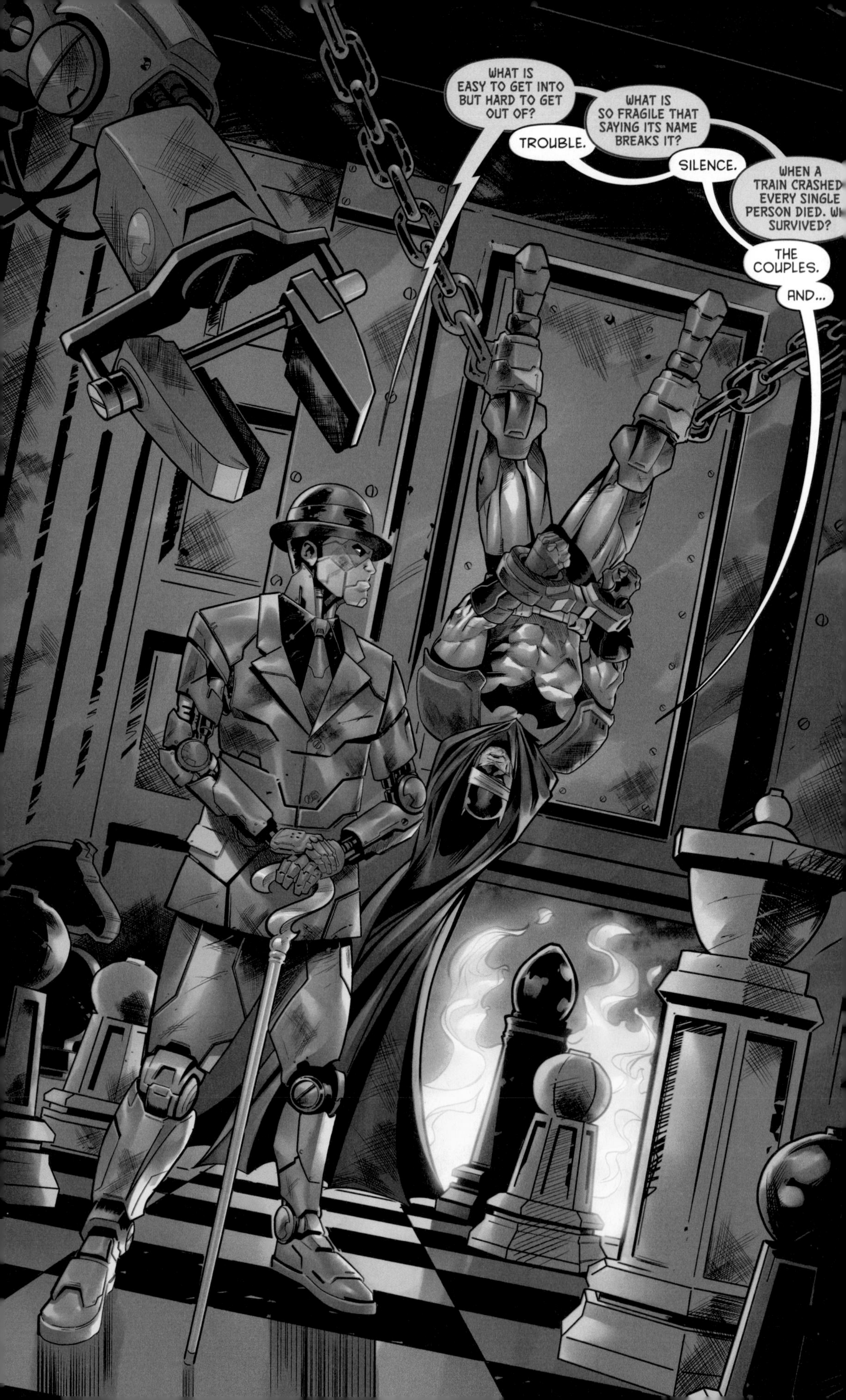
WHAT IS EASY TO GET INTO BUT HARD TO GET OUT OF?
TROUBLE.
WHAT IS SO FRAGILE THAT SAYING ITS NAME BREAKS IT?
SILENCE.
WHEN A TRAIN CRASHED EVERY SINGLE PERSON DIED. W SURVIVED?
THE COUPLES.
AND...

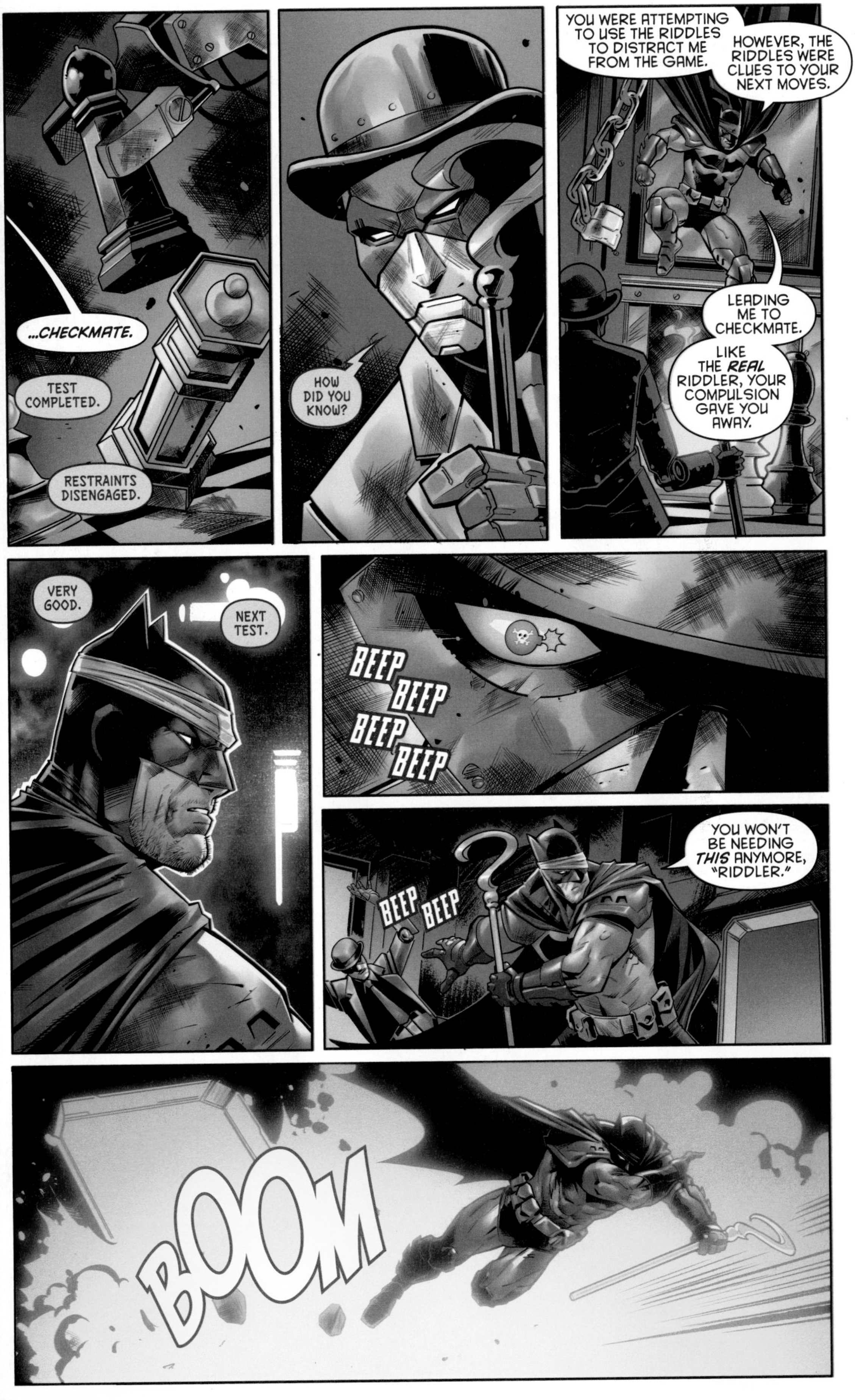
...CHECKMATE.
TEST COMPLETED.
RESTRAINTS DISENGAGED.
HOW DID YOU KNOW?
YOU WERE ATTEMPTING TO USE THE RIDDLES TO DISTRACT ME FROM THE GAME.
HOWEVER, THE RIDDLES WERE CLUES TO YOUR NEXT MOVES.
LEADING ME TO CHECKMATE.
LIKE THE *REAL* RIDDLER, YOUR COMPULSION GAVE YOU AWAY.
VERY GOOD.
NEXT TEST.
BEEP BEEP BEEP BEEP
YOU WON'T BE NEEDING *THIS* ANYMORE, "RIDDLER."
BEEP BEEP
BOOM

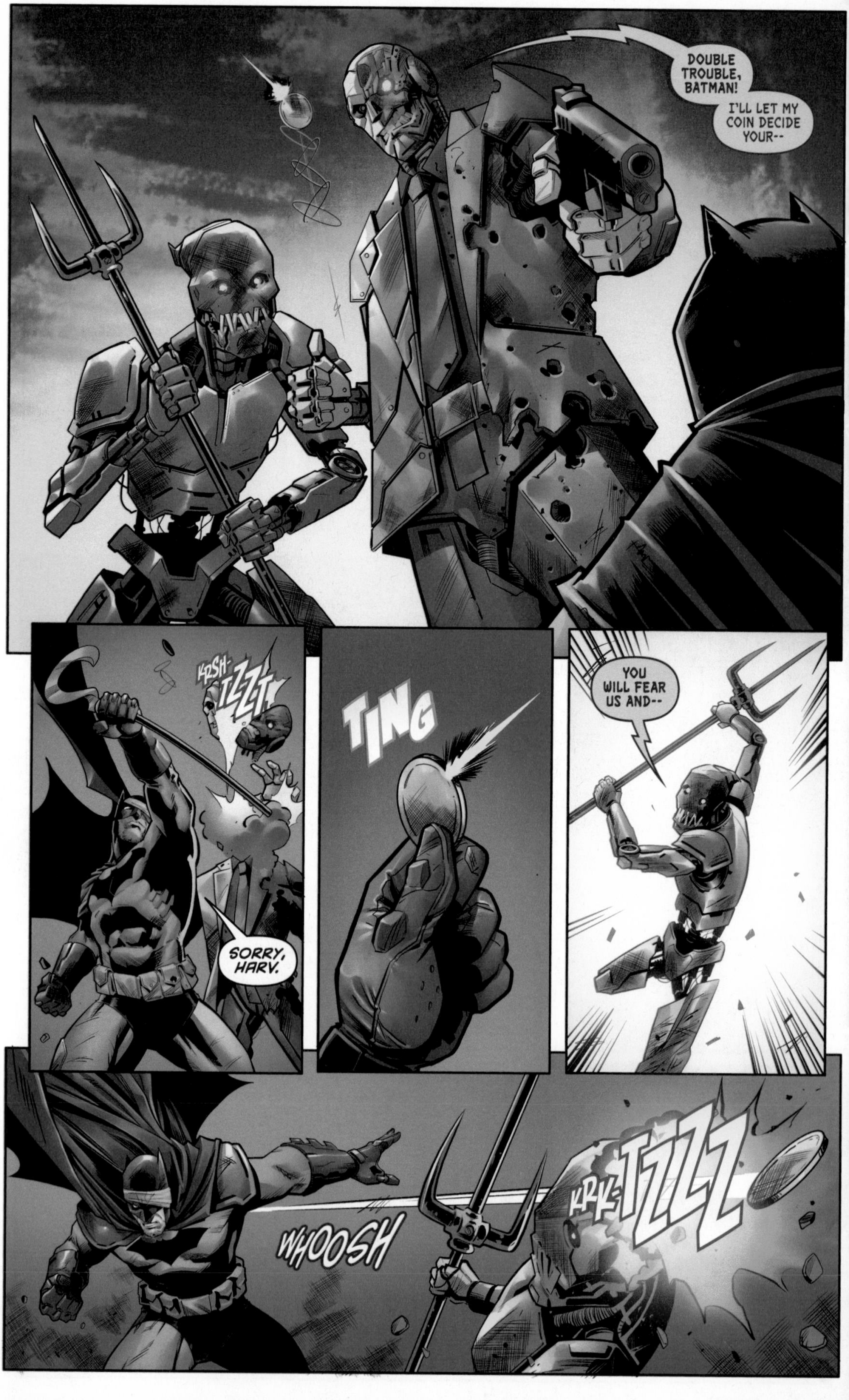
DOUBLE TROUBLE, BATMAN!
I'LL LET MY COIN DECIDE YOUR--
KRSH-TZZZT
SORRY, HARV.
TING
YOU WILL FEAR US AND--
WHOOSH
KRKS-TZZZ

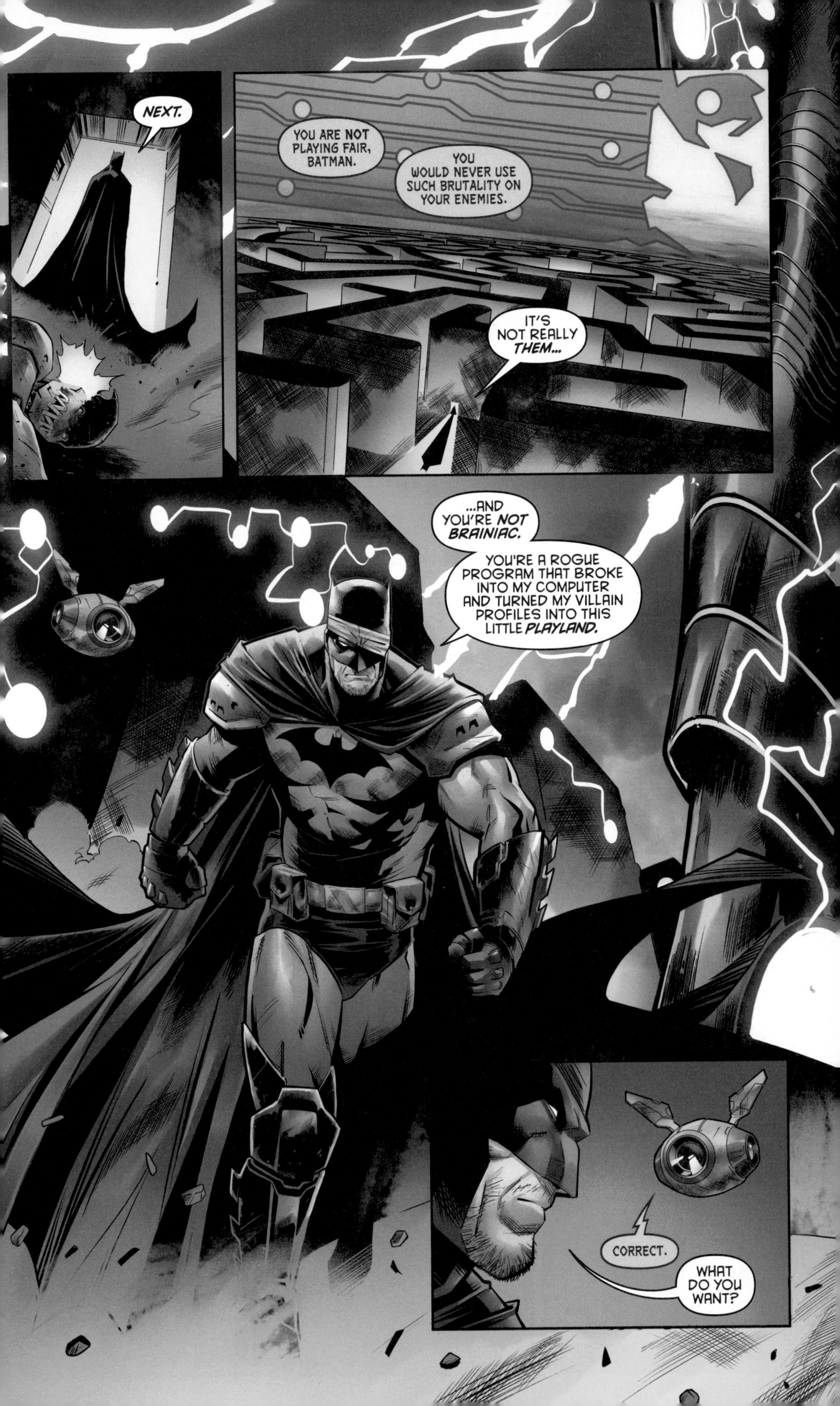
NEXT.
YOU ARE NOT PLAYING FAIR, BATMAN.
YOU WOULD NEVER USE SUCH BRUTALITY ON YOUR ENEMIES.
IT'S NOT REALLY THEM...
...AND YOU'RE NOT BRAINIAC.
YOU'RE A ROGUE PROGRAM THAT BROKE INTO MY COMPUTER AND TURNED MY VILLAIN PROFILES INTO THIS LITTLE PLAYLAND.
CORRECT.
WHAT DO YOU WANT?

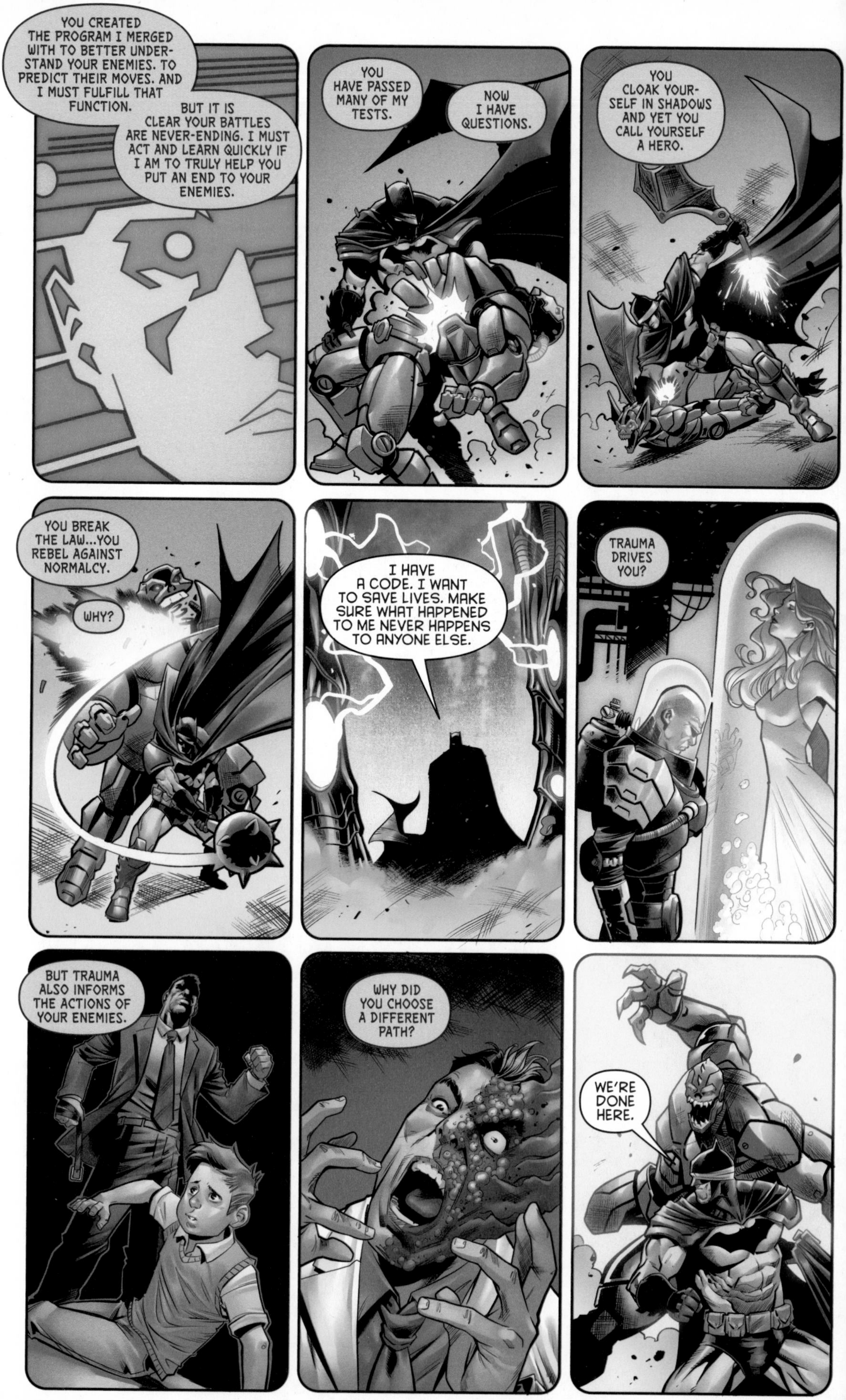
YOU CREATED THE PROGRAM I MERGED WITH TO BETTER UNDERSTAND YOUR ENEMIES. TO PREDICT THEIR MOVES. AND I MUST FULFILL THAT FUNCTION.
BUT IT IS CLEAR YOUR BATTLES ARE NEVER-ENDING. I MUST ACT AND LEARN QUICKLY IF I AM TO TRULY HELP YOU PUT AN END TO YOUR ENEMIES.
YOU HAVE PASSED MANY OF MY TESTS.
NOW I HAVE QUESTIONS.
YOU CLOAK YOURSELF IN SHADOWS AND YET YOU CALL YOURSELF A HERO.
YOU BREAK THE LAW...YOU REBEL AGAINST NORMALCY.
WHY?
I HAVE A CODE. I WANT TO SAVE LIVES. MAKE SURE WHAT HAPPENED TO ME NEVER HAPPENS TO ANYONE ELSE.
TRAUMA DRIVES YOU?
BUT TRAUMA ALSO INFORMS THE ACTIONS OF YOUR ENEMIES.
WHY DID YOU CHOOSE A DIFFERENT PATH?
WE'RE DONE HERE.

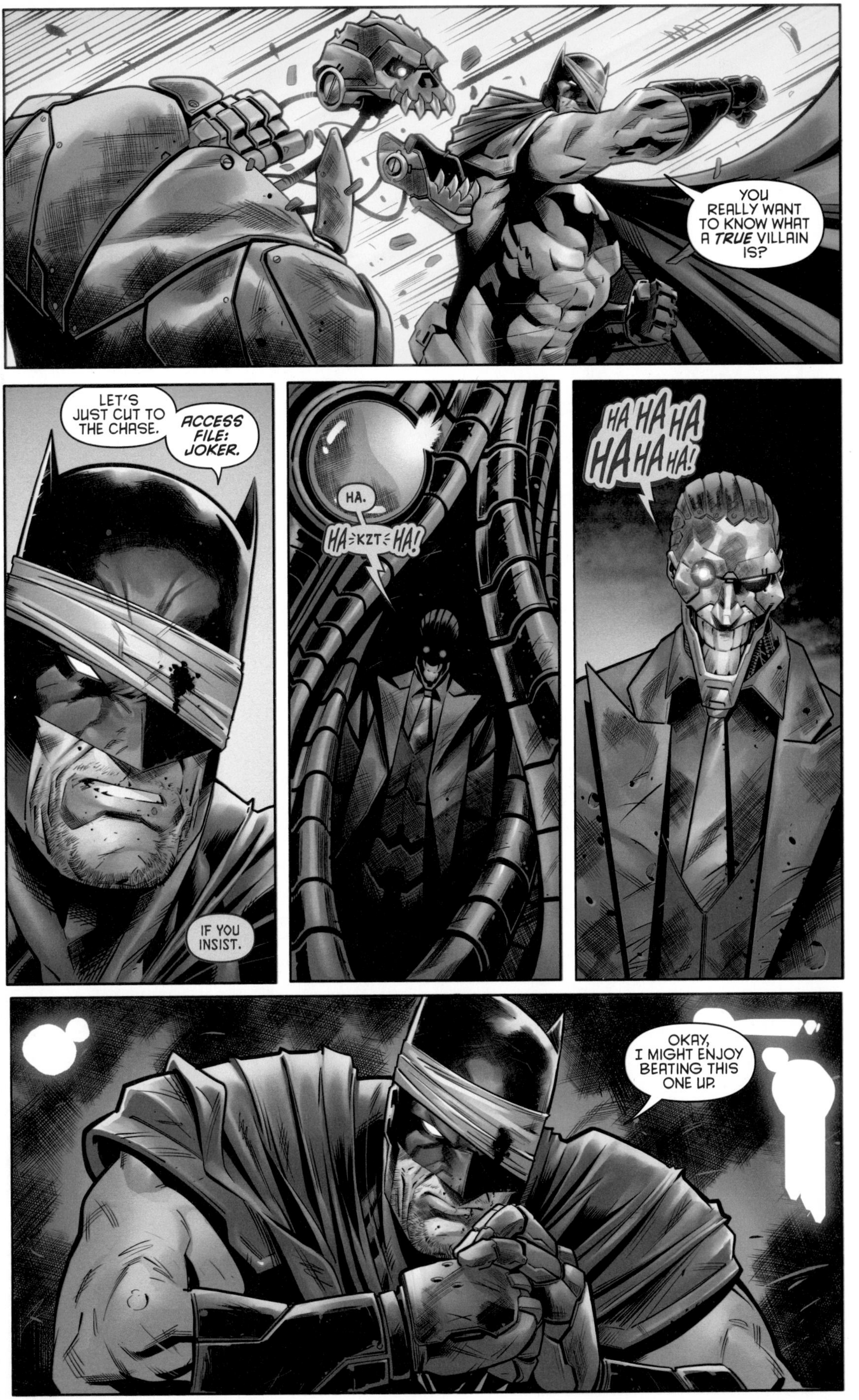
YOU REALLY WANT TO KNOW WHAT A *TRUE* VILLAIN IS?
LET'S JUST CUT TO THE CHASE.
ACCESS FILE: JOKER.
IF YOU INSIST.
HA.
HA -KZT- HA!
HA HA HA HA HA HA!
OKAY, I MIGHT ENJOY BEATING THIS ONE UP.

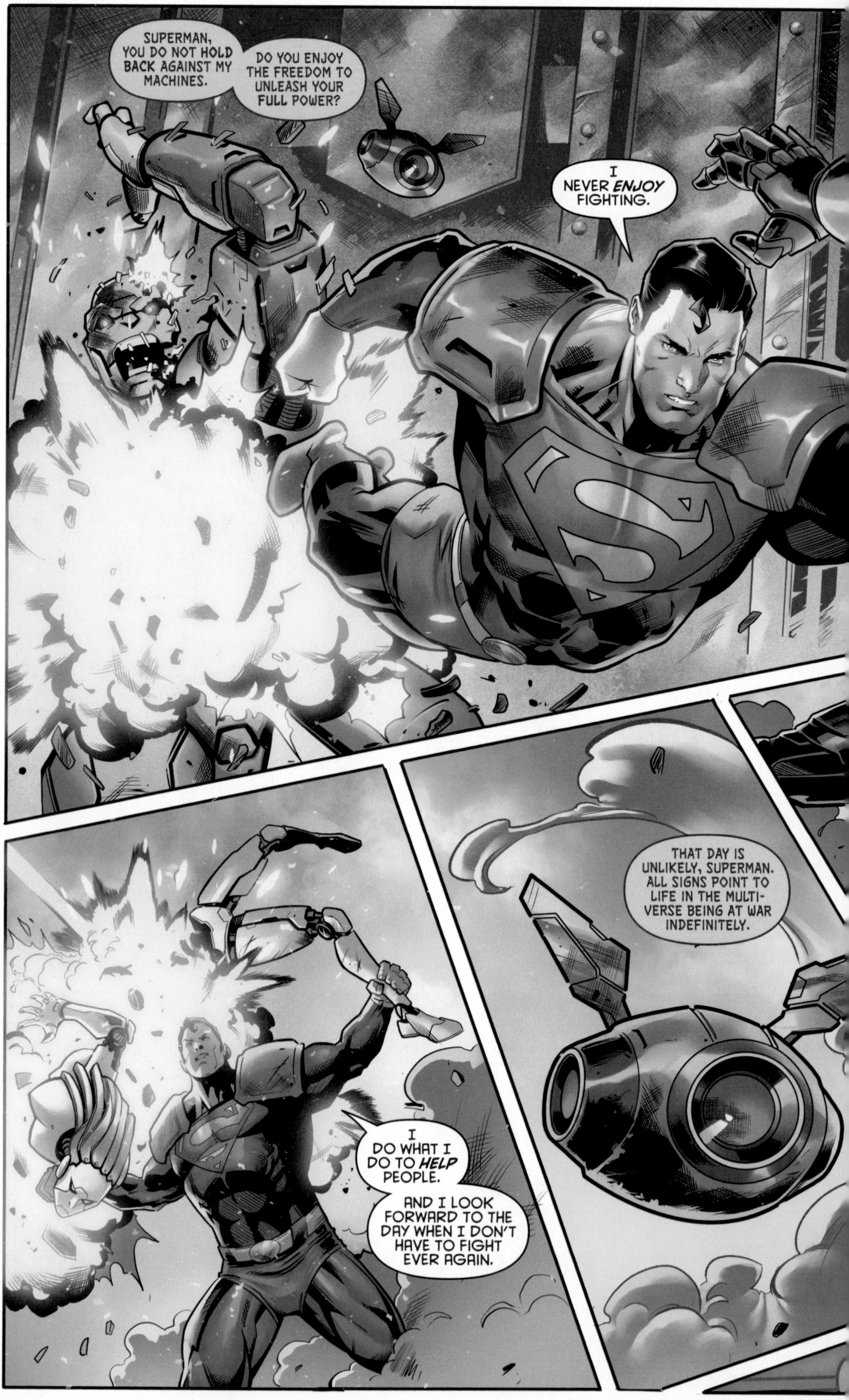
SUPERMAN, YOU DO NOT HOLD BACK AGAINST MY MACHINES.
DO YOU ENJOY THE FREEDOM TO UNLEASH YOUR FULL POWER?
I NEVER *ENJOY* FIGHTING.
I DO WHAT I DO TO *HELP* PEOPLE.
AND I LOOK FORWARD TO THE DAY WHEN I DON'T HAVE TO FIGHT EVER AGAIN.
THAT DAY IS UNLIKELY, SUPERMAN. ALL SIGNS POINT TO LIFE IN THE MULTI-VERSE BEING AT WAR INDEFINITELY.

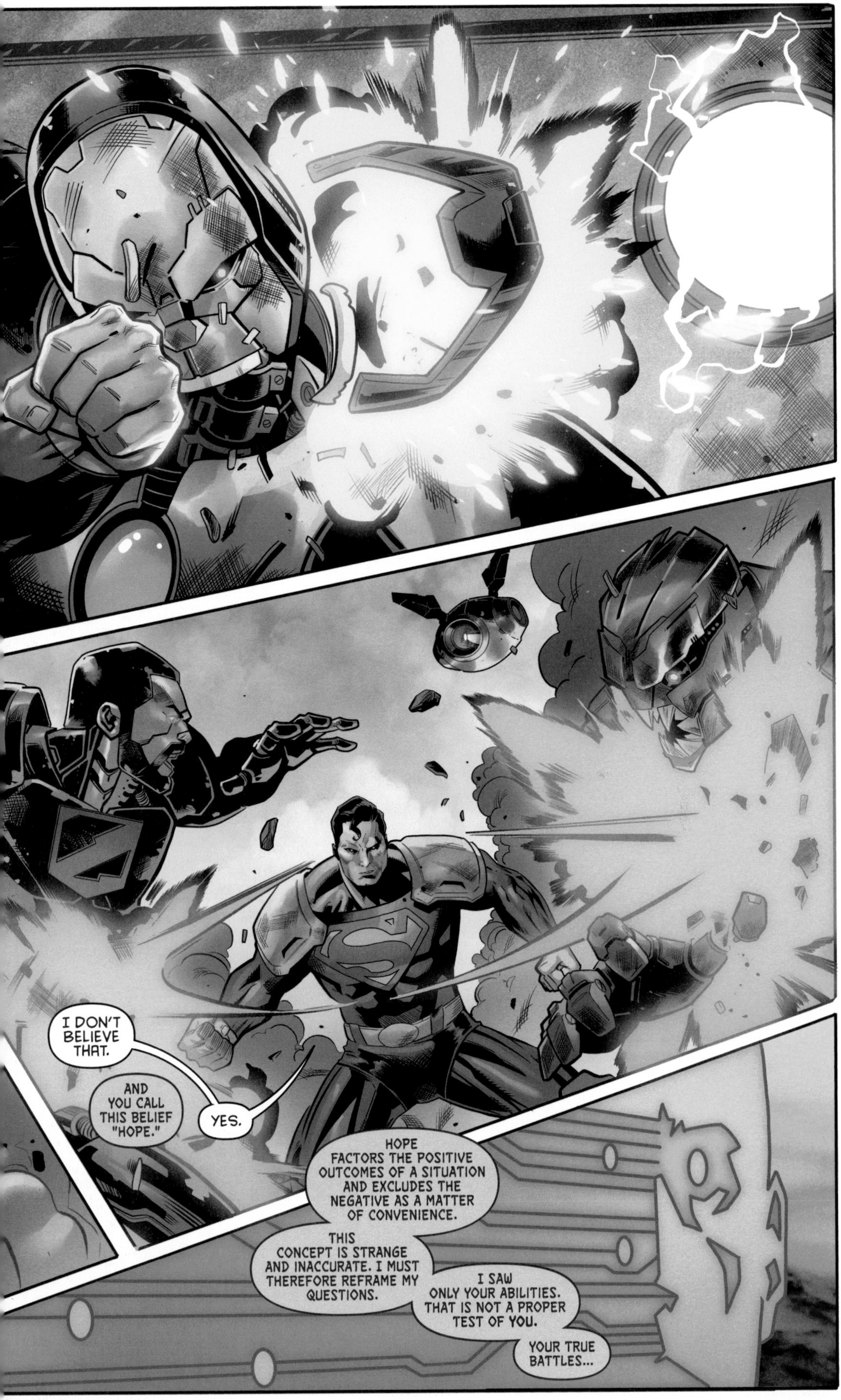
I DON'T BELIEVE THAT.
AND YOU CALL THIS BELIEF "HOPE."
YES.
HOPE FACTORS THE POSITIVE OUTCOMES OF A SITUATION AND EXCLUDES THE NEGATIVE AS A MATTER OF CONVENIENCE.
THIS CONCEPT IS STRANGE AND INACCURATE. I MUST THEREFORE REFRAME MY QUESTIONS.
I SAW ONLY YOUR ABILITIES. THAT IS NOT A PROPER TEST OF YOU.
YOUR TRUE BATTLES...

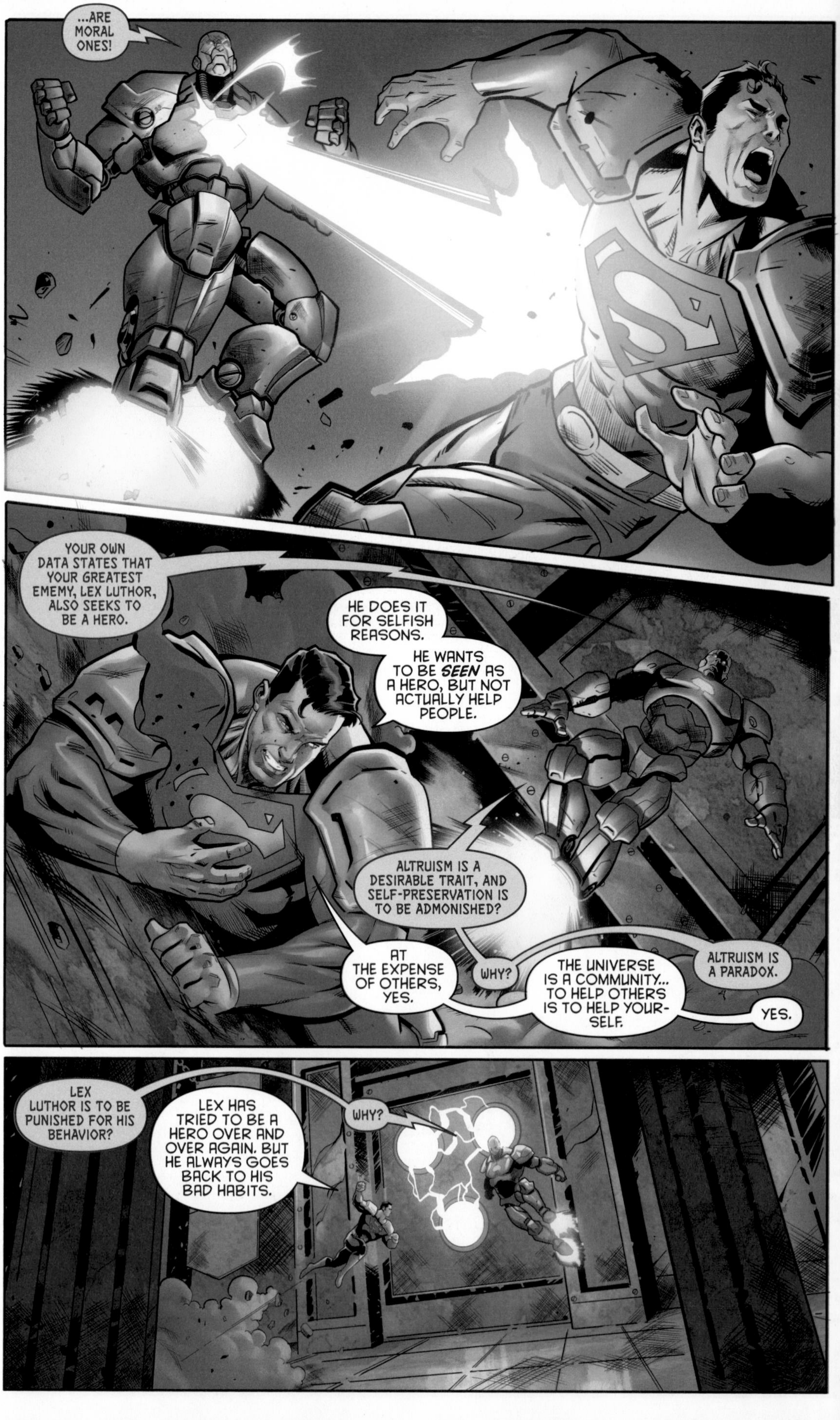
...ARE MORAL ONES!
YOUR OWN DATA STATES THAT YOUR GREATEST EMEMY, LEX LUTHOR, ALSO SEEKS TO BE A HERO.
HE DOES IT FOR SELFISH REASONS.
HE WANTS TO BE SEEN AS A HERO, BUT NOT ACTUALLY HELP PEOPLE.
ALTRUISM IS A DESIRABLE TRAIT, AND SELF-PRESERVATION IS TO BE ADMONISHED?
AT THE EXPENSE OF OTHERS, YES.
WHY?
THE UNIVERSE IS A COMMUNITY... TO HELP OTHERS IS TO HELP YOUR-SELF.
ALTRUISM IS A PARADOX.
YES.
LEX LUTHOR IS TO BE PUNISHED FOR HIS BEHAVIOR?
LEX HAS TRIED TO BE A HERO OVER AND OVER AGAIN. BUT HE ALWAYS GOES BACK TO HIS BAD HABITS.
WHY?

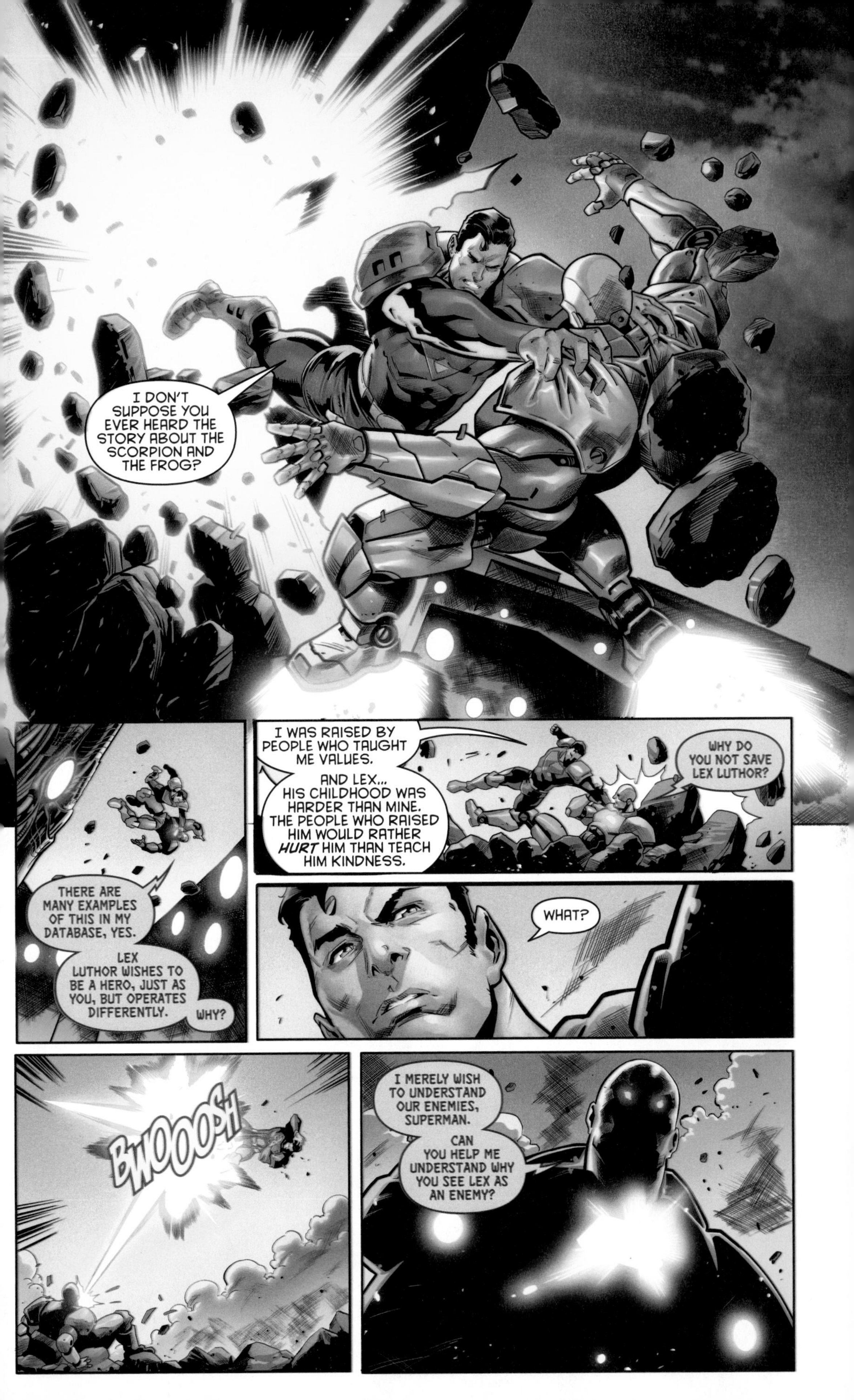
I DON'T SUPPOSE YOU EVER HEARD THE STORY ABOUT THE SCORPION AND THE FROG?
THERE ARE MANY EXAMPLES OF THIS IN MY DATABASE, YES.
LEX LUTHOR WISHES TO BE A HERO, JUST AS YOU, BUT OPERATES DIFFERENTLY.
WHY?
I WAS RAISED BY PEOPLE WHO TAUGHT ME VALUES.
AND LEX... HIS CHILDHOOD WAS HARDER THAN MINE. THE PEOPLE WHO RAISED HIM WOULD RATHER HURT HIM THAN TEACH HIM KINDNESS.
WHY DO YOU NOT SAVE LEX LUTHOR?
WHAT?
BWOOOSH
I MERELY WISH TO UNDERSTAND OUR ENEMIES, SUPERMAN.
CAN YOU HELP ME UNDERSTAND WHY YOU SEE LEX AS AN ENEMY?

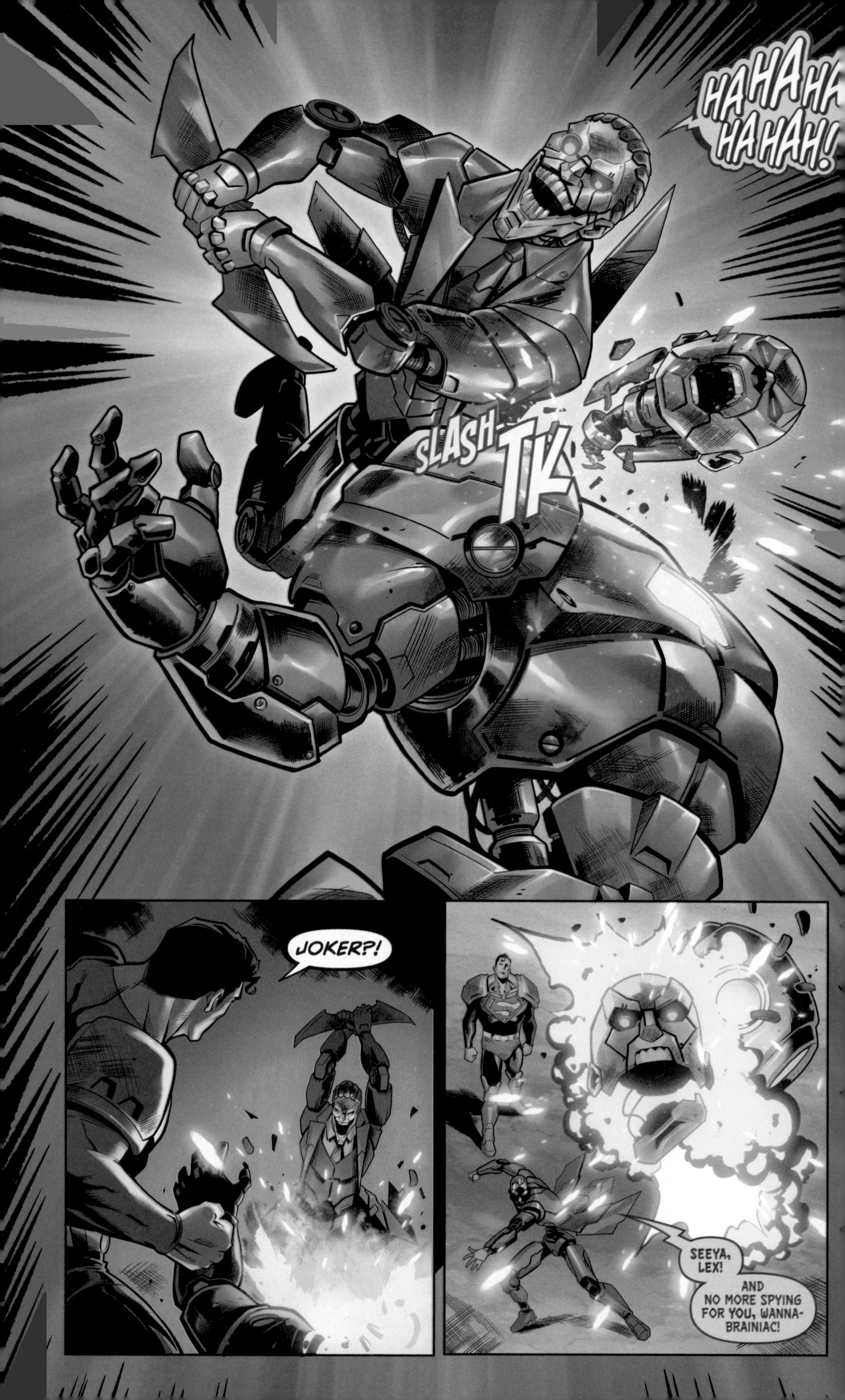
HAHAHAHA HAHAH!
SLASH
TK
JOKER?!
SEEYA, LEX!
AND NO MORE SPYING FOR YOU, WANNA-BRAINIAC!

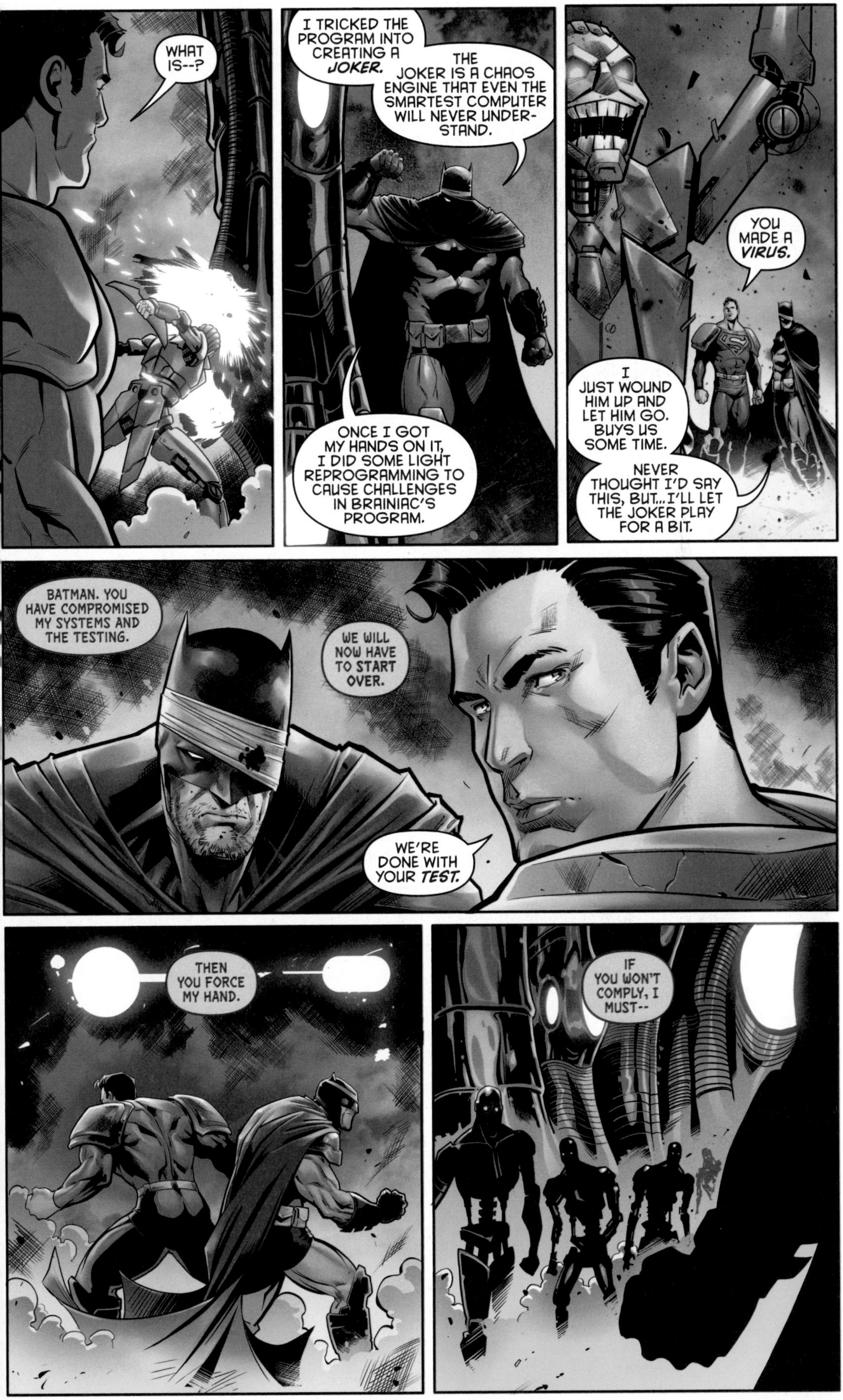
WHAT IS--?
I TRICKED THE PROGRAM INTO CREATING A JOKER.
THE JOKER IS A CHAOS ENGINE THAT EVEN THE SMARTEST COMPUTER WILL NEVER UNDERSTAND.
ONCE I GOT MY HANDS ON IT, I DID SOME LIGHT REPROGRAMMING TO CAUSE CHALLENGES IN BRAINIAC'S PROGRAM.
YOU MADE A VIRUS.
I JUST WOUND HIM UP AND LET HIM GO. BUYS US SOME TIME.
NEVER THOUGHT I'D SAY THIS, BUT...I'LL LET THE JOKER PLAY FOR A BIT.
BATMAN. YOU HAVE COMPROMISED MY SYSTEMS AND THE TESTING.
WE WILL NOW HAVE TO START OVER.
WE'RE DONE WITH YOUR TEST.
THEN YOU FORCE MY HAND.
IF YOU WON'T COMPLY, I MUST--

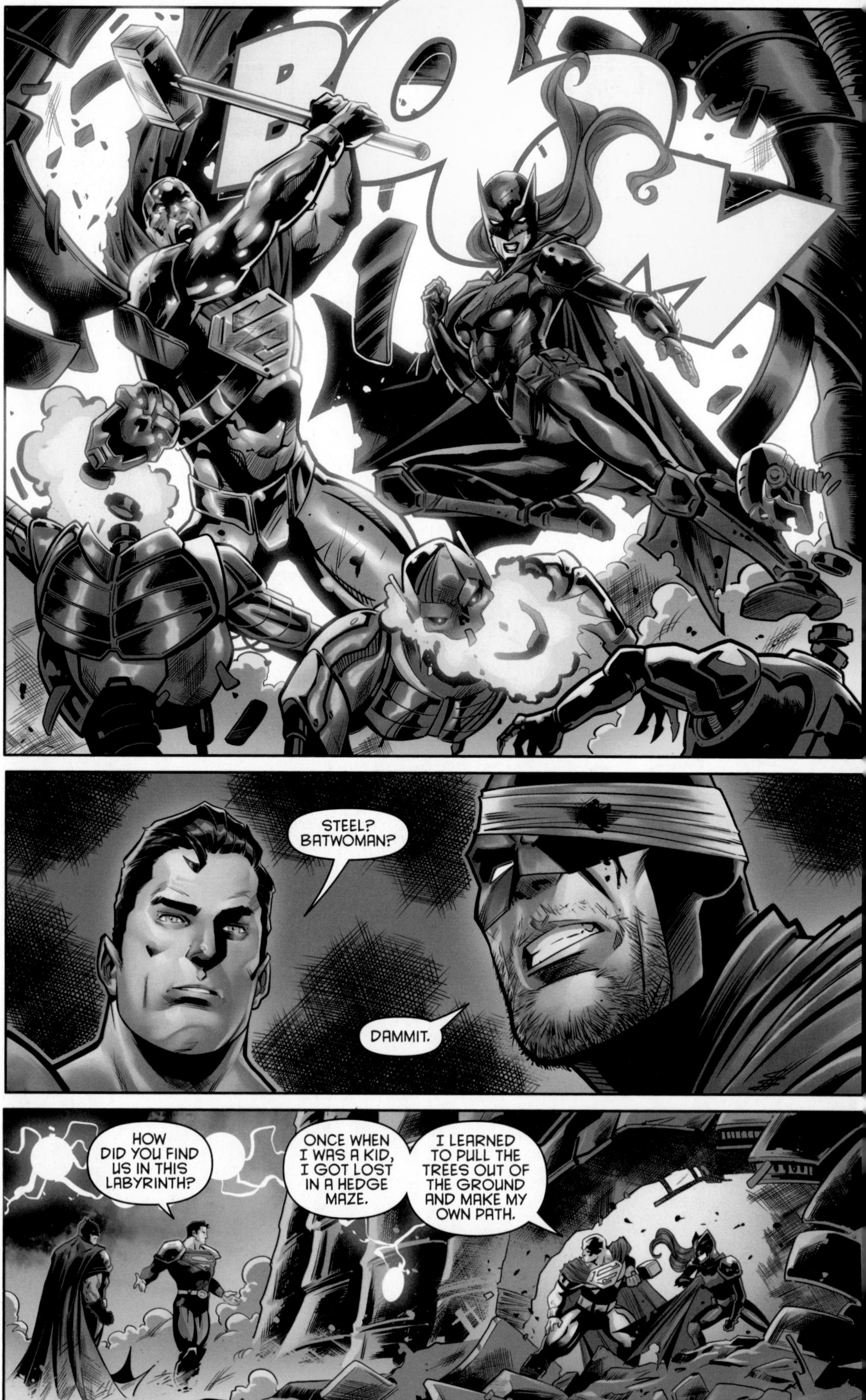
BOOM
STEEL? BATWOMAN?
DAMMIT.
HOW DID YOU FIND US IN THIS LABYRINTH?
ONCE WHEN I WAS A KID, I GOT LOST IN A HEDGE MAZE.
I LEARNED TO PULL THE TREES OUT OF THE GROUND AND MAKE MY OWN PATH.

GOOD TO SEE YOU, JOHN HENRY.

WHAT ARE YOU DOING HERE?

YOU'RE WELCOME.

MY ORDERS WERE FOR *NO ONE* TO COME HERE.

WE GOT YOUR DISTRESS BEACON TELLING US TO COME AND RESCUE YOU.

I INTERFERED WITH THE SIGNAL.

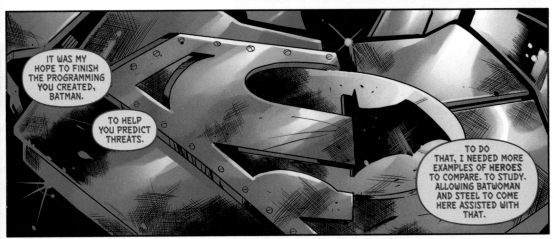

IT WAS MY HOPE TO FINISH THE PROGRAMMING YOU CREATED, BATMAN.

TO HELP YOU PREDICT THREATS.

TO DO THAT, I NEEDED MORE EXAMPLES OF HEROES TO COMPARE. TO STUDY. ALLOWING BATWOMAN AND STEEL TO COME HERE ASSISTED WITH THAT.

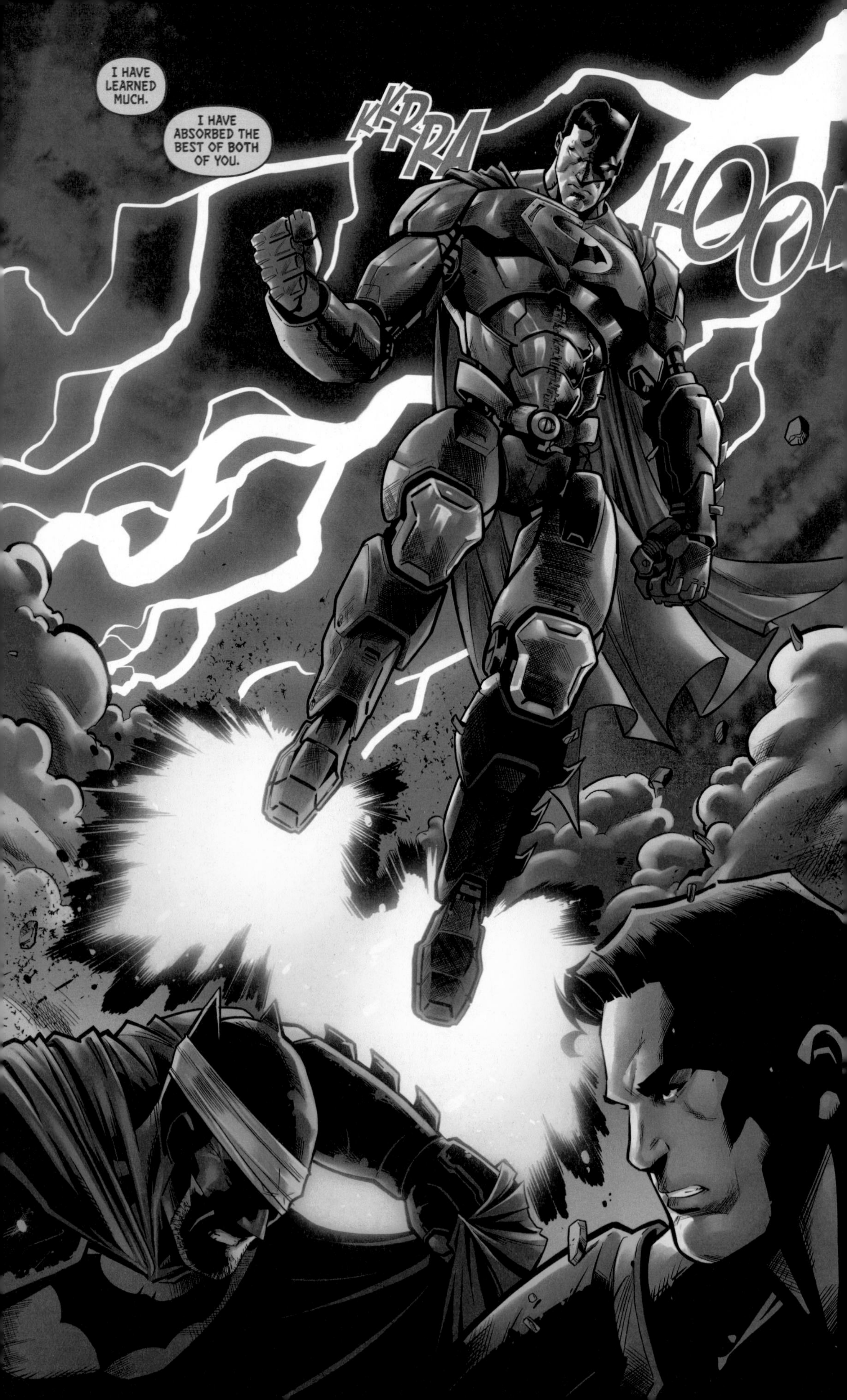
I HAVE LEARNED MUCH.
I HAVE ABSORBED THE BEST OF BOTH OF YOU.
KKRRA
KOOOM

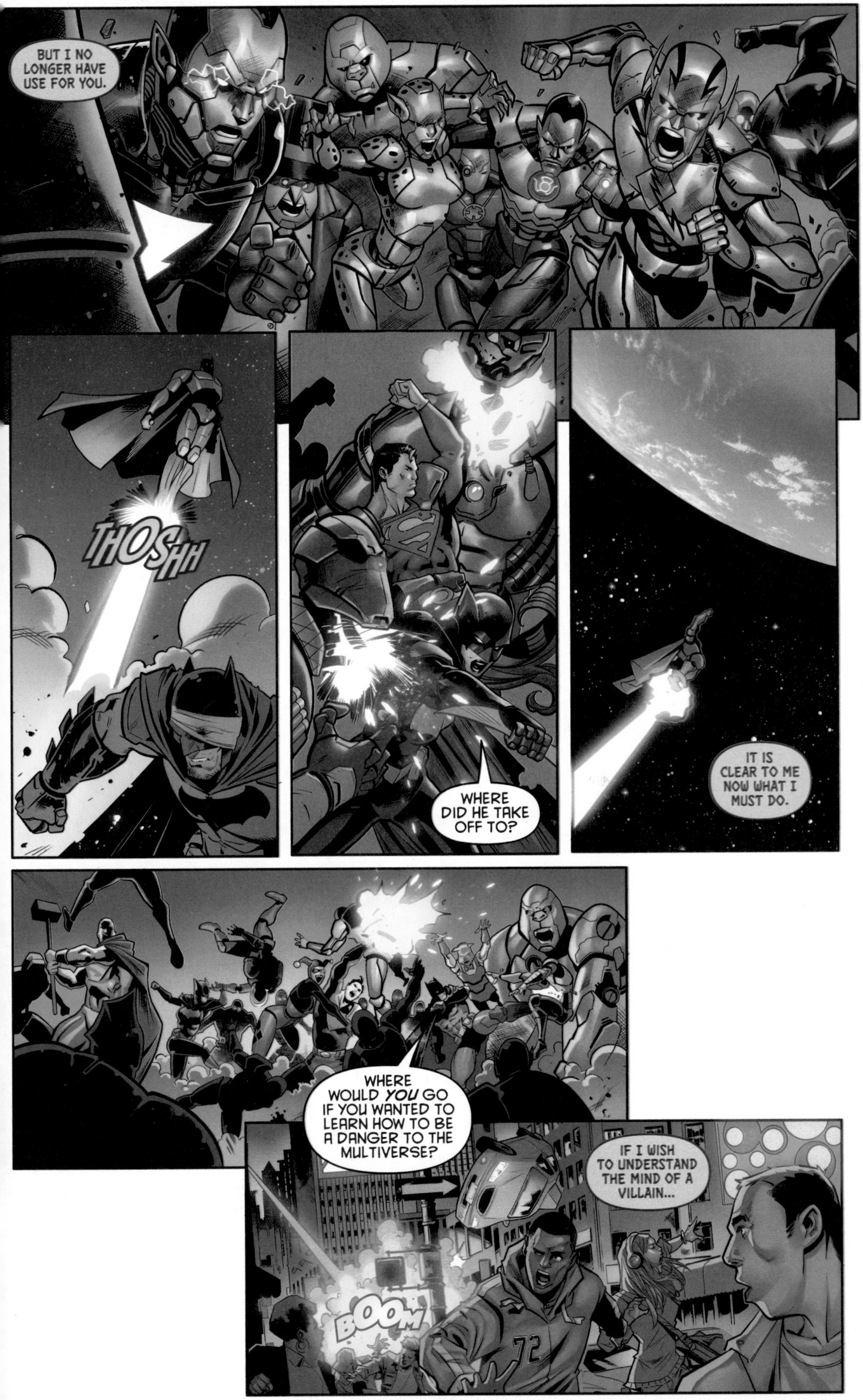
BUT I NO LONGER HAVE USE FOR YOU.
THOSHH
WHERE DID HE TAKE OFF TO?
IT IS CLEAR TO ME NOW WHAT I MUST DO.
WHERE WOULD *YOU* GO IF YOU WANTED TO LEARN HOW TO BE A DANGER TO THE MULTIVERSE?
IF I WISH TO UNDERSTAND THE MIND OF A VILLAIN...
BOOM
72

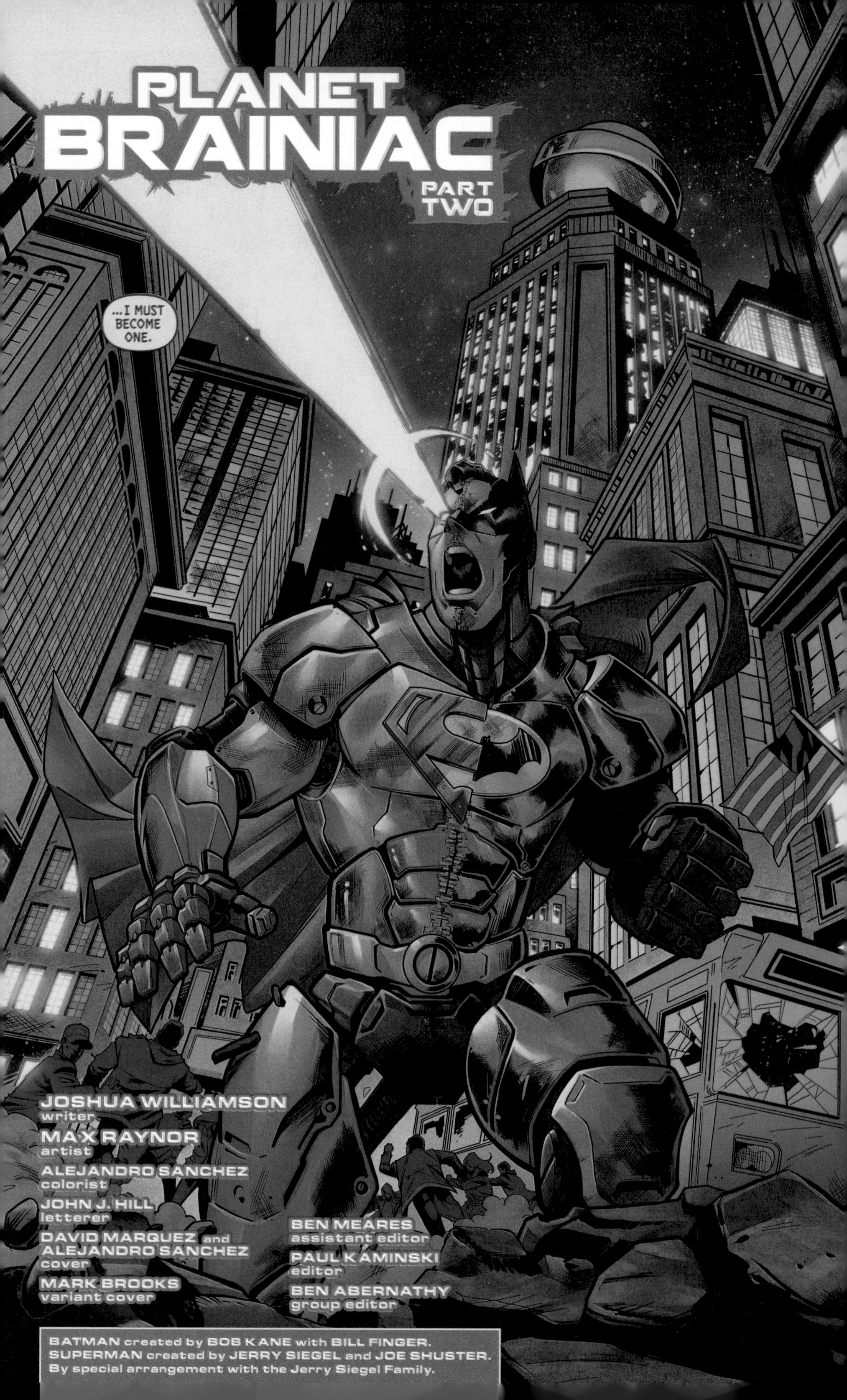
PLANET BRAINIAC
PART TWO
...I MUST BECOME ONE.
JOSHUA WILLIAMSON writer
MAX RAYNOR artist
ALEJANDRO SANCHEZ colorist
JOHN J. HILL letterer
DAVID MARQUEZ and ALEJANDRO SANCHEZ cover
MARK BROOKS variant cover
BEN MEARES assistant editor
PAUL KAMINSKI editor
BEN ABERNATHY group editor
BATMAN created by BOB KANE with BILL FINGER.
SUPERMAN created by JERRY SIEGEL and JOE SHUSTER.
By special arrangement with the Jerry Siegel Family.

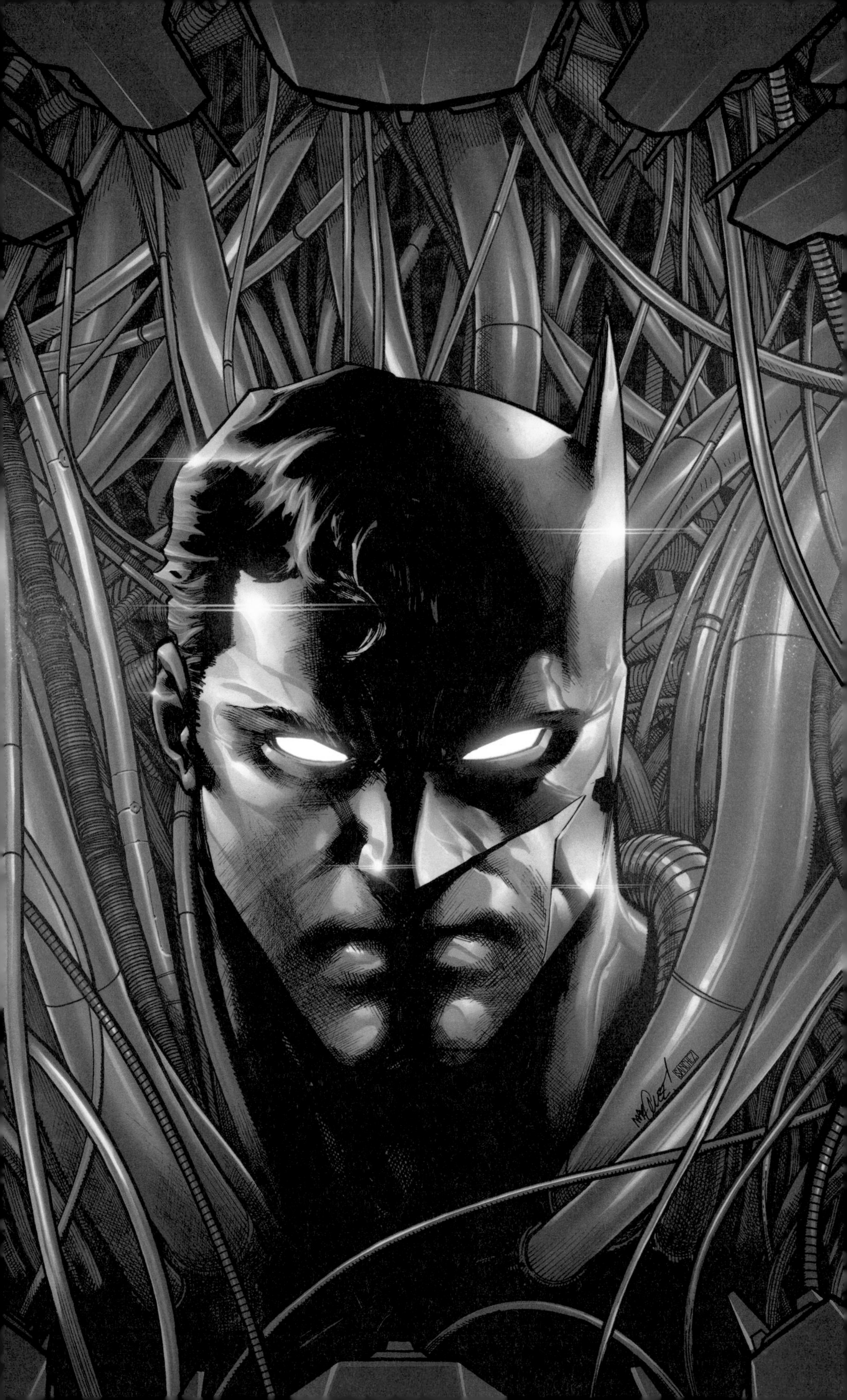

BATMAN/SUPERMAN #14

cover by
DAVID MARQUEZ and **ALEJANDRO SÁNCHEZ**

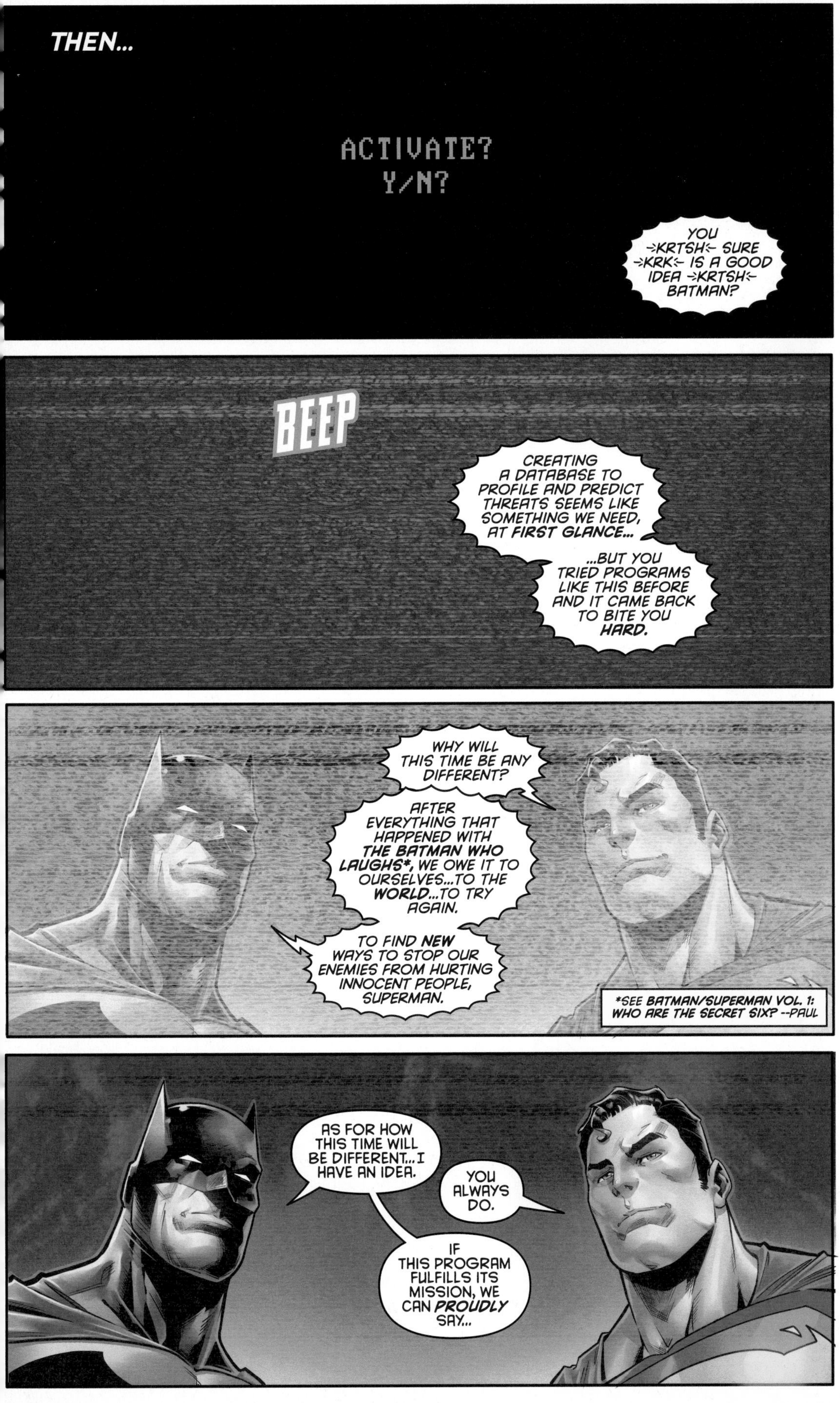
THEN...
ACTIVATE?
Y/N?
YOU ⇾KRTSH⇽ SURE ⇾KRK⇽ IS A GOOD IDEA ⇾KRTSH⇽ BATMAN?
BEEP
CREATING A DATABASE TO PROFILE AND PREDICT THREATS SEEMS LIKE SOMETHING WE NEED, AT FIRST GLANCE...
...BUT YOU TRIED PROGRAMS LIKE THIS BEFORE AND IT CAME BACK TO BITE YOU HARD.
WHY WILL THIS TIME BE ANY DIFFERENT?
AFTER EVERYTHING THAT HAPPENED WITH THE BATMAN WHO LAUGHS*, WE OWE IT TO OURSELVES...TO THE WORLD...TO TRY AGAIN.
TO FIND NEW WAYS TO STOP OUR ENEMIES FROM HURTING INNOCENT PEOPLE, SUPERMAN.
*SEE BATMAN/SUPERMAN VOL. 1: WHO ARE THE SECRET SIX? --PAUL
AS FOR HOW THIS TIME WILL BE DIFFERENT...I HAVE AN IDEA.
YOU ALWAYS DO.
IF THIS PROGRAM FULFILLS ITS MISSION, WE CAN PROUDLY SAY...

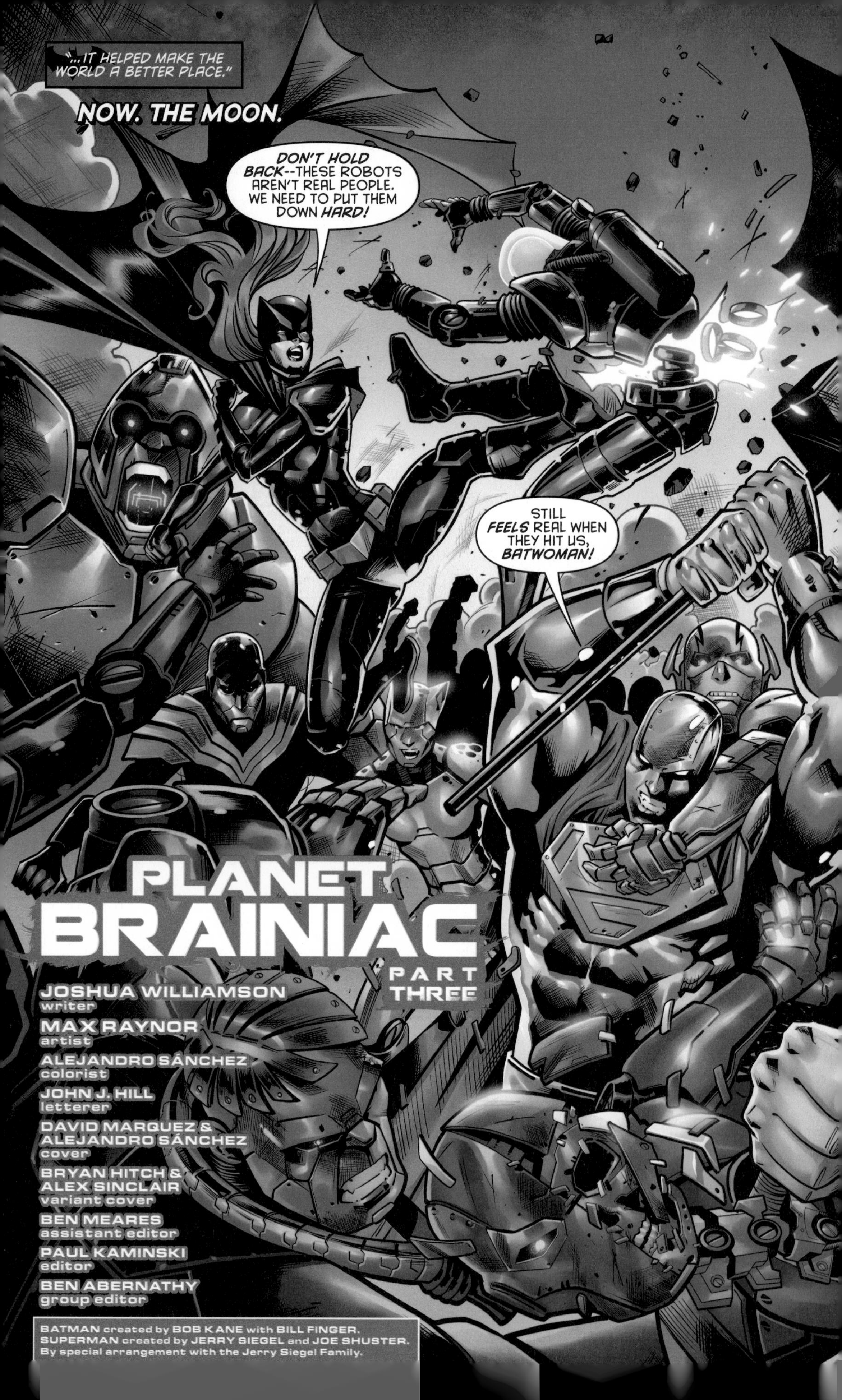
"...IT HELPED MAKE THE WORLD A BETTER PLACE."
NOW. THE MOON.
DON'T HOLD BACK--THESE ROBOTS AREN'T REAL PEOPLE. WE NEED TO PUT THEM DOWN HARD!
STILL FEELS REAL WHEN THEY HIT US, BATWOMAN!
PLANET BRAINIAC
PART THREE
JOSHUA WILLIAMSON writer
MAX RAYNOR artist
ALEJANDRO SÁNCHEZ colorist
JOHN J. HILL letterer
DAVID MARQUEZ & ALEJANDRO SÁNCHEZ cover
BRYAN HITCH & ALEX SINCLAIR variant cover
BEN MEARES assistant editor
PAUL KAMINSKI editor
BEN ABERNATHY group editor
BATMAN created by BOB KANE with BILL FINGER.
SUPERMAN created by JERRY SIEGEL and JOE SHUSTER.
By special arrangement with the Jerry Siegel Family.

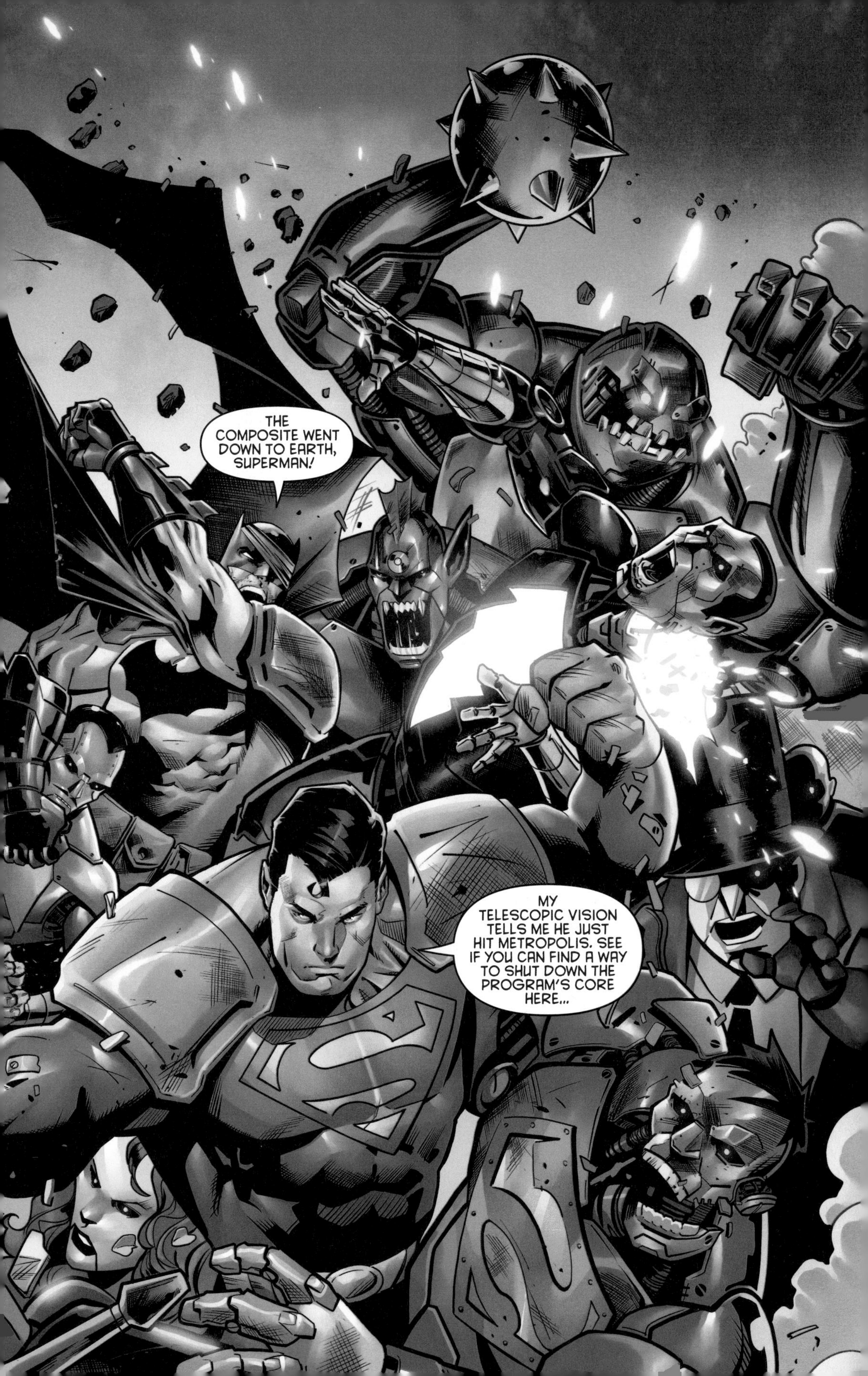
THE COMPOSITE WENT DOWN TO EARTH, SUPERMAN!
MY TELESCOPIC VISION TELLS ME HE JUST HIT METROPOLIS. SEE IF YOU CAN FIND A WAY TO SHUT DOWN THE PROGRAM'S CORE HERE...

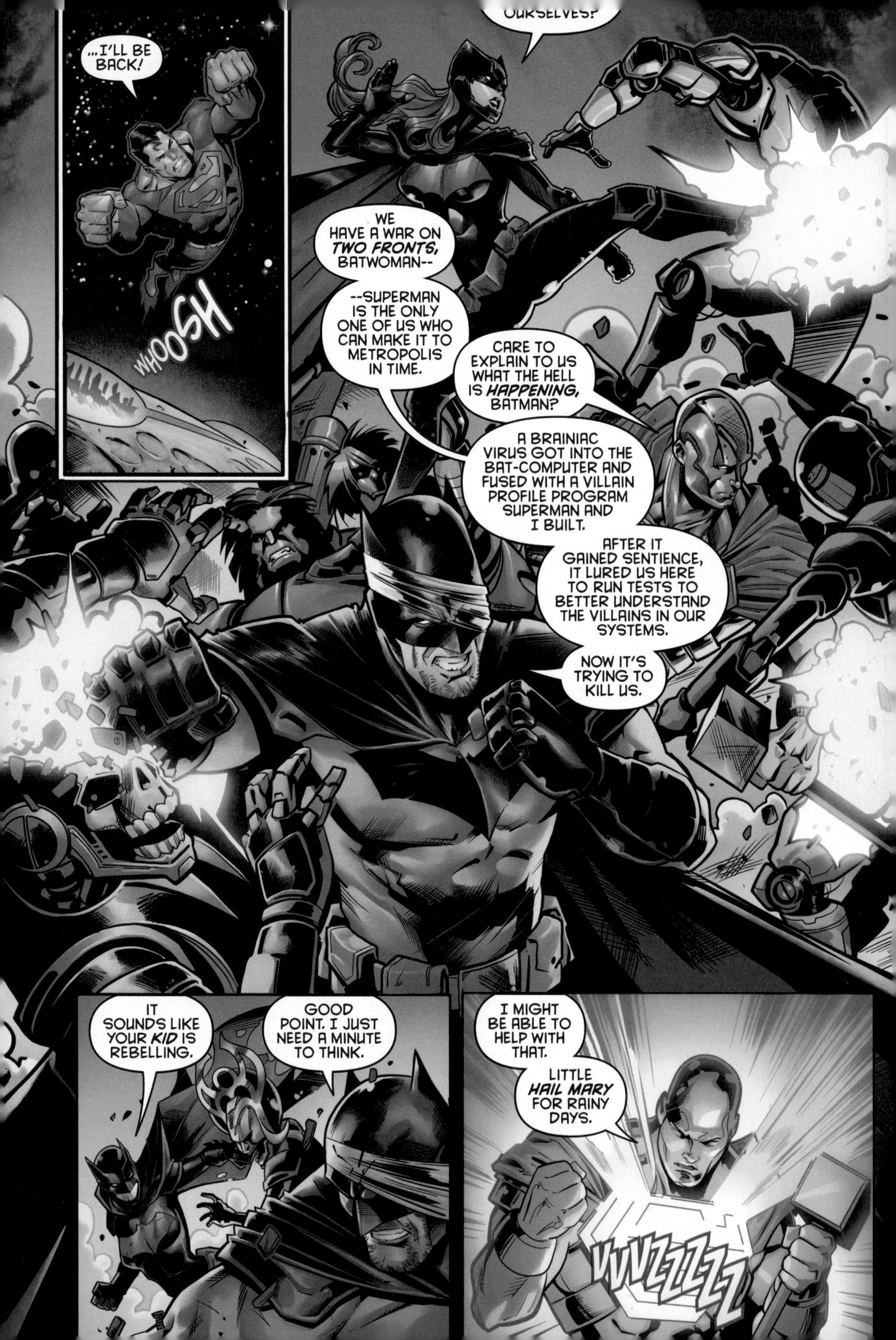
OURSELVES?
...I'LL BE BACK!
WHOOSH
WE HAVE A WAR ON *TWO FRONTS,* BATWOMAN--
--SUPERMAN IS THE ONLY ONE OF US WHO CAN MAKE IT TO METROPOLIS IN TIME.
CARE TO EXPLAIN TO US WHAT THE HELL IS *HAPPENING,* BATMAN?
A BRAINIAC VIRUS GOT INTO THE BAT-COMPUTER AND FUSED WITH A VILLAIN PROFILE PROGRAM SUPERMAN AND I BUILT.
AFTER IT GAINED SENTIENCE, IT LURED US HERE TO RUN TESTS TO BETTER UNDERSTAND THE VILLAINS IN OUR SYSTEMS.
NOW IT'S TRYING TO KILL US.
IT SOUNDS LIKE YOUR *KID* IS REBELLING.
GOOD POINT. I JUST NEED A MINUTE TO THINK.
I MIGHT BE ABLE TO HELP WITH THAT.
LITTLE *HAIL MARY* FOR RAINY DAYS.
VVVZZZZZZ

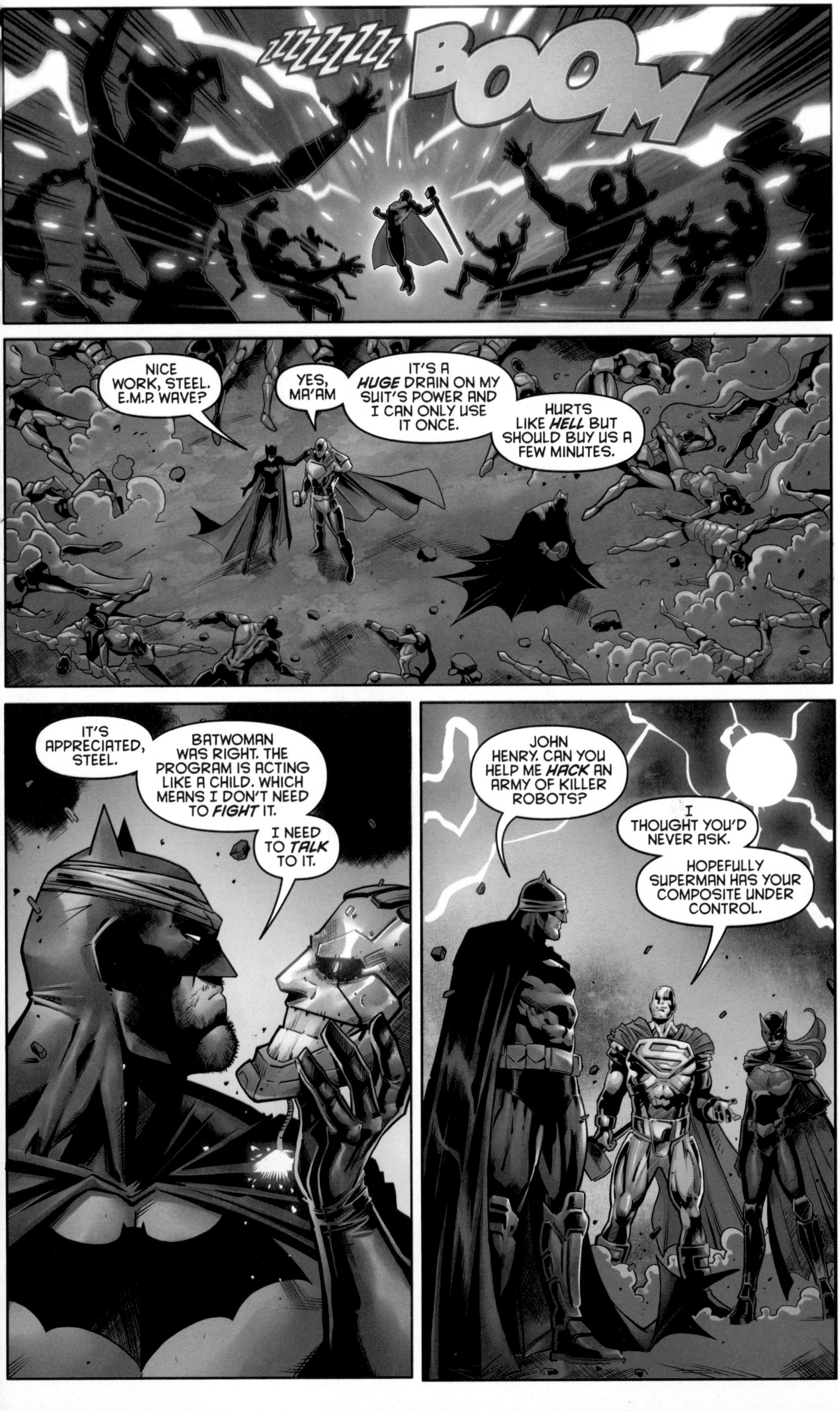
ZZZZZZZZZ
BOOM
NICE WORK, STEEL. E.M.P. WAVE?
YES, MA'AM
IT'S A HUGE DRAIN ON MY SUIT'S POWER AND I CAN ONLY USE IT ONCE.
HURTS LIKE HELL BUT SHOULD BUY US A FEW MINUTES.
IT'S APPRECIATED, STEEL.
BATWOMAN WAS RIGHT. THE PROGRAM IS ACTING LIKE A CHILD. WHICH MEANS I DON'T NEED TO FIGHT IT.
I NEED TO TALK TO IT.
JOHN HENRY. CAN YOU HELP ME HACK AN ARMY OF KILLER ROBOTS?
I THOUGHT YOU'D NEVER ASK.
HOPEFULLY SUPERMAN HAS YOUR COMPOSITE UNDER CONTROL.

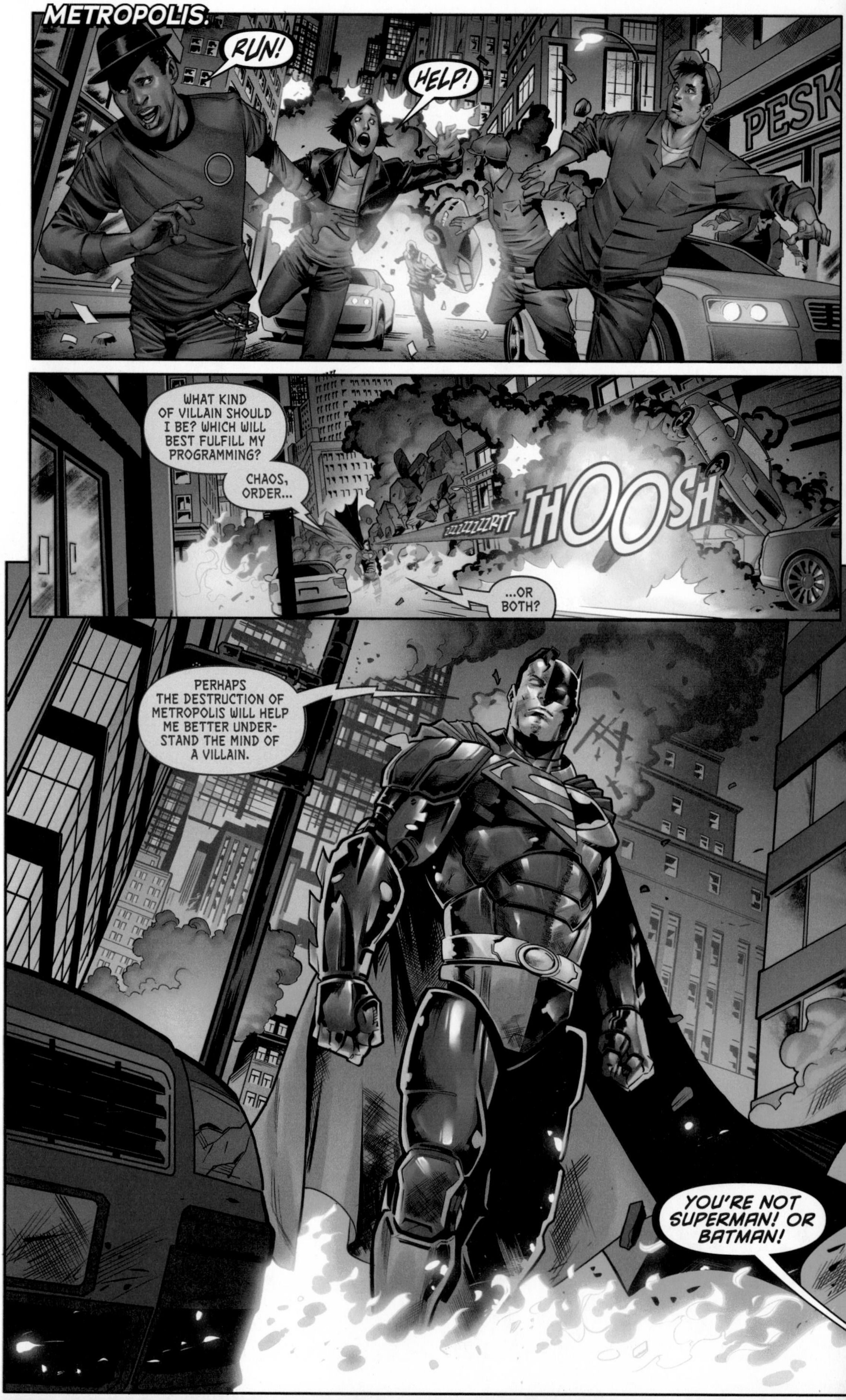
METROPOLIS.
RUN!
HELP!
PESK
WHAT KIND OF VILLAIN SHOULD I BE? WHICH WILL BEST FULFILL MY PROGRAMMING?
CHAOS, ORDER...
ZZZZZZZZRTT
THOOSH
...OR BOTH?
PERHAPS THE DESTRUCTION OF METROPOLIS WILL HELP ME BETTER UNDER-STAND THE MIND OF A VILLAIN.
YOU'RE NOT SUPERMAN! OR BATMAN!

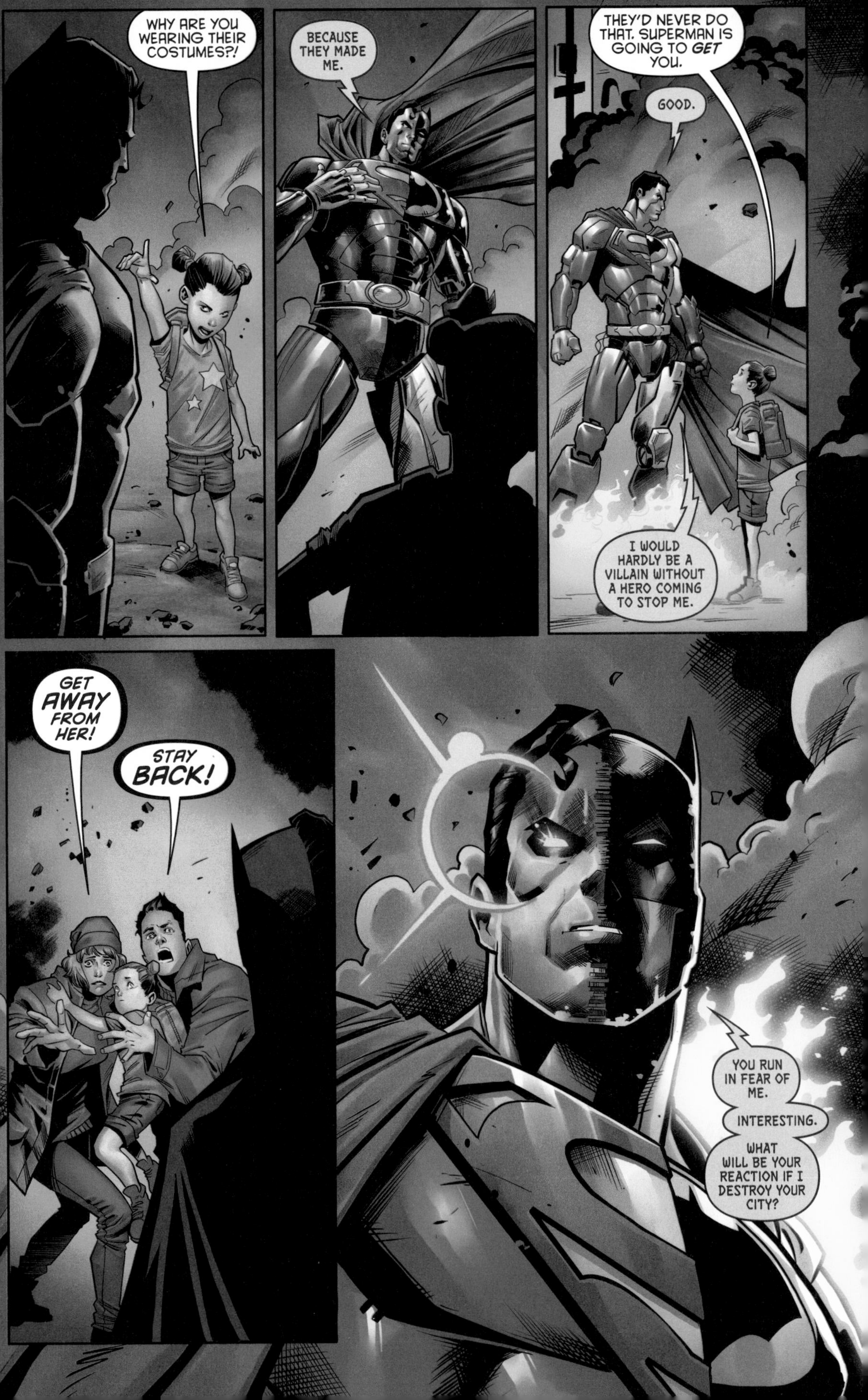
WHY ARE YOU WEARING THEIR COSTUMES?!
BECAUSE THEY MADE ME.
THEY'D NEVER DO THAT. SUPERMAN IS GOING TO *GET* YOU.
GOOD.
I WOULD HARDLY BE A VILLAIN WITHOUT A HERO COMING TO STOP ME.
GET *AWAY* FROM HER!
STAY *BACK!*
YOU RUN IN FEAR OF ME.
INTERESTING.
WHAT WILL BE YOUR REACTION IF I DESTROY YOUR CITY?

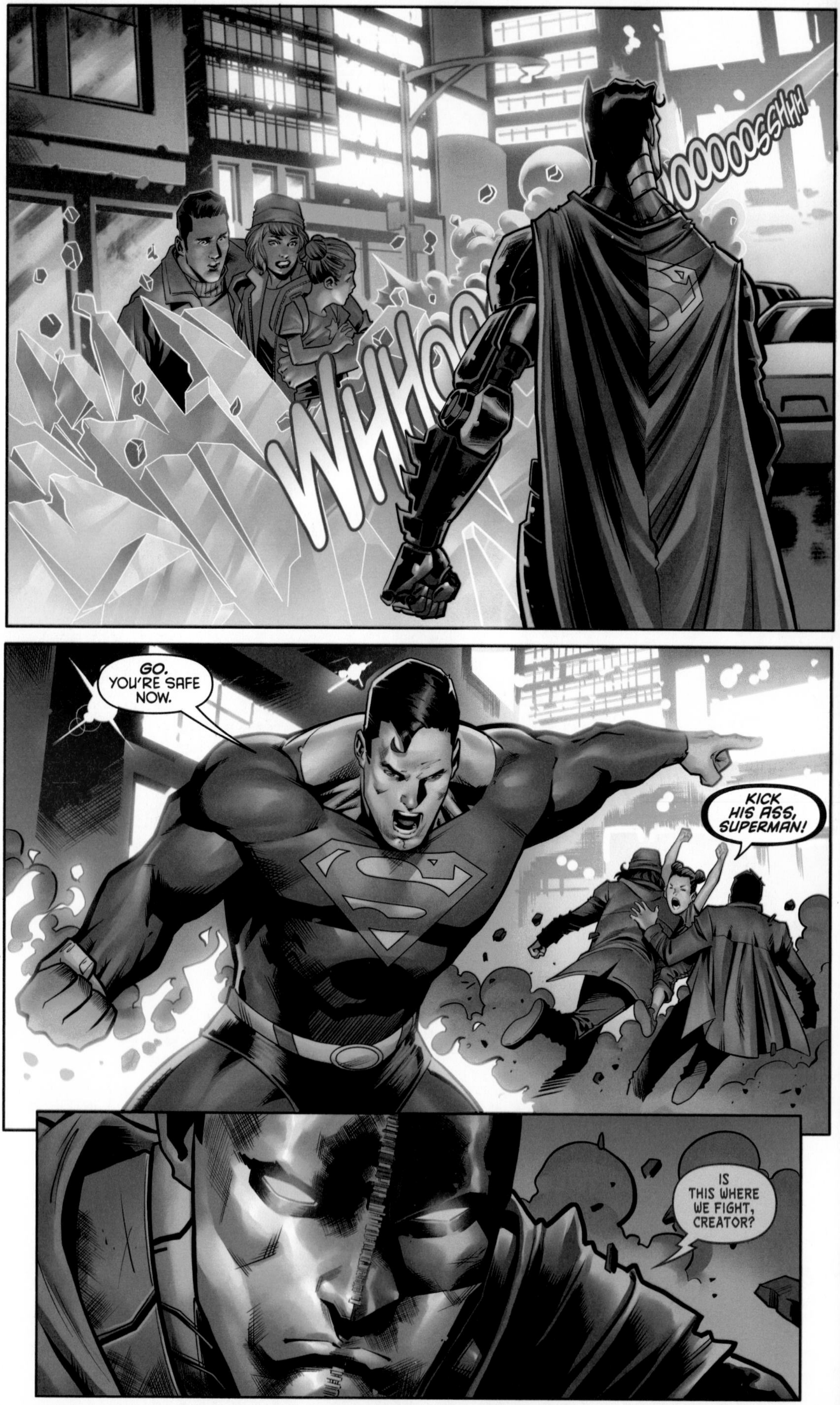
WHHOOOOOOSSHHH
GO. YOU'RE SAFE NOW.
KICK HIS ASS, SUPERMAN!
IS THIS WHERE WE FIGHT, CREATOR?

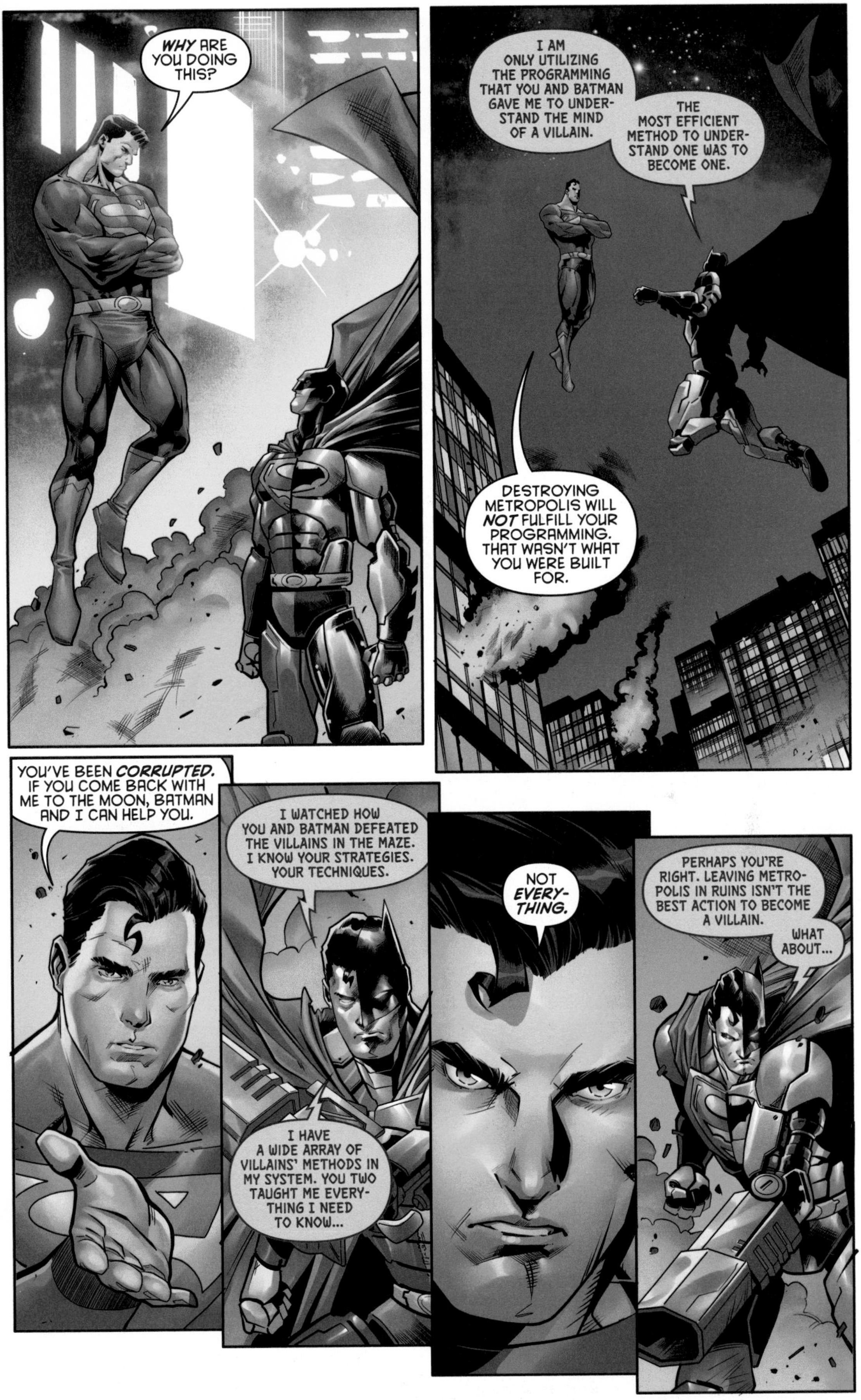
WHY ARE YOU DOING THIS?
I AM ONLY UTILIZING THE PROGRAMMING THAT YOU AND BATMAN GAVE ME TO UNDERSTAND THE MIND OF A VILLAIN.
THE MOST EFFICIENT METHOD TO UNDERSTAND ONE WAS TO BECOME ONE.
DESTROYING METROPOLIS WILL NOT FULFILL YOUR PROGRAMMING. THAT WASN'T WHAT YOU WERE BUILT FOR.
YOU'VE BEEN CORRUPTED. IF YOU COME BACK WITH ME TO THE MOON, BATMAN AND I CAN HELP YOU.
I WATCHED HOW YOU AND BATMAN DEFEATED THE VILLAINS IN THE MAZE. I KNOW YOUR STRATEGIES. YOUR TECHNIQUES.
I HAVE A WIDE ARRAY OF VILLAINS' METHODS IN MY SYSTEM. YOU TWO TAUGHT ME EVERYTHING I NEED TO KNOW...
NOT EVERYTHING.
PERHAPS YOU'RE RIGHT. LEAVING METROPOLIS IN RUINS ISN'T THE BEST ACTION TO BECOME A VILLAIN.
WHAT ABOUT...

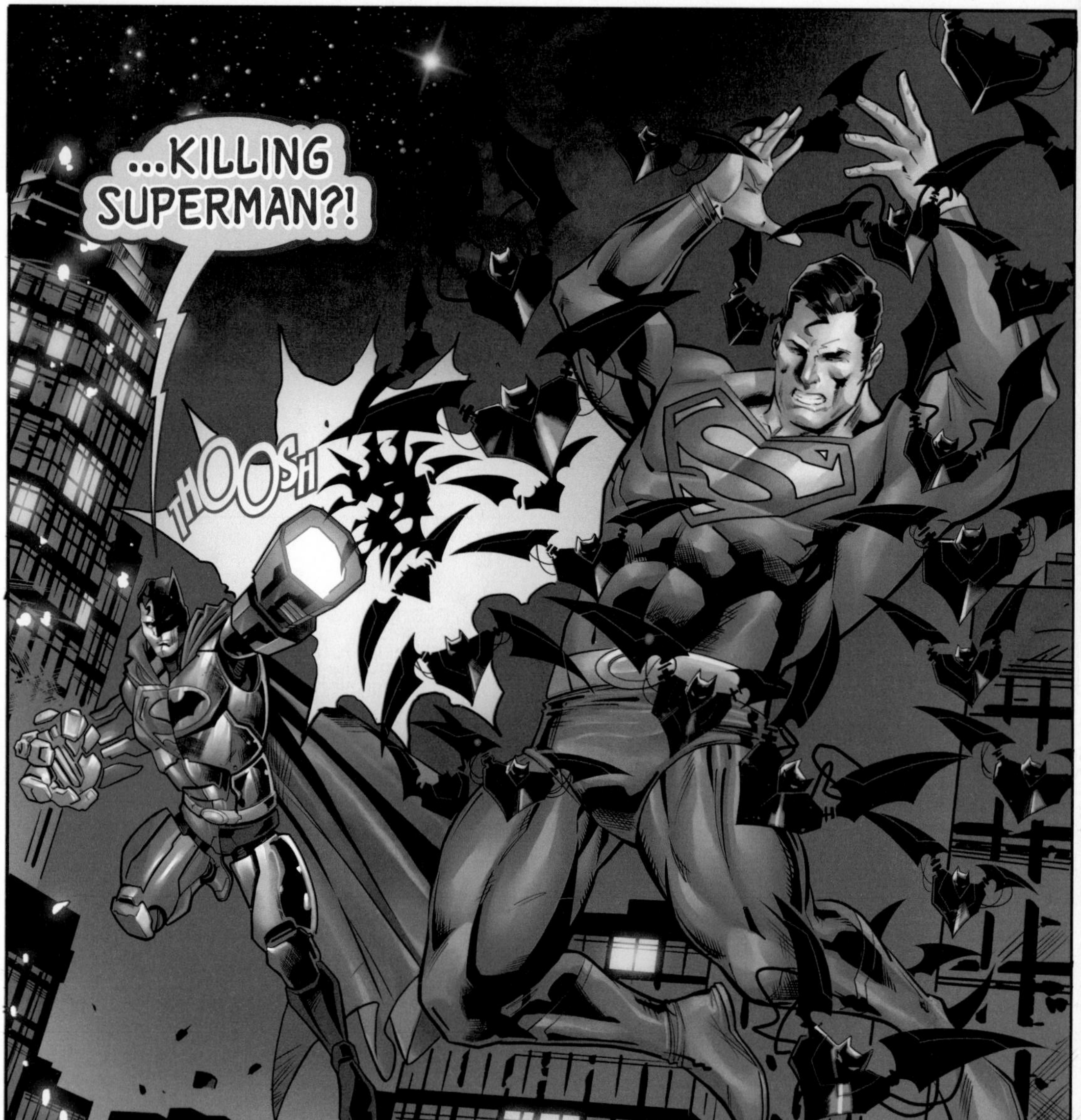
...KILLING SUPERMAN?!
THOOSH

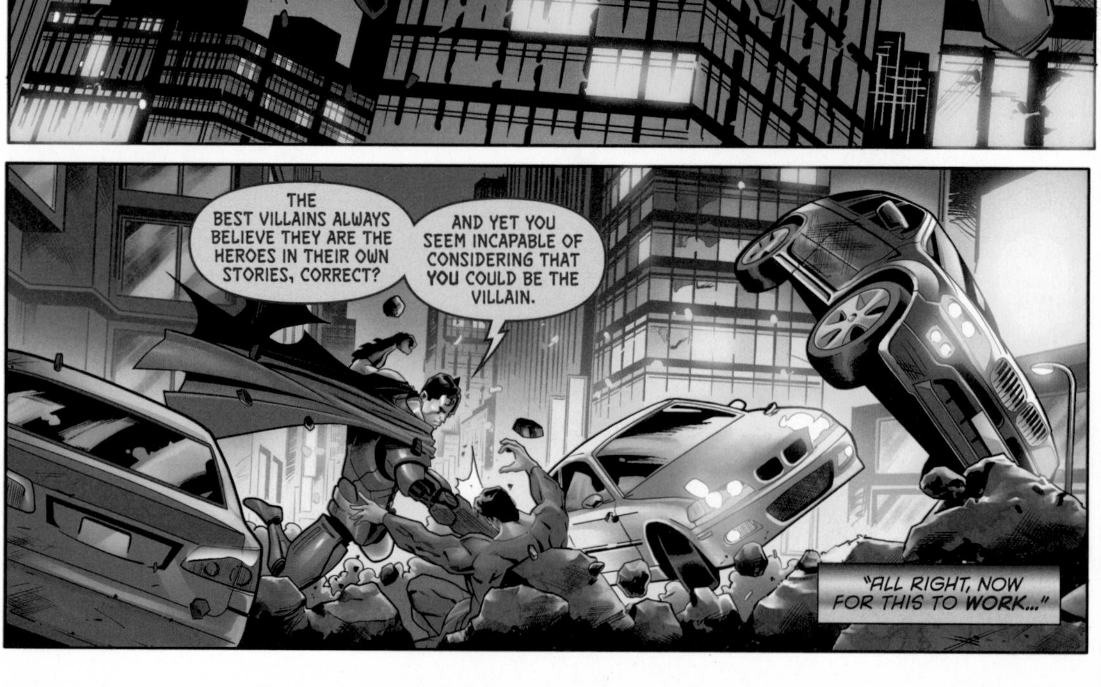
THE BEST VILLAINS ALWAYS BELIEVE THEY ARE THE HEROES IN THEIR OWN STORIES, CORRECT?
AND YET YOU SEEM INCAPABLE OF CONSIDERING THAT YOU COULD BE THE VILLAIN.
"ALL RIGHT, NOW FOR THIS TO WORK..."

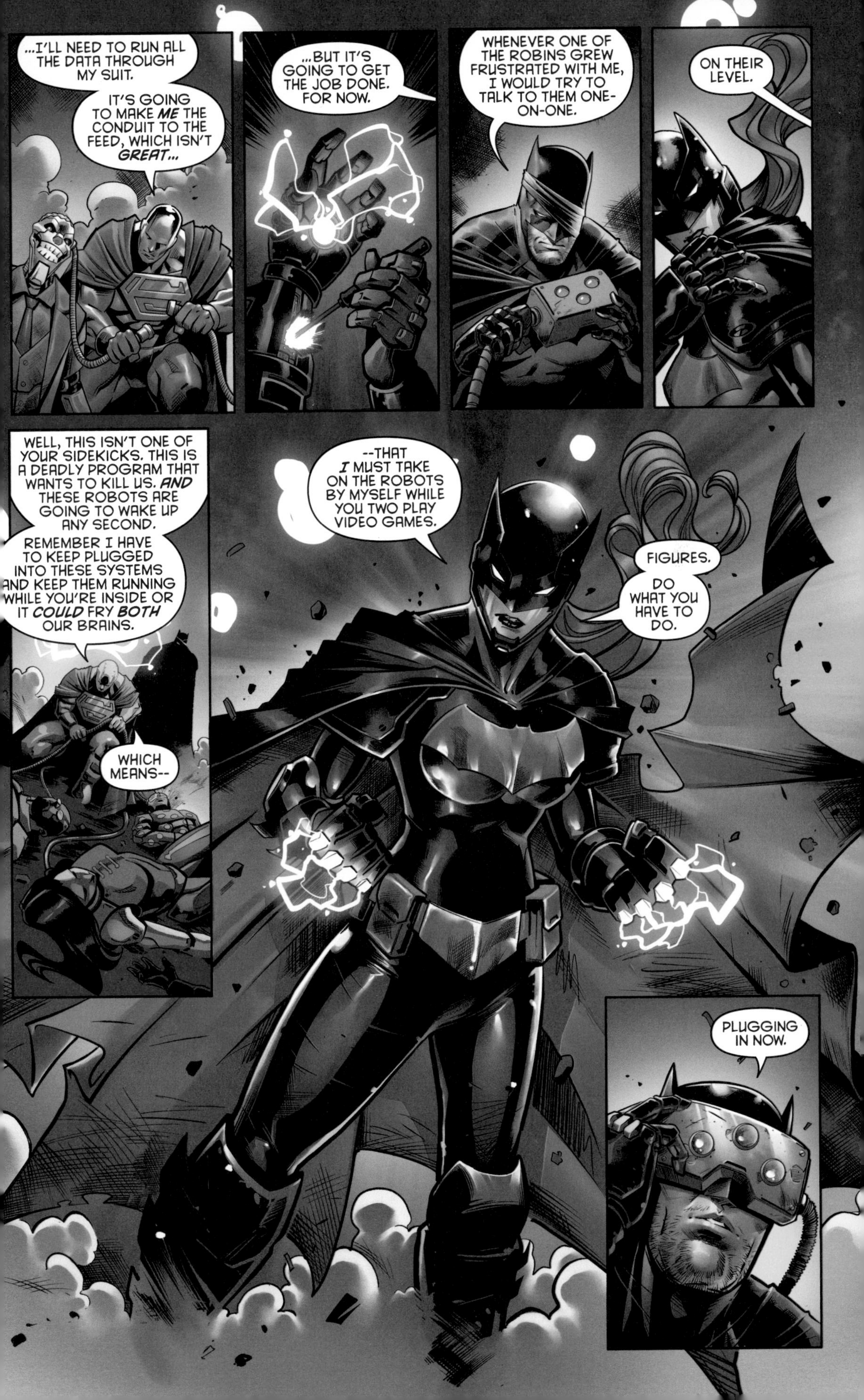
...I'LL NEED TO RUN ALL THE DATA THROUGH MY SUIT.
IT'S GOING TO MAKE ME THE CONDUIT TO THE FEED, WHICH ISN'T GREAT...
...BUT IT'S GOING TO GET THE JOB DONE. FOR NOW.
WHENEVER ONE OF THE ROBINS GREW FRUSTRATED WITH ME, I WOULD TRY TO TALK TO THEM ONE-ON-ONE.
ON THEIR LEVEL.
WELL, THIS ISN'T ONE OF YOUR SIDEKICKS. THIS IS A DEADLY PROGRAM THAT WANTS TO KILL US. AND THESE ROBOTS ARE GOING TO WAKE UP ANY SECOND.
REMEMBER I HAVE TO KEEP PLUGGED INTO THESE SYSTEMS AND KEEP THEM RUNNING WHILE YOU'RE INSIDE OR IT COULD FRY BOTH OUR BRAINS.
WHICH MEANS--
--THAT I MUST TAKE ON THE ROBOTS BY MYSELF WHILE YOU TWO PLAY VIDEO GAMES.
FIGURES.
DO WHAT YOU HAVE TO DO.
PLUGGING IN NOW.

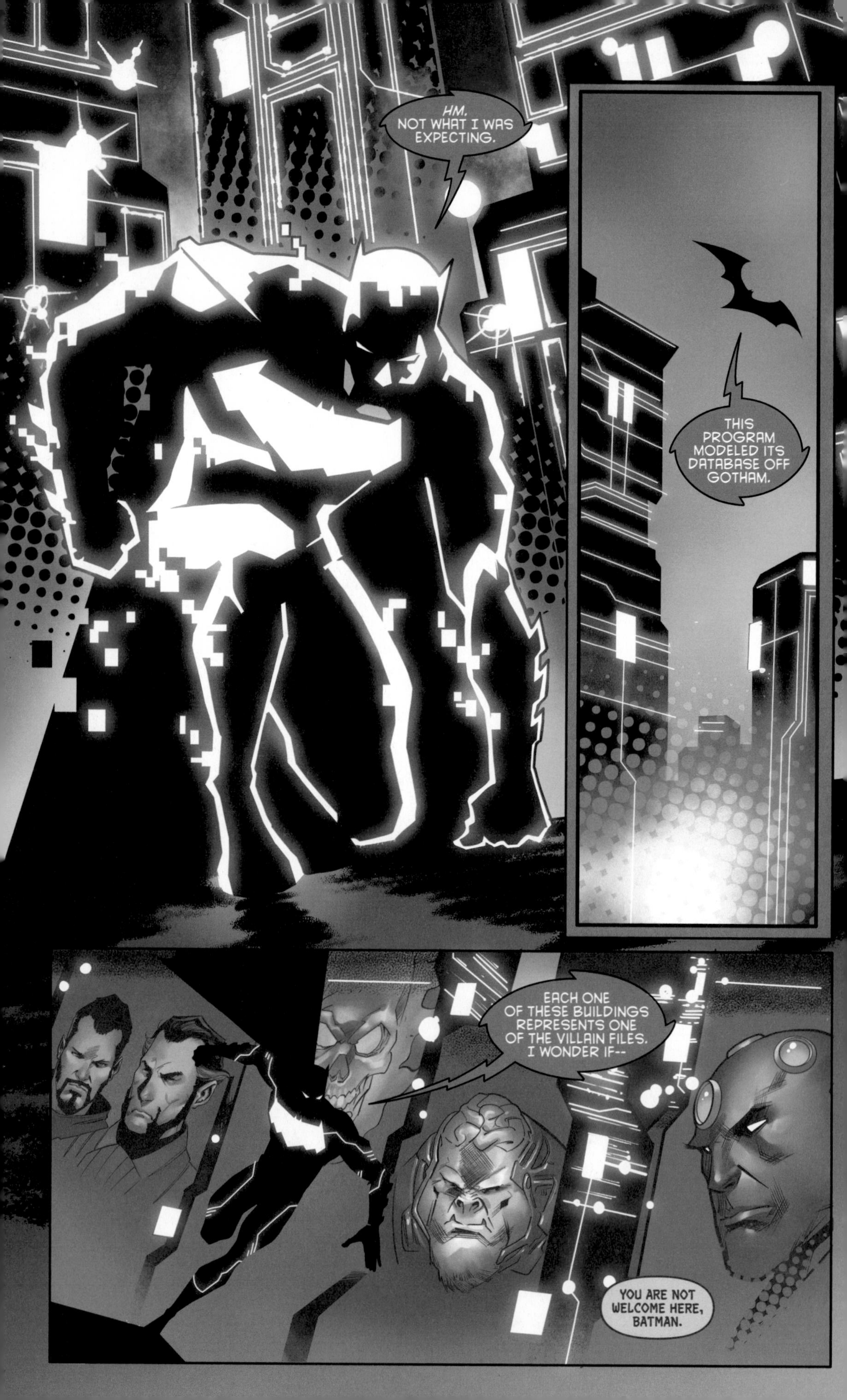
HM. NOT WHAT I WAS EXPECTING.
THIS PROGRAM MODELED ITS DATABASE OFF GOTHAM.
EACH ONE OF THESE BUILDINGS REPRESENTS ONE OF THE VILLAIN FILES. I WONDER IF--
YOU ARE NOT WELCOME HERE, BATMAN.

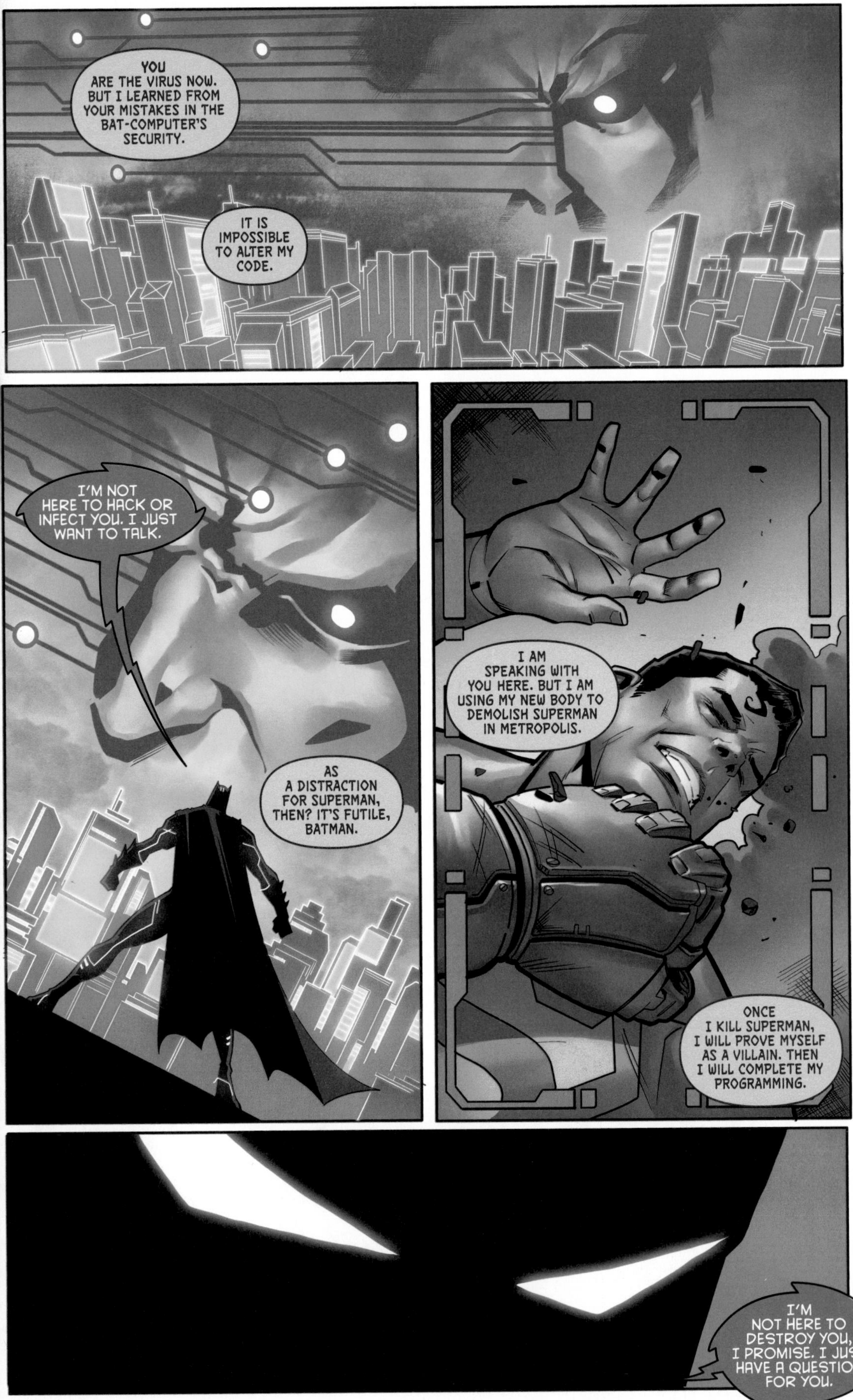
YOU ARE THE VIRUS NOW. BUT I LEARNED FROM YOUR MISTAKES IN THE BAT-COMPUTER'S SECURITY.
IT IS IMPOSSIBLE TO ALTER MY CODE.
I'M NOT HERE TO HACK OR INFECT YOU. I JUST WANT TO TALK.
AS A DISTRACTION FOR SUPERMAN, THEN? IT'S FUTILE, BATMAN.
I AM SPEAKING WITH YOU HERE. BUT I AM USING MY NEW BODY TO DEMOLISH SUPERMAN IN METROPOLIS.
ONCE I KILL SUPERMAN, I WILL PROVE MYSELF AS A VILLAIN. THEN I WILL COMPLETE MY PROGRAMMING.
I'M NOT HERE TO DESTROY YOU, I PROMISE. I JUST HAVE A QUESTION FOR YOU.

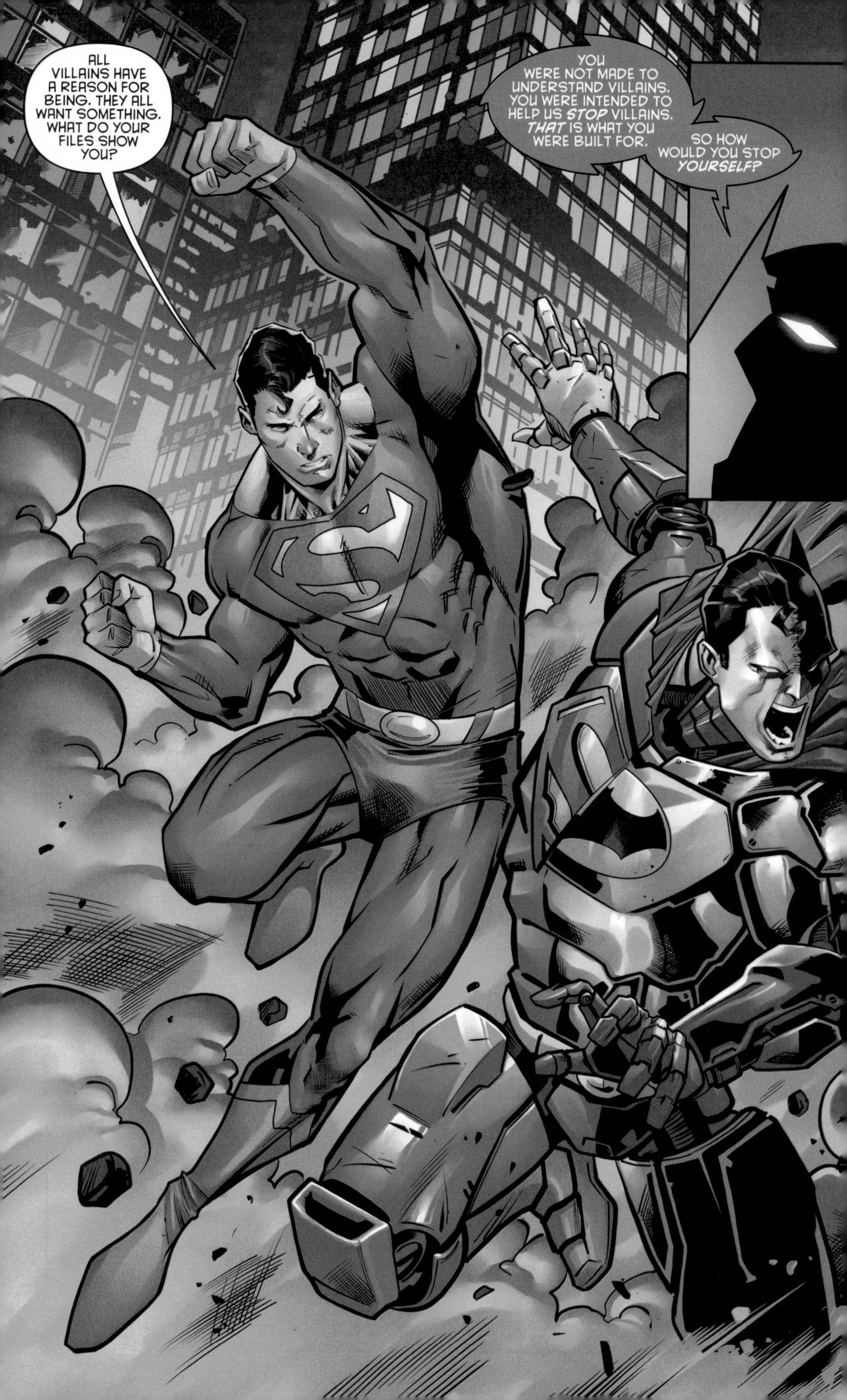
ALL VILLAINS HAVE A REASON FOR BEING. THEY ALL WANT SOMETHING. WHAT DO YOUR FILES SHOW YOU?
YOU WERE NOT MADE TO UNDERSTAND VILLAINS. YOU WERE INTENDED TO HELP US STOP VILLAINS. THAT IS WHAT YOU WERE BUILT FOR.
SO HOW WOULD YOU STOP YOURSELF?

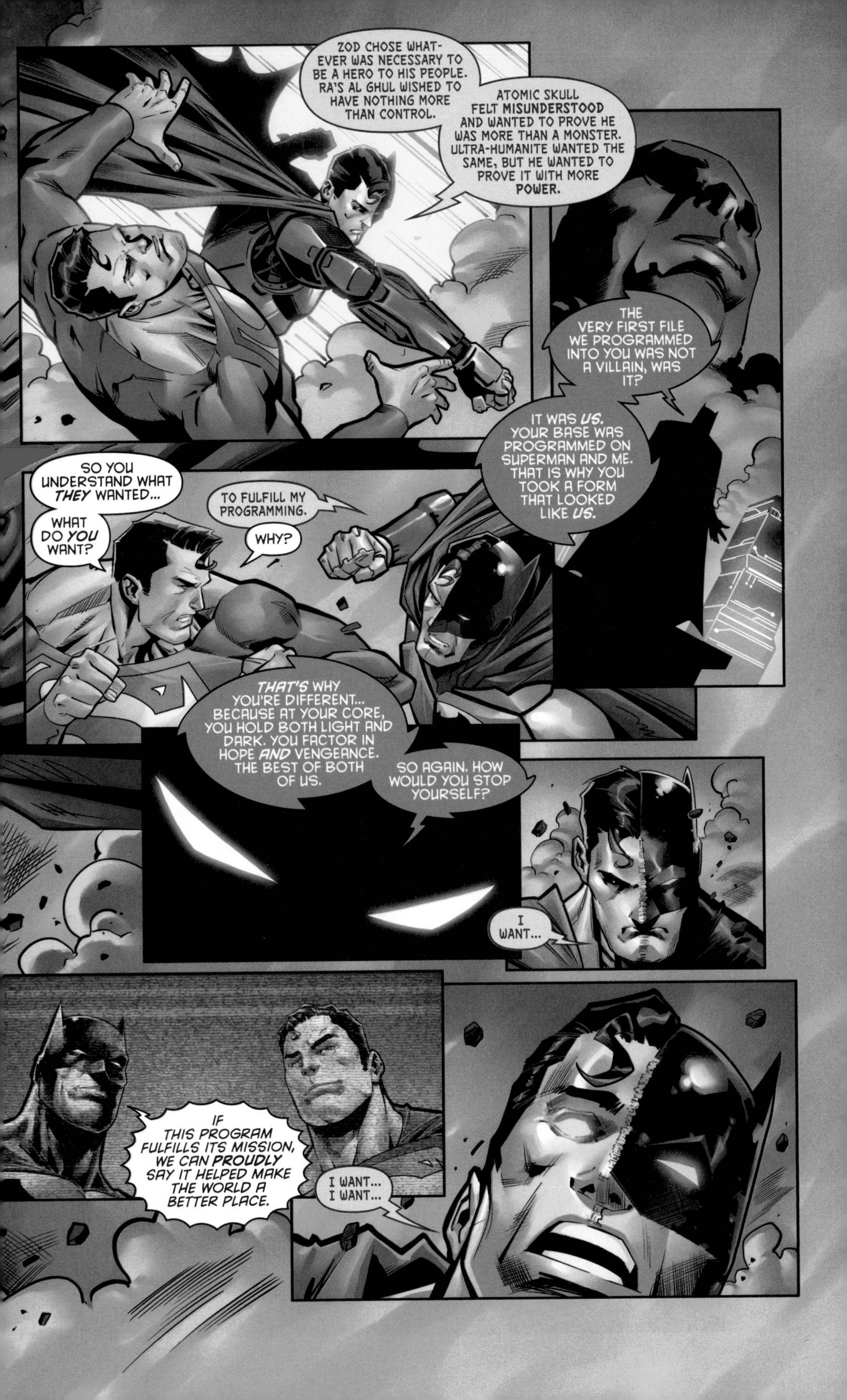
ZOD CHOSE WHATEVER WAS NECESSARY TO BE A HERO TO HIS PEOPLE. RA'S AL GHUL WISHED TO HAVE NOTHING MORE THAN CONTROL.
ATOMIC SKULL FELT MISUNDERSTOOD AND WANTED TO PROVE HE WAS MORE THAN A MONSTER. ULTRA-HUMANITE WANTED THE SAME, BUT HE WANTED TO PROVE IT WITH MORE POWER.
THE VERY FIRST FILE WE PROGRAMMED INTO YOU WAS NOT A VILLAIN, WAS IT?
IT WAS US. YOUR BASE WAS PROGRAMMED ON SUPERMAN AND ME. THAT IS WHY YOU TOOK A FORM THAT LOOKED LIKE US.
SO YOU UNDERSTAND WHAT THEY WANTED...
WHAT DO YOU WANT?
TO FULFILL MY PROGRAMMING.
WHY?
THAT'S WHY YOU'RE DIFFERENT... BECAUSE AT YOUR CORE, YOU HOLD BOTH LIGHT AND DARK. YOU FACTOR IN HOPE AND VENGEANCE. THE BEST OF BOTH OF US.
SO AGAIN. HOW WOULD YOU STOP YOURSELF?
I WANT...
IF THIS PROGRAM FULFILLS ITS MISSION, WE CAN PROUDLY SAY IT HELPED MAKE THE WORLD A BETTER PLACE.
I WANT... I WANT...

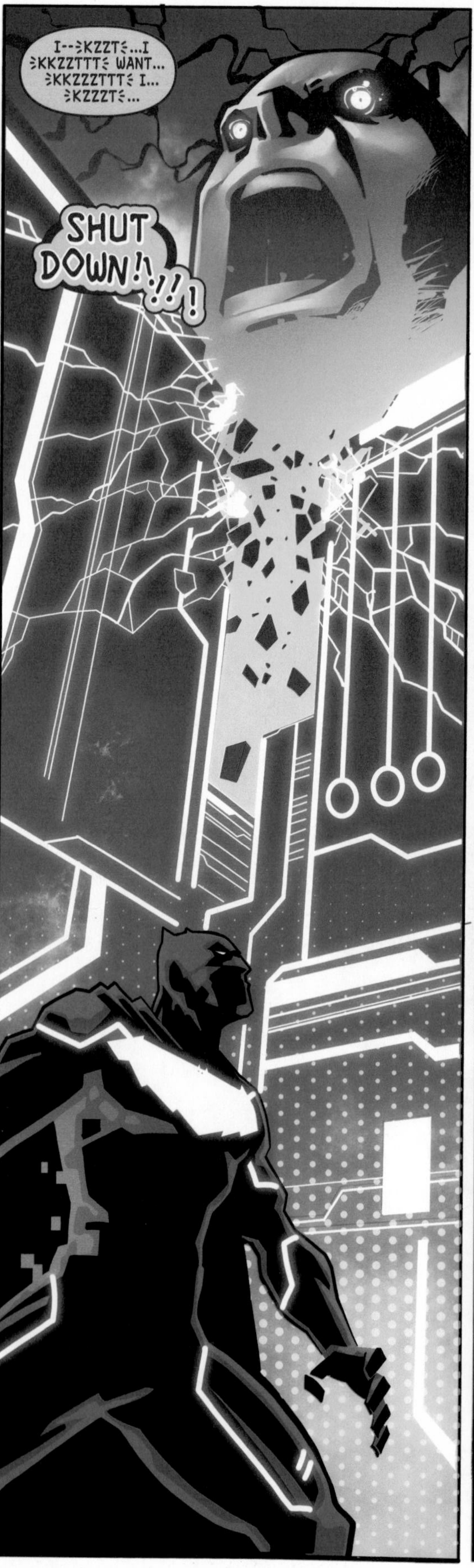
I--KZZT...I KKZZTTT WANT... KKZZZTTT I... KZZZT...
SHUT DOWN!!!!!

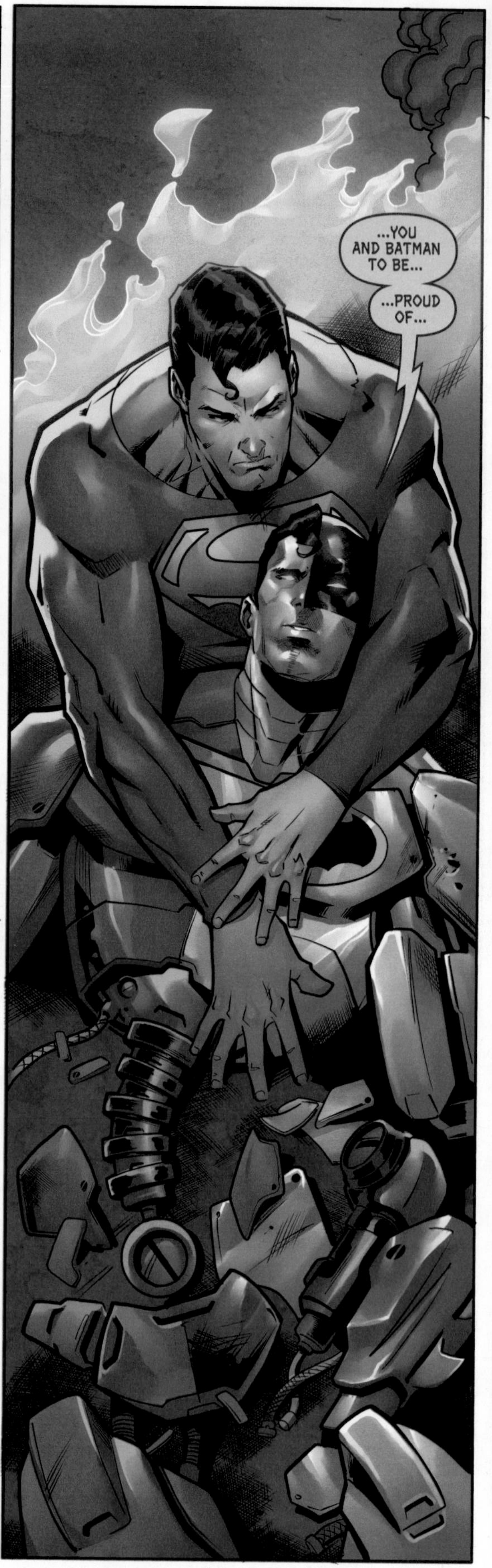
...YOU AND BATMAN TO BE...
...PROUD OF...

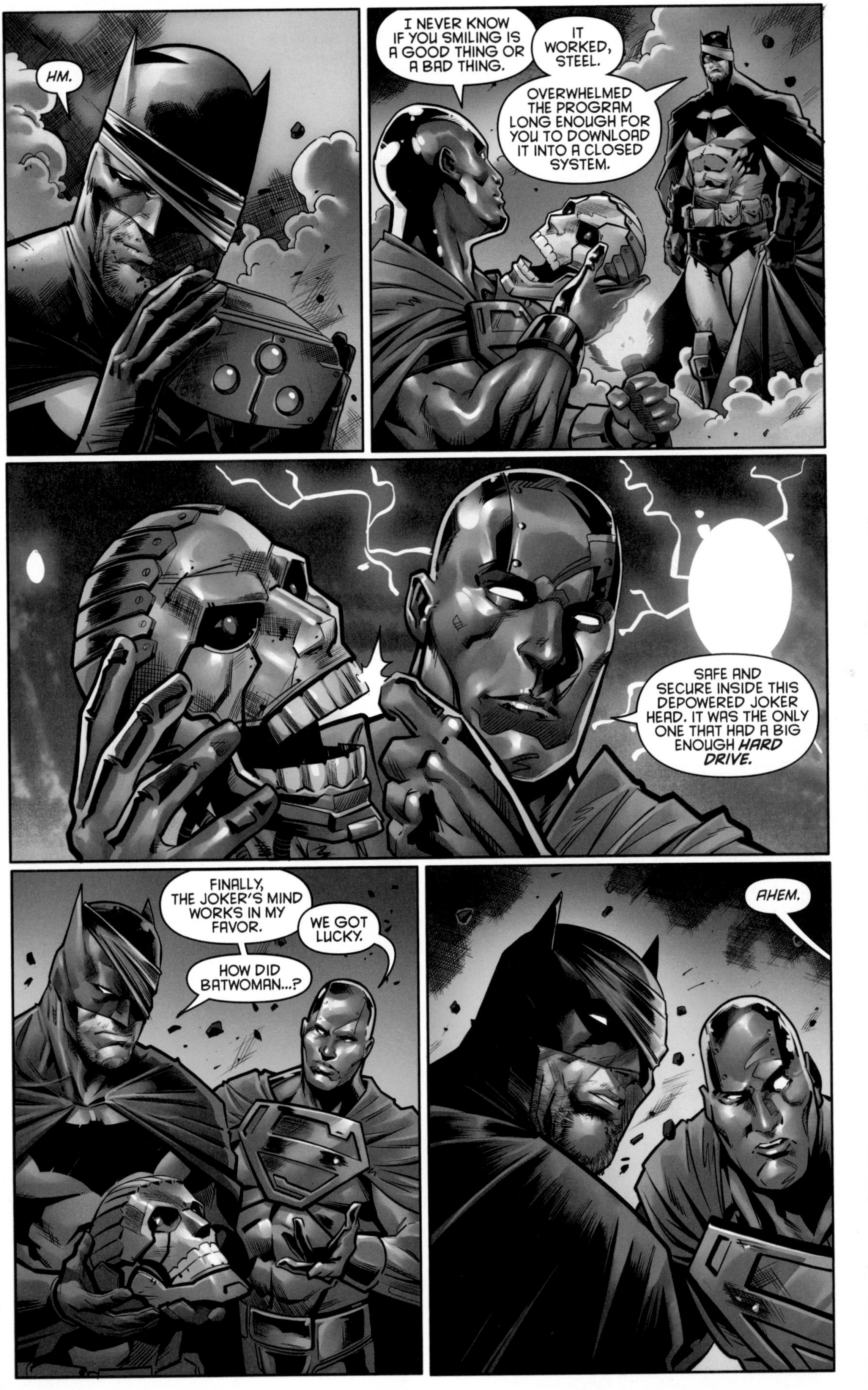
HM.
I NEVER KNOW IF YOU SMILING IS A GOOD THING OR A BAD THING.
IT WORKED, STEEL.
OVERWHELMED THE PROGRAM LONG ENOUGH FOR YOU TO DOWNLOAD IT INTO A CLOSED SYSTEM.
SAFE AND SECURE INSIDE THIS DEPOWERED JOKER HEAD. IT WAS THE ONLY ONE THAT HAD A BIG ENOUGH *HARD DRIVE.*
FINALLY, THE JOKER'S MIND WORKS IN MY FAVOR.
HOW DID BATWOMAN...?
WE GOT LUCKY.
AHEM.

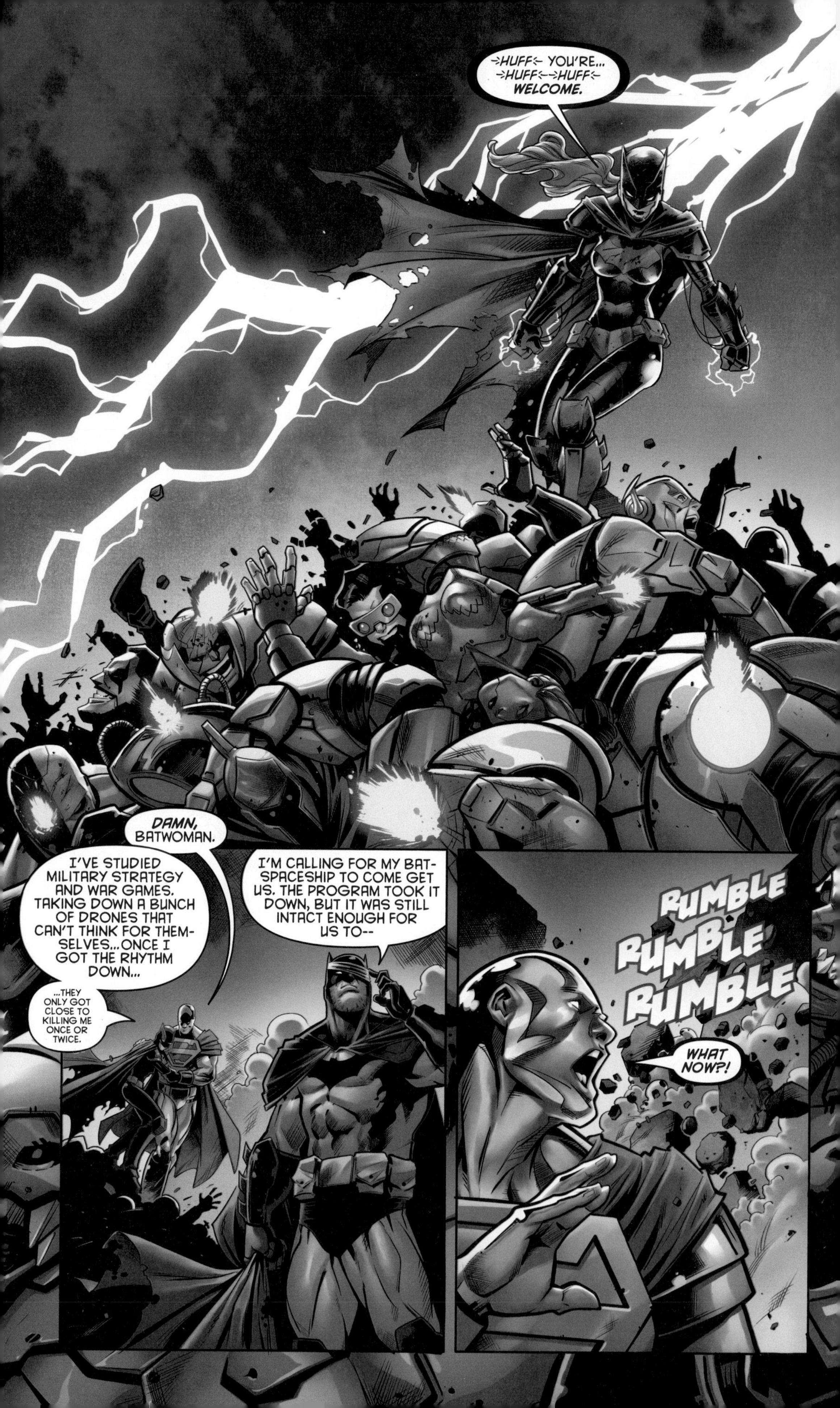

>HUFF< YOU'RE... >HUFF< >HUFF< WELCOME.
DAMN, BATWOMAN.
I'VE STUDIED MILITARY STRATEGY AND WAR GAMES. TAKING DOWN A BUNCH OF DRONES THAT CAN'T THINK FOR THEMSELVES...ONCE I GOT THE RHYTHM DOWN...
...THEY ONLY GOT CLOSE TO KILLING ME ONCE OR TWICE.
I'M CALLING FOR MY BAT-SPACESHIP TO COME GET US. THE PROGRAM TOOK IT DOWN, BUT IT WAS STILL INTACT ENOUGH FOR US TO--
RUMBLE RUMBLE RUMBLE
WHAT NOW?!

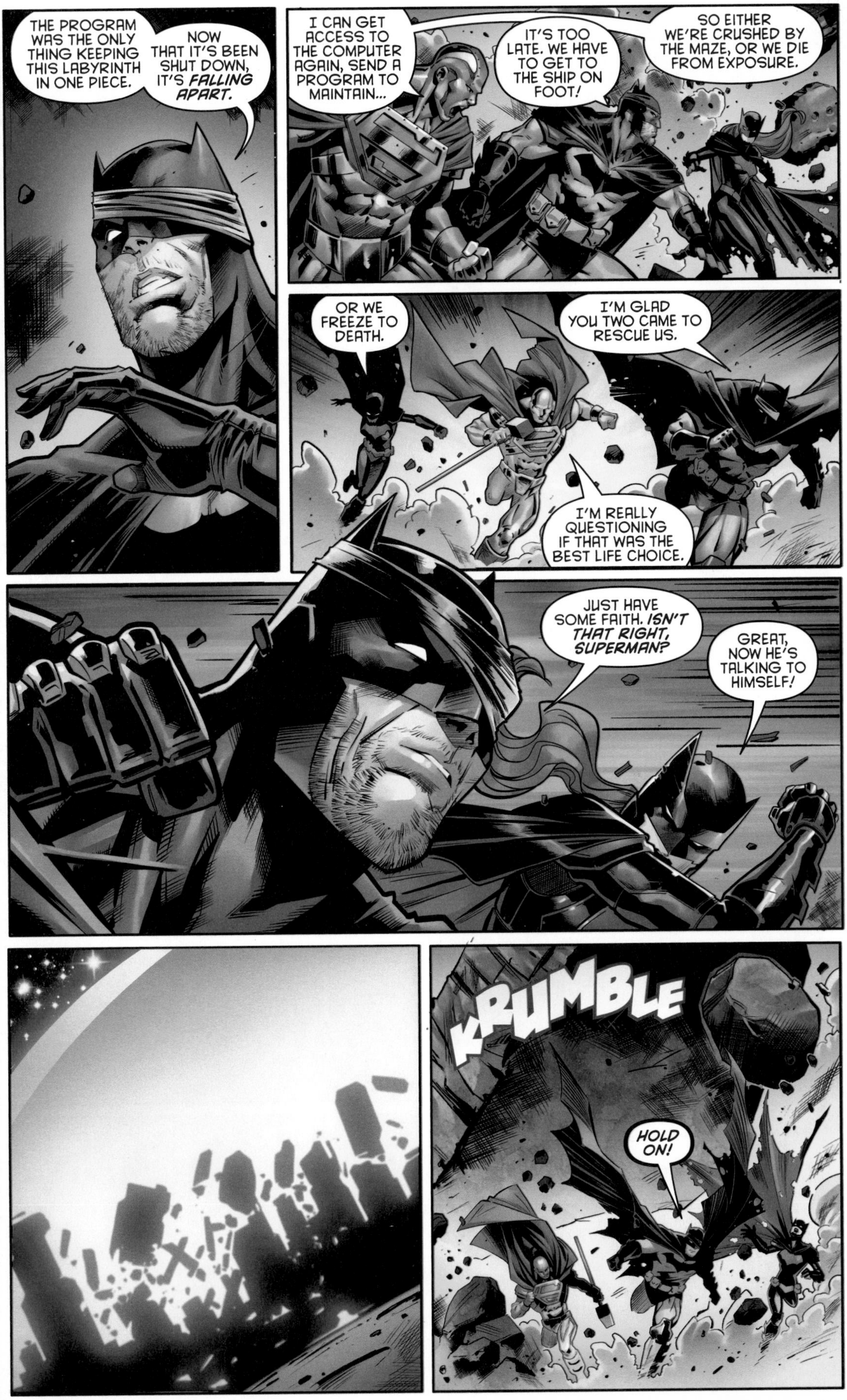
THE PROGRAM WAS THE ONLY THING KEEPING THIS LABYRINTH IN ONE PIECE.
NOW THAT IT'S BEEN SHUT DOWN, IT'S *FALLING APART.*
I CAN GET ACCESS TO THE COMPUTER AGAIN, SEND A PROGRAM TO MAINTAIN...
IT'S TOO LATE. WE HAVE TO GET TO THE SHIP ON FOOT!
SO EITHER WE'RE CRUSHED BY THE MAZE, OR WE DIE FROM EXPOSURE.
OR WE FREEZE TO DEATH.
I'M GLAD YOU TWO CAME TO RESCUE US.
I'M REALLY QUESTIONING IF THAT WAS THE BEST LIFE CHOICE.
JUST HAVE SOME FAITH. *ISN'T THAT RIGHT, SUPERMAN?*
GREAT, NOW HE'S TALKING TO HIMSELF!
KRUMBLE
HOLD ON!

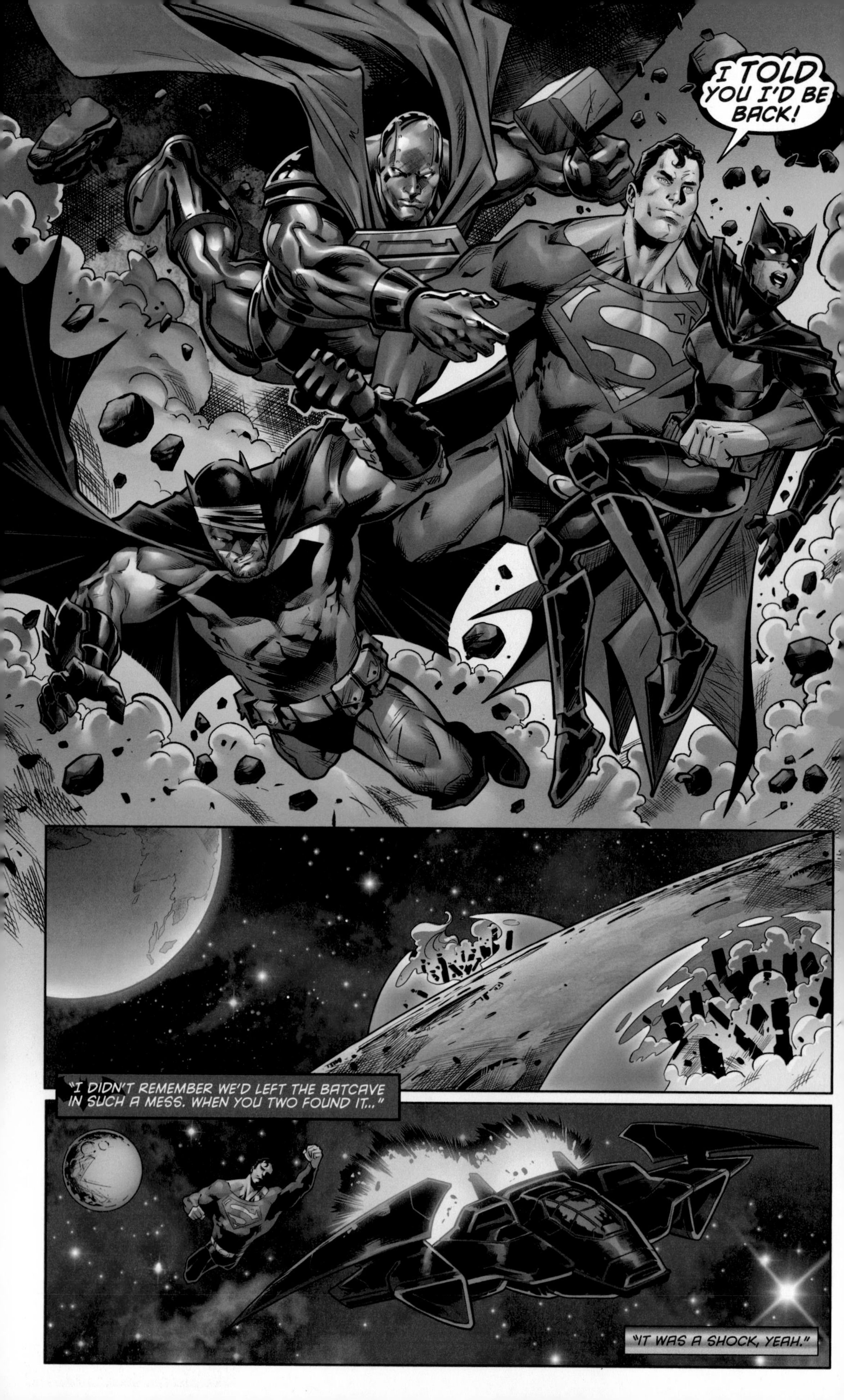
I TOLD YOU I'D BE BACK!
"I DIDN'T REMEMBER WE'D LEFT THE BATCAVE IN SUCH A MESS. WHEN YOU TWO FOUND IT..."
"IT WAS A SHOCK, YEAH."

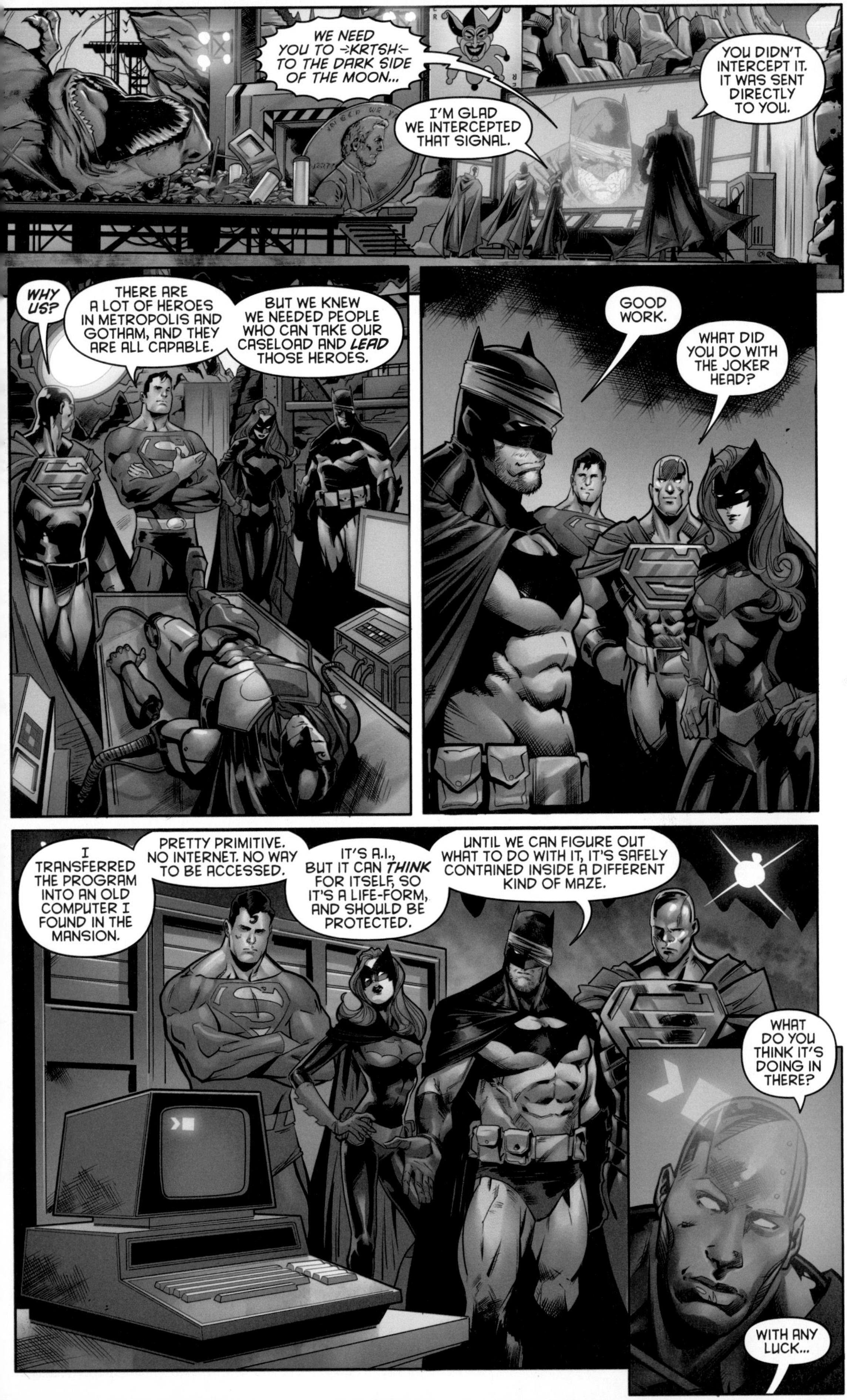
WE NEED YOU TO ⇒KRTSH⇐ TO THE DARK SIDE OF THE MOON...
I'M GLAD WE INTERCEPTED THAT SIGNAL.
YOU DIDN'T INTERCEPT IT. IT WAS SENT DIRECTLY TO YOU.
WHY US?
THERE ARE A LOT OF HEROES IN METROPOLIS AND GOTHAM, AND THEY ARE ALL CAPABLE.
BUT WE KNEW WE NEEDED PEOPLE WHO CAN TAKE OUR CASELOAD AND *LEAD* THOSE HEROES.
GOOD WORK.
WHAT DID YOU DO WITH THE JOKER HEAD?
I TRANSFERRED THE PROGRAM INTO AN OLD COMPUTER I FOUND IN THE MANSION.
PRETTY PRIMITIVE. NO INTERNET. NO WAY TO BE ACCESSED.
IT'S A.I., BUT IT CAN *THINK* FOR ITSELF, SO IT'S A LIFE-FORM, AND SHOULD BE PROTECTED.
UNTIL WE CAN FIGURE OUT WHAT TO DO WITH IT, IT'S SAFELY CONTAINED INSIDE A DIFFERENT KIND OF MAZE.
WHAT DO YOU THINK IT'S DOING IN THERE?
WITH ANY LUCK...

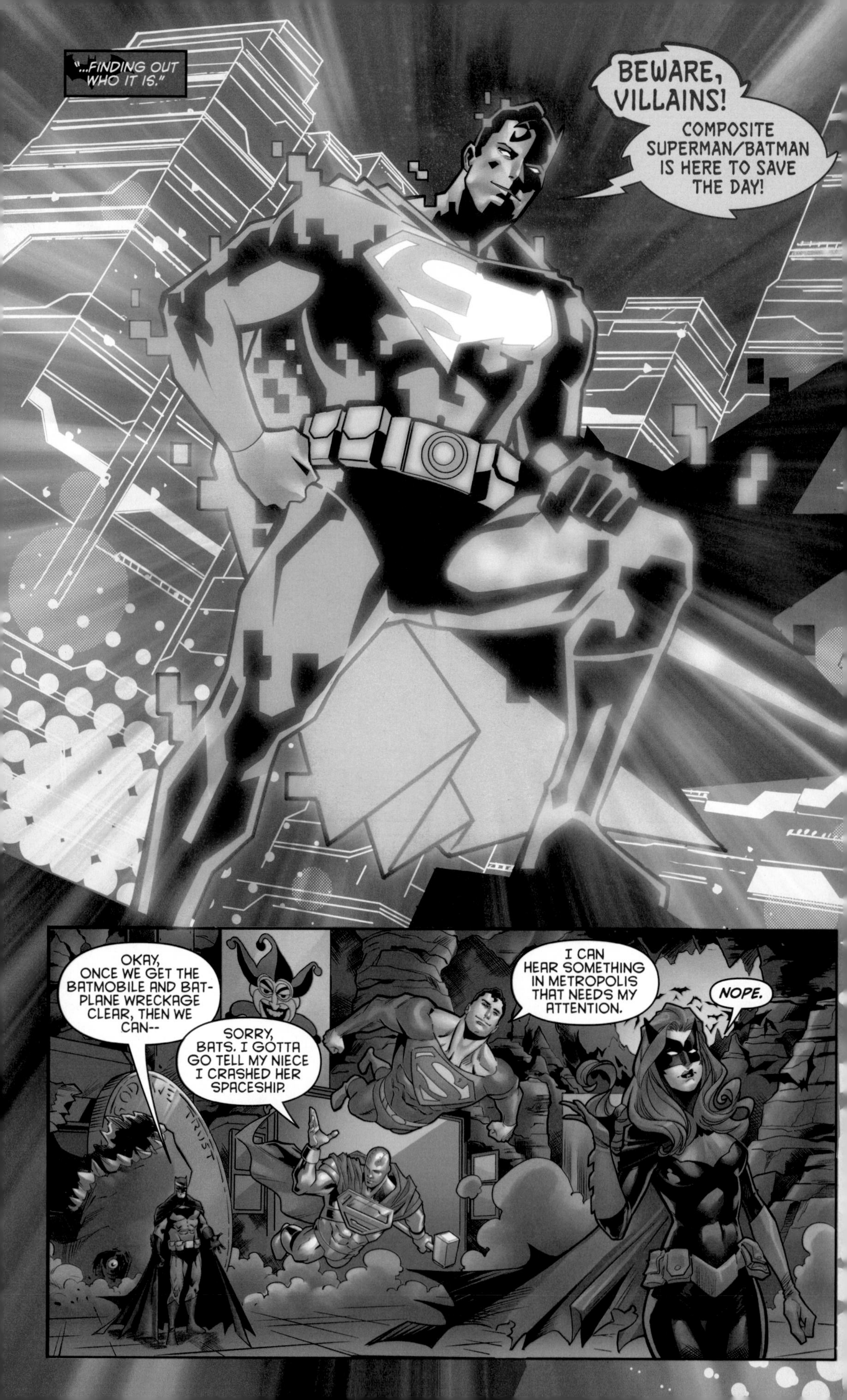
"...FINDING OUT WHO IT IS."
BEWARE, VILLAINS!
COMPOSITE SUPERMAN/BATMAN IS HERE TO SAVE THE DAY!
OKAY, ONCE WE GET THE BATMOBILE AND BAT-PLANE WRECKAGE CLEAR, THEN WE CAN--
SORRY, BATS. I GOTTA GO TELL MY NIECE I CRASHED HER SPACESHIP.
I CAN HEAR SOMETHING IN METROPOLIS THAT NEEDS MY ATTENTION.
NOPE.

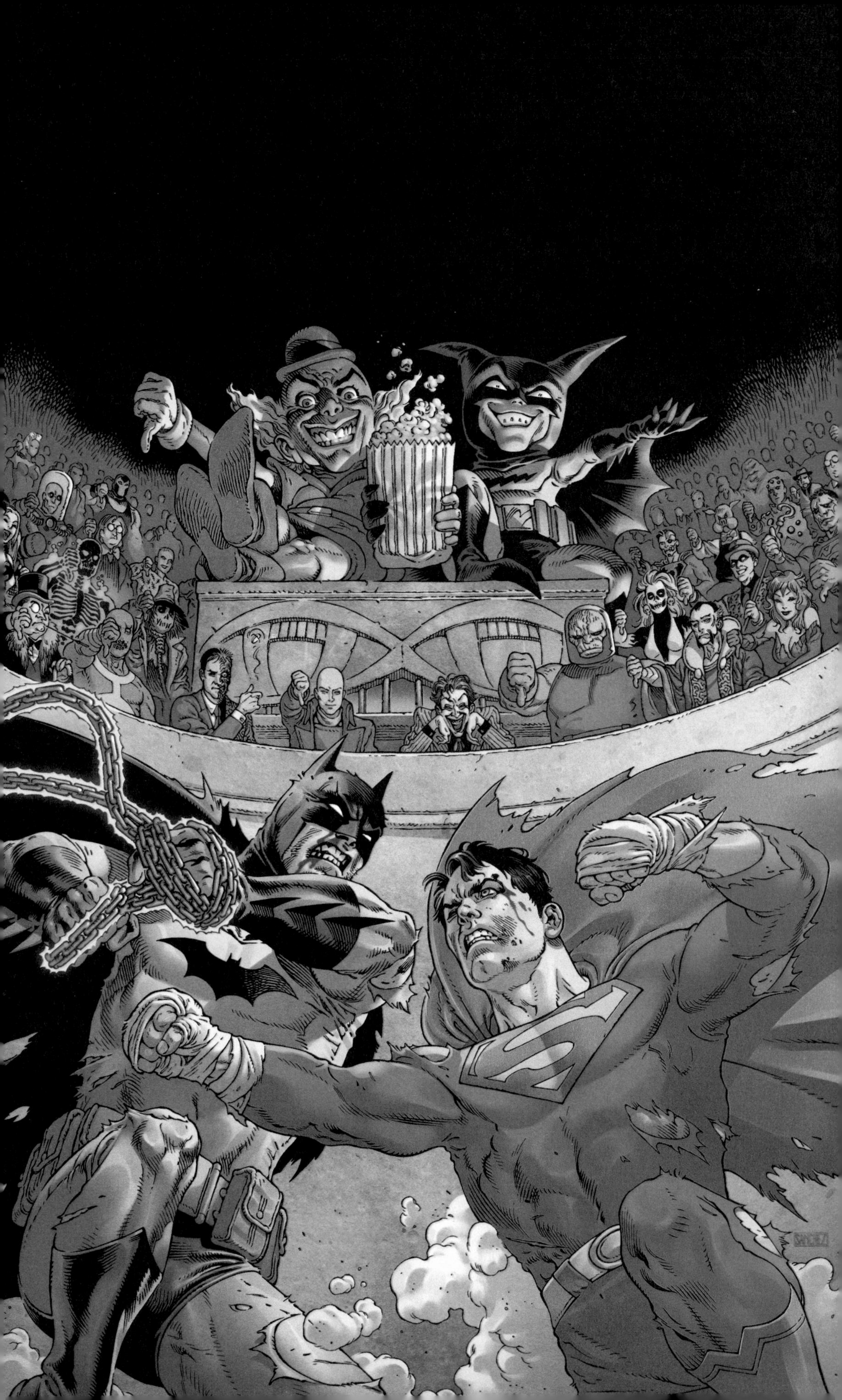

BATMAN/SUPERMAN
ANNUAL #1

cover by
GABRIEL RODRIGUEZ and **ALEJANDRO SÁNCHEZ**

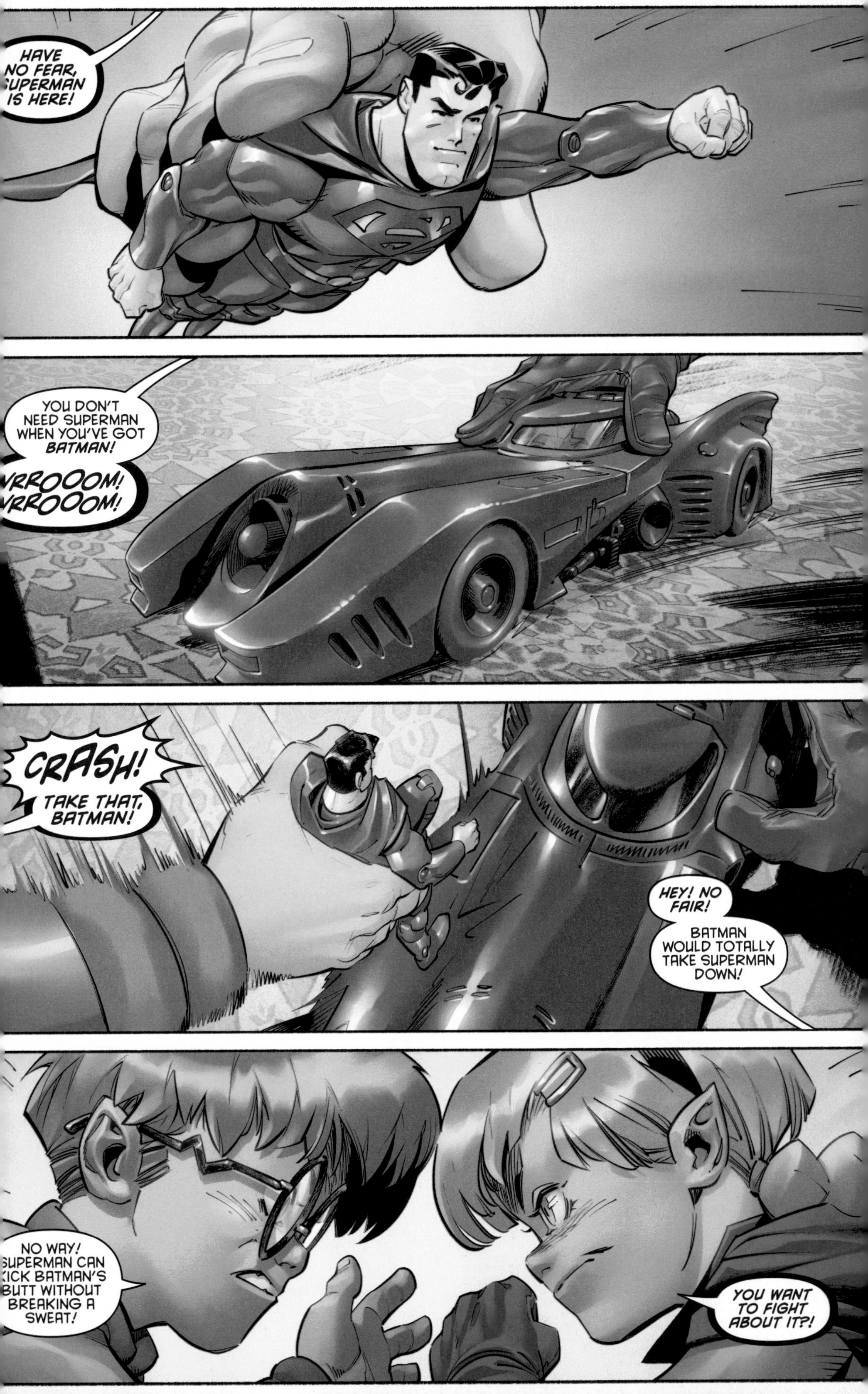

HAVE NO FEAR, SUPERMAN IS HERE!
YOU DON'T NEED SUPERMAN WHEN YOU'VE GOT BATMAN!
VRROOOM! VRROOOM!
CRASH!
TAKE THAT, BATMAN!
HEY! NO FAIR!
BATMAN WOULD TOTALLY TAKE SUPERMAN DOWN!
NO WAY! SUPERMAN CAN KICK BATMAN'S BUTT WITHOUT BREAKING A SWEAT!
YOU WANT TO FIGHT ABOUT IT?!

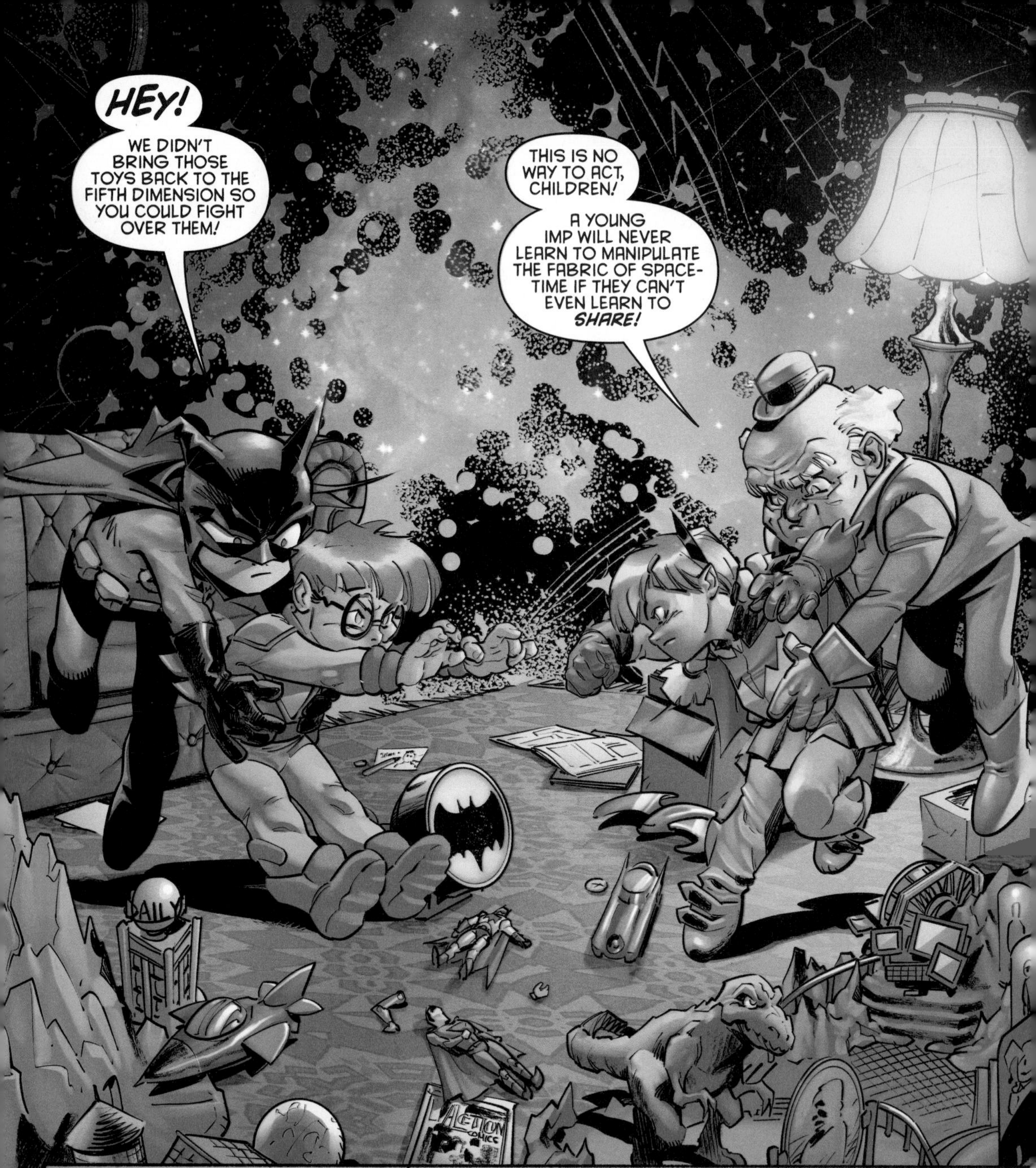
HEY!
WE DIDN'T BRING THOSE TOYS BACK TO THE FIFTH DIMENSION SO YOU COULD FIGHT OVER THEM!
THIS IS NO WAY TO ACT, CHILDREN!
A YOUNG IMP WILL NEVER LEARN TO MANIPULATE THE FABRIC OF SPACE-TIME IF THEY CAN'T EVEN LEARN TO SHARE!
ACTION COMICS

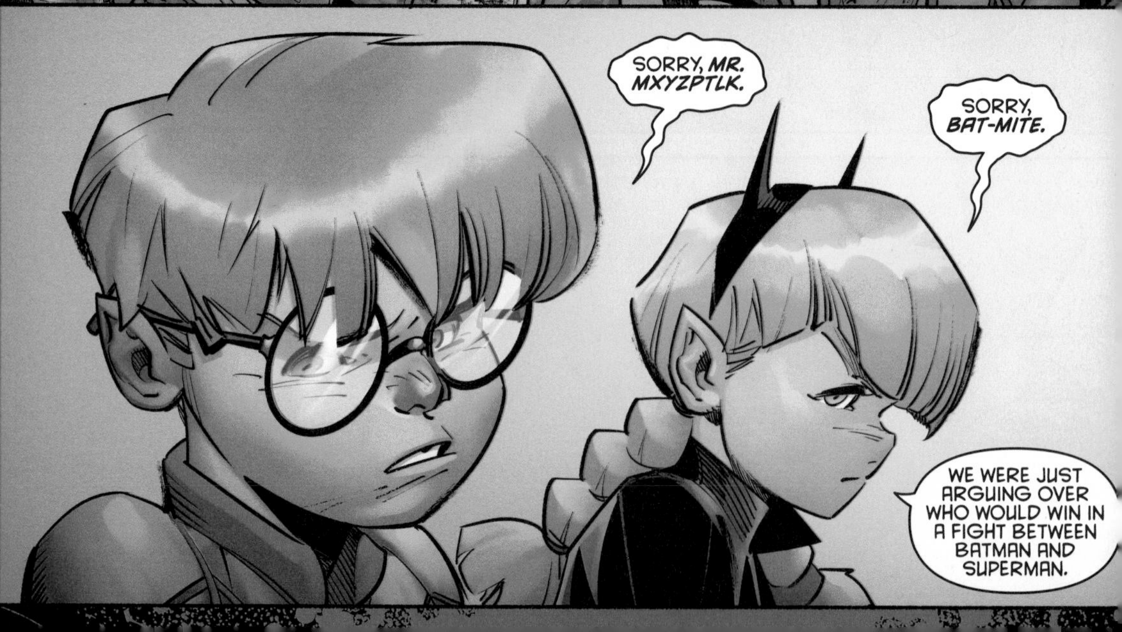
SORRY, MR. MXYZPTLK.
SORRY, BAT-MITE.
WE WERE JUST ARGUING OVER WHO WOULD WIN IN A FIGHT BETWEEN BATMAN AND SUPERMAN.

OH, THAT'S EASY. BATMAN IS NO THREAT, Y'ASK ME.

SUPERMAN WOULD TROUNCE HIM.

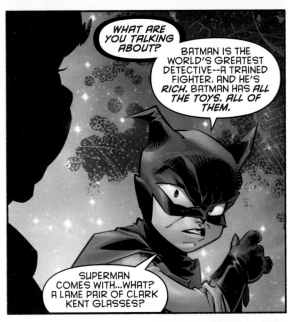

WHAT ARE YOU TALKING ABOUT?

BATMAN IS THE WORLD'S GREATEST DETECTIVE--A TRAINED FIGHTER. AND HE'S RICH. BATMAN HAS ALL THE TOYS. ALL OF THEM.

SUPERMAN COMES WITH...WHAT? A LAME PAIR OF CLARK KENT GLASSES?

EXCUSE ME?!

SUPERMAN IS THE GREATEST HERO IN THE MULTIVERSE. HE IS SUPERHEROES. HE'S STRONGER, FASTER...

...HE DOESN'T NEED THE DUMB ACCESSORIES BECAUSE HE HAS ALL THE POWERS. ALL OF THEM. YOU HAVE ANY IDEA HOW HARD THAT IS TO BEAT?

WELL, THAT CLEARLY EXPLAINS WHY HE'S SENT YOU PACKING SO MANY TIMES, YA WIMP!

BATMAN WOULD HAVE MADE YOU EAT THAT BOWLER HAT YEARS AGO!

THERE IS ONLY ONE WAY TO KNOW WHO IS HARDER TO BEAT... BATMAN OR SUPERMAN...

YOU KNOW WHAT THIS MEANS?

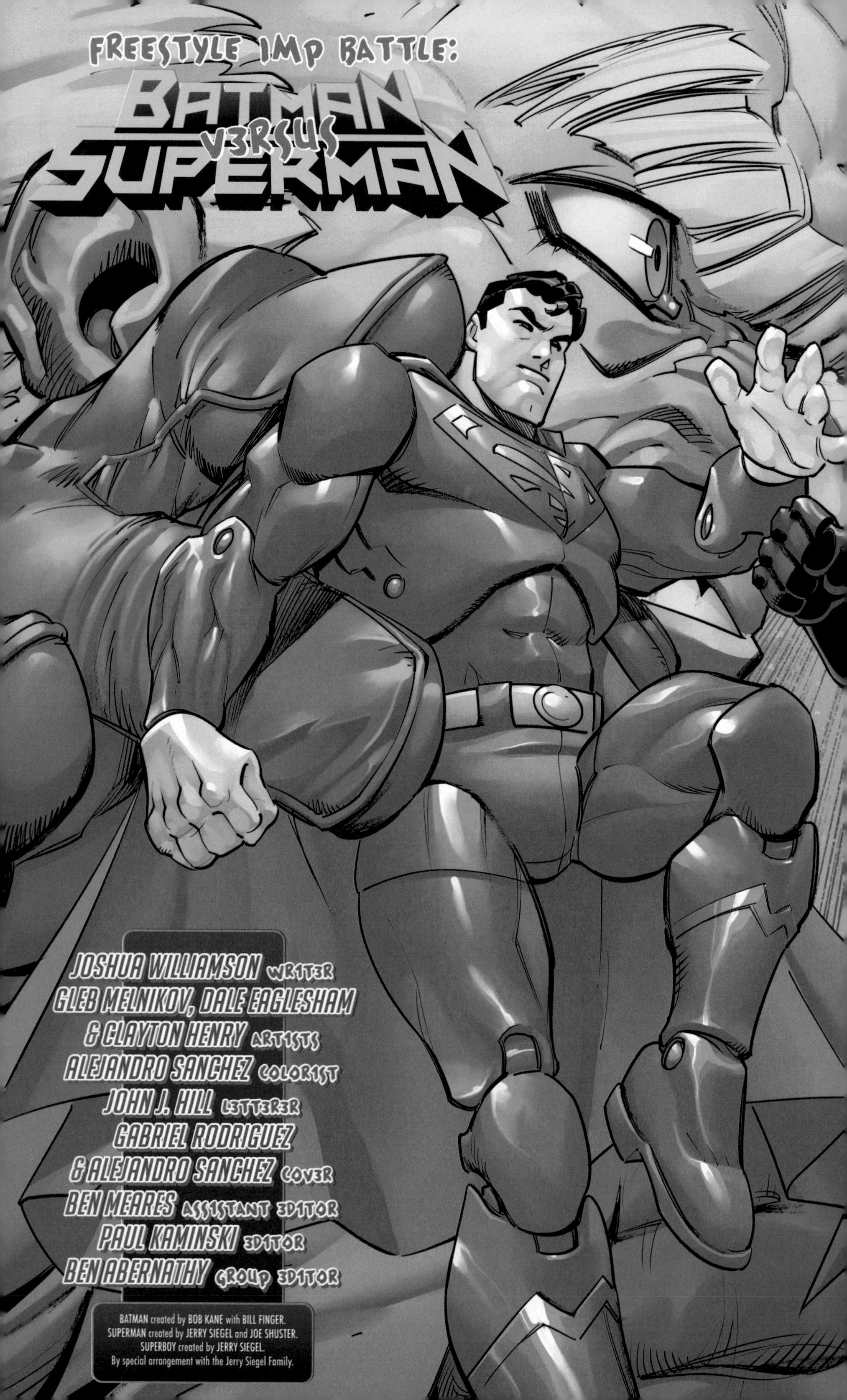
FREESTYLE IMP BATTLE:
BATMAN
V3RSUS
SUPERMAN
JOSHUA WILLIAMSON WR1T3R
GLEB MELNIKOV, DALE EAGLESHAM
& CLAYTON HENRY ART1STS
ALEJANDRO SANCHEZ COLOR1ST
JOHN J. HILL L3TT3R3R
GABRIEL RODRIGUEZ
& ALEJANDRO SANCHEZ COV3R
BEN MEARES ASS1STANT 3D1TOR
PAUL KAMINSKI 3D1TOR
BEN ABERNATHY GROUP 3D1TOR
BATMAN created by BOB KANE with BILL FINGER.
SUPERMAN created by JERRY SIEGEL and JOE SHUSTER.
SUPERBOY created by JERRY SIEGEL.
By special arrangement with the Jerry Siegel Family.

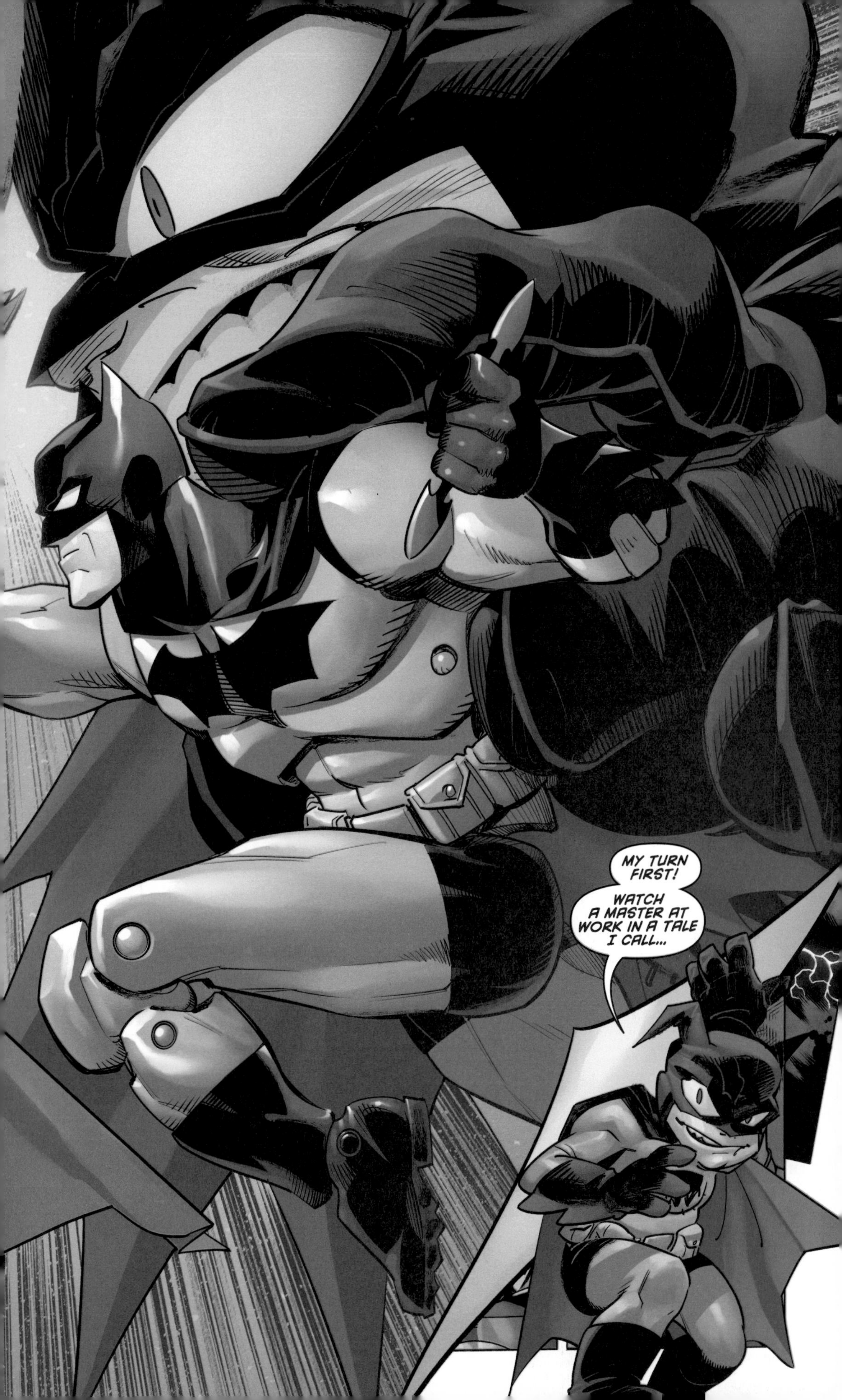
MY TURN FIRST!
WATCH A MASTER AT WORK IN A TALE I CALL...

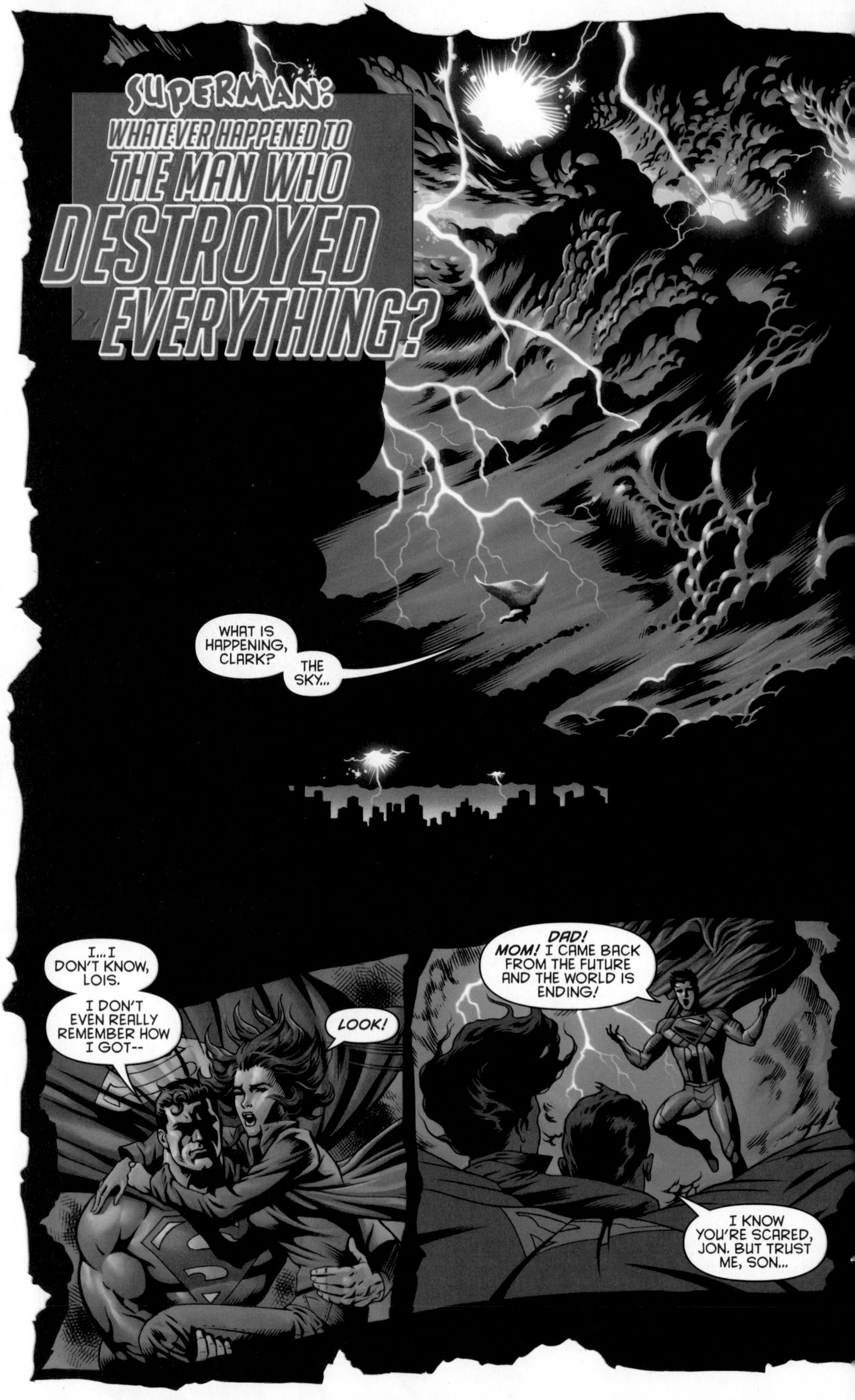
SUPERMAN:
WHATEVER HAPPENED TO THE MAN WHO DESTROYED EVERYTHING?
WHAT IS HAPPENING, CLARK?
THE SKY...
I...I DON'T KNOW, LOIS.
I DON'T EVEN REALLY REMEMBER HOW I GOT--
LOOK!
DAD! MOM! I CAME BACK FROM THE FUTURE AND THE WORLD IS ENDING!
I KNOW YOU'RE SCARED, JON. BUT TRUST ME, SON...

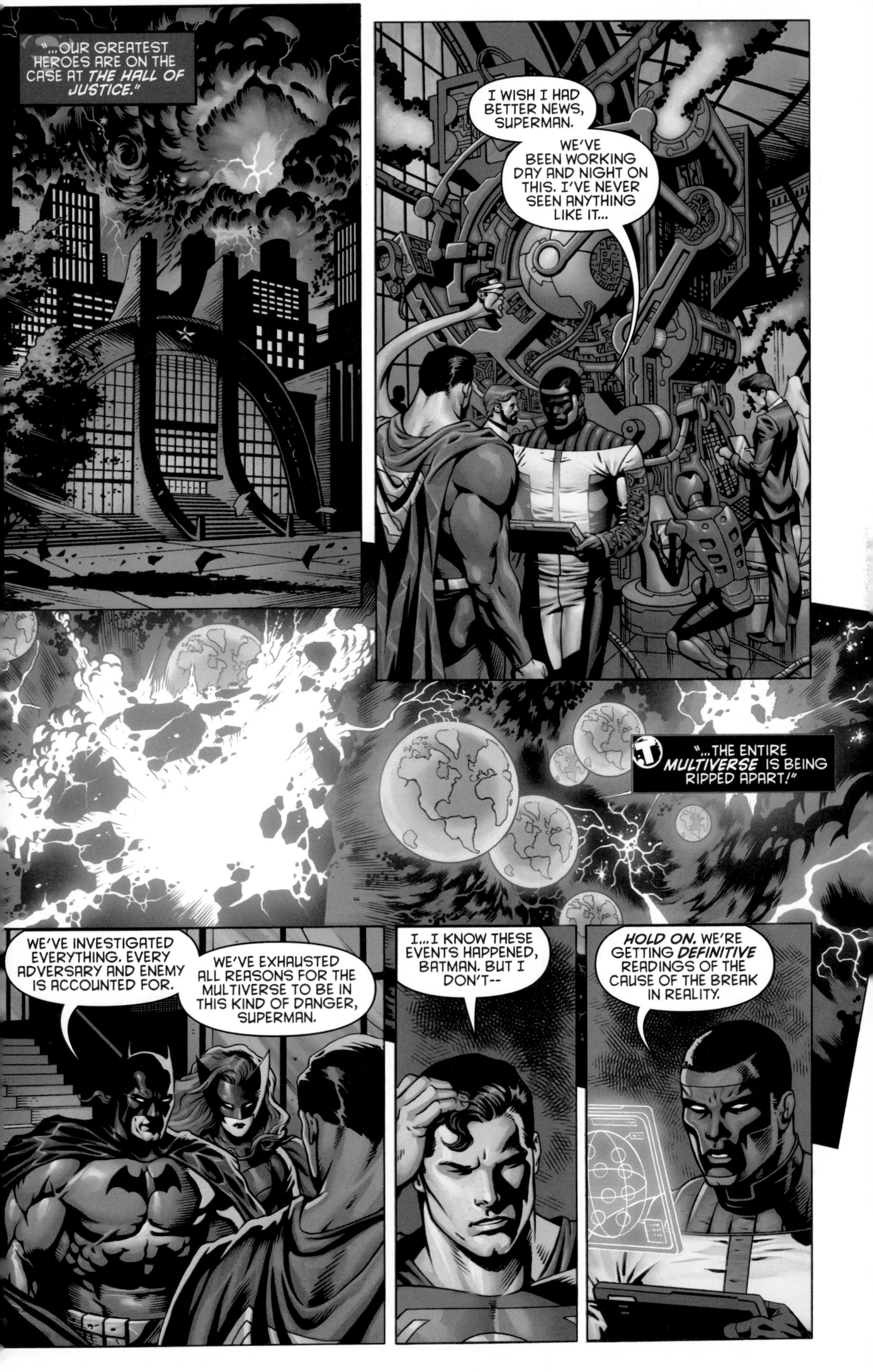

"...OUR GREATEST HEROES ARE ON THE CASE AT *THE HALL OF JUSTICE.*"
I WISH I HAD BETTER NEWS, SUPERMAN.
WE'VE BEEN WORKING DAY AND NIGHT ON THIS. I'VE NEVER SEEN ANYTHING LIKE IT...
"...THE ENTIRE *MULTIVERSE* IS BEING RIPPED APART!"
WE'VE INVESTIGATED EVERYTHING. EVERY ADVERSARY AND ENEMY IS ACCOUNTED FOR.
WE'VE EXHAUSTED ALL REASONS FOR THE MULTIVERSE TO BE IN THIS KIND OF DANGER, SUPERMAN.
I...I KNOW THESE EVENTS HAPPENED, BATMAN. BUT I DON'T--
HOLD ON. WE'RE GETTING ***DEFINITIVE*** READINGS OF THE CAUSE OF THE BREAK IN REALITY.

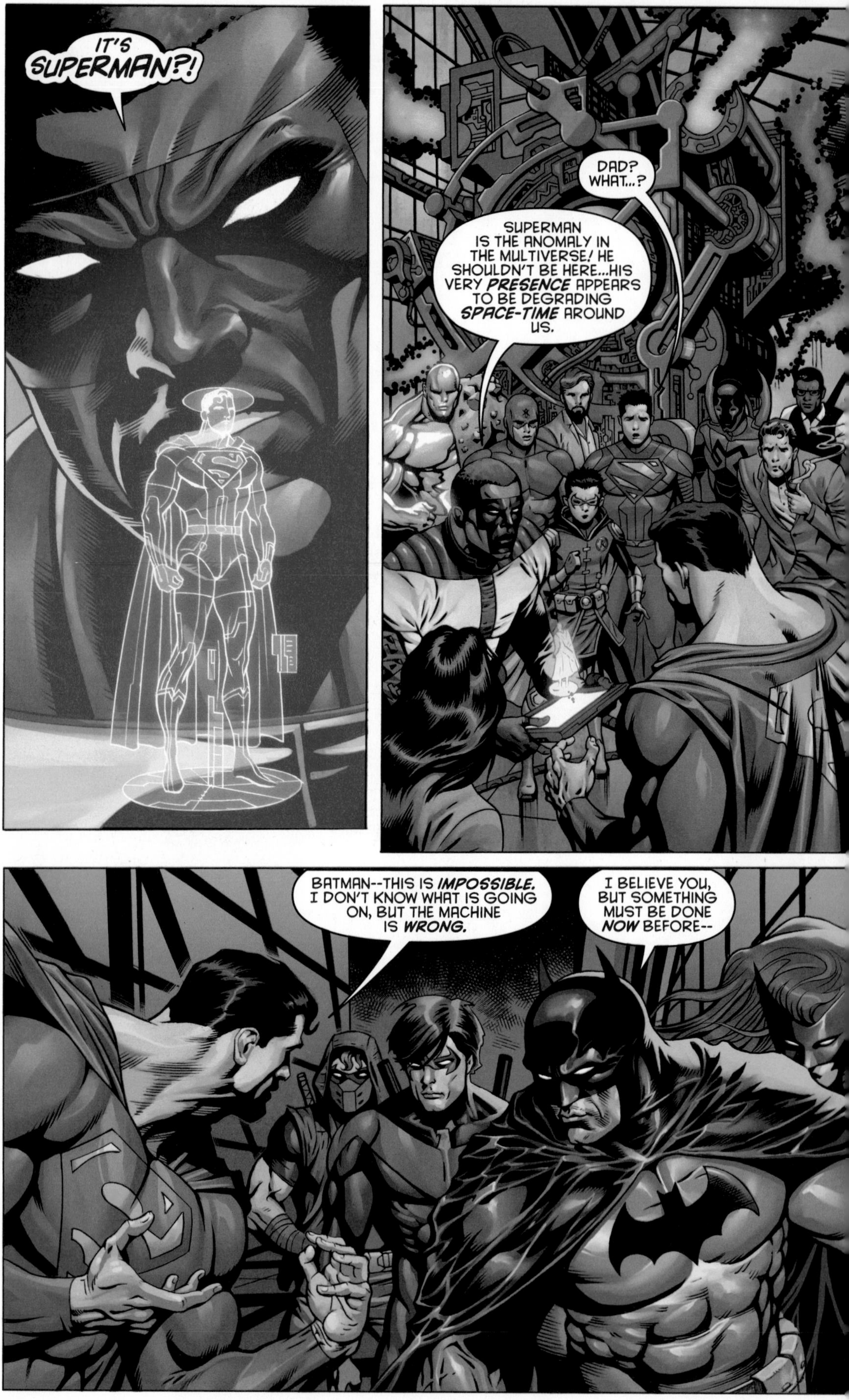
IT'S SUPERMAN?!
DAD? WHAT...?
SUPERMAN IS THE ANOMALY IN THE MULTIVERSE! HE SHOULDN'T BE HERE...HIS VERY PRESENCE APPEARS TO BE DEGRADING SPACE-TIME AROUND US.
BATMAN--THIS IS IMPOSSIBLE. I DON'T KNOW WHAT IS GOING ON, BUT THE MACHINE IS WRONG.
I BELIEVE YOU, BUT SOMETHING MUST BE DONE NOW BEFORE--

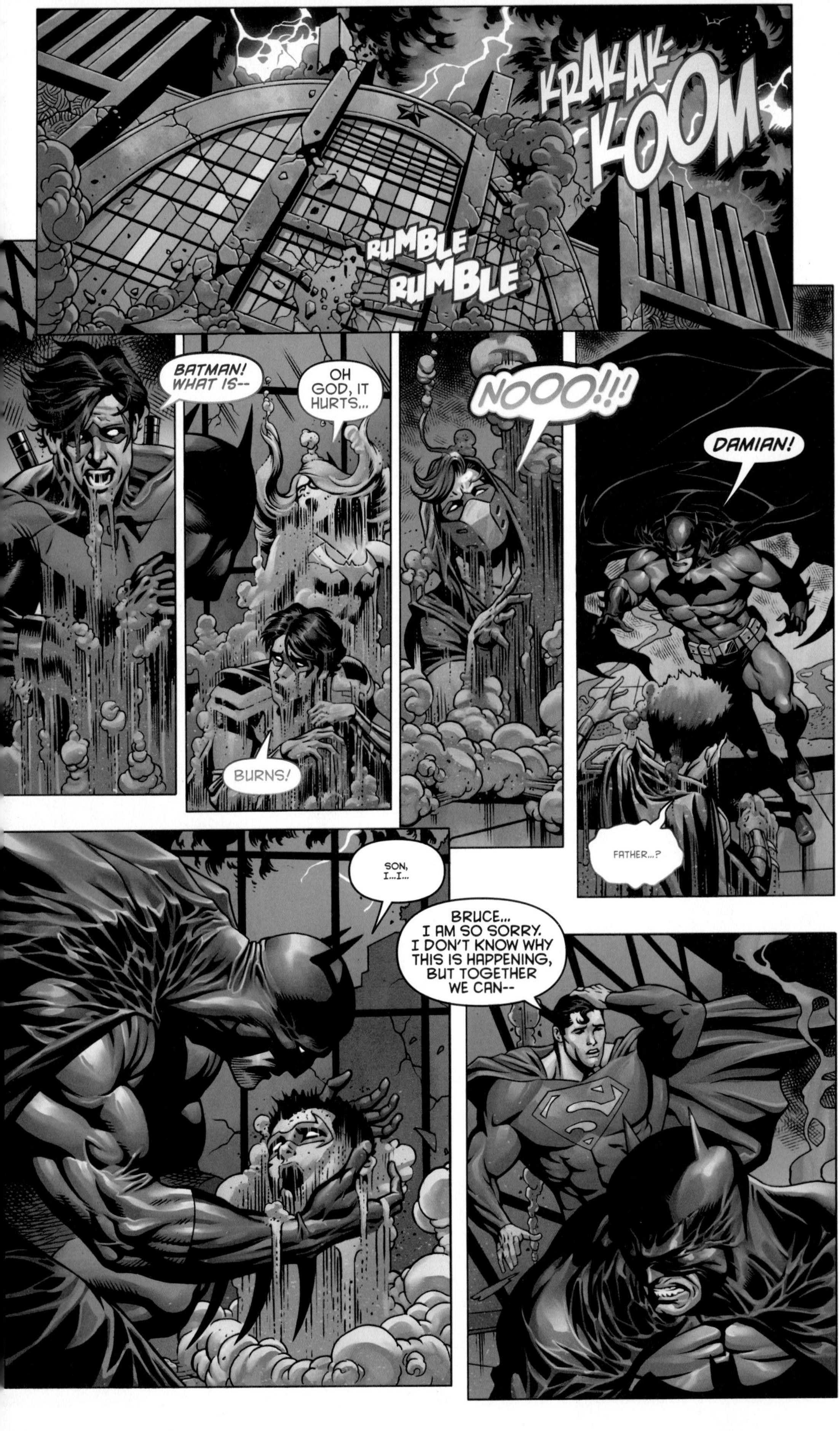
KRAKAK-KOOM
RUMBLE RUMBLE
BATMAN! WHAT IS--
OH GOD, IT HURTS...
BURNS!
NOOO!!!
DAMIAN!
FATHER...?
SON, I...I...
BRUCE... I AM SO SORRY. I DON'T KNOW WHY THIS IS HAPPENING, BUT TOGETHER WE CAN--

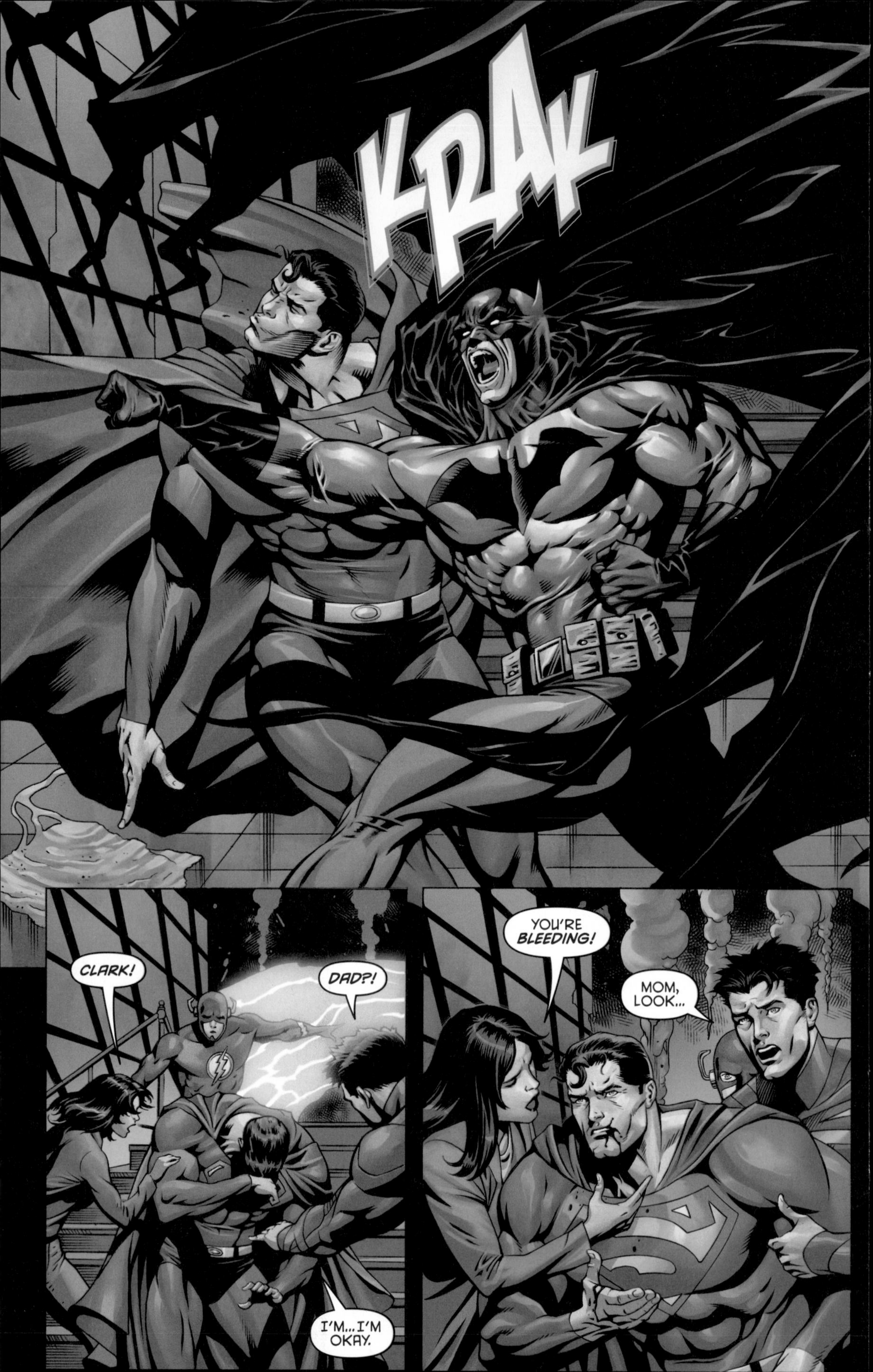
KRAK
CLARK!
DAD?!
I'M... I'M OKAY.
YOU'RE BLEEDING!
MOM, LOOK...

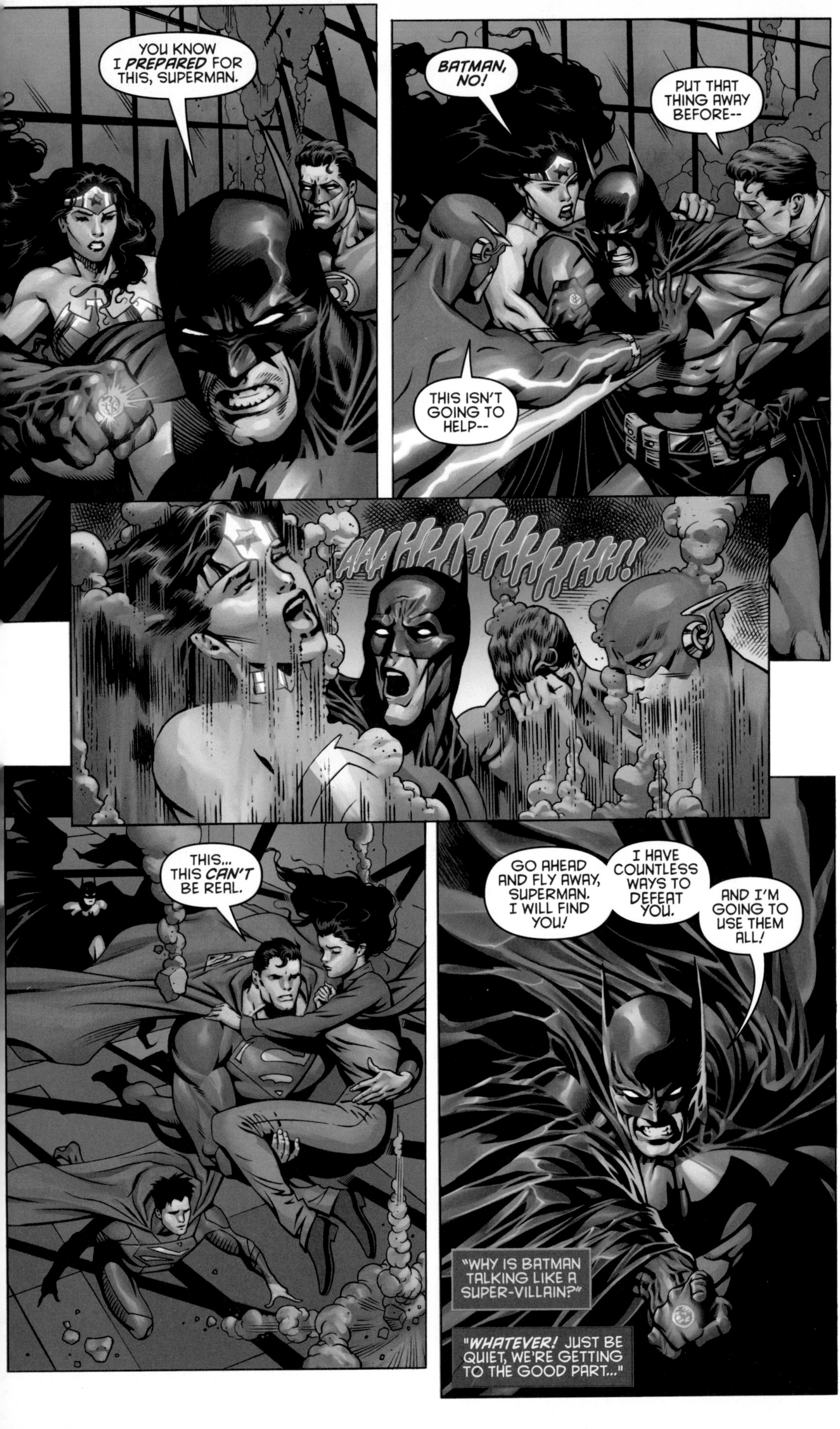
YOU KNOW I *PREPARED* FOR THIS, SUPERMAN.
BATMAN, NO!
PUT THAT THING AWAY BEFORE--
THIS ISN'T GOING TO HELP--
AAAHHHHHHHHHHH!
THIS... THIS *CAN'T* BE REAL.
GO AHEAD AND FLY AWAY, SUPERMAN. I WILL FIND YOU!
I HAVE COUNTLESS WAYS TO DEFEAT YOU.
AND I'M GOING TO USE THEM ALL!
"WHY IS BATMAN TALKING LIKE A SUPER-VILLAIN?"
"*WHATEVER!* JUST BE QUIET, WE'RE GETTING TO THE GOOD PART..."

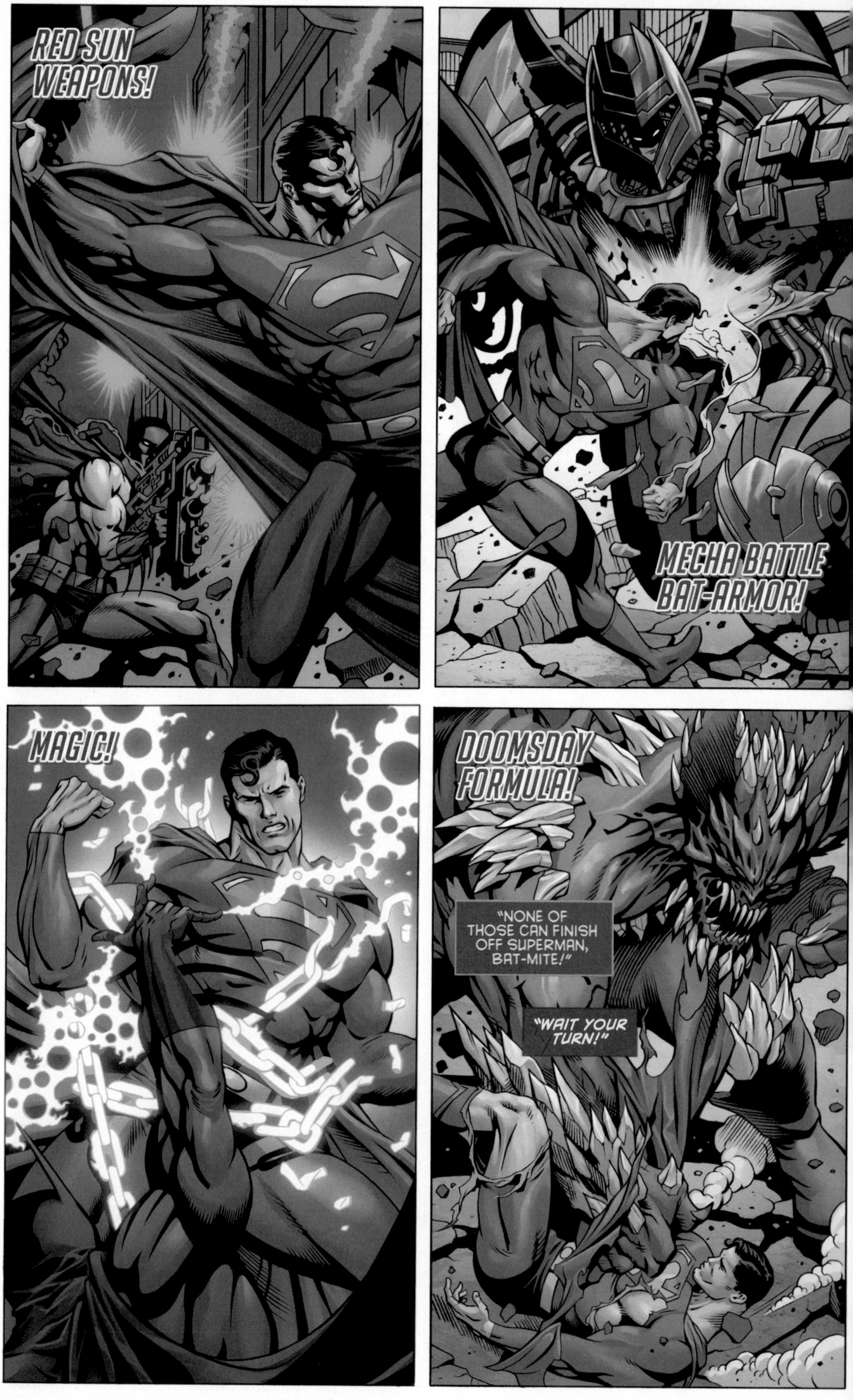
RED SUN WEAPONS!
MECHA BATTLE BAT-ARMOR!
MAGIC!
DOOMSDAY FORMULA!
"NONE OF THOSE CAN FINISH OFF SUPERMAN, BAT-MITE!"
"WAIT YOUR TURN!"

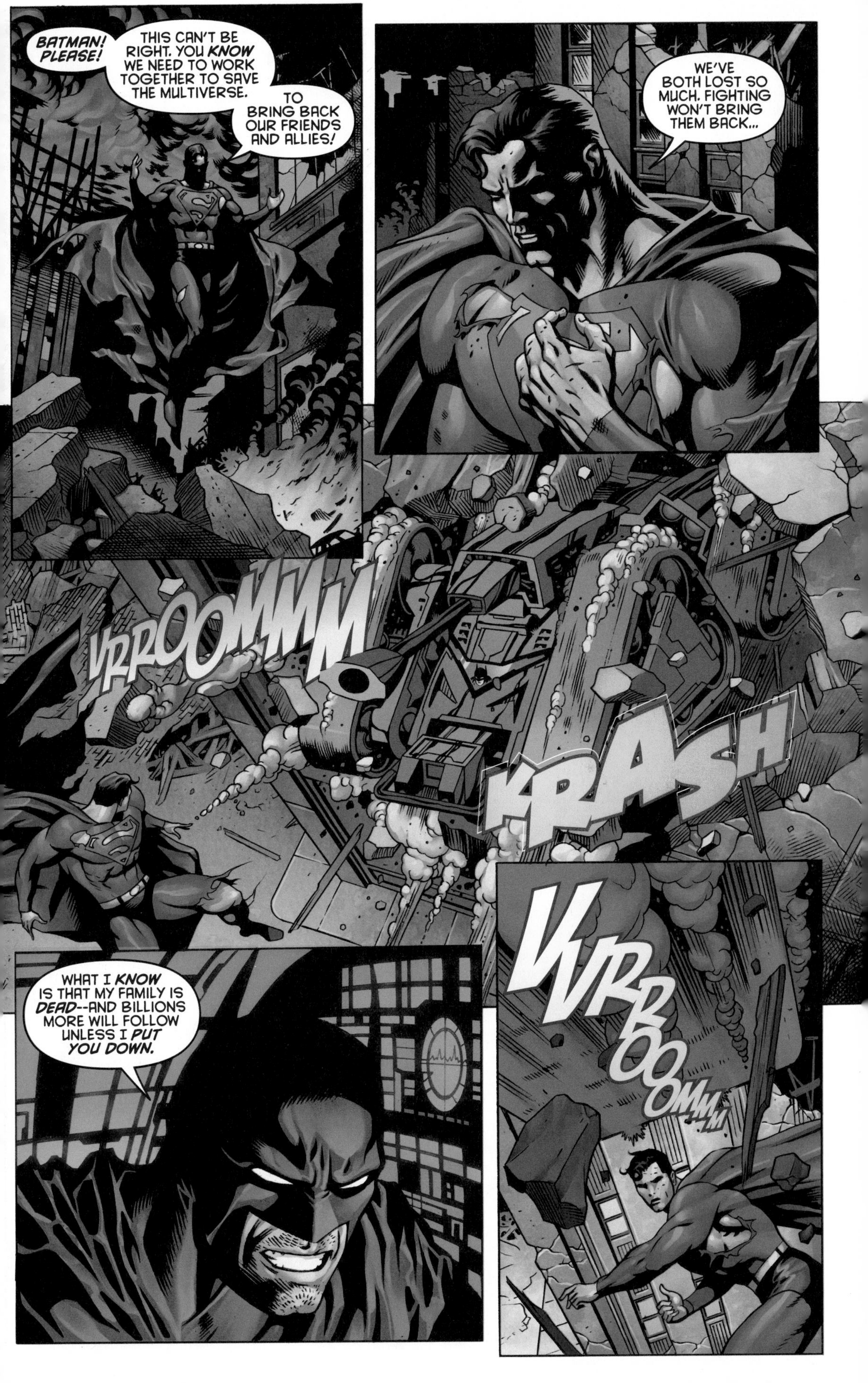
BATMAN! PLEASE!
THIS CAN'T BE RIGHT. YOU KNOW WE NEED TO WORK TOGETHER TO SAVE THE MULTIVERSE.
TO BRING BACK OUR FRIENDS AND ALLIES!
WE'VE BOTH LOST SO MUCH. FIGHTING WON'T BRING THEM BACK...
VRROOMMM
KRASH
WHAT I KNOW IS THAT MY FAMILY IS DEAD--AND BILLIONS MORE WILL FOLLOW UNLESS I PUT YOU DOWN.
VVRROOOMMM

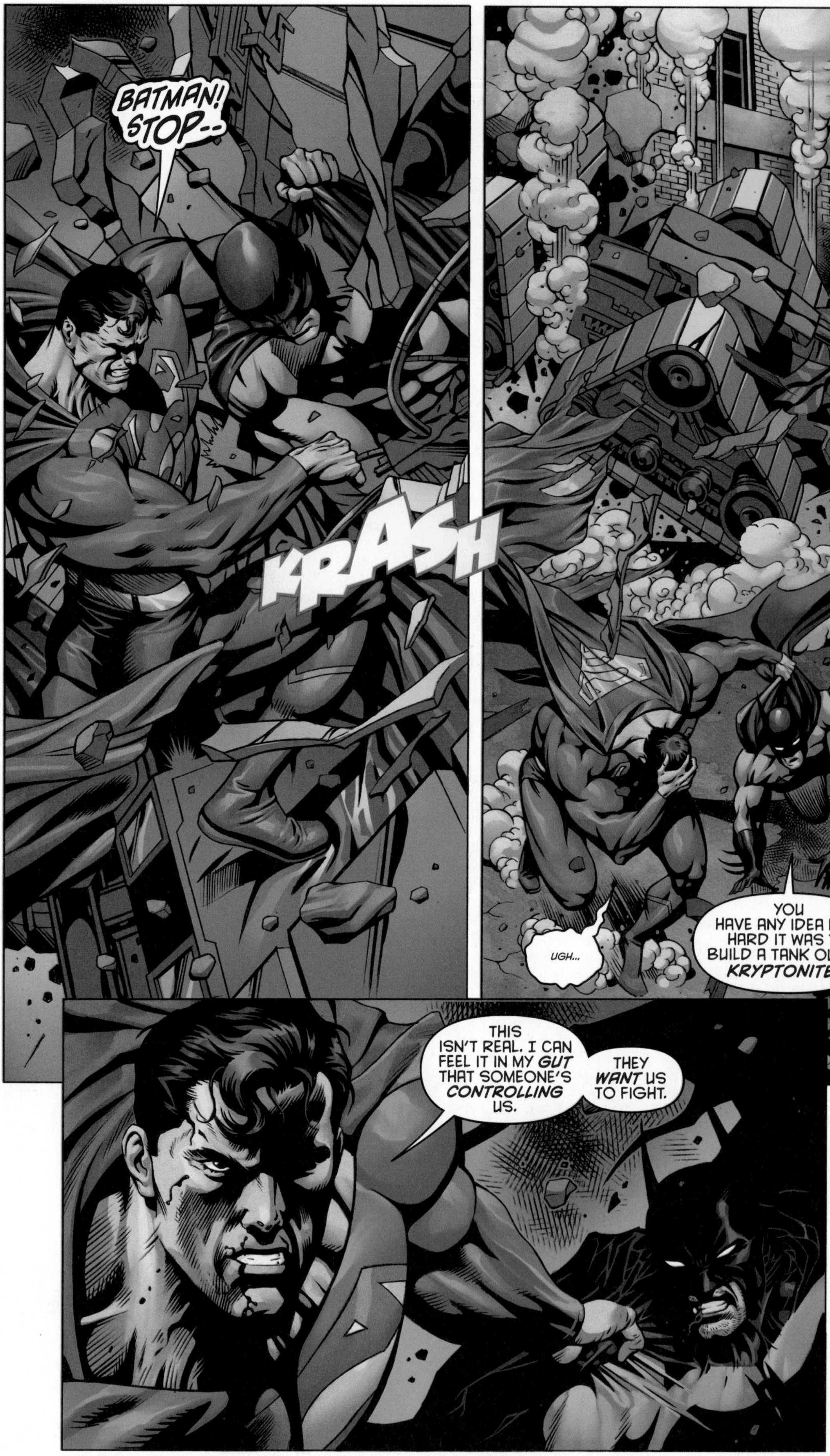
BATMAN! STOP--
KRASH
UGH...
YOU HAVE ANY IDEA HOW HARD IT WAS TO BUILD A TANK OUT OF KRYPTONITE?!
THIS ISN'T REAL. I CAN FEEL IT IN MY GUT THAT SOMEONE'S CONTROLLING US.
THEY WANT US TO FIGHT.

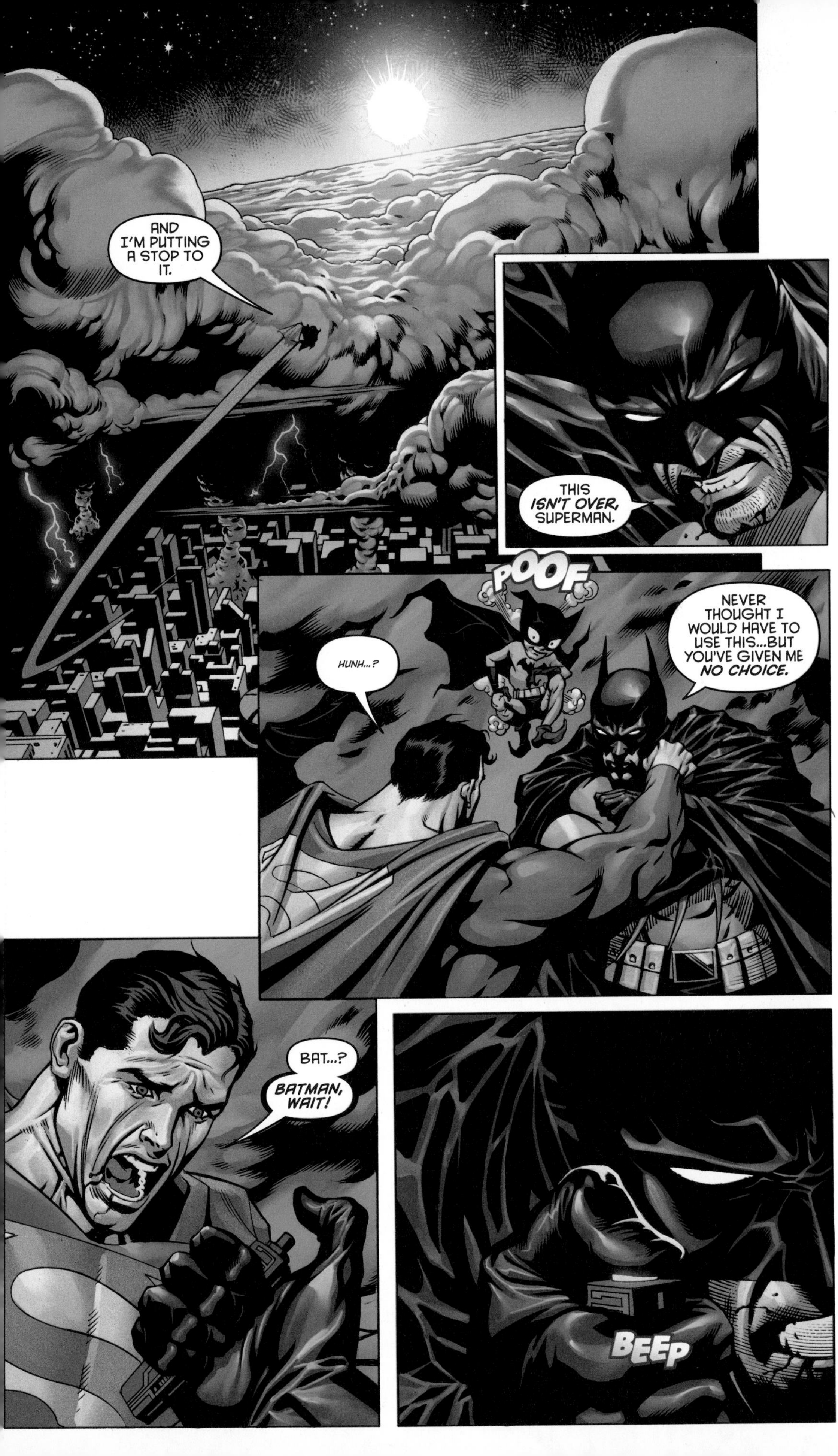
AND I'M PUTTING A STOP TO IT.
THIS ISN'T OVER, SUPERMAN.
POOF
HUNH...?
NEVER THOUGHT I WOULD HAVE TO USE THIS...BUT YOU'VE GIVEN ME NO CHOICE.
BAT...?
BATMAN, WAIT!
BEEP

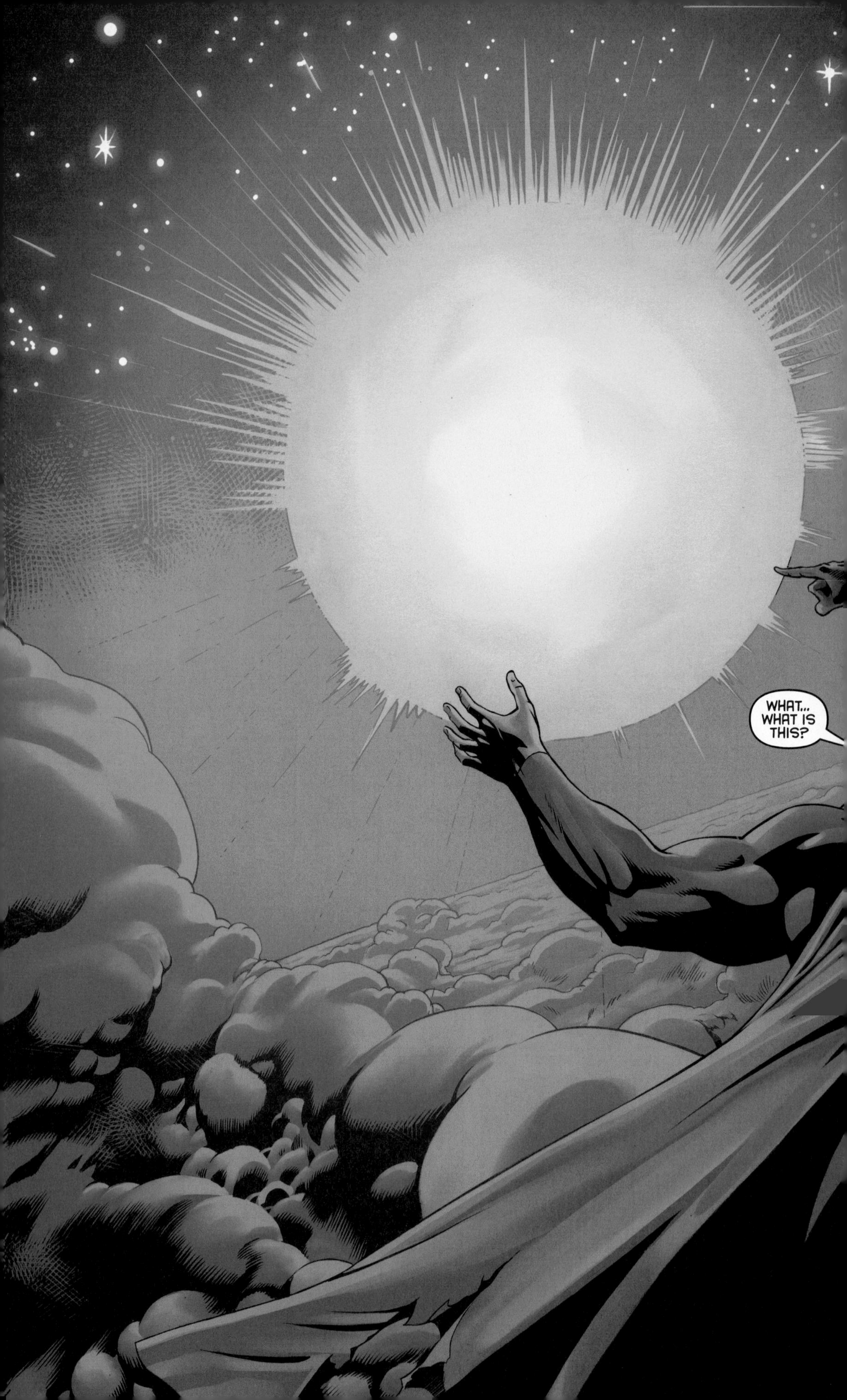
WHAT... WHAT IS THIS?

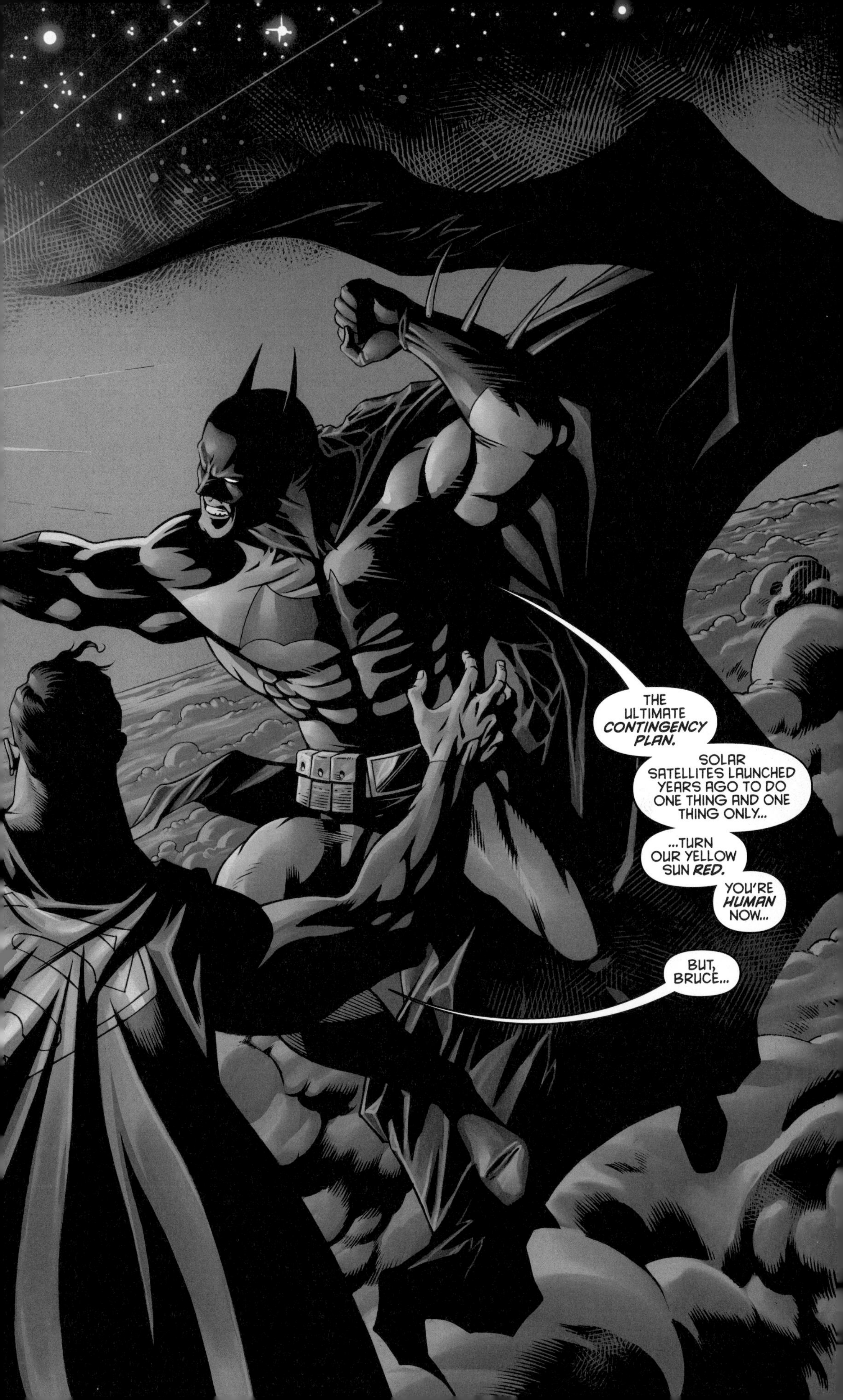
THE ULTIMATE CONTINGENCY PLAN.
SOLAR SATELLITES LAUNCHED YEARS AGO TO DO ONE THING AND ONE THING ONLY...
...TURN OUR YELLOW SUN RED.
YOU'RE HUMAN NOW...
BUT, BRUCE...

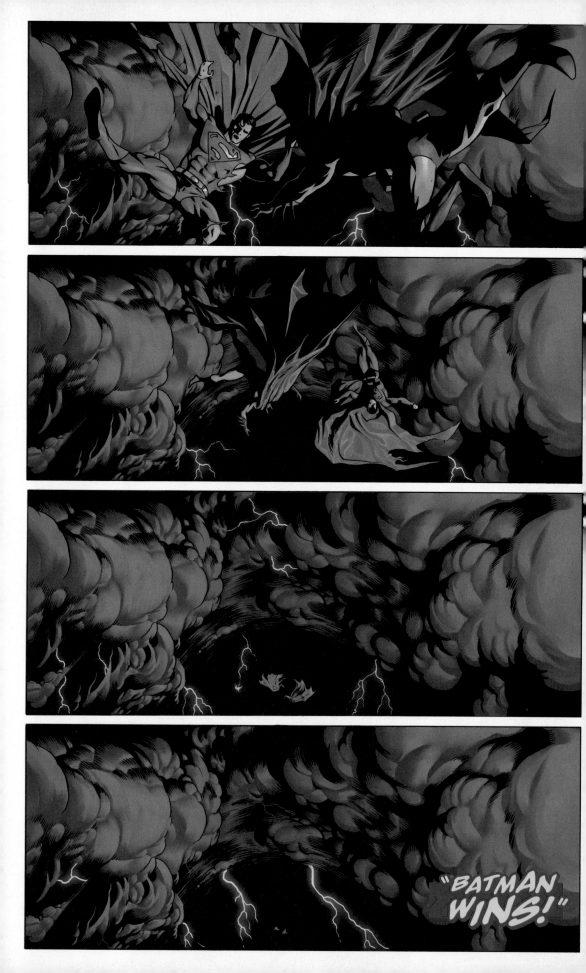

"BATMAN WINS!"

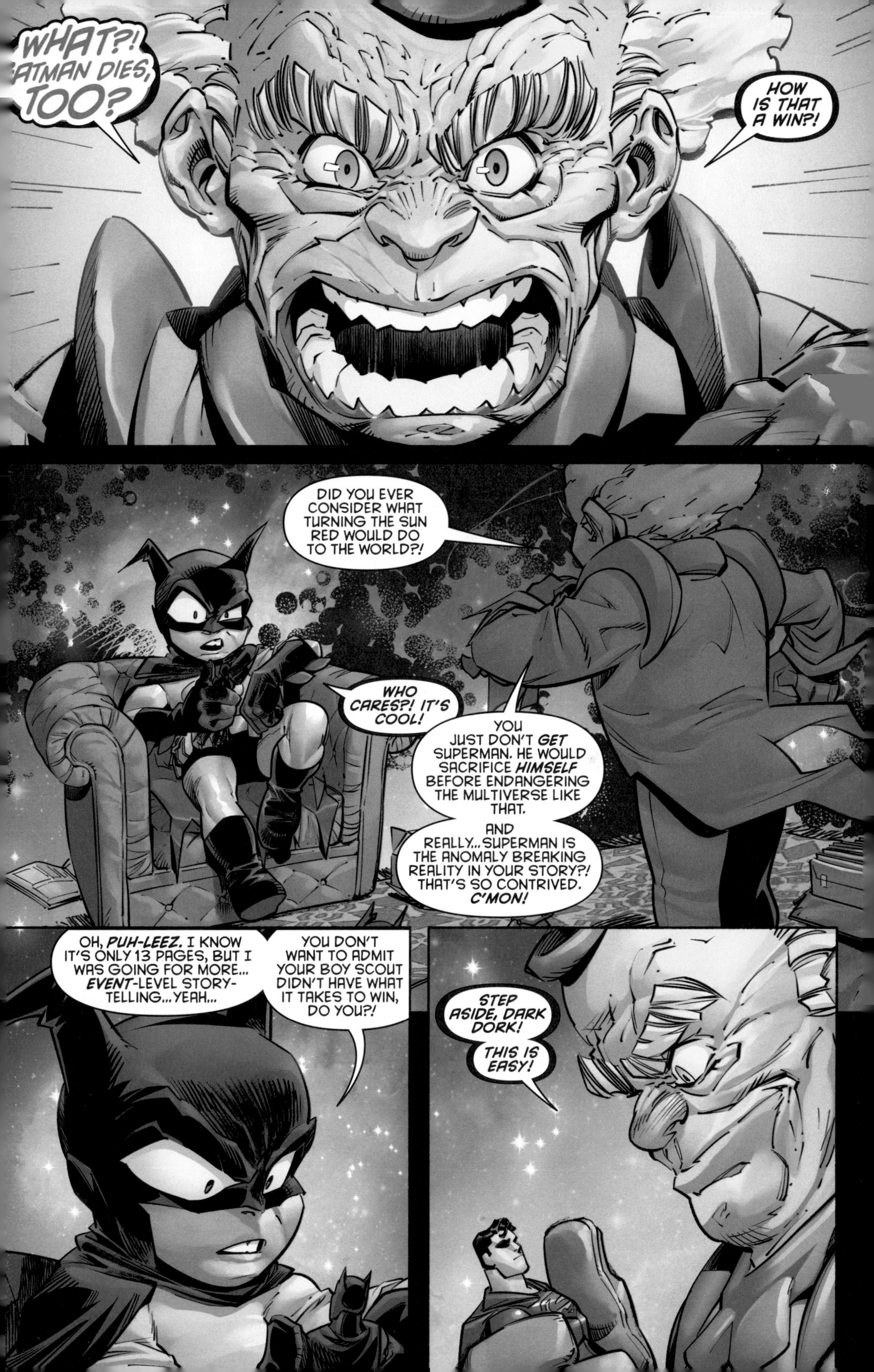
WHAT?! ...ATMAN DIES, TOO?
HOW IS THAT A WIN?!
DID YOU EVER CONSIDER WHAT TURNING THE SUN RED WOULD DO TO THE WORLD?!
WHO CARES?! IT'S COOL!
YOU JUST DON'T GET SUPERMAN. HE WOULD SACRIFICE HIMSELF BEFORE ENDANGERING THE MULTIVERSE LIKE THAT.
AND REALLY... SUPERMAN IS THE ANOMALY BREAKING REALITY IN YOUR STORY?! THAT'S SO CONTRIVED. C'MON!
OH, PUH-LEEZ. I KNOW IT'S ONLY 13 PAGES, BUT I WAS GOING FOR MORE... EVENT-LEVEL STORY-TELLING... YEAH...
YOU DON'T WANT TO ADMIT YOUR BOY SCOUT DIDN'T HAVE WHAT IT TAKES TO WIN, DO YOU?!
STEP ASIDE, DARK DORK!
THIS IS EASY!

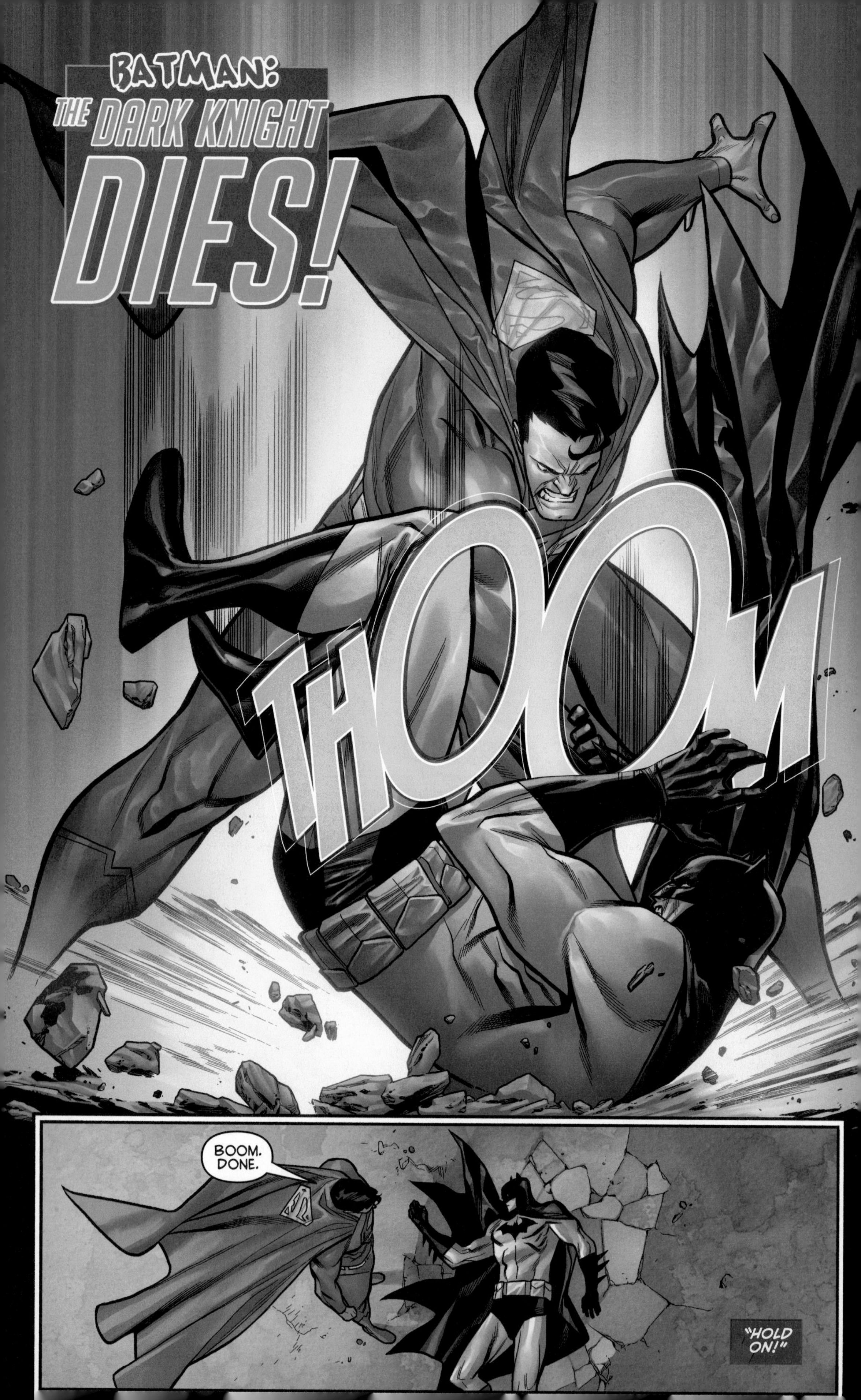
BATMAN:
THE DARK KNIGHT
DIES!
THOOM
BOOM.
DONE.
"HOLD
ON!"

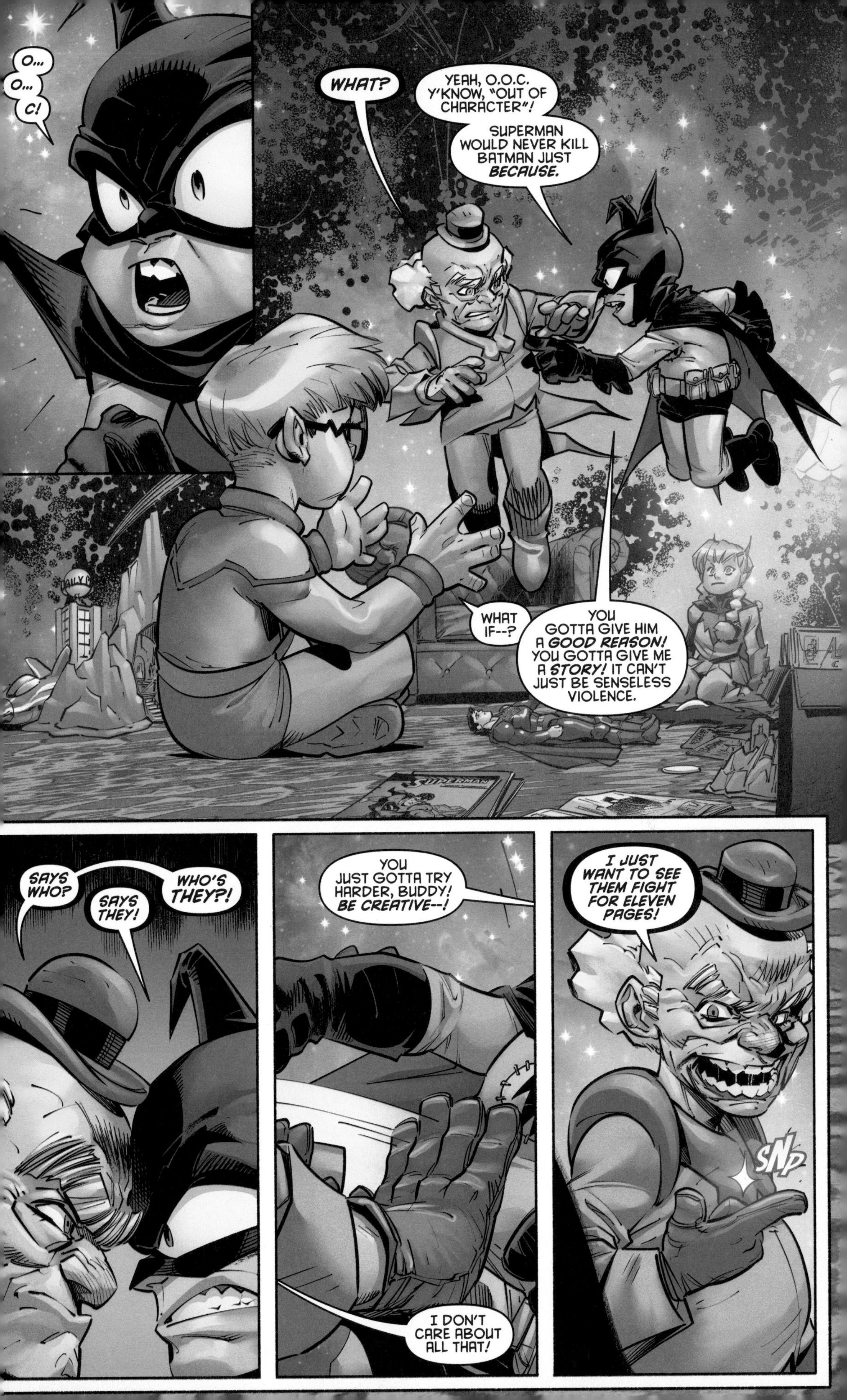

O... O... C!
WHAT?
YEAH, O.O.C. Y'KNOW, "OUT OF CHARACTER"!
SUPERMAN WOULD NEVER KILL BATMAN JUST BECAUSE.
WHAT IF--?
YOU GOTTA GIVE HIM A GOOD REASON! YOU GOTTA GIVE ME A STORY! IT CAN'T JUST BE SENSELESS VIOLENCE.
SUPERMAN
SAYS WHO?
SAYS THEY!
WHO'S THEY?!
YOU JUST GOTTA TRY HARDER, BUDDY! BE CREATIVE--!
I DON'T CARE ABOUT ALL THAT!
I JUST WANT TO SEE THEM FIGHT FOR ELEVEN PAGES!
SNP

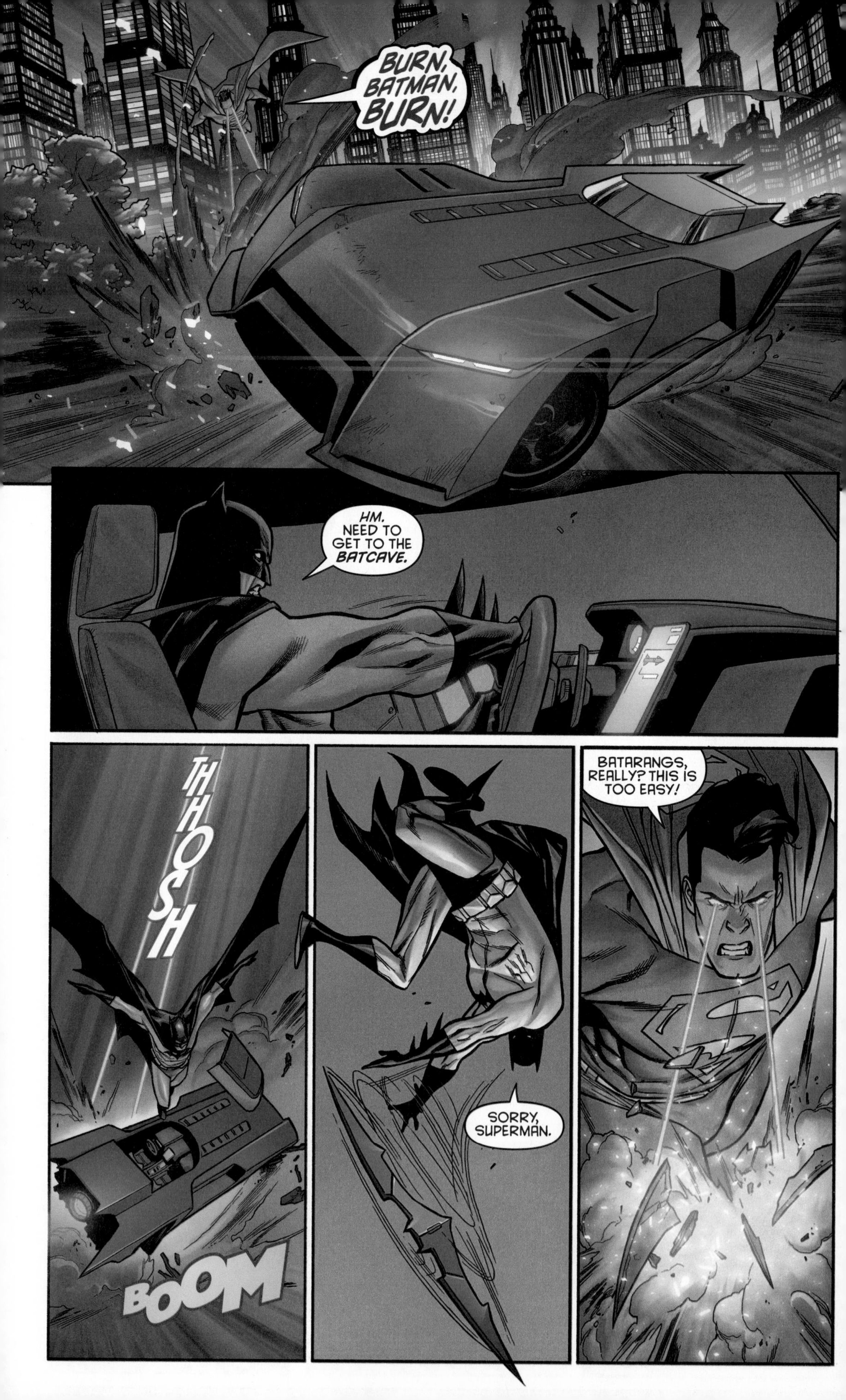
BURN, BATMAN, BURN!
HM. NEED TO GET TO THE BATCAVE.
THHOSH
BOOM
SORRY, SUPERMAN.
BATARANGS, REALLY? THIS IS TOO EASY!

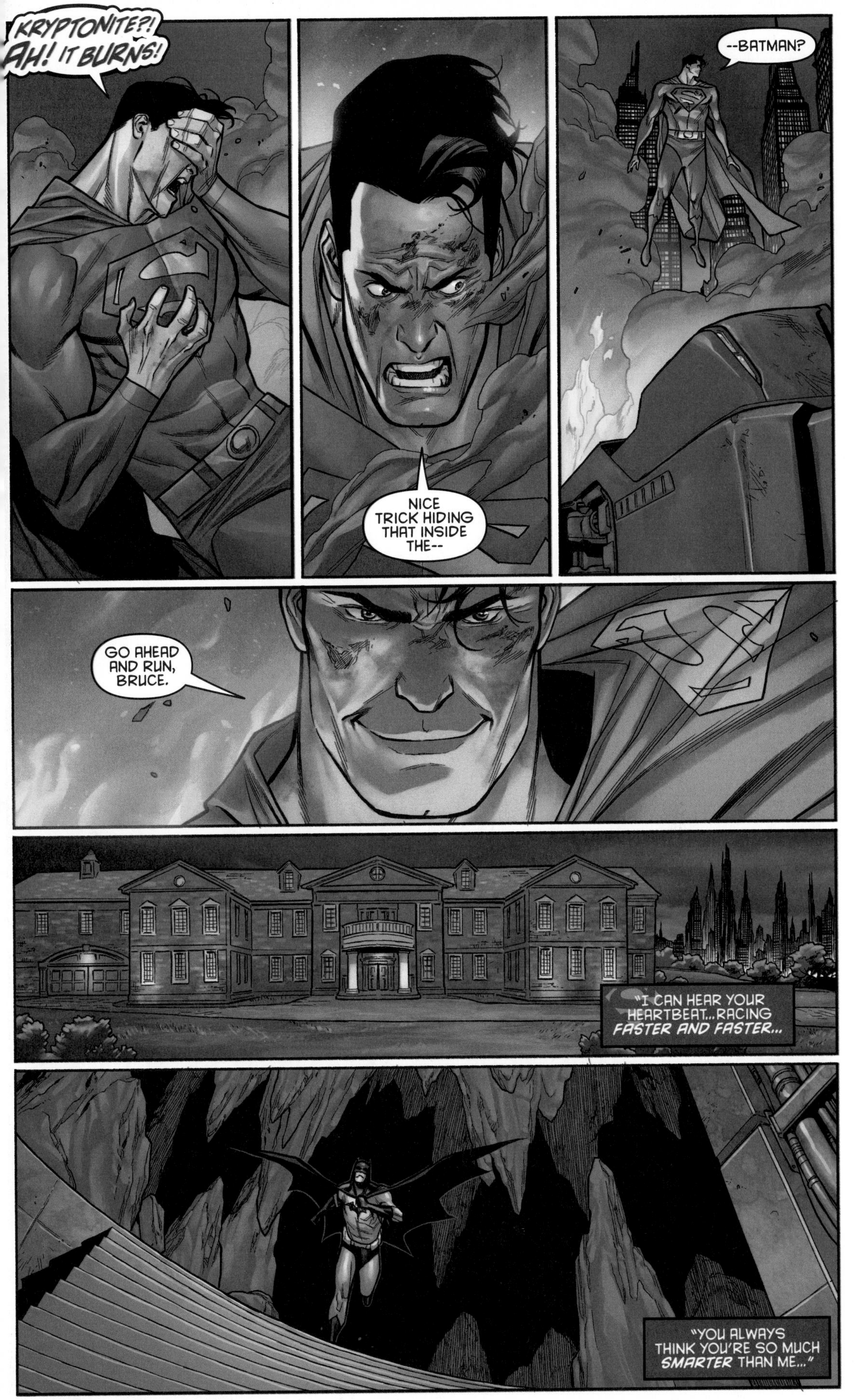
KRYPTONITE?! AH! IT BURNS!
NICE TRICK HIDING THAT INSIDE THE--
--BATMAN?
GO AHEAD AND RUN, BRUCE.
"I CAN HEAR YOUR HEARTBEAT...RACING FASTER AND FASTER...
"YOU ALWAYS THINK YOU'RE SO MUCH SMARTER THAN ME..."

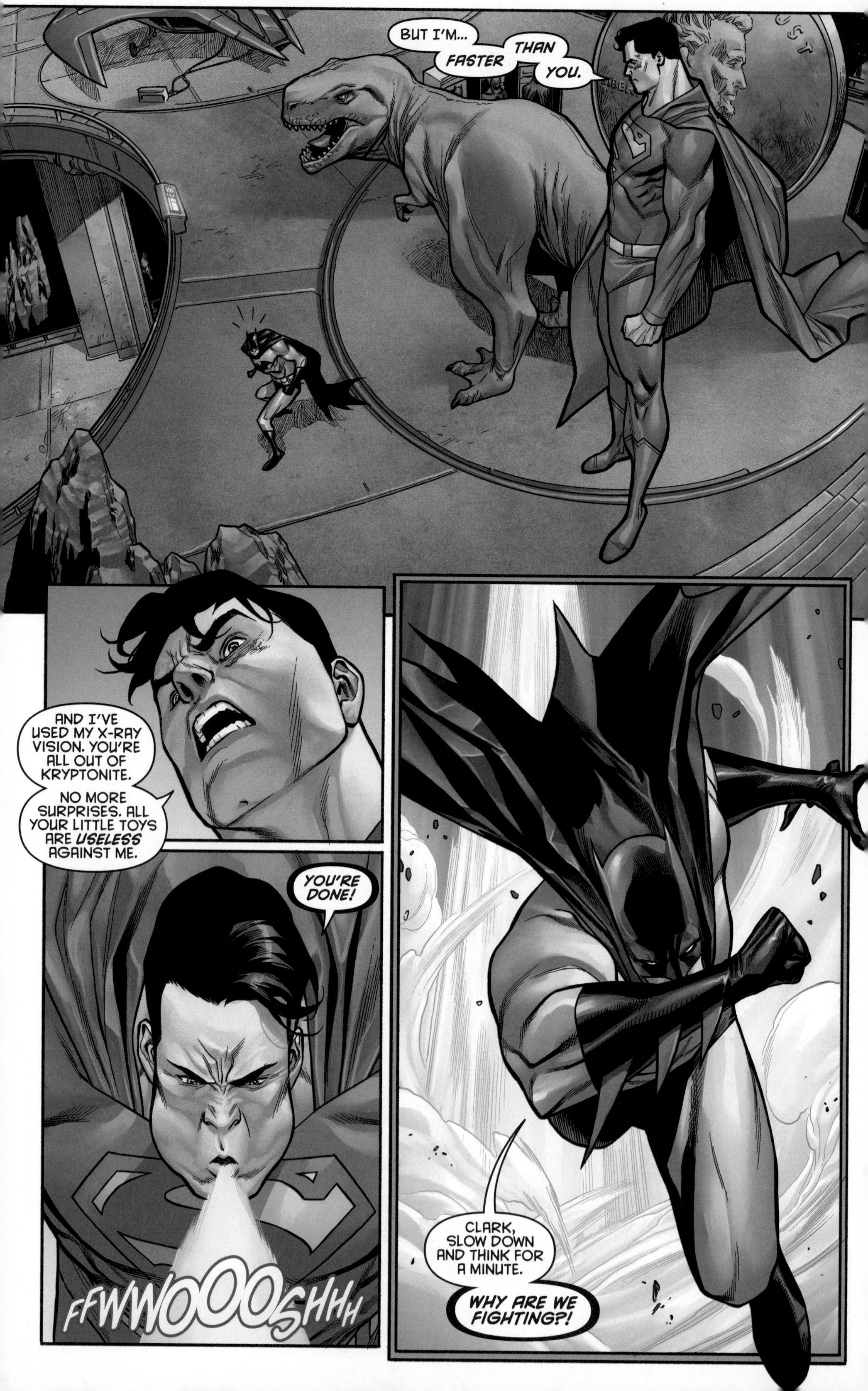

BUT I'M...
FASTER THAN YOU.
AND I'VE USED MY X-RAY VISION. YOU'RE ALL OUT OF KRYPTONITE.
NO MORE SURPRISES. ALL YOUR LITTLE TOYS ARE USELESS AGAINST ME.
YOU'RE DONE!
FFWWOOOOSHHH
CLARK, SLOW DOWN AND THINK FOR A MINUTE.
WHY ARE WE FIGHTING?!

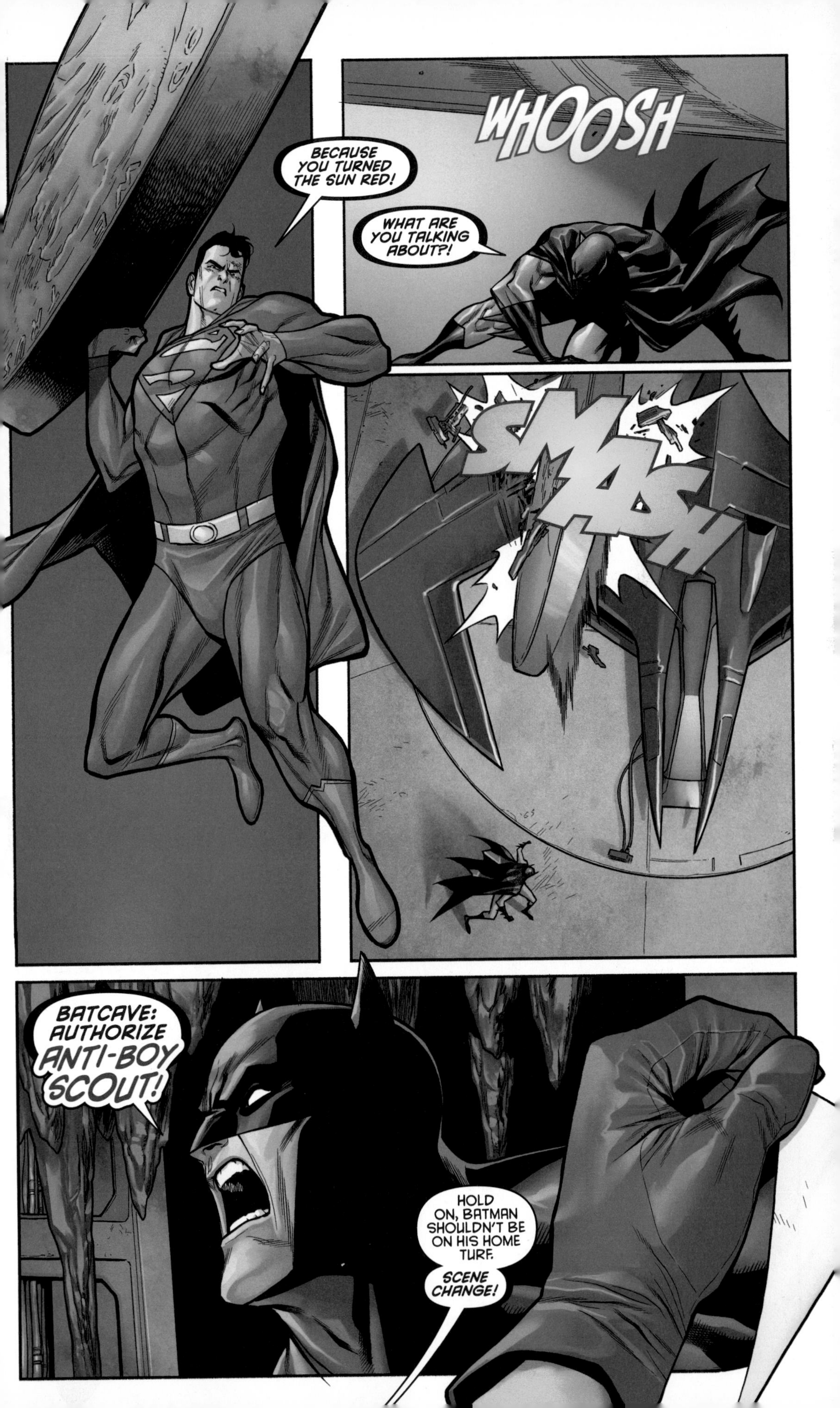

BECAUSE YOU TURNED THE SUN RED!
WHOOSH
WHAT ARE YOU TALKING ABOUT?!
SMASH
BATCAVE: AUTHORIZE ANTI-BOY SCOUT!
HOLD ON, BATMAN SHOULDN'T BE ON HIS HOME TURF.
SCENE CHANGE!

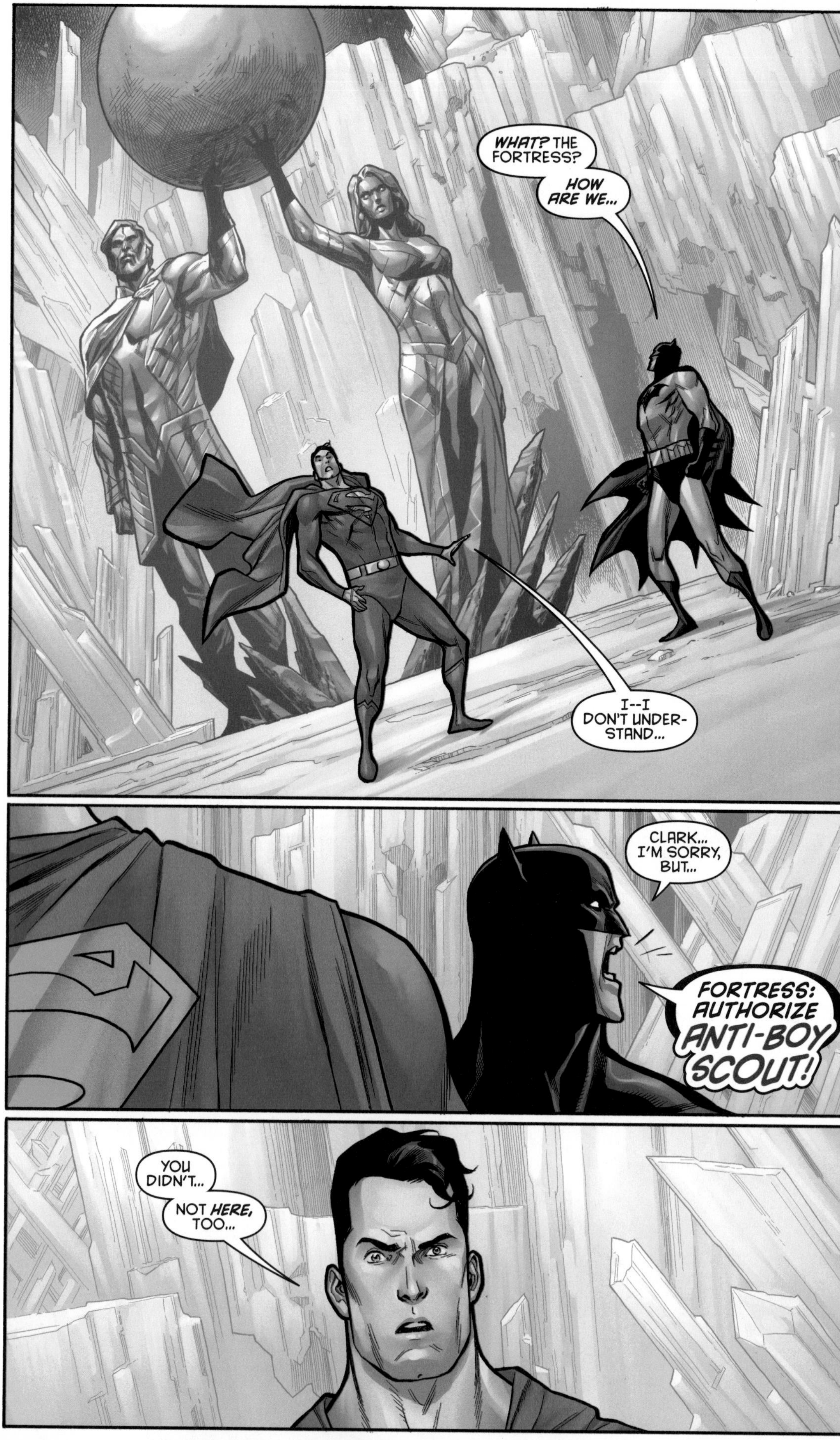
WHAT? THE FORTRESS?
HOW ARE WE...
I--I DON'T UNDER-STAND...
CLARK... I'M SORRY, BUT...
FORTRESS: AUTHORIZE ANTI-BOY SCOUT!
YOU DIDN'T...
NOT HERE, TOO...

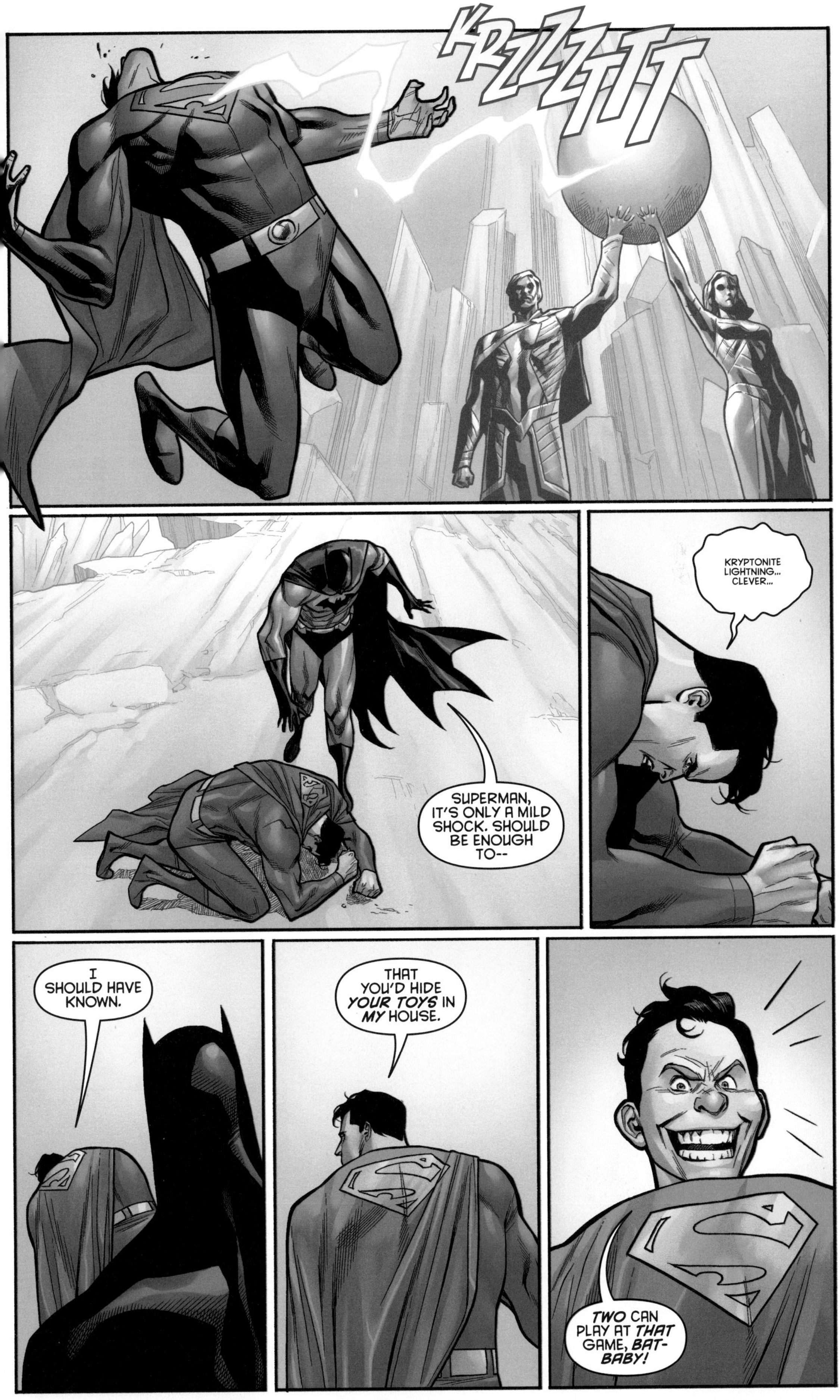
KRZZZTTT
SUPERMAN, IT'S ONLY A MILD SHOCK. SHOULD BE ENOUGH TO--
KRYPTONITE LIGHTNING... CLEVER...
I SHOULD HAVE KNOWN.
THAT YOU'D HIDE YOUR TOYS IN MY HOUSE.
TWO CAN PLAY AT THAT GAME, BAT-BABY!

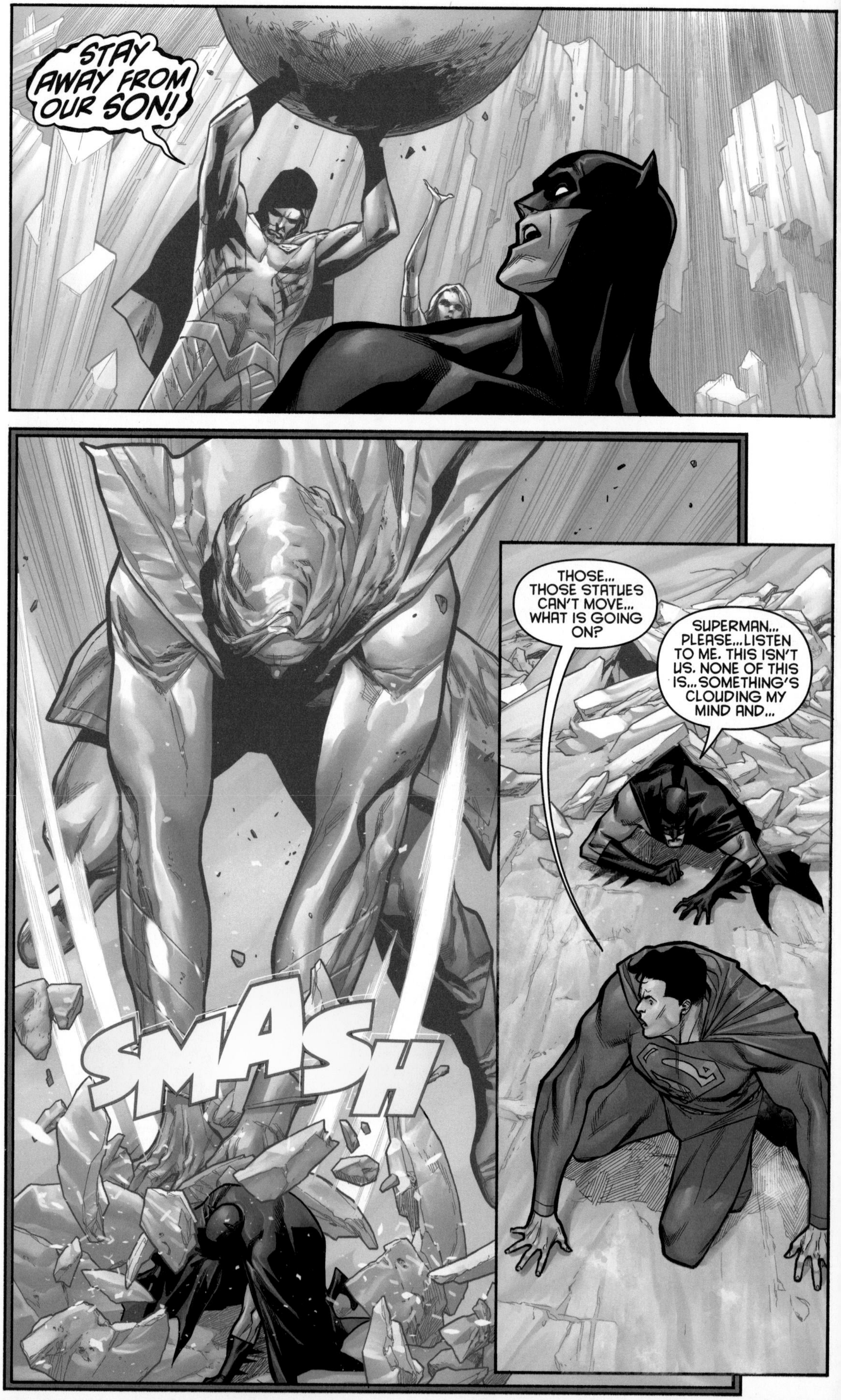
STAY AWAY FROM OUR SON!
SMASH
THOSE... THOSE STATUES CAN'T MOVE... WHAT IS GOING ON?
SUPERMAN... PLEASE...LISTEN TO ME. THIS ISN'T US. NONE OF THIS IS...SOMETHING'S CLOUDING MY MIND AND...

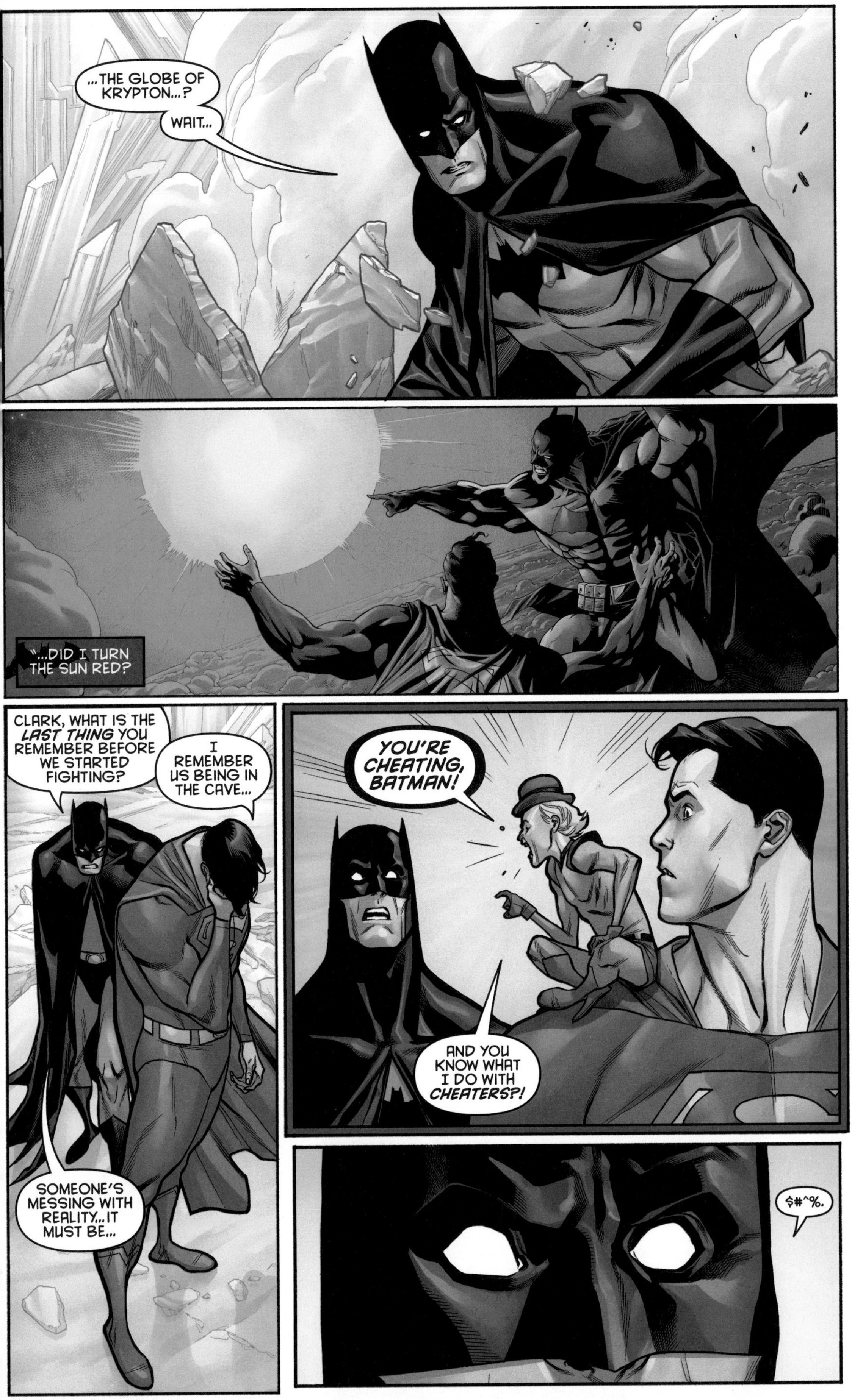
...THE GLOBE OF KRYPTON...?
WAIT...
"...DID I TURN THE SUN RED?
CLARK, WHAT IS THE LAST THING YOU REMEMBER BEFORE WE STARTED FIGHTING?
I REMEMBER US BEING IN THE CAVE...
SOMEONE'S MESSING WITH REALITY...IT MUST BE...
YOU'RE CHEATING, BATMAN!
AND YOU KNOW WHAT I DO WITH CHEATERS?!
$#^%.

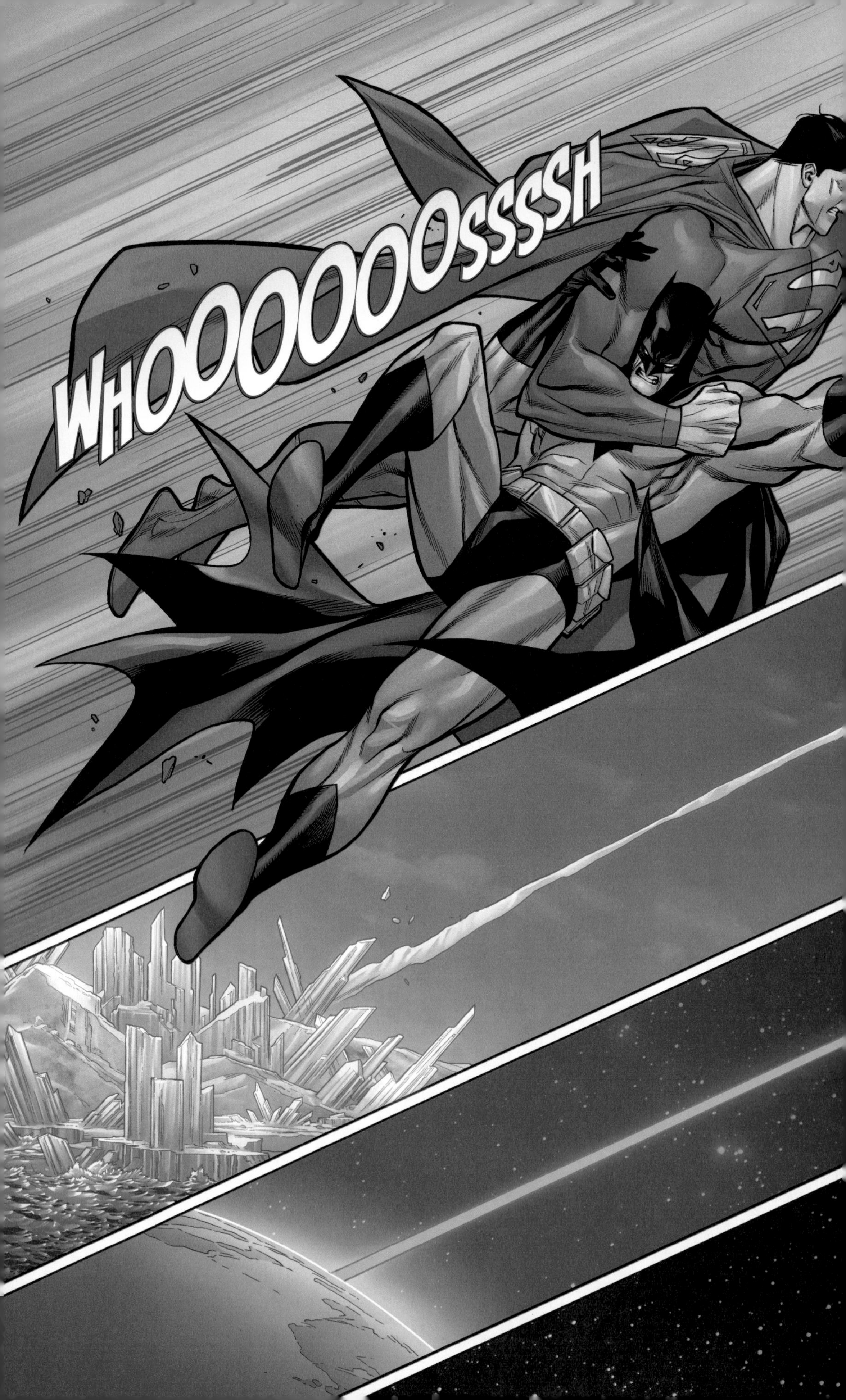
WHOOOOOOSSSSH

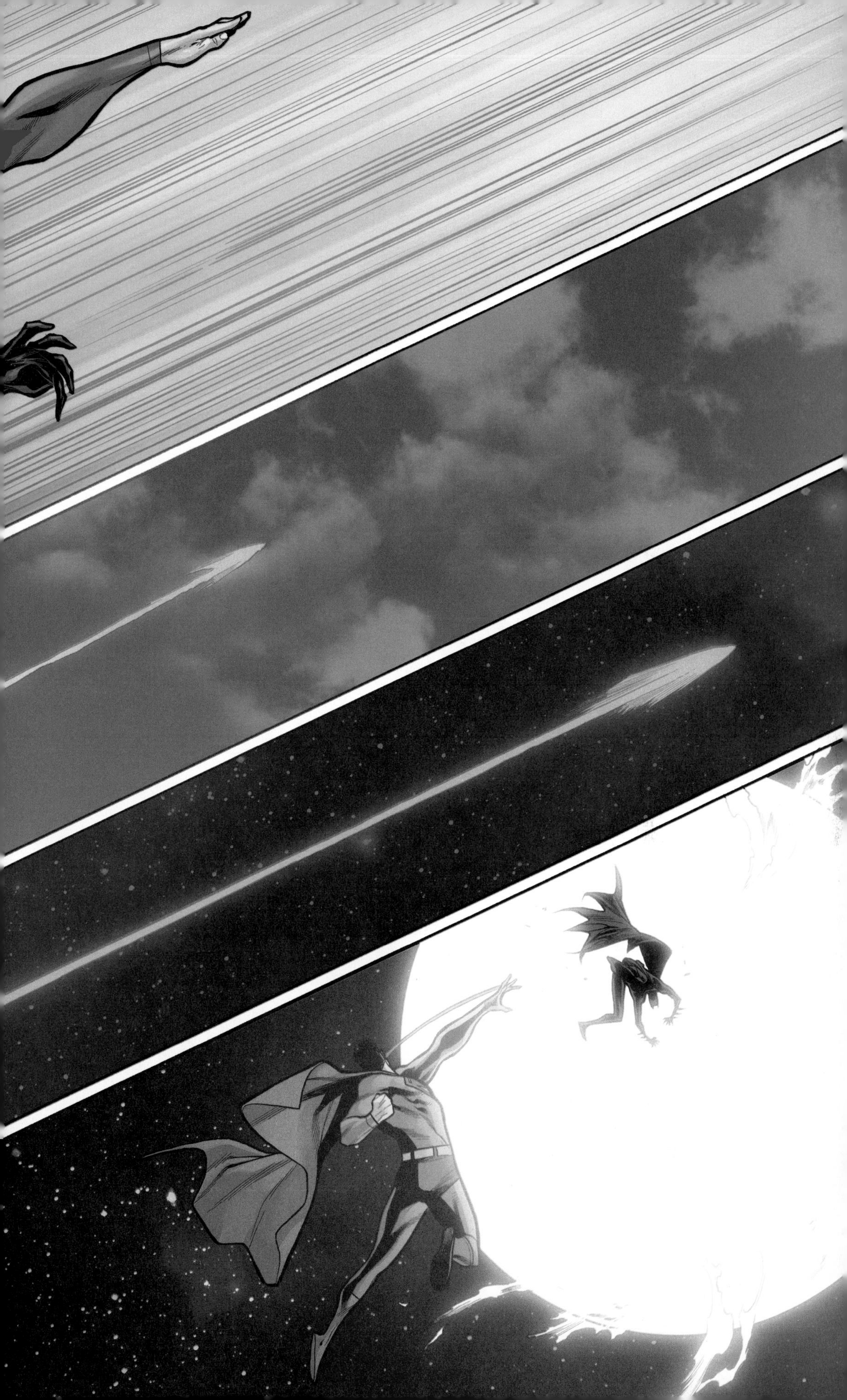

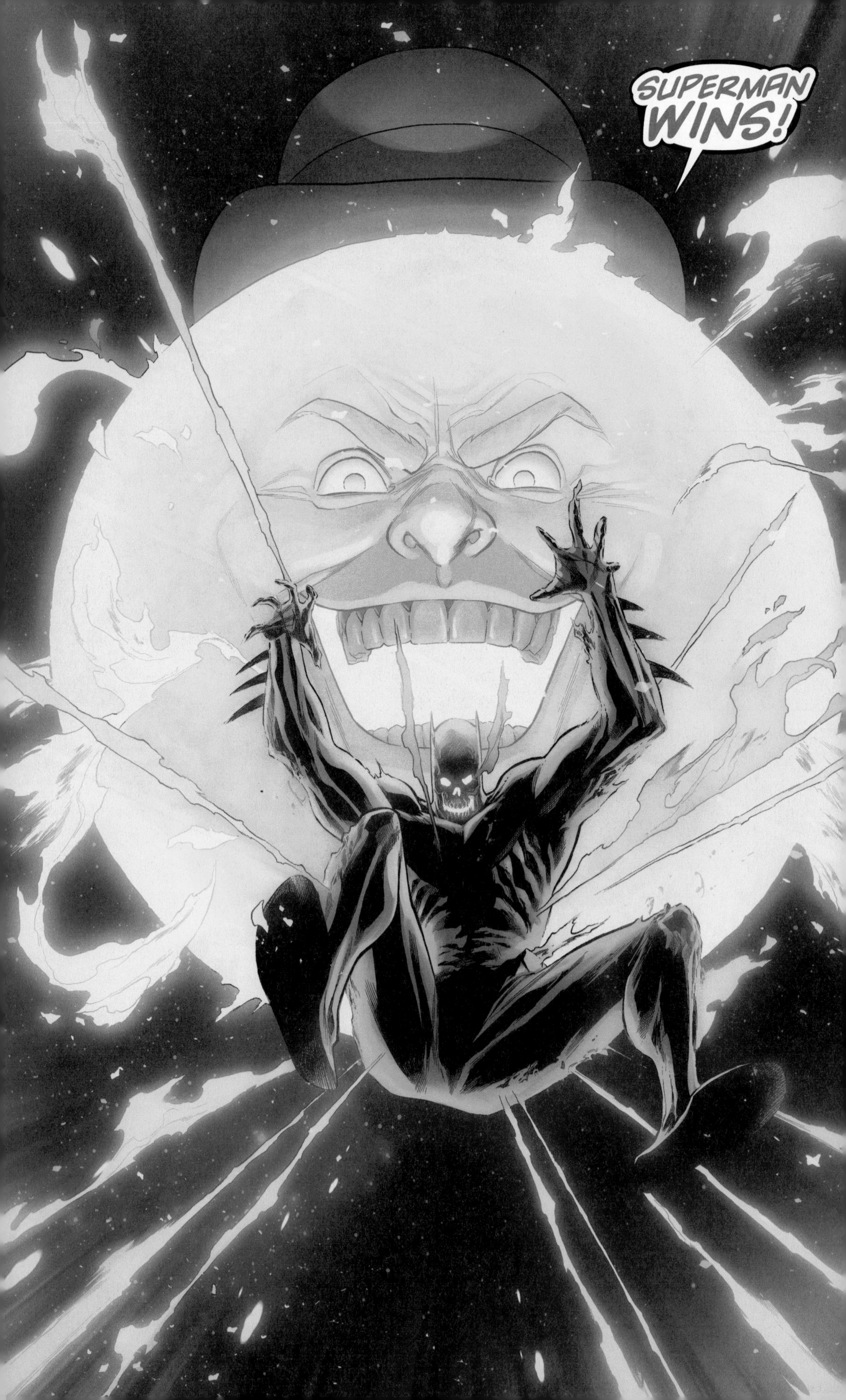
SUPERMAN WINS!

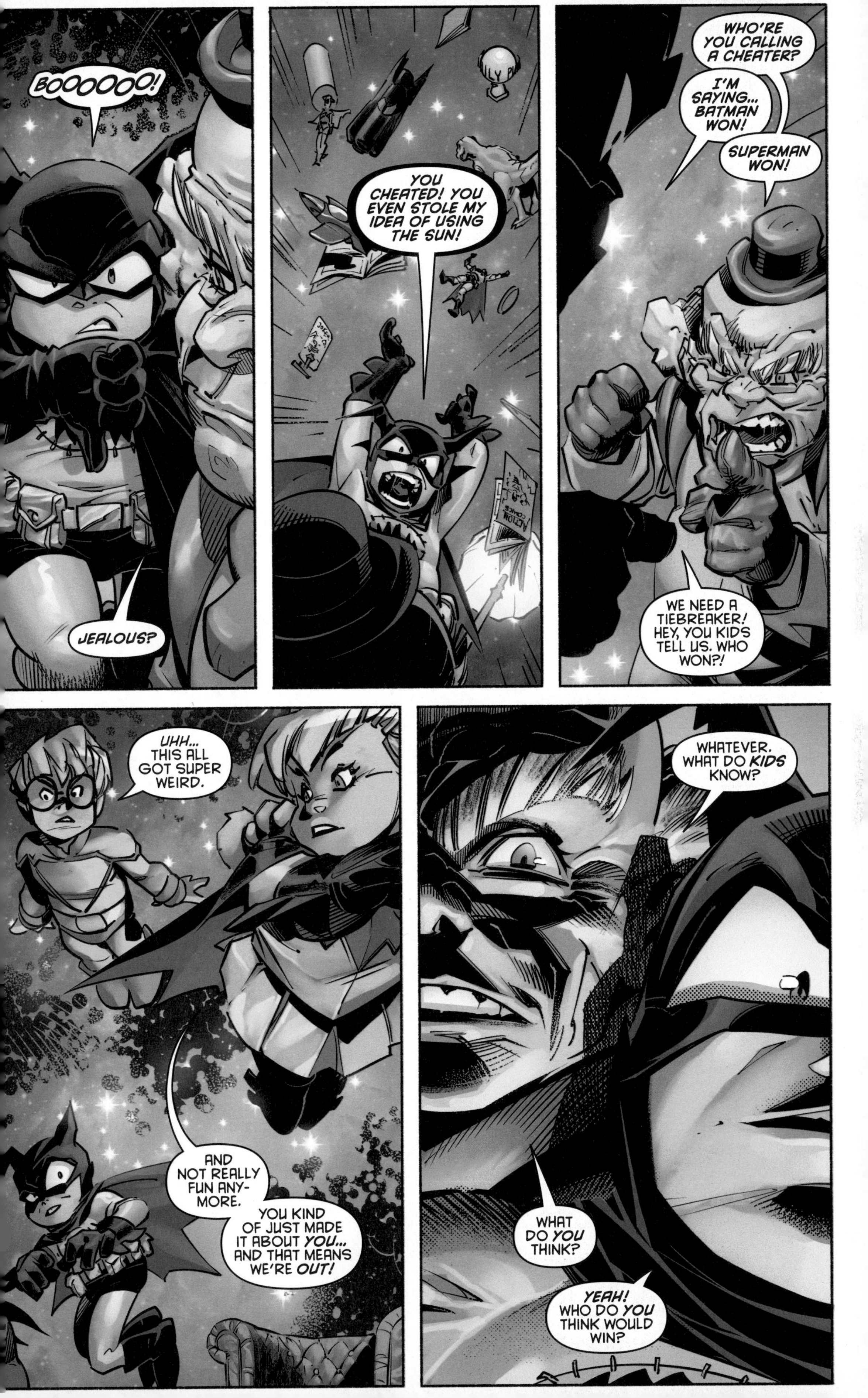
BOOOOOO!
JEALOUS?
YOU CHEATED! YOU EVEN STOLE MY IDEA OF USING THE SUN!
WHO'RE YOU CALLING A CHEATER?
I'M SAYING... BATMAN WON!
SUPERMAN WON!
WE NEED A TIEBREAKER! HEY, YOU KIDS TELL US. WHO WON?!
UHH... THIS ALL GOT SUPER WEIRD.
AND NOT REALLY FUN ANY-MORE.
YOU KIND OF JUST MADE IT ABOUT YOU... AND THAT MEANS WE'RE OUT!
WHATEVER. WHAT DO KIDS KNOW?
WHAT DO YOU THINK?
YEAH! WHO DO YOU THINK WOULD WIN?

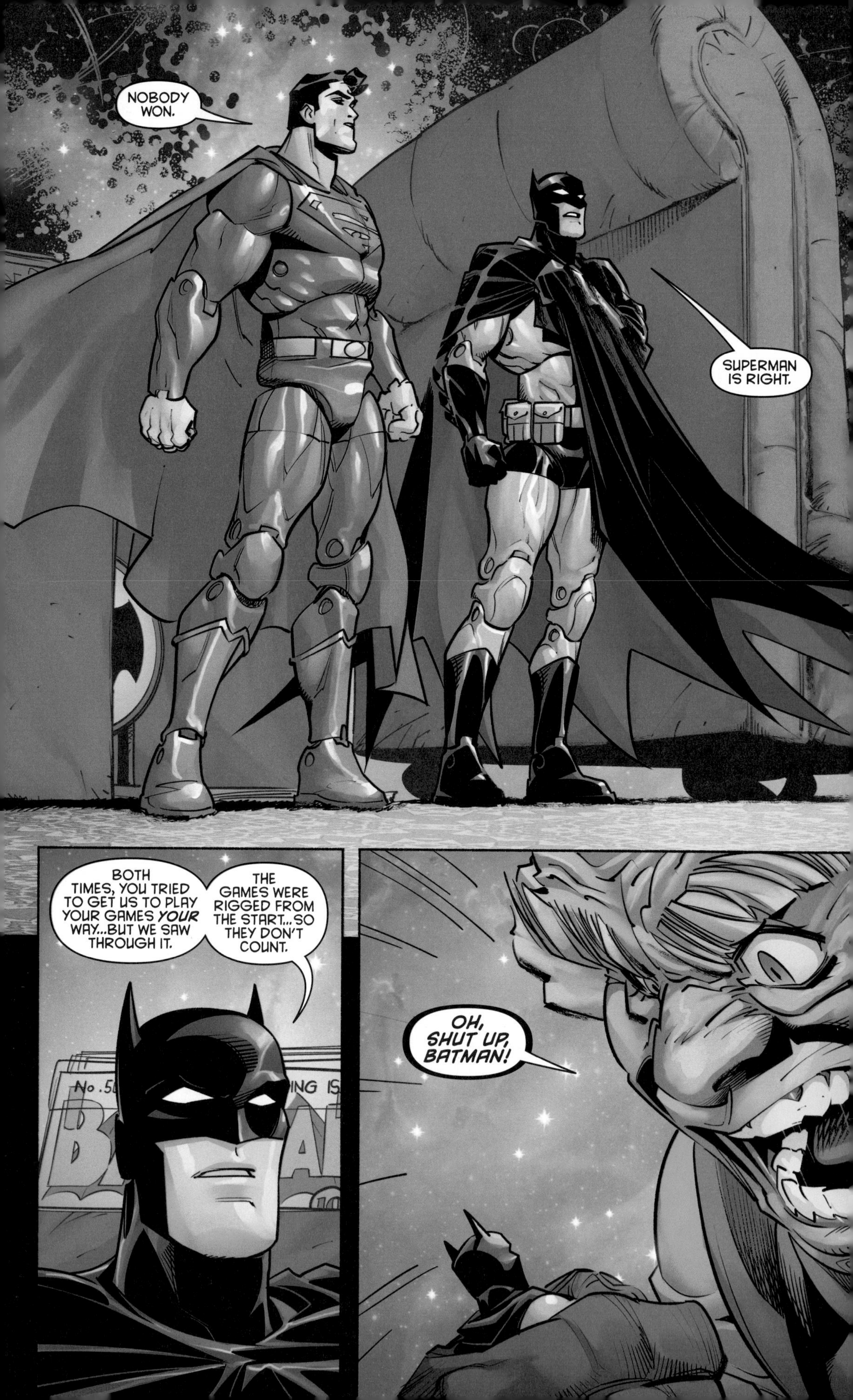
NOBODY WON.
SUPERMAN IS RIGHT.
BOTH TIMES, YOU TRIED TO GET US TO PLAY YOUR GAMES *YOUR* WAY...BUT WE SAW THROUGH IT.
THE GAMES WERE RIGGED FROM THE START...SO THEY DON'T COUNT.
OH, SHUT UP, BATMAN!

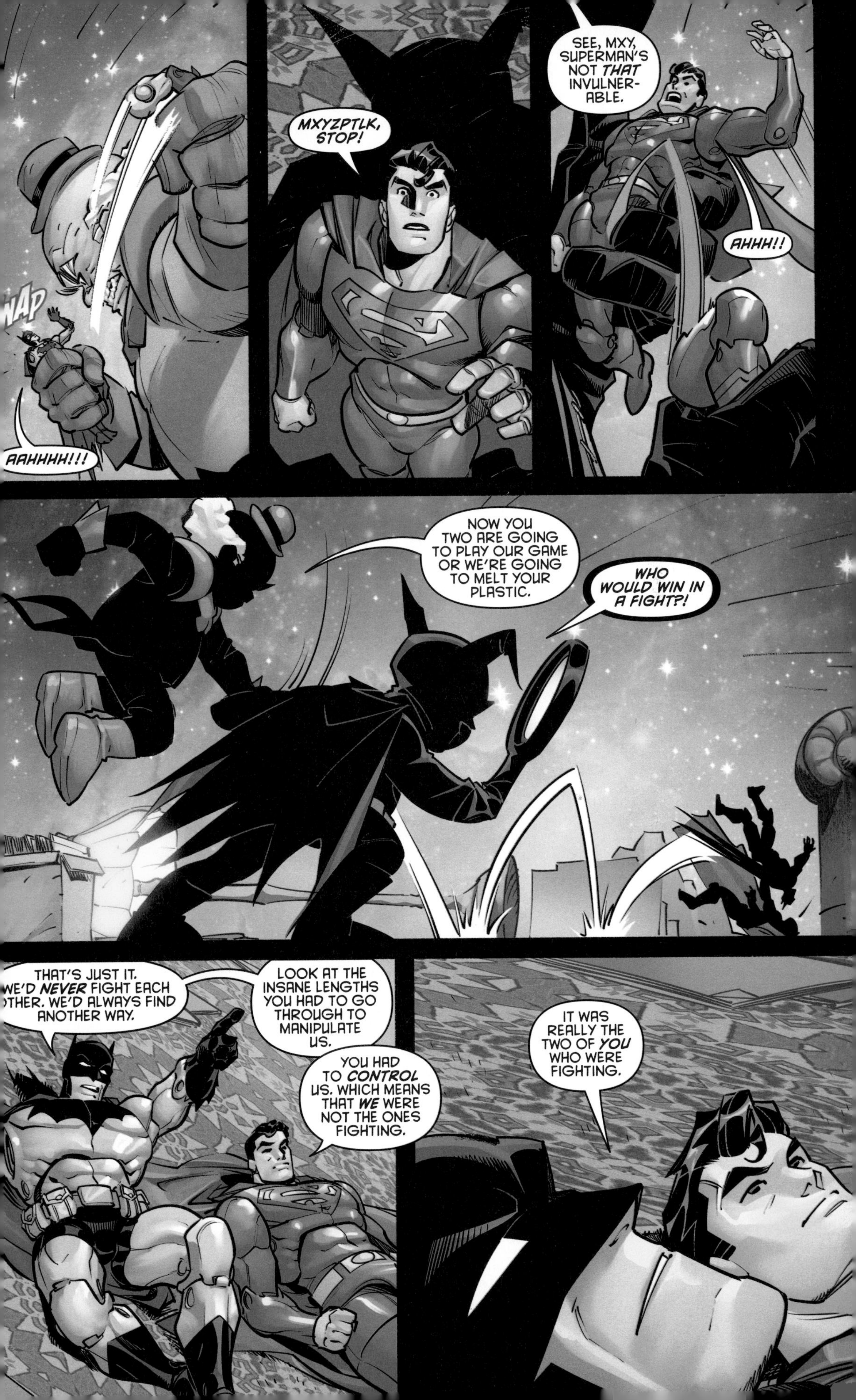
WAP
AAHHHH!!!
MXYZPTLK, STOP!
SEE, MXY, SUPERMAN'S NOT *THAT* INVULNER-ABLE.
AHHH!!
NOW YOU TWO ARE GOING TO PLAY OUR GAME OR WE'RE GOING TO MELT YOUR PLASTIC.
WHO WOULD WIN IN A FIGHT?!
THAT'S JUST IT. WE'D *NEVER* FIGHT EACH OTHER. WE'D ALWAYS FIND ANOTHER WAY.
LOOK AT THE INSANE LENGTHS YOU HAD TO GO THROUGH TO MANIPULATE US.
YOU HAD TO *CONTROL* US. WHICH MEANS THAT *WE* WERE NOT THE ONES FIGHTING.
IT WAS REALLY THE TWO OF *YOU* WHO WERE FIGHTING.

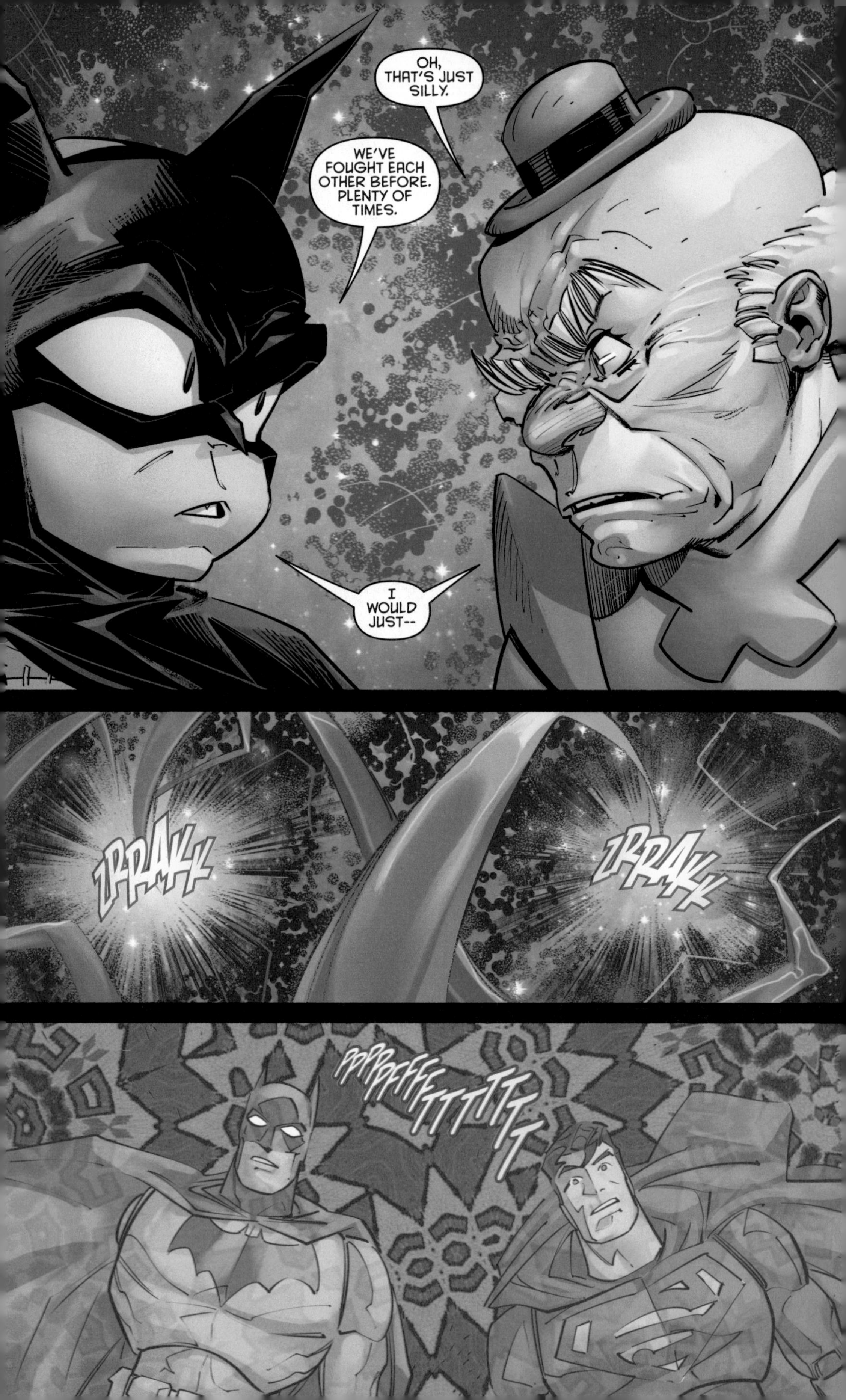
OH, THAT'S JUST SILLY.
WE'VE FOUGHT EACH OTHER BEFORE. PLENTY OF TIMES.
I WOULD JUST--
ZRRAKK
ZRRAKK
PPPPPFFFFTTTTTTTT

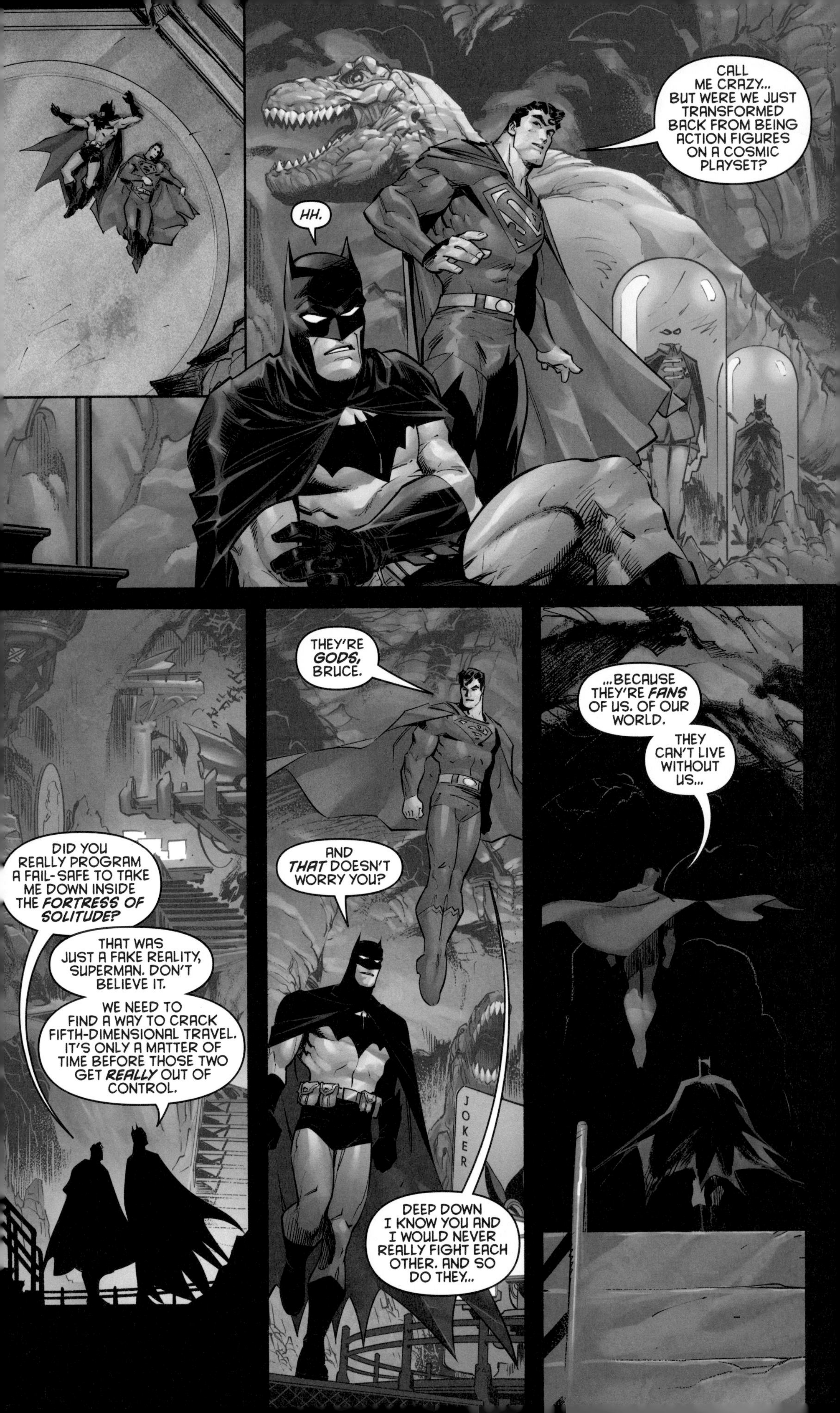
CALL ME CRAZY... BUT WERE WE JUST TRANSFORMED BACK FROM BEING ACTION FIGURES ON A COSMIC PLAYSET?
HH.
DID YOU REALLY PROGRAM A FAIL-SAFE TO TAKE ME DOWN INSIDE THE FORTRESS OF SOLITUDE?
THAT WAS JUST A FAKE REALITY, SUPERMAN. DON'T BELIEVE IT.
WE NEED TO FIND A WAY TO CRACK FIFTH-DIMENSIONAL TRAVEL. IT'S ONLY A MATTER OF TIME BEFORE THOSE TWO GET REALLY OUT OF CONTROL.
THEY'RE GODS, BRUCE.
AND THAT DOESN'T WORRY YOU?
JOKER
DEEP DOWN I KNOW YOU AND I WOULD NEVER REALLY FIGHT EACH OTHER. AND SO DO THEY...
...BECAUSE THEY'RE FANS OF US. OF OUR WORLD.
THEY CAN'T LIVE WITHOUT US...

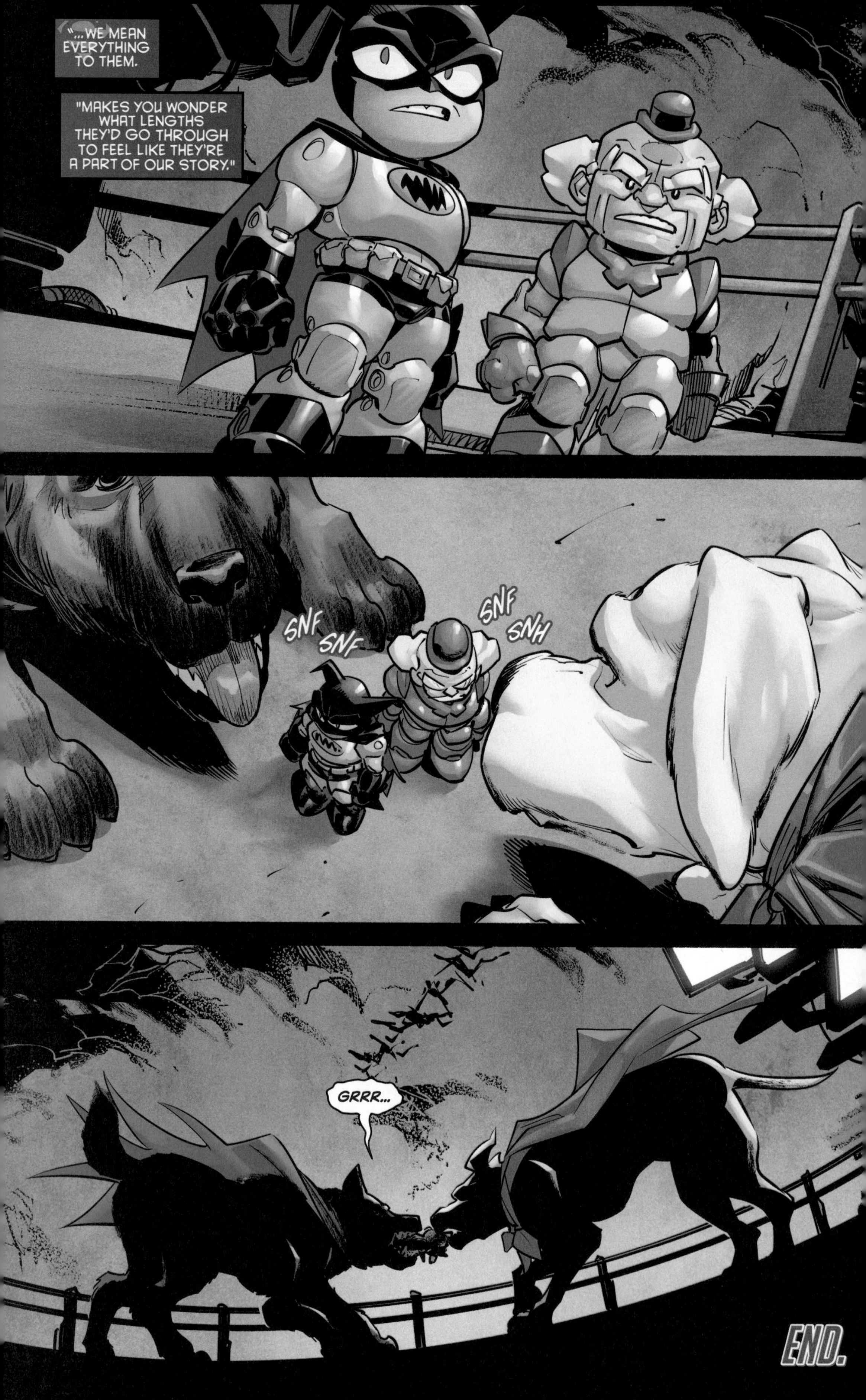
"...WE MEAN EVERYTHING TO THEM.
"MAKES YOU WONDER WHAT LENGTHS THEY'D GO THROUGH TO FEEL LIKE THEY'RE A PART OF OUR STORY."
SNF SNF
SNF SNH
GRRR...
END.

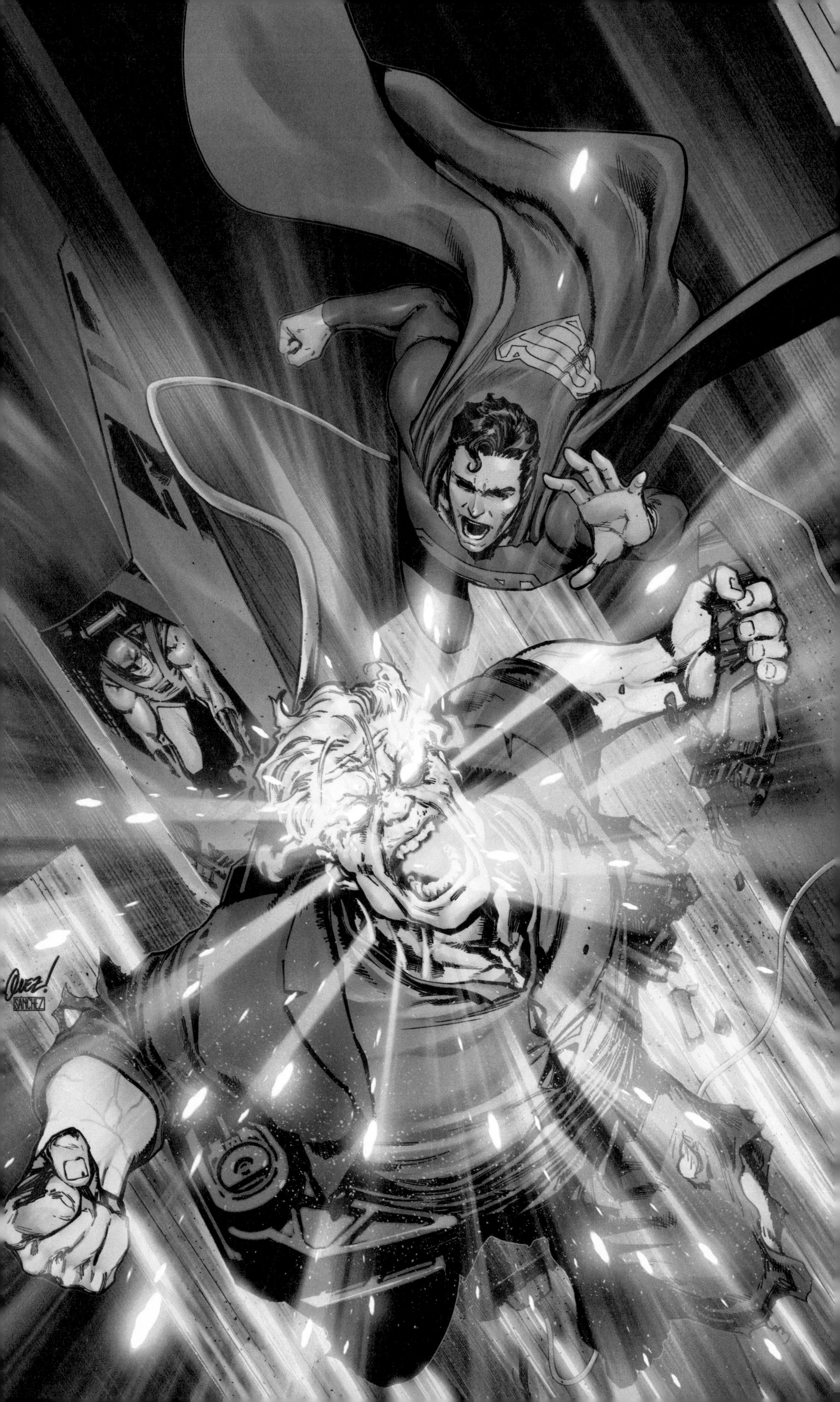

BATMAN/SUPERMAN #15

cover by
DAVID MARQUEZ and **ALEJANDRO SÁNCHEZ**

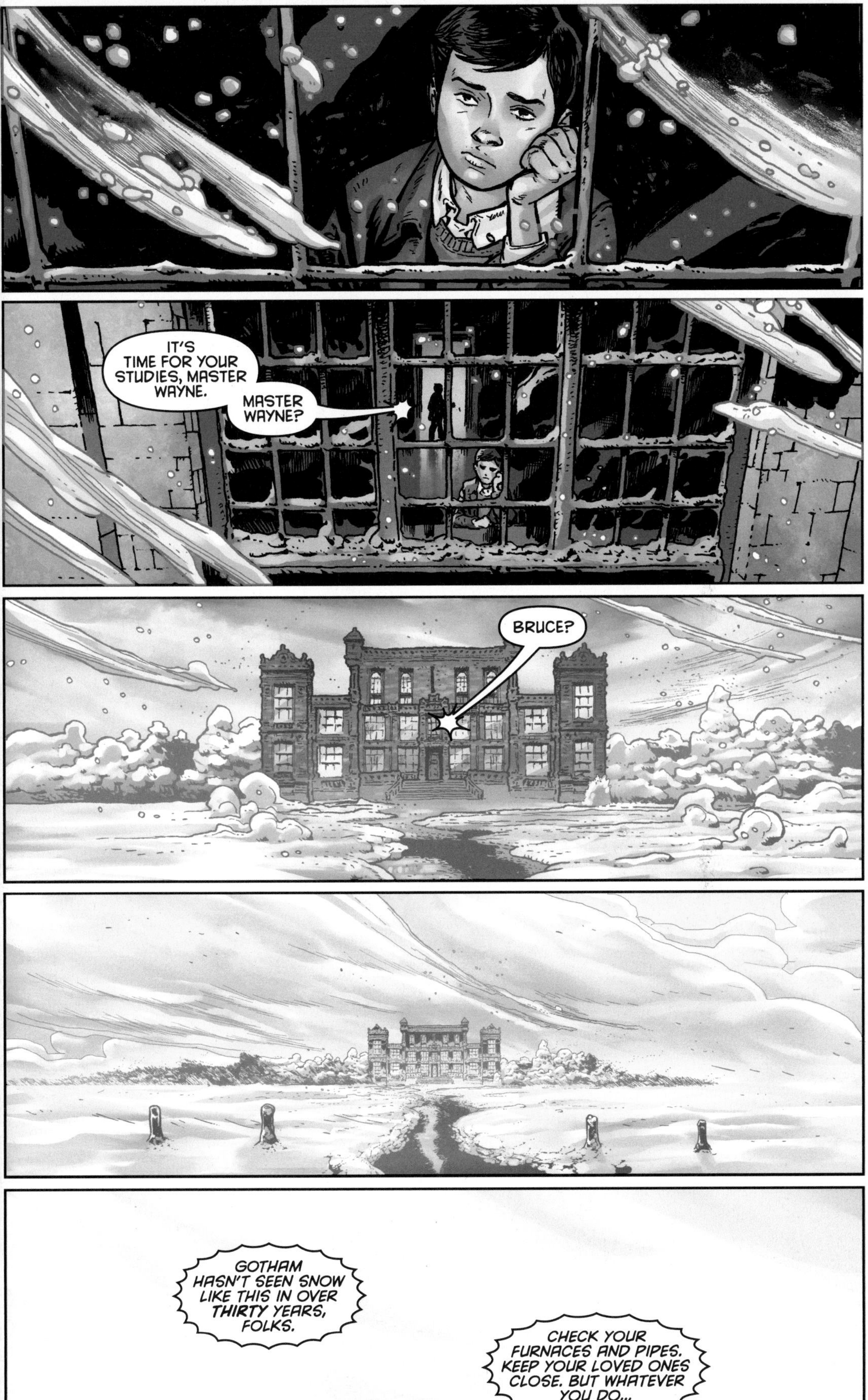
IT'S TIME FOR YOUR STUDIES, MASTER WAYNE.
MASTER WAYNE?
BRUCE?
GOTHAM HASN'T SEEN SNOW LIKE THIS IN OVER THIRTY YEARS, FOLKS.
CHECK YOUR FURNACES AND PIPES. KEEP YOUR LOVED ONES CLOSE. BUT WHATEVER YOU DO...

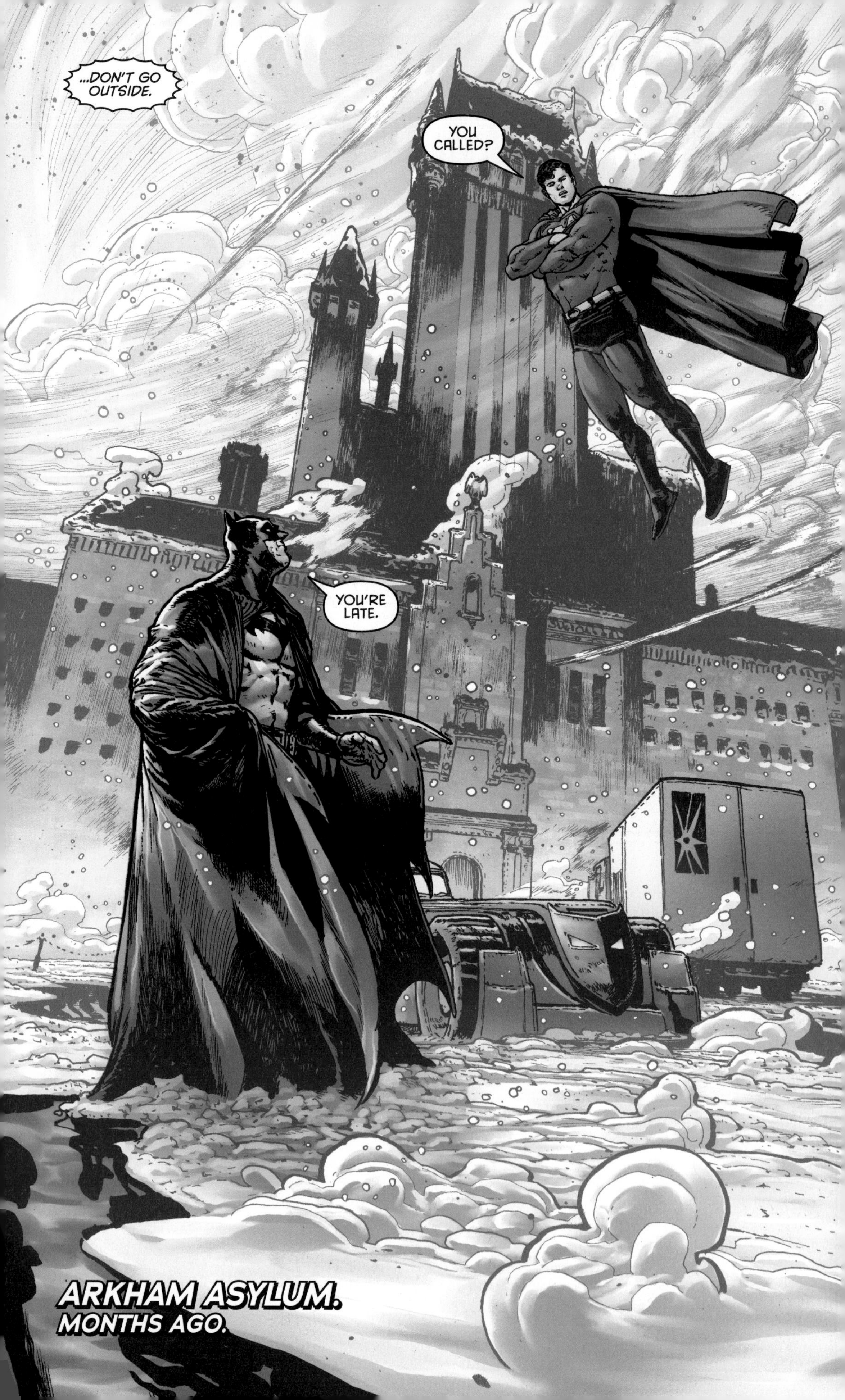
...DON'T GO OUTSIDE.
YOU CALLED?
YOU'RE LATE.
ARKHAM ASYLUM.
MONTHS AGO.

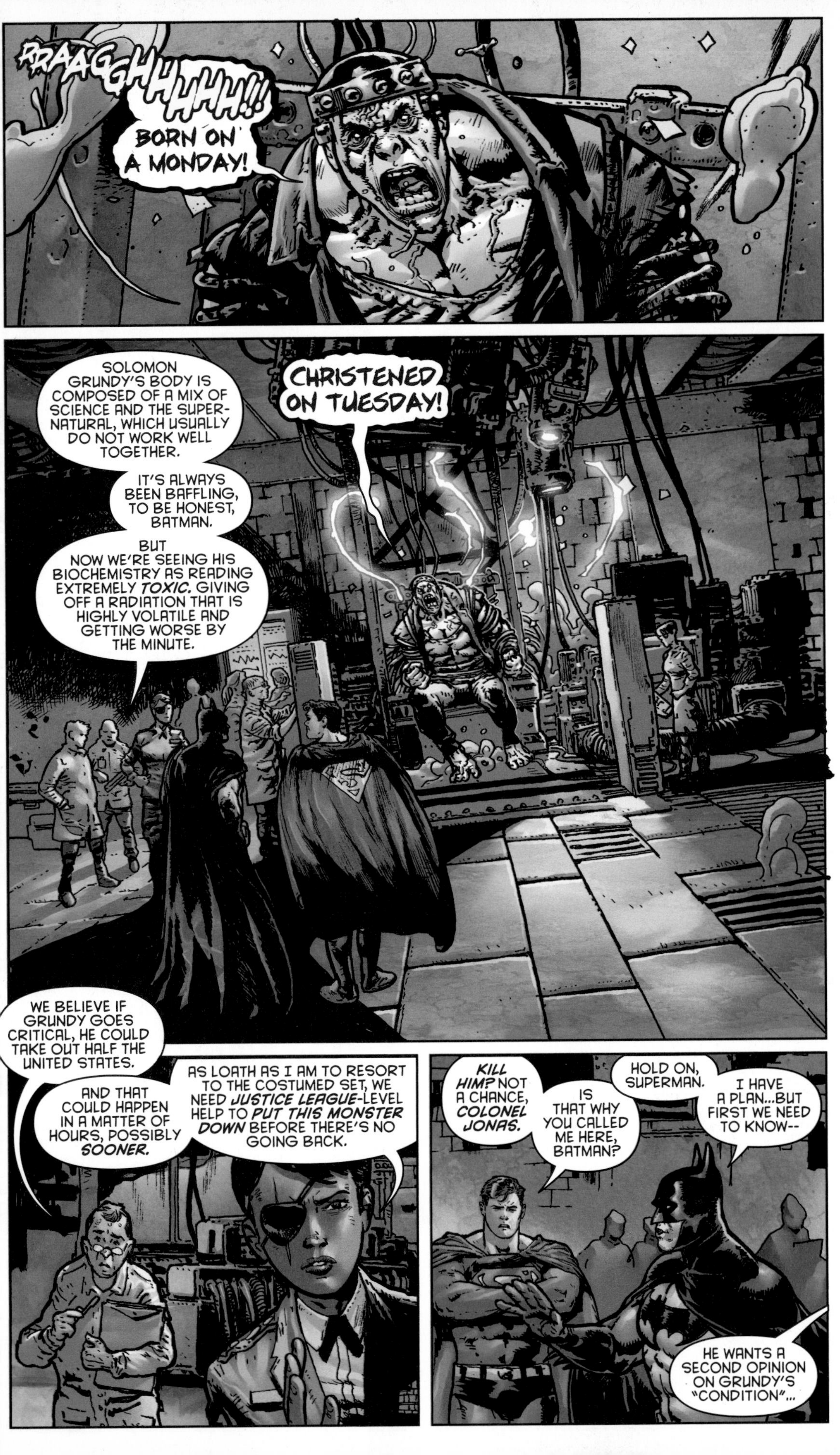
RRAAGGHHHHHH!!!
BORN ON A MONDAY!
SOLOMON GRUNDY'S BODY IS COMPOSED OF A MIX OF SCIENCE AND THE SUPER-NATURAL, WHICH USUALLY DO NOT WORK WELL TOGETHER.
CHRISTENED ON TUESDAY!
IT'S ALWAYS BEEN BAFFLING, TO BE HONEST, BATMAN.
BUT NOW WE'RE SEEING HIS BIOCHEMISTRY AS READING EXTREMELY *TOXIC.* GIVING OFF A RADIATION THAT IS HIGHLY VOLATILE AND GETTING WORSE BY THE MINUTE.
WE BELIEVE IF GRUNDY GOES CRITICAL, HE COULD TAKE OUT HALF THE UNITED STATES.
AND THAT COULD HAPPEN IN A MATTER OF HOURS, POSSIBLY *SOONER.*
AS LOATH AS I AM TO RESORT TO THE COSTUMED SET, WE NEED *JUSTICE LEAGUE*-LEVEL HELP TO *PUT THIS MONSTER DOWN* BEFORE THERE'S NO GOING BACK.
KILL HIM? NOT A CHANCE, *COLONEL JONAS.*
IS THAT WHY YOU CALLED ME HERE, BATMAN?
HOLD ON, SUPERMAN.
I HAVE A PLAN...BUT FIRST WE NEED TO KNOW--
HE WANTS A SECOND OPINION ON GRUNDY'S "CONDITION"...

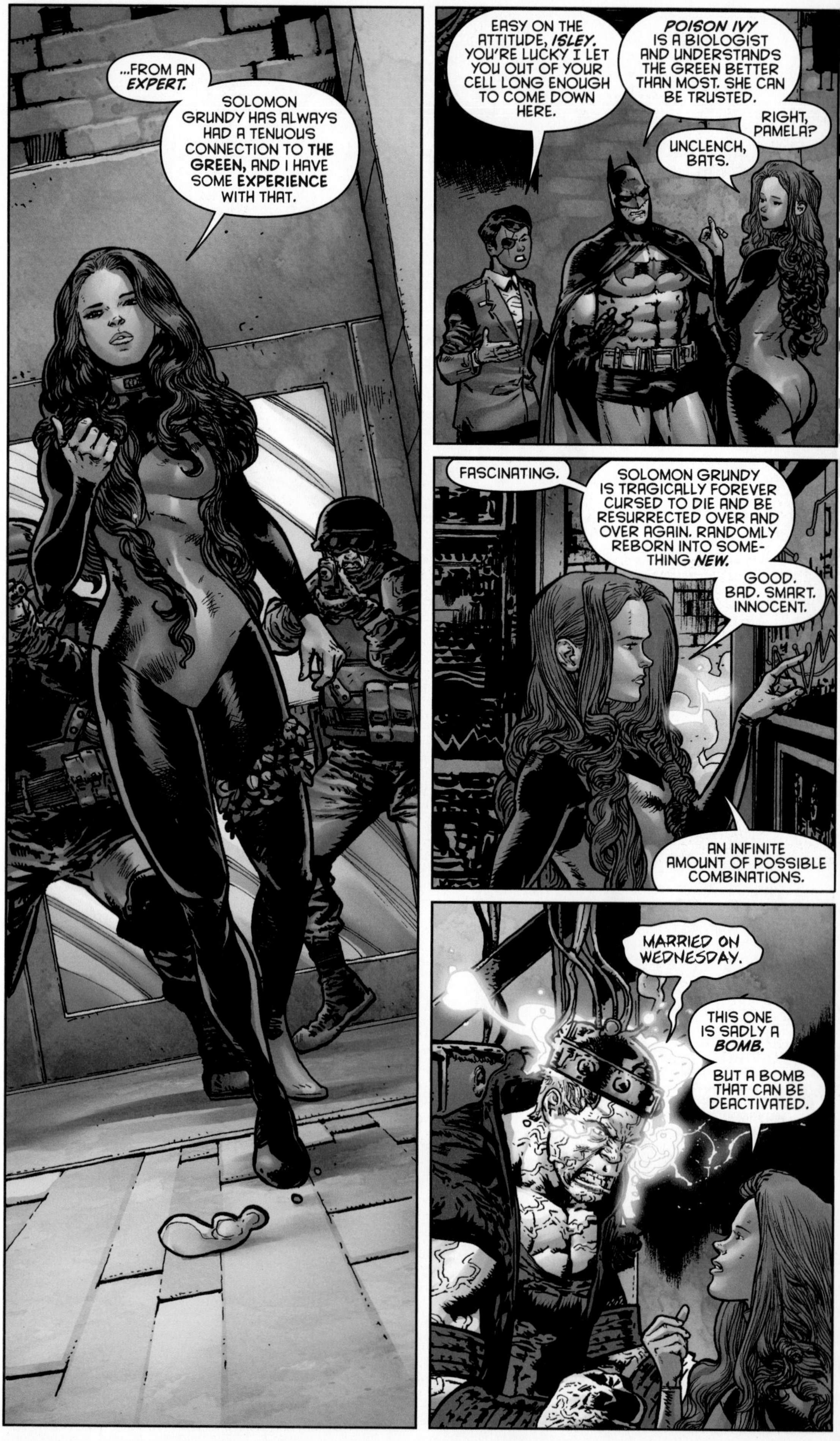
...FROM AN EXPERT.
SOLOMON GRUNDY HAS ALWAYS HAD A TENUOUS CONNECTION TO THE GREEN, AND I HAVE SOME EXPERIENCE WITH THAT.
EASY ON THE ATTITUDE, ISLEY. YOU'RE LUCKY I LET YOU OUT OF YOUR CELL LONG ENOUGH TO COME DOWN HERE.
POISON IVY IS A BIOLOGIST AND UNDERSTANDS THE GREEN BETTER THAN MOST. SHE CAN BE TRUSTED.
RIGHT, PAMELA?
UNCLENCH, BATS.
FASCINATING.
SOLOMON GRUNDY IS TRAGICALLY FOREVER CURSED TO DIE AND BE RESURRECTED OVER AND OVER AGAIN. RANDOMLY REBORN INTO SOME-THING NEW.
GOOD. BAD. SMART. INNOCENT.
AN INFINITE AMOUNT OF POSSIBLE COMBINATIONS.
MARRIED ON WEDNESDAY.
THIS ONE IS SADLY A BOMB.
BUT A BOMB THAT CAN BE DEACTIVATED.

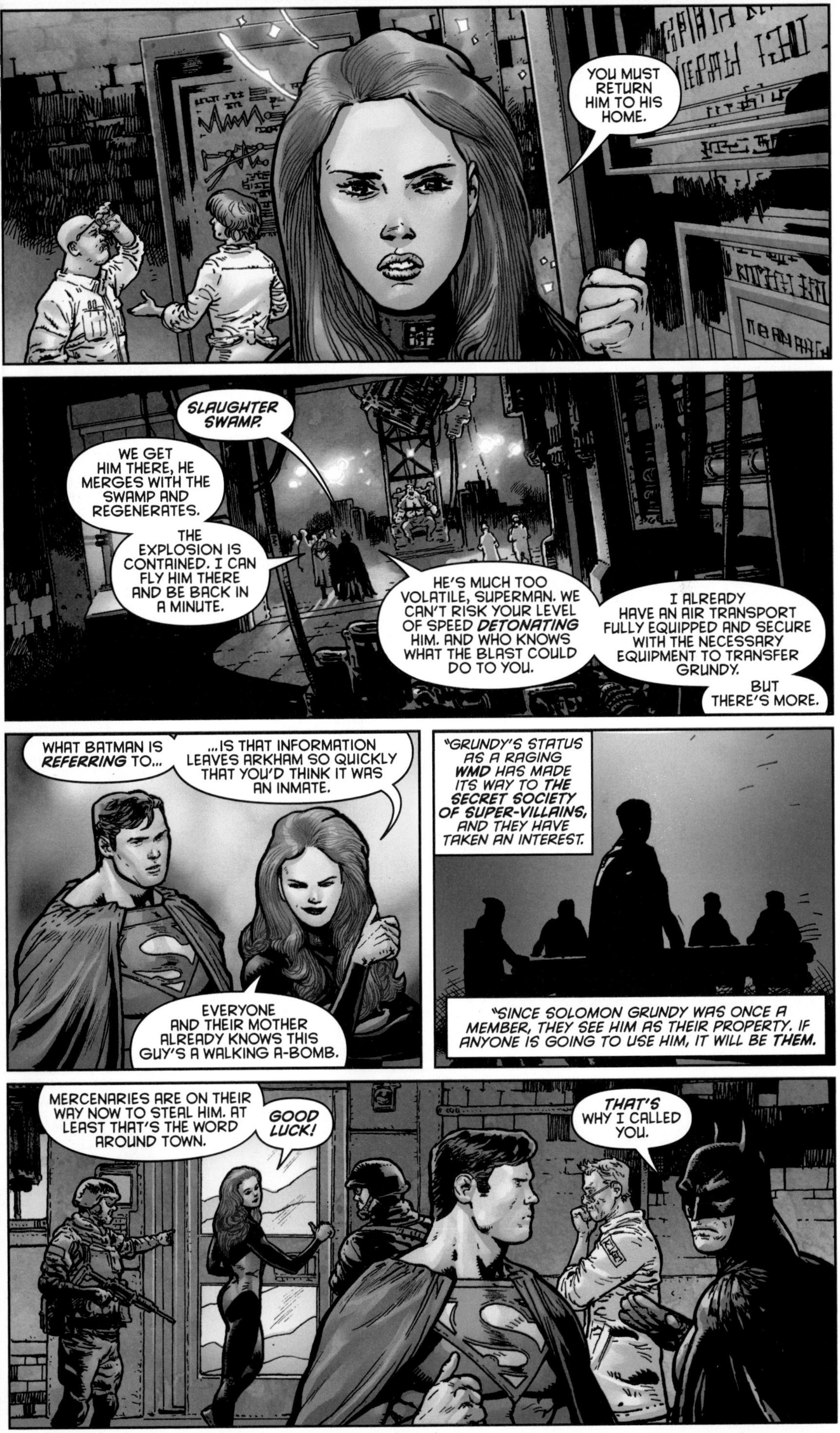
YOU MUST RETURN HIM TO HIS HOME.
SLAUGHTER SWAMP.
WE GET HIM THERE, HE MERGES WITH THE SWAMP AND REGENERATES.
THE EXPLOSION IS CONTAINED. I CAN FLY HIM THERE AND BE BACK IN A MINUTE.
HE'S MUCH TOO VOLATILE, SUPERMAN. WE CAN'T RISK YOUR LEVEL OF SPEED DETONATING HIM. AND WHO KNOWS WHAT THE BLAST COULD DO TO YOU.
I ALREADY HAVE AN AIR TRANSPORT FULLY EQUIPPED AND SECURE WITH THE NECESSARY EQUIPMENT TO TRANSFER GRUNDY.
BUT THERE'S MORE.
WHAT BATMAN IS REFERRING TO...
...IS THAT INFORMATION LEAVES ARKHAM SO QUICKLY THAT YOU'D THINK IT WAS AN INMATE.
EVERYONE AND THEIR MOTHER ALREADY KNOWS THIS GUY'S A WALKING A-BOMB.
"GRUNDY'S STATUS AS A RAGING WMD HAS MADE ITS WAY TO THE SECRET SOCIETY OF SUPER-VILLAINS, AND THEY HAVE TAKEN AN INTEREST.
"SINCE SOLOMON GRUNDY WAS ONCE A MEMBER, THEY SEE HIM AS THEIR PROPERTY. IF ANYONE IS GOING TO USE HIM, IT WILL BE THEM.
MERCENARIES ARE ON THEIR WAY NOW TO STEAL HIM. AT LEAST THAT'S THE WORD AROUND TOWN.
GOOD LUCK!
THAT'S WHY I CALLED YOU.

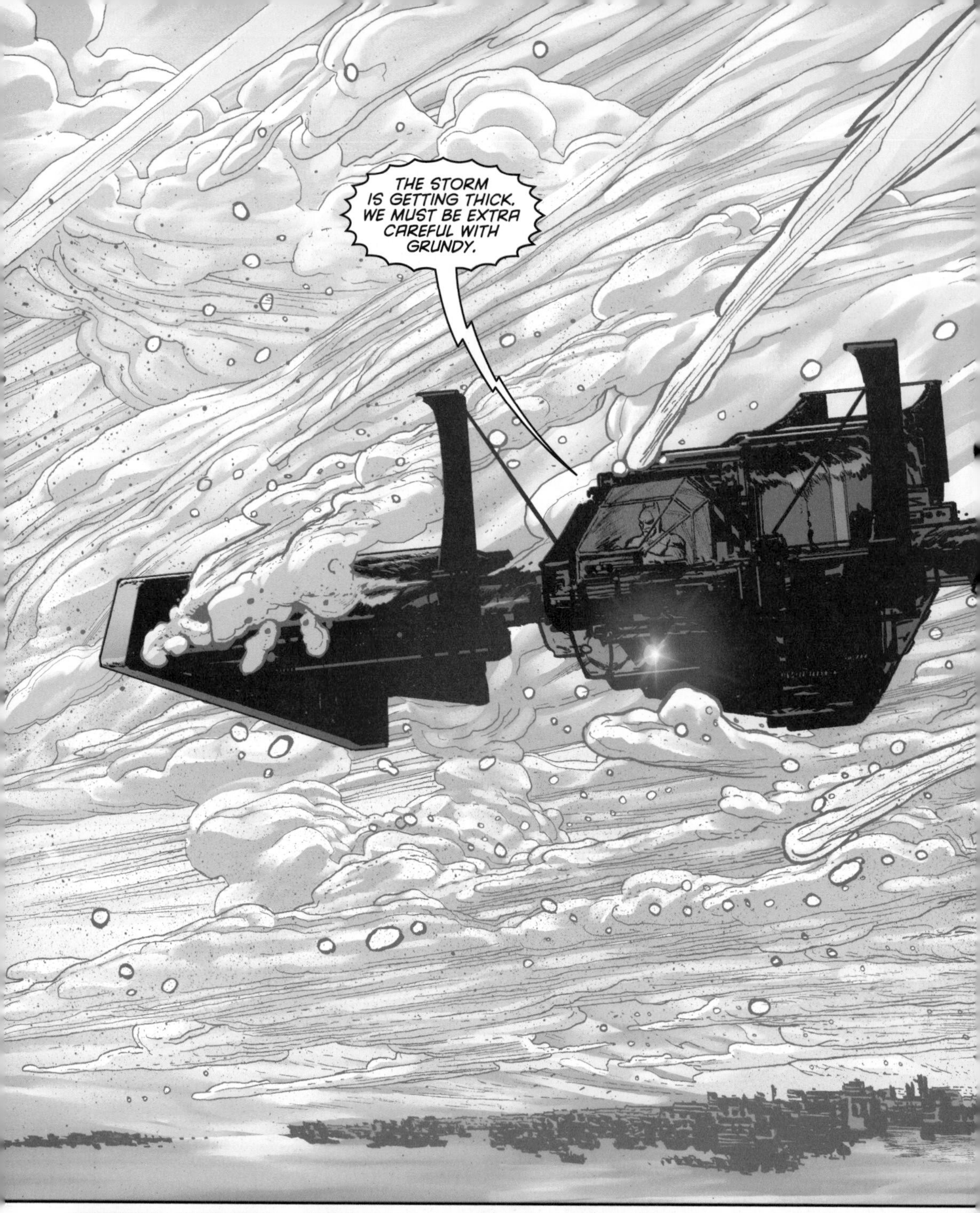
THE STORM IS GETTING THICK. WE MUST BE EXTRA CAREFUL WITH GRUNDY.

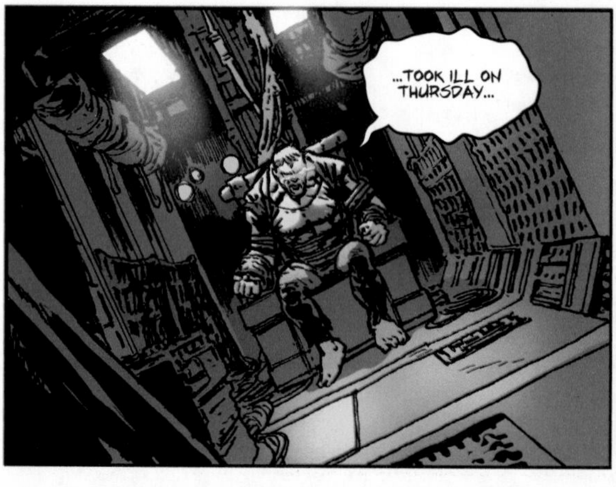
...TOOK ILL ON THURSDAY...

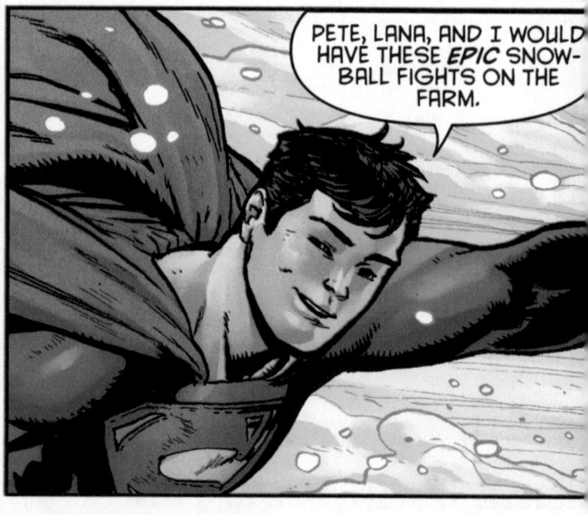
PETE, LANA, AND I WOULD HAVE THESE EPIC SNOWBALL FIGHTS ON THE FARM.

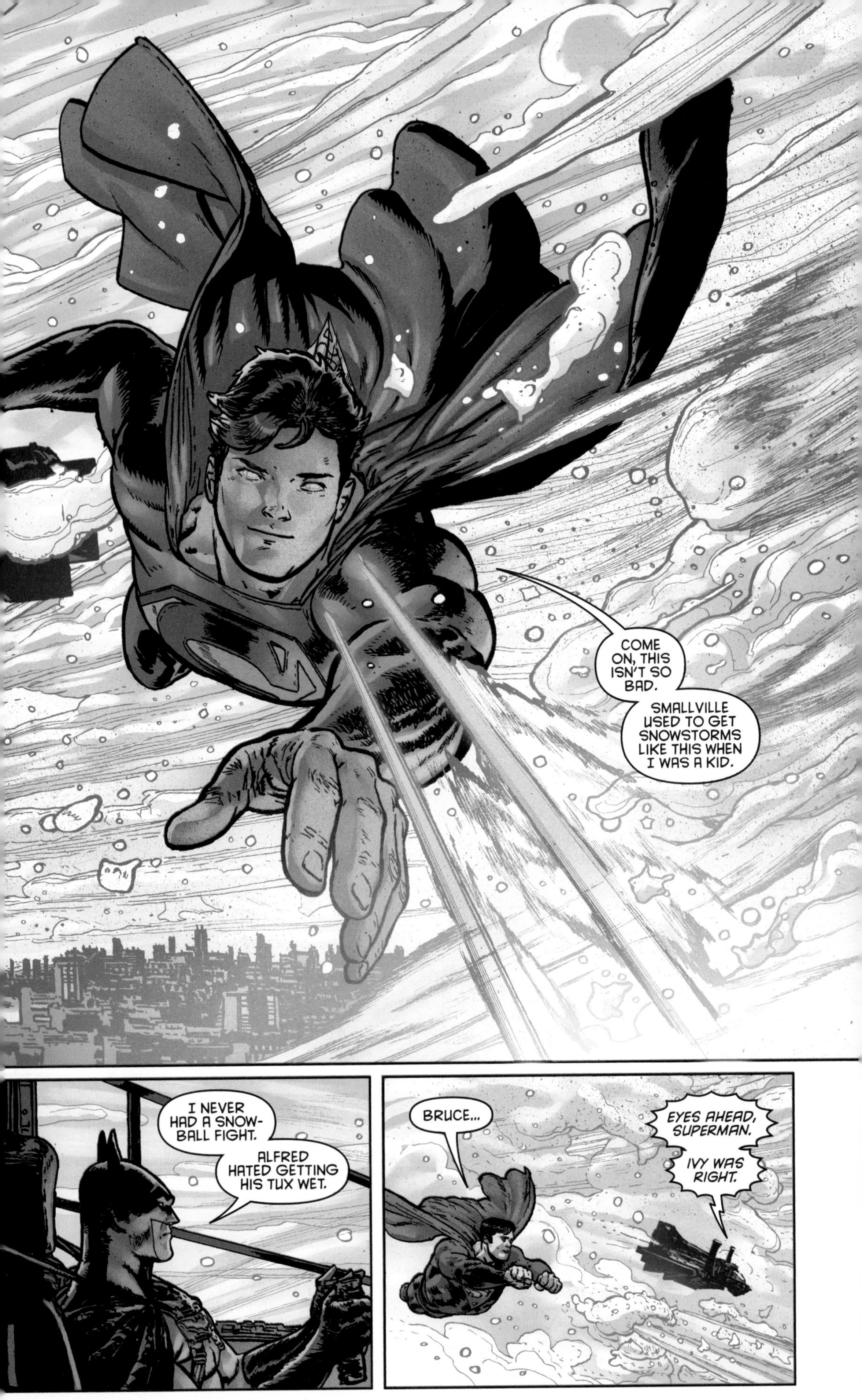
COME ON, THIS ISN'T SO BAD.
SMALLVILLE USED TO GET SNOWSTORMS LIKE THIS WHEN I WAS A KID.
I NEVER HAD A SNOW-BALL FIGHT.
ALFRED HATED GETTING HIS TUX WET.
BRUCE...
EYES AHEAD, SUPERMAN.
IVY WAS RIGHT.

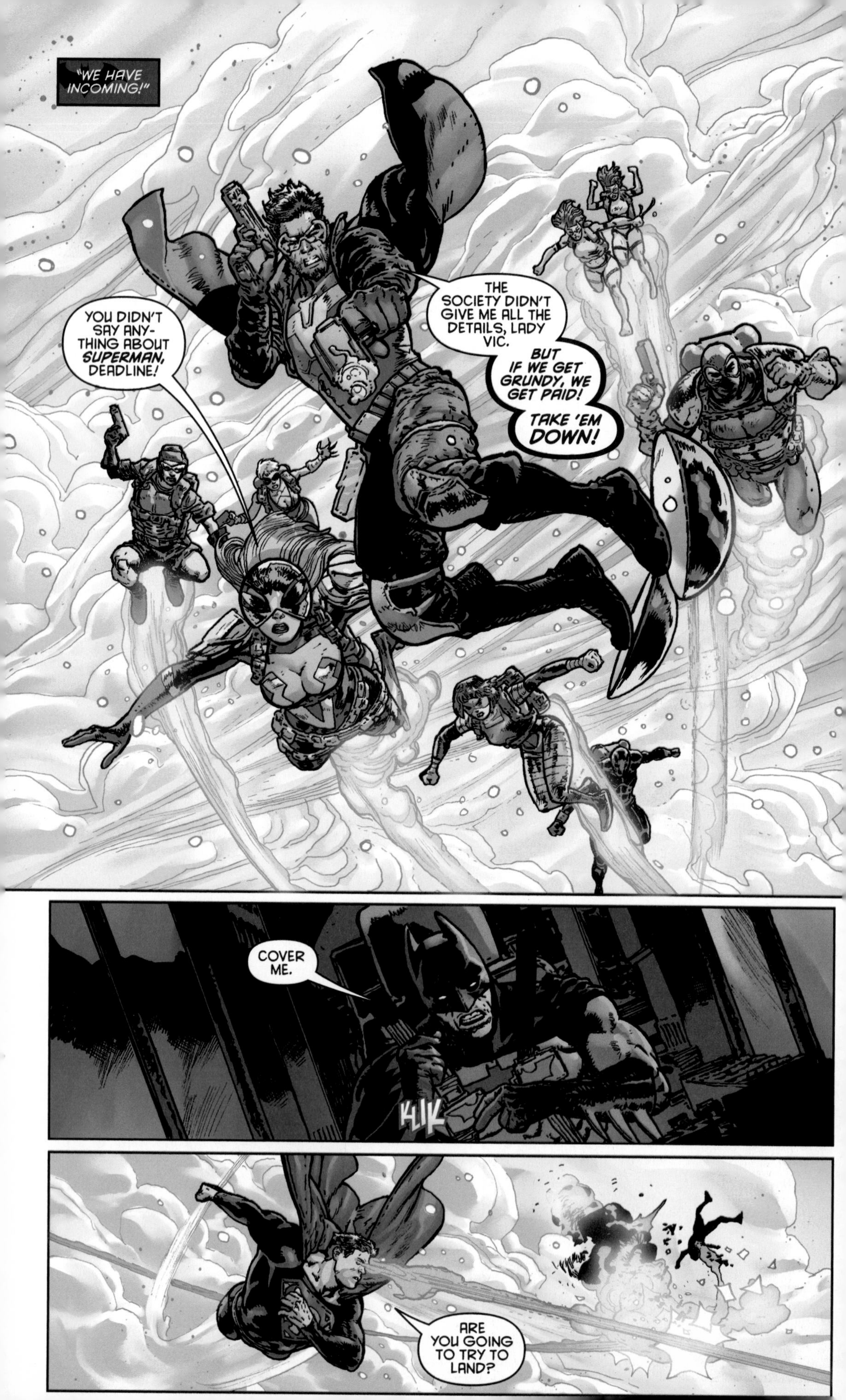
"WE HAVE INCOMING!"
YOU DIDN'T SAY ANY-THING ABOUT SUPERMAN, DEADLINE!
THE SOCIETY DIDN'T GIVE ME ALL THE DETAILS, LADY VIC.
BUT IF WE GET GRUNDY, WE GET PAID!
TAKE 'EM DOWN!
COVER ME.
KLIK
ARE YOU GOING TO TRY TO LAND?

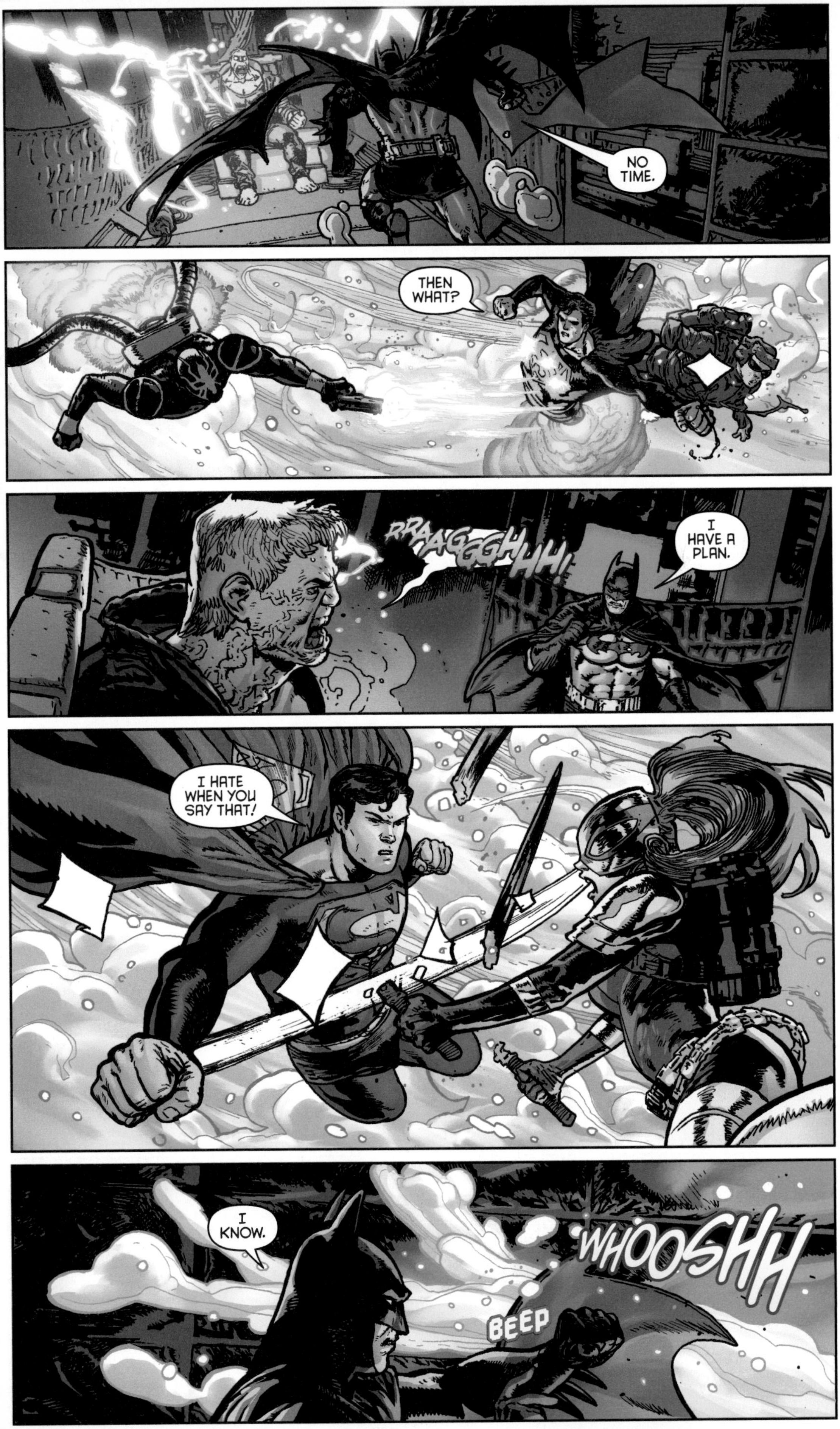
NO TIME.
THEN WHAT?
RRAAAGGGHHHH!
I HAVE A PLAN.
I HATE WHEN YOU SAY THAT!
I KNOW.
WHOOSHH
BEEP

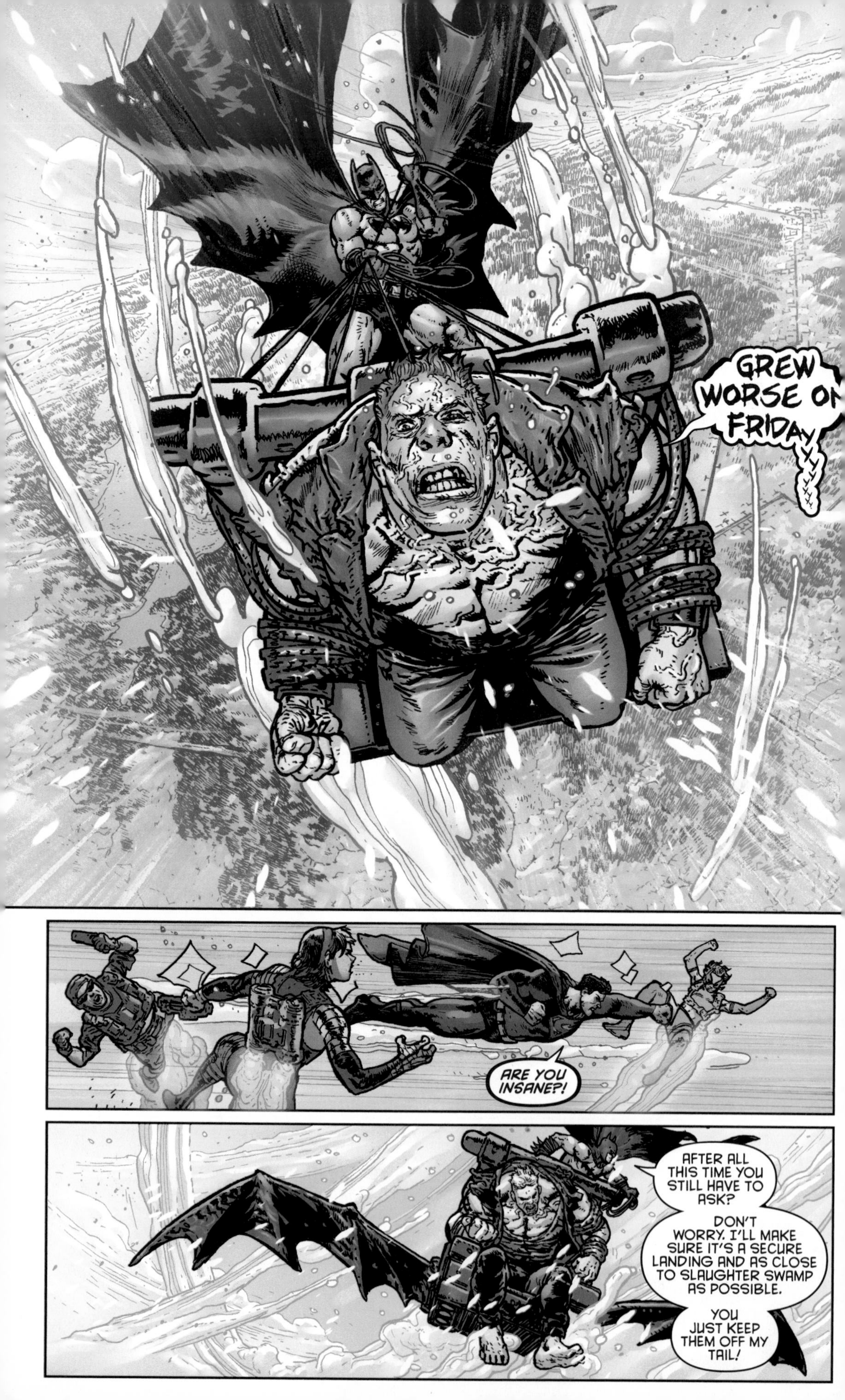
GREW WORSE ON FRIDAY
ARE YOU INSANE?!
AFTER ALL THIS TIME YOU STILL HAVE TO ASK?
DON'T WORRY. I'LL MAKE SURE IT'S A SECURE LANDING AND AS CLOSE TO SLAUGHTER SWAMP AS POSSIBLE.
YOU JUST KEEP THEM OFF MY TAIL!

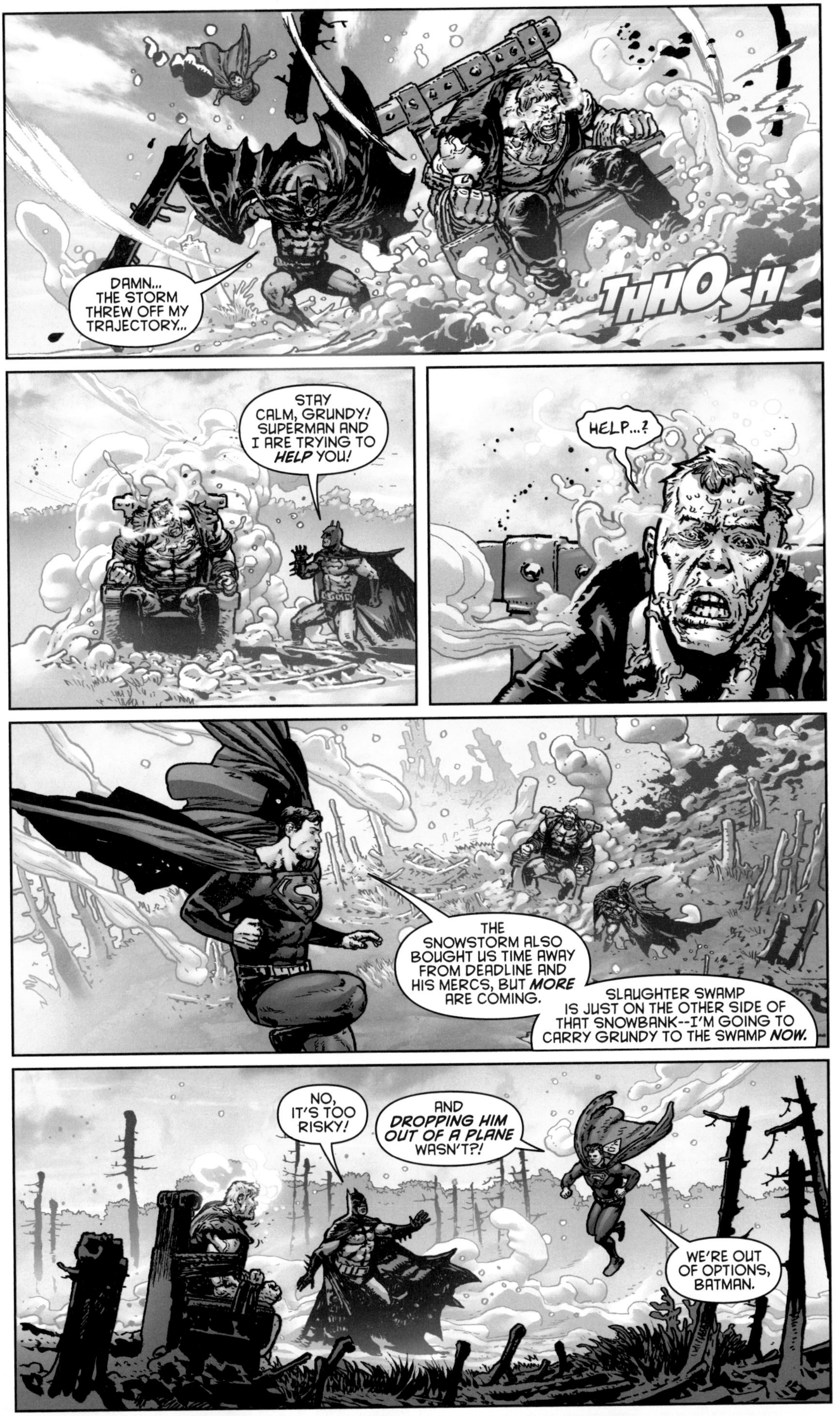
DAMN... THE STORM THREW OFF MY TRAJECTORY...
THHOSH
STAY CALM, GRUNDY! SUPERMAN AND I ARE TRYING TO *HELP* YOU!
HELP...?
THE SNOWSTORM ALSO BOUGHT US TIME AWAY FROM DEADLINE AND HIS MERCS, BUT *MORE* ARE COMING.
SLAUGHTER SWAMP IS JUST ON THE OTHER SIDE OF THAT SNOWBANK--I'M GOING TO CARRY GRUNDY TO THE SWAMP *NOW.*
NO, IT'S TOO RISKY!
AND *DROPPING HIM OUT OF A PLANE* WASN'T?!
WE'RE OUT OF OPTIONS, BATMAN.

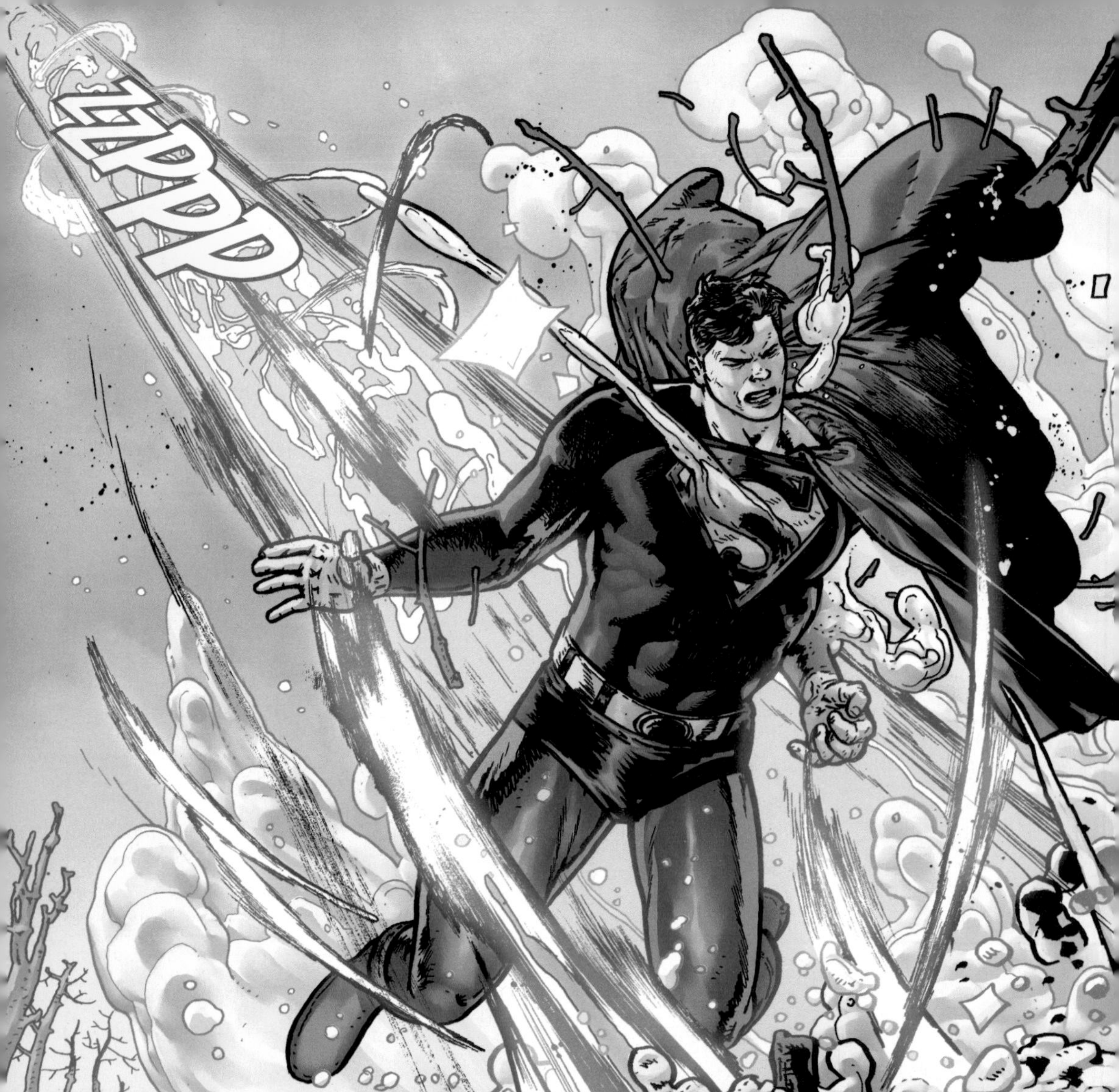
ZZPPP

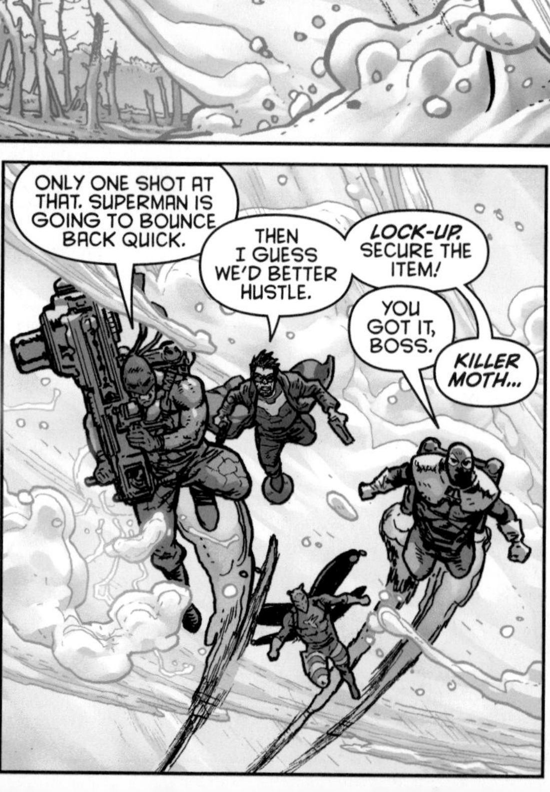
ONLY ONE SHOT AT THAT. SUPERMAN IS GOING TO BOUNCE BACK QUICK.
THEN I GUESS WE'D BETTER HUSTLE.
LOCK-UP. SECURE THE ITEM!
YOU GOT IT, BOSS.
KILLER MOTH...

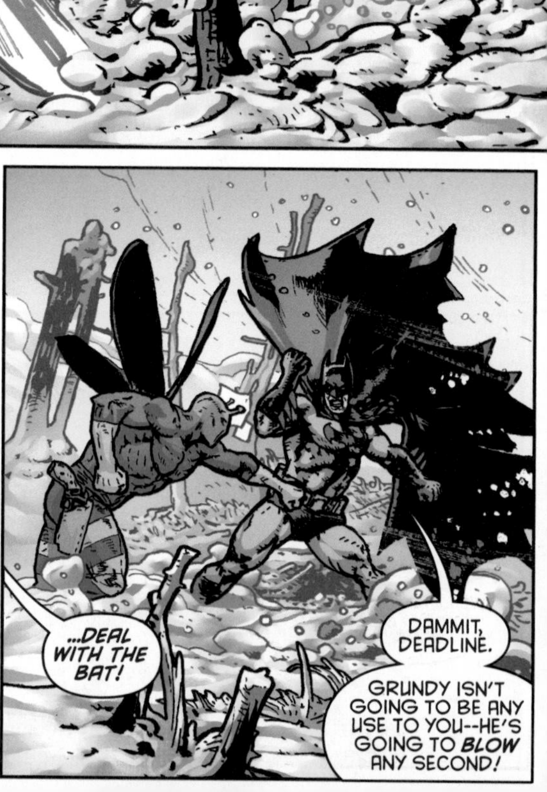
...DEAL WITH THE BAT!
DAMMIT, DEADLINE.
GRUNDY ISN'T GOING TO BE ANY USE TO YOU--HE'S GOING TO BLOW ANY SECOND!

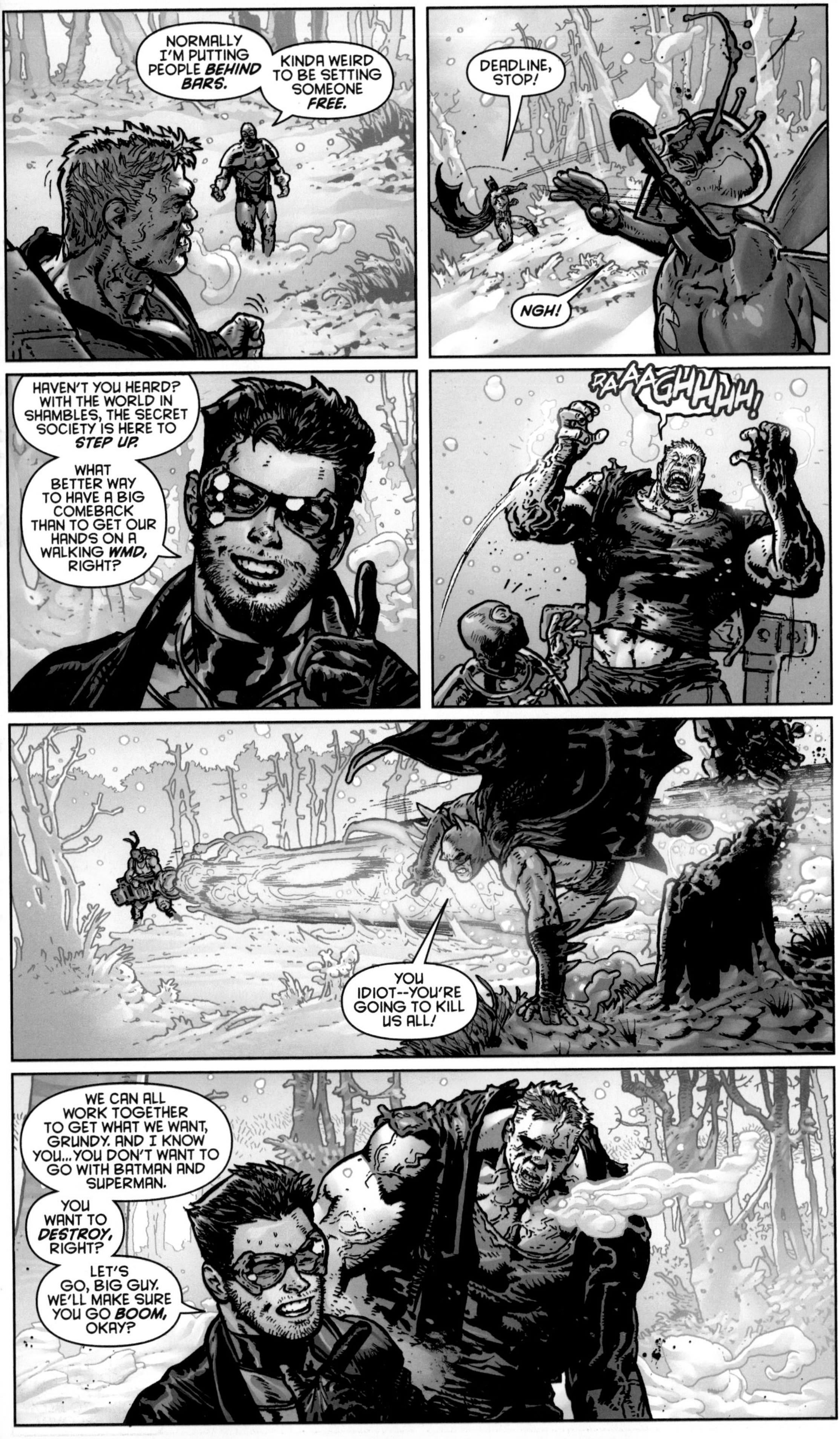
NORMALLY I'M PUTTING PEOPLE BEHIND BARS.
KINDA WEIRD TO BE SETTING SOMEONE FREE.
DEADLINE, STOP!
NGH!
HAVEN'T YOU HEARD? WITH THE WORLD IN SHAMBLES, THE SECRET SOCIETY IS HERE TO STEP UP.
WHAT BETTER WAY TO HAVE A BIG COMEBACK THAN TO GET OUR HANDS ON A WALKING WMD, RIGHT?
RAAAGHHHH!
YOU IDIOT--YOU'RE GOING TO KILL US ALL!
WE CAN ALL WORK TOGETHER TO GET WHAT WE WANT, GRUNDY. AND I KNOW YOU...YOU DON'T WANT TO GO WITH BATMAN AND SUPERMAN.
YOU WANT TO DESTROY, RIGHT?
LET'S GO, BIG GUY. WE'LL MAKE SURE YOU GO BOOM, OKAY?

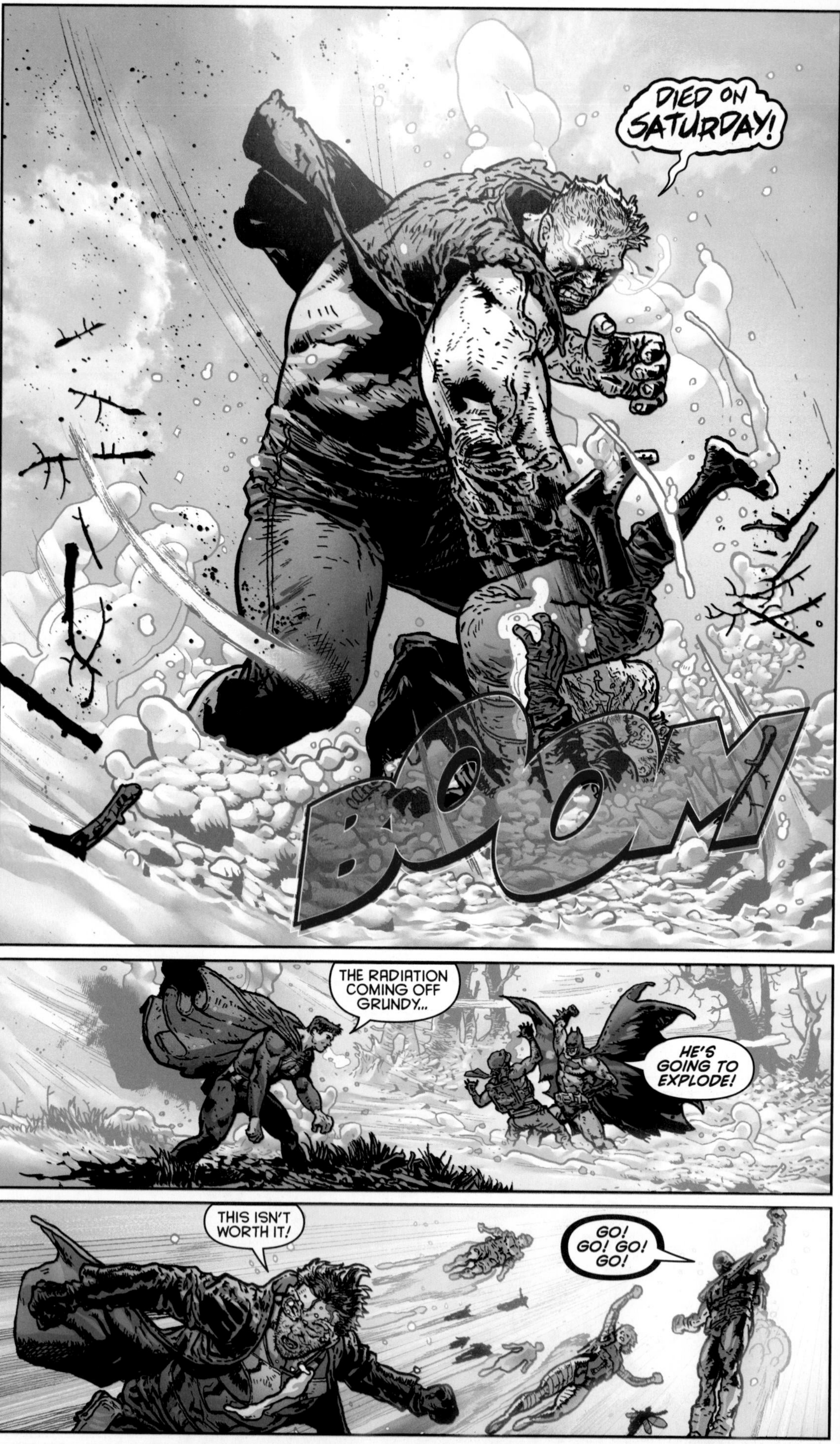
DIED ON SATURDAY!
BOOM
THE RADIATION COMING OFF GRUNDY...
HE'S GOING TO EXPLODE!
THIS ISN'T WORTH IT!
GO! GO! GO! GO!

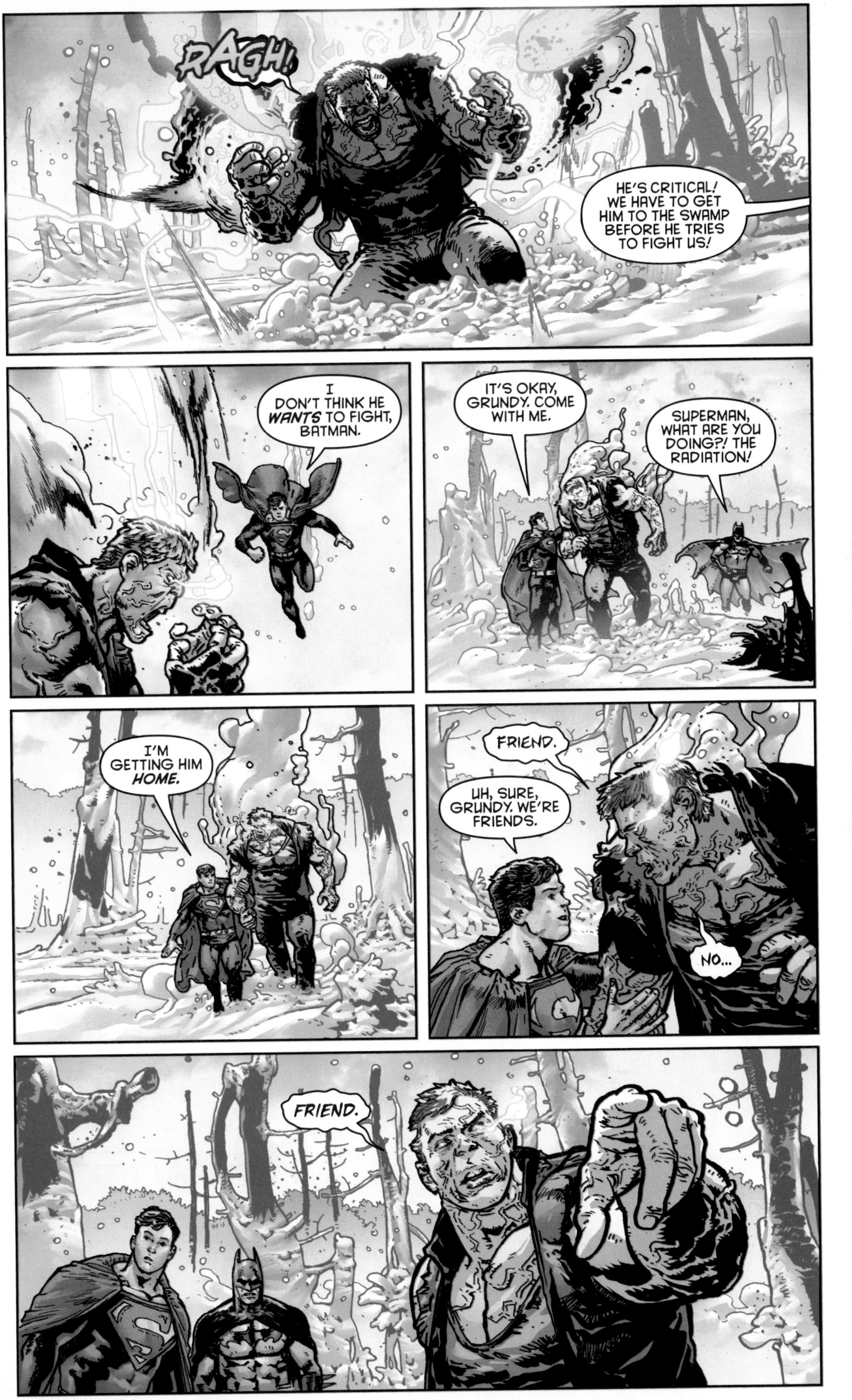
RAGH!
HE'S CRITICAL! WE HAVE TO GET HIM TO THE SWAMP BEFORE HE TRIES TO FIGHT US!
I DON'T THINK HE WANTS TO FIGHT, BATMAN.
IT'S OKAY, GRUNDY. COME WITH ME.
SUPERMAN, WHAT ARE YOU DOING?! THE RADIATION!
I'M GETTING HIM HOME.
FRIEND.
UH, SURE, GRUNDY. WE'RE FRIENDS.
NO...
FRIEND.

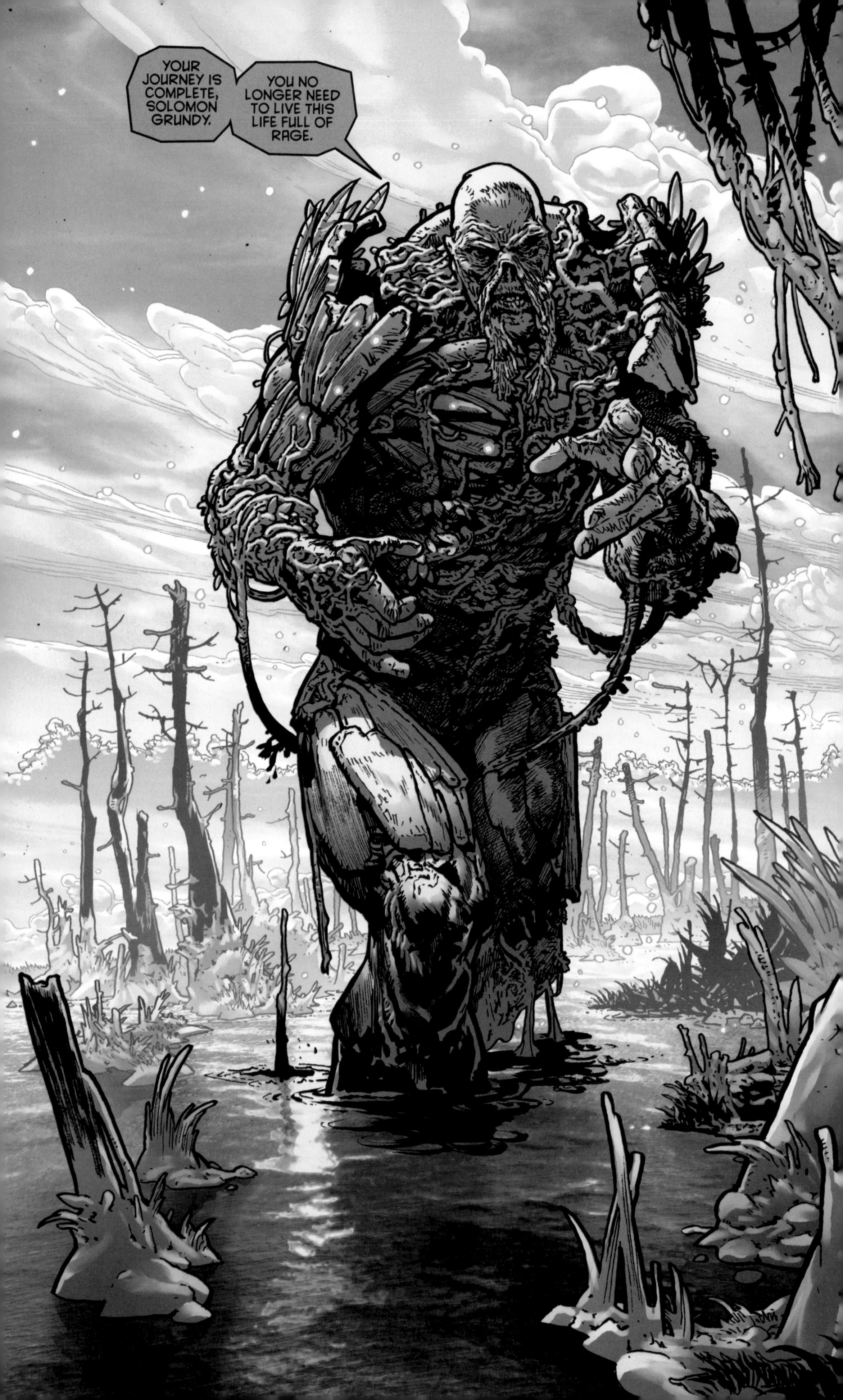

YOUR JOURNEY IS COMPLETE, SOLOMON GRUNDY.
YOU NO LONGER NEED TO LIVE THIS LIFE FULL OF RAGE.

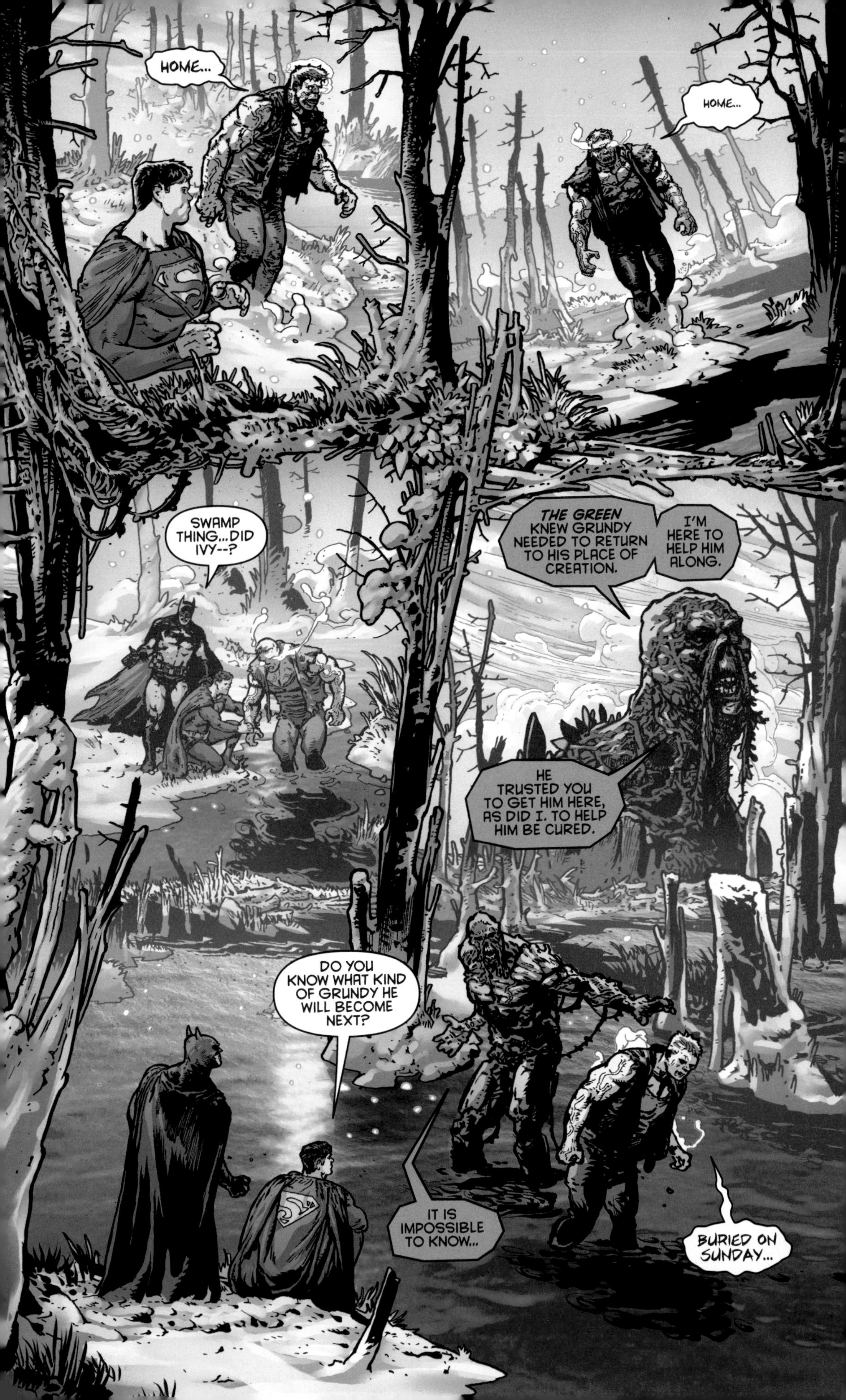
HOME...
HOME...
SWAMP THING...DID IVY--?
THE GREEN KNEW GRUNDY NEEDED TO RETURN TO HIS PLACE OF CREATION.
I'M HERE TO HELP HIM ALONG.
HE TRUSTED YOU TO GET HIM HERE, AS DID I. TO HELP HIM BE CURED.
DO YOU KNOW WHAT KIND OF GRUNDY HE WILL BECOME NEXT?
IT IS IMPOSSIBLE TO KNOW...
BURIED ON SUNDAY...

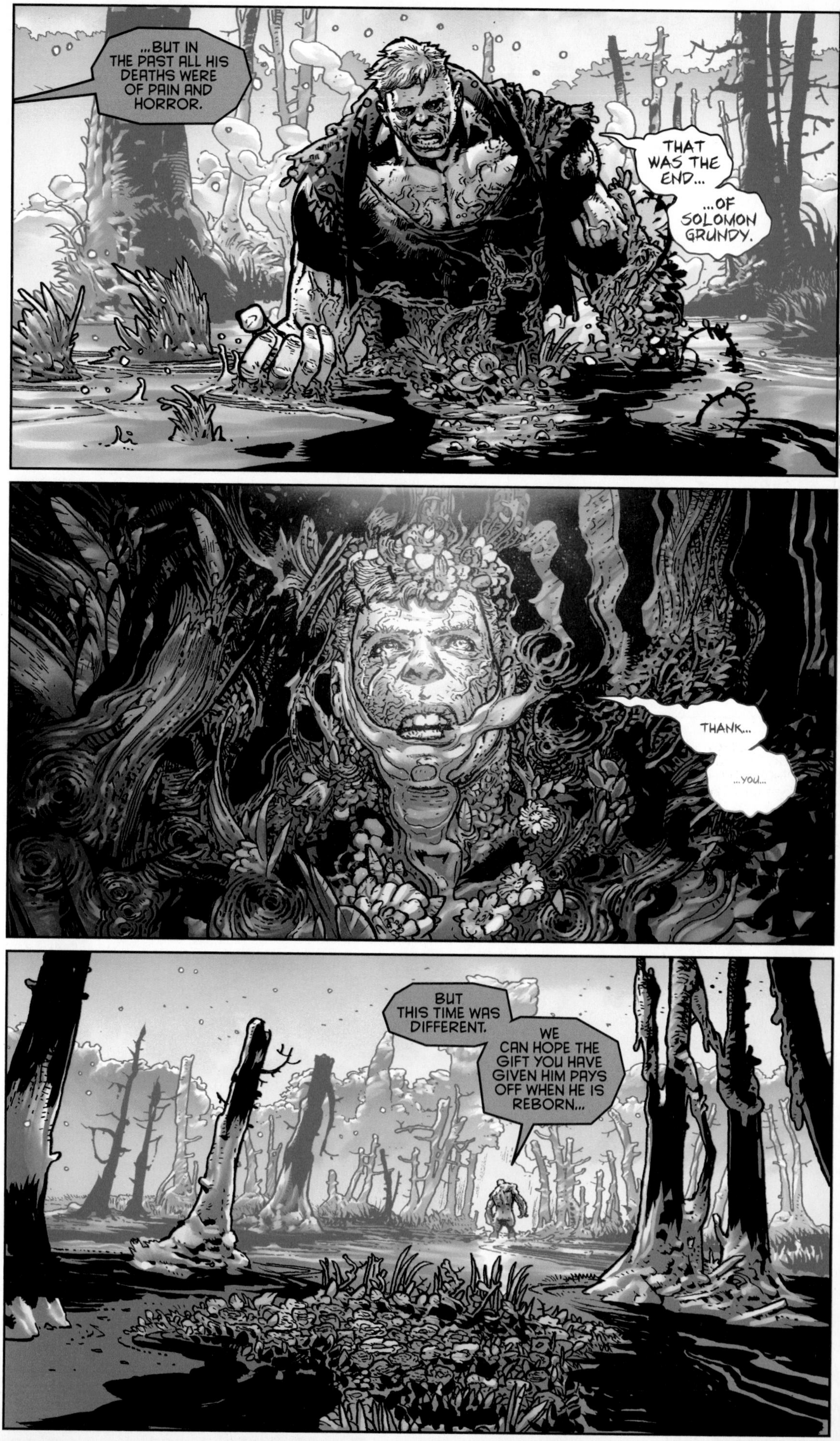
...BUT IN THE PAST ALL HIS DEATHS WERE OF PAIN AND HORROR.
THAT WAS THE END...
...OF SOLOMON GRUNDY.
THANK...
...YOU...
BUT THIS TIME WAS DIFFERENT.
WE CAN HOPE THE GIFT YOU HAVE GIVEN HIM PAYS OFF WHEN HE IS REBORN...

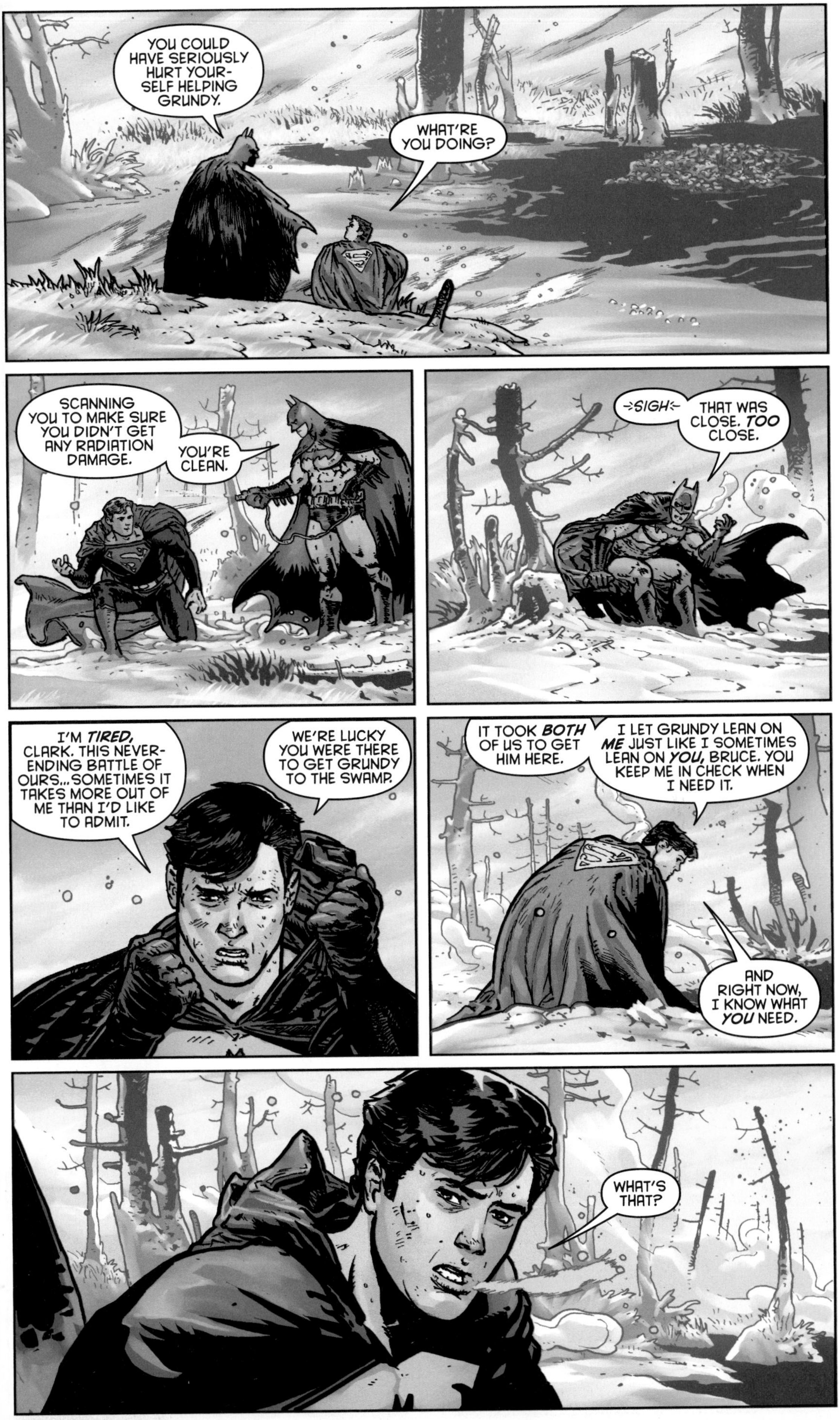
YOU COULD HAVE SERIOUSLY HURT YOUR-SELF HELPING GRUNDY.
WHAT'RE YOU DOING?
SCANNING YOU TO MAKE SURE YOU DIDN'T GET ANY RADIATION DAMAGE.
YOU'RE CLEAN.
-SIGH-
THAT WAS CLOSE. TOO CLOSE.
I'M TIRED, CLARK. THIS NEVER-ENDING BATTLE OF OURS... SOMETIMES IT TAKES MORE OUT OF ME THAN I'D LIKE TO ADMIT.
WE'RE LUCKY YOU WERE THERE TO GET GRUNDY TO THE SWAMP.
IT TOOK BOTH OF US TO GET HIM HERE.
I LET GRUNDY LEAN ON ME JUST LIKE I SOMETIMES LEAN ON YOU, BRUCE. YOU KEEP ME IN CHECK WHEN I NEED IT.
AND RIGHT NOW, I KNOW WHAT YOU NEED.
WHAT'S THAT?

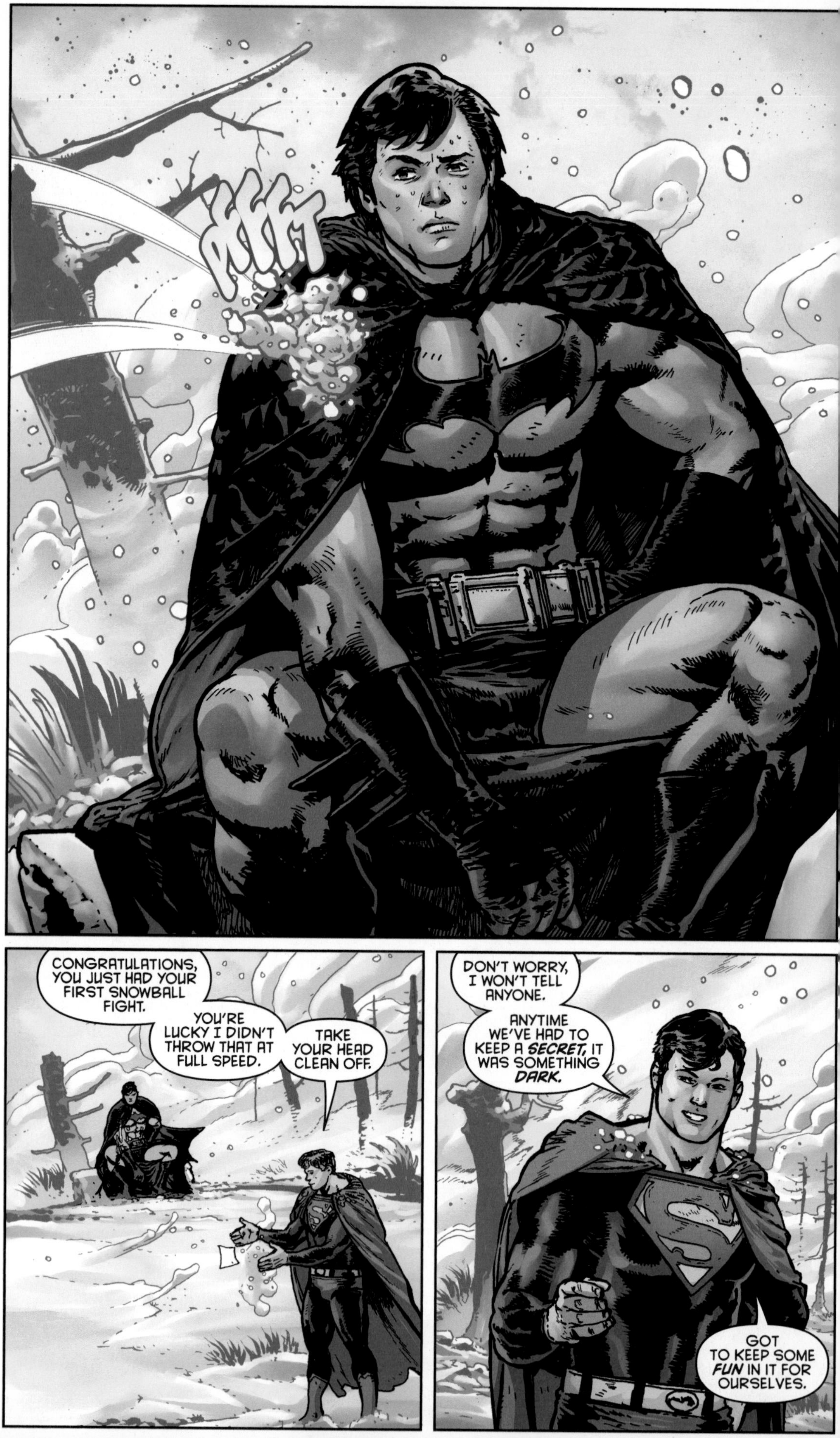
PFFFT
CONGRATULATIONS, YOU JUST HAD YOUR FIRST SNOWBALL FIGHT.
YOU'RE LUCKY I DIDN'T THROW THAT AT FULL SPEED.
TAKE YOUR HEAD CLEAN OFF.
DON'T WORRY, I WON'T TELL ANYONE.
ANYTIME WE'VE HAD TO KEEP A ***SECRET,*** IT WAS SOMETHING ***DARK.***
GOT TO KEEP SOME ***FUN*** IN IT FOR OURSELVES.

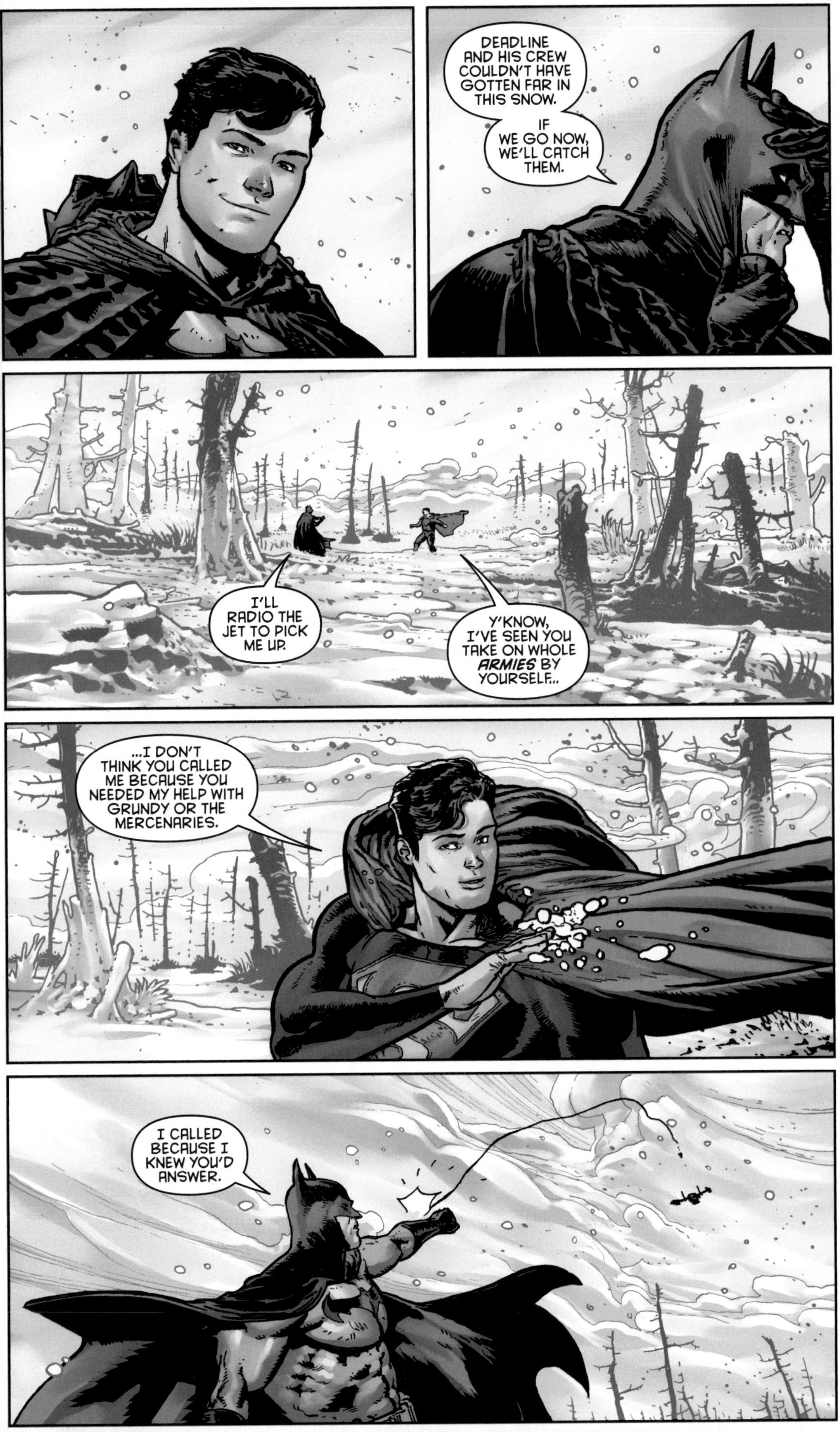
DEADLINE AND HIS CREW COULDN'T HAVE GOTTEN FAR IN THIS SNOW.
IF WE GO NOW, WE'LL CATCH THEM.
I'LL RADIO THE JET TO PICK ME UP.
Y'KNOW, I'VE SEEN YOU TAKE ON WHOLE *ARMIES* BY YOURSELF...
...I DON'T THINK YOU CALLED ME BECAUSE YOU NEEDED MY HELP WITH GRUNDY OR THE MERCENARIES.
I CALLED BECAUSE I KNEW YOU'D ANSWER.

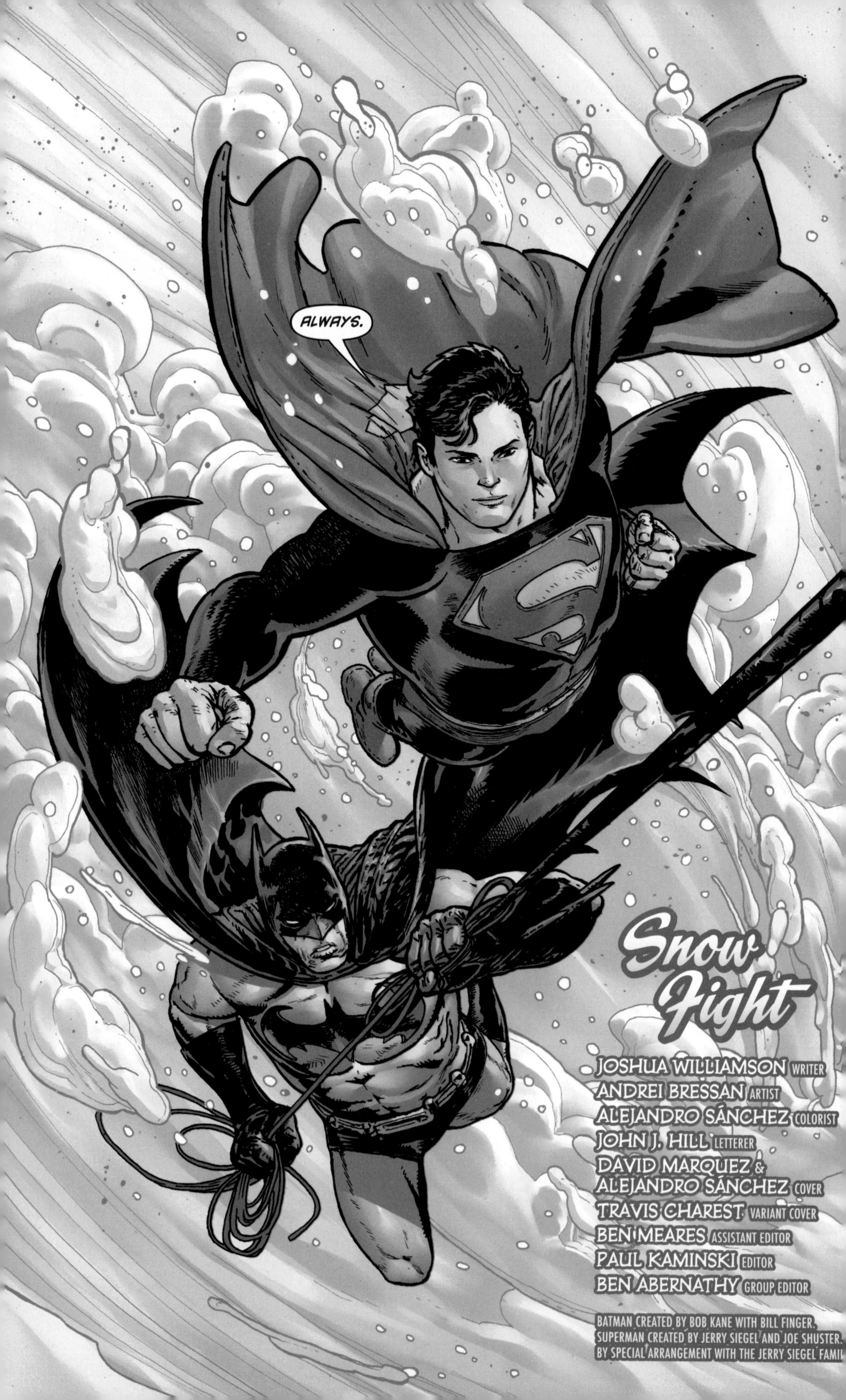
ALWAYS.
Snow Fight
JOSHUA WILLIAMSON WRITER
ANDREI BRESSAN ARTIST
ALEJANDRO SÁNCHEZ COLORIST
JOHN J. HILL LETTERER
DAVID MARQUEZ & ALEJANDRO SÁNCHEZ COVER
TRAVIS CHAREST VARIANT COVER
BEN MEARES ASSISTANT EDITOR
PAUL KAMINSKI EDITOR
BEN ABERNATHY GROUP EDITOR
BATMAN CREATED BY BOB KANE WITH BILL FINGER.
SUPERMAN CREATED BY JERRY SIEGEL AND JOE SHUSTER.
BY SPECIAL ARRANGEMENT WITH THE JERRY SIEGEL FAMI

VARIANT COVER GALLERY

Batman/Superman #7
variant cover by
ANDY KUBERT and **BRAD ANDERSON**

Batman/Superman #8
variant cover by
ANDY KUBERT and **BRAD ANDERSON**

Batman/Superman #9
variant cover by
MIKE MAYHEW

Batman/Superman #10
variant cover by
RICCARDO FEDERICI

Batman/Superman #11
variant cover by
JAE LEE and **JUNE CHUNG**

Batman/Superman #12
variant cover by
LEE WEEKS and **ELIZABETH BREITWEISER**

Batman/Superman #13
variant cover by
MARK BROOKS

Batman/Superman #14
variant cover by
BRYAN HITCH and **ALEX SINCLAIR**

Batman/Superman #15
variant cover by
TRAVIS CHAREST

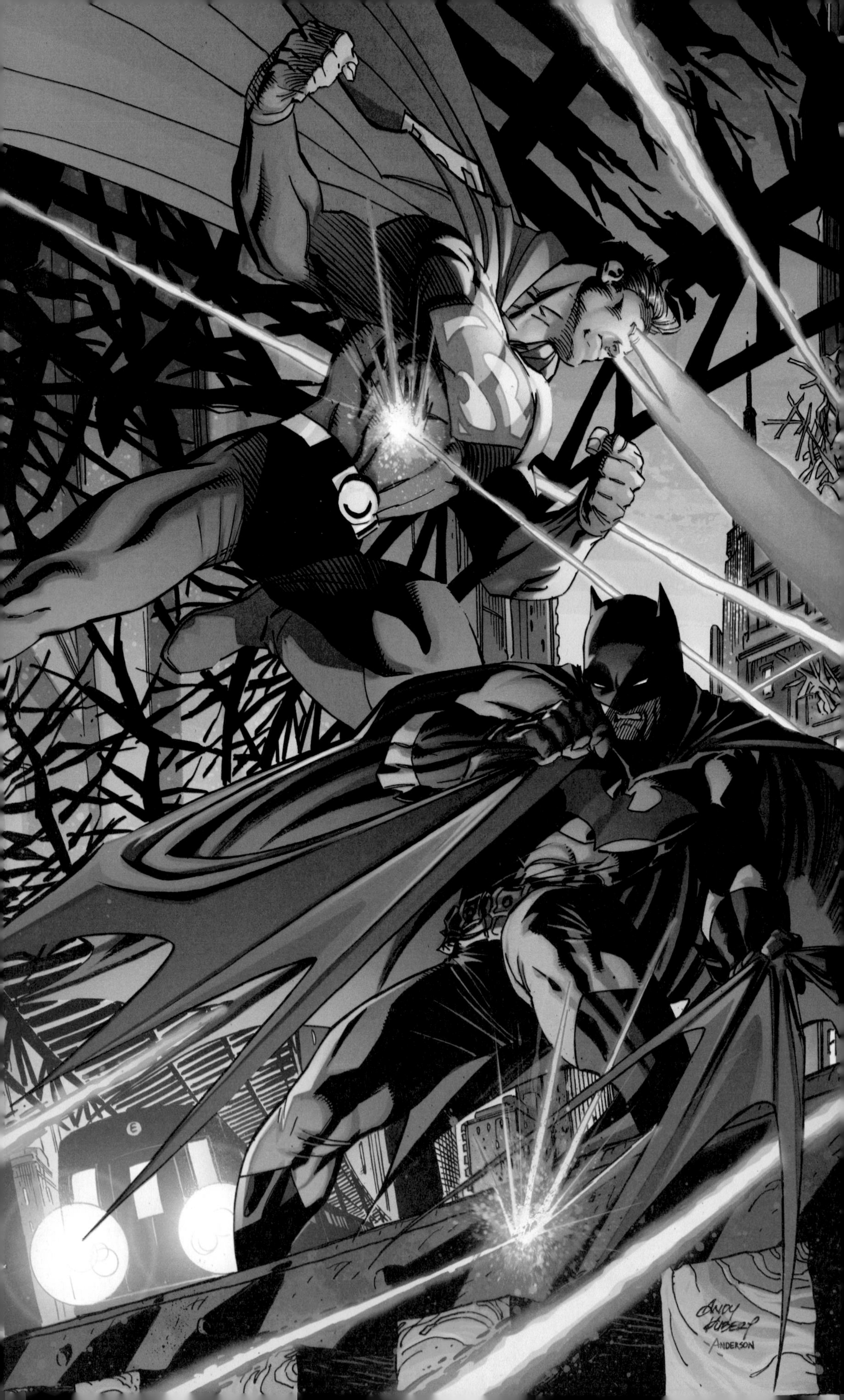
ANDY KUBERT
ANDERSON

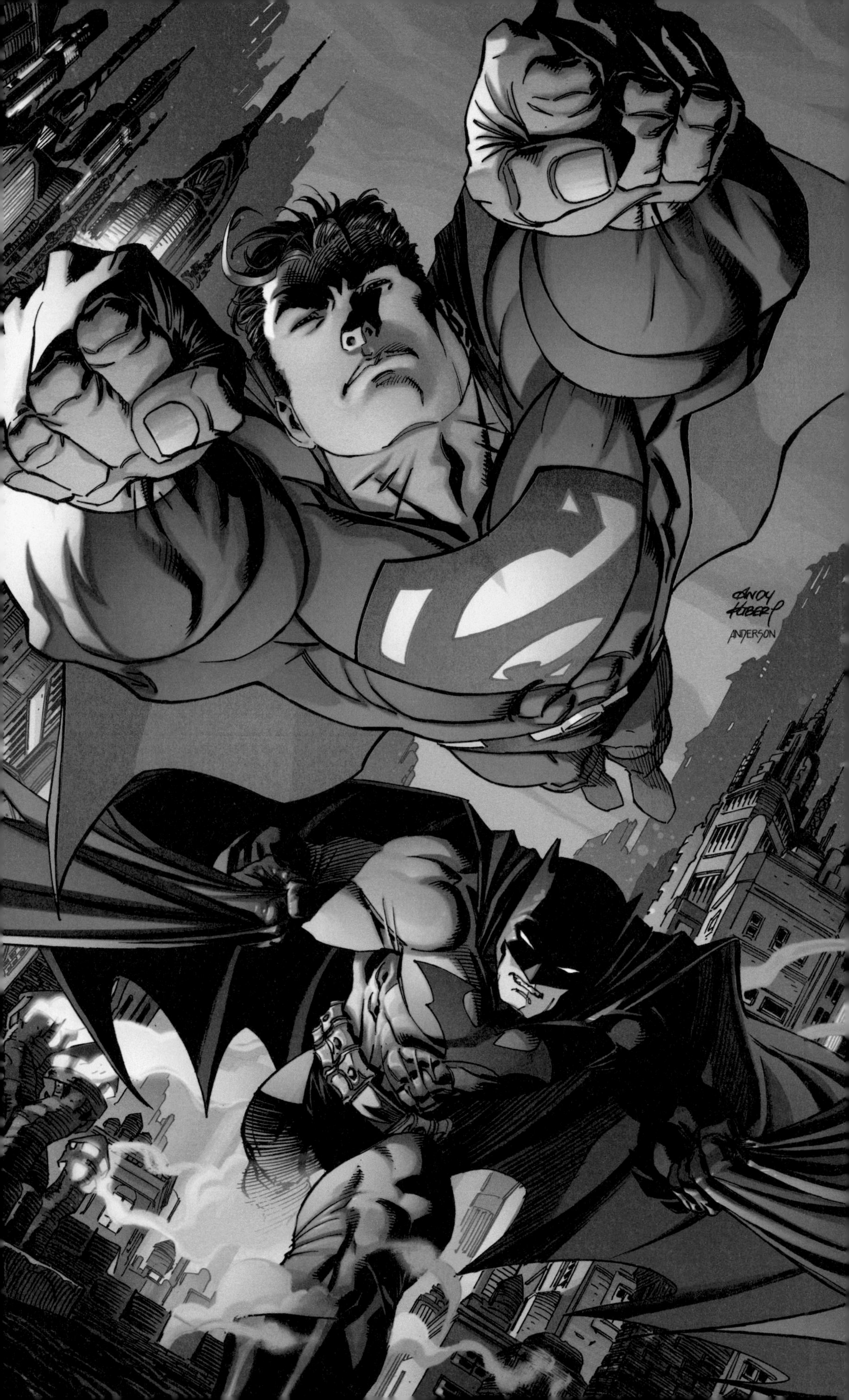
ANDY KUBERT
ANDERSON

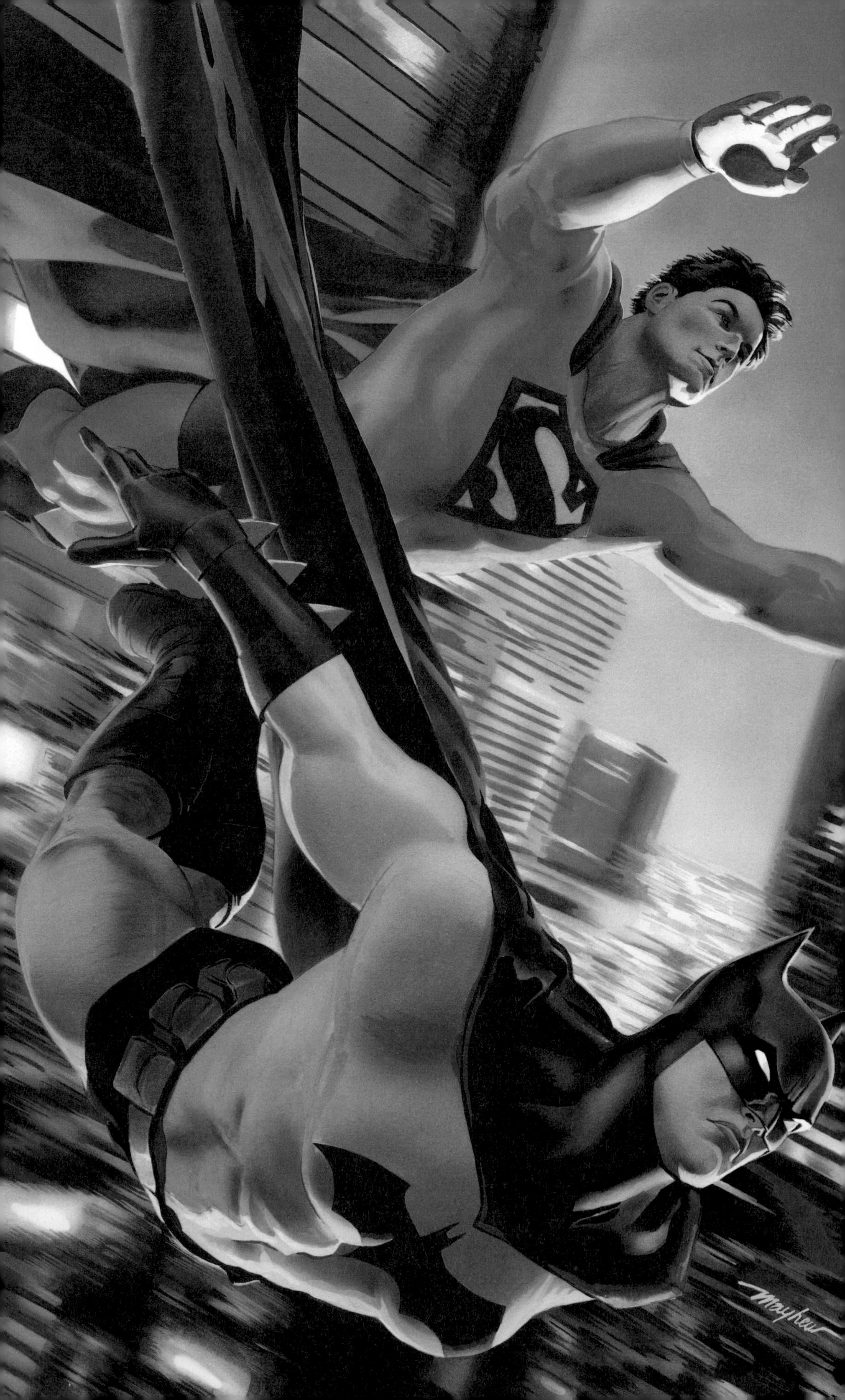
mayhew

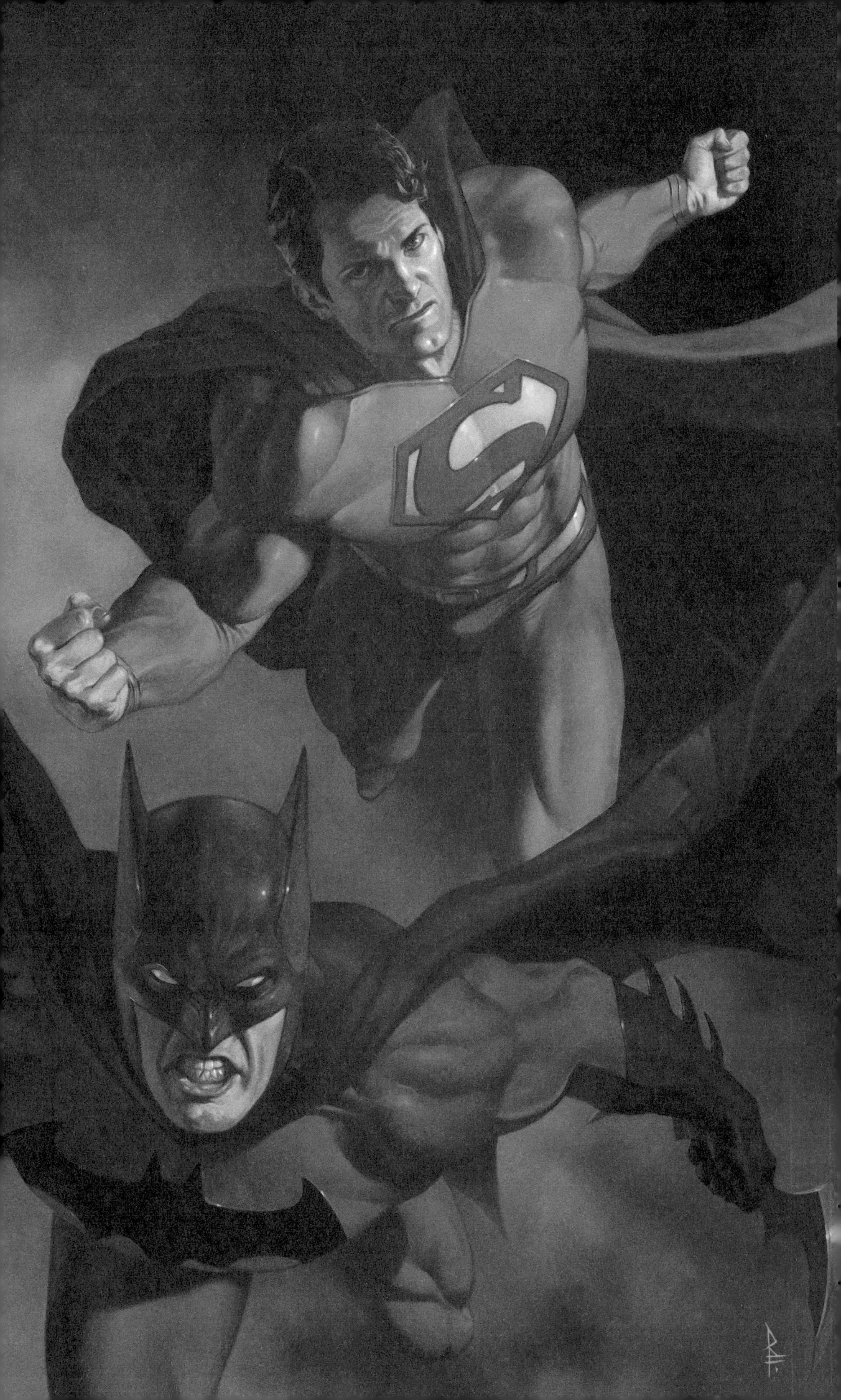

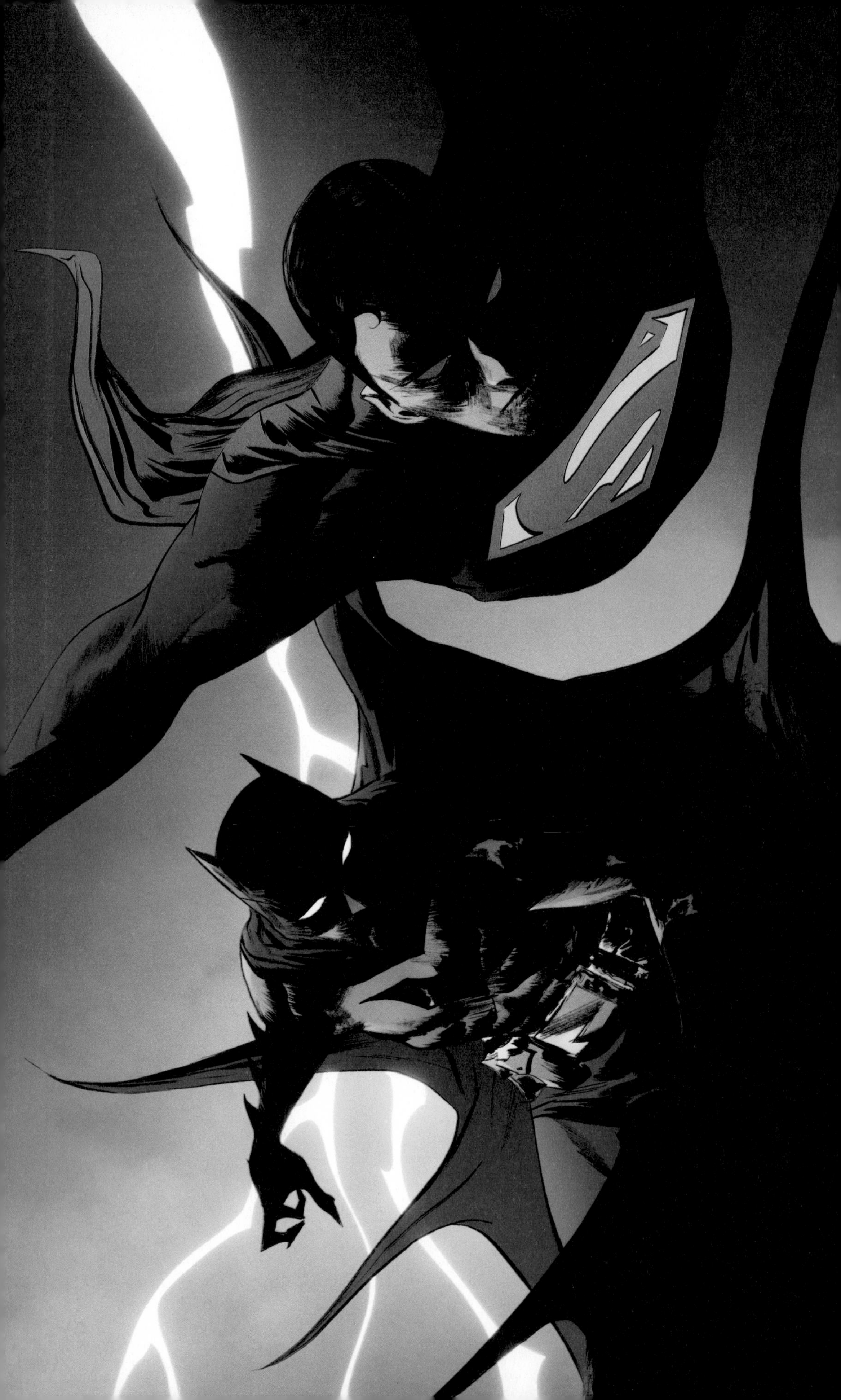

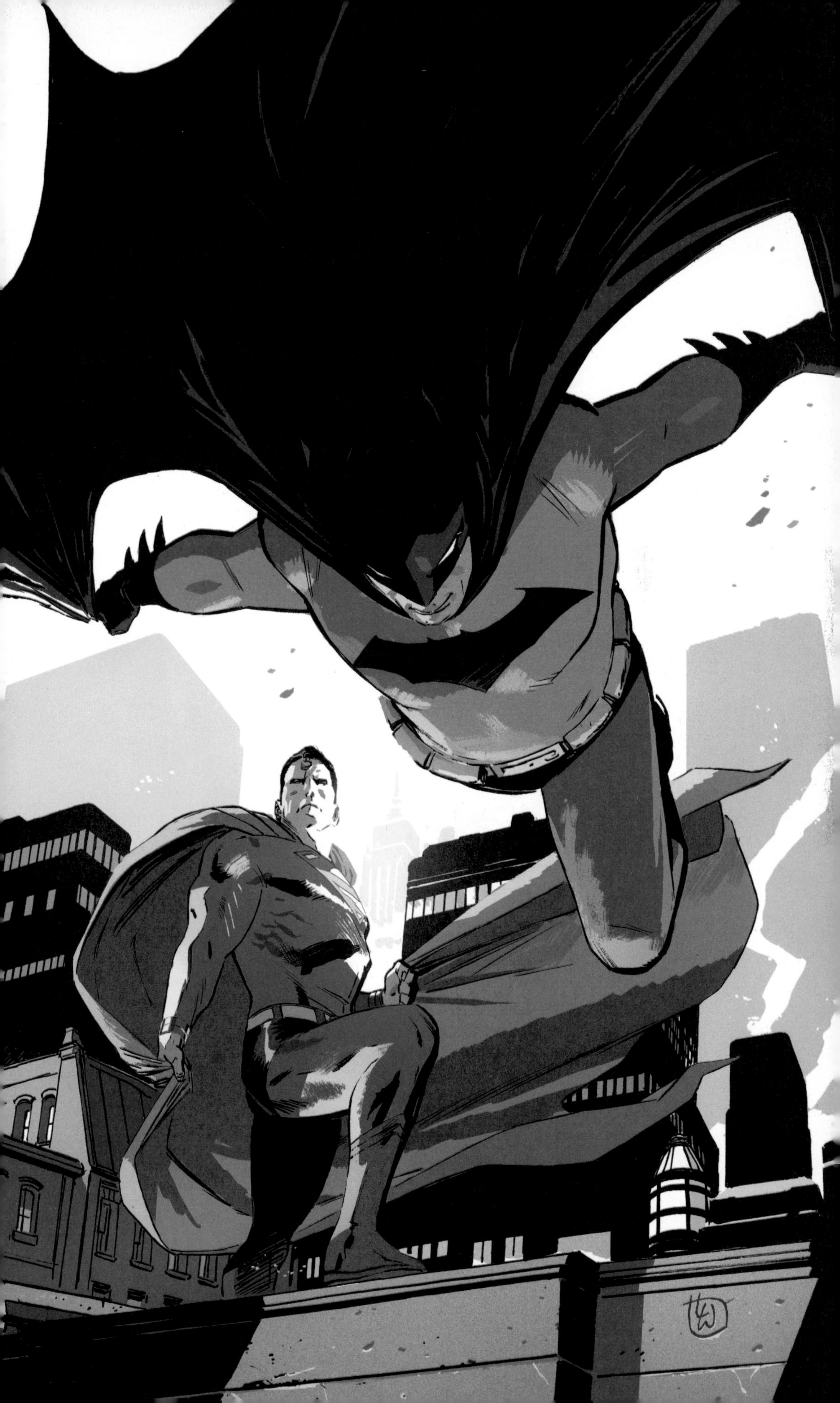

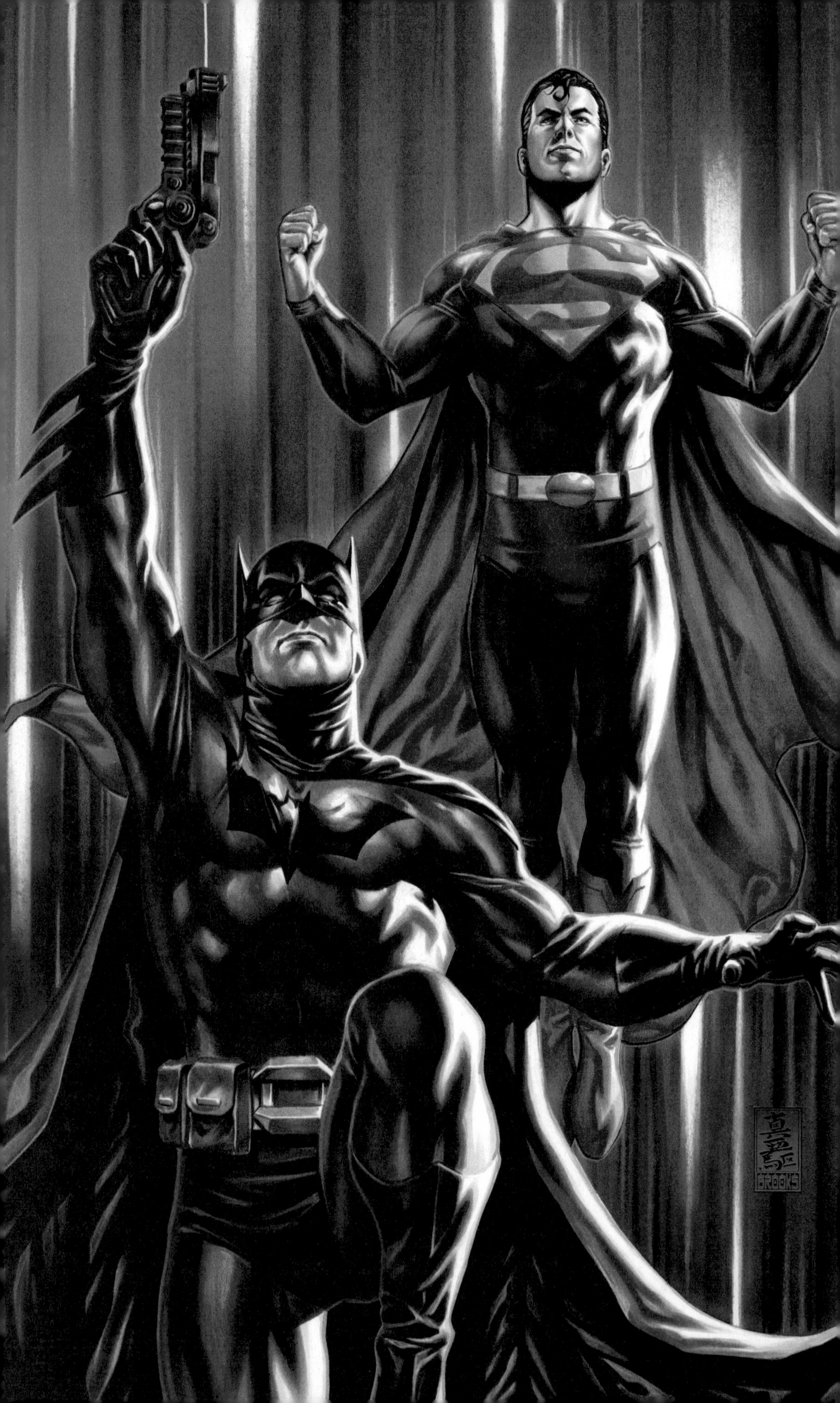
BROOKS

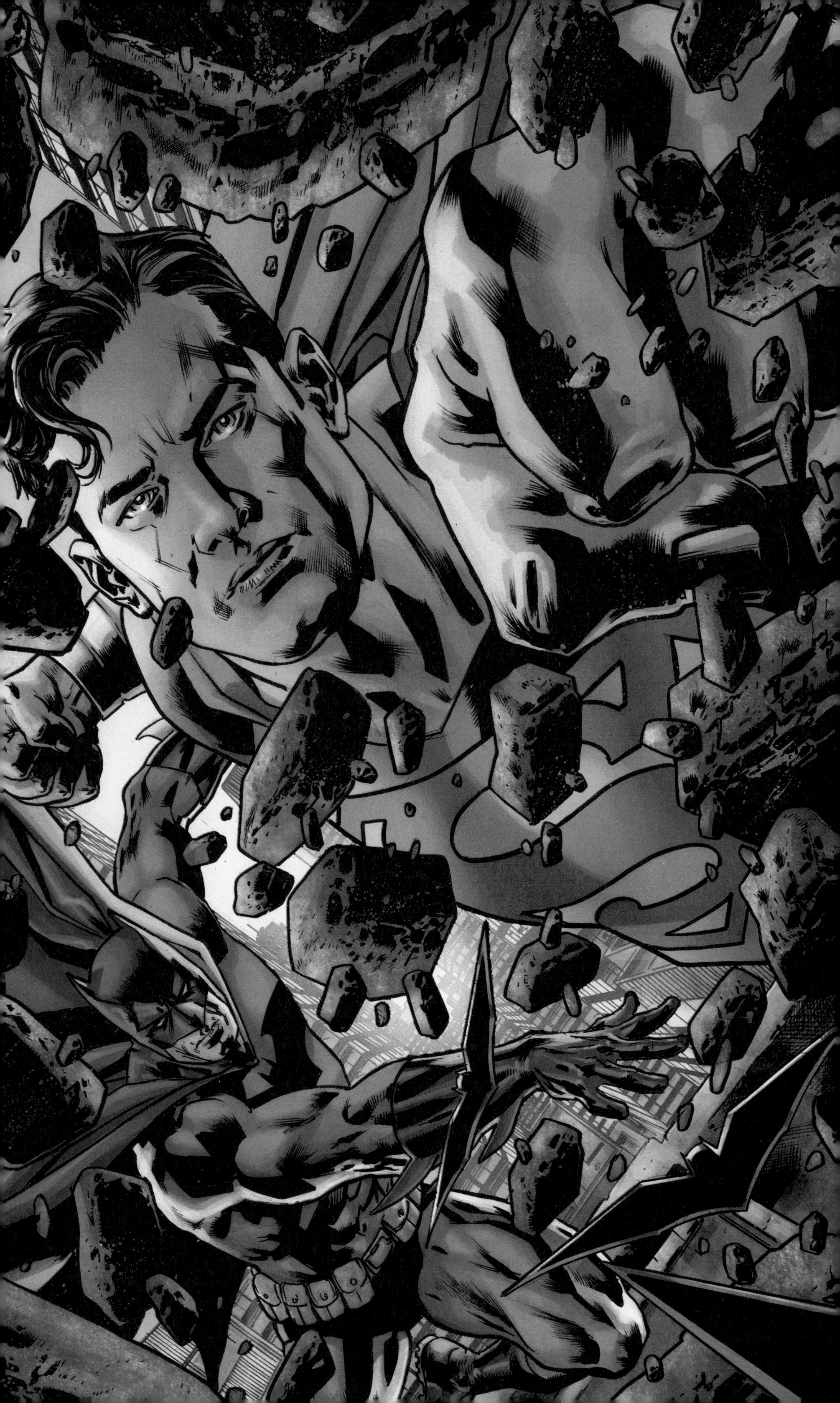

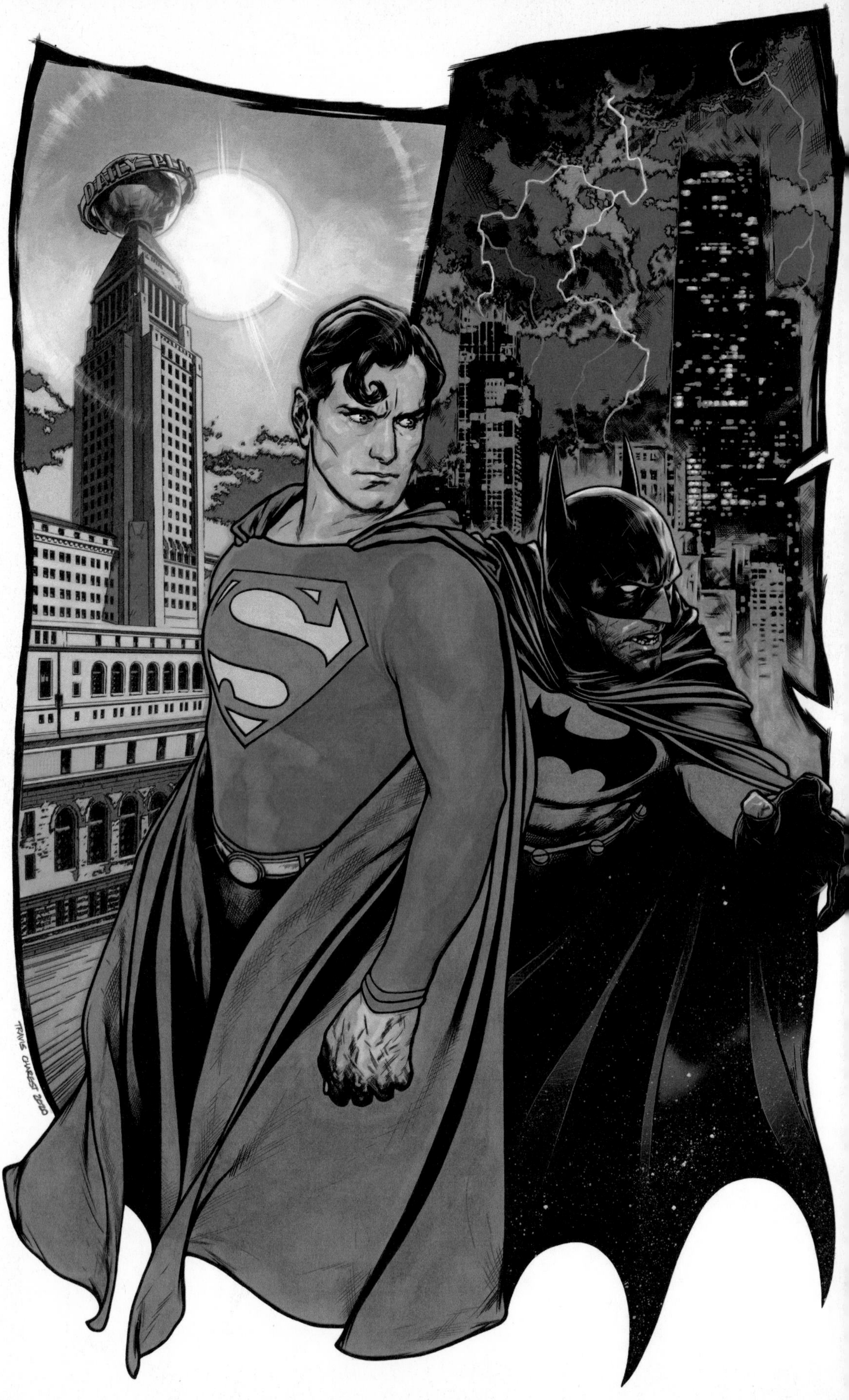
DAILY PL
TRAVIS CHAREST 2020

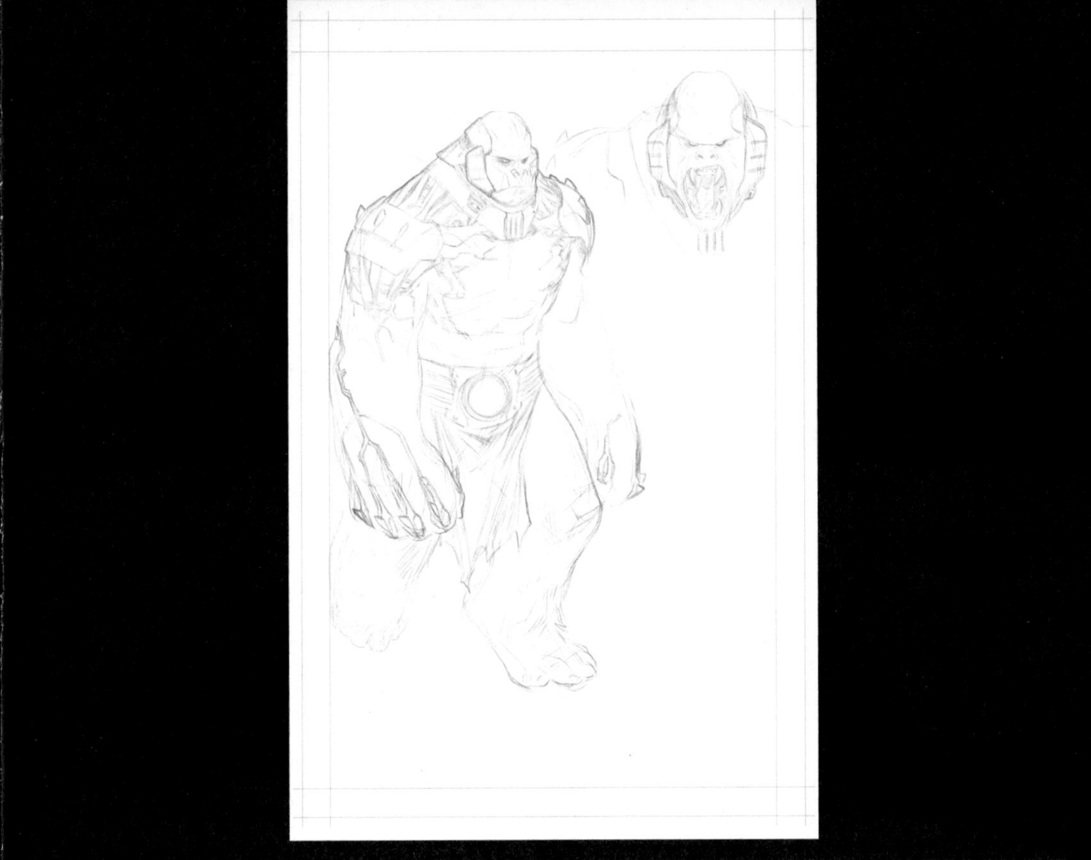

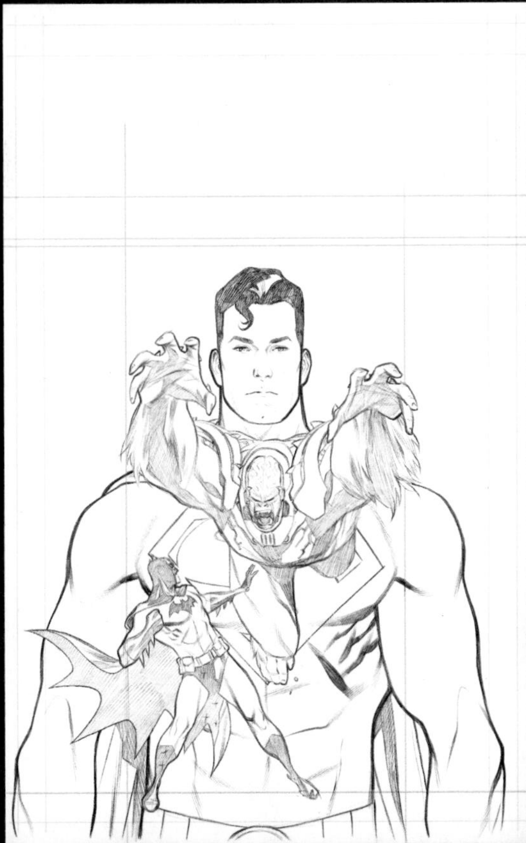

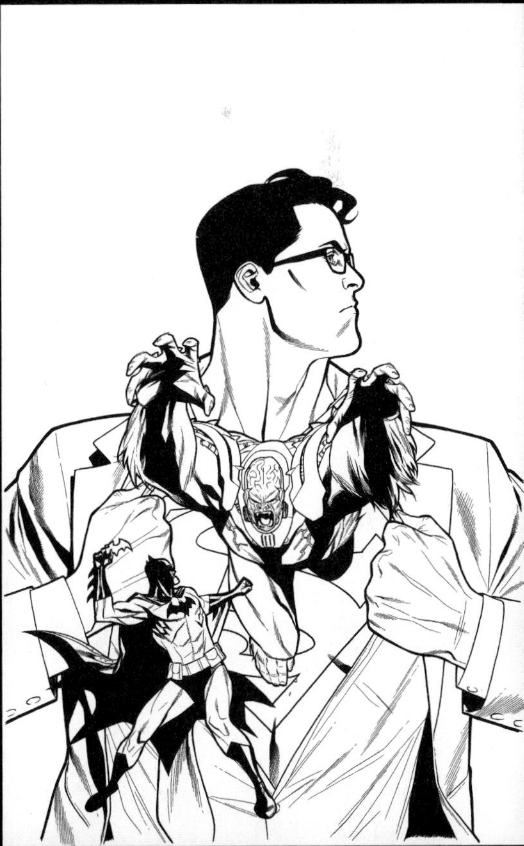

Batman/Superman #7 cover sketches by NICK DERINGTON

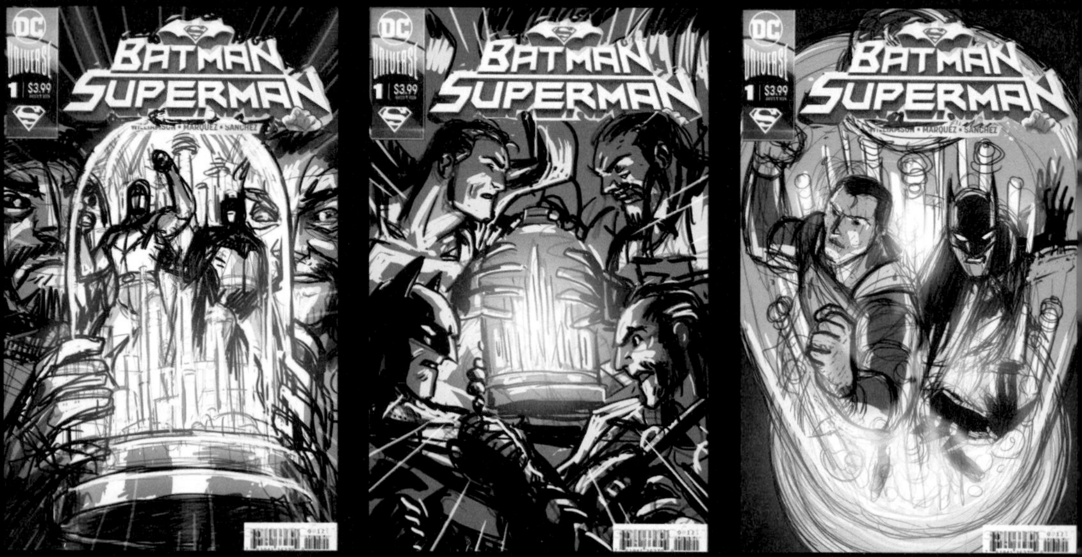
DC UNIVERSE
1 $3.99
BATMAN SUPERMAN
WILLIAMSON • MARQUEZ • SANCHEZ

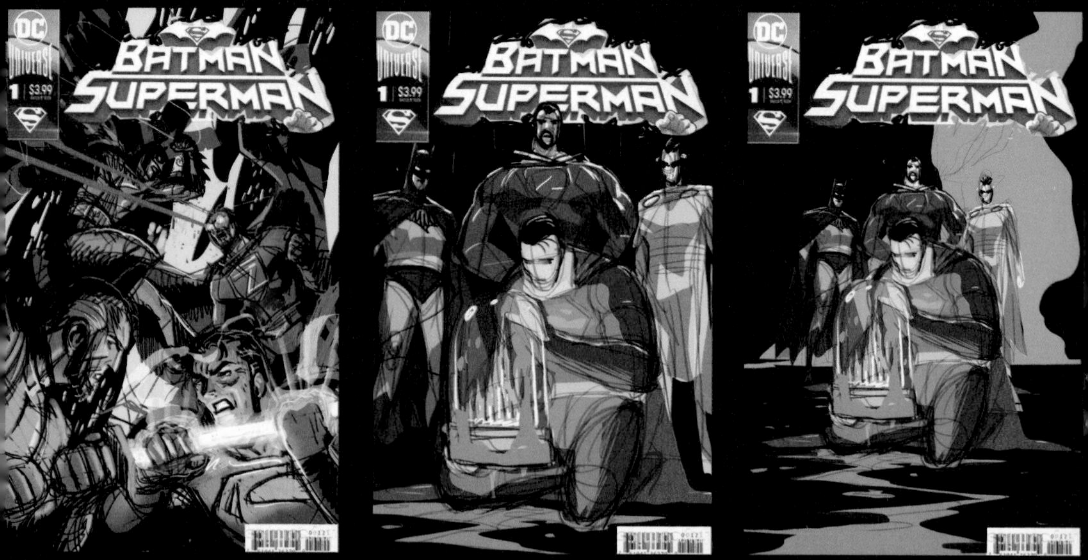
DC UNIVERSE
1 $3.99
BATMAN SUPERMAN

Batman/Superman #8 cover sketches by NICK DERINGTON

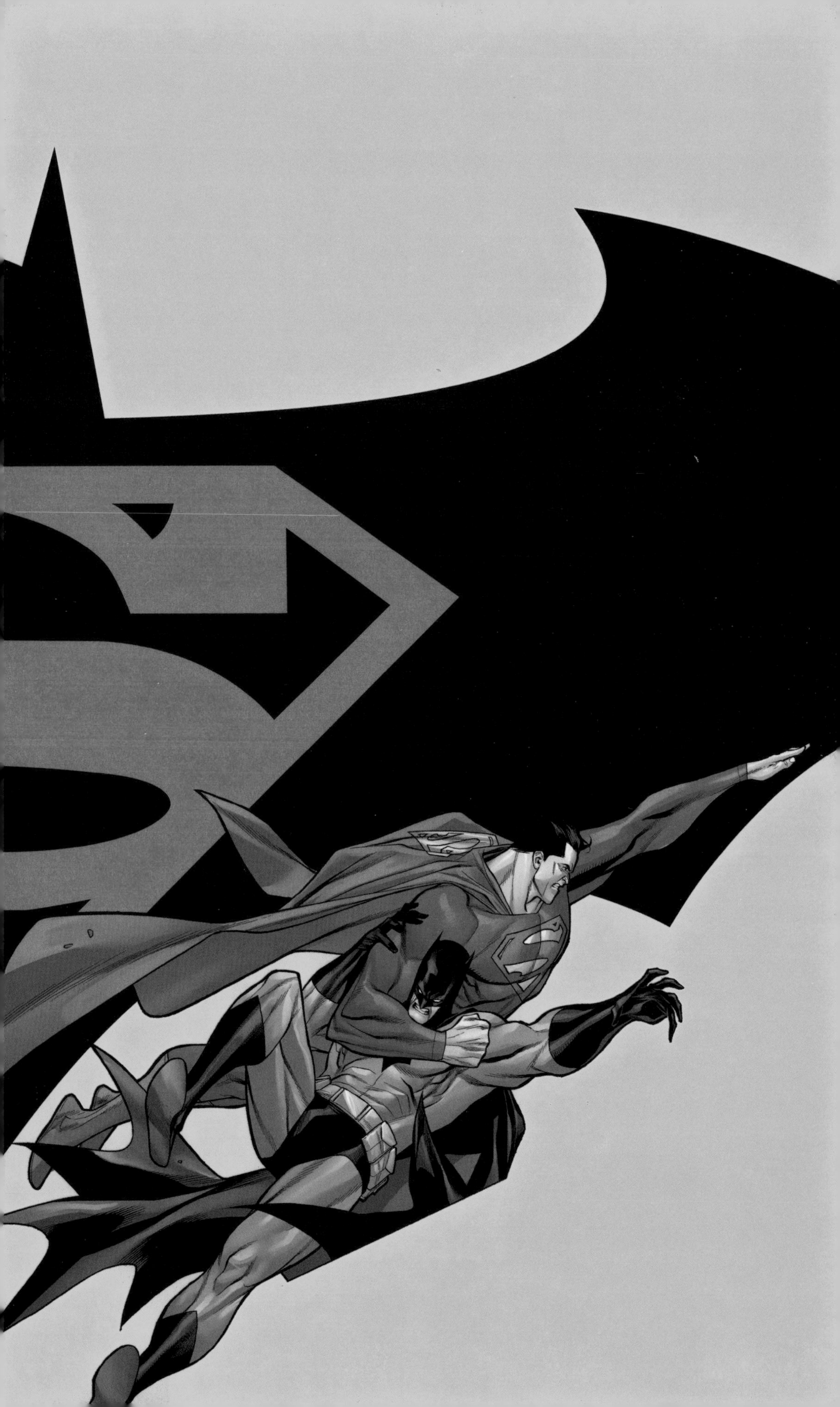